CHRISTIAN COMMUNITY
IN HISTORY

CHRISTIAN COMMUNITY
IN HISTORY

VOLUME **2**

Comparative Ecclesiology

ROGER HAIGHT, S.J.

continuum

NEW YORK • LONDON

2005

The Continuum International Publishing Group Inc
15 East 26 Street, New York, NY 10010

The Continuum International Publishing Group Ltd
The Tower Building, 11 York Road, London SE1 7NX

www.continuumbooks.com

Printed in the United States of America

Library of Congress Cataloging-in-Publication Data
Haight, Roger.
    Christian community in history / Roger Haight.
        p.   cm.
    Includes bibliographical references and index.
    ISBN 0-8264-1630-6 (v. 1 : hardcover : alk. paper)
    ISBN 0-8264-1631-4 (v. 2 : hardcover : alk. paper)
    1. Church. 2. Church history. I. Title.
BV600.3.H35 2004
262′.009 – dc22
                                        2004004006

Contents

Part II
THE CHURCH IN THE MODERN PERIOD

Preface

In the sixteenth century the unity of the church was broken in a way that it had never been before. Surely the Eastern and the Western churches had not been in communion for some time, but each existed in its own sphere apart from the other in the self-collected ways they had for centuries before. In the sixteenth century, churches sharing the same continent and political economy were so divided that they went to war.

Today, in the wake of the ecumenical movement and its unfinished business and in the common Christian consciousness of sharing the religious world with other vital faith traditions, the ecclesial and ecclesiological pluralism that began with the Reformation appears much more benign. In fact, many would make the case today that the pluralism of churches established in the sixteenth century was a spontaneous development that corresponded to the way things should be. The main goal of this comparative ecclesiology is not simply to lay down one after another different ecclesiologies that emerged over the last five centuries, although that describes the volume with empirical accuracy. Its larger intent is to show the richness, vitality, and creativity of the whole church as it moves through history adjusting to new times, places, and cultures. In other words, the object of the study still remains the whole church, but from the sixteenth century forward the church will always be constituted by the churches. The text does not follow that whole church evenly, as in a general history century by century, tracing the development of churches. Rather it jumps to selected authors and texts which represent new things that were or are happening. This strategy allows a certain control of vast data and the ability to enter into some ecclesiological detail while at the same time representing large trends.

The method of this ecclesiology from below directs it to history; it moves through the actual church of history to ecclesiology or an understanding of the church both as it is and as it should be. In the first volume of *Christian Community in History* that passage was fairly explicit because comprehensive ecclesiologies in our sense did not exist. In the chapters which follow ecclesiology itself becomes much more directly the subject matter of the book. But I hope never to lose sight of concrete history and the degree to which these ecclesiologies are historically conditioned.

To make sure of this I have tried to enter into the spirit of each of the churches and ecclesiologies that are studied here with an eye for appreciating what is being said from the point of view of the one writing it and construing it in the positive way in which it was first designed. The presentations are meant to be historically accurate and nonpolemical. But this is far more difficult than it might seem because the outsider inevitably fails to notice the details, the nuances that can shift the focus and with it a world of meaning. For example, how many people notice that Calvin does not generally speak of the "real" presence in the eucharist but of "true" presence? For this reason I take more recourse in the use of quotations than I might do otherwise.[1] And I remain grateful for all the help that I received in this effort to be faithful to the spirit of the many traditions that are reviewed here.

The help and support that I have received in the writing of these two volumes has come in many ways, from many directions, through a variety of people, in different contexts. But I have to single out those who actually spent time with chapters or the whole text of this second volume. These are all experts in their fields and their gift of their expertise is inestimable. They are Dale M. Coulter, Paul Fitzgerald, S.J., Michael Himes, Bradford Hinze, Ghislain Lafont, O.S.B., Frank D. Macchia, Ted Peters, Peter Phan, Jill Raitt, T. Howland Sanks, S.J., and Fredrica H. Thompsett. I am thankful too that the New York

---

1. This will be keenly noticed in chapter 3 on Hooker's apologia of the ecclesiology of the Church of England where I have used the latest critical edition of the *Lawes* that preserves Hooker's Elizabethan English. This immediately dates Hooker and helps guarantee historical authenticity in the reading of the text. The language appears quaint, for most associate it with the poetic imagination of Shakespeare. Although difficult at times, it forces attention to the text, and this stimulates appreciation of the penetrating nuance and classic depth and cogency of this man's thought. What is said here of Hooker applies broadly.

Province of the Society of Jesus supported me during the sabbatical year of 2003–4 so that I could finish this project. I wish to thank as well Gasper F. Lo Biondo, S.J., the director of Woodstock Theological Center at Georgetown University, for accepting me as a Visiting Fellow and putting the resources of the center at my disposal. Thanks too to Leon Hooper, S.J., the director of Woodstock's library and his staff who were consistently gracious and helpful. The companionship of the fellows and staff were a constant blessing. Finally, I thank Frank Oveis, the editor of this project, who has supported it to the end with care and unerring attention, and Gerard Jacobitz, who once again has done a superb job of proofreading and especially indexing the book.

Introduction

The first volume of *Christian Community in History,* subtitled *Historical Ecclesiology,* traced the history of ecclesiology from Jesus to the eve of the Protestant Reformation. What follows continues that history but possesses an integrity of its own so that it can be understood on its own terms. At the same time, readers of the first volume will notice that a change in the strategy of telling the story of ecclesiology in the modern period has been introduced in this work. This is reflected in the subtitle, *Comparative Ecclesiology.* A good way to introduce this work will be to explain how what is going on here continues to be the historical ecclesiology begun in the first volume, but under new circumstances that call for the new strategy. This Introduction will also describe what that strategy consists of and how it unfolds in the chapters which follow.

HISTORICAL ECCLESIOLOGY

The first volume of this work began with considerations of the method for examining the church. The phrase, "historical ecclesiology," was introduced as one that bears the intrinsic paradox of attempting to find the normative in the historical. Historical ecclesiology does not refer simply to studying ecclesiologies of the past, but of retrieving the truth within them that has a claim on Christian consciousness. The church of the past is always grasped simultaneously in two languages, the one of historicity and the other of theology which mediates a perennial, because transcendent, truth. This theoretical concept takes flesh in a process or method of research, interpretation, and writing. It uses history to recapture and stress the particularity of the church in each period. It uses a sociological imagination and a sociological model of organizations to help appreciate the elements and dynamics of the organized church.

1

It carefully integrates the theological self-understanding that constitutes the community within historical reality so that the two dimensions interpret each other: the historical imperfectly actualizes the theological ideal, and the theological keeps calling for adjustments in the actual church.

Concretely, each chapter was developed in a way that insured the three levels of analysis were always implicitly in dialogue with and mutually critical of each other. A given chapter began by eliciting a sense of the historical period in which the church existed. This was followed by an analysis of a series of texts that represented both the social organization of the church and its theological self-understanding. A third section of each chapter consisted in constructing a portrait of the church at a given period, a process which could also be regarded as constructing a more or less explicit ecclesiology out of the life of the church and witness to the church at a given time. This resulted in a construction of ecclesiologies in the different epochs by synthesis, beginning with the first 150 years, through the period of the early church and the fathers, to the medieval period in which the basic structure of the Roman Church was formed.

A SHIFT IN STRATEGY

Everything changed with the Protestant Reformation in the sixteenth century. The institutional unity of the European Church was shattered, and a new age of the history of the church in West began. After the sixteenth century the unity of the church will always consist in a plurality of churches, formally so called and institutionally independent. Moreover, the plurality of churches generated a multiplicity of different ecclesiologies such as had never been seen before in the church in such formal and explicit terms. This too marked a turning point and the beginning of a new era of the church.

Ecclesiology began to develop into a formal, self-conscious discipline in the course of the late Middle Ages. Of course the church had been the subject of serious reflection by organizers, administrators, bishops, theologians, and the equivalent of canonists from the beginning. But ecclesiology became more of a formal area of reflection and subdiscipline of Christian theology in the course of controversies between emperors and popes, and especially during the conciliarist crisis. Obviously there were differences in understanding the church, but the pluralism implicitly reflected in Torquemada's papalist ecclesiology over against a conciliarist spirit are differences within a relatively large institutional paradigm about which there was consensus. In the sixteenth century ecclesiology broke the boundaries of that paradigm and rapidly developed: it became radical and comprehensive in the differences in self-conception and organization, and because ecclesiology became polemic and apologetic, the critical rationales for the church became clearer and more acute. Over against the Roman ecclesiology that had been in place, the Reformation offered several distinct and theologically well-reasoned alternatives.

One of the reasons for a shift in the strategy of a historical ecclesiology lies in this fact that ecclesiology became a central concern of theology in the sixteenth century and thereafter. One does not need to construct ecclesiologies of the sixteenth century because ecclesiology had become a formal discipline, and the churches were systematically portraying their nature, organizational structure, and mission. One stage of the constructive strategy used in the first volume thus becomes unnecessary. One does not have to construct comprehensive ecclesiologies of the churches because various authors of the period provide them. Such a construction also becomes less feasible. Given the massive amount of data relative to Europe, the Reformation movement, and the development of each church, it becomes impossible to control the developments on the ground in a single work.[1] But that is a purely pragmatic concern, whereas the principle is decisive: the only way to understand the whole church when it is divided into a plurality of churches is by a comparative ecclesiology.

In sum, this volume continues to use the same method that was used in the first volume, but it contains a shift of strategy that is significant. The point of historical ecclesiology from below is to move

---

1. George Huntson Williams, *The Radical Reformation*, 3rd ed. (Kirksville, Mo.: Sixteenth Century Journal Publishers, 1992), offers a good example of massive historical research into the dynamics of the movement of the left wing of the Reformation. Although historians speak of "the Reformation," it should also be recognized that it consisted of a number of discrete movements, in Wittenberg and Saxony, in Geneva and then beyond, in England, and so on. Each had distinctive issues that formed a center of gravity and a different theological, moral, and political tone.

from history, through the actual church of history in order to arrive at an ecclesiology or an understanding of that concrete church. In the chapters which follow the focus shifts so that ecclesiology itself becomes much more than before the subject matter that commands attention. But this strategy does not neglect concrete history nor the fact that these ecclesiologies emerged out of history. The methodological strategy that will be employed, therefore, remains a subset of historical ecclesiology and is specified by the label "comparative ecclesiology."

COMPARATIVE ECCLESIOLOGY

Comparative ecclesiology should be understood in the context of the larger framework of historical ecclesiology that was develop at the head of the first volume of this work and alluded to at the beginning of this Introduction. Comparative ecclesiology consists in analyzing and portraying in an organized or systematic way two or more different ecclesiologies so that they can be compared. This is less a formal definition of an established method in ecclesiology and more a description of the strategy employed in this second volume of a historical ecclesiology. A brief account of three features of the method will provide a fairly clear account of what it entails.[2]

First, history and other social sciences enter into the process of comparative ecclesiology. Differences among the churches and their ecclesiologies are largely a product of history. This means that the very process of portraying a distinct ecclesiology requires attention to the historical field of social forces that helped produce it. In the chapters which follow, because of the constraints of space, attention to historical background and detail had to yield somewhat to the complexity and nuance which accrued to ecclesiology itself as it developed in the course of the sixteenth century, but it is not neglected.

Second, a crucial step in writing the ecclesiology of a given church consists in selecting the sources. This whole work has been based mainly on written sources, especially the analysis of key authors. In

---

2. The work of Dennis M. Doyle, *Communion Ecclesiology: Visions and Versions* (Maryknoll, N.Y.: Orbis Books, 2000) can be considered a work of comparative ecclesiology.

this second volume, in order to be able to manage the sheer amount of data, the analysis turns to single authors who have themselves developed extensive ecclesiologies. The main criteria for the choice of this figure are the degree to which the author is representative of the particular church tradition, and thus bears some intrinsic authority, and also the actual effects of that authority, that is, the measure in which the ecclesiology has helped determine the tradition through its being studied or through its actualization. As previously noted, the fact that individual authors have written comprehensive ecclesiologies short-circuits the task of having to interpret church developments, for these representative figures have assumed that task.

It would be of some interest to take stock of the relative authority of the figures chosen and the function their ecclesiologies play in their respective traditions. Luther and Calvin, for example, became the equivalent of founders of particular churches or ways of being church; others are influential figures who enjoy various degrees of authority. In all cases where the representative texts are by individual authors, their authority is not ultimately normative, but representative of a tradition as source and inspiration. Perhaps an author or text might carry the authority of a classic. For example, Luther's ecclesiology is not the equivalent of Lutheran ecclesiology, but it bears authority, continues to inspire, and may function as a criteriological witness in certain cases. But even when the texts or the visions they contain become classics, they remain historical; they transcend historical particularity through their particularity and specificity. Thus the biography of key agents and authors behind the texts is not unimportant, and the chapters which follow keep the historical background and the biography of each author in view. This volume remains historical ecclesiology. But insofar as the authors take on representative value, they begin to function as types. The comparative ecclesiology which follows, therefore, is intrinsically tensive: it combines the historical particularity of the ecclesiologies of specific authors with a representative function that resembles in some respects the pure ideality of types.

A third feature of comparative ecclesiology consists in the strategy of organizing and presenting the thought of different theologians according to a common pattern or template. Thus, for example, the common pattern used in the first volume of this work drawn from the sociology of organizations is used as a common grid for the presentation of each of these ecclesiologies. This hermeneutical device is not reductive, however, but gives an explicit place to theological self-understanding and interpretation. This pattern serves as a bridge for comparison and contrast, even when that task is not undertaken formally and methodically. But this interpretive superstructure does risk distorting a particular author since it may block from view the genesis of thought or a perspective or approach that may be crucial for understanding the particular genius of a given ecclesiology. To offset that possibility as much as possible, the systematic laying out of a given ecclesiology is introduced by an account of the historical background and an analytical, narrative account of the genesis of the texts in question.

The implied comparison among the ecclesiologies developed in this volume are not drawn out in an explicit way for several reasons. A first reason flows from the theoretical goal of this work, which is not to stress the differences among ecclesiologies, but rather, after having displayed them in their difference, to see each one as part of the one tradition of the whole church. The emphasis in presenting the ecclesiologies which developed during and after the Reformation falls on the internal logic of each ecclesiology in turn and its coherence, and how it is consistent with the tradition widely construed. Differences are the first accent, but they cannot be the final word. A more practical reason why the actual comparison is not undertaken is that it could not be done in one volume, or could only be accomplished superficially with the broadest abstractions. But that would distract from the power of this second volume which consists in laying down one after the other successive ecclesiologies, leaving implicit discussion of their differences, but building a large horizon for understanding the depth of a tradition that can sustain many different arrangements within the one church.[3] The church has become a multicolored tapestry of ecclesiologies, or a large river that

---

3. By way of exception chapter 4 contains an explicit comparison between two historical and particular ecclesiologies, but represented as types, through a creative adaptation and application of the two types of Troeltsch, "sect" and "church," to yield ecclesiological principles.

has branched out in the delta of the sixteenth century, so that it is simply no longer possible to think that a single church could carry the full flow of Christian life in a single organizational form.

DIVISION AND OUTLINE OF THE WORK

This volume takes a form that reflects the historical development of the church across the modern period. The first four chapters are dedicated to four distinctly different churches and ecclesiologies that were generated in the sixteenth century along with the Roman Church. Luther's full ecclesiology is spread across many writings and in some measure has to be constructed from a selection of his works. Some of his basic principles had enormous influence across all Reformation ecclesiologies. Calvin's ecclesiology is particularly comprehensive and well developed, and his ecclesiological principles had effects well beyond what came to be known as churches in the Reformed tradition. The Church of England gradually developed a distinctive ecclesiology which was given its first comprehensive formulation by Richard Hooker in the last decades of the sixteenth century. The label of "free church" is attached to two distinct ecclesiologies which bear the family resemblances of the radical reformation: the Mennonite and Baptist Churches as these were reflected in the ecclesiological writings of Menno Simons and John Smyth respectively. Rounding off the sixteenth century, chapter 4 also considers the ecclesiology of the Roman Church immediately after the Council of Trent as that is portrayed in the short but considered, semiofficial, and influential text of the Tridentine Catechism. The consideration of the sixteenth century is concluded with a typology representing two ends of the spectrum of ecclesiologies that rimmed the ecclesiological horizon at the end of the sixteenth century. Rather than summing up ecclesiology they show the wide territory between the two poles. Historical ecclesiology always challenges accurate portrayal by types.

A good half or more of this volume deals with the sixteenth century. Reflection on some things that are often taken for granted justify this emphasis. The pluralism in ecclesiology that Christians are used to in the twenty-first century really began only in the sixteenth century. It is crucial to analyze how that happened even though the question of why it happened is not formally addressed. Today one can understand pluralism in a nontoxic and positive way; if pluralism is understood and actualized in a certain way, it represents how the church should be today. But this was not the general understanding in the sixteenth century, and only a few people, such as Hooker, could look on pluralism positively, and then only in different places, not in a single town or nation. Laying out five distinct ecclesiologies, each with a positive rational and internal coherence, demonstrates how the forces of history operate, displays the differences of these several self-understandings of church, and also reveals to the eyes of a twenty-first-century Christian how many things these churches had in common despite the nontolerance of the century in question.

Chapter 5 deals with nineteenth century, post-Enlightenment European ecclesiology in the persons of Friedrich Schleiermacher and Johann Adam Möhler representing Protestant and Roman Catholic forms of the church. Historically the Protestant missionary movement and the papacy of Pius IX may have had more concrete impact on these churches than these two thinkers. But these two ecclesiologies are classically modern ecclesiologies and as such have continued relevance. They formulated for the first time themes that would come to dominate twentieth-century-church development.

Finally, chapters 6 and 7 deal with ecclesiological developments in the twentieth century. In some ways the developments in the church in the twentieth century have an imposing size that rivals the sixteenth century. The ecumenical movement in some measure at least reversed the vectorial forces of fission into those of fusion. The Roman Catholic Church suddenly opened itself in dialogue with the other churches and the world. Liberation theologies addressed the historical dimensions of salvation and fostered new ecclesiastical forms. The Orthodox Church, so many of whose churches suffered persecution and repression during the twentieth century, helped initiate the ecumenical movement and began to flourish after its own liberation at the end of the century. And as the church underwent a new surge in growth in the continents of the developing world, pentecostalism led the way and has created another new form of church.

Some may feel that the Roman Church is not sufficiently repre-sented in this second volume. This impression, possibly, is caused partly by where the last volume leaves off and this volume begins. The last two chapters of the first volume provide a substantial ac-count of the medieval church that was stamped with the form of the Gregorian reform. It will be shown in chapter 4 of this vol-ume that despite the fact that the Council of Trent was a watershed defining the early modern Roman Catholic Church, there is consid-erable continuity between it and the church of late-medieval times. Surely this church underwent major developments in the modern period, and the Gregorian church was seriously modified by Vati-can II. But consideration of these developments helps to underline the subject matter and structure of this work, because these develop-ments did not alter substantially the Gregorian form of the Roman Church. In fact, a case can be made that its Gregorian "form" in many respects still remains the defining force in the current Roman Catholic Church.[4] While the basic form of the Roman Church has remained relatively constant, surely not without major developments but steady in its organizational structure and self-understanding, a whole pluralistic world of structurally different ecclesiologies has ap-peared. The final two chapters will show that just as the Catholic Church has begun to adjust to the modern world of Christian plural-ism, the context is on the verge of changing again, just as radically, to a postmodern, globalized world of the multicultural with eccle-siologies across Christian traditions and new ones reflecting this diversity. In sum, comparative ecclesiology does not undermine the basic thrust of historical ecclesiology but sharpens its tensions and makes it considerably more interesting.

---

4. Ghislain Lafont, *Imagining the Catholic Church: Structured Communion in the Spirit* (Collegeville, Minn.: Liturgical Press, 2000), 37–64, 213.

Part I

THE CHURCH IN THE
SIXTEENTH CENTURY

Chapter 1

Luther's Ecclesiology

"Revolution" is the proper word to characterize the development of the Western church during the course of the sixteenth and early seventeenth centuries. In no period in the history of the church did it go through such a thoroughgoing transformation; no other period even comes close to the radicality of the change wrought during the extended Reformation period. Before the sixteenth-century Reformation the Western church enjoyed institutional unity. At best the term pluralism, if it is appropriate at all, might refer to the division between the Eastern and Western churches, but they occupied separate territories. Within the Western church it might be used to indicate differences in cultures, or regional character, style, and ethos, or schools of theological opinion, or splinter groups branded heretical. But the institutional church in the West was not pluralistic. By the end of the period in question pluralism refers to a divided Western church, churches separated from each other within a shared political and cultural sphere, but unable to share local spaces, and seriously at odds to the point of going to war. Western Christianity became a name for a collection of different churches.

This chapter traces the emergence of the ecclesiology of Martin Luther, the man who led the evangelical movement in its earliest years. But before turning to Saxony, the city and university of Wittenberg, and the man regarded as the initiator of the Reformation, the stage must be set with some consideration of the historical context in which the movement unfolded. The chapter then turns attention to Luther and begins by tracing the development of Luther's ecclesiology in a narrative, biographical, and bibliographical style. This is designed to communicate a sense of the development of Luther's reconception of the church, to connect it squarely with his historical situation, and to introduce the texts selected to represent it. Given this basis, the third part of the chapter consists in a schematic, analytical portrayal of Luther's ecclesiology. The chapter concludes with some general reflections concerning Luther's view of the church and some principles that will be important for understanding the church at any given time.

EUROPE AND THE WESTERN CHURCH AT THE BEGINNING OF THE SIXTEENTH CENTURY

This brief introduction to Europe and the Western church at the end of the Middle Ages is intended to jog the reader's memory. The description of the church of the late Middle Ages which concluded the first volume of this work may also serve as an introduction to the church in the sixteenth century. This overview offers no theory of the cause of the Reformation, but a depiction of the situation in a series of data raises up some elements of the period that allowed it to happen.[1] This question of how such a massive change in the religious situation of Europe could have happened in such a compacted period of time can find an answer, not in a single proposition, but in the broadest possible terms in three fundamental conditions. The first was the virtually universal desire for reform "in head and members" that was documented in the course of the characterization of the ecclesiology of the late Middle Ages. The second was the de-absolutization of the hold that the Roman Church had on the theological imagination and the spirituality of a good number of Europeans. The third was the extended process of the formation of new churches that is documented in the span of this and the next three chapters. The theme running through this introduction to the development of ecclesiology in the sixteenth century highlights factors that tended to relativize the institutional church in place. These may

---

1. A number of works have been helpful in this characterization of Europe at the eve of the Reformation: Euan Cameron, *The European Reformation* (Oxford: Clarendon Press, 1991); Owen Chadwick, *The Early Reformation on the Continent* (Oxford: University Press, 2001); C. Scott Dixon, *The Reformation in Germany* (Oxford: Blackwell, 2002); Alister E. McGrath, *Reformation Thought: An Introduction* (Oxford: Basil Blackwell, 1988). These four works are referred to in the text by the initials of the authors, EC, OC, SD, and AM respectively and to the page of their texts.

be divided into two sources: the one, outside the church, from the secular sphere of Europe, the other from factors internal to the life of the church.

Europe

It may be helpful to distinguish the political structures that characterized Europe from social and cultural issues. Analysis of these dimensions of social existence reveal distinct aspects that had a bearing on change in the church.

Political structure. Relative to the population, historians reckon that about 80 million people lived in Europe at the start of the sixteenth century. Ninety percent of them "lived in small hamlets or scattered farmsteads, their lives shaped by the agricultural cycle. Of the remainder less than half lived in one of the hundred or so towns which by 1600 exceeded 20,000 inhabitants" (EC, 4). These simple but sweeping demographics indicate that for 90 percent of Christians the delivery of religious services in the rural churches was pretty much the same as it had been in the Middle Ages.

Europe, however, was no political monolith, and Rome did not provide a political center. The phrase, "a balance of powers," might better describe the interactions across the continent. Spain, France, and England had developed into relatively stable, monarchical nation states. "Northern Italy" and "Germany" pointed to collections of interacting political entities under the overarching embrace of the Holy Roman Empire. On June 28, 1519, Charles, Duke of Burgundy and King of Spain, was elected emperor of the Holy Roman Empire; he would preside over the formative stages of the Reformation (SD, 1–3). "In 1521 there were eighty-five free cities of the empire" (OC, 83).[2] On the ground, the Reformation developed in the cities or large towns; it was largely spearheaded by educated people; the role of the university was important; and there were exceptions to all of these general principles. In the end, then, the political and social framework for the Reformation has to be thought of in terms of difference: regions, nations, empire, principalities, local movements; cities, towns, universities, villages; even the peasants wanted change.

---

2. Chadwick describes the city as a framework for understanding the unfolding of the Reformation in OC, 82–113.

The systems of church and society were thoroughly intertwined. After the Gregorian reform the church became a much more solid and autonomous organization. But this did not lessen the interpenetration of jurisdictions. Besides mediating grace and the norms of morality, the church directed many phases of secular life such as education and welfare. Reciprocally, many ecclesiastical decisions that affected life in town and city involved king, prince, or city magistrates. A comparison of papal power vis-à-vis secular rule in the thirteenth century and the beginning of the sixteenth would show that papal authority had declined and secular rulers felt less bound by it (AM, 24–25). The pope oversaw the whole of the church, but he could direct its operations at a distance only by working with secular rulers. "Relations between church and state in the century before the Reformation were carried out in an atmosphere, not of continuous hostility, so much as of regular haggling and negotiation.... The clergy's special status survived exactly as long as lay rulers were willing to accept and uphold it, and no longer" (EC, 29). If the power of secular rulers was secure, they "could abrogate the popes' powers whenever they chose" (EC, 55).

The relative autonomy and strength of nations, principalities, or free cities mean that the process by which the Reformation unfolded involved secular rulers as much as religious thinkers and ecclesial authorities. From the perspective of the reformers, they needed the help of secular rulers; generally they "allied themselves with regional or civic powers in order to effect their programme of reform" (AM, 5). In many instances the radical reformation proved to be an exception to this general rule when some groups defined themselves over against society. But the general pattern of how the Reformation progressed showed that it depended on the weakened authority of the papacy and the relative protection supplied to religious thinkers by secular rulers.

A typical pattern of how the Reformation spread shows the role played by townspeople and magistrates. First a preacher begins to expound the new ideas; the people become sympathetic; crowds demonstrate over certain specific issues; magistrates or a prince decides church policy for the town and for the region, whether or not an absentee bishop went along (OC, 94–96).

Society and culture. Another facet in the overall process by which the church lost its "absolute" hold on people's allegiance can be attributed to a steady growth of education. Education correlates with critical ability. Schools and universities produced literate citizens and contributed to the growth of a managerial class of schooled tradespeople and magistrates. "The growth of an educated laity — one of the more significant elements in the intellectual history of late medieval Europe — led to increasing criticism of the church on account of the obvious disparity between what the church *was* and what it *might* be" (AM, 4–5).

The renaissance in letters and arts has to be counted as a major factor that fed into the possibility and the actual unfolding of the Reformation. This subject is both too well known and too massive to develop, but also too important to neglect. It will be helpful at least to list several ways in which the influence was felt. Among the most important of these is the structure of the imagination which fueled the Renaissance: the return to the sources of Western wisdom. This pattern of learning and the inner conviction that sustains it bear enormous significance for the very logic and the possibility of the Reformation. The sources of Western culture are the classics, and the classics of the church are the scriptures and the early Fathers. As these sources were made known in new edition and translation, they both inspired with their content and provided critical distance with their difference. Internalization of this hermeneutical pattern of learning and conviction simultaneously generated a critical and reforming attitude as past norms revealed distortion by historical accretion and urged return to what was pristine and genuine. "The fundamental belief motivating the magisterial Reformers was that Christianity could best be reformed and renewed by returning to the beliefs and practices of the early church" (AM, 15).

This abstract description of a differentiated consciousness was played out in the outburst of printed editions of the Bible after the invention of the printing press in the mid-fifteenth century. Early in the sixteenth century a printed edition of Augustine's works made his thought more available and his influence more direct. In fact, the texts of the Bible, and Augustine, undercut or failed to support some teachings that were in place. The Bible thus served as a wedge of relativization (OC, ch. 2): at several specific places the New Testament seemed directly to contradict current doctrine taught by the church (AM, 39–40). This contributed to a weakening of an absolute hold that contemporary teaching may have possessed.

The literary forms of the new style of learning were more concrete, understandable, appealing, and applicable. Prescinding for the moment from content, the historicist medium of reasoning bore a significant contrast with the abstract, deductive, and logical style of scholasticism in its various schools. In other words, scholasticism itself, which was the intellectual medium of church teaching, had a rival source and logic for establishing truth.

Erasmus still stands as the most significant figure who symbolizes in his person and work these tensive alternatives.[3] The very point of his early work, *In Praise of Folly*, consisted in an ironic reversal born by satire, and the church figured prominently among his targets. His *Enchiridion* offered a straightforward, christocentric and morally based spirituality for the engaged Christian. The real impact of this latter work began in 1515 when "it became a cult work, apparently going through twenty-three editions in the next six years. Its appeal was to educated lay men and women, whom Erasmus regarded as the true treasure of the church" (AM, 37). Erasmus remained loyal to the church in place, but his historicist and religious consciousness allowed him to relativize its institutions.

Historians single out the invention of the printing press as something of a *sine qua non* of the Reformation. The printing press "changed the religious and intellectual history of Christendom" (OC, 1). It "meant that the propaganda of the Reformation could be produced quickly and cheaply" (AM, 12). The printing press also allowed wide diffusion and helped put in the hands of many the text of the Bible and of important early theologians such as Augustine. In other words, without the printing press these sources would not

---

3. Chadwick summarizes the career of Erasmus and his direct bearing on the events and the movement that turned out to be the Reformation in OC, 37–68.

have contributed to the Reformation so extensively their important theological content.[4]

Finally, one has to recall the discovery of a new world for Europeans by Columbus, and the way it introduced a new horizon of thinking. The world was bigger than was previously thought. With this discovery a new missionary movement was launched which should have changed thinking about the church more than it actually did. In fact the new missionary movement had very little if any impact on ecclesiology, even though the vitality of Christian faith was acted out in far-reaching missions to the West and to the East. The interecclesial conflicts in Europe so occupied the churches in the sixteenth centuries that ecclesiologies became hardened, and this ultimately impeded a qualitative development that one might expect from a missionary movement's exposure to new cultures.

The Church

Euan Cameron softens the spontaneous tendency to exaggerate the problems of the church in order to explain the Reformation. This approach often leads to reading the opposite of what came to pass in the Reformation into the church on the eve of the Reformation (EC, 9). Cameron, however, theorizes that the church succeeded well enough in providing the means and environment of religious services but became vulnerable in the secondary features of its existence as an institution (EC, 20). Some areas were the residue of the church's involvement in every aspect of social life. As church and society grew more differentiated, the presence of clergy in positions of secular power began to be resented and resisted (EC, 21–24). "Issues of money, its collection, distribution, and expenditure, cause[d] much of the church's 'vulnerability' at this period" (EC, 24). Money intended to support church ministry was diverted from that end: to houses supporting men and women living in community, to institutions which appropriated the tithes from the parishes, to the support of absentee ministers or clerics not ordained to the priesthood (EC, 24–27). "This monetary tangle harmed the church's image with lay

---

4. From the beginning of printing and the first printed edition of the Bible in 1456 the book that occupied the printer's attention most was the Bible. (OC, 1)

people: an impoverished local priesthood seemed to offer poor service for the money which it demanded; much of what was levied effectively 'disappeared' into enclosed monasteries or the arcane areas of higher education or administration" (EC, 26–27). Abuse of clerical privilege was an irritant (OE, 27–29). An inflated church bureaucracy, trade in benefices, and a complex legal system all devoured funds. But generalizations have to be made with caution. On the assumption that the term church referred to the institution that was concretized in the hierarchy and clergy, how did it appear? "The secular clergy was a vast and heterogeneous body, containing at one extreme the wealthy vicar-general with a fistful of benefices on the brink of appointment to a bishopric, and at the other the impoverished curate or chaplain performing basic priestly services for an insecure stipend barely more than a farm-laborer's wage" (OE, 35). This is the same church as in the late Middle Ages. But there were changes in degree and in levels of toleration. We can divide the discussion of a certain relativization along the lines of papacy, clergy, and laity.

Papacy. Volume one showed that in the course of the late Middle Ages the pope lost considerable ability to single-handedly control the church in regimes at a distance. Along with this loss of political power the renaissance papacy elicited complaints about its secularity and loss of moral integrity. There is no reason to think that the scandal inside the church would be any less at the start of the sixteenth century than it would be today if the facts were known. But they were known by some, whether the sophisticated Erasmus or the young friar Martin Luther.

Priesthood and clerical status. The clerical system, governed by law, allowed a large group of men to live off the funds generated through the arrangement of tithes in the parishes, and myriad taxes and entitlements. That the system needed reform is evidenced by the conciliar legislation in the fourteenth and fifteenth centuries as well as Trent. The clergy as a class or group were the object of general criticism. Criticisms of failure in clerical celibacy, lack of education, or clerical privilege were conditioned by circumstance; others were more systemic. Too many people distant from pastoral ministry were being supported by the system of tithes which drew money from the congregations. Too much land was controlled by the church. "The most urgent worry of secular society was the steady, relentless way in which the church took over more and more property, especially landed property, which then remained under the 'dead hand' of church ownership and could no longer be taxed" (EC, 59).

Lay piety. An account of the religiosity of the period requires particular delicacy involving distinctions between city, town, and village, attention to the culture of the time, and sensitivity to the theology of the period. By some measures, religiosity was healthy and vital. The tradition of the *devotio moderna* as represented in the *Imitatio Christi* and the spirituality of social participation of Erasmus's *Enchiridion* display spiritual vigor; the confraternities organized this spiritual energy into social action. Behind this spiritual vitality, however, three currents ran together in an unhealthy mix.

The first was a theology that leaned toward Pelagianism as seen in the well known maxim: "To those who do what is in them, God will not deny his grace" (EC, 85). When this is understood in the teleological framework of scholasticism, it lends itself to a spirituality of moral striving. A second theme equally in need of fine distinctions concerned superstition and what counted as such. One group's superstition is an integral part of another's coherent worldview. "All levels of society readily believed in various kinds of superstition, magic, prophecy, and other supernatural intrusions into the order of creation. These were not 'deviant, perverted,' or 'aberrant' forms of thought; they were an integral part of the overall picture" (EC, 17).[5] The third current of understanding may be called "objectification." This refers to a certain quantification of religious practice as a measure of God's grace. The theory and practice of indulgences is important as an issue to which Luther reacted and which caught people's attention. It is more significant as representative of objectification in the style of spirituality.

---

5. Cameron describes the religion of the people of Europe at the beginning of the sixteenth century at EC, 9–19. His overall reflection is that the language of decay and corruption is somewhat anachronistic. "One must stop talking about 'decay' or 'flaws' *except* to the extent that they were deplored (and not just by a high-minded clique of late medieval reformers) at the time." EC, 18.

The system of indulgences may be explained telescopically as something that developed in stages of practice and theological rationalization. The penitential system arrived at in the Middle Ages consisted in confession of sins to a priest, absolution by the priest, and the performance of acts to demonstrate repentance and to serve as a punishment for the sin against God. One step in the process of objectification was taken when it was agreed that "if the penitent could not do it a friend could do it instead" (OC, 74). On the one hand, mere acts of penance cannot effect remission of sin without internal repentance; on the other hand, the church had the power to forgive sin given it by Christ. Indeed, application of the fruit of penitential acts could be dispensed by the church for both the living and the dead. The dispensation of remitting a person from punishment due to sin on the basis of performed acts of penitence was coupled with the doctrine of purgatory. This produced a system in which by virtuous actions one could build up a quantity of remission for punishment due to sin for oneself and for others who had died. An indulgence was a grant or application by the church of remission of punishment due to sin for acts of virtue. They were as credible as was the belief that loved ones were suffering the severe pain of purification in purgatory. The problem of indulgences was magnified when they were offered for sale to become a regular or irregular source of income for the church. Indulgences gradually became "a big source of extra revenue in the church" on which the church depended (OC, 75). This is perhaps the most noteworthy example of an objectification of the sacramental principle run wild. Merit became detached from explicit human intention and thus able to be applied to another.

On the one hand, the practice of special indulgences granted by Rome fit in with a long term practice and spirituality of the people; on the other hand, there is evidence that early in the sixteenth century certain people had become conscious or at least were beginning to feel that "indulgences as sold in Germany were a racket" (OC, 94).

In larger terms, the structure of Christian spirituality in the West at the beginning of the sixteenth century may be pictured in terms of a cycle of sin, absolution, the performance of penance, and grace. This year to year cycle as marked by yearly confession and communion was reinforced by the sacrifice of the mass which stood at the center of sacramental piety. The church proved itself "in the 'communication of grace': the sacraments in general, and the 'sacrifice' of the mass, with its benefits for the souls of the living and the dead, in particular" (EC, 90). This yearly cycle was wrapped in a larger worldview in which human beings were born into sin, baptized into grace, and died into punishment in purgatory before final salvation in heaven.[6] For the Reformation to take hold, this worldview and the role of the church in it had to be relativized, and this could only be done if it were replaced by an alternative.

Reformation as a collection of different movements with different thematics.[7] Rather than thinking of the Reformation as the unified phenomenon the single word suggests, it may be more useful to underline the differences that marked the movement. As an umbrella term it covers a group of different movements, interconnected in various degrees by attraction and repulsion, which left Europe at the end of the sixteenth century divided into many different churches with different ecclesiologies. A kind of teleological retrojection impels the idea that Luther intended the kind of Reformation that occurred, and others simply joined his movement. In fact, it is really quite difficult to determine when the radical divisions that occurred actually took hold. The four chapters that follow will focus on distinct movements that led to the formation of specific churches with distinct ecclesiologies. Each had different thematics underlying it, each took a distinctly different direction. The sources of Luther's ecclesiology are the Saxon city of Wittenberg, the university, the study of theology and the Bible, and a concern for lived spirituality. Calvin was a lawyer and an emerging humanist, self-taught in theology and scripture, whose talents combined textual scholarship and social organization. The Church of England was created as a national church by a legislative act of parliament. The ecclesiologies generated under the leadership of Menno Simons and John Smyth, in different situations, shared enough in common for some of their descendent churches to consider uniting. Roman Catholic ecclesiology of the sixteenth century was not far from that outlined by Juan de

---

6. This cycle is mapped by Cameron in *European Reformation*, 79–93.
7. This idea is briefly developed by McGrath, *Reformation Thought*, 6–11.

Torquemada the century before, even though the church underwent considerable reform in many of its institutions during or in the wake of the Council of Trent. These differences merely typify the extraordinary ecclesiological developments of the sixteenth-century Western church.

HISTORICAL DEVELOPMENT
OF LUTHER'S ECCLESIOLOGY

Luther was born in 1483 into the late medieval church when the renaissance papacy flourished. He died in 1546, on the eve of the Council of Trent, convened for the most part because of the religious revolution of which he was the prophet or charismatic leader. Like any human life, the experiences, events, and actions of Luther make up an elaborate network of contingencies and particularities. Change a couple of details and modern Europe may have been different. Yet his theology and ecclesiology also bear a historical consistency and a religious coherence that have proven to be classic. This first section provides the historical linkage of Luther's ecclesiology to the late Middle Ages and to the world of Europe in the first half of the sixteenth century. The narrative shows the polemical character of its genesis: Luther's ecclesiology emerges out of a reaction against the abuses he perceived in the system which obtained. The following analytical part of the chapter will represent Luther's ecclesiology in a positive and constructive way. The two questions addressed here are basic and far-reaching and have to be discussed even though a few pages really cannot do them justice: where does Luther's ecclesiology come from? How does it develop historically?

Formation of Theological Foundations

The story of Luther's early life is well known. He entered the religious monastery of the Augustinians in Erfurt in 1505 at the age of twenty-two, was ordained two years later, and directed toward becoming a university professor. The Augustinians in Erfurt were engaged in university work, but Luther's superior arranged for his position at the university in Wittenberg, which was newly founded by the imperial elector Frederick the Wise of Saxony. Luther had had a strong dosage of scholastic philosophy and theology in the nominalist tradition of Gabriel Biel, and taught philosophy at Wittenberg for a term as a visitor, but he developed no love for it. When permanently installed at Wittenberg in 1512, Luther received the Doctorate, took up the role of professor of scripture, and began lecturing on the scriptures. In early 1517 Luther, already the leader of a reform in theological method based in scripture, proposed a series of theses against scholastic theology. Later in the year he addressed his famous ninety-five theses against indulgences. These theses spread abroad in printed form, and Luther was called to account for them. He had a dramatic encounter with the papal legate, Cajetan,[8] in Augsburg in mid-October, 1518. He publicly debated John Eck in Leipzig in early July 1519. Luther was not passive before these events but carried on a full schedule of teaching, preaching, and prolific writing. But these are the works of the outer man; a lot more was going on inside.

Interpreters of Luther often place a good deal of weight on some of his innermost experiences as keys for understanding his thought. Luther had a deep sense of sin, especially his own sin and unworthiness before God. The regular practice of confession, the ordinary means of finding God's forgiveness, did not work for Luther. Within this framework God was perceived as judge, transcendent and righteous, in various complex ways an object of fear. Much more should be said to circumscribe more accurately the various manifestations of this constellation of experiences and Luther's failed efforts at achieving either perfection or peace or a sense of full acceptance by God. But it may be more important simply to note the engaged, if not existentially intense, character of Luther's spirituality. His piety holistically encompassed his person, his basic attitudes, his life.

A biographical or psychological interpretation of Luther completely misses the point of the religious truth of what he stands for. To counter such a reductionism one can point to several other layers of experience and conviction in which Luther underwent a transition during the early years of teaching at Wittenberg. These transitions

---

8. Thomas de Vio Cajetan (1469–1534): Thomistic theologian, Dominican, and cardinal.

help to understand what went on in Luther's life from the time he began teaching scripture in Wittenberg through 1519, and they help form the foundations of his ecclesiology.

A first transition consisted in a theological transformation of his experience that raised it to a new level through the mediation of scripture. This transition can be interpreted in different ways. But in fact Luther loved scripture early on, perhaps before his becoming an Augustinian, and as he grew more expert in it and received more consolation from it the scriptural word of God more and more became the interpreter of his experience. The central role of scripture cannot be stressed too much in an understanding of Luther: his study, his teaching, his preaching, his reform of theology in the university, his way of thinking theologically, and the positions that he held. Speaking both descriptively and theologically, Luther's experiences were transformed by the word of God in scripture. In terms of a differentiated consciousness and the scholarly processes of reason, Luther should be related to the world of renaissance scholarship rather than scholastic metaphysics, the theological world of revelation and faith mediated through texts and studied by historical research and exegesis.

Luther was made Doctor of the Holy Scripture in 1512 and probably began teaching in the winter semester of 1513–14. In the course of the next few years he lectured on the Psalms, then on Romans in 1515 and/or 1516. He then lectured on Galatians, and these lectures were followed by a course on Hebrews in 1517 and/or 1518. In the course of studying and teaching scripture, these texts "became for him *the* theological way of speaking, i.e., the critical norm against which he measured the theology of his time."[9] One thus finds in Luther's lectures formulations of God's righteousness, human sinfulness, and the righteousness of the sinner who recognizes and acknowledges his or her sinfulness.[10]

---

9. Martin Brecht, *Martin Luther,* I-III (Philadelphia: Fortress Press, 1985–93), 1, 131. Cited hereafter by volume and page number.

10. "Between 1513 and 1516 a definite change certainly took place in Luther's image of God. No longer did he find himself in continual confrontation with the judging God. He knew that God did not reckon sins to the believer who confessed them, and to this extent he experienced forgiveness." Brecht, *Luther,* 1, 136.

A second transformation can be distinguished in the gradual formation of what Brecht calls "the reformatory discovery."[11] By this he means the center or kernel of Luther's theology, the principle of justification by grace through faith. From one point of view, this may be regarded as a simple experience or revelation or principle concerning God's mercy, grace, forgiveness, actual acceptance of the human person received in faith by the mediation of the Spirit of God. But as such it is so dense and existentially explosive in religious meaning that one must imagine that Luther did not receive it all at once but grew into it over an expanded period of time. In fact interpreters do not know exactly when or exactly how or in what measure Luther came into full possession of this spiritual and theological conviction, this revelation. But one could hardly be wrong in believing that it grew in clarity and importance through the times when he lectured on the scriptures, attacked nominalist scholastic theology for its Pelagianism in 1517, reacted against the theology and spirituality involved in what in effect was the selling of indulgences, and took up the defense of his theses with scripture as his major weapon or theological resource.

Brecht defends the view that Luther came into full possession of his "reformatory discovery" or the understanding of justification by grace through faith in 1518, that is, later than was formerly hypothesized. The premise in all of this is christocentrism and the manner in which God's relation to human existence is constituted by Christ. "The gospel now says that the God of righteousness is the God of mercy. He does not punish, but he gives, and he justifies precisely through faith in the gospel. Luther had attained a new understanding of the gospel and at the same time a new image of God. Thereby the situation of the sinner had changed completely. An enormous burden had been removed."[12] Several texts of 1518 mark a decisive formulation of this conviction. For example, the sermon of February 1518 entitled "Two Kinds of Righteousness" makes Christ the communication of God's righteousness to us, so that the righteousness of

---

11. Brecht, *Luther,* 1, 221–37.
12. Brecht, *Luther,* 1, 226. The conclusion is based on Luther's commentary on his theses on indulgences (1517) which was put into final form between February and May of 1518. See ibid., 224–27.

God no longer stands over against the human but is a righteousness that saves, God's love given to human beings in gratuitous mercy.[13] The understanding of Christ as God's word of forgiveness, offered in pure grace and internalized by pure faith, became in a way the centering standpoint for all of Luther's theology. It developed into the concentrated kernel of the Christian message itself, so that it formed the liberating source of his other theological moves.

Although this will be expanded in the course of the chapter, it may be useful to specify how this fundamental principle can be so generative. The church is frequently defined by Luther as the fellowship of those who hear the word of God and accept it by faith, so that justification by faith lies at the basis of Luther's ecclesiology.[14] But this appropriation of Christ by faith for Luther entailed a realistic presence of Christ within the believer. Luther characterized this presence in *The Freedom of a Christian* (1520) with the analogy of the iron in the fire, so that the fire became internal to the iron, and the analogy of the union of husband and wife such that in their love there were exchanges of status in identity and power.[15] The presence of Christ to the Christian thus provides a deep structural analogy for God's being present to the community objectively though the appropriated word of scripture and the sacraments.

A third transition occurred in Luther's appreciation of the church during this early period of his theology. The doctrine of justification by faith, the positive basis of all of his theology, provided him with a criterion for judging various other systems in place. It gave him perspective to view and evaluate the scholastic theology of his time, the devotional practices of the church, and finally the church itself. It also furnished leverage to criticize them. More technically it

---

13. Martin Luther, "Two Kinds of Righteousness," *Luther's Works*, 31 (Philadelphia: Muhlenberg Press, 1960), 297–306. See Brecht's analysis of this sermon as well as Luther's 50 theses on *The Investigation of Truth and Comfort for Anxious Consciences* (1518), Brecht, *Luther*, 1, 229–30, 235–36.

14. Bernhard Lohse, *Martin Luther's Theology: Its Historical and Systematic Development* (Minneapolis: Fortress Press, 1999), 278.

15. Martin Luther, *The Freedom of a Christian* (1520), *Luther's Works*, 31, 333–77. Cited in the text as Freedom. The place of these metaphors or analogies in Luther's anthropology are analyzed in R. Haight, *The Experience and Language of Grace* (New York: Paulist Press, 1979), 79–104.

gradually supplied him with a basis for reflection and a set of theolog-ical axioms for cutting through the doctrines in place, reformulating the grounds for Christian spirituality and practice, and revisioning the theological understanding of the nature of the church. One has to understand Luther's ecclesiology within the context of his more general breakthrough in understanding the basic Christian message.

One place where one can see this logic at work is the sermon that Luther gave on June 29, 1519, the feast of St. Peter and St. Paul, in Leipzig immediately before his debate with John Eck. The sermon deals with the relationship between the doctrine of justification and the doctrine of the church. The context is set by the question of the role of the papacy in the church which Eck was urging against Luther.[16] Luther spent some time studying this issue in the spring prior to the debate. The result consisted in positioning the many aspects of the doctrine of the church in relation to the center, justi-fication by grace through faith. In Brecht's assessment, the sermon allowed Luther "to express in a few sentences that what was essential was justification, while the ecclesiastical office, in contrast, had only functional significance."[17] This concise statement, however, has far reaching significance, applying not only to institutional structure in the sense of organization but also to the dynamics of sacraments. The power and office of the keys was not bestowed on a person or a single office but is a gift to the whole community of faith. The sacraments do not work independently of the faith of the one receiv-ing them but are mediated precisely through that living and engaged faith. These basic points indicate that a really foundational logic is being announced here; church institution is being turned outside-in so that the essence of the church lies not in organizational structures but in a community constituted by Christ in the faith of the commu-nity members. We shall see that Luther does this while preserving

---

16. For the sermon, see Martin Luther, "Sermon Preached in the Castle at Leipzig on the Day of St. Peter and St. Paul, Matt. 16:13–19, June 29, 1519," *Luther's Works*, 51 (Philadelphia: Muhlenberg Press, 1950), 53–60.

17. Brecht, *Luther*, 1, 319. It will become apparent later that the "only" in this sentence is unwarranted; it is an example of how a polemical context can elicit am-biguous language. Luther accords the functional mediation of the church considerable importance.

institutional structure but lessening its importance by comparison with the Church of Rome.

There was a fourth transition. After the debate in Leipzig Luther wrote two texts that summarized his position on the church and its hierarchical structure and indicated that he stood squarely within the only church he knew.[18] Some time later, perhaps in 1520, Luther began to move from criticism of the church from within it, as one criticizing one's own family, to a position that transcended the institution, as one criticizing an organization from the outside. The reference here is to the institutional church which hierarchically depended upon Rome. In terms of a distinction that Luther would use later, he began to think in terms of a "spiritual" church that allowed him to stand outside of the Roman or papal church. It is not necessary to try to pin down the time when this transition occurred; on this there are different views.[19] Nor does the point require that Luther was aware of a transition described in such bald terms. But this transition was made at some time, and it is likely that *The Babylonian Captivity of the Church* (1520) reflects its completion.

In sum, Luther's ecclesiology evolved out of his religious, academic, and ministerial life. External events drove this development from the outside, but spiritual experience and academic study of the word of God in scripture decided its outcome. The center of his ecclesiology, when it is objectively formulated, is the doctrine of justification by grace through faith, an internalized conviction that became a principle of criticism of church practice and doctrine and the source of his theology. By some time in 1520 Luther's ecclesiology was being formulated from a standpoint that transcended the institutional boundaries of the Roman Church, so that the ecclesiology being developed became an alternative to what was in place. Also, even at this early period, some of his more constructive reflections on the church emphasize the role of the Spirit in a trinitarian view of the church.

LUTHER'S ECCLESIOLOGY

---

18. See Brecht, *Luther*, 1, 325 for a summary statement of Luther's position in these texts.

19. Brecht, *Luther*, 1, 322.

Ecclesiological Developments from 1520 to 1530

The last section responded to the question of where Luther's ecclesiology came from; the question now is the way it developed.
Themes which would prove to be foundational to Luther's ecclesiology appeared early during the formative years. But while the
development of the church and Luther's ecclesiology which followed
were organic to those beginnings, they were hardly necessary: other
developments from those premises were and are possible.[20] Charting
the development during this next period aims at identifying some of
Luther's more important ecclesiological decisions and writings, sup-
plying them with a connection with his career as a reformer, and
providing a historical context for their content. Some of the mile-
stones in Luther's life over the next decade offer a good place to
begin.[21]

The year 1520 for Luther was full. He was attacked by theological adversaries, threatened with excommunication from Rome, but
supported by some humanists, defended at home in Wittenberg, and
provided political safety by Frederick the Wise, elector of Saxony, his
ruling prince. During this year Luther continued his work as university professor and preacher, and wrote some of his most important
and well-known essays. Luther was finally excommunicated early
in 1521 and later was given safe conduct to appear before emperor
Charles V at the Diet of Worms. There, on April 18, 1521, he pronounced before all Christendom his famous words: "I cannot and I
will not retract anything, since it is neither safe nor right to go against
conscience. May God help me. Amen."[22]

Instead of immediately returning to Wittenberg, it was thought for
safety's sake that Luther go into hiding for a period, and so he did

---

20. Jared Wicks, "Holy Spirit-Church-Sanctification: Insights from Luther's Instructions on the Faith," *Luther's Reform: Studies on Conversion and the Church*
(Mainz: Verlag Philipp von Zabern, 1992), 197–220, shows the consistency of the
development of Luther's ecclesiology from the early period through the 1520s.

21. Roland Bainton gives a brief account of the crucial ten years between 1520
and 1530 in which the Reformation movement took hold, including the events and
negotiations leading up to the Augsburg Confession. Roland H. Bainton, *Here I Stand:
A Life of Martin Luther* (New York: Abingdon-Cokesbury Press, 1950), 305–25. Cited
in text as HIS.

22. Brecht, *Luther,* 1, 460.

for ten months at Wartburg castle where he was by no means idle. Once back in Wittenberg in 1522 Luther continued his work as professor, pastor, writer, and main catalyst of the movement. He wrote to mobilize the princes and the congregations toward reform and in reaction against spiritual extremism and the peasants revolution; he lived at first in the familiar surroundings of the Augustinian monastery, and then he married and formed his own family; he visited the churches in the region and wrote catechisms; and he addressed a series of topics in writing, thereby constructing a coherent ecclesiology. A catalogue of some of these important texts according to the areas or topics addressed shows how the initial insights were gradually fleshed out in the course of meeting contingencies and problems as they arose, and in going back to them again for further refinement.[23]

One of the first tasks of the reform movement was to get it going, and Luther addressed this exigency at various levels. He wrote a public appeal to the secular rulers of Germany for them to initiate reforms in church and society in 1520. On the one hand, he undermined the foundations of Roman authority and, on the other, invoked both Christian faith and nationalism for the cause.[24] While at Wartburg in 1521 he wrote to the Augustinians at Wittenberg urging them to take concrete steps in reforming the liturgy.[25] In response to the difficulties that a particular but typical community was having in establishing an evangelical church order and ministry he wrote a seminal statement on the autonomy of the congregation and its right to call its pastor and authorize its ministry.[26] Analogously, but in very different circumstances, he wrote to the Bohemian church in Prague

---

23. If it is viewed structurally, in terms of a social process, the development of church structures in the Lutheran evangelical church appears analogous to the development of structures in the early church.

24. Martin Luther, *To the Christian Nobility of the German Nation concerning the Reform of the Christian Estate* (1520), *Luther's Works*, 44 (Philadelphia: Fortress Press, 1966), 123–217. Cited in the text as Nobility.

25. Martin Luther, *The Misuse of the Mass* (1521), *Luther's Works*, 36 (Philadelphia: Muhlenberg Press, 1959), 133–230. Cited in the text as Misuse.

26. Martin Luther, *That a Christian Assembly or Congregation has the Right and Power to Judge All Teaching and to Call, Appoint, and Dismiss Teachers, Established and Proven by Scripture* (1523), *Luther's Works*, 39 (Philadelphia: Fortress Press, 1970), 305–14. Cited in the text as Right.

encouraging it to move beyond a concept of the sacramental ordination of priests, and to accept congregational responsibility for calling and authorizing the tasks of ministry.[27]

Luther had to establish the nature of the church over against the universal institution which was pressing in against the reforming impulse. He did this early on, and one can see in his work conceptions analogous to those used in the conciliarist controversy the century before: Luther knew the work of Jean Gerson. Luther's appeal was to the ground of the church in faith. The church was a "spiritual" or faith-based community and communion, and not identical with the universal institution, the Roman or papal church.[28] He took up the theme again the next year but emphasized this time the doctrine of the priesthood of all believers.[29]

Another major question that Luther had to address concerned the sacraments, both each sacrament in itself and what may be called the sacramental system. Consideration of the medieval church indicates how closely the institutional church (clergy, priesthood, office) was intertwined with sacraments. The sacraments in their turn were the lifeblood of personal and congregational piety. Luther addressed the individual sacraments of baptism, eucharist, and penance in sermons in 1519.[30] But in 1520 he pushed well beyond his initial insights in a programmatic essay in sacramental theology that cut the sacraments back from seven to two or three.[31] It was noted earlier that many feel that Luther crossed a threshold with this essay.

Luther addressed at several junctures during this period the central issue of the priestly or clerical structure of the church. The status of

----

27. Martin Luther, *Concerning the Ministry* (1523), *Luther's Works*, 40 (Philadelphia: Muhlenberg Press, 1958), 7–44. Cited in the text as Ministry.

28. Martin Luther, *On the Papacy in Rome against the Most Celebrated Romanist in Leipzig* (1520), *Luther's Works*, 39, 55–104. Cited in the text as Papacy.

29. Martin Luther, *Answer to the Hyperchristian, Hyperspiritual, and Hyperlearned Book by Goat Emser in Leipzig — Including Some Thoughts Regarding His Companion, the Fool Murner* (1521) *Luther's Works*, 39, 143–224. Cited in the text as Emser.

30. Martin Luther, *The Sacrament of Penance* (1519), *Luther's Works*, 35 (Philadelphia: Muhlenberg Press, 1960), 9–22; *The Holy and Blessed Sacrament of Baptism* (1519), LW, 35, 29–43; *The Blessed Sacrament of the Holy and True Body of Christ, and the Brotherhoods* (1519), LW, 35, 49–73. Referred to in the text as Penance, Baptism, and Eucharist respectively.

31. Martin Luther, *The Babylonian Captivity of the Church* (1520). *Luther's Works* (1520), 36, 11–126. Referred to in the text as Babylonian.

priests and the meaning of priesthood lay embedded in issues already mentioned: sacraments, office, hierarchy, the institutional structure of the church. In response to this tangle of issues Luther boldly proclaimed the priesthood of all believers. The doctrine, for Luther, had the clearest warrant in scripture and bore significant implications for understanding the church.[32]

Another foundational premise of Luther's ecclesiology consisted in the fact that the center of gravity of his ecclesiology rested in the congregation, the local community in the sense of a parish or set of parishes in the region of the larger town or city. In a way, the reform movement consisted in the beginning of winning over one community after another. This certainly did not mean that Luther failed to consider the broader regional or universal church, in the sense of an episcopal see or Christendom. But from the beginning, for example, in his discussion of excommunication in a sermon of 1519 or 1520, the frame of reference was the parish community, and he supported excommunication for the good of the sinner.[33] Other works already mentioned support the autonomous congregation as the foundation of the whole church.[34]

Also very early, in 1520, Luther provided a careful formulation of the Christian foundations for spirituality or Christian life and ethics" in his classic essay *The Freedom of a Christian*. Because spirituality was so closely implied in his theology of grace, salvation, and justification by faith, this essay lent a distinctive character to Luther's ecclesiology. In 1524 Luther had a significant exchange with Erasmus on the nature of free will in the Christian conception of human existence, and this interchange provided the grounds for a sharp distinction of conceptions of the dynamics of Christian life.[35]

---

32. The priesthood of all believers is discussed in Babylonian, Misuse, Right, and Ministry, *passim*.

33. Martin Luther, "Sermon on the Ban" (1520), *Luther's Works*, 39, 7–22. Cited in the text as Ban.

34. The autonomy of the congregation and congregational polity are discussed by Luther in Right and Ministry.

35. Desiderius Erasmus, *On Free Will* (1524) and Martin Luther, *The Bondage of the Will* (1524) in *Luther and Erasmus: Free Will and Salvation* (Philadelphia: Westminster Press, 1969).

Between October 1528 and January 1529 Luther did a series of visitations of various cities and congregations. He was somewhat taken aback by the understanding of the Christian faith that he found there: "Good God, what wretchedness I beheld!" he wrote in the preface of *The Small Catechism* that he wrote to meet the problem.[36] The two catechisms, small and large, indicate what Luther believed were the essentials of the Christian faith expressed in a straightforward way to be used in families and seminaries respectively.

Finally, the documents related to the Diet of Augsburg summoned by Charles V in an effort to heal the divisions in Christendom can serve as a way of summing up this decade of development of Luther's ecclesiology. The Diet opened on June 20, 1530, and although Luther did not attend, he participated from a nearby city. Prior to its opening Luther composed a work that catalogued aberrations in church life which he had addressed in a reforming spirit, ranging from theological issues to practices in the life of the parish. The work was a virtual "state of the church" address that underlined the reforms that were needed.[37] A more constructive document was "The Augsburg Confession" submitted by the Lutheran evangelicals to the Diet. Although not a document written by Luther himself, he had a hand in it. It provides a compact summary of established evangelical positions and a second series of matters that are disputed.[38]

Developments from 1530 to Luther's Death in 1546

Right after the Diet of Augsburg, during July and August, Luther composed a strong polemical essay on the use of authority in the church.[39] It was meant to head off any possibility of compromise with a Roman understanding of binding and loosing when it comes

---

36. Martin Luther, *The Small Catechism* (1529), *The Book of Concord: The Confessions of the Evangelical Lutheran Church*, ed. Theodore G. Tappert (Philadelphia: Fortress Press, 1959), 337–56; *The Large Catechism* (1529), in ibid., 357–461. Cited in the text as Small Cat. and Large Cat. respectively.

37. Martin Luther, *Exhortation to All Clergy Assembled at Augsburg* (1530), *Luther's Works* 34 (Philadelphia: Muhlenberg Press, 1960), 9–61. Cited in the text as Exhortation.

38. *The Augsburg Confession*, in *The Book of Concord*, 23–96. Cited in the text as Augsburg.

39. Martin Luther, *The Keys* (1530), *Luther's Works*, 40, 325–77. Cited hereafter in the text as Keys.

to church law. "The power of the keys did not bestow authority upon the pope; it was given for the comfort and admonition of sinners."[40] Once again one sees the congregational premise at work in this view of the authority of the church.

Early in 1532 Luther wrote to government officials, cities, and the nobility to control Anabaptist preachers who were moving into the territory of Luther's churches.[41] The letter has to be understood in context: a given region could be governed by only one religious authority; a pluralism of different churches in a given area was not possible. Also, the commingling of "church and state," an intertwining from the medieval period, was taken for granted. In the work Luther displayed a concern for unity and order in the church: the preachers were disrupting the order of the churches. The hinges of his ecclesiological argument were the need of the call and the commission of the community to preach the gospel. Luther was aware that the same arguments could be leveled against his own reform movement, and he responded that he always operated openly and with a call and commission of a community, as a scholar and church leader. He still maintained the priesthood of all believers, "but from now on his earlier understanding of the ministry of all who had been baptized receded completely into the background."[42]

Although there was considerable discussion in the early 1530s among the churches in the evangelical movement about the eucharist and the real presence of Christ in the sacrament, it is not clear what occasioned Luther's essay of 1533, *The Private Mass and the Consecration of Priests*.[43] It is a polemical work against the Roman Church in which he lays bare the systemic interconnection between absolute ordination, ordination as a power to consecrate, the mass as sacrifice, a work, and private masses cut off from the faithful. In contrast

---

40. Brecht, *Luther*, 2, 401.

41. Martin Luther, *Infiltrating and Clandestine Preachers* (1532), *Luther's Works*, 40, 383–94. Cited in the text as Infiltrating.

42. Brecht, *Luther*, 2, 447. "In his attempt to support the ministers against the sectarians, Luther retreated greatly from his earlier views of the maturity of the congregation." Ibid.

43. Martin Luther, *Luther's Works*, 38 (Philadelphia: Fortress Press, 1971), 147–214. Cited hereafter in the text as Priv Mass.

Luther returns to his sacramental theology, explains ordination as a call to ministry, and describes what goes on in the eucharist in the evangelical church.

On June 2, 1536, Pope Paul III summoned a council to convene in May of 1537 in Mantua, in which church leaders and secular leaders alike would participate, as well as representatives from the Smalcald League and the churches of Saxony.[44] In preparation for such a council, the elector of Saxony wanted "a final and definitive theological statement from Luther."[45] Wary because of what happened to Hus, Luther studied the Council of Constance. He then composed a series of articles grounded in the doctrine of justification which distinguished between points on which he would make no compromise and others that could admit of discussion.[46] The result is a kind of theological testament of Luther and a fairly extensive schematic outline of the basic elements of his ecclesiology in contrast to his view of these elements in the Roman Church.

The council at Mantua was postponed, and Luther became convinced that one would never be called. But he remained interested in the question and studied the first four ecumenical councils of the church with the question of exactly what such councils did, that is, their function and purpose. The result was a significant work published in 1539 entitled *On the Councils and the Church.*[47] In it Luther rounded out his ecclesiology with an account of the nature of the church, a position on the powers and usefulness of councils, and another list of the signs or criteria of the true church. He also presented a schematic outline of the three spheres or orders of social life: the family, the state, and the church. These orders seemed to model town or city life; they contained no need for a universal hierarchical church. Local church, regional church, and Christendom coexisted in a certain uneasy tension in Luther's imagination.

---

44. The Smalcald League was an alliance of evangelical churches, not including Luther's church in Wittenberg, that was formed in late 1530.

45. Brecht, *Luther,* 3, 178.

46. Martin Luther, *The Smalcald Articles* (1537), *The Book of Concord,* 287–318. Cited hereafter in the text as Smalcald.

47. Martin Luther, *Luther's Works,* 41 (Philadelphia: Fortress Press, 1966), 3–178. Cited hereafter in the text as Councils.

Finally, in 1541 Luther was provoked to respond to a certain Henry of Braunschweig/Wolfenbüttel.[48] The term "Hanswurst" from the title refers to "a German carnival figure, carrying a long leather sausage around his neck and wearing a colorful clownlike costume."[49] The work was a particularly strong personal attack, but in it Luther defended the Lutheran movement as representing the true church defined by criteria; he also responded to the question of whether or not the Lutherans left the church or divided the church. These were basic issues that went to Luther's fundamental understanding of the church. The text shows that Luther conceived the evangelical church as identical with the true ancient church, whereas the Roman Church was a false church because of the corruption introduced by human innovations and novelties.

In sum, this series of texts shows that Luther's understanding of the church continually developed over the almost three decades of his leadership of the reform movement, while at the same time remaining constant in some basic fundamental principles. The next section offers a fuller systematic account of his ecclesiology.

AN ANALYTICAL ACCOUNT OF LUTHER'S ECCLESIOLOGY

The discussion now turns to the task of representing Luther's ecclesiology holistically and analytically. The last section showed how Luther's ecclesiology developed by an interaction with the church practices of his time. From that history one can gain a sense of how Luther's ecclesiology developed on the ground by his initial interactions with the church in place and the movement's continual response to the Roman Church's resistance to his proposals. Because of Luther's and the Lutheran evangelical movement's continual development during this period, the analytical description which follows should not be taken as a fixed and static system. It was

---

48. Martin Luther, *Against Hanswurst* (1541), *Luther's Works*, 41, 185–256. Cited hereafter in the text as Hanswurst.
49. Eric W. Gritsch, "Introduction," in ibid., 182.

anything but that.[50] Also, this synthetic statement avoids polemical interpretation and resists going into what some might take as important details on several topics. The sketch which follows, then, simply aims at proposing an alternative ecclesiology to the one that developed in the Middle Ages. To facilitate this contrast the outline for this analysis is not drawn organically from the internal logic of Luther's theology. Rather, according to a pattern of organizational theory, it takes up in succession the nature and purpose of the church, its organization, the members who make it up, its activities, and its relationship with its environment. This template is used in the hope that the adjustment of Luther's views to the heuristic schema used across both volumes of this work does not substantially distort his view of the church.

The Nature and Mission of the Church

We begin with Luther's understanding of the nature and mission of the church. This generalized understanding encompasses all that follows and at the same time will be further qualified and clarified by the subsequent topics.

Nature of the church. Luther defines the church in simple, direct terms, and yet the answer to the question of the nature of the church remains subtle and nuanced. One reason for the subtlety lies in the fact that the one word "church" refers to a corporate reality that exists at a variety of social and theological levels. In other words, the church contains several distinct dimensions. The most common designation for the church is the assembly of Christians, the "com-

---

50. Interpretation of Luther on major points involves situating him within several matrices or fields of tension. For example, should one emphasize the changes Luther introduced or the things that he presupposed would remain in place? Should one attend more to his polemical stances articulated in controversy or to his constructive expositions, as in the catechisms? How should one evaluate the importance of what Luther tolerated or approved in an emergency over against what he expected in normal and peaceful circumstances? How is one to adjudicate the relative weight of positions formulated at different stages in his career, or in relationship to different audiences or opponents, or in response to different problems that he faced? Finally, should one depict Luther as a radical to show his distinctiveness, or draw him toward the center in today's more ecumenical atmosphere? The interpretation which follows proceeds from a sensitivity to these tensions and an inability adequately to meet their challenge in a short space.

munion of saints," the coming together or the union of those people
who believe in Christ and possess the Holy Spirit (Councils, LW 41,
143–44). The church "ought to be called 'a Christian congregation or
assembly,' or best and most clearly of all, 'a holy Christian people.'"
But the church is less a communion and more a community. It is a
community of saints, "that is, a community composed only of saints,
or, still more clearly, 'a holy community'" (Large Cat 2.3. p. 417).

This communion of saints has several boundaries, but two perspectives play an important role in Luther's ecclesiology: one is the
local congregation and the other is the whole Christian movement.
Of the two, the primary referent for the church in Luther's ecclesiology is the congregation. The church theologically is constituted by
Christ and the Holy Spirit, and sociologically constitutes itself most
fundamentally on a congregational or parish level. This appears most
clearly in texts where Luther mobilizes the formation of evangelical
churches (Right, LW 39, 305; Ministry, LW 40, 10–11). It also becomes apparent when Luther describes what is supposed to happen
existentially in the holy community as the result of the operation
of the Spirit and faith in Christ (Large Cat, 2.3, p. 418; Councils,
LW 41, 145–46). This point will come up again in the discussion of
church organization. But for now it should be noted that Luther also
designates the whole Christian movement as church. The church
universal is the communion of those who confess Jesus Christ. The
essence of this whole church is constituted by faith, not by physical
proximity as in the congregation or by institutional or juridical bonding as in the Roman Church. Rather it is a spiritual community, the
communion of saints (Papacy, LW 39, 65–69).

The basic definition of the church and the two distinct social referents of the term lead to further questions and complications, so that
the ambiguity of the term "church" prompted Luther at times to pre-
fer the expression the "people of God." For example, when Luther
referred to the church as a spiritual or invisible reality, he did not
mean to undercut its historical and social actuality, but to insist, especially but not exclusively on the universal level, that what bound
Christians together was faith and the working of the Spirit of God
that could not be reduced to external institutional bonds (Papacy, LW

39, 65–71).[51] Second, within the whole or universal church, Luther distinguished between true and false churches. He used various sets of criteria to measure the difference. From the beginning he appealed most generally to the gospel or word of God and the sacraments: baptism, eucharist, and the gospel are the three external signs of the church. "Wherever there is baptism and the gospel no one should doubt the presence of saints.... " (Papacy, LW 39, 75). Later he developed lists of seven (Councils, LW 41, 148–65) and then ten criteria.[52] A third important qualification has to do with membership, and it will be taken up further on. But simply on the level of a broad definition of the nature of the true church Luther distinguished among members. "There are many Christians who are in the physical assembly and unity but through their sins they exclude themselves from the inward spiritual unity" (Papacy, LW 39, 66). This is reminiscent of Augustine's distinction of the inner sanctified church, the true church within the empirical church, the Dove.[53]

To sum up, Luther's most basic and simple understanding of the church contains all the nuance that is found in Augustine and the canonists of the Middle Ages. Its distinctive character rests in defining the church primarily in theological terms of being grasped existentially by Christian faith and refusing all sociological reduction of the church to external organization. The true church can be found within the Roman Church; the true church has historical existence, order, and organization, but cannot be reduced to this.

Theological understanding of the church and its mission. Attention to Luther's constructive account of the church in the catechetical works provides a balanced view of Luther's theological grounding of its nature and mission and tends to shift the interpretation from a christocentric to a trinitarian view. This does not displace the

---

51. In the end, to perceive the church as church requires faith because the reality transcends empirical historical existence. "The church is a high, deep, hidden thing which one may neither perceive nor see, but must grasp only by faith, through baptism, sacrament, and word." Hanswurst, LW 41, 211.

52. The ten which include the seven were: baptism, eucharist, the true keys, preaching office and the word of God, the ancient creed, the Lord's prayer, obedience to temporal authority, respect for the divine institution of marriage, cross or persecution, and nonviolence toward and prayer for others. Hanswurst, LW 41, 194–99.

53. *Christian Community in History*, 1, 227. Cited hereafter as CCH.

importance of justification by faith's attachment to Christ for understanding the church; rather the role of Christ is expanded to include
the work of the Spirit in the church, and this is placed in the larger
context of the narrative trinitarian doctrine of the economy of salvation. "The foundation of Luther's teaching on the church is therefore
the trinity, which effects our salvation by the earthly missions of Son
and Holy Spirit."[54]

Luther explains the theological character of the church in his treatment of the third article of the creed on the Holy Spirit. The proper
work of the Spirit is sanctification; that sanctification occurs within
the church; the work of the Holy Spirit, then, is to bring about the
church, bestow on it the gifts it needs to perform its task in history,
and to use it as the means or instrument of its own work of sanctification. The point is that the understanding unfolds in the terms
of the narrative of salvation. "Just as the Son obtains dominion by
purchasing us through his birth, death, and resurrection, etc., so the
Holy Spirit effects our sanctification through the following: the communion of saints or Christian church, the forgiveness of sins, the
resurrection of the body, and the life everlasting. In other words, he
first leads us into his holy community, placing us upon the bosom of
the church, where he preaches to us and brings us to Christ" (Large
Cat 2.3, p. 415).[55] There is a definite order to the doctrines; they
constitute a narrative sequence which is more than a chronological
sequence. The first two articles of the creeds on creation and Christ's

---

54. Jared Wicks, "Holy Spirit-Church-Sanctification," 201. The account of Luther's
theological understanding of the church offered here is in line with Wicks's proposal.
Lohse gives some prominence to the "body of Christ" as a basic doctrine of Luther
consequent upon his view that Christ is the head of the church. Christ as head appears
polemical against the papacy, but constructively it entails the church as the body of
Christ. But at the same time, "just as Luther understood the church as Christ's body,
so he saw it as the special work of the Spirit" (Lohse, *Martin Luther's Theology,* 280).
Lohse thus recognizes Luther's trinitarian view of the church in the pattern of the
economy of salvation.

55. This expresses the basic economy of salvation. Christ effected human salvation
through the actions that Luther spells out in his redemption theory; the Spirit brings
the believer to Christ through the church and in the church. The Father is creator, the
Son is Redeemer, the Spirit is Sanctifier, and sanctification is a process that is ongoing,
historical, developmental: but always with the dialectical structure that is contained in
justification by grace through faith, the dialectic of sin and forgiveness.

salvific work are followed by Spirit, church, forgiveness of sin, resurrection, glory. "Luther emphasized the relevance of the third article by contrasting it with the Father's and the Son's already completed works of creation and redemption. Sanctification by the Holy Spirit is the work that is presently being carried out in a continuous, ongoing manner."[56] The Spirit carries out what Christ effected and the Spirit does this by means of the church: "What Christ merited by his passion, that the Holy Spirit carries out through his church. Consequently the work of the church is the forgiveness of sins. For she announces the gospel, baptizes, and offers the forgiveness of sins."[57]

The question of the purpose or mission of the church draws one more deeply into the large framework of the economy of salvation. Luther's conception of the mission of the church accompanies his theory of redemption, what Christ did for our salvation, and the role of the Holy Spirit in the economy of human appropriation of that salvation. The Christian church functions as the historical mediator of salvation in Christ. The economy of salvation refers both to the macrohistorical project of God dealing with humanity and to God's dealing with individuals within the Christian community. On the large historical stage, there is no salvation outside of Christ and thus outside the church. "For where Christ is not preached, there is no Holy Spirit to create, call, and gather the Christian church, and outside it no one can come to the Lord Christ" (Large Cat 2.3, p. 416).[58] Within the church as well, salvation consists in a process or economy of God dealing with human beings. "The Holy Spirit must continue to work in us through the Word, daily granting forgiveness until we attain to that life where there will be no more forgiveness. In that life are only perfectly pure and holy people, full of goodness and righteousness, completely freed from sin, death, and all evil, living in new, immortal, and glorified bodies" (Large Cat 2.3, p. 418). In his

---

56. Wicks, "Holy Spirit-Church-Sanctification," 206.

57. Luther, cited by Wicks, ibid., 209, from Luther's catechetical sermons of 1528.

58. "But outside the Christian church (that is, where the Gospel is not) there is no forgiveness, and hence no holiness. Therefore, all who seek to merit holiness through their works rather than through the Gospel and the forgiveness of sin have expelled and separated themselves from the church" (Large Cat 2.3, p. 418). But note that Luther found Christ at work in the Old Testament, and so the historical Christian church cannot be said to limit the working of Christ.

early writings the theme of justification dominates Luther's imagination, and that remains a permanent structure of his thinking: *simul justus et peccator.* But one is not sinner in the same sense before and after baptism, and in his later writings he speaks about a holy church. The Holy Spirit works within people, vivifying, sanctifying, renewing life, not leaving people passive in sin, but urging new life by abandoning the old life and abounding in good works. Objectively, holiness applies only to God; but through the Spirit the church's mission is to become a holy community (Councils, LW 41, 143–44).[59]

The Organization of the Church

Luther did not focus his attention on the organization of the church. To begin with, a universal church order already existed, and he did not envisage creating a new institution in a region all at once. Rather he believed that parishes and priests would gradually embrace the reform: "But if individual cities adopt it for themselves the example of one will soon be followed by another" (Ministry, LW 40, 40). Moreover, he distinguished theologically the so-called spiritual church from its objective institutionalized form; he was always wary of an objective human institution usurping the power of Christ and the Spirit over the Christian conscience (Emser, LW 39, 119–20). Despite this, however, organization became more important as the movement began to separate from the Roman Church and matured as an alternative church. The center of gravity of the organization remained the congregation or parish.

The local church. It was explained earlier how the local church, in the sense of the congregation, provided the foundation of Luther's ecclesiology. The organization of the parish relates organically with his engaged theology of the Word, where "Word" refers both to Christ,

---

59. What is the holiness effected by the Spirit through the church? Fundamentally, the Spirit sanctifies by bringing believers to Christ so that by attachment to him they attain new life. Wicks enumerates four dimensions of the holiness that is thus mediated through the church. "It is, first, the forgiveness of sins by means of God's word of grace; second, the personalization of one's relation to God, by the Holy Spirit's imprinting of the love of God upon a believing heart; third, the penitential life, expelling sin and renewing daily behavior in accord with God's commandments; and, fourth, the expectation of complete sanctification in resurrection unto eternal life." Wicks, "Holy Spirit-Church-Sanctification," 212.

to the scriptures, and by extension to the preached word, all of which expressed and mediated God's communication to human existence. Behind his view of church structure, then, lie Luther's view of Christ saving and salvation mediated to humankind through the scriptural word. This occurs concretely in the church community, but only because the word of God itself creates the community. "It is not God's word just because the church speaks it; rather, the church comes into being because God's Word is spoken" (Misuse, LW 36, 144–45). At ground level, Christ and the word of scripture directly rule and direct the church. Scripture and the word of God are viewed as over against human words and human traditions (Right, LW 39, 306–7). This is the basic evangelical principle relative to the church. Put in organizational terms, the foundational institution does not consist in a set of officers or clergy, but in the written word of scripture which then has to be preached.

Another way into the foundations of the organization of the congregation lies in Luther's doctrine of the priesthood of all believers, the call to ministry, and ordination (Emser, LW 39, 151–74). Negatively, the priesthood of all believers stands over against the division between clergy and laity that had become hardened after the Gregorian reform.[60] We will see later how Luther perceived this distinction as deeply systemic. With the doctrine of the priesthood of all believers he undermined the clerical system as that was understood in the Roman Church.[61] Positively, the doctrine of the priesthood of

---

60. Luther held that "all Christians are truly of the spiritual estate, and there is no difference among them except that of office." This central conviction of Luther is grounded in the priesthood of all believers: "we are all consecrated priests through baptism. . . . " Neither externals nor office can make a person into a spiritual being; this comes with baptism and faith. "It follows from this argument that there is no true, basic difference between laymen and priests, princes and bishops, between religious and secular, except for the sake of office and work, but not for the sake of status. They are all of the spiritual estate, all are truly priests, bishops, and popes" (Nobility, LW 44, 127–29). The context for these statements was the empowering of lay princes with spiritual authority. See Paul Althaus, *The Theology of Martin Luther* (Philadelphia: Fortress Press, 1966), 313–18 for the linking together of baptism, priesthood of all the faithful, church membership, and corporate responsibility.

61. Luther is explicit about this on exegetical grounds: "in the New Testament there is no outward, visible priest. . . . We have only one single priest, Christ, who has sacrificed himself for us and all of us with him." According to Hebrews, " 'Every priest is appointed in order that he might pray for the people and preach' (Heb 5:1). Thus every Christian on his own may pray in Christ and have access to God. . . . " "Indeed,

all believers provides the foundation of autonomy of each Christian congregation. The community as "A Christian Assembly or Congregation has the Right and Power to Judge All Teaching and to Call, Appoint, and Dismiss Teachers, [and this is] Established and Proven by Scripture" (LW 39, 305–14). This congregational autonomy of the priesthood of all believers that comes from hearing the word in faith constitutes a distinct alternative to the ecclesiology that was in place because it breaks down the position of the clergy both theologically and organizationally.[62]

The primacy of the word grounds the office of preaching, and the priesthood of all believers and the autonomy of the congregation imply that the office of ministry is filled by the call or the selection and appointment by the community. All are empowered and have the right and duty to preach, teach, and pray in the name of the community, but only those who are called and appointed to do so are legitimated by the community to exercise this right. The autonomy of the congregation includes the selection of its ministers from within (Right, LW 39, 309–14). The congregations "possess full freedom and means to drive away unworthy ministers and to call and appoint only such worthy and devout men as they choose" (Ministry, LW 40, 10).

The origin and authority of ministry. The analysis up to this point has relied on Luther's early writings where the priesthood of all believers is prominent. But there is a tension in Luther's theology relative to the source and authority of ministry in the church, and scholars divide in the way they resolve it. Sometimes Luther grounds ministry "from below," in the congregation, which confers it to the

---

Christ alone and no other is the mediator and teacher of all men." "Thus it follows that the priesthood in the New Testament is equally in all Christians. . . ." Luther thus reviews the references to the term priest and shows that there is no ordained priesthood in the New Testament. Misuse, LW 36, 138–41.

62. "Here we take our stand: There is no other Word of God than that which is given all Christians to proclaim. There is no other baptism than the one which any Christian can bestow. There is no other remembrance of the Lord's Supper than that which any Christian can observe and which Christ has instituted. There is no other kind of sin than that which any Christian can bind or loose. There is no other sacrifice than of the body of every Christian. No one but a Christian can pray. No one but a Christian may judge of doctrine. These make the priestly and royal office." Ministry, LW 40, 34–35; also Babylonian, LW 36, 116.

minister by delegation.[63] At other times he stresses that the office of ministry of the word was instituted by Christ and that ministers serve on the basis of a call which distinguishes their ministry and establishes it within a context of a succession in ministry from the apostles.[64] Gerrish "resolves" this tension by admitting and explaining its existence, introducing some distinctions that soften the seeming contradiction, and then subordinating one element of the tension to the other.

First, because Luther's position developed over a period of time in which he argued polemically against two opposite extremes, one should expect a certain tension in his thought. He appropriates the view that perhaps the bipolarity of this position is "a safeguard against the opposite tendencies of Rome and congregationalism, each of which...isolates one of the two distinct lines of thought" (Gerrish, PM, 101). But, second, some distinctions help to make sense of the tension. Luther seems to have had a strong distinction between "power" and "use of a power." All have a power of priesthood, but it remains a potency unless certain conditions are fulfilled, for example, a state of emergency or other special circumstances. Another distinction relates to whether the power of the priesthood is exercised privately, that is, within the community in an unofficial and nonpublic way, or by an official in public office. It is one thing to be a priest, it is quite another to hold the office of pastor in the parish (Gerrish, PM, 98–99, 102).

Third, in the light of these circumstances and distinctions, Gerrish sees one pole as a function of historical contingency, the other as the theological rule, but at the same time recognizes the tension in Luther's thought. In his view "the notion of delegation is qualified by Luther's understanding of the church as the communion of

---

63. "The authority which the entire congregation, and every individual in it, possesses is thereby delegated to the one whom they choose from their midst or who is called by a superior.... Then he administers his office in the place of all and as the representative of the entire community." Althaus, *Theology of Martin Luther*, 325.

64. For a delineation of the problem see Lohse, *Martin Luther's Theology*, 286–97. Brian A. Gerrish, "Priesthood and Ministry: Luther's Fifth Means of Grace," *The Old Protestantism and the New: Essays on the Reformation Heritage* (Chicago: University of Chicago Press, 1982), 94 and passim, defines the problem and analyzes it at length. Cited in the text as PM.

saints, acting under Christ's commission, as well as by the other, more prominent notion of the ministry as a divine institution" (Gerrish, PM, 101). This applies as well to Luther's notion of calling, ordination, and installation into ministerial office. The passages that affirm delegation in situations of emergency do not represent what Luther preferred in a normal situation (Gerrish, PM, 102). But the tension must still be maintained. "In Luther's view ordination is only a public confirmation of calling, and what is received in calling is not some special gift of grace or power but a commission" (Gerrish, PM, 104). Ordination ratifies or notarizes calling, but calling occurs within the community. On the one hand, the minister does not stand over against the community in such a way that they could not remove him if he failed to preach God's word. Succession did not guarantee pure preaching of the word. On the other hand, Luther saw the public office of the minister as an office established by God, and ministers were in an apostolic succession. "A call issued through the church . . . is a call from Christ himself."[65]

Luther's theology of ministry has to be understood in the light of these tensions. His theology of ministry should be called functional but not "merely" functional. The ministry of the leader of the congregation is functional because he is chosen by the community precisely to exercise a power possessed by the whole community. This functionality appears most vividly over against the clerical system of absolute ordination and assignment of a priest to a congregation from the outside. According to Luther, "the priests, as we call them, are ministers chosen from among us. All that they do is done in our name; the priesthood is nothing but a ministry" (Babylonian, LW 36, 113). "The duty of a priest is to preach, and if he does not preach he is as much a priest as a picture of a man is a man. . . . It is the

---

65. Althaus, *Theology of Martin Luther*, 332. Lohse sums up the status of the ordained minister in this way: the office is one of ministry; its criterion is functional; if a congregation judges the minister unworthy, it can dismiss the minister or pastor (294). "For Luther, ordination denoted an actualizing of the choice and calling to ministerial office. It confirmed the legitimacy of the call; it was an assignment to office in the church, not only in the congregation, as well as a blessing on the office." Although ordination did not bestow an indelible character, it was not to be repeated. Lohse, *Martin Luther's Theology*, 294–95, cited at 295.

ministry of the Word that makes the priest and the bishop" (Babylonian, LW 36,115). Luther reasoned that "when a bishop consecrates
it is nothing else than that in the place and stead of the whole community, all of whom have like power, he takes a person and charges
him to exercise this power on behalf of the others" (Nobility, LW 44,
128).[66] In principle, then, the priesthood of all the faithful implies
that "a priest in Christendom is nothing else but an officeholder. As
long as he holds office he takes precedence; where he is deposed, he is
a peasant or a townsman like anybody else. Indeed, a priest is never
a priest when he is deposed" (Nobility, LW 44, 129).[67]

But ministry and organizational structure cannot be called
"merely" functional because the community is constituted by the
word of God, and the word of God must be preached. Ministry is
"the office of the word and its calling, or the call to the pastoral office
or the care of souls..." (Priv Mass, LW 38,192). And ordination
"should consist of, and be understood as, calling to and entrusting
with the office of ministry; Christ and his church, wherever it is
in the world, have and must have this power, without chrism and
tonsure, just as they must have the word, baptism, the sacrament
[of the Lord's Supper], the Spirit, and faith" (Priv Mass, LW 38,
197). Luther held that the public ministry of the word, established
by ordination, was "the highest and greatest of the functions of the
church, on which the whole power of the church depends, since the
church is nothing without the Word and everything in it exists by
virtue of the Word alone" (Ministry, LW 40, 11). The pastor of the
congregation, therefore, exercises or mediates the constitutive power

---

66. To illustrate this, Luther proposes that a community has within itself the power
and right to ordain for itself both bishop and priest. The power to ordain comes from
the common mind and will of the community itself and by election and a charge by
the community to preach and administer the sacraments. He proves this by pointing
to the early practice of electing a bishop (as in the cases of Augustine, Ambrose, and
Cyprian) and the example of the ability of a lay person to baptize as an illustration of
the principle. Nobility, LW 44, 128.

67. The functionality of ministry becomes evident in Luther's description of the
practical process of choosing a pastor. Every town or Christian community should
select one of their equally spiritual priests, "the oldest or rather the most learned and
most godly," "to be their servant, official, caretaker, and guardian in regard to the gospel
and the sacraments, just as a mayor in a city is elected from among the common mass
of all citizens." Emser, LW 39, 155, 157.

of the word of God. This constitutive character of ministry appears
in relief against the background of disintegrating forces that threaten
the unity and integrity of the congregation itself. "If we did not hold
fast to and emphasize the call and commission, there would finally
be no church. For just as the infiltrators come among us and want
to split and devastate our churches, so afterwards other intruders
would invade their churches and divide and devastate them. There
would be no end to the process of intrusion and division, until soon
nothing would be left of the church on earth" (Infiltrating, LW 40,
386). The pastor, called and installed by the community to preach
the word of God, is the keystone of the congregation. Thus the later
Luther, in his insistence on the objectivity of the office of ministry,
transcended without abandoning his earlier focus on the congregation
and resituated it within the broader context of a regional or universal
church.

Luther listed the various tasks of ministry. The primary ministry
is preaching and teaching the Word, and to that ministry "everything
accomplished by the Word in the church is entrusted.... In as much
as the office of preaching the gospel is the greatest of all and certainly
is apostolic, it becomes the foundation for all other functions, which
are built upon it..." (Ministry, LW 40, 36).[68] Obviously the task and
responsibilities of a pastor were not slight, and Luther wanted the
best men of the community in the office. He wanted ministers to
be educated and trained (Councils, WP 41, 176). He wanted a married
clergy because celibacy neither respects scriptural teaching on
the institution of marriage nor does it respect women, but encourages adultery and fornication (Misuse, WP 36, 206; Exhortation, LW
34, 40–44). Luther gave a good deal of latitude to the pastor of a

---

68. One of Luther's lists of ministries is the following: "Mostly the functions of
a priest are these: to teach, to preach and proclaim the Word of God, to baptize, to
consecrate or administer the eucharist, to bind and loose sins, to pray for others, to
sacrifice and to judge of all doctrine and spirits. Certainly these are splendid and royal
duties. But the first and foremost of all on which everything else depends, is the teaching
of the word of God. For we teach with the Word, we consecrate with the Word, we bind
and absolve sins by the Word, we baptize with the Word, we sacrifice with the Word,
we judge all things by the Word. Therefore when we grant the Word to anyone, we
cannot deny anything to him pertaining to the exercise of his priesthood." Ministry,
LW 40, 21.

congregation on matters of detail in the order of worship and discipline.[69] He did not favor women in ministry on the basis of nature and divine dispensation (Councils, LW 41, 154–55). And despite the spiritual equality of ministers with all in the common priesthood, he expected ministers to occupy an honored position in the community and spoke of this duty to respect the minister under the heading of the fourth commandment (Large Cat, 1.4, 387).

The larger church. To what extent did Luther understand the larger church, the church that extended beyond the congregation to the whole Christian movement, as a structured or organized reality? Or, more concretely, how did he view bishops, the papacy, and councils? At various times and contexts Luther's language may be more or less accepting of various aspects of these institutions. The description which follows has to remain rather general in character.

Bishops. According to Luther, bishops in New Testament "are honorable, married, mature, good men, learned in the word of truth, many in a single city, who are chosen by the neighboring bishops or by their own people. They might be the very ones whom we now call parish priests, and their chaplains and deacons . . . " (Misuse, LW 36, 158). They are elders elected not to rule but to serve the sheep. Luther attempted to introduce an evangelical office of bishop but failed for various reasons so that "the episcopal functions as a whole devolved on the princes."[70] But he could make no religious sense out of the external trappings of contemporary bishops: their vestments and the ceremonies with which they surrounded themselves, their retinues, their wealth, in short, episcopacy's whole external mien. Insofar as people invest religious value in these externals the episcopacy becomes "not only apart from God's will but contrary to his divine command and institution" (Misuse, WP 36, 157). But Luther was willing to accept an administrative role for bishops, a power that did not interfere religiously with the ministry of the gospel within the congregation. Episcopal jurisdiction would be administrative but

---

69. "A person who is commissioned as a minister of the gospel ought, however, to be able to conduct himself successfully in these matters, if he follows the teaching of Him by whom he was anointed. Now it is enough if by prayer and devotion we obtain from God such a ministry and if we are worthy, when we obtain it, to keep it and to rejoice in it." Ministry, LW 40, 44.

70. Lohse, *Martin Luther's Theology*, 278.

not religious, i.e., not binding on consciences before God. Thus he could accept the bishops in place, so long as they allowed evangelical freedom in parishes. Luther said explicitly that "we do not want to arrogate to ourselves their [pope and bishops] ecclesiastical rights and authority; rather, if they did not compel us to accept unchristian articles of faith, we would readily be consecrated and governed by them and would also assist in maintaining their rights and authority" (Priv Mass, LW 38, 147; also Exhortation, WP 34, 52).[71]

The papacy. Luther had much to say about the papacy across the span of his career. Sometimes he addressed the pope, at other times the office of the papacy; sometimes the office itself was targeted, at other times the papacy symbolized the whole Roman system. Early he came to the conclusion that God did not establish or prescribe the papacy. He deabsolutized the office of the pope in *Nobility* in 1520 (LW 44, 126–39); he interpreted the Petrine texts in the New Testament as meaning that the power bestowed on Peter was communicated through him to the entire church, and the rock upon which the church was built was Christ himself. Peter was not given jurisdictional authority over the other apostles (Papacy, LW 39, 86–103).

Luther provided a concise statement of his position on the papacy in 1537 (Smalcald, 2.3, pp. 298–301). "The pope is not the head of all Christendom by divine right or according to God's Word, for this position belongs only to one, namely, to Jesus Christ. The pope is only the bishop and pastor of the churches in Rome and of such other churches as have attached themselves to him voluntarily or through a human institution (that is, a secular government [the pope's temporal rule])" (298). Thus the pope has usurped authority, and all that he has done on that basis is injurious to the church and conflicts with the basic article on the redemption of Jesus Christ. As Luther sees it, Christendom does not need a papacy: "the papacy is a human invention, and it is not commanded, it is unnecessary,

---

71. The Augsburg Confession proposes these basic Lutheran maxims regarding bishops: (1) they cannot legislate against the gospel; (2) they cannot proclaim laws with a burden of sin nor laws encouraging the merit of grace through works; (3) they should make regulations to promote church order, unity, and love; (4) they may in no way dominate or coerce the churches in the sense of congregations. Augsburg, 86–94.

and it is useless. The holy Christian church can exist very well without such a head.... The papacy is of no use to the church because it exercises no Christian office. Consequently the church must continue to exist without the pope" (299). In fact the church "cannot be better governed and maintained than by having all of us live under one head, Christ, and by having all the bishops equal in office (however they may differ in gifts) and diligently joined together in unity of doctrine, faith, sacraments, prayer, works of love, etc" (300). This describes the way the early church and the apostles got on. In effect Luther thus recommends pluralism in the institutional organization of Christendom.[72]

Councils. Luther's attitude toward and position on the status and power of councils in the universal church also fluctuated in the course of his career. In 1520 he tried to mobilize secular rulers to call a council. His reasoning there had a conciliarist tone; he argued from the common good of the whole Western church as a unity (Nobility, LW 44, 136–39). His statement in 1539 was more considered and reflects a matured judgment (Councils, LW 41, 123–42). He recognized the institution of a council and listed what he considered its powers: it can define no new articles of faith, but can condemn them should they arise; it can enjoin nothing on conscience, but can condemn evil works; it has no power to impose new ceremonies but can condemn them; it possesses no power over secular law and government, but has power to condemn laws in the church on the basis of scripture; it lacks the ability to bind consciences with laws, but can create profitable ceremonies and procedures that promote common good order.

In sum, a council is like a consistory that issues judgments according to scripture. Sometimes a problem becomes large and a council

---

72. Luther's hostility to the papacy never waned. The papacy remained a principal barrier, along with clerical celibacy, communion in both kinds, and the objectified form of the mass, to any possibility of ecclesial reconciliation between the evangelical churches and the Church of Rome. He consistently thought of the papacy as the "anti-Christ" and an institution used by Satan. In these views and the harsh language expressing them, Luther's principle motivation was pastoral, the protection of souls from a destructive spirituality promoted by the papal system. He was also convinced that the church did not need the office. Scott H. Hendrix, *Luther and the Papacy: Stages in a Reformation Conflict* (Philadelphia: Fortress Press, 1981), 144–59.

is needed on a universal level, as in the case of Arius. It also makes transient disciplinary laws for transient matters, but always according to the ancient faith normed by scripture. Permanent, commonly possessed institutions like scripture and the catechism are worth all the councils and the Fathers. A council can condemn on matters of faith, but not on transitory external matters of discipline. Thus the nature and function of a council fit coherently into his ecclesiology.

The Members of the Church

As in the medieval period, "everyone" in Europe with the exception of the Jews and the encroaching Turks was a member of the church. Membership came with birth into society. But as the Reformation movement took hold and alternative churches made their appearance, membership in the true church became a question, and for some it required a decision. Luther's ecclesiology required a distinctive theology of membership. This is found in the topics of baptism and excommunication.

Luther discusses baptism in his *Babylonian Captivity* in 1520 (Babylonian, 57–81).[73] The foundation of Luther's theology of baptism lies in scripture and his insight into justification by faith as opposed to works. Baptism is the foundational sacrament because it is the sacrament of the basic faith of the Christian. He appeals to Mark 16:16: "he who believes and is baptized will be saved." This text contains the sum and substance of the Christian life: the divine promise of salvation the response to which is faith. Therein are contained the center of Christian existence and the whole of it, for baptism is precisely the sacrament of faith. Luther strongly rejects the tendency to leave baptism behind in the course of life as sin has been committed. The turning to all sorts of works, including masses and efforts at satisfaction, to extricate the self from sin forget that baptism sets up a permanent structure that is always operative. Not static, this structure consists in the interactive relationship between believing sinner and graciously forgiving God. The Christian "could not lose his salvation, however much he sinned, unless he refused

---

73. This followed his sermon on baptism of 1519. A good summary of Luther's doctrine on baptism is found in Large Cat 4, 436–46.

to believe. For no sin can condemn him save unbelief alone" (60). Being baptized into this structure transcends all organizational or institutional frameworks for church.[74]

Luther highlights Paul's metaphor of death-resurrection, of baptism being a burial into Christ's death so that with him we are risen, to explain baptism. He prefers this image to "washing" or "cleansing." For the dialectic of death and rising is not just a temporally sequential pattern but the intrinsic structure of the Christian life correlating analogously with Luther's views on law and gospel, sin and grace, as patterns of life. "Thus, you have been once baptized in the sacrament, but you need continually to be baptized by faith, continually to die and continually to live" (69). Although infant baptism is not prescribed in the New Testament, Luther has no doubts about its appropriateness. The fundamental character of baptism also relates it to the elementary characteristic of the Christian life, namely, freedom. And in this light, he recommends the abolition of all vows that seem to imprison the Christian, that is, public vows that link the Christian life to works that have to be accomplished. This baptismal spirituality will recur further on in the context of fundamental Christian ethics.

Turning to excommunication or the ban, these generally synonymous terms refer to exclusion from fellowship in the church, and depriving or excluding one from the eucharist (Ban, LW 39, 7). Because there are two levels of fellowship, Luther finds two different kinds of excommunication. "The first kind of fellowship is inward, spiritual, and invisible, for it is in the heart. It means that through faith, hope, and love a man is incorporated into the fellowship of Christ and all the saints — as signified and given in the sacrament. . . . No man, be he bishop or pope, nor any creature or even angel may either grant or take away such fellowship" (Ban, LW 39, 7). Excommunication on this level, if it is to be so termed, can

---

74. Baptism communicates the entire grace of God, not part of it, but the whole of it. This gift is meaningful and operative throughout the entirety of a Christian's life, not merely at the time of the sacrament. It is the very structure of the Christian life as being forgiven by God in Christ. Luther's doctrine of baptism is "nothing else than his doctrine of justification in concrete form." Althaus, *Theology of Martin Luther*, 353–56, citation at 356.

only be self-imposed as when people exclude themselves from the inner spiritual unity of faith (Papacy, LW 39, 66).

"The second fellowship is outward, physical, and visible. It means that a man is allowed to participate in the holy sacrament, to receive it and to partake of it together with others" (Ban, LW 39, 8). External excommunication has no influence *per se* on the inner relationship of the Christian before God. In 1520 Luther held that a bishop or pope might exclude someone from this fellowship because of his sins. Later, he approved of excommunication within the context of the congregation and on the presupposition of serious public sin that gave scandal. He found justification for the practice in the New Testament (Ban, LW 39, 8–9) and construed its purpose as positive, for the improvement of the sinner and the protection of the community.

Luther spoke of judgment of sin and forgiveness in terms of the power of the keys, the binding and loosing that Christ bequeathed to the church. This topic too contains various levels and nuances that overlap with excommunication. First of all, loosing concerns forgiveness of sins as in the practice of confession. Luther endorsed the practice of private confession but criticized the fact that the ministry of forgiveness had become a power communicated to the clergy. For Luther, any Christian could be a confessor; all Christians could hear the confessions of other Christians and seek pardon from Christ through the mouth of others (Babylon, LW 36, 81–91).

The power of the keys also refers to the power of the congregation to excommunicate and admit back into the community. "It means to ban and to absolve from the same, to excommunicate and to release from excommunication" (Keys, LW 40, 359). The meaning of binding is public judgment by the community on public sin, and cutting a person off in some degree from the community. Loosing means absolving the repentant sinner and receiving him or her back into the community.[75] In sum, membership in the church has two levels,

---

75. Luther sums up this teaching on the keys in this way: "In conclusion, we possess these two keys through Christ's command. The key which binds is the power or office to punish the sinner who refuses to repent by means of a public condemnation to eternal death and separation from the rest of Christendom. And when such a judgment is pronounced, it is as a judgment of Christ himself. And if the sinner perseveres in his sin, he is certainly eternally damned. The loosing key is the power or office to absolve the sinner who makes confession and is converted from sins, promising again eternal

internally and externally defined, that are interrelated but remain distinct.

The Activities of the Church

One understands organizations largely on the basis of the activities they engage in. The central activity of the church is worship; the church began when Christians came together, assembled for worship and prayer. This section gives a brief account of the distinctive character of Luther's sacramental theology that underlies his theology of worship. But religious organizations also exist to preserve and mediate basic norms and values for human existence, and these translate into ethics and patterns of spiritual life. The structure of Luther's spirituality and ethics is also quite distinct from the teleological framework employed by Aquinas. This too is included in the activities of the church.

Assembly for word and sacrament. The principal activity of the Christian church is assembly for worship. This more than anything else holds the congregation together. Luther placed the word and the office of preaching at the center of both the self-understanding of the church and its organization. Preaching God's word, mediating the content of scripture to the congregation, is the basic ministerial activity. This correlates with the place scripture held in Luther's theology and the leverage it provided him in launching the Reformation movement. While this emphasis on preaching and teaching did not undermine or subtract from the importance of the eucharist, a major shift of emphasis was going on. Compared with the theology and especially the practice of the medieval church the relative importance between preaching and the eucharistic sacrament, the two components of the church's worship service, were altered. Mediating the

---

life. And it has the same significance as if Christ himself passed judgment. And if he believes and continues in this faith he is certainly saved forever. For the key which binds carries forward the work of the law. It is profitable to the sinner inasmuch as it reveals to him his sins, admonishes him to fear God, causes him to tremble, and moves him to repentance, and not to destruction. The loosing key carries forward the work of the gospel. It invites to grace and mercy. It comforts and promises life and salvation through forgiveness of sins. In short, the two keys advance and foster the gospel by simply proclaiming these two things: repentance and forgiveness of sins (Luke 24:47)." Keys, LW 40, 372–73.

word of God became the organizing center of worship. This practical development fits consistently with Luther's sacramental theology and ethics.

Teaching and preaching. Bainton outlines the various ways in which Luther made the church into a vehicle for instructing the people in their faith. First, he translated the Bible into a splendid German and continued revising it. As a people's Bible, it was richly illustrated with woodcuts. Second, he commissioned catechisms and then wrote two himself. Families were strongly encouraged to catechize their children. He took a direct hand in revising the liturgy. He loved church music, wrote it, and published a hymnal (HIS, 326–47). The center of the reforming spirit, however, was found in the sermon, in preaching. "All the educational devices . . . found their highest utilization in the pulpit. The reformers at Wittenberg undertook an extensive campaign of religious instruction through the sermon" (HIS, 348). There was a whole staff of clergy or teachers to do this; there were multiple sermons and instructions on the catechism, even during the week, and Luther himself preached constantly.[76]

Sacramental theology. It may be helpful to begin with a constructed outline of Luther's sacramental theology before considering his theology of the eucharist.[77] Luther defines the structure of a sacrament in the context of a discussion of the eucharist as having three dimensions. "The first is the sacrament, or sign. The second is the significance of this sacrament. The third is the faith required with each of the first two. These three parts must be found in every sacrament. The sacrament must be external and visible, having

---

76. Bainton provides samples of Luther's sermons (HIS, 350–57). They mixed the doctrinal and the practical. In an example that carries the imagination into the church where Luther was preaching, we hear him urging the people to contribute to the church to support the ministers: "So far the common chest has cared for these, and now that you are asked to give four miserable pennies you are up in arms. What does this mean if not that you do not want the gospel preached, the children taught, and the poor helped? I am not saying this for myself. I receive nothing from you. I am the prince's beggar. But I am sorry I ever freed you from the tyrants and the papists. You ungrateful beasts, you are not worthy of the treasure of the gospel. If you don't improve, I will stop preaching rather than cast pearls before swine." HIS, 352.

77. Althaus, *Theology of Martin Luther,* 345–52 gives an overview of the general principles of Luther's sacramental theology.

some material form or appearance. The significance must be internal and spiritual, within the spirit of the person. Faith must make both of them together operative and useful" (Eucharist, LW 35, 49). This understanding of a sacrament follows Augustine's classic understanding of the sacrament's objectivity; Luther however underlines the importance of the role of faith in appropriating the sacrament fruitfully.

Luther preserves the "objectivity" of the sacrament, that is, its holiness and effectiveness by God's power and not from the power of the minister. He insists on the action of God in the sacrament as distinct from the sacrament being a human action of the minister. "Our action only offers and bestows such baptism, ordained and constituted by Christ's command and institution. For this reason he alone is and remains the one true, eternal baptizer who administers his baptism daily through our action or service until the day of judgment. So our baptizing should properly be called a presenting or bestowing of the baptism of Christ, just as our sermon is a presenting of the word of God" (Priv Mass, LW 38, 199).[78] The objectivity of the sacrament is grounded in its being instituted by Christ, with the promise that God acts in it. This fundamental structure also applies to the ministry of the word and preaching.[79]

But the objectivity of God's action and promise must be met by faith, and this emphasis on faith is a distinctive emphasis of Luther's sacramental theology, although it in no way contradicts a previous tradition. "But our signs or sacraments . . . have attached to them a word of promise which requires faith, and they cannot be fulfilled by any other work. Hence they are signs or sacraments of justification, for they are sacraments of justifying faith and not of works. Their

---

78. "For our faith and the sacrament must not be based on the person, whether he is godly or evil, consecrated or unconsecrated, called or an imposter, whether he is the devil or his mother, but upon Christ, upon his word, upon his office, upon his command and ordinance; where these are in force, there everything will be carried out properly, no matter who or what the person might happen to be." Priv Mass, LW 38, 200–01.

79. It is interesting to note that Luther also applies this objectivity to the office of ministry and authority within the church, especially that of the pastor. "Offices and sacraments always remain in the church; persons are daily subject to change. As long as we call and induct into the offices persons who can administer them, then the offices will surely continue to be exercised." Priv Mass, LW 38, 201.

whole efficacy, therefore, consists in faith itself, not in the doing of a work" (Babylonian, LW 36, 65–66). In explaining this further Luther puts full emphasis on faith as the mediation of efficacy or what Augustine and Aquinas understood as fruitfulness: "Thus it is not baptism that justifies or benefits anyone, but it is faith in that word of promise to which baptism is added" (66). He resists all theological interpretations that move toward an objective efficacy of the sacrament apart from the mediation of faith, that which medieval theology characterized as occurring *ex opere operato*. Luther combined the objectivity of God's presence and action with the personal character of the engagement between God and human beings. The doctrine of *ex opere operato* would represent a clinging only to the sign and not the promise, a movement away from faith and toward turning sacraments into works.

Eucharistic theology. Luther left the basic structure of the mass intact, with the exception of the canon which contained references to the celebration as a sacrifice. Many of the outward accouterments remained the same, from vestments to the arrangements of the sanctuary. "Even the elevation of the elements was retained until 1542" (Bainton, HIS, 340). In place of the canon Luther inserted an exhortation to receive communion. But within the basic structure there was a shift of emphasis. The mass was in German; the scripture readings assumed a more central role in the service; the homily became longer; the whole tenor of the service shifted in the direction of instruction, teaching, the didactic (HIS, 340).

Given his reaction against Roman practice and the debates over the eucharist within the Reformation movement itself, it may seem ludicrous to broach Luther's eucharistic theology in a few words. But the point here is the church and how eucharist is integral to Luther's ecclesiology.[80] His theology differed from Roman theology and practice at several points. First, he promoted communion under both species. Second, he quarreled with the concept of transubstantiation

---

80. Three short constructive treatments of the eucharist by Luther are Eucharist, LW 35, 49–73, Babylonian, LW 36, 19–57, and Large Cat, 5, 447–57. Luther's historical development is especially relevant to his theology of the Lord's Supper. See Althaus, *Theology of Martin Luther,* 375–405, where he distinguishes stages in this development.

and preferred to speak of what can be called consubstantiation.[81] Third and most forcefully he objected to the mass being considered a sacrifice and functioning as a work through which grace and satisfaction could be earned.[82] This is of a piece with the way Luther insightfully analyzed the systemic interconnection between priestly ordination, private masses, works-satisfaction in 1533.[83]

Luther (in Babylonian, LW 36, 37–57) sums up his eucharistic theology in terms of promise, sign, and faith. The mass "is a promise of the forgiveness of sins made to us by God, and such a promise as has been confirmed by the death of the Son of God." The Word of God is a promise; it is received and becomes efficacious by faith (39). The bread and wine is the body and blood of Christ; it is the sign containing and confirming the promise of the forgiveness of sin. " 'As often as you partake of them, remember me, proclaim and praise my love and bounty toward you, and give thanks' " (40). As far as Luther is concerned "the whole power of the mass consists in the words of Christ, in which he testifies that forgiveness of sins is bestowed on all those who believe that his body is given and his blood poured out for them" (43). "Thus, in the mass, the word of Christ [that is, in the scripture readings and preaching] is the testament, and the bread and wine are the sacrament. And as there is greater power in the word than in the sign, so there is greater power in the testament than in

---

81. Luther (in Babylonian, LW 36, 29–35) defends the same real, substantial presence as in the doctrine of transubstantiation (29), but also admits that a Christian is free to hold either position (30). Supported by Pierre d'Ailly, he argues that real presence is protected in the same degree. He also provides an image: "In red-hot iron, for instance, the two substances, fire and iron, are so mingled that every part is both iron and fire. Why is it not even more possible that the body of Christ be contained in every part of the substance of the bread?" (32) Scripture provides no warrant for accidents without the substance, and this is difficult to explain metaphysically (34). He also appeals to hypostatic union as an analogy: as two natures in one person, so that the human nature is not swallowed by the divine but is united to it as an entirely integral nature, so too, two substances coexist in the eucharist.

82. All are priests; all offer sacrifice, because sacrifice is offering oneself to God as Paul says (Rom 12:1). There is one high priest, Christ. Christ sacrificed himself once for all. That sacrifice is remembered in the eucharist, not repeated. And each one, in taking on Christ's life, offers the self as a living sacrifice to God. There are no grounds in the scriptures for the current mass being a sacrifice. (Misuse, LW 36, 145–48) In *The Smalcald Articles* Luther argued strongly against current use of the mass as contradicting the office and work of Christ and as an essential difference between the evangelicals and Rome. Smalcald 2.2, 293–97.

83. Priv Mass, LW 38, 147–214.

the sacrament; for a man can have and use the word or testament apart form the sign or sacrament" (44). Thus Luther's theology of the eucharist holds together word and sacrament (sign), but gives primacy to the word. At the same time he remained absolutely firm on the real presence of Christ in the sacrament.

Relative to eucharistic practice, Luther recommended frequent communion: "It is Christ's will, then, that we partake of it frequently, in order that we may remember him and exercise ourselves in this fellowship according to his example" (Eucharist, LW 35, 56; Babylonian, WP 36, 46). He expected that the effects of communion with Christ would be felt in the community. First of all, it creates fellowship between the Christian and Christ in which was effected that wonderful exchange with Christ: "This fellowship consists in this, that all the spiritual possessions of Christ and his saints are shared with and become the common property of him who receives the sacrament" (Eucharist, WP 35, 51).[84] It builds the congregation into a community of love. In this way it nurtures the Christian life by urging the Christian to love of neighbor, especially the needy. "As love and support are given you, you in turn must render love and support to Christ in his needy ones" (Eucharist, WP 35, 54). This leads to a consideration of Luther's conception of the Christian life and ethics.

Ethics. The interest here does not lie in any of Luther's particular positions on moral dilemmas but in the evangelical framework that he mapped out for the unfolding of Christian spirituality and life. The strong, internally consistent conception of the Christian life that prevailed in northern Europe during the fifteenth century, the *devotio moderna,* combined a deep moral structure with the teleological ethics developed in scholasticism. The evangelical character of Lutheran spirituality stands out by contrast.

The background lies in Luther's criticism of nominalistic scholastic theology for its implicit Pelagianism. He recalls the maxim cited

---

84. The Lord's Supper had a central importance for Luther in both his spirituality and his theology. The logic for this centrality derives from the words of institution which included the words "given for you." In the reception of the Lord's Supper there occurred the "happy exchange" of redemption and salvation: "Christ becomes ours, and sin is no longer reckoned to us." Lohse, *Martin Luther's Theology,* 312–13, cited at 313.

earlier, "A man is able to keep and fulfil God's commandments through his own natural powers, if he does as much as in him lies" (Misuse, LW 36, 214). This doctrine denies the need of grace and makes Christ's redemption unnecessary. The scholastics also say: "Man (if he does as much as in him lies) is certainly able to merit the grace of God, not that he deserves it, but because it is appropriate" (Misuse, LW 36, 215–16). Once again, we have no need of the mediator. By contrast Luther sums up his anthropology in a word: "Because man is conceived and born in sin and is a child of wrath he can do nothing but sin and daily fall deeper and deeper into the wrath of God, until he finally hears and believes that Christ is his Savior and has died for him to redeem him from his sins. Through this hearing, the Spirit of God comes into his heart and he is permeated with God's grace and life, so that he loves God, praises and hallows his name, rests and keeps still and lets God accomplish His own work in him. Thus, no one can fulfil these three commandments [worship God, hallow his name, keep the Sabbath] without Christ" (Misuse, LW 36, 217). No merit, no fulfilling the law without grace, no good works leading to faith or to salvation, but a bondage of the freedom of the will relative to salvific activity. In place of human freedom turning to God, Luther posits faith in the gospel, accepting God's word of forgiveness in Christ; and from out of this faith, through gratitude, the Christian serves God and neighbor in love.[85]

From this framework Luther criticized what he saw as a spirituality of works in countless forms and practices of the late medieval church. He criticized indulgences, various penances employed to gain satisfaction for sin, various devotions to every imaginable saint, pilgrimages, relics, Marian devotions as undercutting Christ, the "brotherhoods [confraternities] in which indulgences, masses, and good works are apportioned" (Nobility, LW 44, 193).[86] But one of his most important critiques was directed toward monasticism because of the long history of that institution and the ideals of the vows that

---

85. Luther's classic statement of the distinction between faith and works, and the priority of justification by grace through faith alone to all good works is found in Freedom, LW 31, passim.

86. A large part of *Exhortation to All Clergy Assembled at Augsburg* (1530) is a catalogue of problems Luther saw in contemporary Christian life. LW 34, 9–61.

it enshrined. Monastic life, according to Luther, was not a true service of God; if it were, all would have to become monks, since all
men have the same commandment to serve God. Monasticism is
no state of perfection; the vows constrict Christian liberty and often
conceal a spirituality of works and merit.[87] There is no difference
among people as regards true service of God, since it is measured by
God's commandments which apply to all.

In contrast to monasticism Luther appeals to an ordinary Christian life of virtue in the world as opposed to isolation, and a life
regulated by the commandments rather than the so-called counsels
or vows (Councils, LW 41, 124–30). While he retained a respect for
monks who were truly blessed with the gift of celibacy, the standards
for the Christian life are the ten commandments. They were contained in *The Small Catechism,* and Luther wanted them learned by
everyone as children; they were commented on for the clergy in *The
Large Catechism.*[88] Early in the career of the reformer, justification by
faith so commanded his attention that one sees little description of
the virtuous life in those writings. Later, as we have seen with respect
to the role of the Holy Spirit in the church, he freely speaks of sanctification through one's life in the world. The Spirit sanctifies daily
life according to the first and second tables of the law. A sign of the
church is that in it the Spirit sanctifies and people grow in "holiness"
until the end when no forgiveness is needed. The commandments or
law are needed to indicate lawful obligations and how far the Spirit
has advanced in sanctification. But in all of this the structure of
sin and grace, of justification by faith, and of action springing from
faith are maintained (Councils, LW 41, 166–67). In sum, externally
the ethics of the Christian in Luther's congregation may have resembled that of the Christian in the late medieval parish, but the
theological understanding of what was going on was considerably
different.

---

87. A good statement of the Lutheran case against monasticism is found in *The
Augsburg Confession,* a. 27, 70–80.

88. On one level this is in perfect continuity with the catechisms of the late medieval church; on another level the holistic framework for understanding the place of
the commandments in the Christian life has been altered.

Church and Society

Organizational theory studies the way an institution relates to its environment. How does the church in Luther's ecclesiology relate to society? The question includes such issues as the relation of the Lutheran church to Christendom, its conception of society, and the church's place among other social and political institutions. Luther did not set out to effect great changes in these matters but in fact they occurred.

Christendom but a pluralism of churches. Luther's congregationalism does not mean that he gives up the idea of a universal church. Just as in the Middle Ages, and along with the Roman Church, Luther accepts Christendom, the fact and the idea that the whole of society was Christian. But in the medieval period the church included a single vast institutional structure which had a strong jurisdictional influence on social life. For Luther the universal church is a *communio sanctorum*, bound by an internal common faith and similar external signs, but not a universal institution. He reconceives the church within an imaginative framework that builds upon the congregation as the base, and the region or diocese or sphere of a prince's rule as the effective administrative unit. He appeals to the nobles or princes or magistrates to initiate, or allow, or organize the reform movement.[89] He sometimes appeals overtly to nationalistic loyalties. The times did not allow for different churches in one town, city, or politically united region. But Luther's ecclesiology allowed for and effected a pluralism of churches within Western Christendom.

According to Troeltsch, the influence of the church on society is spiritualized.[90] This is certainly the case relative to the whole of Christendom, since the church surrenders its "universal" or "international" institutional structure. But this is true even on the regional level. The church does not influence or deal with society through power or institutional pressure. In fact the organization of the church is given over to the princes or secular authority of each locale. This

---

89. For example, "Nobility," "Ministry," and "Infiltrating" are all addressed to people in positions of secular authority.
90. Ernst Troeltsch, *The Social Teaching of the Christian Churches* (New York: Harper Torchbooks, 1960), 512.

happened because of the vacuum of power created when the Lutheran churches gave up the ecclesiastical institutional authority that transcended local churches and regions. Thus the church in this ecclesiology becomes a territorial church, similar to that of the early Middle Ages, where organizational life was controlled by a unified and unifying secular rule. As Troeltsch put it, "In theory, the church was ruled by Christ and by the Word; in practice it was governed by the ruling princes and the pastors."[91] We shall return to this from another perspective below.

Three orders of society. Luther sees the church analytically as part of the universal order of things. He conceives of society as consisting in three distinct orders, which could also be called elements of society, or structures of social life, or governments, or spheres of life, or sets of rules, duties, or laws. These three orders were constituted by God. The first is the home or family or the personal rule of life. The function of the family is to produce members of society; it is where life is created and nourished at its most elemental level. The second is the state or secular rule. Its function is to govern society and to promote and protect the land and the life of the people. The third is the church where Christ and the Spirit rule. Presumably, although Luther does not say it in this context, its function is to sanctify; it is the medium of salvation. "These are the three hierarchies ordained by God, and we need no more..." (Councils, LW 41, 177).[92] "The home must produce, whereas the city must guard, protect, and defend. Then follows the third, God's own home and city, that is, the church, which must obtain people from the home and protection and defense from the city" (Councils, LW 41, 177).

The three orders, theoretically, are distinct, but they operate harmoniously. Luther picks up medieval distinctions of kinds of law, each with its basis in God, and associates them with these three spheres of society. Divine law is exercised by the church, natural law governs the home and family, and temporal laws are made by divinely authorized government. Luther's imaginative framework in this construct is drawn from and corresponds with the city or town of

---

91. Troeltsch, *The Social Teaching,* 520.
92. We need no more refers to the law and government of the pope which is superfluously superimposed upon these three orders.

the period in a very concrete way. There is the church at the center, together with its school. There is the citizen's or burgher's house. There is city hall or the prince's castle. And God is over all. Through the word of God and the school the church influences Christian society (Councils, LW 41, 176–77).

The two kingdoms. Luther's famous doctrine of the two kingdoms certainly has a bearing on the church, but less than one might think, and it must be understood with a good deal of nuance. "The intent behind the differentiation between the two kingdoms or two governments, both of which exist side by side in Luther, is to distinguish human existence 'before God' and 'before the world,' and to that extent to grasp with acuity the spiritual and temporal in their relation to as well as in their difference from each other."[93] The distinction operates on different levels. Relative to the person, it distinguishes activity relative to oneself in relation to God and relative to others in society. It distinguishes spiritual or religious activity from temporal activity. Still more generally, then, it applies to the relation between the church and the state. In this latter application its roots go back to Augustine's views on the church and the empire and the medieval history of competition between *sacerdotium* and *imperium*. Relative to the Christian life, therefore, the Christian lives in the two spheres; they are autonomous and distinct, and the Christian is responsible to both. Against the "fanatics" he maintained that the world needed secular rule and could not be governed by the gospel.[94] The church and the secular sphere make up two distinct kingdoms, the one bearing on our relation to God, the other made up of autonomous human relations governed by civil authority and temporal relations, the one ultimately an inner sphere or accountability, the other an external responsibility.[95] The church relates to society in a

---

93. Lohse, *Martin Luther's Theology*, 115. The intent of the distinction is thus quite close to the point of Luther's distinction between law and gospel and the sphere of relationships within society and to God. Ibid., 315.

94. Ibid., 320.

95. *The Augsburg Confession* puts it this way: "Actually, true perfection consists alone of proper fear of God and real faith in God, for the Gospel does not teach an outward and temporal but an inward and eternal mode of existence and righteousness of heart." Augsburg, 16, pp. 37–38.

new way relative to the medieval church. The church exercises its influence through the word of God which affected and animated people
and flowed through them by their lives into the world and society.[96]
Church over against society. Theoretically the very different orders of church and state are harmoniously related. Both are ordained
by God. But in fact they do not relate so smoothly. The seventh mark
of the true church is persecution, suffering, the cross.[97] Persecution
and suffering come from the hands of "the world," "the devil," and
"the flesh" or temporal sphere. This occurs not in a minority church
as in Tertullian, but in Christendom. Thus, in fact, the secular or
temporal sphere is in some measure alien to the spiritual sphere;
it is a sphere of competition, coercion, force, in general guided by
worldly if not sinful motives. Meant to protect the church, temporal authority often opposes the church (Councils, LW 41, 164–65).
The church in its turn stands over against society because it represents the sphere of Christ's values and is persecuted by evil elements
in the world. Yet the church, or more precisely the Christian in the
church, should sanctify public life of city and town by its members
living the Christian life in the world. In fact, however, this turns out
to be difficult or impossible. The Christian, then, has to endure the
world. A certain split or dichotomy obtains between the Christian
ideal and way of life, on the one hand, and the temporal sphere, on
the other. The church in Luther, like the early church, is not a vehicle for transforming society but the persecuted victim in or of society.
If one looked upon the church as the kingdom of God, in Luther's
ecclesiology this would have lost its triumphalism relative to civil
society or temporal rule and been marked by a theology of the cross.

But not over against the princes. The church's being over against
society, therefore, should not be interpreted in an active or aggressive
sense. The sphere of government and secular authority enjoys autonomy given by God, and Luther consistently taught obedience in all

---

96. Wilhelm Pauck, *The Heritage of the Reformation* (Glencoe, Ill.: Free Press of
Glencoe, 1961), 53.

97. The Christian people "must endure every misfortune and persecution, all kinds
of trials and evil from the devil, the world, and the flesh...in order to become like
their head, Christ" (Councils, LW 41, 164). Luther also points to continuity with the
persecution of the early church. Hanswurst, LW 41, 197.

that is not sin. The authority enjoyed by government extends to all who exist in the temporal sphere or estate, including spiritual leaders. He believed that "since the temporal power is ordained of God to punish the wicked and protect the good, it should be left free to perform its office in the whole body of Christendom without restriction and without respect to persons, whether it affects pope, bishops, priests, monks, nuns, or anyone else" (Nobility, LW 44, 130; Augsburg, 16, 37–38). To support his position Luther cited Paul on temporal authority in Romans 13 (Nobility, LW 44, 131). The work of secular rulers "should extend without hindrance to all the members of the whole body to punish and use force whenever guilt deserves or necessity demands, without regard to whether the culprit is pope, bishop, or priest" (131). In terms of structure, for the historical contexts are completely different, Luther's position appears analogous to the situation under Constantine, Justinian, and Charlemagne, where it was a matter of course. He also shares some ideas, analogously, with Marsilius of Padua who proposed his views polemically against the reigning system.

Holy community? One can ask whether in Luther's ecclesiology the church is to be considered a holy community. Or, better, what does the confession of the creed which calls the church holy mean? The quality of holiness in Luther always refers to God, so that the Spirit sanctifying the church is holy, and doctrine and sacrament are holy because they are authored by God and God acts in them. Yet the holiness of the church also refers derivatively to the moral character of its corporate life, as in the early period when the church stood over against society, and in the ideal which is reflected in different ways in the Donatist church and monastic communities. The section on ethics hinted at the issue when it suggested that Luther's Christians probably did not appear different than the members of the Roman Church. Did the power of sanctification of the Spirit in the community produce a distinctively "holy" or "moral" people? Luther favored the discipline of excommunication; he was also a realist in his appraisal of human nature. The holiness of the word and the purity of doctrine transcend its ministers and are effective despite them (Hanswurst, WP 41, 218). Yet, at the same time, those who teach and preach falsehood or impure doctrine do not or cannot remain in the church; or they are in the church but not of the church. "Accordingly, we draw this distinction: not all are Christians who pretend to be Christians" (219). In the end, then, Luther adopts the distinction between the empirical and the inner true church, a distinction that leaves the historical church existing in society in a manner not very distinct from what is not the church in its social behavior.

REFLECTIONS ON LUTHER'S ECCLESIOLOGY

Luther's reform movement turned out to be the most important event in the history of the Western church since the legitimation of Christianity by Constantine. Before Luther the Western church existed as a united institution that spanned western Europe, not without some dissident groups. After Luther the Western church was divided into different churches, and pluralism would be a mark of its existence ever after. Following the account of the development of Luther's ecclesiology and the analyses of its contents, these reflections comment on aspects that arise from a comparison with the previous history.[98] These reflections are not offered as an argument, nor do they add up to a thesis. But as a series of observations they will serve as a summary and contribute to an understanding of what happened in the evangelical movement. In relation to all that could be said to this point they may appear random or arbitrary but not without application.

The Logic of Luther's Reform

Edward Schillebeeckx developed a category from the critical theorists which he called a negative experience of contrast.[99] This common

---

98. These reflections are implicitly comparative. They presuppose a knowledge of the history of ecclesiology that led up to the sixteenth-century reformation. Volume one of this work thus operates as the backdrop of what follows.

99. Edward Schillebeeckx, *Church: The Human Story of God* (New York: Crossroad, 1990), 5–6, and more fully in *The Understanding of Faith: Interpretation and Criticism* (New York: Seabury Press, 1974), 91–101. For commentary see Patricia McAuliffe, *Fundamental Ethics: A Liberationist Approach* (Washington, D.C.: Georgetown University Press, 1993), 3–19, and Kathleen Anne McManus, *Unbroken Communion: The Place and Meaning of Suffering in the Theology of Edward Schillebeeckx* (Lanham, Md.: Rowman and Littlefield, 2003), passim.

everyday experience can also run deeply to transform a person's life. It consists in the recognition of a given situation, event, action, or institution as negative, more or less deeply flawed or destructive of life, especially human life. Some negative situations one knows instinctively and viscerally to be such that they simply should not be. The very experience presupposes some positive knowledge, an implicit awareness or more, of the way things should be, in more or less detail. Without some such perception, the negativity could not appear as such. This experience also includes resistance against the negativity, a desire if not an actual impulse to right the wrong, to negate the negation, to change things. One could make the case that some such experience lies behind any and every movement of reform, for these three elements describe the very intention of reformation.

In Luther this negative experience of contrast took the form of religious scandal. Such religious scandal can be discerned beneath much of Luther's negative polemic. For example, his attack on the system of priesthood, laws, and the mass as a sacrifice in *The Misuse of the Mass* reveals fundamental and deeply held Christian values which he believes are being actively negated by the system in place (LW 36, 199–230). Occasionally this negative experience of contrast finds explicit formulation precisely as religious scandal. Christ said that the gates of hell would not prevail against the true church. The true church is clearly not the church of the papacy that is in place; the empirical church is one against which the gates of hell have prevailed. The true church, then, has to be a spiritual reality: "a spiritual place standing in the Spirit, invisibly built upon the rock of Christ" (Emser, LW 39, 222). This logic of scandal helps to explain the force of Luther's polemic and the courage of the reformer.[100]

---

100. The extensiveness of the need for reform and the norms by which this is to be measured have not been discussed here. That major question exceeds the scope of this chapter. The view represented here is tensive. On the one hand, as Cameron points out, one does not have to go to the extreme of thinking that there was nothing of true Christian value in the church at the beginning of the sixteenth century in order to understand the Reformation (above). On the other hand, the logic of scandal, described as a negative experience of contrast, built on the pervasive desire for reform that was abroad and fueled Luther's movement. It ran deeply in the reformer himself.

The Method of Luther's Reform

How was Luther's reform movement able to succeed against such odds, when so many earlier attempts had failed, and when so many improbable things had to fall into place? The question is not aimed at eliciting a synthesis of the many historical, political, and sociological influences that fed into the Reformation. But it may be helpful to analyze the structure of the theological imagination that was operative in Luther's writing and action: what had to happen? What did happen?

Relativization of institution. One thing had to happen: the institution into which Luther and the whole of western Europe was socialized had to be relativized. The institutions of the Roman Church monopolized the religious side of life. The Roman Church exercised a dominating power in social life, directed religious practice in the central ritual of the mass and in all sorts of other practices, and employed a language of absolutism that controlled the imaginative framework of religious conversation. The relativization of such a controlling social framework for understanding self, world, and God cannot happen all at once.

Scripture as leverage. What enabled Luther to relativize what had to appear as an absolute institution? Luther's biography and his theological texts indicate that the lever was scripture and the experience that it mediated to Luther's own religiosity: the encounter with the Christ of grace. Scripture assumed the role of the absolute, the norm which itself could not be normed, the objective principle from which judgments could be made about the structures in place, and ultimately the institution as a whole. Besides its varied objective content, however, scripture mediated to Luther an existential religious encounter with God in Jesus Christ, God's Word. What dominates this experience, not a one-time experience, but a prevailing or transcending experience, has to do with how it defines the quality of what it means to be a Christian. It shapes the contours of Christian faith itself, and how faith becomes a norm to criticize all objective manifestations or practices of religion. For Luther this faith stood over against and judged "works" of religion insofar as they were mechanical, nonintentional, and thus "inanimate objects," as he says in

The Freedom of a Christian. Evangelical experience, mediated by the word, includes the engagement of faith consciously receiving God's grace.[101]

One can point to several examples of how Luther wielded the lever of scripture to pry open the absolute system he faced. He confronted scholastic theology with a scriptural revival, indulgences and works with the redemption of Christ and grace, the authority of the papacy with the authority of scripture, and the seven sacraments in place with a need for their grounding in the scriptural promise of Christ. Another example is the way he used his conception of the office and work of Christ to criticize a whole array of systemically interconnected practices. Of the doctrine of redemption, of Christ's work and our appropriation of forgiveness by grace through faith, Luther says: "On this article rests all that we teach and practice against the pope, the devil, and the world" (Smalcald, 2.1, p. 292). This interpretation and engaged experience of grace allowed him to critically perceive the systemic interconnection between objective and absolute ordination, the practice of private masses, the objectification of this practice in the trafficking of masses, and clerical leadership of the church (Priv Mass, LW 38, passim) In short, scripture mediated to Luther a kind of primal religious encounter which relativized all objective practices or works that were cut off from it.

A New Imaginative Framework

Can one appropriate the language of "ecclesiology from below" to describe Luther's constructive theology of the church? Not without making cultural and contextual adjustments. Luther's movement was begun in a university town and was led initially by theologians. But is was responsive to the piety and spirituality of the people at large. The suggestion that this is ecclesiology from below opens up analogies between the development of Lutheran churches and ecclesiology and the formation of the early church. The way the reform

---

101. I use the term "experience" in this account with a hesitation about whether it can capture without misleading the faith encounter referred to by it. It is used "neutrally" with respect to the modern discussion of the role of experience in theology. Also, the normative character of scripture was itself structured by Luther's appropriation of Paul's teaching on justification by faith.

movement spread through local churches, and the way Luther's ecclesiology found its focal point in the congregation, bear a structural analogy to the development of the early church. In fact, Luther believed the evangelical churches that characterized his ecclesiology were replicas of the church of the apostles and the ancient early church communities (Smalcald, 2.4, p. 300).[102] The development of the Lutheran church, however, significantly differs from that of the early church because a church was already in place, and this situation elicited a vigorous polemic regarding elements that needed reform and reappropriation. But here too one finds a rough analogy with the Christian argument with Judaism. In any case, the process by which Luther's ecclesiology developed exemplifies the principle of functionality: offices and structures are not ends in themselves but function to respond to religious exigencies. Structures or institutions always relate to the mediation of the word and the spiritual effects of encountering grace.[103]

A Significantly Different Ecclesiology

Luther's ecclesiology represents a reformation of the Christian church inherited from the period leading up to his time. It should be expected that in some respects Luther's ecclesiology will run parallel with that of the Roman Church and in others run in a different direction. One could indicate the traditionalism of Luther by pointing to what he preserved from the medieval church. But it is equally important to signal that Luther's ecclesiology significantly differs from what was in place. Several basic points prove it to be a genuine alternative to the Roman Church. First, the congregational focus means that the local community constitutes the primary organizational point of reference for the church. The word "church" does not refer to the institutionalized universal church.[104] Second, the sacra-

---

102. Writing on the true church he said: "Thus we have proved that we are the true, ancient church, one body and one communion of saints with the holy, universal, Christian church." Hanswurst, LW 41, 199.

103. Jaroslav Pelikan, *Spirit Versus Structure: Luther and the Institutions of the Church* (New York: Harper & Row, 1968), 8–12.

104. At the same time, the word "church" can indicate the whole Christian movement precisely in distinction from the local congregation. This is the significance of the

mental system, with the eucharist or mass at the center, but with sacraments that nurtured the whole of life and spread out into other tangible forms of devotion, yields place to another center, the Word, and preaching the word of scripture. Third, the clerical structure of leadership, founded on absolute ordination as a permanent, ontologically constituted status of clerics who form a class distinct from the laity, is conditioned by and held in tension with the priesthood of all believers. Finally, institution and structure, office and established practice, are delegitimized as having religious value in themselves: they are judged on the basis of their function in mediating God's grace through Christ. These moves, together with their ramifications, add up to a new ecclesiology.

Cameron describes this change as moving from a hierarchy made up of sacrificing priests to various orders of preaching ministers. He describes the *terminus a quo* in terms of the priesthood that emerged out of the Gregorian reform: "the priesthood was set apart from and above other Christians, by the 'indelible character' of sacramental ordination, its legal privileges, ritual celibacy, clerical dress and tonsure, and above all by the sacrificial and miraculous ritual of the mass."[105] This priestly structure of the clergy was defined theologically, sociologically, and culturally, and it constituted a deeply ingrained system of ecclesial life. Luther's priesthood of all believers constituted an alternative church structure and thus a new practical understanding of the church. On one level the priestly minister was an equal member of the community all of whom were priests. On another level, that of office, the authority of the minister was mediated to him by a call from God to a divinely established office of ministry, but this also is mediated through the community. The minister is not called to a state in life or status but to an office of preaching and ministering. The size of the change or difference in systems is massive: from a universal system of government (pope, cardinals, archbishops and metropolitans, bishops) to church organizations in cities and regions; from the priest who was set aside, to a cadre of ministers equal to

---

tension in ministry between delegation by the local community and office instituted by Christ for the whole church.

105. Cameron, *European Reformation*, 148.

all others but judged on their ability to minister; from a whole network of social relationships involving land, property, and legal ties, to a more simplified but demanding task of ministering: preaching the gospel, administering the sacraments, and caring for people in the congregation. The conception and practice of ministry changed fairly radically.[106]

Lack of a Deep Historical Consciousness on All Sides

Wilhelm Pauck reminds us of some of the ironies on both side of the polemics between the Roman Church and the Lutheran evangelicals. Relative to Luther he indicates that in his own mind Luther was not an innovator. He was sure that what he established was continuous with the ancient tradition of the church. The Roman Church was the innovation that developed through history by a series of human decisions. The irony is that, despite these convictions: "As a matter of fact . . . the Protestant churches, formed under the direct or indirect influence of Luther's Reformation, were new historical creations, just as Luther's own church was."[107] One has here another example of the past or the traditional being introduced into new circumstances with revolutionary results. Relative to the Roman Church, Pauck says that it thought that Luther was the innovator, that it represented the ancient tradition, and that Luther broke tradition and seceded from the church. But the irony here is that this judgment too lacked a historical consciousness. The Roman Church did not view itself as a creation of history and a product of human decisions, but as being established the way it was in the sixteenth century by divine law. Thus only in post-Enlightenment times are we able to see the intrinsically historical nature of human existence and critically grasp the tension between old and new in relation to continuous historical change. Whatever church order prevails at any time is a product of human historical decisions.[108]

---

106. Ibid., 148–51.
107. Pauck, *Heritage*, 58.
108. Ibid., 58–59.

PRINCIPLES FOR
A HISTORICAL ECCLESIOLOGY

Something new in the Western church happened with Luther. In the first volume of this work principles for a historically conscious ecclesiology were drawn from the development of the one church which possessed a shared or common ecclesiology, at least in some measure at any given period. It is true that despite efforts the churches of the East and the West could not achieve communion; their differences were territorial, social, cultural, and theological. But in the context of the pluralism of churches and ecclesiologies opened up in sixteenth-century Europe, these differences seem less radical. Luther's ecclesiology proposes an alternative to the ecclesiology of the Roman Church at the beginning of the sixteenth century. This concluding section draws on Luther's ecclesiology and formulates principles for an ecclesiology as such, principles that are significant not just for a Lutheran communion but for the whole church. Because of the difference of Luther's ecclesiology from that of the Roman Church, and because of the polemical context in which it was developed, these principles will often appear dialectical. Such is the dynamics of the constructive side of comparative ecclesiology.

On the necessity and structure of reform. Constant reform of the church is necessary; the phrase *ecclesia semper reformanda* is a cliché today; few are unaware of it. The whole church in the late Middle Ages also knew that the church at that time needed reform. But such reform requires leadership, right conditions, tactful strategy, and so on, and these do not present themselves upon demand. When leadership of the church postpones gradual reform, issues tend to back up like water behind a damn before it breaks.

While all may agree on the necessity of periodic if not constant reform, less consensus will be formed around the method. In fact there is no single method: the Gregorian reform proceeded "from above," the Lutheran movement came "from below," as represented by academics, lower clergy, and influential laity. But one finds imbedded in Luther's program a structure, already alluded to, that offers possibilities. The reference is not to the logic of scandal, for this is more descriptive, but to Luther's employment of scripture and a foundational Christian experience and doctrine as the leverage of reform. The first volume of this work explained in what sense scripture functions as the constitution of the Christian community. The canon provides the classical, normative statement of the original faith, which all communities possess in common, and upon which Christian reflection doubles back as it advances in history. But one also needs a principle of interpretation that defines or lies close to the core of Christian faith. For Luther this was the doctrine of redemption and grace. Some such doctrine or set of doctrines are necessary to provide the ability to cut through the historical accretions, the elements that obscure or block the power of the gospel. No complex organization can assign to all its elements the same absolute status. Reformation requires a *reductio ad simplicitatem,* which is no reductionism, but a retrieval of an inclusive "heart of the matter," the forgotten basic truth or truths, that by comparison assign to elements picked up along the way their rightful status.

On the necessity of pluralism and division. The ecclesiology of Luther differs significantly from that of the Roman Church. Lutheran evangelical churches were also different.[109] From our viewpoint today, conditioned deeply by a consciousness of human historicity, one can see that this pluralism was inevitable then even as pluralism defines the Western church today. Moreover, the pluralism led inexorably to division. Although no one in the sixteenth century saw either pluralism or division as necessities, the conditions for their breaking out openly were being prepared during the whole course of the late Middle Ages, geopolitically, politically, culturally, and religiously. Historical and political forces, practically speaking, made the outbreak of reformation necessary, if not through Luther, then through another. This is not of course a metaphysical necessity. Rather it consists in the historical and social imperative that a single complex and centralized jurisdictional institution encompassing the whole of western Europe be flexible and differentiated, especially at the periphery. As long as it was not, the development of pluralism into the division that the reformation movement led to was inevitable. Pauck's observations

---

109. I have suggested that the churches who adopted the reform probably did not look all that different from those which did not. But the point still obtains: different self-understandings made practices that looked alike really different.

just cited aim at showing that what was inevitable in the sixteenth century is by no means so today, because pluralism need not mean division.

Reappearance of a conciliarist principle. Luther's conception of the church spontaneously employed a distinction that Ockham had emphasized, that became common in conciliarist theory, and that was given its clearest formulation by Dietrich of Niem.[110] In Dietrich's language the distinction differentiated the universal church and the apostolic church. The universal church was the whole movement of Christians united in faith in God through Jesus Christ; the apostolic church was the institutional structure that held all the faithful together as an organization. In effect, it was the hierarchy. This distinction had its origins in the canonical tradition prior to formal conciliarist theory, and it functioned widely as axiomatic in conciliarist thinking. Once this distinction is made, and the relationship between the two aspects of the church is probed, it inevitably leads to relativizing the organizational structure of the church to the service of the community of people united in faith. This is exactly how it functions in Luther's ecclesiology. It also exemplifies how occasionally a sociological principle and a theological insight can coalesce as one.

Functionality of office. Luther's historical reason, as distinct from an Aristotelian metaphysical reason,[111] retrieved the functionality of church office and ministry. In his appeal to the New Testament, the formation of the early church, and the priesthood of all believers, he showed how ministries evolved out of the communities as instruments to communicate the word. In so doing he provided the principle of the functionality of church office uncommon theological depth. He exploited the analogy between the function of church ministry in evangelical congregations with the formation of church

---

110. Dietrich of Niem was a Roman conciliarist theologian writing just prior to the Council of Constance. The distinction is discussed in chapter 6 on conciliarism in the first volume of this work. See CCH, 1, 375–85.

111. Brian A. Gerrish, *Grace and Reason* (Oxford: Clarendon Press, 1962), 136–37, 168–70. Gerrish's thesis is that Luther's hostility to Aristotle and scholastic theology should not be interpreted as evangelical faith opposed to reason. Luther adopted another form of reason, that of the historian and biblical exegete, to subvert any identification of rational, metaphysical speculation with revelation.

ministry in the church of the New Testament period. He held fast
to the office of ministry as historically instituted by Christ and as
such an office of divine foundation transcending each congregation.
He grounded the functionality of the office of ministry theologically
in the mediation of the Word of God, Christ and scripture, as that
which constitutes the church. In other words, the idea of ministry
being "merely" functional in Luther's ecclesiology is impossible. He
balanced objective office and functionality. Luther shows the actual,
formative, and constitutive character of ministry for the church: the
church is insofar as ministry functions in mediating God's word.

Change in the conception of the nature of the church. What was
"the holy catholic church" which the reformers could believe in after
the unified institutional Roman Church no longer defined it? The
most generally accepted designation or definition of the church was
the community of the faithful. On the one hand, this was no new
doctrine because it is consistent from Augustine onward through the
Middle Ages, even though it could be thoroughly nuanced. But on the
other hand, when this definition is pronounced in reaction against
the Roman Catholic, hierarchically ordered, institutional church, it
had a new meaning. In contrast to institutional unity, the universal
visible church became "the aggregate of the regional churches, the
'essential' body within which Christ was preached."[112] But this pluralism of churches raised the question of authenticity, and this was
answered by a series of marks or notes, either the four developed
by Augustine against the Donatists, or the two criteria of Luther at
one point, preaching of the word and authentic administration of the
sacraments, or a larger set of marks which distinguished to the satisfaction of different parties that the true church did indeed exist and
was found in their own community. The situation thus consisted
not only in a pluralism of churches but a pluralism of conceptions of
what an authentic church was. Reality had changed, and ecclesiology
was catching up with it.[113]

Observations on church and world. The relationship between
the church and the world will change in a situation of pluralism

---

112. Cameron, *European Reformation*, 147.
113. Ibid., 145–48.

among churches. In the course of the history of the church up to the sixteenth century, the church assumed different stances relative to the world outside its boundaries and to the world within its boundaries defined as a secular sphere. Different groups within the church also related to society differently. In the light of this history one has to expect that different churches will assume characteristically different relationships to the world at different times and in different places. For example, the very shift to a congregational and regional polity means that a church will not have the broad institutional power base to influence society on a macro level that the Roman Church possessed in the Middle Ages. A thoroughgoing historical consideration of the church will reveal that a particular and distinctive dynamic relationship to the world is a major factor for defining ecclesial identity.

To conclude, Luther led the Reformation movement of the sixteenth century and forged a coherent ecclesiology whose broad lines were adopted by the Lutheran communion of churches. But the impetus for reform and the directions the movement would take were hardly exhausted by his efforts. We turn now to the reform inspired and led by John Calvin.

Chapter 2

Calvin's Ecclesiology

Just as Thomas Aquinas was Augustinian in his theology, because all Western theologians at the start of the thirteenth century were, yet with magnificent difference, so too John Calvin was Lutheran, so that basic Lutheran themes resonate in his theology. But in areas where difference prevails ecclesiology must rank among the top. This chapter aims at representing Calvin's ecclesiology, though not in deliberate counterpoint to Luther. One of those differences, however, consists in Calvin's explicit development of an integral ecclesiology, where integrity points to a combination of theological reason and social organization. "Calvin was able to forge an alliance between religious thought and action which made Calvinism a wonder of its age."[1] But this means that ecclesiology functioned as the medium or agent for the power of Calvin's ideas. In it one finds a delicate balance of self-understanding, theological grounding, ecclesial organization in ministry and polity, catechism, preaching, worship, discipline, sacrament, education, spirituality, relation with city and state, and European vision.

This chapter follows the same structural pattern as the others. The first part outlines the manner in which Calvin's ecclesiology emerged from his life situation and developed historically. An analytical account of Calvin's ecclesiology follows, one using a sociological-theological pattern different from Calvin's own presentation. This may provide a fresh perspective with a minimum of distortion. The

---

1. Alister E. McGrath, *A Life of John Calvin: A Study in the Shaping of Western Culture* (Oxford: Basil Blackwell, 1990), xii. McGrath endorses Troeltsch's view that only at two points has Christianity decisively transformed human civilization: "during the Middle Ages, through the scholastic synthesis of Thomas Aquinas, and in the early modern period, through Calvinism." Ibid.

third part presents some interpretive reflections that may help situate Calvin in a broader framework. The fourth part tries to harvest from the developments of the church seeded by Calvin some principles that will be valuable in understanding the whole church in any given situation.

THE DEVELOPMENT OF CALVIN'S ECCLESIOLOGY

Calvin lived a relatively short life of fifty-five years accomplishing *multum in brevi.* He experienced a number of turning points in his life, but these three periods measure distinct phases of his career: his early life of preparation leading to his conversion and the writing of the *Institutes,* his first abortive efforts at reform in Geneva leading to a brief stay in Strasbourg, and his final push to success in Geneva.

Early Life and Conversion

John Calvin was born Jehan Cauvin on July 10, 1509, in Noyon, a small cathedral city with two monasteries and four city parishes, about sixty miles north and a bit east of Paris. His father, Gérard, worked in the cathedral, making the ways of the church familiar to the family: his older brother would become a priest. As for John, he received benefices from the church which enabled his father to send him to the University of Paris in 1523 at the age of fourteen, or possibly earlier, with the intention that he would eventually study theology and make a career in the church.[2]

---

2. Calvin did not communicate a great deal of information about himself or his early life, and much of the biography, especially concerning this early period, is constructed by various inferences. For example, the exact dates of Calvin's initial period of study in Paris are uncertain. McGrath puts it bluntly: "The fact, however, is that we simply do not know with any degree of certainty when Calvin went up to Paris" (Ibid., 22). I have used the following sources for this account: William J. Bouwsma, *John Calvin: A Sixteenth-Century Portrait* (New York/Oxford: Oxford University Press, 1988); Bernard Cottret, *Calvin: A Biography* (Grand Rapids: Eerdmans; Edinburgh: T & T Clark, 2000); William G. Naphy, *Calvin and the Consolidation of the Genevan Reformation* (New York / Manchester: Manchester University Press, 1994); McGrath, *A Life of John Calvin;* T. H. L. Parker, *John Calvin: A Biography* (Philadelphia: Westminster Press, 1975); Williston Walker, *John Calvin: The Organizer of Reformed Protestantism, 1509–1564* (New York: Schocken Books, 1969, orig. 1906); François Wendel, *Calvin:*

Paris would play a significant role in the formation of young Calvin. As a student of Collège de Montaigu he was subjected to a traditional education in the arts, perfected his Latin, and internalized habits of scholarship. Perhaps more important for Calvin's development than any teacher or subject was the intellectual fermentation in the city and university during this period. Traditional nominalist philosophy and theology were being challenged by the humanists; historical methods of scholarship were being applied to the scriptures; the evangelical movement was in the air. Calvin as a boy in Paris was destined for but not a student of theology, and no evidence establishes that he ever formally studied the discipline. But Paris was one of Europe's whirlpools for these intellectual currents. Having completed his study in the arts, his father decided that the young man should study law, and around 1528 he moved to Orléans to that end. The motive according to Calvin focused on career possibilities and financial reward.[3]

Roughly speaking, during the period from 1528 to 1531 Calvin was engaged in the study of law, first at Orléans and then for a year at Bourges and then returning to Orléans. "Early in 1531, Calvin graduated as *licencié ès lois* from the University of Orléans."[4] He was twenty-two years old. But other things were going on during this period of legal studies. He was attracted to the project of the humanists and he learned Greek. "The study of law had led Calvin on to a love of letters. Presumably in an attempt to gain a reputation as a humanist scholar, he dedicated two years of his life to writing a commentary on Seneca's *De clementia*, which he published at his own expense in April 1532."[5] As it turned out, the study of law and letters provided Calvin with some of the essential tools for his future work: he developed an understanding of society and institution and a critical historical method of dealing with ancient texts.[6]

The Origins and Development of His Religious Thought (New York: Harper & Row, 1963).

3. But in fact Calvin's father was engaged in a financial or business conflict with the church at Noyon at this time which eventuated in his excommunication, a fact that feeds speculation about the motives of both Calvin and his father during this period.

4. McGrath, *A Life of Calvin*, 60.

5. Ibid.

6. See Wendel, *Calvin*, 27–37 for a discussion of the significance of Calvin's humanism as reflected in his commentary on Seneca's work.

Between the spring of 1532 and the winter of 1534 Calvin underwent two momentous changes: he converted to the evangelical movement and he gained the theological expertise that is demonstrated in the *Institutes* (1536). Calvin may have spent the academic year of 1532–33 in Orléans in a post at the university that allowed him time to study. In the fall of 1533 he was in Paris when, on October 31, Nicholas Cop, the newly elected Rector of the University of Paris, gave an inaugural address that appeared so tainted with evangelical ideas that he had to flee the city. Calvin too, clearly sympathetic to the movement, also sought refuge with a friend who possessed a large library.[7] There Calvin occupied himself with issues of theology and the evangelical movement.

But what of the conversion? When did it occur? And how? What were the reasons that drove Calvin to embrace the ideals of reform? These questions penetrate deeply into the roots of Calvin's whole theology, and a great deal of effort has gone into answering them. But we do not know much more than Calvin himself confided in two basic texts. They shed considerable light on the structure of his conversion, if not its time, place, and concrete circumstances. The first describes a "type" of conversion which interpreters feel cannot be far from Calvin's own experience. The passage posits a person born and instructed into the Roman Church. Gradually, however, the mode of worship and the ways of Christian life in the church failed to sustain a peaceful conscience.

> The more closely I examined myself, the sharper the stings with which my conscience was pricked; so that the only solace which remained was to delude myself by obliviousness. Yet as nothing better offered, I was pursuing the course which I had begun, when a very different form of doctrine started up, not one which led us away from the Christian profession, but one which bought it back to its source and, as it were, clearing away the dregs, restored it to its original purity. Offended by the novelty, I lent an unwilling ear, and at first, I confess, strenuously and passionately resisted.... One thing in particu-

---

7. Louis du Tillet, canon of Angoulême and rector of Claix.

lar made me averse to those new teachers, namely, reverence for
the Church. But when once I opened my ears and allowed myself to be taught, I perceived that this fear of derogating from the
majesty of the Church was groundless. For they reminded me
how great the difference is between schism from the Church,
and studying to correct the faults by which the Church herself
is contaminated.[8]

He subsequently felt scandalized by his former life, condemned it,
and humbly appealed to God's forgiveness.

In the second text, which is authentically autobiographical and
written in 1557, he describes himself in this way:

And first, since I was too obstinately devoted to the superstitions of Popery to be easily extricated from so profound an abyss
of mire, God by a sudden conversion subdued and brought my
mind to a teachable frame, which was more hardened in such
matters than might have been expected from one at my early period of life. Having thus received some taste and knowledge of
true godliness, I was immediately inflamed with so intense a desire to make progress therein, that although I did not altogether
leave off other studies, I yet pursued them with less ardour. I
was quite surprised to find that before a year had elapsed, all
who had any desire after purer doctrine were continually coming to me to learn, although I myself was as yet but a mere
novice and tyro.[9]

But what was "the year" in which this took place? A good guess is
1533–34 because in early May of 1534 he surrendered his benefices
to the Canons of the cathedral of Noyon.[10]

It is not clear where Calvin resided during the remaining months
of that year, but after evangelical demonstrations in several French
cities in October led to a severe backlash, Calvin decided to leave

---

8. John Calvin, "Reply by John Calvin to the letter by Cardinal Sadolet to the Senate and People of Geneva," *Calvin: Theological Treatises* (London: SCM Press, 1954),
250–53, citation at 251–52. Cited hereafter as Reply by page number of this edition.

9. John Calvin, *Commentaries*, IV, "The Author's Preface," *Commentary on the
Book of Psalms* (Grand Rapids: Baker Book House, 1981), xl–xli.

10. Wendel, *Calvin*, 42.

France. He settled in Basle in early 1535. In August of that year Calvin signed the dedicatory letter to the King of France introducing his *Institutes of the Christian Religion* which were published the following year in March when Calvin was not yet twenty-seven years old.

The *Institutes* (1536), a major theological work, immediately established Calvin as a significant evangelical theologian.[11] The work contains Calvin's first public statement on the nature of the church. He drew from many sources: scripture, the fathers, especially Augustine, contemporary evangelical theologians such as Bucer, Zwingli, and Melanchthon, but especially Luther. The structure of this first version of the *Institutes* generally followed the outline of Luther's Small Catechism.[12] While most of the *Institutes* (1536) are drawn up into the edition of 1559 which will be studied more closely in the next part of this chapter, some notes on his earliest ecclesiological thinking will help in understanding how he developed.

In his introductory letter to Francis I Calvin explained the purpose of the *Institutes* to summarize, especially for the French, "certain rudiments" of the true faith and "the nature of the doctrine" contained in the evangelical movement. He also reduced the basic errors of the Roman Church concerning the nature of the church to two: the view that the form of the true church "is always apparent and observable," and that this visible form is identified with "the see of the Roman Church and its hierarchy." By contrast, the evangelicals hold that "the church can exist without any visible appearance, and that its appearance is not contained within that outward magnificence...." The true church appears rather in "the

---

11. The term *institutio* or institution or institutes is associated with education and teaching. The *Institutes of the Christian Religion* was thus a textbook of the Christian Religion or of Christian Religious Education. Cottret, *Calvin,* 112–13; Bouwsma, *John Calvin,* 17.

12. The six chapters treated: (1) law and the commandments, (2) faith in terms of the creed, (3) prayer with an exposition of the Lord's Prayer, (4) the sacraments, (5) the five false sacraments of the Roman Church, echoing Luther's *Babylonian Captivity,* and (6) Christian freedom, ecclesiastical power, and political administration, three aspects of the public order in a Christian city or state. John Calvin, *Institutes of the Christian Religion (1536),* ed. H. H. Meeter Center for Calvin Studies (Grand Rapids: Eerdmans, 1986). Cited hereafter as *Institutes* (1536) by chapter and paragraph.

pure preaching of God's Word and the lawful administration of the sacraments."[13]

Calvin's most constructive reflections on the church appear in Chapter II, where he treats the fourth part of the creed (II.21–34). There one sees that already in 1536, before contact with Geneva, Calvin had formulated some basic notions that became typical of his ecclesiology. The nature of the church, catholic and holy, is such that it includes all the elect, angels and humans, dead or alive (II.21). He closely links membership in the church with election and salvation (II.23–24, 31). He defends the power of excommunication to protect the holiness of the church in its faith and sacrament (II.26–28). He develops the ideas of visible and invisible church and the communion of saints (II.29–30). Calvin devotes a separate chapter to sacramental theology and the sacraments of baptism and the Lord's Supper. Interestingly, he presents some detailed recommendations for the order of worship, especially relative to the Lord's Supper (IV.53).

Chapter VI, entitled "Christian Freedom, Ecclesiastical Power, Political Administration," deals with Christian life, lived in freedom before God and neighbor, but within the context of the twofold government or rule in human existence: the inner and the outer, the spiritual and the temporal. "The one we may call the spiritual kingdom, the other, the political kingdom" (VI.13). He develops delicate balances between Christian freedom and public responsibility. He relativizes church power to being a vehicle of God's authority, and at the same time insists on the necessity of church order. And he develops a theory of civil government that remains quite consistent in later editions of the *Institutes*.

In all, with the first publication of the *Institutes* in 1536, Calvin had traveled far and accomplished a great deal since he had left Paris as a teenager to begin the study of law eight years earlier. And he had yet to embark on his life's work in Geneva for which he is remembered.

---

13. Calvin, "Epistle Dedicatory to Francis, King of the French," *Institutes* (1536), 1, 6.

Geneva and First Efforts at Church Organization

The second phase of Calvin's career, from 1536 to 1541, contributed significantly to the formation of his ecclesiology. These years included an initial residence in Geneva during which he worked with Guillaume Farel at organizing a church which only recently had decided to embrace the reform. But his first work there ended in failure, and from 1538 to 1541 he served as pastor of a French church in Strasbourg. One must begin this phase of Calvin's life with an introduction to Geneva.

Geneva in the early sixteenth century. Calvin organized the church in Geneva, but Geneva helped shape the ecclesiology that emerged in and with that church. Three elements of the city in particular had a direct bearing on the church: its recent political history, its governmental structure, and the various competing factions in the city.

Geneva was a city of about ten thousand people, with a trading economy, ruled temporally and spiritually by a prince-bishop right up into the 1530s.[14] The city related to the Swiss in cities to the north and east and to the French to the west. Since the mid-fifteenth century the duchy of Savoy virtually appointed and controlled the bishop; but increasingly Genevans looked to the Swiss as a counterweight to the Savoyards. In the 1520s the Reformation spread to Zurich and Bern, but the main source of energy in Geneva during the 1520s and early 1530s came from a desire for political autonomy, so that in various respects acceptance of the evangelical movement functioned as a way of gaining political leverage for independence, or at least always in tandem with that goal. The ruling city council gradually assumed more governing authority from the bishop and church canons in the course of the 1520s. In 1535, under the influence of Farel, the city magistrates suspended the celebration of the mass. In May 1536, the city finally decided for the reform, and the move solidified their independence from the bishop and Catholic Savoy, even though it left them vulnerable to the influence of Bern. Relative to Calvin and the organization of a reformed church, this recent history meant that the

---

14. E. William Monter, *Calvin's Geneva* (Huntington, N.Y.: Robert E. Krieger, 1975), 2, puts the population of Geneva at 10,300 in 1537.

magistrates of the newly independent city were resolved "not to sub-
stitute the tyranny of a reformer for that of a Catholic bishop."[15] The
church could only be built through a process of symbiosis with the
city; concretely this meant give and take with the city magistrates.

Geneva's city government evolved over decades and gradually assumed more authority until the city became an independent republic.
It consisted in a series of councils at the center of which were four ex-
ecutives or syndics. These four were the leaders of the Small Council
consisting of twenty five members. This was the main administrative body of government, and it met in city hall three times a week.
A Council of Sixty, consulted by the Small Council in important
matters especially regarding foreign affairs, played a minor role in
government. The next important entity was the Council of Two
Hundred which met once a month. This deliberative body considered legislation and also, once a year, elected the members of the
Small Council. Then, finally, a General Assembly, or gathering of
all the male citizens of Geneva, assembled twice a year or when a
crisis demanded it. This body elected the four syndics that led the
government.[16]

As a matter of course every social-political body and every government will harbor a variety interests: different factions live by different
group loyalties. Part of the city was more loyal to France, or to the
Savoyards whose language was closer to the Genevans' than was
French, while others favored alliances with the Swiss in Fribourg or
Bern. Some would be Catholic in their sympathies while others obviously welcomed the reform. Any given issue could generate different
sets of competing interests. A faction of Genevans who favored the
reform professed loyalty to Farel; others wanted closer affiliation with
the church of Bern. Many of the reformers, including Farel, Calvin,
and many of the ministers, were not Genevans. The organization of
the new evangelical reformed church at Geneva, then, could only be

---

15. McGrath, *A Life of John Calvin*, 85. As Wendel puts it, "the civil authorities had
no wish to find themselves confronted by a new ecclesiastical authority, which would
soon have tried to make itself independent of the political power." Wendel, *Calvin*,
52–53.

16. This description is drawn from Parker, *John Calvin*, 55–56 and Wendel,
Calvin, 50.

negotiated slowly: it required patient interaction between a newly autonomous city government, which always retained some power over the church, and the suasive powers of the new church leaders. This made the challenge confronting Calvin formidable.

Calvin's first efforts at church leadership. The story of Calvin's being enlisted as a church organizer in Geneva rivals the story of Augustine's conversion. After his *Institutes* were published in March of 1536 Calvin traveled to Ferrara for a relatively brief visit and afterward, during the summer, traveled to Paris to take care of family business. In Paris he persuaded his younger brother and sister to accompany him to Strasbourg. But because of warring armies, he had to take a longer southern route which entailed an overnight in Geneva. Farel, who had been leading the evangelical movement in Geneva since 1532, learned of Calvin's arrival, and along with others met with him, and prevailed upon him to stay in Geneva. Calvin was reluctant until Farel, as Calvin put it later, detained him at Geneva, not so much by counsel and exhortation "as by a dreadful imprecation, which I felt to be as if God had from heaven laid his mighty hand upon me to arrest me.... [Farel] proceeded to utter an imprecation that God would curse my retirement, and the tranquility of the studies which I sought, if I should withdraw and refuse to give assistance, when the necessity was so urgent. By this imprecation I was so stricken with terror, that I desisted from the journey which I had undertaken."[17] This incident induced in Calvin the lasting conviction that he was sent by God to Geneva, and that his work there was God's work.

Thus in August of 1536 Calvin began his career as an organizer of the church in Geneva. The city hired him in the official position of "Reader in Holy Scripture to the church in Geneva,"[18] that is, teacher; but he would soon assume as well the positions of preacher and pastor, and he assisted in the task of church organization. Such church organization was quite lacking: there was little more than regular preaching in the city when Calvin arrived. But Calvin and Farel together lost little time in putting some fundamental documents in

---

17. Calvin, "The Author's Preface," *Commentary on the Book of Psalms*, xlii–xliii.
18. Wendel, *Calvin*, 50; McGrath, *A Life of Calvin*, 96.

place that would help shape the identity of a church. On November 10, 1536, they submitted to the Small Council a "Confession of Faith" that was clearly intended to define the new church as evangelical and weed out those who had not opted for the reform. It proposed that there is only one true church, which exists wherever the gospel is "purely and faithfully preached" and the sacraments "properly administered." "Hence the churches governed by the ordinances of the pope are rather synagogues of the devil than Christian churches."[19]

Early in 1537 the city's General Assembly elected four syndics who were sympathetic to Farel, and on January 16 the body of ministers of the church of Geneva presented to the Small Council certain articles of faith which would serve as a structural basis for the church. Presumably Calvin wrote these articles.[20] They were not laid out schematically, and altogether they contain a number of distinct provisions. In effect they amounted to petitions addressed to the magistrates of the city, since neither the ministers nor Calvin had the authority to enforce them. But they pointed a clear direction for the church as it was emerging in Calvin's planning and negotiation with the city. Some of the major provisions were as follows: (1) Monthly celebration of the Lord's Supper, a provision which was not accepted. (2) The discipline of excommunication, for "if there is in us any fear of God, this ordinance must have place in our Church" (Articles, 51). (3) The ministers petitioned the Small Council to appoint persons who "should be dispersed and distributed in all the quarters of the city, having oversight of the life and government of each of them." This group was to report to the ministers, and this could lead in serious matters to excommunication (Articles, 52). (4) The ministers asked that all the people of the Genevan church witness to the confession of faith of 1536 as a test of their loyalty to the reform. It explicitly asked the magistrates to lead the way (Articles, 53). (5) The articles urged the singing of psalms at assemblies for

---

19. "Confession of Faith which all the citizens and inhabitants of Geneva and the subjects of the country must promise to keep and hold," *Calvin: Theological Treatises,* ed. J. K. S. Reid (London: SCM, 1954), par. 18, p. 31.

20. John Calvin, "Articles concerning the Organization of the Church and of Worship at Geneva proposed by the Ministers at the Council," *Calvin: Theological Treatises,* 48–55. Cited as Articles by page number of this edition.

worship and asked that choirs of children be set up to lead the others in song. (Articles, 51–52). (6) The articles prescribed instruction for children in the basics of the faith, and that periodically they be examined by the ministers (Articles, 52). (7) And, finally, the articles asked that the magistrates set up a committee including ministers which would design ordinances concerning marriage relative to common cases and then judge and decide the various cases that had arisen (Articles, 54–55).

During the first part of 1537 Calvin also wrote a catechism in French, entitled *Instruction in Faith*, intended primarily for the instruction of children, but in the end far too difficult for them.[21] But it served as another pillar of support for the formation of the church. Early paragraphs define a Christian vision in terms of a basic anthropology and scheme of redemption as they treat knowledge of God, true religion, human existence, free will and sin, and restoration to salvation and life. This is followed by sections paralleling his *Institutes*. The last section dealing with the powers of the pastors of the church and civil magistracy emphasize the functional character of the office of ministry: it exists as a mediation of the Word and the sacraments, and its power and authority lie in the Word. But like Luther in his commentary on the fourth commandment Calvin underscores the authority of the ministers: "Of no slight importance is the fact that the Lord testified once for all that when they are received, he is received; likewise when they are rejected, he is rejected. And in order that their ministry will not be contemptible they are equipped with a notable commandment of binding and loosing..." (Instruction, 30, p. 36).

These aggressive moves of Calvin and Farel met with resistance. "Genevans did not like being forced to attend sermons, any more than they liked the threat of excommunication."[22] Many were not willing to sign on to the Confession of Faith, and the magistrates

---

21. Calvin translated this catechism into Latin in 1538 so that it would be widely accessible in Europe and help in solidifying the various churches of the Reformation movement. I. John Hesselink, *Calvin's First Catechism: A Commentary* (Louisville: Westminster John Knox Press, 1997) contains a translation of the Latin version. Cited in the text as Instruction by paragraph and page.

22. McGrath, *A Life of Calvin*, 99.

were not eager to lead the way. "In July they rejected the plan for discipline, reserving to themselves the supervision of public morals. . . ."[23] It would be years before Calvin won for the church the right of excommunication. The election of the syndics in early 1538 reflected the backlash: they were sympathetic to Bernese ways of ordering the church. In the spring of that year the magistrates legislated that in certain concrete matters the church of Geneva would follow the church of Bern. Calvin reacted against what he took as interference in the autonomy of the church. And the magistrates responded in turn: "The Small Council, the Two Hundred and the General Assembly held meetings in succession, and solemnly confirmed the adoption of the Bernese ceremonies. Calvin, Farel and another minister were deprived of their functions and ordered to leave the town within three days."[24]

Pastor of a French church in Strasbourg (1538–41.) Calvin thought first of returning to Basle and scholarly activity, but finally yielded to the request that he become the pastor of a church of French refugees in Strasbourg. He arrived in Strasbourg in September 1538. The experience of being a pastor of a church of between four and five hundred members, where he preached or lectured every day, confirmed him in a life of ministry that seemed to have been undermined at Geneva.[25] He accomplished much in three years. He learned how to organize a parish congregation both from the other churches in Strasbourg and in a way that corresponded to his concerns for singing the psalms, catechetical instruction, discipline, and reserve concerning who would participate in the Lord's Supper. He also participated in ecumenical exchanges with other churches and leaders of the reformation movement. "By 1541, Calvin had gained considerable practical experience of church management and had given much thought to the theory of church and civil

---

23. Wendel, *Calvin*, 52.

24. Ibid., 56. Naphy stresses the political character of this event. "The ministers in no way played a major role in the 1538 events. They were simply caught up in a political dispute in Geneva which revolved around the issue of the Republic's relationship with its military protector, Berne." Naphy, *Calvin and the Consolidation of the Genevan Reformation*, 222.

25. Parker, *John Calvin*, 67–70.

polity and discipline (in which he was considerably influenced by Bucer)."[26]

The multifaceted relationship between Calvin and Martin Bucer (1491–1551), former Dominican and leader of the church in Strasbourg, was significant and profound.[27] Bucer helped Calvin in his initial steps as the new pastor of a church. He was the catalyst in Strasbourg for stimulating his developing ideas about liturgy, eucharistic theology, church organization, and questions about order and discipline. Bucer encouraged Calvin's marriage, and he urged Calvin's return to Geneva when the invitation came. Their relationship transcended personal acquaintance and reached the level of revered mentor and father figure. After Calvin returned to Geneva, while he awaited the reaction of the city magistrates to his plan for the church, Calvin spoke plainly of his devotion to Bucer: "And if in any way I do not answer your expectation, you know that I am under your power, and subject to your authority. Admonish, chastise, and exercise all the powers of a father over his son." He closed the letter with this phrase: "Adieu, my much honored father in the Lord."[28]

Calvin continued to write prolifically at Strasbourg. His works during this period included his translation of the French catechism into Latin. He finished a new edition of his *Institutes* in 1538 and it was published the following year. He translated it into French in 1541. In March of 1541 he published a commentary on *Romans*. And in the same year he wrote his *Little Treatise on Holy Communion* in which he sought "to interpret the relevant biblical data in a new way, more or less independently of the Roman, Lutheran or Zwinglian explanations."[29]

In 1539 Calvin wrote his *Reply to Sadoleto*, a work that bears some significance for understanding the development of Calvin's concept

---

26. McGrath, *A Life of Calvin*, 102.

27. Historians emphasize the many lessons Calvin learned in Strasbourg and in particular the impact that Bucer had in his development. See Cottret, *Calvin*, 132–56; Bouwsma, *John Calvin*, 21–24; Alexandre Ganoczy, *Calvin: Théologien de l'Eglise et du Ministère* (Paris: Editions du Cerf, 1964), 184.

28. Letter of John Calvin to Bucer, October 15, 1541, in Jules Bonnet, ed., *Letters of John Calvin* (New York: Burt Franklin, 1972), 294–95.

29. Wendel, *Calvin*, 62.

of the church.[30] Sensing disarray in the church at Geneva, Cardinal
Sadoleto addressed the magistrates and citizens of the city of Geneva
inviting their return to the Roman Church. It became clear that no
one could better answer the letter than Calvin, even though he was
in Strasbourg. In responding, Calvin was forced to face the most fundamental criticisms of the reform movement in a public way. This
meant that he reached for what he took to be foundational principles
of Christianity and the church.

First of all Calvin reminds Sadoleto that the reform movement had
achieved some important results: it returned to civil rulers what is
theirs by God's design, the temporal authority appropriated by clerics;
it had also broken the system of ecclesiastical wealth and returned
ministers to a frugal lifestyle (Reply, 226–27). Second, Christian piety
is being realigned away from too much concern with the self and
happiness to dedication to the glory and sanctity of God: "For we are
born first of all for God, and not for ourselves" (Reply, 228). Third,
the reformers did not leave the church, any more than prophets do
when they seek to reform it. The very charge misunderstands the
nature of the true church. Here Calvin shows his conviction that
the reformed churches lie closer in identity to the early church than
does the Roman Church (Reply, 224–45, 229, 231, 249). But, fourth,
Calvin emphasizes that moral issues in no sense or degree constitute
the motive that drives the reform of the church. For Calvin the Spirit
governs the church,[31] but always as bound by the Word (Reply, 229–
31), so that the real problem in the Roman Church consists in the
fact that the Word has been buried, and the pastoral office for mediating the Word subverted (Reply, 241). Fifth, then, the unity of the
church needs grounding in Christ the head, and cannot lie in solidarity with leaders who subvert Christ's truth. "Nor did I think that I
dissented from thy Church, because I was at war with those leaders"
(Reply, 249). Along the way Calvin lists what might be called the

---

30. *Calvin: Theological Treatises*, 221–56. Cardinal Jacopo Sadoleto was bishop of
Carpentras in southern France. Sadoleto=Sadolet. See n. 8, above, for the full title of
this work.
31. "There is then nothing of Christ in him who does not hold the elemental principle, that it is God alone who enlightens our minds to perceive his truth, who by his
Spirit seals it on our hearts, and by his sure testimony of it confirms our conscience."
Reply, 244.

three pillars of the church: "doctrine, discipline, and the sacraments; and to these a fourth is added: ceremonies, by which to exercise the people in offices of piety" (Reply, 232). These themes are subsumed into Calvin's systematic ecclesiology in the *Institutes* of 1559.

Meanwhile, back in Geneva the tensions with Bern continued as the two cities sought to define more exactly their political relationship. In the course of 1539 and 1540, in a series of events, the pro-Bernese faction in Geneva appeared to be working at cross purposes to the interests of their own city, and this gradually undermined the premise of the disgrace of Farel and Calvin in 1538. But the church remained in disarray. Thus in 1540 the magistrates decided to invite Farel and Calvin back to Geneva. Farel could not come; Calvin did not want to come. But once again he was persuaded to consider the move as God's will. With that understanding he again entered the city of Geneva on September 13, 1541.

Full Development of Calvin's Ecclesiology

If the *Institutes* of 1559 represent the "full development" of Calvin's ecclesiology, he only arrived there through time and historical struggle. We have seen his conviction that the New Testament and the early church provided some kind of blueprint for the church; but its actualization in Geneva required negotiation and compromise. Rather than represent that development in detail, what follows indicates how it occurred by chronicling some significant texts and events.

The "Ordinances." The "Draft Ecclesiastical Ordinances" were commissioned by the city magistrates upon Calvin's return, and he drafted them in committee with the other ministers and six members of the Small Council. Once submitted they went through some revisions in the Small Council and the Two Hundred before being accepted by the General Assembly on Nov. 20, 1541.[32]

Calvin intended this relatively short document to serve as a kind of constitution of the church; it is written in a dry, legal language of prescription. These Ordinances greatly surpass his earlier Articles;

---

32. John Calvin, "Draft Ecclesiastical Ordinances (September and October, 1541)," *Calvin: Theological Treatises*, 58–72. Reference in the text is to page number in this edition.

the three years in Strasbourg had made a difference. Whether or not the basic ideology or theology of the church was fully worked out, one can see in these provisions a holistic account of the structure of the Christian church. A detailed account of the provisions outlined here will be subsumed into the representation of Calvin's ecclesiology in the section which follows, but a brief abstract statement of the content and its significance is appropriate.

First of all, Calvin posits the four orders of ministry, which are pastors, teachers, elders, and deacons, in some detail, thus laying down for the first time his conception of the structure of ministry. He is, moreover, quite detailed in his stipulations for the choice, examination, authorization, induction, and continued oversight of the pastors and the ministers generally. He also clearly delineated the functions of the other ministers. The Ordinances then go on to legislate on the sacraments, baptism and the Lord's Supper, and on marriage, Christian burial, the visitation of the sick, visiting prisoners, catechizing children, and a detailed specification of how the consistory of elders and ministers were to be chosen and exercise their task of "oversight of the life of everyone" (Ordinances, 63).

The Ordinances define a new stage in Calvin's developing ecclesiology. They implicitly subsume into a schematic, constitutional structure convictions that had developed through previous years of study, experience, and reflection. Three large and embracing conceptions help to collect some of these foundational notions that are implied in this text.[33] One resides in a heightened awareness of the role of ministry in the church. Calvin goes to great length to surround ministry, especially that of the pastor, with institutional supports that will guarantee a high standard of spiritual and moral leadership and service. Second, in contrast to the monarchical bishop, Calvin posits a corporate form of government of the local church; one might call it "collegial," in the sense of a ministerial group, even though this is not Calvin's language. Ministry is a team effort, and it unfolds within a structure that contains checks and balances exercised through mutual responsibilities of the ministers for various aspects

---

33. I draw these from Harro Höpfl, *The Christian Polity of John Calvin* (Cambridge: Cambridge University Press, 1982), 90–102.

of church ministry and for each other. Third, the role of discipline, that is, "a comprehensive censorship of morals,"[34] which in his letter to Sadoleto Calvin judged to be one of the pillars of the church, finds expression in the several institutions and stipulations designed to promote and ensure it. If one adds to these the more obvious overall fact of a tight ecclesiastical structure, one can see that the distinctiveness of Calvin's evangelical ecclesiology is beginning to appear.

Other writings. Calvin spent the rest of his life in Geneva preaching, organizing the church, writing, teaching, negotiating with the city magistrates, and with other churches and reformers. His ecclesiology evolved in the mix of his larger theology, the city of Geneva, and the actual church of Geneva. In lieu of an analysis of this development, a list of some of Calvin's writings will signal the movement. In 1542 Calvin wrote a book of services whose full title removes any need for commentary on its contents and their place in the life of the church: "The manner of praying in the French Churches, both before the preaching and after, together with French Psalms and Canticles sung in the said Churches; followed by the order and form of administering the Sacraments of Baptism and of the Supper."[35] Calvin hoped this standardization in worship would be relevant to the reform movement in France. In 1543 he published another edition of the *Institutes* which in its ecclesiology consolidates and explains some of the moves made with the Ordinances.[36] The "Catechism of the Church of Geneva" was finished in 1544 and consisted in a long exposition of the faith in the form of questions and answers between the minister and the child. Calvin expected that children would gradually memorize the catechism over a long period of time.[37] Legislation passed by the city government further structured the re-

---

34. Ibid., 101.
35. Parker, *John Calvin*, 86.
36. Benjamin Charles Milner, in his "Introduction" to *Calvin's Doctrine of the Church* (Leiden: Brill, 1970), 1–5, indicates that the broad lines of Calvin's ecclesiology were in place in the 1543 edition of the *Institutes*, and that most of the development in his ecclesiology after that found expression in his commentaries to which Calvin gave much of his energy. Milner's work draws heavily from the commentaries.
37. Calvin, *Calvin: Theological Treatises*, 88–139.

gional church that was dependent on Geneva. In 1546 the "Draft Order of Visitation of the Country Churches" established a routine annual visitation by a team of four members appointed by the Small Council and thus a close relationship between the city church and the surrounding rural area. Only vaguely reminiscent of the episcopal visitations in the medieval church, these aimed at fact-finding and were not juridical in nature. In 1547 the "Ordinances for the Supervision of Churches in the Country" extended the order of the church in Geneva to the churches in the countryside. Certain provisions furnish insight into the life of the church in the villages.[38]

Other events. Two events among many had a bearing on the development of the church in Geneva. The one was the trial and execution of Michael Servetus for heresy which transpired in the late summer and fall of 1553. Although space prohibits discussion of this famous incident, it illustrates the symbiotic character of the church and the city of Geneva: the magistracy took the lead in pursuing the affair.[39] The other case, more directly relevant to the church vis-à-vis the city and involving a prominent citizen, began during this same period and lasted into 1555. Philibert Berthelier had been excommunicated by the church's consistory, but he petitioned the Small Council for permission to present himself at the Lord's Supper, thus presuming the council had the power to overrule the church. The council ruled in Berthelier's favor, but counseled him not to present himself on this occasion. For Calvin, however, this was a matter of principle. "On communion Sunday, 3 September, at the end of his sermon, Calvin reaffirmed the non-competency of the council in excommunication and warned any who were excommunicated not to present themselves."[40] The council took up the matter again and

---

38. These last two documents are found in Calvin, *Calvin: Theological Treatises,* 74–75, 77–82. Calvin consolidated the authority of the church ministerially in two ways: first, he built a unified Company of Pastors who were talented and educated. Prior to 1546 the body of the pastors was small and "marked by constant instability, dissension and chaotic changes in personnel" (Naphy, *Calvin and the Consolidation of the Genevan Reformation,* 79). Second, he gathered a group of supportive elders on the consistory. Ibid., 223.

39. The intricate relationship of church and city government is illustrated best in the consistory which will be examined in the second part of this chapter.

40. Parker, *John Calvin,* 124. See also McGrath, *A Life of Calvin,* 121–23.

seemed to reverse itself within a matter of weeks: excommunication lies with the consistory. Berthelier appealed, and the Two Hundred ruled in his favor: "And as for the Supper, the *Consistoire* has not the power to forbid anyone without the commandment of the Council."[41] The ministers in their turn rejected this interpretation of the Ordinances, and the city sought help from the opinion of other churches, but this step proved to be inconclusive. In late 1554 a commission took up the matter, and in early 1555 the Small Council voted to honor the Ordinances as ordaining that the church, or the consistory, had the power of excommunication. Shortly thereafter the political tide turned in Calvin's favor so that 1555 is often considered the end of deep resistance to Calvin's policies and the beginning of the more cooperative relationship between church and civil government, each with its own competency, that Calvin actually sought.

The Academy and the Institutes (1559–60). These two events of 1559 mark a kind of apogee in Calvin's career. Calvin had always been interested in Christian education, both for citizens and for ministers, but the city either had other more pressing problems or lacked the finances. But in 1558 the Small Council was won over to the building of an academy. Inaugurated in 1559, within five years it had a thousand students in the Collège and three hundred on the higher level of the Academy. Calvin enlisted the service of Théodor de Bèze as its leader and was fortunate to receive a corps of professors who had recently been dismissed by the Bernese magistrates in 1558 from the school in Lausanne because of their sympathy for Calvin's ideas, especially on predestination.[42] The school became a European center for training in evangelical theology and ministry. Needless to say, the final edition of the *Institutes* in Latin of 1559 and its slightly different French translation in 1560 were the climax of Calvin's theological career. The *Institutes* will serve as the main but not the exclusive source for the representation of Calvin's ecclesiology that follows.

---

41. The formula comes from the Two Hundred, cited by Parker, Ibid., 125.

42. Ibid., 126–29; Wendel, *Calvin*, 105–06. See Gillian Lewis, "The Geneva Academy," *Calvinism in Europe: 1540–1620*, ed. Andrew Pettegree, Alastair Duke, and Gillian Lewis (Cambridge and New York: Cambridge University Press, 1994), 35–63.

AN ANALYTICAL ACCOUNT
OF CALVIN'S ECCLESIOLOGY

We turn now to an analytical account of Calvin's ecclesiology. This sketch proposes a clear outline of Calvin's understanding of the church; many subtle and significant matters of detail are passed over unnoticed. The goal is holistically to represent the integrity and coherence of Calvin's view of the church. The method reinterprets Calvin insofar as it does not follow the order of his own presentation in the *Institutes* (1559).[43] Rather, Calvin's ideas are fitted into the scheme that has been used to explore other churches or ecclesiologies. This includes the following aspects of the church: its nature and mission, its organizational structure, the members that make it up, the activities they perform, and its relationship to its environment. While this report thus runs parallel to the last chapter on Luther, it does not dwell on comparisons beyond casual notations.

The Nature, Mission, and Powers of the Church

Calvin's understanding of the nature of the church in general theological terms includes its mission in history and the powers it possesses in order to maintain itself and pursue its mission.

The nature of the church. In his characterization of the nature of the church Calvin employs some of the same distinctions as Luther. For example, "the communion of saints" can serve as a definition of the church, "for it very well expresses what the church is" (4,1,2). This church has various aspects and Calvin distinguishes between a visible and an invisible church. In some measure this distinction compares with that of Augustine: the invisible church consists of all the elect, both in heaven and on earth; this church includes all the saved and is an object of faith whose members are known only

---

43. John Calvin, *Calvin: Institutes of the Christian Religion*, I and II, ed. John T. McNeill, trans. Ford Lewis Battles (Philadelphia: Westminster Press, 1955). References in the text are to this edition by book, chapter, and paragraph or subheading. Calvin's order of discussion of the church is arranged in this way: "the church, its government, orders, and power; then the sacraments; and lastly, the civil order" (4,1,1). Wendel, in *Calvin*, stays close to the *Institutes* in representing Calvin's theology of the church. The same is true of Wilhelm Niesel, *The Theology of Calvin* (London: Lutterworth Press, 1956), 182–245.

to God (4,1,2; 4,1,7–8). One may differentiate this invisible church from the visible church, the huge multitude of those spread over the earth who profess to worship one God and Christ (4,1,7). For this visible church is a mixed body which includes many hypocrites. The invisible church remains visible only to God, while the visible church empirically stands in relation to human beings in the world (4,1,7). Calvin draws the distinction between the invisible and the visible church from scripture (4,1,7). But one should not construe this distinction as involving a separation between these two churches here on earth.[44]

Calvin implicitly distinguishes as well between the universal church visible here on earth and the local church. The universal church consists of the whole of those that confess Christ; it is catholic and universal because it is one; all are united to Christ in one faith, hope, and love, and animated by the same Spirit (4,1,2). But no institutional structure holds this universal community together such as, for example, the papacy. In contrast to such an encompassing institution, Calvin focuses his view of the visible church on the local or regional church. For example, the church of Geneva consisted of a few city congregations and the rural congregations dependent upon the city.

Concerning the marks or signs of the true church, Calvin writes that "Wherever we see the Word of God purely preached and heard, and the sacraments administered according to Christ's institution, there, it is not to be doubted, a church of God exists" (4,1,9).[45] These criteria, basically the same as those used by Luther, serve a double function: they define the whole universal church, the true church of Christendom among all the nations as united in word and sacrament. Calvin was very concerned about this universal unity; he viewed the whole church of Christendom as one (4,1,9). But, second, these marks also define the authenticity of any local church. Calvin was against the tendency in the Reformation of breaking unity, of splitting

---

44. Milner, *Calvin's Doctrine of the Church*, 69.

45. Calvin has an existential-historical or actualist understanding of these marks that transcends objectively true preaching and right administration of the sacraments. The word must be truly heard and the sacraments faithfully received. The actual or existential occurrence of these marks constitute the true church. Ibid., 132–33.

off into separate churches.[46] If these two essential marks were found, even in the face of some fault in administration, there should be no schism over unessential matters (4,1,12).[47] Thus he admitted a certain pluralism among different local communities (4,1,9). But as a man of the mid-sixteenth century he could not have accepted a pluralism of churches locally. The idea of different or separate churches in one place was not yet thinkable. The struggle of Geneva for the reform reflected the either/or option available at the time.

An accurate appreciation of Calvin's conception of the nature of the church, however, must center on its theological character. The church forms an integral part of Calvin's understanding of the cosmic-historical economy of God dealing with humankind. "The church is not so much an institution in history in which the restoration of order has been accomplished, as it is itself the history of that restoration."[48] Two metaphors, taken together, best capture Calvin's theology of the church: the kingdom of Christ and the body of Christ.[49] They interrelate dynamically as sanctification and justification. Under the umbrella of the "kingdom of Christ" one may situate the themes of order and discipline, that is, government of the church and jurisdictional regulation of morals. The image of the "body of Christ" correlates with justification, that is, the forgiveness of sin effected by Christ's death and its appropriation by faith. The Holy Spirit, or Calvin's pneumatology, provides the dynamic principle in both of these images. The Holy Spirit causes faith and binds the believer to Christ. The Spirit holds the members of the church together as one body. The Spirit, as the principle and cause of regeneration and sanctification, thus plays the role of creator of the church.[50] In sum,

---

46. "With insistence and vehemence Calvin denounces the schismatic temper, while he carefully distinguishes fraternal admonition from schism." John T. McNeill, *The History and Character of Calvinism* (New York: Oxford University Press, 1967), 215.

47. For Calvin, unity in essentials applied more to doctrines and worship than to church organization. He was especially intent on preserving certain fundamental "aspects of doctrine which are essential to salvation." Niesel, *The Theology of Calvin*, 196. See *Institutes*, 4,2,1.

48. Milner, *Calvin's Doctrine of the Church*, 47.

49. Milner traces the significance of these two images and their correlate themes in ibid., 168–79, 179–88 respectively.

50. Ibid., 58.

the church as external means of salvation does not occupy a position outside or added on to Calvin's fundamental theological vision but constitutes it as an integral part.[51]

The mission of the church. Calvin clearly conceived the purpose or mission of the church: the church functions as the external means of salvation. This key idea forms the title of the fourth book of the *Institutes:* "The External Means or Aims by Which God Invites Us Into the Society of Christ and Holds Us Therein." In God's providence the institutional church provides the external historical medium of salvation; Calvin cites Cyprian to the effect that there is no salvation outside the church (4,1,4). In another defining phrase, as seen above, the church is the body of Christ and Christ its sole head. But Christ's headship must channeled through historical means, through ministers and church organization.[52]

The powers of the church. The church in history has been charged to be the instrumental means or medium of salvation and sanctification of humankind. To accomplish this task it has been given certain powers to accomplish its goal. These powers reside in the institutions and offices of the church, and the next section will delineate the organizational structures by which they are exercised or implemented. But at this point it will be helpful to explain these powers abstractly as functions of the church's mission. Calvin insists on the spiritual character of this power; ecclesial power differs totally from the power of the state or civil government to use force or coerce. This spiritual power aims at building up the church, the body of Christ, so that it can perform its mission (4,8,1). What are these three powers?

Doctrine. The first role of the church and hence its first power is to teach and proclaim true doctrine. The church possesses the

---

51. The visible, organized church is a practical, ministerially functional institution. Because ministry is a central concern, images for the church, such as the church as mother, have a practical side corresponding to ministerial nurturing, teaching, forming the members. Ganoczy, *Calvin,* 221–22.

52. Although the reformers did not generally attend to foreign missions at this time, Calvin did approve two ministers to accompany an abortive mission expedition to Brazil (G. S. M. Walker, "Calvin and the Church," in *Readings in Calvin's Theology,* ed. Donald K. McKim [Grand Rapids: Baker Book House, 1984], 228–29). R. Bruce Beaver, "The Genevan Mission to Brazil," *The Heritage of John Calvin,* ed. John H. Bratt (Grand Rapids: Eerdmans, 1973), 55–73 gives an account of the mission.

authority, then, to lay down articles of faith and to proclaim them (4,8,1). But in saying this Calvin strongly insists that "The power of the Church...is not infinite but subject to the Lord's Word and, as it were, enclosed within it" (4,8,4). Ministers no more than the Apostles can exceed God's Word (4,8,9). Rather, ministers serve as instruments or channels of God's sovereign word; they do not speak for themselves.

Legislation. The question of legislation is a tricky issue for Calvin theologically speaking. On the one hand, the Reformation itself reacted against the system of canon law and other prescriptions in the Roman Church that bound people's consciences, so that obedience was taken as necessary for salvation. This legalism had destroyed the freedom of the Christian conscience before God. Yet, on the other hand, law, which reflected God's sovereign will, reflected a high value for Calvin; he appreciated the necessity of community life being disciplined and regulated. He had to balance these two practical necessities. He does so by setting the question in direct and explicit terms: whether the church can "lawfully bind consciences by its laws" (4,10,1). Can the church initiate *human traditions* relative to how God is to be worshiped and relative to the life of the religious community that also bind in conscience?

With characteristic subtlety Calvin answers this question with a Yes and a No. Human laws cannot bind the conscience directly before God, precisely because they are human laws. Only God, God's law, God's Word, can bind the conscience directly. But human laws within the church may require obedience indirectly even though *of themselves* they are neither binding nor necessary for salvation. This is so because of God's general will that Christians obey the lawgiver. In such a case, one is not bound by the specific law or the human tradition or regulation, but by a general obligation to obey the lawgiver or authority (4,10,4–5).

Thus it remains true that only God can bind consciences directly. But the church still has the power to regulate church discipline by law. All societies need some form of regulation, and the church requires order as well (4,10,27). Such laws aim at regulating ceremonies and worship and the whole orderly life of the community (4,10,28–29). But the church may also change this discipline so that different orders may obtain in different churches (4,10,31–32). In sum, specific regulations or laws within a church regarding discipline may be human and relative to a given need or practice; but they may also command obedience according to the general will of God that whatever is done be done in order (4,10,30).

Jurisdiction and discipline. Calvin devotes two chapters to the power of jurisdiction and the discipline that flows from its exercise (4,11–12). Jurisdiction pertains to the regulation of the moral life of the community. As any society, so too the church requires a spiritual polity. The regulation of the organization will be carried out by courts of judgment which investigate, judge, and censure immoral behavior or vice in the community. Calvin finds the scriptural basis for this in the power of the keys in the gospels of Matthew and John; to bind and loose is to excommunicate and receive back into the church (4,11,1–2).

Given these powers, we turn now to the organization of the church which possesses these powers and the institutions by which it exercises them.

The Organization of the Church

For the most part the churches of the Reformation on the continent began as city churches that included the dependent towns and villages. The organization of the church in Calvin's ecclesiology thus focuses on the urban church. Its polity departs from the monarchical arrangement of the bishop who was also a prince but does not quite reach a congregational polity. In addition to Calvin's view of the local church's ministries this section also treats his views on bishops, popes, and councils.

The local church. The distinctiveness of Calvin's ecclesiology begins to appear in the sphere of church organization. Ultimately the eternal Word of God alone rules and governs the church. But within history the Word of God, by God's own design, requires human agents or ministers to become channeled or mediated to people's lives. Departing from Calvin's language here, but not his conception, this could be called the sacramental principle: the church is the sacrament of God's Word in history. God uses ministers, sacraments, and organizations instrumentally. Therefore these ministers stand in

HUGE CONCERT/RESPONSIBILITY — Similar to views.
                                                    God's views.

the place of God; they "represent his person," as the bishop did in
Ignatius of Antioch (4,3,1). All owe obedience to them as to God,
even when they possess little personal worth.[53] Calvin thus sides
with Augustine against the Donatists in this respect, and an organized ministry becomes the chief historical sinew or bond by which
the whole body is held together (4,3,2).[54]

Calvin sometimes spoke of the clergy and people as two "orders"
(4,12,1). He was willing to consider ordination to the ministry a
sacrament, like baptism and eucharist (4,19,28; 4,19,31), but did
not because the evangelical churches did not commonly share this
doctrine. Also, Calvin took care to lay down strict criteria for who
would be chosen as a minister. As a result, while Calvin accepted the
principle of the priesthood of all believers, this was in turn limited
and controlled by an objective institutional or organizational principle.[55] This organization he drew from the New Testament; it was
not based on pragmatic principles or human law, but was willed by
God and not "free." The church was to have an objective institutional
structure by which it would be ruled and governed. The four offices
of the church's structure laid out in the *Institutes* corresponded with
the Ordinances of 1541 which were still in effect in 1559. The representation in the *Institutes* is more general and theological, and
it is interesting to appeal to the Ordinances as instantiation of the
doctrine.[56]

Pastors. The office of pastor is the first and central ministry in the
congregation. Calvin tends to think of it as the permanent office that
replaced the temporary office of apostle (4,3,5–6). The pastorate has

---

53. Calvin bestowed a great deal of authority on ministers, i.e., insofar as they
mediated the Word of God or Christ the head of the church. Few, if any, ecclesiologies
exalt ministry to a higher position. Eric G. Jay, *The Church: Its Changing Image through
Twenty Centuries* (Atlanta: John Knox Press, 1980), 174.

54. Ganoczy synthesizes Calvin's theology of ministry drawing from his commentaries and sermons. He establishes that ministry is first of all a *diakonia*, a dedication
to service of the community. Second, ministry is christocentric in the sense of an extension into the community of the mediatorship of Christ. Third, its efficacy stems from
the power of the Holy Spirit; ministers cooperate with God in mediating salvation.
Ganoczy, *Calvin*, 224–43.

55. Ernst Troeltsch, *The Social Teaching of the Christian Churches* (New York:
Harper Torchbooks, 1960), 591–92.

56. Ganoczy, *Calvin*, analyzes the various facets of the offices of pastor (300–366),
doctors or teachers (366–71), elders (371–81), and deacons (381–86).

a divine origin and basis: it is a divinely instituted office.[57] The pastor's centrality stems from his being "the one mouth" mediating the word of God that holds the congregation together (4,3,1; 4,3,3). The pastor has the main task of preaching the word and administering the sacraments; to this Calvin adds being in charge of teaching, instructing in true godliness, discipline, warning people of vice or sin, and exhorting them (4,3,4). This office of preaching is the highest in the church (4,3,3).

Teachers or doctors. Teachers or doctors have a more limited function. They take on responsibility for purity of doctrine, which means scriptural interpretation, no charge for discipline, sacraments, admonishing, or exhorting (4,3,4). Teachers thus correspond by a rough analogy to the transient ministry of evangelist in the New Testament period. The office of pastor and teacher can be held by one person and the offices in some measure overlap.

The elders. The third office is that of elder. It corresponds to the power of governing the church which Calvin finds in Paul (4,3,8 [Rom 12:7–8; 1 Cor 12:28]). "Governors were," he says, "elders chosen from the people, who were charged with the censure of morals and the exercise of discipline along with the bishops" (4,3,8). "Each church, therefore, had from its beginning a senate, chosen from godly, grave, and holy men, which had jurisdiction over the correcting of faults" (4,3,8). The office of elder, then, is the office of government in the church. The elders form with the pastors a consistory or tribunal which oversees and judges the public and even the private moral life of the community.

The deacons. Finally, the office of deacon bears responsibility for the church's dealing with the poor. Speaking of the primitive church, Calvin says: "The care of the poor was entrusted to the deacons" (4,3,9). In the *Institutes,* corresponding to the Ordinances, Calvin distinguishes two distinct functions of deacons: "the deacons who distribute the alms" and the deacons devoted "to the care of the poor and the sick" (4,3,9). Women can fulfill this public office of caring for the poor (4,3,9).[58]

---

57. Ibid., 365.
58. By surveying each of the church offices and showing how the distinct spheres of authority supported and complemented each other William G. Naphy makes the point

The *Institutes* give explicit attention to the calling, the authorization, and the ordination of ministers, because in Calvin's view the supremely important selection of ministers has to be done carefully and according to order. A candidate needs an inner call and an outer call manifested at least in sound doctrine and a holy life. Choosing ministers is carried out seriously and reverentially, not by one person but "by the consent and approval of the people," with other pastors presiding as moderators. But ultimately ministers do not serve on the basis of the decision of the candidates or of the church but of God's choice which uses ecclesial authority as its instrument. Succession and continuity in the pastoral office, therefore, refers to God constantly raising up ministers of God's word. The appointment of ministers is a "symbol of a process which is radically transcendent."[59] The ordination or installation in office can but does not have to involve laying on of hands (4,3,10–16). The procedures established in the Ordinances concretized these general prescriptions and the concerns behind them. For example, the election of ministers went through stages: a candidate was first elected by the ministers; then, second, presented to the Small Council who evaluated and certified the candidate; and, third, presented to the people for their common consent

---

that, ideologically, there was no separation or tension between church and state in Calvin's Geneva. Relative to the pastors, despite their being foreign, they were consistently supported by the magistrates when they clashed with the locals ("Church and State in Calvin's Geneva," in *Calvin and the Church: Papers Presented at the 13th Colloquium of the Calvin Studies Society, May 24–26, 2001*, ed. David Foxgrover [Grand Rapids: Published by the Calvin Studies Society by CRC Product Services, 2002], 16–17). Relative to the elders and the consistory: "While other Calvinistic church structures tended to draw their eldership from prominent members of the local congregation, who might be magistrates, largely at the suggestion of the ministers and prominent laymen, the Genevan consistory had an eldership which was a representative, elected body of magistrates" (ibid., 20). Relative to the doctors, the magistrates were supportive of education, and the Ordinances "made it clear that the office pertained to the school system for boys and girls and culminated in a *collège*. The office existed and was maintained and supported in a spirit of concord both by the church and the state" (ibid., 21). Relative to the diaconate, "Calvin drafted the *Ordinances* very much as he did the republic's civil constitution. He simply codified and regularized a pre-existing situation. . . . Or, as Prof. Kingdon said in his response to this essay: 'in effect Calvin did not create but rather consecrated or sacralized an institution that had already been created in Geneva to handle the problems of the poor and unfortunate.' Once again, the church and state worked as one to institute and maintain a unified ecclesiastical and secular system of bureaucracy and authority in Geneva." Ibid., 22.

59. Ganoczy, *Calvin*, 365.

(Ordinances, 59). To insure the continual quality of ministers in doctrine and life, especially the pastors, those in the city met weekly to discuss doctrine and reconcile disputes; they met every third month, if there were need, to raise questions of the conduct of ministers as measured by lists of faults to be avoided (Ordinances, 61). The order to be observed by those who supervised the moral life of the community was regulated. The Ordinances laid out the various duties of deacons and routinized them. In sum, then, Calvin's ecclesiology calls for concrete and detailed procedural organization. Because of his ecumenical interests Calvin admitted the validity of a variety of church orders. But that the community should be specifically ordered in some way represented a high value for a church that is marked as one and holy.

The larger church. Calvin had critical opinions on the larger structures that organized the universal church. Did he conceive of the Christian movement as a whole retaining some institutional form?

Bishops. Calvin made no case against the order of bishops in principle.[60] In his view the presbyters of the earliest Christian communities chose one of their number to be a bishop who acted as a principle of unity (4,4,2). Early bishops generally were elected from the community. He cites with approval Cyprian's conception of the episcopacy as a whole in which each bishop participates (4,6,17). He was satisfied that "the ancient bishops did not intend to fashion any other form of church rule than that which God has laid down in his Word" (4,4,4). The problem with the episcopacy lay in the fact that this office of ministry gradually became corrupted or extinguished.[61] But despite the general situation, if and when authentic episcopal ministry prevailed in service to God's Word and sacraments, it would be a valid office. "For I willingly grant them," he wrote, "that they have a godly and excellent office, if only they would fulfill it" (4,5,11).[62]

---

60. Calvin's positive regard for episcopacy can be read in his acceptance of the office in the Church of England; he also recommended an episcopal organization for the church in Poland. McNeill, *Calvinism*, 217.

61. Calvin charts that corruption in 4,5. It consisted in the domination of the one bishop over the other presbyters, and giving the position a divine sanction rather than a human, political status. Milner, *Calvin's Doctrine of the Church*, 147–48.

62. Ganoczy traces the evolution of Calvin's views on the episcopal function in the church and on the office of the bishop in *Calvin*, 271–85, 295–97, 387–96.

The papacy. By contrast, Calvin finds no warrant for the office of the papacy in either principle or fact. It cannot be established on the basis of the Petrine texts or the writings of the Fathers in the early history of the church. The head of the universal episcopacy is Christ (4,6,17). His overview of the history of the development of the papacy discredits the institution (4,7).[63]

Councils. Calvin proposes a nuanced view of councils. They have scriptural warrant broadly speaking, and he accepts the teachings of the first four councils. Councils are to be endorsed in principle: "We indeed willingly concede, if any discussion arises over doctrine, that the best and surest remedy is for a synod of true bishops to be convened, where the doctrine at issue may be examined. Such a definition, upon which the pastors of the church in common, invoking Christ's Spirit, agree, will have much more weight than if each one, having conceived it separately at home, should teach it to the people, or if a few private individuals should compose it" (4,9,13). But councils only carry valid authority in the measure that they mediate God's Word in scripture; they have not always assembled in Christ's name; and so they do not command blind obedience, but must be judged critically according to God's Word (4,9).

In sum, one can say that Calvin's ecclesial organization focuses on the local or regional church. In contrast to episcopal government, Calvin's ministerial structure spreads authority among a group of ministers, with specific roles and sometimes overlapping responsibilities, who relative to each other exercise mutual reinforcement and oversight.

The Members of the Church

Speaking generally and allowing for exceptions, just about all of the people of Geneva were members of the church. Calvin's theology of baptism which constituted membership in the church will be outlined in the next section. Among these church members one can

---

63. Calvin's logic in the chapters tracing the historical origin and development of episcopacy and papacy is intended to show the discontinuity between the early church and the current structure of the Roman Church. In contrast to this is his conviction that the church organization he proposes reflects more exactly and authentically the church in the period of the New Testament and the Fathers.

imagine the whole range of degrees of internalized religious and moral seriousness and commitment. Neither Luther nor Calvin were sanguine about the inherent goodness of the human person; they both had strong anthropological doctrines of sin and insisted on the ability of the church to excommunicate public sinners. Yet Luther saw the church as an agent of God's sanctifying power and spoke of the effect of the Spirit in the community as sanctification. The church should become more holy in the sense of its corporate morality. But Calvin much more strongly emphasizes church discipline as a characteristic of the church and built into his ecclesiology an institution for promoting good moral conduct, that is, the consistory. Both the conception of the consistory and its actual practice set up two tensions which are intrinsic to Calvin's ecclesiology. The first tension subsists between the existential holiness of a church in terms of general moral conduct and its being a church coterminous with the whole of society. The second is the relation between the church as overseer of public behavior in relation to the same function enjoyed by society and government. Although both of these issues help define membership in the church and the character of the church in Calvin's ecclesiology, they may be more fruitfully discussed within the framework of the church and society. But for the moment attention falls on the activities of the church.

The Activities of the Church

In this theological and organizational analysis of Calvin's ecclesiology the category of "activities" performed by the members refers to the most typical actions performed *ad intra,* namely, religious worship and ethical behavior insofar as it is construed as the Christian life. Religious assembly in Calvin's church offers a good place to begin.

Worship. Calvin, no less than Luther, located Jesus Christ, the Word of God, at the center of Christian self-understanding. The Word of God thus had the central role in his theology and the practical life of the church, though not without the work of the Spirit. The designation, "Word of God," had multiple references and meanings: the eternal Word of God, the incarnate Word of God as Jesus Christ, the Word of God mediated by scripture and thus, analogously, as scripture itself, and even the Word of God contained in preaching the gospel. It is fitting, then, to treat worship in Calvin's ecclesiology synthetically around the themes of word and sacrament, and to begin with his theology of the preached sermon.

The order of worship. Thomas Parker gets at the heart of what goes on when the community assembles with the question of what makes the word preached by the pastor the Word of God.[64] The question generates a dialectical response, as in a sacramental theology, where the human activity and created signs mediate a transcendent reality. Neither the preacher nor the preaching is the transcendent, divine Word of God, but each is an instrument of it. The Word of God is mediated and activated within the encounter of the preaching. Scripture, preaching, sacraments are all instrumental accommodations by which God communicates to humans as to children. By the principle of accommodation, then, God speaks through the minister's words (4,1,5). This occurs when what the preacher says remains faithful to the source and norm of God's Word, namely, Jesus Christ and his message as scripture represents them. "In the Holy Scriptures and in the proclamation that faithfully interprets the Holy Scriptures, God himself speaks, declaring his existence, his purpose, his will, redemptively revealing human existence to itself as the creature of God, as the sinner, as the redeemed."[65]

The members of the church in Geneva assembled for Sunday worship to hear this Word of God and to respond with praise and thanksgiving. Liturgy used the language of the people (3,20,33). It was to be celebrated with modest and straightforward reverence and decorum (4,10,29). Calvin ordered the regular service in such a way that the sermon, with subject matter drawn from scripture in a continuous reading through a book of the Bible, provided the centerpiece of the service, with prayer and singing both leading up to it and then responding to it. The service began with a confession of sin by the pastor in the name of the congregation and an absolution, followed by a singing of the commandments, the Lord's Prayer, a sung psalm, and extemporaneous prayer by the pastor. The sermon then provided the focal point of the congregation's encounter with God. The sermon

---

64. Parker, *John Calvin*, 90. I take this condensed theology of preaching and description of the order of worship from Parker, 84–91.

65. Ibid., 90.

was followed by bidding prayers for public figures and for the faithful themselves, a short reflection on the Lord's Prayer, the singing of a psalm, and dismissal.[66] One can discern in this order how the theology of the Word has been transposed into a ritual vehicle for religiously affective meaning and a concrete experience of God.

But one should not gain the impression that the Sunday assembly amounted to an intellectual experience, as if God were mediated to the mind in a conceptual rendering of God's Word. Parker highlights the role of singing in Calvin's conception and implementation of worship. He recognized how music mediated an affective response to reality, and this had a major role in the way he conceived liturgy. Singing "both lends dignity and grace to sacred actions and has the greatest value in kindling our hearts to a true zeal and eagerness to pray" (3,20,32). He also had a theology of singing. His understanding of scripture as the Word of God meant that one could conceive of God as the author of the lyrics when one sang the psalms. And his theology of the use of creatures, which will be addressed further on, allowed him to employ the power of music to mediate the response of gratitude and joy to the power of God's Word. Thus Calvin exploited the affective immediacy of singing "to incite us to pray to and to praise God, to meditate on his works, that we may love, fear, honor, and glorify him."[67]

Sacraments. Calvin has a well developed general sacramental theology and specific treatises on baptism and the Lord's Supper in the *Institutes.* What follows does not reproduce their exceptional nuance,[68] but is intended to illustrate two things: that Calvin proposes

---

66. This description condenses the already schematic outline provided by Parker, ibid., 86–87. It should be noted that Calvin's preference was for a weekly celebration of the Lord's Supper, but in imitation of Zurich and Bern the magistrates approved only a quarterly Lord's Supper.

67. Parker, quoting Calvin, at ibid., 88.

68. I have studiously avoided the intricacies of sacramental theology, especially as manifested in the eucharistic controversies in the early medieval period and here in the sixteenth century. Calvin addressed issues surrounding the Lord's Supper many times beginning with the *Institutes* of 1536, and a detailed representation of his views requires at least differentiation of Calvin from Zwinglian, Lutheran, and Roman theologies. It is important to recognize the limited intention of the broad synthetic strokes that follow. Milner, *Calvin's Doctrine of the Church,* 110–32, provides a concise account of Calvin's sacramental theology, with some attention to the neuralgic points of the efficacy of a sacrament, infant baptism, and true presence in the eucharist. For a fuller account

a coherent sacramental theology which integrates into itself his theology of the Word and the Holy Spirit, and that he preserves the priority of Christ's action in the sacrament and the truth of Christ's presence in the eucharist precisely as effected by the Spirit.

Calvin begins his treatise on sacraments by reminding the reader that sacraments are related to preaching as another aid to faith. They consist in outward signs that seal, confirm, and actualize God's Word and promise in our lives (4,14,1). The key to understanding the function and the substance of a sacrament lies in a series of tensions that Calvin uses to describe them. The meaning of a sacrament lies in the tension between the scriptural and preached word and the sacrament or sign; without the word the sign would be mute (4,14,3). One must also distinguish between the sign as such and the "matter" or substance of the sign: Christ and encounter with Christ the Word constitute the substance of every sacrament (4,14, 15–16). Still another intricate dialectical understanding is required to appreciate the roles of the Word, the Spirit, and faith in sacramental encounter: God instructs through the Word, so that Christ the Word is the cause of sacramental efficacy. The Word in the sacrament, however, is only operative in and through faith: Calvin explicitly denies an efficacy of the sacrament outside of faith (4,14,17). But, finally, faith is activated by the Holy Spirit; the Holy Spirit illumines the human subject from within so that Word and sacrament can enter in or be appropriated (4,14,8; 4,14,17). In sum, the material sacraments are genuinely instrumental in the communication of Christ the Word to the faithful recipient.

Given his general sacramental theology, Calvin's definition of baptism appears straightforward. "Baptism is the sign of the initiation by which we are received into the society of the church, in order that, ingrafted in Christ, we may be reckoned among God's children" (4,15,1). Calvin lists three effects of baptism. The first consists in the sealing, confirming, reassuring character of the sacrament: it provides, not forgiveness of sin, for this is effected by the Word and

---

of Calvin's eucharistic theology see Kilian McDonnell, *John Calvin, the Church, and the Eucharist* (Princeton: Princeton University Press, 1967) and B. A. Gerrish, *Grace and Gratitude: The Eucharistic Theology of John Calvin* (Minneapolis: Fortress Press, 1993).

not the water, but certainty of forgiveness of sin, not just for the past but into the future (4,15,1–3). Thus the sacrament only becomes effective when the child reaches the age when he or she can elicit the faith without which there can be no efficacy. Second, baptism grafts a person into Christ's death and generates in the Christian a new righteous life. (4,15,5) Third, baptism signifies sanctification, being imbued with the Holy Spirit to actualize the new life in Christ. Baptism thus signs forth the basic Christian mystery of human purgation and regeneration of which the Father is the cause, the Son the matter or substance, and the Spirit the effecting agent (4,15,6). Calvin, siding again with Augustine against the Donatists, denies that the efficacy of baptism depends on the merit of the minister (4,15,16). Despite the strong role of faith in his theology of the sacraments he defends infant baptism. Somehow, if among the elect, infants are regenerated by God's power (4,16,17–20).[69]

Calvin developed a distinctive and particularly subtle theology of the Lord's Supper. His first move, logically, establishes the imaginative framework of understanding: the fundamental metaphor for the eucharist is a meal (4,18,7).[70] The Lord's Supper consists of bread and wine "which represent for us the invisible food that we receive from the flesh and blood of Christ" (4,17,1). The sacrament nourishes, sustains, and preserves the life begotten in us by baptism, and represents a pledge of God's continuing liberality (4,17,1). It should be administered frequently, at least once a week, something that Calvin did not achieve in the Genevan church (4,17,43). The sacrament effects union with Christ and thus confers upon our mortality immortality (4,17,2). The sacrament accomplishes this by mediating the true presence of Christ to the believing subject (4,17,3). Calvin "localized" the risen Christ in heaven, and thus he could not speak

---

69. In the end, Calvin does not tie salvation to baptism. Infants who die without baptism may still be saved. "God declares that he adopts our babies as his own before they are born, when he promises that he will be our God and the God of our descendants after us. Their salvation is embraced in this word" (4,15,20). See McNeill, *Calvinism,* 218.

70. In explicit contrast to the mass in the Roman Church. The *Institutes,* 4.18 is given over to other problems he finds in Roman eucharistic theology. Calvin had a great love of the Lord's Supper: it was the bond of charity that held the community together as the body of Christ. Bouwsma, *John Calvin,* 219; Walker, "Calvin and the Church," 223.

of Christ the Word's presence in physical and material terms relative to the bread and wine, as the terms transubstantiation and consubstantiation might have suggested. He thus insisted on the eucharist as instrument of the true spiritual presence of Christ to the mouth of faith by the power of the Holy Spirit. In the end he did not explain this presence, except by negation: "as may neither fasten him to the element of bread, nor enclose him in bread, nor circumscribe him in any way . . . " (4,17,19). "To summarize: our souls are fed by the flesh and blood of Christ in the same way that bread and wine keep and sustain physical life" (4,17,10).[71]

Ethics. Calvin's ethics affords a locus for responding to the question of the activities of the members of the Christian church. Something could be deduced from the various lists of vices to be avoided and virtues to be cultivated from the writings of Calvin. But here the focus falls on the larger questions of the positive function of the law, the role of sanctification in his theology of the Christian life, and some principles of Christian spirituality.

The law and sanctification. Calvin was educated as a lawyer and a humanist. One might expect in him a humanistic appreciation of the value and role of law within the human community. And so it was, but always within the larger context of the Christian economy of salvation. Law for Calvin means the whole religion given by God to Moses. It also designates the decalogue or the revealed moral law.[72] And law refers as well to the various bodies of positive civil and religious ceremonial law. Focusing specifically on the moral law, Calvin characterizes three distinct functions for it within the divine economy. The first operates dialectically in a negative and positive Pauline

---

71. He then puts this in the terms of his general sacramental theology: "But if it is true that a visible sign is given us to seal the gift of a thing invisible, when we have received the symbol of the body, let us no less surely trust that the body itself is also given to us" (4,17,10). Calvin describes the order of the service of the Lord's Supper in 4,17,43.

72. Dowey shows that for Calvin the decalogue and the natural law were identified, and that Jesus' ethical teachings were in line with the Mosaic law. Thus the law of the Old Testament and the New Testament are both intimately related to the prescriptions of natural law (Edward A. Dowey, *The Knowledge of God in Calvin's Theology* [New York: Columbia University Press, 1952], 228–30). "The moral law of scripture, summarized in the commandments, is an attestation of the natural law which God has engraved in all men's hearts." McNeill, *Calvinism,* 224. Also Milner, *Calvin's Doctrine of the Church,* 77.

fashion: the law condemns us by displaying human sinfulness, but in so doing moves human beings to seek grace (2,7,6–9).[73] Second, the law instills fear; as such it is an outward restraint and "necessary for the public community of men" (2,7,10), but is not salvific. The third use of the law, for believers, pertains more closely to its proper purpose: "the law points out the goal toward which throughout life we are to strive" (2,7,13). Here its function becomes positive because, freed from fear of the law by the salvation wrought in Christ and appropriated by faith, another force becomes operative in Christian life, namely, the Holy Spirit through whose power the Christian desires to follow God's will and seeks direction (2,7,12).

Calvin's view of the law meshes perfectly with his doctrine of sanctification. Luther had a doctrine of sanctification in the power of the Spirit, but Calvin places an emphasis on this aspect of Christian salvation that in the end contributes to a significant difference in their ecclesiologies. Calvin begins his analysis of the way we receive the grace of Christ with a discussion of faith which he defines thus: "a firm and certain knowledge of God's benevolence toward us, founded upon the truth of the freely given promise of Christ, both revealed to our minds and sealed upon our hearts through the Holy Spirit" (3,2,7). The regeneration of human existence occurs within this faith, and Calvin begins his analysis of it with repentance.[74] To schematize his teaching here, repentance, which is a distinct dimension of faith, involves [1] conversion, a turning around, so that "departing from ourselves, [2] we turn to God, and having taken off our former mind, we put on a new one." More precisely repentance "consists in [3] the mortification of our flesh and of the old man, and [4] in the vivification of the Spirit" (3,3,5). Calvin uses the language of breaking the bonds of sin, so that sin loses its domination over the Christian (3,3,10). The fruit of this repentance, finally, lies in sanctification and a holy life. The Spirit, which began the course of faith in us, sustains this whole movement. "Now we can understand the nature

73. "The law is like a mirror. In it we contemplate our weakness, then the iniquity arising from this, and finally the curse coming from both . . ." (2,7,7).

74. Regeneration or rebirth in Christ includes both justification and sanctification. But whereas a certain logic would place justification "before" sanctification, Calvin distinctively lays out the dynamics of sanctification flowing into the Christian life (3,3–10) before he deals with justification (3,11–19)

of the fruits of repentance: the duties of piety toward God, of charity toward men, and in the whole of life, holiness and purity. Briefly, the more earnestly any man measures his life by the standard of God's law, the surer are the signs of repentance that he shows" (3,3,16). This forms the theological underpinnings of Calvin's conception of the Christian life.

Principles of the Christian life. Calvin's short treatise on the Christian life occupies five chapters of the *Institutes* (3,6–10). He allows a large place for asceticism and self-denial, the disciplining of self for the glory of God, bearing the cross, and contemplation of a future life. But certain principles that treat the way Christians should deal with the world need to be highlighted, for they lend a distinctive note to Calvin's ecclesiology by defining the spiritual activity of its members in society and the world.

First, creatures should be used and not avoided. Things of this world should be used insofar as they are a help in the Christian life. A criterion for how they should be used is their inner teleology; they should be used according to the end given them by God, not only pragmatically but also for enjoyment. Things should be used moderately, not abused, and with recognition given to God their giver (3,10,1–2).

Second, things should be used in the light of eternity, with neither excessive indulgence nor excessive care or worry if one has little material possessions. Moderation in all things supplies the key here (3,10,3–5).

Third, Calvin lays down the principle of stewardship: the things of this world "were so given to us by the kindness of God, and so destined for our benefit, that they are, as it were, entrusted to us, and we must one day render account of them" (3,10,5). The distribution of goods in the community should be governed by love.

And, fourth, the principle of vocation or calling voices the conviction that "each individual has his own kind of living assigned to him by the Lord. . . ." God has "appointed duties for every person in his particular way of life" (3,10,6), so that every single task one performs will "be reckoned very precious in God's sight" (3,10,6). This dovetails with Calvin's view of special providence and harbors a powerful religious idea: every action is foreseen by God and has religious significance. McNeill summarizes the point nicely: the Christian life "is laden with responsibilities, and these extend to every task and every hour. There is no realm of life that is exempt from obligation of service to God and man.... We are not our own: every Christian is to live as one dedicated."[75] The third part of this chapter will draw out in more detail the significance of Calvin's ethics and spirituality for his ecclesiology.

Church and Society

It remains to give an account of Calvin's view of how the church relates to its environment or to the world. A distinction between the manner in which church affects society generally and the way it relates to civil government in particular helps to clarify Calvin's refinement in these matters. In general it must be said that Calvin had to deal with Geneva, and the city influenced his views. But it does not follow that he took these actual conditions as ideal or exemplary.[76]

Church and society. The church had a major impact on Genevan society, and Calvin intended this symbiosis. One can begin to appreciate the "size" of the impact of the church on a society such as Geneva's simply by considering the church's ministries. First of all, the church possessed the pulpit, the major vehicle of mass communication in a city where people had "the legal duty to attend sermons on Sundays."[77] The pastors and the teachers taught catechism to all the youth of the city; the church sponsored and the city paid for the Academy for the education of ministers and citizens. The pastors and the elders served on the consistory, yet to be described, which had oversight over the moral behavior of all in the church and hence the city. And the deacons and their agencies dealt with the poor and the sick of the city. In terms of religious understanding, moral discipline, and material support for those who needed it, the church,

---

75. McNeill, *Calvinism,* 221.
76. Calvin saw the order of the church in Geneva as exemplary, but this did not extend to the government of Geneva nor to the relationship between the church and the city government. Höpfl, *The Christian Polity of John Calvin,* 150–51.
77. Höpfl, *The Christian Polity of John Calvin,* 199.

represented by a more or less unified body of ministers, brought considerable influence to bear on common social life. The degree of the impact seems comparable to the church in the town or city of the high Middle Ages.

It is clear that Calvin wanted a church that would have an impact on society. Another question is whether the church that was in place had the impact that Calvin wanted. On the one hand, an interpreter can write that "Calvin's ideal remained that of a society in which citizenship was equated with church-membership."[78] On the other hand, there was little other choice available to him, but he could envisage other values. " 'We are always wanting a multitude,' he observed, 'and evaluating in that way the condition of the church. It would be more desirable for us to be few and for the glory of God to shine in us all.' "[79]

Church and state. Relative to the political sphere of civil government Calvin expressed his views in the last chapter of the *Institutes*, both in the first version of 1536 and the last in 1559–60. One sees many of the distinctions that were used in the medieval debates between the rights of popes and emperors, bishops and princes, spiritual and temporal power. Although many of his basic ideas were formulated before his arrival in Geneva, one can sense that he was thinking from the perspective of the evangelical churches making their way where they could in protected environments. Calvin was also scandalized by the church in the past appropriating to itself the functions of secular rule. Thus one can interpret Calvin both with reference to the macro politics of Europe and also in terms of city and town. In the latter case one sees a conception of the church that opens up to life in the public sphere. One finds no strong distinction between private and public morality; the Christian does not merely submit to or tolerate the state, for it is a positive good ordained by God; church and government cooperate in God's economy of the world.

The autonomy and role of civil government. The Christian lives under two distinct governments: the one pertains to the soul or the inner spiritual life, the other pertains to civil or social justice and

---

78. Walker, "Calvin and the Church," 221.
79. Bouwsma, *John Calvin*, 217–18, citing Calvin's commentary on Isaiah 4:3.

outward morality. But freedom in the religious sphere does not mean anarchy in the civil sphere. Rather the Christian bears responsibility to civil government and authority (4,20,1). Civil government is not polluted; it does not pertain to worldly matters that are foreign to Christians. Rather God wills human government as an essential part of human life itself (4,20,2).[80] The magistrates or rulers "have a mandate from God, have been invested with divine authority, and are wholly God's representatives, in a manner, acting as God's vice-regents" (4,20,4). The office of ruler is a holy calling, "the most sacred and by far the most honorable of all callings in the whole life of mortal men" (4,20,4). This language is Calvin's own; it is strong, direct, and unambiguous; it indicates the overwhelmingly positive view he had of civil rule. As to the reactions of Christians to rulers, they simply owed obedience, and Calvin extends this even to unjust rulers (4,20,25).[81] He thus makes a clear distinction between office and the actual ruler. In sum, civil government is autonomous. It does not derive from the church. It forms part of God's providential will for human society as such and thus remains quite distinct from formal religious authority. Both God's will and one's religious response to God include obedience to civil authority.

Civil government aims to regulate the outward behavior of society. This extends to guaranteeing both the rights of God in society and the rights of human beings. Thus the purpose of civil government includes the responsibility to ensure and protect the worship of God and thus the church. And second, its purpose is to guarantee and protect the second table of the law, reconciling people among themselves, shaping social behavior, ensuring general morality, peace, order, tranquility.[82] Unlike the church, civil government can exercise force and

Church/State together

---

80. As to the best form of government, McNeill comments as follows: "Broadly, he holds the best defense against tyranny to lie in a form of government in which aristocracy (the rule of the best) is mingled with democracy." Many is better than one, for they can help and correct each other. McNeill, *Calvinism*, 224–25. See 4,20,8.

81. Except in some extreme situations where obedience to a ruler would entail disobedience to God. (4,20,32)

82. "Yet civil government has as its appointed end, so long as we live among men, to cherish and protect the outward worship of God, to defend sound doctrine of piety and the position of the church, to adjust our life to the society of men, to form our social behavior to civil righteousness, to reconcile us with one another, and to promote general peace and tranquility" (4,20,2). See also 4,20,9.

coercion to attain these ends; it can wage war, execute criminals, and so on.

Cooperation of church and civil government. Calvin distinguished two autonomous and distinct spheres of governing human life. Spiritual and temporal power were not the same, and each sphere was autonomous in the sense of being irreducible to the other. As in the medieval period both were theologically grounded; both functioned at the behest of God's will. But they were designed by God to work together cooperatively. They were surely not intended by God to be two spheres competing with each other for hegemony. In Calvin's view they cooperated under God's Word in fashioning a Christian society.

In practice the relationship between church and magistracy in Geneva was not always so harmonious, nor could it be when two distinct authorities share responsibility relative to a single Christian society. In theory, the "church does not assume what is proper to the magistrate, nor can the magistrate execute what is carried out by the church" (4,11,3). But as long as a single church and society were bound together as one, with a Christian church that was involved in the public or social arena and concerned with public behavior, tensions could hardly be avoided. In fact, several areas were subject to competing interests so that tension was constantly felt. One example lay in the appointment of pastors and other ministers. But the main point of overlapping concerned the city's control of public morals and the church's control of public morals through the consistory. It took fourteen years for Calvin to win for the church the autonomous right to excommunicate. In a Christian commonwealth, the Word of God will ultimately be supreme because the magistrate or ruler, if he is godly, will also be a member of the church which judges according to God's Word (4,11,4).

These concrete tensions, however, did not dim the vision; they were precisely to be negotiated within the context of the encompassing framework of cooperation. By treating the church and civil government in the same book under the same title Calvin was maintaining that both church and government functioned as two " 'external media' whereby the grace of God is distributed to the world.... "[83] Both agencies, with distinct powers given by God, use them "for the disciplining of the same congregation or body of inhabitants ... to obedience to the same body of laws which covered both piety and righteousness."[84]

We now turn to the consistory, a development of the ecclesiastical court that exemplified the coincidence of authorities and the resultant tensions that typifies Calvin's ecclesiology.

The consistory. The consistory may be the most famous element of Calvin's ecclesiology and the least understood. It was not completely distinctive, for analogous institutions appeared in other ecclesial polities, including its predecessor in many respects, the ecclesiastical court of the Roman Church. Because its records from Calvin's time proved to be extremely difficult to decipher, only recently has new light been thrown on the actual functioning of this institution. The importance of the consistory lies in the fact that a better understanding of its functioning provides a clearer idea of the actual church that lay behind Calvin's ecclesiology and an appreciation of what "discipline" really meant. Appreciating these also provides insight into the tensions involved in the church-society relationship and the relation between the ideal and the actual church. What follows juxtaposes a prescriptive account and a historical account.

The consistory in the Institutes *and the Ordinances.* The consistory was a committee or tribunal of ministers of the church, pastors and elders, which exercised the power of spiritual jurisdiction of the church by oversight of the public and in some cases private moral behavior of the members of the church.[85]

The Ordinances laid down the constitution of the consistory in Geneva. Besides the pastors, it consisted of the elders, twelve men, two from the Small Council, four from the Council of Sixty, and six

---

83. Höpfl, *The Christian Polity of John Calvin*, 191.

84. Ibid., 193. This refers to the external forum. The true Christian was internally disposed, the unrighteous conformed only externally. But since Christianity in Calvin's Geneva was the only publicly confessed religion, none had a right to complain about the civil enforcement. Ibid.

85. The consistory is discussed in the *Institutes* at 4,12, 1–13. I will fill out the theological description found there with some of the practical implementations that are codified in the Ordinances.

from the Two Hundred, all prudent and of good character. They were to represent every quarter of the city so they could have all-embracing oversight. The Small Council designated the members of the consistory in consultation with the pastors and then presented them to the Two Hundred who approved or actually elected them. They were then inducted into office, for this was a church ministry, by taking an oath of service. The elders were not ordained. Each year they presented themselves to the magistracy for review. Calvin's Ordinances recommended that they not be "changed often without cause, so long as they discharge their duty faithfully" (Ordinances, 64).

The consistory was to operate in the following way: it would meet once a week to discuss whatever disorder there might be in the church along with the remedies (Ordinances, 70–71). It might act, first of all, by referring cases to the pastors: pastors admonish and exhort. Or the elders themselves might admonish people privately, or they might rely on family members, or they might impose a fine for various actions. If there were no success, a person might be summoned by the consistory, perhaps in the presence of witnesses. Finally, if there were no reform in a serious matter, the consistory could excommunicate, that is, cut people off from the Lord's Supper. All of this procedure could apply to private matters (4,12,2). In the case of public scandal, the consistory could proceed directly with public rebuke (4,12,3). The narrative section of this chapter indicated how Calvin had to fight to gain the autonomous power of excommunication as inherently belonging to the church.

Calvin viewed this procedure as spiritual power, quite distinct from civil power of coercion, because the church possessed no physical power and always appealed to a person's freedom (4,11,3). The justification of this power, aside from scripture, rested in Calvin's conviction that it essentially complemented the preaching of the Word. If the preaching of the Word were taken seriously, then people had to allow themselves to be judged by that Word (4,11,5). As to the purpose or goal of this power of jurisdiction, Calvin saw it as threefold: negatively, public sinners in the church would disgrace the church and desecrate the Lord's Supper. Second, wicked people in the church would corrupt others. Third and more positively, the discipline aimed at stimulating repentance in the person concerned

(4,12,5). Calvin strongly insisted that the whole process unfold in a constructive manner and be done with such moderation that no one would be injured (Ordinances, 70).

The significance of all three powers of the church, but especially spiritual jurisdiction, is that they add up to a view of the church as a holy community.[86] The Word of God is the soul of the church; discipline constitutes the sinews by which members are held together (4,12,1). When Calvin addressed the Anabaptists or separated churches, he said their ideals sounded perfectionist and unrealistic; the church is a mixed body and it is impossible to have a perfect or holy church (4,1,13). But at the same time Calvin *did* see the church advancing in holiness; "it is daily advancing," "it makes progress from day to day" (4,1,17). Through the consistory and the ministry exercised through this institution Calvin provided an environment that would help actualize or stimulate this growth in the church.

The historical functioning of the consistory.[87] Although this historical description overlaps the theological-prescriptive account just given, it puts some flesh on the skeletal structure without the fat of the actual cases. The consistory met every week on Thursdays for three to four hours in the former cloister of the canons of the Cathedral of St. Peter which came to be known as the Hall of the Consistory.[88] It was made up of "about twenty-five members: twelve elders, elected each year, and, *ex officio*, all the pastors of the city. Depending on the period, there were between nine and twenty-two pastors. . . . It also had an 'officer' with the duty of summoning people

---

86. The category is used by Ernst Troeltsch, and I shall return to it in later reflections on Calvin's ecclesiology.

87. This historical account of the consistory is drawn from Robert M. Kingdon, "The Geneva Consistory in the Time of Calvin," *Calvinism in Europe: 1540–1620*, ed. Andrew Pettegree, Alastair Duke, and Gillian Lewis (Cambridge and New York: Cambridge University Press, 1994), 21–34; idem, "The Institutional Matrix," *Adultery and Divorce in Calvin's Geneva* (Cambridge, Mass.: Harvard University Press, 1995), 7–30; idem, "Preface," *Registers of the Consistory of Geneva in the Time of Calvin*, I, 1542–44, ed. R. M. Kingdon et al. (Grand Rapids and Cambridge: Eerdmans, 2000), x–xvi; Thomas A. Lambert and Isabella M. Watt, "Introduction," *Registers of the Consistory of Geneva in the Time of Calvin*, I, xvii–xxxiv; E. William Monter, "The Consistory of Geneva, 1559–1569," *Bibliothèque d'Humanisme et Renaissance* 38 (1976): 467–84.

88. Kingdon, "The Geneva Consistory," 22; Lambert and Watt, *Registers*, xxix.

before the consistory and a secretary whose task was to transcribe the minutes of its weekly sessions."[89]

"The presiding officer of the consistory was one of the four syndics for the year. The remaining members sat on two benches. One of the benches was made up of the pastors on the city payroll, assigned to parishes within the city and in a number of villages in the city's hinterland which the municipal government controlled. Calvin, as permanent Moderator of the Company of Pastors, sat at the head of this bench. The other bench was made up of commissioners or 'elders,' chosen once a year in the elections in which the entire government was shaped, but often reelected to the position for a number of consecutive years. The slate of those nominated each year to be elders . . . was prepared by the outgoing Small Council every year before the elections. Unlike the other slates, however, the slates of deacons and elders were prepared under the terms of the ecclesiastical ordinances, in consultation with the pastors. When the consistory was fully operational, at the height of Calvin's career, it consisted of twelve elders and a number of pastors that varied but averaged between ten and twelve."[90] There were also distribution requirements for elders mentioned earlier so that each of the councils were represented as were geographical districts. The registers of the consistory make it clear that all twenty to twenty five members did not have to be there every session. The syndic was in charge of the meeting and led the questioning, but Calvin often dominated the proceedings as the members of the consistory deferred to him. Apart from his personality, he was the single most educated and famous religious leader and legal expert in the city. His credentials were overpowering.[91]

The historical records indicate that the typical outcomes of a case before the consistory fall into three categories. The first was a ritual scolding or remonstrance formulated usually by one of the ministers or by Calvin.[92] The second level was excommunication, barring a

---

89. Kingdon, *Registers*, xi.
90. Kingdon, *Adultery*, 13–14.
91. Ibid.,17.
92. Some people appeared before the consistory as petitioners rather than defendants. Many of the cases were quarrels among family members, relatives, complaints between acquaintances, clearly "low-voltage" issues. Most of the cases ended in reprimands. Monter, "The Consistory of Geneva," 471.

Wow,

person from at least the next quarterly communion or more. This was a punishment that was feared for either religious reasons or for its effect of humiliation or separation from the community, and it could lead to banishment if people did not seek reinstatement.[93] In a third level of action, if the offence was judged to involve a crime, it could be referred to the Small Council for a secular punishment.[94]

After some years of studying what the consistory actually did, Kingdon has formulated an assessment of its function in the church and the city. From the perspective of modern Western societies which value freedom and privacy, the consistory was surely an invasive institution. The editors of the Registers calculate that the consistory summoned between 6 and 7 percent of the adult population of the church every year, and in 1569 it reached as many as 15 percent.[95] But its role was not purely negative or repressive. The consistory had three broad functions: "it served as an educational institution, as a compulsory counseling service, and as a kind of court."[96] Most people are familiar with the third function. After a consideration of the cases in the registers during Calvin's life time, however, it appears that the consistory was considerably more than a piece of a repressive disciplinary system. Sometimes it functioned as a court of appeal, at other times as a court of arbitration. It "did indeed try to act as an educational institution and as a counseling service."[97] The many cases of family and neighborly fights that ended in reconciliation show that discipline for Calvin and these early Genevans could not be reduced to social control. The consistory "was also a genuinely caring institution. It really tried to assist everyone in its

---

93. It should be recalled that the consistory did not have a free hand to excommunicate apart from the consent of the magistrates until 1555. Thereafter the numbers of excommunications grew rapidly: in 1551 there were four; in 1557 almost 200; in 1569 there were 535. But most excommunications were for short durations, perhaps one communion service. Signs of repentance were expected so that the ban could be lifted. (Ibid., 476–77) Some of the cases in the city that ended in excommunication involved, in order of predominance: scandals and lying, domestic quarrels, quarrels with others, fornication, rebellion toward elders, superstition, blasphemy, theft, gambling, dancing, profane songs, usury. Ibid., 479.

94. Kingdon, *Adultery*, 18–21.

95. Lambert and Watt, *Registers*, xvii–xviii; Monter, "The Consistory of Geneva," 484.

96. Kingdon, "The Geneva Consistory," 24.

97. Ibid., 34.

city-state to live the kind of life it thought God intended people to
live....In Calvin's Geneva there was always someone available to
help."[98]

Church and state in the light of the consistory. What can be
said of the relation between the church and civil government in the
light of the controversy over the power of excommunication? Naphy responds to that question by removing it from the context of a
church-state battle: "one cannot consider the struggle about excommunication purely as a clash between the church/ministers and the
state/magistrates. Instead it is a question of jurisdiction and place in
the institutional structure of the state between one bureaucratic body,
the consistory, and another, the *Petit Conseil.*"[99] There was a conflict
between the consistory and the Small Council, but it was not a conflict between church and state, because the consistory for its part
served the city, and the government for its part never wavered in its
support of its ministers. "The debates about the final right to appeal
against an excommunication, however, was more about the correct
relationship between the two political institutions and the 'turf wars'
of two sets of magistrates than a clear fight between the church and
the state" (27). "Instead it was a disagreement between one institution of the state, the consistory, and another, the *Petit Conseil.* I
cannot stress this point strongly enough," insists Naphy. "The consistory had twelve elected magistrates on it, representing all three
councils. There is every reason to believe that these politicians —
and that is what they were — saw their presence as a sufficient check
on the power of the ministers" (26). The Small Council "held that
the consistory was a lower level of the republic's bureaucratic and
institutional structure and that appeals were possible depending on
the sentence. Thus, admonition and remonstrance were decreed and
delivered on the spot by the ministers and magistrates of the consistory. However, the application of excommunication (rather than its
recommendation), much like the recommendation to the criminal
courts for further punishment, was seen to be a matter left finally
to the *Petit Conseil*" (26). The view of church-state relations that

98. Ibid.
99. Naphy, "Church and State," 26. Page references in the text of this paragraph are
to this article of Naphy.

emerges from this analysis of the consistory is one of a unity of church and state, with a distinction but no separation within certain public spheres of authority, and a deliberate balance of powers where each sphere of authority in some measure held the other in check. The whole thing worked out politically in terms of the issues and the persons involved in their various capacities.

REFLECTIONS ON CALVIN'S ECCLESIOLOGY

Calvin's ecclesiology as it unfolded during his career as theologian and church father in Geneva became a source for the spread of a reformed tradition into different areas in Europe where it took on a variety of distinctive differences. A comparison of these different forms would provide a method for discovering the many implicit potentialities of Calvinist structures.[100] This section is restricted to underlining the more obvious themes that lie practically speaking on the surface of what has been sketched so briefly here. They are geared simply to emphasize distinctive traits which can contribute to the sense of pluralism in ecclesiology.

Almost in passing, François Wendel contrasts three of Calvin's proclivities with regard to church in contrast to the Lutherans that Calvin knew during his three year period in Strasbourg.[101] They are instructive, for they all seem to come from and represent Calvin himself and thus help in defining other distinctive elements. First of all, Calvin thought that the German theologians neglected church discipline; at least they did not accord it the importance he gave it. Second, they reproduced much more closely the Roman liturgy than Calvin thought necessary or proper. By contrast, Calvin believed that the order of worship that he followed resembled more closely patterns which he found in the New Testament itself. Third, Calvin believed that Lutheran churches allowed themselves to become strictly dependent upon civil political power and authority, particularly where the princes incorporated the churches into their political administration.

---

100. As in McNeill, *Calvinism.*
101. Wendel, *Calvin,* 64–65.

Calvin vs Luther

By contrast Calvin wanted a church autonomous and free to act in its own sphere, not independently from the state as we have seen, but in tandem with it, with its own prerogatives. These three themes do not exhaust the differences between the French and German evangelical churches, but they indicate trajectories.

The Roman Church and the Anabaptist Churches can rightly claim to be the natural foils for understanding Calvin's ecclesiology by contrast. But one can also note some major differences between Calvin's and Luther's understanding of the church as that was described in the last chapter. Five themes help differentiate Calvin from Luther in matters ecclesiological. Each one helps open up a sensitivity to the distinctiveness of Calvin's ecclesiology.

(1) The first has to do with *law*. Calvin had a more positive view of law than Luther. Although Calvin too stood against what he considered to be a Roman legalism that bound consciences, he introduced law into the church. He saw the positive need for discipline and an ordered and structured church life. This has bearing on what one might call ecclesial spirituality.

(2) A second theme, not far from law, more broadly revolves around institution. Although Calvin saw the church as a free community in the sense that it was spiritual and based on faith, still the church was also an institutional structure. It was both a spiritual community and one structured by an objective institution; both a voluntary community and at the same time a compulsory organization. Calvin allowed for a great deal of variety in church institution; his definition of the true church shows that he did not espouse a single, normative church polity. But the church had to have some definite institutional structure in a given place, its ministerial structure was not completely free, and Calvin found objective institutionalized ministries in the New Testament.[102] Church polity and ordinance did not bind Christian conscience, for only God's Word reached directly into the human soul. But indirectly the people in the church were expected

---

102. Jay notes negatively that Calvin's attempt to find a scriptural basis for his order of ministry succeeds no better "than that of the papist, episcopalian, or congregationalist . . . of his own tradition." Jay, *Church*, 174. But one can also say positively, on the premise of the pluralism of church order in the New Testament, that they are all equally successful.

to obey the ministers; they shared an institutional authority that ultimately went back to God's will.

Third, because the autonomy of church administration concerned Calvin deeply, his structuring of the various orders of the clergy into a semiautonomous entity gave the church more power in its *involvement in society*. No church, as a public institution, can fail to be involved and to have an impact on society. The difference here lies in scope and power. Like the medieval church, Calvin's church is deeply involved in society and the temporal sphere. The quality of this involvement plays out on two distinct levels. On the level of personal spirituality, in Calvin's view, church members should perceive themselves as involved in the world, and not hostile to participation in temporal, social life. Transcending the world transpires through discipline and use of the world for the glory of God. This has direct bearing on Christian spirituality, and we shall return to it further on. On the social level, the church as institution has an impact on the world. As a distinct institution, explicitly grounded in the Word of God, the church brings its message and its spiritual power to bear on the public order through its various ministries to peoples minds, their moral conduct, and their material needs when they fall through the cracks of society.

The relation between the church and society always contains ambiguities or tensions. Such tensions are readily apparent in Calvin's consistory. In some respects these tensions are inevitable. They are not new in the case of Geneva. But in the case of Calvin's church, modernity was beginning to take hold, and when they are viewed through the lens of the consistory in a city church, they appear with a clarity that is instructive. Some examples of these tensions are these: is the consistory an ecclesiastical institution or a mechanism of city government?[103] Clearly it was both in fact: it governed or regulated life in the city. But Calvin thought of it as a church ministry; it functioned as a conscience of the church and thus the city. Were the elders clergy or lay ministers? Although the company of pastors were consulted, the elders were actually appointed by the city magistrates

---

103. Kingdon refers to the consistory as part of the government of Geneva (*Adultery,* 11). Lambert and Watt refer to it as an ecclesiastical institution. *Registers,* xxx.

and not ordained; but Calvin understood them to be authorized by the New Testament as an office of the ministry of the church. Theologically the pastors were to be chosen by the company of the pastors and approved by the people; in fact, they were appointed by the Small Council upon nomination by the pastors. The syndic chaired the consistory, but Calvin and the pastors had considerable influence. How should one describe the relation between clergy and laity? One commentator speaks of Calvin's "clericalism" in which the clergy were positioned above the laity.[104] Another commentator can write that Calvin "to a far greater degree than Luther wiped out all distinctions between clerks and laity."[105] On spiritual and temporal power: the church wielded spiritual authority or power which is quite distinct from the power of civil government to force or coerce. Yet the consistory regularly handed over those who deserved punishment to the government. The power of excommunication itself is a spiritual jurisdiction and judgment, but no one would deny its coercive power in a monolithically religious city-state. All of these tensions were vital during the medieval period. They became much more acute when the church's boundaries were more intimately drawn to define a local or regional church.

Fourth, Naphy shows that there was much more cooperation between the government or the magistrates of the city of Geneva and the church than is usually depicted. Calvin drafted what was in effect the constitution of the church in his Ordinances. He was also charged "to lead the committee designed to draft Geneva's first post-independence constitution."[106] A survey of the design and workings of the four offices of church ministry with city's government illustrates "the unified nature of the relationship. Moreover, it highlights the immense area of overlap between the ecclesiastical and political realms. Finally, and most importantly, the Genevan republic and the

---

104. Bouwsma, *John Calvin*, 219–20.
105. Ganoczy, *Calvin*, 379, citing Wendel.
106. Naphy, "Church and State," 14–15. These actions of the magistrates indicated a good deal of initial trust. Naphy's view in this essay seems to have evolved from language used in his earlier work where he indicated that the magistrates were less open to Calvin's reform measures; Calvin's "vision of the correct relationship between the church and state in Geneva differed radically from that of the magistrates who recalled him." Naphy, *Calvin and the Consolidation of the Genevan Reformation*, 222.

Genevan church can be seen as a single, national unity comprising much of the same personnel and the same space. The composite, undifferentiated, and national character of the consistory is simply the most obvious expression of this."[107] The consistory in Geneva was unique; it was not the standard model. "In Geneva the consistory was as much an expression of state and magisterial power as it was religious and ministerial authority."[108]

Fifth, Calvin was personally concerned about the *universal church*, and some aspects of his ecclesiology show it. He energetically participated in ecumenical efforts and strove to prevent the splitting up of churches; he exported the Reformation beyond his own sphere as Geneva became the center for the whole Reformation movement. Although he rejected the current papal mode of an institutional unity of the universal church, Calvin elicited concern for the unity of all churches through intercommunion. He saw a possible role for councils. His view of the universal church transcended congregationalism. His model for the universal church approached the Cyprianic communion of churches but without the necessity of an episcopal structure of collegiality but open to the possibility of it.

The theme of the relation of the church to the world provides a context in which the most distinguishing characteristics of the church in Calvin's ecclesiology begin to appear. One could list several distinct ideas and motifs from Calvin's theology that support this particular feature of his ecclesiology: Calvin's idea of the transcendent and sovereign will of God, providence, his view of sanctification, the unity but nonreducibility of religion and morality, the spirituality of the use of creatures, stewardship and calling, and so on. The great difference of Calvin's church from the medieval church in this regard lay in the fact that the Roman Church was a universal institution. It operated from the Roman center and dealt with the macropolitics of Europe. The local church makes up the basic unit of Calvin's church. In this respect, he proposes an ecclesiology from below. The church's universality, if institutionally organized, would consist in a federation of churches in communion, united as one church by the

---

107. Naphy, "Church and State," 22.
108. Ibid., 20.

two marks of Word and Sacrament. But in the town or city with its environment the church constituted human society. It was in no way envisaged as apart from society. Its whole purpose as the means of salvation also implied that it was a leaven of society, an institutional force in forging a specifically Christian society.

Unpacking this further, the church's involvement with society unfolds on the two distinct if inseparable levels already mentioned. The one pertains to the spirituality of the individual members of the church; the other relates to the church as a social entity. Beginning with the level of personal spirituality, one can notice how explicitly in Calvin's theology engagement in the world enters into the self-understanding of Christian existence. Calvin's broader theology brings to his ecclesiology the foundations for a personal spirituality of engagement, even professional engagement, in the world and society. Calvin's doctrine that human laws cannot bind the conscience directly before God radically relativizes human institutions generally. The individual whose conscience primarily relates to God, especially as revealed by the Word, gains leverage over human prescriptions. "Thus does the individual in relation to the divine Word tower above his social context and its obligations and through his conscience experience the obligation to judge that social matrix by a higher norm."[109] This principle did not save conscientious objectors from being expelled from Geneva. But without it Calvin, by his own testimony, would never have been converted.

The doctrines of providence, election, sanctification, the third use of the law, vocation, the use of creatures reinforce this. One's sanctification occurs in and through one's life in the world. Thus for Calvin one's occupation or work consisted in more than the neutral context or sphere of activity in which one was set by divine providence. In Calvin one's calling becomes a means of sanctification; one moves toward sanctification *through* it and not just in it. "Because of his knowledge of his own election, each individual knew that the roots, so to speak, of his own individuality and its unique powers

---

109. Langdon Gilkey, *Reaping the Whirlwind: A Christian Interpretation of History* (New York: Seabury Press, 1976), 185.

were grounded in God's eternal will, an astonishing base for particular individuality with its unique and idiosyncratic characteristics and powers. Moreover, because the meaning of historical life is thus channeled *through* his individual activity, so related to God's will, his vocation is a creative role given to *him*, subject to *his* creative interpretation, and so 'open' for the determination by his own creative will."[110] Calvin's emphasis on special providence brings God's will to bear upon the specificity and uniqueness of each person's action. Calvin's church member is "filled with a deep consciousness of his or her own value as a person, with the high sense of a Divine mission to the world, of being mercifully privileged among thousands, and in possession of an immeasurable responsibility."[111]

The ideas of calling, providence, and election thus merge. As a Christian, the follower of Calvin is "drawn irresistibly into a wholehearted absorption in the tasks of service to the world and to society, to a life of unceasing, penetrating, and formative labor."[112] The reason for this is not a positive view of human nature, not in Calvin,[113] nor an optimism about history. He had a radical view of sin and human corruption. Rather it finds support in the absolute glory of God, election, the necessity of trusteeship and service to God's glory, God's will, and responsibility in the use of creatures.[114] The idea of progressive sanctification from the germ of election and justification strengthens the vision. In sum, Calvin absolutely transcends the bland assertion that no separation divides the church and social life or that the Christian ethic and life in the world are connected. Engagement in the world, in one's daily life as carpenter and citizen, shop-keeper, tradesman, or magistrate, constitute a spirituality of service ultimately willed by God in and through which one's unity with God becomes strengthened and actualized.

---

110. Ibid.

111. Troeltsch, *The Social Teaching*, 617. See the way Bouwsma, *John Calvin*, strings together Calvin's theology of *work* (198–99), *calling* (199–200), *stewardship* joined with an idea of the *common good* (201–03) as the climax of Calvin's teaching on social ethics.

112. Troeltsch, *The Social Teaching*, 589.

113. See T. F. Torrance, *Calvin's Doctrine of Man* (Grand Rapids: Eerdmans, 1957) who lays out Calvin's anthropology in detail.

114. Troeltsch, *The Social Teaching*, 589–90.

Calvin showed a bias for protecting society and the church over the rights of individuals. "Calvin's instincts were for the good of the public, but too often the good of the individual — which must be protected if in the long run the public is to benefit — was not protected." A number of cases show that the public "was protected, but not the individual."[115] But Graham is also clear that Calvin acted like a person of his time; his acquiescence in torture or the death penalty or other measures against individuals was not extraordinary. "'All the blessing we enjoy,' he proclaimed, 'have been entrusted to us by the Lord on this condition, that they should be dispensed for the good of our neighbors.'"[116] He saw all people bound together in society under certain relationships, as it were, of nature. Calvin put the community before the individual functionally, but also in the end spiritually. "The rich 'must one day give a reckoning of their vast wealth, that they may carefully and faithfully apply their abundance to good uses approved by God.'"[117]

Richard captures Calvin's framework for understanding spirituality in the basic theological categories of creation, anthropology, sin, and restoration through Christ, Spirit, and church. In the beginning the world and human beings were created so that in them the glory of God might shine forth as in a mirror. The order of the universe radiates God's wisdom and power; human existence especially was to reflect the image of God. Sin broke the order of creation and history; sin effaced the glorious image of God. But Christ is the turning point of restoration. "Adam was the first created after the image of God, and reflected as in a mirror the divine righteousness; and that image having been defaced by sin must now be restored in Christ. The regeneration of the godly is indeed . . . nothing else than the formation anew of the image of God in them. . . ."[118] Restoration of the image, righteousness, and glory of God in creation and human existence itself is being accomplished in and through those justified and

---

115. W. Fred Graham, "Church and Society: The Difficulty of Sheathing Swords," in *Readings in Calvin's Theology*, ed. Donald K. McKim (Grand Rapids: Baker Book House, 1984), 284–86.

116. Bouwsma, *John Calvin*, 201, citing Calvin, 3.7.5.

117. Ibid., 202, citing Calvin's Commentary on John 6:13.

118. Lucien J. Richard, *The Spirituality of John Calvin* (Atlanta: John Knox Press, 1974), 113, quoting Calvin's commentary on Ephesians 2:24.

sanctified by Jesus Christ and the Holy Spirit. Religious piety consists in being integrated into and living within God's new restored order of creation and history. The primary motive for this is not personal salvation, although that is not undermined, but the glory of God. This is manifested, first, when people obey the commandments of proper worship of God against all idolatry. Second, in many ways more tellingly, a true religious piety shows itself in an outgoing love and concern for others. In this way, Calvin's spirituality transcends all asceticism geared to personal self-fulfillment and moves it toward an engagement in society that will restore the image of God in creation itself.[119]

Finally, the eschatological dimension or perspective that Calvin brought to spirituality is also significant. John H. Leith sums up this relevance in three points and adds a fourth as a kind of summary.[120] First of all, the eschatological promise of fulfillment grounds the importance of human life. Second, an eschatological perspective frees the tragedies of human existence from their ultimate tyranny; the negativities of existence can in the end be made positive. Third, an "eschatological perspective provides a vantage point from which history can be judged."[121] That is, the kingdom of God represents a criterion for judgment. Finally, in sum: "The eschatological hope is the conviction that the eternal will of God will carry to completion the work which it has begun...."[122] This eschatological perspective entails a theology of history and the church plays a central role in it. "Calvin's interpretation of the eschatological defeat of Antichrist as an ongoing process imparts a vigorous dynamic to his view of

---

119. Ibid., 111–22, 174–80. One can see in Calvin's thought at this point a certain analogy with the shifts that Erasmus introduced relative to the *devotio moderna* that was common in Northern Europe in the fifteenth century. See CCH, I, 395–98, 401–6. Richard develops these continuities at pp. 122–29. Gene Haas reacts against the view that Calvin's ethics were conceived individualistically, or in the context of the individual before God, by charting the many ways the church shaped a Christian life in and for society. For Calvin "the church plays a vital role in molding the moral life of the believer, but, alternatively, ... the believer cannot make progress in the Christian life without involvement with fellow believers in the ecclesial community." "Calvin, the Church and Ethics," in *Calvin and the Church*, ed. David Foxgrover, 72–91 at 74.

120. John H. Leith, *John Calvin's Doctrine of the Christian Life* (Louisville: Westminster / John Knox, 1989), 162–65.

121. Ibid., 163.

122. Ibid., 165.

the task of the church in the world."[123] Through the preaching of God's word the church is "already effecting in history the dawning of that future day of the return of Christ."[124] "Because the final victory is already occurring in the present defeats suffered by the Antichrist, the kingdom of God is already being established in the world. Such present victories anticipate and lead to the final victory of Christ over Antichrist. The church and its activity are an essential part of the eschatological movement of history from advent to return."[125]

These foundations for a spirituality of daily life expand outward into a more comprehensive vision of the impact of the church on the world on the level of society. It has become clear that in Calvin the church functions as more than an organ of inner, personal, and spiritual salvation. He saw it as an effective means for christianizing a community. For Calvin scripture reveals doctrine, promulgates an ethics, and proffers a message of an all-embracing religious purpose that governs life in the world.[126] Scripture, the word of God, is not only God's word of forgiveness; it is also moral command; it echoes God's will. Thus the church, mediating that word, has legislative and disciplinary power. One must continually recall that everyone in a given place was a member of the church; this is still Christendom with no pluralism of churches in a single locale. In that context, in the intraecclesial sphere, public sinners proved themselves unfit to be part of the church or share at the Lord's Supper. But this automatically entailed the same constituency in broader secular terms. Thus the purification of the church means the purification of society; the church in being church also christianizes society. Calvin intentionally held together quality and quantity, something often taken as impossible to do, to have a holy community of the masses. Calvin of course knew as well as anyone that ecclesiastical discipline cannot make people righteous, "but this in no sense restricts [the

---

123. David E. Holwerda, "Eschatology and History: A Look at Calvin's Eschatological Vision," in *Readings in Calvin's Theology*, ed. Donald K. McKim (Grand Rapids: Baker Book House, 1984), 334.

124. Ibid., 334.

126. Troeltsch, *The Social Teachings*, 600–604.

church's] competence as an agency which facilitates the task of sanctification."[127] The church does not compete with the state here: civil discipline and law generally accomplish the same end, not just of repressing disorder, but of providing possible paths of sanctification. Also, as in the case of personal spirituality, here too the church influences society with more than just the political power of regulating conduct. The church possesses a theological conception of reality and history, and it mediates God's purposes, God's will, God's glory in history. As Troeltsch says, "the whole range of life [is placed] under the control of Christian regulations and Christian purposes."[128] The word of God governs the whole of life, and the whole of life becomes part of the church's purview. Calvin did not imagine a triumph of righteousness, a regeneration of society, or a new social order of justice in this world. Such would be incompatible with his conception of human sinfulness. He thought rather in terms of constant struggle, and at the same time expected that the church would bear visible fruit in the social life of a community.[129]

In the end, Milner provides the broadest generalization on Calvin's doctrine of the church when he reinterprets the grand vision underlying the *Institutes* in order to assign to the church an integral part in it. The structure consists of the narrative or drama of the original order of creation, the fall, and the economy of restoration. The dynamics of restoration are accomplished by the Word, through the working of the Spirit, mediated by the external means of the church.[130] Situating the church in this cosmic-historical scheme implies three things. First, the church consists in a historical movement effected by the Spirit. This means that the idea of a fixed institution

---

127. Höpfl, *The Christian Polity of John Calvin*, 191.
128. Troeltsch, *The Social Teaching*, 591.
129. Höpfl, *The Christian Polity of John Calvin*, 194.
130. Milner, *Calvin's Doctrine of the Church*, 193. Interpreters constantly repeat that Calvin's ecclesiology is christocentric. Ganoczy is one voice in a chorus that affirms this christocentrism "because its guiding principle is the doctrine of the mystical Body of Christ" (Ganoczy, *Calvin*, 184). While one can hardly deny that in some sense the Christian church is "christocentric," it is far more accurate to say that Calvin's ecclesiology is centered in the trinity. The economy of salvation, represented in the doctrines of the Creator, the Redeemer, and the sanctifying Spirit that uses the church as its instrument, provides Calvin with a narrative framework for understanding the church in history between creation and the eschaton.

or a static structure finds no place in Calvin's thinking. Second, the conception implies that sanctification constitutes the defining element of the church, or that for which the church exists. In the end, the essential does not lie in doctrine, creed, tradition, ritual, or polity; all these serve the restoration of the *imago Dei* in history. But, third, this means that the church bears an essential relation to history and the unfolding of society. The church does not belong apart from or at the margins of society. Rather Calvin's political activism arises out of the theological purpose of the church.[131]

PRINCIPLES FOR
A HISTORICAL ECCLESIOLOGY

The classic character of Calvin's ecclesiology could be illustrated by showing how some of its basic principles subsist in and energize the ecclesiologies of quite different churches. This chapter, however, concludes with an effort to abstract from Calvin's ecclesiology some principles for a historically conscious theology of the church that should be relevant for understanding the church in any given time. As such these have to be general and in some cases purely formal principles that make up consistent loci or points of tension in any ecclesiology. The criteria used in the selection of these principles lie in the estimate that they are both distinctive in Calvin and have universal relevance.

Theological principle supporting the role of the church in human history. Calvin expresses as well as any other theologian the theological principle that defines the role of the church in human history. This could be called the principle of incarnation, or the sacramental principle, or the principle of divine accommodation.[132] By contrast, it is imaginable that God could deal with each human being individually by his or her use of reason, or some direct contact, or illumination of the mind. But God has chosen to deal with human beings historically, in and through agents in the world, and the church has become the medium or "means" of God's communication to humankind of what was effected in the event of Jesus

131. Ibid., 194–95.
132. On divine accommodation to the human see Dowey, *Knowledge of God*, 3–17.

Christ. This conception, shared of course by other theologians, gives the church an intrinsic role in the divine economy and dialogue with human beings in history. It establishes theologically a responsibility to be exercised within the church by its ministers and leaders, along with a basis for their authority relative to the members at large.

Theological principle of the relation of Word and Spirit in the church. Because of the pressure of space, the preceding exposition barely alluded to the distinctive theology of the Spirit in Calvin, but it has bearing on his ecclesiology as Milner shows. It was indicated that the theological foundation of the church in the New Testament rests on Jesus as the Christ and the Holy Spirit. Calvin's theology of the complementary roles of Word and Spirit develop that foundation with considerable subtlety. Calvin reinforces his christocentric theology of the Word with a developed theology of the Spirit as divine illuminator and internal witness to the Word of God, the principle of the appropriation of God's revelation, and the sanctifier who leads to holiness. This threefold construction provides the church with more intrinsic theological support from another perspective. The church cannot be reduced to the organization of Christian people in community. Calvin supplies ecclesiology with profound theological warrant in the trinitarian summary of God's dealing with humankind in history.

Origins of the church and pluralism of church polity. Few areas in ecclesiology provide more room for controversy than the justification of a particular conception of church polity and ministry. Calvin proves to be of particular interest here because of the importance he placed on church structure, his historical knowledge, and the distinctive church polity he ultimately produced. Consider the last two of these in tandem. Calvin was convinced that the church structure as he laid it out represented a fairly close appropriation of the structure of the church in either the New Testament or the early church. In fact, he used this replication as an argument against the abuses which had been introduced historically into the Roman Church. This represents the classic argument of an appeal to origins and the normativity of the primitive church. But in fact Calvin constructed a distinctive ecclesiology. The ensemble of the four orders of ministry, their actual responsibilities, their interrelationships, and the location of authority in the whole mix appears to be quite new in history. This tension is not noticed as an argument against Calvin's arrangement, but as an example of the process of appropriation. In fact, Calvin's retrieval does approach quite accurately the spirit and content of the New Testament church. It would be of interest to study more closely how Calvin, who recognized the development of a monarchical episcopacy in the early church, argued that it should be abandoned for a more "corporate" exercise of church authority. But the process of Calvin's reasoning retains far more value than its actual results: the way he handles the tensions between continuity and change, how he defines the criteria for change across history, where he applies them, and how he used the large analogy that must obtain between the church in the first and second centuries along the shores of the Mediterranean and the church in sixteenth-century Geneva.

What Calvin demonstrates in this process and what may be raised up to a level of principle in historical ecclesiology can be gathered up in a series of propositions. One is that the New Testament church continues to exercise a normative claim on the ecclesiology of the Christian churches. Churches should reckon with it. Another is that there is no clear cut, consistent New Testament polity that can be applied today. The appropriation of the New Testament must include adjustments for the present historical situation and environment of the church. And third, the tensive unity of these two principles generates a third: the New Testament can be seen to validate different church polities at any given time. On the one hand, no version of the organization of the church in the New Testament can exclude all others; on the other hand, the pluralism of the New Testament witness to the church can stimulate different arrangements. Thus watching what Calvin does, beyond what he says, introduces one right into the heart of historical ecclesiology.

Church organization and historical environment. The principles announced in the last paragraph extend further to questions of inculturation, adaptation of church organization and polity to historical environment, what can change and what cannot, the unity among churches which have developed different organizational patterns and offices of ministry. These are big issues, and Calvin does not resolve them singlehandedly. But he exemplifies them. For example, inculturation. People have noted a certain resemblance between the order in Calvin's church and Geneva's political order, and a parallelism between his thinking on ecclesiastical and civil polity in general, particularly his preference for aristocracy over monarchy.[133] It would be useful to track down these resemblances in a more exact fashion, but the point can be made without so doing. Calvin in some measure bore a historical consciousness, recognized the necessity of adaptation to historical context and culture, and realized that differences in church organization should not stand for church division except in essential matters. What were essential would of course have to be debated, as they were, for example, in the controversies over the eucharist. But to engage in debate itself presupposes a form of unity. Calvin took church organization seriously, but he did not endow particular organizations with ultimacy. Church office at the end of the day was functional; it existed for ministry, and ministry was for mediation of the Word of God. Division among churches over church organization has little support in Calvin.

The tension between objective and existential holiness of the church. This tension was displayed in the development of the early Latin church as reflected in the ecclesiologies of Tertullian, Cyprian, and Augustine.[134] The church as a small community in a larger pagan world measured its holiness in the quality of the life of its members; in the larger church of Augustine, holiness resided more in the objective forms of the church which mediate God's grace than in the lives of the mass of its members. Troeltsch incorporates this tension in his characterization of the contrasting types of church he called "church" and "sect."[135] Upon analysis Calvin can be seen to dramatize this tension since he seems to want to maintain the church as a necessary society, to which all in a particular place belong, from birth with infant baptism, and at the same time retain the quality of existential uprightness typical of the Anabaptists, a voluntary association of people committed to moral discipline, but in this case encouraged through the institution of the consistory. In effect Calvin breaks the mold of the two distinct types in this respect, and makes the tension

---

133. Höpfl, *The Christian Polity of John Calvin*, 153–54.
134. See Robert F. Evans, *One and Holy: The Church in Latin Patristic Thought* (London: SPCK, 1972).
135. Troeltsch, *The Social Teachings*, 331–43.

overt and palpable. A church holy only in its objective forms offers an empty claim; a church which claimed holiness only on the basis of its members' lives, given the reality of sin, will be judged fraudulent. Churches and their ecclesiologies have to deal with this tension.

Ideals and actualities of ecclesial life: the character of a church. A tension between the ideals of a church and the actuality of its existence subsumes the last point on sanctification into a broader or more generalized formulation. Every church will contain a tension between its ideals and its performance along a variety of axes: understanding of doctrine, profession of faith, fidelity in prayer and worship, active commitment to church activities. Calvin believed that discipline in the general moral comportment of the members of the church was a high value, and the consistory was a means of actualizing the value. But another church may be much more acquiescent or tolerant or understanding of moral failure, at least on a public level, and not feel compelled to establish an institution like the consistory. All of this seems self-evident as matter of fact, but the question it raises goes to principle: how do churches adjudicate these various tensions between ideals on one side and recognition of finitude and sin on the other? For the most part this tension seems to be decided by the church's character. Or, to emphasize the descriptive or even tautologous nature of what is being said here, the way these tensions are resolved determines a certain reproducing "character" of a church. Many social and historical data may flow into the constellation of factors that determine a church's character; the sources of the different characters of churches include social, cultural, historical, and other elements.[136] In sum, one must expect that different churches will each take on or adapt a distinct character because of their relation to their environment and the many historical and social factors that shape their members. And this character will influence more strongly than some universal doctrine how the various tensions between ideal and possibility are managed.

---

136. H. Richard Niebuhr's *The Social Sources of Denominationalism* (New York: World Publishing, A Meridian Book, 1957), in analyzing denominations also gets at what I am calling the character of churches. Another term that suggests the same thing over a period of time is "tradition," not in the technical theological sense, but in the sense of a consistent character or bearing in history.

The relation of the church and the world. The last section developed at some length the way many theological and organizational factors come together in Calvin's theology and ecclesiology to form a powerful statement of the church's involvement in society. Such an understanding of the church's social commitment would be consistent with other ecclesiologies as well. For example, Calvin's ideas do not conflict seriously with the self-understanding of the Roman Church in the medieval period on this issue. But appreciation and retrieval of these themes in different places and in later periods will require major reinterpretation and reformulation. In the West, separation of church and state and the recognition of religious pluralism change the premises of the church's public engagement with society. When the church finds itself in the position of a small social minority, as in the early church, or in India or China today, its position vis-à-vis society cannot be immediately comparable to the church of Christendom. In an ecclesiology from below the most basic principles must always be appropriated contextually. But we have by no means exhausted the possibilities offered to the church by Western culture in the sixteenth century. We thus take up the Church of England as representative of another new and distinctive ecclesiology.

Chapter 3

The Church of England

During the sixteenth century England...declared its independence of Rome; the English church was brought increasingly under state control and the king assumed its earthly headship. Monasteries, chantries and religious guilds were dissolved, and much of the wealth of the church was confiscated by the government. This included not only land owned by religious orders, but also objects from parish churches: bells, communion-ware made from precious metals, and richly decorated vestments worn by priests when celebrating Mass. The number of saints' days was drastically reduced; pilgrimages to shrines were forbidden and the veneration of relics condemned; statues and wall-paintings were defaced and roods were pulled down. Prayers and Masses for the dead, along with the use of palms and ashes, were banned, and Latin services were replaced by a vernacular liturgy. These changes constituted the English Reformation, part of a wider European movement.[1]

This dramatic portrayal of the English Reformation begins imaginatively with what was in place and depicts it largely as a process of tearing down. Looking backward from the end of the reign of Elizabeth I in 1603, however, one can read the English Reformation as a slow historical construction of a distinctive Christian church. That history was jerky, not smooth; the Reformation was accomplished by a series of "revolutionary" decisions constituting real reversals. But by the end of the sixteenth century the Church of England had developed into a church among the churches of Western Christianity, with a coherent, integral ecclesiology.

---

1. Doreen Rosman, *From Catholic to Protestant: Religion and the People in Tudor England* (London: University College London Press, 1996), 18.

This chapter will expand on this proposition, but a mere glance reveals large differences between the Church of England, the Church of Rome, and the churches inspired by Luther and Calvin. This is a national church, not a world church, not a regional church, and not an urban church. Its size and scope in terms of territory and members set it off from all three of the other churches. This church had no single reformer whose spirit informs it in a defining way; in fact no single distinctive characteristic that might define this church would win a consensus. This church was not created or formed all at once, or even in a relatively short period of time. It emerged out of a long series of events that gradually contributed pieces of a church that would continue to grow after its first solidification during the reign of Elizabeth I.

The whole medieval church in England provided the collective subject that became transformed into the Church of England. But that narrowly focused story is unintelligible apart from the wider history of Europe, religious and secular. Much of this has to be left as supposition. This chapter represents the ecclesiology of the Church of England in the sixteenth century in a manner analogous to the last two chapters. It begins by narrating the key historical events that together constituted the English Reformation. It then repairs to the comprehensive characterization of the church provided at the end of the century by Richard Hooker in his eight volume work on the polity of the Church of England for a systematic presentation of its ecclesiology. The concluding two sections consist in a set of broad reflections about this ecclesiology, implicitly relating it to other understandings of the church, and a set of distinctive principles or instances of ones highlighted in past chapters that may be useful for a constructive ecclesiology at any given time.

DEVELOPMENT OF
THE CHURCH OF ENGLAND

The few pages which follow offer such an abbreviated account of the development of the Church of England that it may be no history at all. They do not represent the motives or causality of the events as they unfold, nor a theory that in some measure explains what happened. But they gather together some major events and products of human decision that proved to bear constitutive value for the formation of this church on the symbolic and institutional levels.[2] Space requires, then, that this account be narrowly focused on what might be called religious history, as it rushes by the international political pressures of this period in English history: the periodic fiscal crises of government because of war or internal economic situations that drove decisions; the regional competitions; the influx of new religious ideas in a country and church that, we now see, was passing from the "Middle Ages" to the "modern period";[3] the direct role of various figures, political and religious, in the unfolding of particular events; the place of the university and theologians in the mix; the faith of the people as in a social history from below. The role of the historian includes analyses of these complex factors and various judgments that explain or account for the twists and turns of history. While this may be lacking, the story still recalls a truly distinctive context and series of events that led to the Church of England.

To perform this task with some clarity and dispatch a set of three interlocking frameworks mark stages in the development, even though the simplicity of this formula may deceive. The first schema is temporal: we follow the development of the Church of England through the monarchies of Henry VIII (1509–47), Edward VI (1547–53), Mary (1553–58), and Elizabeth I (1558–1603). The reigns of

---

    2. The following works have been consulted for this narrative: David Daniell, *William Tyndale: A Biography* (New Haven and London: Yale University Press, 1994); A. G. Dickens, *The English Reformation*, 2nd ed (London: BT Batsford, 1989); Susan Doran, *Elizabeth I and Religion 1558–1603* (London and New York: Routledge, 1994); Christopher Haigh, *English Reformations: Religion, Politics, and Society under the Tudors* (Oxford: Clarendon Press, 1993); David Knowles, *Bare Ruined Choirs: The Dissolution of the English Monasteries* (Cambridge/New York: Cambridge University Press, 1976); Peter Lake, *Moderate Puritans and the Elizabethan Church* (Cambridge: Cambridge University Press, 1982); Diarmaid MacCulloch, *Thomas Cranmer: A Life* (New Haven and London: Yale University Press, 1996); *The Boy King: Edward VI and the Protestant Reformation* (New York: Palgrave, for St. Martin's Press, 1999); Rosman, *Catholic to Protestant*.
    3. These periods did not exist, nor did any clear threshold. Whatever reality they have was created by the corporate historical decisions of the period. Yet the phrase still carries the broad meaning that something bigger was going on, and this particular segment of history was part of it.

Henry, Edward, and Elizabeth may also be regarded as three stages of development which loosely correlate with three principal structural forms which supported and provided a specific character to the Church of England: royal supremacy, the Book of Common Prayer, and the Thirty-Nine Articles of Religion. Other major actors and a whole congeries of factors contribute to all of these stages. But this straightforward map helps to understand how these building blocks were gradually set in place. Hooker's analytical account of the structure they supported will thus be provided with a historical context.

Royal Supremacy (Henry VIII)

The church in England at the eve of the Reformation is an obvious place to begin this narrative. One might characterize this church generally as the church of the late Middle Ages. Rosman provides an extended description of the everyday life in this church; she indicates that the English church was not in a state of decline, but showed signs of great vitality in the building of churches, pilgrimages, new fraternities, printing of religious material in the vernacular, sermons and so on. "It was this enthusiasm about religion that prompted calls for abuses to be reformed. Critics came from within the church."[4] Their criticism, moreover, touched actual problems, or the Reformation would never have taken hold in England.

Many of the factors that called out for change were the legacy of the medieval church. The influence of Wyclif lived on in England in the Lollard movement of lay preachers that carried his ideals: clergy should be in their parishes preaching God's word, and the people should have God's biblical word in English. Wyclif wanted a literate clergy who lived poorly; in fact, many clergy in the countryside lived in poverty, were ignorant, worked other manual jobs on the side, and compromised their celibate status. The system of benefices allowed absentee priests to pay low salaries to their vicars who had little education but learned the job by apprenticeship.[5]

---

4. Rosman, *Catholic to Protestant*, 19.
5. Dickens, *English Reformation*, 68–74.

By the early 1520s the ideas of Luther were prevalent enough in England that Henry VIII felt the need to publicly defend the seven sacraments against the German reformer, for which he was rewarded with the title of *Defensor Fidei* by the pope in 1521. But Luther's ideas were discussed more objectively in the universities, and they gained a sympathetic hearing among many. Luther's critique took aim at practices of the Roman Church as such and thus found targets in England as well: the objectification of piety in pilgrimages and devotions, clerical celibacy, monastic wealth, subordination to Rome, the mixture of the religious with temporal power.[6] Luther's doctrine of justification by faith and his appeal to scripture appeared especially threatening. While Wyclif provided a pied à terre in England for Lutheran ideas, attention of the universities to humanism and the return to sources contributed more directly to the evangelical movement.

The story of Tyndale and the English Bible provides insight into the initial phase of the English Reformation.[7] Copies of the translation of the Bible into English accomplished by Wyclif and his associates circulated in England as subversive literature since the late fourteenth century. To understand a situation in which the availability of the Bible in one's own language would appear disadvantageous, one must think in the broad symbolic terms of mediated religious authority. The Bible represented God's inspired word and made directly available, in a seemingly comprehensible language, what often appeared disconnected or at odds with the authoritative teachings of the church. Subversion of ecclesiastical authority, therefore, exactly

---

6. Ibid., 46–60.

7. See Benson Bobrick, *Wide as the Waters: The Story of the English Bible and the Revolution It Inspired* (New York: Simon & Schuster, 2001). The chapter on William Tyndale, 79–136, is especially instructive. William Tyndale (c. 1494–1536) had studied at Oxford and Cambridge, was influenced by Luther and the evangelical movement, and in the 1520s dedicated his life to translating the Bible into English. Working on the continent, his translation of the New Testament began arriving in England in 1526. Once discovered, the church orchestrated a serious attack on selling, possessing, and reading the English New Testament, and it had to be smuggled into the country. The vernacular New Testament was closely associated with Luther and hence with heresy. Tyndale's English New Testament gave people the whole New Testament in their own language and "opened the gates of the flood of biblical knowledge which has been freely available to us ever since." Daniell, *Tyndale*, 134, 174, 279.

describes the threat of the English Bible.[8] Tyndale thus played an important role in the beginnings of the evangelical movement in England.

Two other factors, more mundane and set against the background of the a strong nationalist spirit in England, provided some of the momentum toward the Act of Supremacy. One issue involved governmental finances and taxes. The church owned one quarter of the land of England prior to the Reformation.[9] That wealth was subject to taxation by Rome, and each year tax payments, annates, left the country for Rome. There was never a time in the late Middle Ages when English rulers did not regret the loss of that revenue. The other issue concerned the divorce of Henry VIII from his Spanish wife, Katherine of Aragon. Henry wanted a male heir, Katherine seemed unable to give him one, he and his canon lawyers found grounds for divorce in scripture, a case many think would have been granted had Katherine not been the aunt of Emperor Charles V. Henry began pursuing the case in the late 1520s but without success.

Two men assisted Henry VIII during the 1530s as he gradually turned toward reformation of the church. Thomas Cromwell served as Henry's executive officer from 1532 until 1540 and was the most influential man in the realm after Henry himself. Thomas Cranmer was consecrated archbishop of Canterbury in 1533, a position in which he served until his execution by Mary in 1556.[10] Cranmer also became Henry's friend. Both were his allies as Henry moved by steps against the dependence of the English Church on Rome. Henry worked for the most part legally through parliament. In 1532 the

---

8. Tyndale worked on the continent until he was captured by the anti-reformation faction in Belgium and strangled before being burned as a heretic in 1536. Henry VIII resisted the English Bible during the 1520s and with his Chancellor since 1529, Thomas More, worked to contain the influx of copies smuggled into the country.

9. Rosman, *Catholic to Protestant*, 11. MacCulloch estimates it at two fifths. *Cranmer*, 166.

10. Cranmer (1489–1556), a Cambridge don up to the late 1520s, after some experience in diplomacy, became deeply engaged in the political campaign for the annulment of Henry's marriage in 1529. He participated in various missions to the continent, used the occasions to learn more of the reform movement, and became acquainted with reformers including Bucer in 1531. Cranmer was appointed archbishop of Canterbury in October 1532, through the influence of the Boleyn family, while he was on a mission to the court of the emperor. He was installed in 1533 upon his return to England. MacCulloch, *Cranmer*, 41–78.

First Act in Restraint of Annates conditionally withheld their payment to Rome while their very existence was negotiated. In 1533 parliament passed the Act in Restraint of Appeals which declared the English Church's competence to solve such cases as marriage problems and bequests without appeal to Rome, in effect declaring the sovereignty of the national church. The Second Act in Restraint of Annates of 1534 then outlawed the payment of annates to Rome, and those funds were diverted to the government. It also withdrew from the pope while awarding to the king the power to nominate, in effect to appoint, candidates to be elected and consecrated bishops. Finally, later that same year, parliament passed the Act of Supremacy which made the ruling monarch the "Head of the Church." For many this did not appear a radical step because tension between pope and temporal ruler, with encroachments in each direction, had characterized the church since the Gregorian reform. At this point doctrine and the sacramental life in the parishes were unaffected; Supremacy was accepted, or at least not resisted, by the bishops and lower clergy alike. Yet from another perspective everything changed, including the very referent of the term "church." The Church of England was now an autonomous church. Henry had accomplished a twofold revolution: he broke the English Church off from Rome, and he subjugated it to the English Crown by law in parliament.[11] This was a political or juridical revolution.

It remains to chronicle some of the major events and developments in the Church of England during the remaining thirteen years of Henry's rule. The dissolution of the monasteries and their expropriation must rank as the most massive and dramatic move of Henry's reign. 1535 saw a visitation of the religious houses throughout the realm. Then, in 1536, the Act for the Dissolution of the Lesser Monasteries, later extended to all religious houses of men and women, began a process lasting four years of dismantling religious life in England. The stated reasons for this action pointed to various kinds of religious abuse or laxity, but historians generally agree that the real reason was economic. The intent was to endow the

---

11. Dickens, *English Reformation,* 106.

monarchy with land and to gain sufficient income to pursue interests abroad. But the need for ready cash encouraged the sale of the land to the gentry. Many of the religious were pensioned off and taken in, but the end of the monastic movement in England did not occur without much pain and considerable disruption of the religious life of the towns dependent on the monasteries.[12]

Before Tyndale's death in 1536, Henry VIII became convinced of the positive role of an English Bible and promoted it. In 1535 the first full English Bible was finally published under the auspices of Miles Coverdale. But it was not satisfactory and another was commissioned, and in 1539 the so called Great Bible appeared. There were to be copies in every church in England. Also beginning in 1535 a number of official documents were published which sought to state a broad unifying consensus within this first stage of the emerging Church of England. The Ten Articles (1536), issued by authority of the convocation of bishops, showed that the church was still the Catholic church but with a salutary internalization of certain Lutheran evangelical themes. They affirmed the normativity of scripture and the early councils, three sacraments, the doctrine of real presence as well as the language of justification by faith; they also respected images, the honoring of saints, certain medieval rites and ceremonies, and prayer for the dead.[13] This was followed in 1537 with "The Bishops' Book," a practical handbook of instruction based on the Ten Articles.

Struggle lay behind all these developments, between the party of Cranmer, who advanced the evangelical cause as best he could,

---

12. David Knowles, *Bare Ruined Choirs: The Dissolution of the English Monasteries* (Cambridge/New York: Cambridge University Press, 1976), tells this story.

13. The Ten Articles were a statement produced by convocation with an introduction by the king representing "the first attempt at defining what Henry VIII's Church now believed." The ten were divided between five on doctrine and five on ceremonies. Behind the doctrinal propositions were a set of seventeen compromise conclusions known as the Wittenberg Articles which had been developed in conference with Lutherans in the winter and spring of 1536. The Ten Articles, which committed the English Church to the doctrine of justification by faith, proved to be divisive: there was no meeting of minds between evangelicals and conservatives, and the two convocations, Canterbury and York, had different tempers. "All subsequent doctrinal statements, during the entire course of the English Reformation up to 1563, were thrashed out in private committees of bishops and theologians, with Convocation having little or no say in them." MacCulloch, *Cranmer,* 161–65.

and those who resisted, such as Stephen Gardiner (1483–1555), bishop of Winchester. Thus in 1539 the pendulum seemed to swing back as the king pressed the passage by parliament of the Act of Six Articles which sharply reasserted certain Catholic conceptions and practices: transubstantiation, clerical celibacy, auricular confession among others. Henry insisted on the Catholic character of the church. In 1543 the manual "The Bishops' Book" was revised and published as "The King's Book." Incorporating Henry's views and using more precise theological language, it represented a certain but not total distancing from Lutheran ideas.[14] At Henry's death in 1547 the Church of England was an autonomous national church with open ties to the Reformation churches on the continent and, although shorn of monasticism, still very identifiably a Catholic church.

The Book of Common Prayer (Edward VI)

The deepest changes in the church in England occurred during the six and a half year reign of Edward VI. The boy king was educated in the spirit of the Reformation and surrounded by a Council of Regency that encouraged development in this direction. Also, by the late 1540s ideas from John Calvin's Geneva were beginning to challenge the Lutheran influence. Haigh sums up the reforming events of Edward's reign: "In 1547 there were new reformist Injunctions and new evangelical *Homilies*; endowed prayers were suppressed, and the laity allowed communion in both bread and wine. In 1548 church images were pulled down, and an Order of Communion introduced English prayers to the Latin mass. In 1549 the Latin rites were replaced by a half-Protestant Book of Common Prayer, and the clergy were permitted to marry. In 1550 altars were exchanged for communion tables, and a new Ordinal provided Protestant pastors rather than Catholic priests. In 1551 the episcopate was remodeled and a corps of missionary preachers created. In 1552 there was a decisively Protestant second Prayer Book. In 1553 redundant mass equipment was confiscated, the Protestant theology of the church

---

14. E. J. Bicknell, *A Theological Introduction to the Thirty-Nine Articles of the Church of England*, 3rd rev. ed. (London: Longmans, Green, 1955), 8–10.

defined in Forty-Two Articles, and a Catechism published to teach the new religion."[15]

In December of 1547 Parliament passed the Act for the Dissolution of Chantries, that is, the chapels, colleges, hospitals, fraternities, guilds, and other religious entities that were endowed with property for the performance of religious rites. The action was aimed at wiping out superstitious practices at various shrines and pilgrim sites and was sweeping in its scope: even religious objects, such as monstrances and art work, were confiscated. Whereas the monasteries and religious houses operated in a more self-contained manner, the effects of this suppression reached more widely into the common religious life and popular piety of the people, altering the spiritual fabric of society.[16] "Within three years of Edward's accession all images had been removed from churches ... and in most cases windows had been reglazed and walls whitewashed."[17]

In 1549 Cranmer's First Prayer Book addressed the spiritual vacuum created by the radical curtailment of popular piety. It had been in preparation for some time, but in earnest after the death of Henry. The development of the Book of Common Prayer unfolded within a context of struggle between those desirous "of worship after the pattern of Protestant orders of worship and those who would reform it after the pattern of medieval worship."[18]

---

15. Haigh, *Reformations*, 168. MacCulloch believes that the group of evangelicals "knew from the start in 1547 exactly what Reformation it wanted: whatever hesitations occurred were primarily attributable to the need to disarm conservative opposition.... There was an essential continuity of purpose in a graduated series of religious changes over seven years. These changes were designed to destroy one church and build another, in a religious revolution of ruthless thoroughness. Thomas Cranmer was the one man who guaranteed the continuity of the changes, and he was chiefly responsible for planning them as they occurred, although more practical secular politicians decided the pace at which they should be put into effect." MacCulloch, *Cranmer,* 365–66.

16. Dickens, *English Reformation*, 230–42. This movement also had many characteristics of a land-grab.

17. Rosman, *From Catholic to Protestant*, 44. "In many respects Protestants were right to assume that if they destroyed the shrines and representations of saints they would put an end to prayer directed towards them." She points to the fact that fraternities suppressed in 1547 could have been reconstituted in Mary's reign but generally were not. Ibid., 46.

18. John E. Booty, "History of the 1559 Book of Common Prayer," *The Book of Common Prayer 1559* (Charlottesville: University Press of Virginia, 1976), 346–47. Cited hereafter as "History." MacCulloch describes Cranmer's work on the Prayer Book

Cranmer provided the creative genius for the Prayer Book. During the reign of Henry VIII he facilitated a gradual introduction of the English Bible into liturgical use. In the 1540s he worked on the reform of the breviary and the production of a book of sermons to be used in the parishes; he "engaged in a reform of the medieval Processional. In 1544 he produced an English Litany in response to the King's request."[19] The death of Henry opened the way to further development of the liturgy.

In the Fall of 1548 Cranmer worked with a committee to draft the first Prayer Book. Parliament debated it during December and "passed a uniformity act, to which was appended the Book of Common Prayer, on January 21, 1549, and the first copies were on sale by March 7. The book was to be in use by Whitsunday, June 9, and was to displace all other orders of worship."[20] The Prayer Book was introduced with decisiveness: in December 1549 all the old service books were ordered to be destroyed; in London altars were replaced with "the Lord's board after the form of an honest table decently covered."[21]

The Prayer Book was new and the subject of much criticism from the left and the right and from those opposed to all change. Thus work on revision began almost immediately. Among those consulted were Martin Bucer and other European reformers living in England.[22] In April of 1552 a second Prayer Book was legislated to go into effect on All Saints Day. It contained some significant changes, especially relative to the Lord's Supper or "Order of Communion," and in this respect moved away from the medieval and toward a more Protestant and scriptural understanding and practice. The Prayer Book of 1552,

---

in terms of his part in the writing and editing, what help he had, what his sources were, the content, and the particular genius that he contributed to the work. *Cranmer,* 395–421.

19. Booty, "History," 349–50.

20. Ibid., 353.

21. Douglas Harrison, "Introduction," *The First and Second Prayer Books of Edward VI* (London: Dent, 1975), xiii. Cited hereafter as Harrison, "Introduction."

22. MacCulloch notes the strong influence Bucer had on Cranmer's theology generally, but especially on his eucharistic theology (MacCulloch, *Cranmer,* 380–81). "The opinions of both Bucer and Martyr very significantly influenced the revision of the Prayer Book, although Cranmer did not slavishly follow their recommendations in all things." Ibid., 505.

however, did not last long because Edward died the following year and Mary forbade its use. But Elizabeth I would reinstate it in 1559.

The Book of Common Prayer brought together in one book in English a broad variety of the prayers used in the church, most importantly the public prayers used by the clergy to lead community worship. It integrated into these prayers the reading of the scriptures. The traditional reading or singing of the hours and the readings of the breviary were distributed into the orders of Morning Prayer and Evening Prayer. And readings from the whole of the scriptures were fitted into the year's calendar. The book contained the Litany which was prescribed for various liturgical celebrations, as well as the collects, epistles, and gospels to be read at Holy Communion throughout the year. The order of Holy Communion was set forth along with the rituals for baptism, confirmation (including a brief catechism analogous to those of the medieval period), matrimony, visitation and communion of the sick, burial, the thanksgiving of women after childbirth, and a rite of commination against sinners.

What are some of the principles that guided the revision and editing of traditional prayers? The Preface indicates closeness to scripture as a criterion. The Prayer Book leaves out "many things whereof some be untrue, some uncertain, some vain and superstitious," so that everything may be the pure Word of God or grounded in it.[23]

The section entitled "Of Ceremonies, Why Some Be Abolished and Some Retained" offers some rationale for the construction of the Prayer Book (BCP, 18–21). It begins with a premise that a certain common order for the whole church is a good thing. Second, the ceremonies chosen possess a power of edification. Third, the Prayer Book explicitly tries to chart a middle course between love of novelty and attachment to the past with ceremonies thought pleasing to God. Simplicity became a criterion of selection, a desire to cut through sheer accumulated excess in custom and ceremonial devotion. In sum, the selection aimed at "those ceremonies which do serve to a decent order and godly discipline, and such as be apt to stir up the dull mind of man to the remembrance of his duty to God by

---

23. "Preface," *The Book of Common Prayer* (BCP), 16. References are to pages in the text of the Booty edition cited above.

some notable and special signification whereby he might be edified" (BCP, 19). Certain ceremonies were eliminated when they appeared to be superstitious, or when they occasioned offerings of money and thus could be used for financial gain, or when the practices burdened people's consciences without cause.

One can begin to measure the enormous significance of the Book of Common Prayer for the Church of England by seeing the many needs it met and levels at which it functioned. On a general social and political level it simplified and standardized the rites and ceremonies of worship, and it offered a comprehensive, unified, ecclesial piety in English. The Prayer Book formed a bridge to the past insofar as basic ritual structures of the past were drawn up into it. "As constructed, the Book of Common Prayer contained all the services needed for the regular weekday and Sunday worship of the church and occasional services to meet pastoral needs, emphasizing the great events of life: birth, marriage, sickness, and death. The Prayer Book, preserving tradition, thus provided for various understandings of the passage of time: the church year of the propers; secular time in the daily offices; the course of a lifetime in the occasional services; and the dynamic view of time in the Holy Communion with its remembering (*anamnesis*) of events past, in the light of things to come (the messianic banquet), whereby Christ's presence is realized and human existence transformed in the present."[24]

On the personal and religious levels, the Prayer Book needed time to fill the void left with the sudden changes in the Edwardian church; it was not broadly or nationally influential during Edward's reign. The full effects of the revised liturgy would only gradually be felt and internalized during the Elizabethan period. The book became pervasive in the Elizabethan church and thus in society as a common point of reference with which all were familiar. Everyone was supposed to go to church; and every church used the Book of Common prayer for all their ceremonies. One was influenced by the book even if one was a dissenter from the Elizabethan church. Just the shift to English carried consequences.[25] Besides the value of prayer itself,

---

24. Booty, "History," 355.

25. A dimension of its impact can be understood against the background of the medieval mass where two parallel activities were going on, the actions of the priest

the services taught the faith: "learning by reading and being read to, by means of Scripture, preaching, the recitation of basic formularies, and the formal teaching of the catechism heard recited over and over again at Evening Prayer."[26]

Finally, on the theological level, the English Reformation, no less than the movements inspired by Luther and Calvin, was driven by the return to scripture and the religious primacy of the word of God. Cranmer's design of the Book of Common Prayer displayed this operative principle and goal of giving the word of God a central place in the common worship of the Church.[27]

To sum up, the Book of Common Prayer turned out to be attractive to devotion and able to preserve Catholic elements in a way that both embodied some and withstood other evangelical influences. In the end "Cranmer's accomplished liturgical work survived [Mary's] persecution to afford a solid basis for Elizabeth's resumption of the Edwardian experiment. More than any other factor this work gave a distinctive and unique flavor to the national Church."[28] More sharply, the English rite contained in the Prayer Book was "the Archbishop's great legacy to history."[29]

The Thirty-Nine Articles (Elizabeth I)

Mary I reigned from 1553 to 1558: she reestablished the bond with Rome, celibacy of the clergy, and the liturgy and sacraments of the medieval church.[30] She also persecuted the reformers. With the reign

---

and the devotional activity of the people: "the great moment of union of priest and people coming at the elevation of the consecrated host." By contrast, the commonness of the rite of the Prayer Book also connotes "the priest and people attending to the same aspects of the liturgy together. Hence the repeated emphasis not only on the vernacular but on clerical audibility...." Judith Maltby, *Prayer Book and People in Elizabethan and Early Stuart England* (Cambridge: University Press, 1998), 40–41.

26. Booty, "History," 378.

27. Ibid., 360.

28. Dickins, *English Reformation*, 385.

29. MacCulloch, *Cranmer*, 397.

30. In Haigh's view: "The Marian reconstruction of Catholicism was a success" (*Reformations*, 236). It was not an aberration as many historians portray it. He counters the standard view by saying the old religion was still strong; the Protestants remained a significant minority movement. Perhaps not a total success in only five years. "But the evidence from the parishes is of considerable and continuing support for traditional services and celebrations...." The main failures in Mary's reign were political and economic, whereas in terms of the church there were signs of a revival of religion on

of Elizabeth the Reformation regained momentum again, and by its end the Church of England was firmly established. At the beginning of Elizabeth's reign "the majority of men and women in England and in Wales were Catholic in belief," and the task was to win them to the new church.[31] "In this, the government had considerable success. By the end of the reign English Catholicism had shrunk to a very small sect (constituting about 1 or 2 per cent of the population), practicing a household religion which posed little threat to the monarch or the Church."[32] The solidification of the Church of England was a gradual process over the period of Elizabeth's long reign involving many religious battles with puritans on the left and Catholic missionaries on the right. Among many, three elements of the Elizabethan settlement deserve special notice: the legal foundation, the doctrinal framework of the Thirty-Nine Articles of Religion, and the Puritan constituency.

The essential elements of Elizabethan religious policy were set in place during the first session of parliament of her reign in 1559 with the passage of the Act of Supremacy and the Act of Uniformity. This did not happen spontaneously. It began with a House of Lords that favored the status quo, including all the bishops. But with political pressure, and the queen's acceptance of the title of "Supreme Governor" of the church instead of "Supreme Head," the legislation was passed on April 28, 1559, and after it all the bishops save one took the Oath of Supremacy. The uniformity was of course directed toward use of the Book of Common Prayer, in this case the second Edwardian Prayer Book with a number of revisions in a restorationist direction. For example, the 1559 Prayer Book included a more

---

the parish level (Ibid., 236). Haigh credits the success of Mary's claim on the throne to alienation of people because of the government's intense unpopularity in the wake of its confiscations of property and possessions of the parishes. Ibid., 183.

31. Doran, *Elizabeth I*, 48. The changes during the Edwardian and Marian periods were met by a good deal of absenteeism from religious services. MacCulloch accepts as a possible explanation the suggestion of historians such as Eamon Duffy and others that the medieval Western church "had intimately engaged the population in a complex and rich life of devotional practice. If that is so, it was not so much indifference as trauma which emptied the pews in the early Reformation: a polarization of religious attitudes, not an abandonment of religion." Where Edward's church succeeded, Mary's church stimulated an analogous reaction. MacCulloch, *Boy King*, 108.

32. Doran, *Elizabeth I*, 48.

traditional understanding of eucharist and called for the use of the ornaments and vestments that was in place in the second year of Edward's reign. Elizabeth also promulgated the Royal Injunctions of 1559, regulations governing church life, which generally moved in a conservative direction. For example, they included directives regarding distinctive dress for clergy in their everyday wear; they encouraged church music; unleavened bread was allowed for Communion. The injunctions were also directed toward the education of clergy, required monthly sermons in the parishes, and allowed clerical marriage. They formed the basis for a royal visitation of the church throughout the country beginning in the summer of 1559.[33]

After the Act of Supremacy and the Book of Common Prayer, the third essential element of the new Church of England lay in its collection of basic doctrines in the Thirty-Nine Articles of Religion.[34] These articles had a history that began with the Ten Articles of 1536. These were developed into the Forty-Two Articles written by Cranmer in 1553. These Forty-Two Articles were carefully revised, amended in convocation, and then passed by the convocation of bishops in 1563. They passed into statutory law by an act of parliament in 1571. The Articles thus reach back into the Edwardian period and Cranmer's construction, but they became a constitutive dimension

---

33. Ibid., 14–17. Haigh, in *Reformations,* characterizes Elizabeth's reform in several facets that make it distinctive. First, it was top down, an imposition of her convictions and will and not based on popular demand from below. Second, over and above supremacy, it consisted mainly in a restoration of Edwardian provisions. Third, the reformation was to be accomplished in once-for-all legislative action in 1559, as distinct from a longer, drawn out program of reform by increment (239). Fourth, when this met resistance Elizabeth and her allies "achieved their majority by the intimidation and imprisonment of bishops, and by buying off the nobles; they had been helped by episcopal vacancies, unfilled since 1557 because of Pole's dispute with the pope" (241). The legislation was followed by a visitation where the clergy were summoned and asked to subscribe to "the supremacy, the Prayer Book, and the Injunctions" (243). The subscription was uneven, but generally less than half the clergy subscribed in person (243–44). At the same time, some places witnessed reaction against Catholic practices with iconoclasm: pictures, images, altars, and roods were destroyed.

34. "The Articles, together with the Book of Common Prayer, are the foundation of Anglican theology." Oliver O'Donovan, *On the Thirty Nine Articles: A Conversation with Tudor Christianity* (Exeter: Paternoster Press, 1986), 9. Some would question whether the Thirty Nine Articles have the same importance as Supremacy and the Book of Common Prayer in the formation of the Church of England.

of the church under the leadership of Elizabeth and her archbishop of Canterbury, Matthew Parker.[35]

The analysis of the ecclesiology of Richard Hooker will implicitly comment at length upon the Articles, but it may be helpful schematically to represent the ecclesiology, to which over half the articles are directed, under four headings.[36]

The nature of the church (Art 19). The whole church is the *congregatio fidelium*, the whole worldwide community of the faithful. This phrase from the medieval tradition flourished in conciliarism. It is not quite clear whether the idea of an "invisible church" is operative here. The second part of Article 19 refers to local churches as if they were parts of the universal church indicating a clear conception of a "whole-part distinction." The basis of the church is the word of God, that is, scripture (Art 20). The criteria for the true church are, as in Luther and Calvin, the ministration of word and sacrament.

Organization or polity (Art 23, 36, 37). The Articles do not define the offices of ministry in the church, but these are presumably the archbishops, bishops, priests, and deacons in Art 36. At the same time the ruling monarch is the supreme governor of the church. Spiritual authority and the authority of mediating word and sacrament reside in the clergy; but the external authority of government within the church, especially in temporal matters, order, and discipline, resides in the monarch, because the church is coterminous with the realm. The models at work here go back to the early church. One can find analogies with a Cyprianic episcopalism in the communion with other churches outside England, combined with a Constantinian or Justinian view of the integration of church and state.

Authority of the church. The authority of the church is seen in two spheres, in doctrine and discipline: (1) *Doctrine* (Art 20–22). The

---

35. It might be helpful to loosely differentiate the nature of Articles by contrast with Creeds or confessions of faith. Whereas Creeds arise spontaneously as attempts to define the essential and universal character of Christian faith in a short, unexplained, positive way that can act as a universally accepted criterion of the faith, Articles often aim at collecting a distinctive set of doctrines within the universal faith in a way that is not necessary and could possibly be temporary and changing, expressed in a more explanatory form in a situation of crisis or conflict. Bicknell, *A Theological Introduction to the Thirty-Nine Articles*, 18–20.

36. The 39 Articles, in parallel with the 42 Articles, are found in O'Donovan, *39 Articles*, 133–55.

church has authority in matters of the doctrine of faith. But the basis and norm for this is scripture or the word of God. Councils are not infallible; their authority is derived from scripture. To discredit Trent, the articles maintain that councils cannot be summoned apart from the will of monarchs. (2) *Discipline* (Art 24, 26, 32–35). The teaching here is summed up with the following sentence: "Every particular or national church has the authority to ordain, change, abolish, ceremonies or rites of the Church, ordained only by human authority, so that all things be done to edifying" (Art 34).

Church and state (Art 37–39). The relation between church and state is really defined by the polity of the church. The unity of church and state includes a distinction of spheres of authority. The formula resembles a national or territorial church analogous to the church in the early medieval period under Charlemagne, but without his obedience to Rome.

In 1560 or 1561 John Jewel wrote an extensive explanation and defense of the Church of England that won wide acceptance and authority. Its second part is a positive confession of faith that depends upon and integrates into itself the Forty-Two Articles. It can thus be read as a paraphrase of the Thirty Nine Articles which were at this time being retrieved for presentation to the bishops. The essay can be considered an extensive paraphrase of the Articles of Faith.[37] Does this apology and do the Articles of Religion define a *via media* between Rome and continental Protestantism? This common conception meets some resistance. From the historian's perspective, this later view, applied back on the events, makes it appear as though a deliberate policy governed the formation of the church, in contrast to the actual series of contingent, practical decisions that finally constituted the church.[38] From the theologian's perspective, the theological positions of the English reformers were not "middle," and it is also difficult to decide the positions between which this so-called middle is to be located.[39]

---

37. John Jewel, "Part II," *An Apologie of the Church of England*, in *English Reformers*, ed. T. H. L. Parker (Philadelphia: Westminster Press, 1966), 20–33.

38. Doran, *Elizabeth I*, 21.

39. O'Donovan, *39 Articles*, 14.

The Elizabethan church, however, was set in place and took hold within the framework of a tension between those hankering for the ways of the medieval church and those influenced by the Reformation on the continent, especially after Mary's reign, when the hundreds of English exiles influenced by Calvin's ideas and practices returned. They formed a basis for the Puritans who made their presence felt all during Elizabeth's reign. Frequently Puritans are understood over against the Church of England, and Hooker's work is addressed polemically against them. But at this time Calvinist theology and ideas were quite prevalent in the Elizabethan church, and the Puritans should be located within it. "Puritans were Protestants, both lay and clerical, whose religious enthusiasm and zeal marked them off from their more lukewarm contemporaries. They were a self-conscious group who were totally committed to purging the Established Church of its popish 'superstitions' and bringing a biblical morality to English society."[40] The term "Puritan" was first coined during the 1560s to describe those who resisted the 1559 Prayer Book, and continued to be used relative to those who did not follow all the rubrics. But by the end of the sixteenth century "Puritan" was usually a pejorative reference to religiously zealous Protestants, of a Calvinist sort, who followed a godly life-style that distinguished them from their neighbors, without withdrawing from the church itself.[41]

Peter Lake constructs the identity of "moderate puritans," that is, puritans who were far from separatists and should be defined positively as being "principled members of the most godly and committed section of English protestant opinion, and [by] their active

---

40. Doran, *Elizabeth I*, 24.
41. Ibid., 25. Puritans emphasized the doctrine of predestination; they wanted a church that enforced morality and showed forth the quality of the elect; they had a sense of evil and a pessimistic anthropology. "Puritans were not members of a separatist sect standing outside the Church of England, nor were they members of an opposition group in the House of Commons. They cannot be distinguished from conformist Protestants by their belief in a predestinarian theology, or in a Presbyterian form of church government, or in a capitalist social theory. It was only the intensity of their religious experience, their style of personal piety and their commitment to further religious reform that gave them a particular identity and earned them their pejorative nickname." Ibid., 29–30.

role within the established church."[42] By studying a variety of such figures, Lake builds a profile not through a set of formal doctrines but from the lives of important figures and the practical divinity drawn from their preaching. The core of their worldview "was provided by an all-encompassing concern with the potentially transforming effects of the gospel both on individuals and on the social order as a whole.... The doctrinal position that lay behind this attitude was uncompromisingly Calvinist."[43] It amounted to an "insistence on the transformative effect of the word on the attitudes and behavior of all true believers. It was this, applied to the public sphere, and particularly to the person of the magistrate and the councillor, that lay behind the puritan campaigns for further reformation in church and state and the concomitant attempts to purge the social order of its sins and corruptions."[44] The substance lay less in doctrines and more in a dynamic spirituality that wanted the word of God to be effective in the world.

In conclusion, by the end of Elizabeth's reign, the Church of England was an autonomous church, quite distinct from the church in England of the late Middle Ages. In a way, the transformation of the church corresponded with the passage from the Middle Ages to the modern period. The church was in one respect uniform, but it contained a pluralistic constituency. Moreover, it had developed a consistent, coherent, and distinctive ecclesiology which is reflected most clearly and in detail in the writings of Richard Hooker.

RICHARD HOOKER'S ECCLESIOLOGICAL SYNTHESIS

We now take up the work of Richard Hooker as a source for a comprehensive but in no sense detailed representation of the ecclesiology

---

42. Lake, *Moderate Puritans*, 4.

43. Ibid., 279. Lake wants to correct views "of 'puritanism' as an entirely oppositionist force...continually teetering on the edge of open separation" (Ibid., 280). Not that there was no opposition to Prayer Book conformity, but the core of the moderate puritan position was not critique of the liturgy, or of polity, or of the doctrinal consensus. It lay rather in the view that being a Christian had to make a difference; the godly had to be able to "recognize one another in the midst of a corrupt and unregenerate world." Ibid., 282.

44. Ibid., 282.

of the Church of England at the end of the sixteenth century. Before
explaining his thought and its promising yield, a few words about
this theologian are in order.

Richard Hooker was born in March of 1554 in or near the city of
Exeter. At the age of fourteen he went off to Corpus Christi College,
Oxford, with the support of John Jewel, then bishop of Salisbury. He
was awarded the B.A. degree in 1573, the M.A. in 1577, and was designated a full fellow in 1579.[45] The intellectual climate of theology at
the time of Hooker's education varied, echoing the situation within
the church. Archer notes that "the Catholic influence was strong
down through the reign of Elizabeth, though the reformed religion
prevailed."[46] Yet Hooker's tutor preferred the theology of Calvin.

Hooker's scholarly life unfolded within the larger context of ministry. Some time before the end of 1581 Hooker was ordained in
the Church of England. Late in 1584 he was briefly assigned to a
parish at some distance from Oxford, and then three months later
Hooker received a royal appointment as Master of the Temple church
in London which catered to lawyers and students of the law. The
religious situation in London at the time was marked by the controversies between the Puritans and the established church. Hooker's
new church neatly replicated the general situation since the former
master's assistant, Walter Travers, who shared a Puritan perspective,
had expected the assignment, did not get it, but nevertheless stayed
on in the church as reader and preacher. By arrangement Hooker
preached in the morning and his reader in the afternoon to the effect
that the "pulpit spake pure Canterbury in the morning, and Geneva
in the afternoon."[47] The difference in perspective became a public
controversy in a matter of months, and it finally came to an end
the following year with the silencing of Travers by the archbishop of
Canterbury.

It is not exactly certain at what time Hooker decided to write his
life's work, *Of the Laws of Ecclesiastical Polity*, or when he actually

---

45. Stanley Archer, *Richard Hooker* (Boston: Twayne, 1983), 1–4. I draw the
biographical data on Hooker from this work.

46. Ibid., 4.

47. Ibid., 11, quoting Thomas Fuller, *History of the Worthies of England*, ed. P. A.
Nuttall (New York: AMS Press, 1965), I, 423.

began the project. Some think Hooker began his work in 1586, when he was still at the Temple and engaged in controversy with Travers; Booty thinks some time later. "In 1588 he married Joan Churchman, the daughter of an affluent London businessman. It was sometime after this that he began to write the eight books of the *Laws,* supported in part by the Churchman family and, from 1591, by Queen Elizabeth I, who presented him with the sub-deanship of Salisbury Cathedral, the prebendary of Netheravon, and the living of Boscombe."[48] In any case, he finished the first four books in January 1593, and they were published later that year. Book five was published in 1597, and the remaining three books were published after Hooker's early death in 1600. Archer characterizes the work as "the most comprehensive defense of the Elizabethan religious settlement of its time, the culmination of four decades of challenges to the church by Puritans and Catholics."[49]

In a lengthy preface to *Of the Laws of Ecclesiastical Polity* Hooker describes the context, aims, and structure of the work.[50] The preface addresses those within the Church of England who wish to reform

---

48. John Booty, *Reflections on the Theology of Richard Hooker: An Elizabethan Addresses Modern Anglicanism* (Sewanee, Tenn.: University of the South Press, 1998), 2.

49. Ibid., 19. Hooker engaged the issues of the debate in the Elizabethan period to create a "new synthesis at the center of which [was] a distinctive and novel vision of what English Protestant religion was or, rather, ought to be." "If he had any rival to the title of founder of Anglicanism, it could only be the author of the Prayer Book itself." Philip B. Secor, "In Search of Richard Hooker: Constructing a New Biography," *Richard Hooker and the Construction of Christian Community,* ed. Arthur Stephen McGrade (Tempe, Ariz.: Medieval and Renaissance Texts and Studies, 1997), 24–25, echoing Peter Lake, *Anglicans and Puritans? Presbyterianism and English Conformist Thought from Whitgift to Hooker* (London / Boston: Allen & Unwin, 1988), 146.

50. Richard Hooker, *Of the Laws of Ecclesiastical Polity,* I-III, ed. W. Speed Hill (Cambridge, Mass,. and London: Belknap Press of Harvard University Press, 1977–81). The eight books of Hooker are contained in these three volumes. References to the work in the text are by book, chapter, and paragraph. The following works have been helpful in interpreting Hooker: John E. Booty, "Hooker and Anglicanism, in *Studies in Richard Hooker: Essays Preliminary to an Edition of His Works,* ed. W. Speed Hill (Cleveland and London: The Press of Case Western Reserve University, 1972), 207–39; *Reflections on the Theology of Richard Hooker;* Robert K. Faulkner, *Richard Hooker and the Politics of a Christian England* (Berkeley: University of California Press, 1981); John S. Marshall, *Hooker and the Anglican Tradition: An Historical and Theological Study of Hooker's Ecclesiastical Polity* (London: Adam & Charles Black, 1963); W. B. Patterson, "Hooker on Ecumenical Relations: Conciliarism in the English Reformation," in *Richard Hooker and the Construction of Christian Community,* 283–303;

its laws and ecclesiastical order.[51] It is, therefore, a polemical work responsive to the charges of the other side in controversy. But it is not acrimonious; Hooker aims at cool analysis and appeal to evidence: "It is no part of my secret meaning to draw you hereby into hatred or to set upon the face of this cause any fairer glasse, then the naked truth doth afford" (Pref, 7, 1). Hooker describes the conflict within the Church of England as one between the church as it had been formed under Elizabeth I and those committed to the form of a church in the pattern of John Calvin and Geneva.[52]

Hooker mentions along the way several goals of the work. One is to defend the Church of England in its present form against the attacks of the reformers, to show the truth of the matter and that their attacks on the present structure are wrong (Pref,1,2; 7,1). His larger goal is for peace and harmony within the church, "to live as if our persons being manie our soules were by one" (Pref,9,3). The best way to achieve this is by calm, dispassionate, rational analysis of each issue and each charge, point by point, argument by argument with all exactness possible (Pref,9,1; 7,1).[53]

Hooker outlined the structure of the whole work in the preface (Pref,7). Its eight books are divided logically into two parts of four books each. The first part deals with fundamental issues and general

---

Philip B. Secor, "In Search of Richard Hooker," 21–37; Debora Shuger, " 'Societie Supernaturall': The Imagined Community of Hooker's *Lawes*," in *Richard Hooker and the Construction of Christian Community*, 307–29; Ramie Targoff, "Performing Prayer in Hooker's *Lawes:* The Efficacy of Set Forms," in *Richard Hooker and the Construction of Christian Community*, 275–82. Bibliographies of material on Hooker are found in Egil Grislis and W. Speed Hill, "Richard Hooker: A Selected Bibliography, 1971–1993," in *Richard Hooker and the Construction of Christian Community*, 385–405, and for material prior to 1971 Grislis and Hill, "Richard Hooker: An Annotated Bibliography," *Studies in Richard Hooker*, 279–320.

51. The "laws of the church" refer broadly to its whole organizational structure: "The lawes of the Church, whereby for so many ages together we have beene guided in the exercise of Christian religion, and the service of the true God, our rites, customs, and orders of Ecclesiticall government are called in question . . . " (1,1,3).

52. In a substantial section Hooker shows his knowledge of Calvin and his ministry in Geneva (Pref,2); he maintains that Calvin's organization of the church corresponded exactly to what the situation there and at that time demanded (Pref,2.4), but it is far from proved to be a universally normative structure (Pref, 4,5).

53. Hooker's ecclesiology possessed no official status; it did not, for example, represent Puritan positions. Major portions did not appear until deep into the seventeenth century. But as an extraordinary, synthetic ecclesiological *summa* it represents the center of the Church of England at the close of the sixteenth century.

principles that regulate the criticisms of the reformers. According to the first four books, these are:

1. the nature and kinds of law,

2. whether scripture should rule all our actions,

3. whether a God-given, unchanging, foundational governing structure can be found in the New Testament,

4. whether the Church of England is corrupted by popish rites, orders, and ceremonies.

The second part and the next four books deal with four issues that are more specific to the controversy within the English church. They are:

5. the prayers and sacraments of the church and the power of orders,

6. stated as the question of the jurisdiction of elders in the reformed churches, but in fact dealing with repentance in the church,

7. the power and honor due to bishops, and

8. the sovereign power or jurisdictional authority in the church. (Pref, 7)

The center of the eight books of the *Lawes* is Book 5 which is laid out as a commentary on the Book of Common Prayer. This indicates where Hooker located the platform upon which the church was constructed.

The interpretation of Hooker's ecclesiology which follows diverges from Hooker's order of presentation, which has the Prayer Book at its center, preceded by introductory matters to some extent imposed upon him by controversy. In this presentation understandings of various elements of the church are fitted into the loci used in the other chapters of this book. It will thus treat in succession the nature of the church, royal supremacy as defining its relation to the state, the members of the church, the ministerial and organizational structure of the church, the activities of the church, and finally its relation to society.

The Nature of the Church

Hooker understood the nature of the church in strictly theological terms. His preferred theological metaphor for the church is the "mystical body of Christ." This church is one: which means it is a single reality that is unified, although it contains masses of human beings in this world and the next. "That Church of Christ which we properly terme his body mysticall, can be but one..." (3,1,2). The huge collective body of people is mystical "because the mysterie of their conjunction is removed altogether from sense" (3,1,2). The mystical church refers to those members who are already with Christ in a new life and also those on earth, because their internal dispositions "are not object unto our sense" but known only to God (3,1,2). In some respects, then, Hooker uses the term "mystical" to express what other theologians mean by the invisible church, but it reaches much further. The distinction between the visible and mystical church roughly corresponds with a historical-sociological approach to the church and a theological consideration of the same church. The following account of Hooker's conception of the nature of the one single church attends to these two distinct levels.

The visible church. The visible church is a distinct society of human beings held together by common faith and the external bonds of creed, ritual, and offices. Speaking sociologically, Hooker distinguishes the church as a society from an assembly which is united existentially in the performance of a common action.[54] He understands a Church, as "a societie, that is, a number of men belonging unto some Christian fellowship, the place and limites whereof are certaine. That wherein they have communion, is the publike exercisen of such dueties, as those mentioned in the Apostles actes, *Instruction, Breaking of bread,* and *Prayers* (3,1,14).[55]

---

54. "In this sense the Church is alwaies a visible society of men, not an assembly, but a societie. For although the name of the Church be given unto Christian assemblies, although any multitude of Christian men congregated may be tearmed by the name of a Church, yet assemblies properly are rather things that belong to a Church. Men are assembled for performance of publike actions, which actions being ended, the assembly dissolveth it selfe and is no longer in being, whereas the Church which was assembled, doth no lesse continue afterwards then before" (3,1,14).

55. Hooker prefers to speak of polity when dealing with the visible aspect of the church generally, because government seems too limited or restricted to the task

The visible church is the church in history, "a sensiblie knowne company," according to its social forms. "And this visible Church in like sorte is but one, continued from the first beginning of the world to the last ende" (3,1,3). This continuous church includes both those before and those after Christ, and the name, the Church of Christ, most properly applies to the latter. Three bonds holds this visible church together as one: "The unitie of which visible body and Church of Christ consisteth in that uniformitie, which all severall persons thereunto belonging have, by reason of that *one Lorde* whose servantes they all professe them selves, that *one faith* which they al acknowledge, that *one baptisme* wherewith they are all initiated" (3,1,3). Hooker develops each one of these elements; together they define the criteria of membership. The first is adherence to the person of Jesus Christ as savior (3,1,4); the second is profession of the faith which he communicated to humankind (3,1,5); the third is baptism because "entered we are not into the visible Church before our admittance by the doore of baptisme" (3,1,6).

With these defining criteria, Hooker can make some clear judgments about membership in the church. First, he clearly affirms that: "In whomsoever these things are, the church doth acknowledge them for hir children; them onely she holdeth for aliens and strangers, in whom these thinges are not found" (3,1,7). He probes the meaning of this with the question whether one can belong both to Satan and the church of Christ? Relative to the mystical church such is not possible for ultimate spiritual attachment to both would be contradictory. But members of the visible body of Christ may be alienated from God (3,1,8). The simple identification of spiritual union with Christ and membership in the visible church stems from a failure to distinguish between the mystical and visible church and a visible church that is either sound or corrupted (3,1,9). This can be seen in the case of the excommunication of individuals from a specific church. Take the case of heresy or crimes that are not repented. Either of these exclude one from the mystical body of Christ. They also constitute a separation from the sound segment of the visible church. But neither

---

of ruling; polity, by contrast, is broader and refers to "both governement and also whatsoever besides belongeth to the ordering of the Church in publique" (3,1,14).

the one nor the other separate one cleanly from the visible church. In Hooker's view excommunication "neither shutteth out from the misticall nor cleane from the visible, but onely from fellowship with the visible in holy dueties" (3,1,13).

This principle, that deficiency with regard to the three criteria of membership is not the same as a lack or absence of them, expands the understanding of the unity and continuity of the historical church. Those churches which are deficient in various ways are still in and of the church; and a church that reforms itself, does not become another church (3,1,10). With reference to Rome, for example, one reformed church does not break the fellowship of being church with another church for lack of the latter's reformation. "Notwithstanding so far as lawfullie we may, we have held, and doe hold fellowship with them [Rome]" (3,1,10). He goes so far as to claim that "we must acknowledge even heretikes them selves to be though a maimed part, yet a part of the visible Church" (3,1,11).[56]

Hooker thus had a clear rationale for the unity of the whole visible church, the distinction of churches within the whole, and a dialectical whole-part consistency of the historical church. "For preservation of Christianitie there is not any thing more needfull, then that such as are of the visible Church have mutuall fellowship and societie one with another. In which consideration as the maine body of the sea being one, yet within divers precinctes hath divers names; so the Catholike Church is in like sort devided into a number of distinct societies, every of which is termed a Church within it selfe" (3,1,14).[57]

---

56. "Heretikes therefore are not utterly cut of from the visible Church of Christ" (3,1,11). They may and should be separated from them with sound faith, but they are not as infidels who reject the very principles of Christian faith.

57. "As therefore they that are of the misticall body of Christ have those inward graces and vertues, whereby they differ from all others, which are not of the same body; againe whosoever appertaine to the visible body of the Church, they have also the notes of externall profession, whereby the world knoweth what they are: after the same manner even the severall societies of Christian men, unto everie of which the name of a Church is given with addition betokening severaltie, as the Church of Rome, Corinth, Ephesus, England, and so the rest, must be indued with correspondent generall properties belonging unto them, as they are publique Christian societies. And of such properties common unto all societies Christian it may not be denied, that one of the verie chiefest is Ecclesiasticall Politie" (3,1,14).

The mystical church. Hooker discusses the foundations of the mystical church in his sacramental theology. Sacraments draw their power ultimately from the incarnation of the divine Son in Jesus Christ: God is in Christ by the personal incarnation of the Son who is true God (5,51). On the basis of the incarnation, Hooker discusses the personal presence of Christ everywhere, and this leads him to the specific question of the "union or mutuall participation which is betweene Christ and the Church of Christ in this present worlde" (5,56). In this discussion Hooker presents the theological grounding of the church in the trinity and the incarnation.

Hooker works from a metaphysical premise that causes are in their effects, and the effect subsists in the cause. This bears out in creation. All things are the offspring of God: "they are *in him* as effects in theire highest cause, he likewise actuallie is *in them,* thassistance and influence of his deitie is *theire life*" (5,56,5). But beyond creative presence Hooker considers God's efficacy of salvation. Human beings are offspring of Adam by nature, but children of God by grace and favor (5,56,6). One can conceive this election as sons and daughters of God unto salvation on two levels, the one in the eternal foreknowledge of God, the other in its being actually effected in and through the church. Thus Hooker says that we are united with God "onlie from the time of our actuall adoption into the bodie of his true Church, into the fellowship of his children. . . . Our beinge in Christ by eternall foreknowledge saveth us not without our actuall and reall adoption into the fellowship of his Sainctes in this present world" (5,56,7).[58] This mysticism of mutual coinherence of the Christian in Christ and Christ in the Christian finds expression in trinitarian language. Christ is in us by the Spirit: "Seinge therefore that Christ is in us as a quickninge Spirite, the first degree of communion with Christ must needes consist in the participation of his spirit..." (5,56,8).

---

58. Hooker enjoyed an ontological and mystical conception of the church participating in the divine reality of Christ: "For in him wee actuallie are by our actuall incorporation into that societie which hath him for their head and doth make together with him one bodie (he and they in that respect havinge one name) for which cause by vertue of this mysticall conjunction wee are of him and in him even as though our verie flesh and bones should be made continuate with his. Wee are in Christ because he knoweth and loveth us even as partes of him selfe. No man actuallie is in him but they in whome he actuallie is" (5, 56, 7).

Three elements in Hooker's vast mystical vision of the church stand out. First, he retains a distinction between God as creator and as savior, and between union with God as creature and graced, and thus a sense of election.[59] Second, the whole Christ is present in every part of the church so that every distinct church is wholly church. "Christ is whole with the whole Church, and whole with everie parte of the Church, as touchinge his person which can no waie devide it selfe or be possest by degrees and portions" (5,56,10). But, third, his vision of the church is vast, historically differentiated, and at the same time mystically inclusive and united: it is made up of all who "belonge to the mysticall bodie of our Savior Christ and be in number as the starres of heaven, devided successivelie by reason of theire mortall condition into manie generations, are notwithstandinge coupled everie one to Christ theire head and all unto everie particular person amongst them selves, in as much as the same Spirit, which annointed the blessed soule of our Savior Christ, doth so formalize unite and actuate his whole race, as if both he and they were so manie limmes compacted into one bodie, by beinge quickned all with one and the same soule" (5,56,11). Hooker would not be outdone in the grandeur of his conception of the church.

Relation of the Church to the State: Royal Supremacy

Previous chapters examined the relation of the church to society and state as a concluding topic of analysis. Hooker too deals with the relation between church and the kingly power in the last of eight books. But the Act of Parliament declaring Royal Supremacy was the first major legal step in the long process of the English Reformation, and the king's position of head of the church is one of the most distinctive characteristics of this ecclesiology. This could be exaggerated: for many at the time it was a question of jurisdiction. But as the church developed in the course of the sixteenth century, the identification of the church precisely as a national church took on more importance

---

59. "It must be confest that of Christ, workinge as a creator, and a governor of the world by providence, all are partakers; not all partakers of that grace wherby he inhabiteth whome he saveth. Againe as he dwelleth not by grace in all, so neither doth he equallie worke in all them in whome he dwelleth" (5,56,10). This means that some are holier than others and God's grace effects more in some than in others.

for the self-understanding of the church as such.[60] Hooker divided his consideration into those dealing with general principles and then specific powers of the king relative to the Church of England.

General principles. The first three chapters of Book 8 deal with general principles defining the framework for understanding the specific powers of the king in the Church of England. They are always at work in all of Hooker's arguments, sometimes tacitly, sometimes quite explicitly. What follows are some of the most important.

First, Hooker had a hierarchical imagination which may be illustrated in the following conception: God's law requires that wherever many interact socially, the lower is to be bound to the higher, and their interconnection will unite each to the other and to all so that all act as one (8,2,1). Also, he holds up uniformity in society and religion as an ideal for overcoming the disadvantages that come from differences in substantial matters (8,3,5).

Second, the rationale behind all talk of royal supremacy rests on the assumption of the coextensiveness of the commonwealth and the Christian church (8,3,5). Objections to this arrangement always depend on the distinction or separation between the church and the civil commonwealth. For his part, Hooker concedes the distinction or difference between the church and the commonwealth; they are not identical. But he argues from the fact of their unity and coincidence that all in England belong to the same church, and the whole church is made up of the English (8,1,2).[61]

Third, one might identify the basic insight as the need for a supreme unifying authority in a society. This view in its turn stems from a conception of the common good, the universal *bonum publicum*. It presupposes that there are a number of different spheres of authority within a single society. It further stipulates, however, that

---

60. This is not merely a question of size, of English reformers doing in a nation of four million what Calvin did in a city of ten to thirteen thousand. The differences in cultural, historical, social, and psychological frameworks of understanding alter everything.

61. He finds a model for this unity in the kings of Judaism. True, the early church and Roman Empire were two separate societies; and at the present time the Roman Church divides jurisdiction so that it does not depend on the civil ruler; but the Church of England follows the pattern of Israel in which "the self same people whole and entire, were both under one chief Governour, on whose supreme authoritie they did depend" (8,1,7).

there must be one overall [monarchical] authority that coordinates these authorities, and points them to the common good (8,3,4). This common good of human beings transcends the needs of the body and includes concern for spiritual fulfillment (8,3,5). From the point of view of religion and Christianity, no one will deny that the church requires discipline and coercion (8,3,5).

Fourth, Hooker conceives of royal supremacy in religion in terms of dominion. Spiritual power refers to performing actions that have to do with religion itself; dominion or supreme power is that which has no power above it that can overrule it within a certain sphere. "When therfor Christian Kings are said to have spirituall dominion or supreeme power in Ecclesiasticall affaires and causes, the meaning is, that within their own precinctes and territories they have authoritie and power to command even in matters of *Christian Religion,* and that there is no higher, no greater, than can in those causes over command them, where they are placed to raigne as *Kings*" (8,2,1).

Fifth, however, one must attend to Hooker's frequently repeated principle that royal power is best when it is limited by law. He consistently reiterates how kingly dominion is better the more it is qualified and conditioned and limited by law (8,2,1). "Happier that people, whose lawe is their *King* in the greatest things then that whose *King* is himself their lawe" (8,3,3).

Sixth, Hooker's arguments relative to the specific powers of kings aim not as establishing them as the divinely mandated or only order of the church, but as a possible church polity. He finds no positive scriptural command for royal supremacy. This is a human arrangement, but God approves and supports lawfully appointed rulers, and they act as God's lieutenants and with God's power or authority (8,3,1; 8,3,6).

Seventh, Hooker summarizes his overall view in three points as follows: in matters of religion kings may have lawful authority and may lawfully exercise dominion and the temporal sword within the sphere of religion. But at the same time some kinds of actions have an intrinsically religious or spiritual character and are denied to kings: "actions of the power of order and of that power of jurisdiction which is with it unseperably joyned, power to administer the worde and Sacramentes, power to ordaine, to judg as an Ordinarie, to binde and loose, to excommunicate and such like." However, the ruler can exercise dominion within the sphere of religion in many other matters, and they should be regulated by laws of ecclesiastical affairs that have been agreed upon with uniform consent (8,3,3).

Specific powers and exemptions of the king. Hooker enumerates six distinct titles, powers, or prerogatives of the king relative to the church: three, the title Head of the church, the power to call assemblies, and exemption from juridical process or punishment, are less significant; the other three, the power to make ecclesiastical law, to appoint bishops, and of universal jurisdiction, require more explanation.

The main objection against calling the king the "Head of the Church" comes from the conviction that only Christ holds that position as was seen in the last section. But Hooker explains that the meaning of this title is utterly different "in order, measure and kinde" (8,4,5). "Wee in terming our Princes *Heads of the Church* doe but testifie that we acknowledg them such Governours" (8,4,1). Little controversy surrounds the proposition that kings can summon assemblies since Constantine provides such a prominent precedent. As for suffering ecclesial judgment, princes will have their judgment in heaven, not on earth (8,9,2). An agency within the realm simply cannot have coercive power over the sovereign (8,9,6). But at the same time, Hooker grants that the simple priest, let alone higher clergy, can excommunicate a king, that is, forbid him communion as a notorious sinner (8,9,6).

The power of kings to make ecclesiastical law. Hooker offers a sustained argument to make this point. Some of his premises are these: that church and commonwealth are coterminus; that all societies, including the church, have within themselves the right of self-government or to make laws for themselves; it follows that the subject making church law is the whole church itself;[62] such legislation cannot be made by the clergy alone, but must involve the

---

62. Based on the analogy of all societies, "so we affirme that in like congruitie the true originall subject of power also to make church lawes is the whole intire body of that church for which they are made" (8,6,1). In a word, "the whole body of the *Church* [is] the first originall subject of all mandatorie and coercive power within it self..." 8,6,3.

consent and ratification of the laity;[63] they must also involve the will of the king;[64] and, finally, parliament is where all these elements come together. The parliament of England, in a sense, is England itself assembled, for it includes the church through convocation, the king, and the people by representation. Parliament is "that wherupon the very essence of all goverment within this kingdome doth depend. It is even the bodie of the whole Realme . . . " (8,6,11).

But parliament includes the king as king, and laws cannot be made without the king. Negatively, if a king did not have the power of veto, he would not have the dominion that constitutes kingship. Positively, the church gives to the king the power to make laws for itself because of the king's universal authority.[65] "In devising and discussing of lawes wisdome is specially required, but that which establisheth and maketh them is power, even power of dominion the Cheiftie wherof amongst us resteth in the person of the *King*" (8,6,12).

The power of kings to appoint bishops. The making of a bishop involves his consecration, his election, and his appointment to a specific see. The king does not consecrate bishops, but he appoints them and this appointment subverts their canonical election. The practices in Hooker's time "make voyd whatsoever interest the people aforetime hath had towardes the choice of their own *Bishop* and also restraine the very act of canonicall election usually made by the *Deane* and *Chapter* . . . " (8,7,3). The election of bishops "is now

---

63. No matter how good any laws may be, it is "the generall consent of all that giveth them the forme and vigor of lawes . . . but lawes could they never be without consent of the whole *Church* . . . " (8,6,11).

64. Thus Hooker argues that "no *Ecclesiasticall* lawe be made in a *Christian Commonwealth* without consent as well of the laitie as of the Clergie but least of all without consent of the highest power" (8,6,7).

65. Hooker construes the power of the king in specifically church matters as analogous to that of Constantine wherein the church gave him as supreme ruler of the empire the power to make laws for Christianity, and he, being a Christian, used this authority and power for the benefit of the church. The point is that the imperial dignity of the emperor is what enabled him to make prescriptions into law for the whole commonwealth and religion (8,6,11). It is not that the laws ultimately receive their force from the power which the king gives to parliament and the people. Rather laws receive their force "from power which the whole body of this *Realme* being naturally possessed with hath by free and deliberate assent derived unto him that ruleth over them. . . . So that our lawes made concerning religion do take originallie their essence from the power of the whole *Realme* and *Church* of England then which nothing can be more consonant unto the lawe of nature and the will of our *Lord Jesus Christ*" (8,6,11).

but a matter of forme. It is the *Kings* meer graunt that placeth and the *Bishops* consecration which maketh *Bishops*" (8,7,3).

Hooker justifies this practice by long and extensive precedent, the role of the bishop in the situation of the unity of church and commonwealth, and the role that the bishop plays in society. Hooker relates this whole matter to the investiture controversy in the wake of the Gregorian reform and takes a position that investiture by the prince was the correct thing to do (8,7,5). But he also admits the dangers that kings could appoint unqualified or unworthy bishops.

The juridical power of kings: universal jurisdiction. The Church of England has no office or ministry with universal jurisdiction (8,8,1). Rather the king possess that power and authority by virtue of his universal dominion. The point of this jurisdiction is to support local church jurisdictions and to serve as an avenue of appeal.[66] Such jurisdictions were formerly claimed by the pope, but with the provision of royal supremacy it has been "annexed" by the English crown (8,8,4).

Some argue that the king is incompetent in spiritual or religious matters. But Hooker shows that the practice of judicial oversight is not usually exercised directly, but the whole system works through tiered levels of expertise. Distinctions obtain "between that ordinarie jurisdiction, which belongeth to the Clergie alone and that Commissionarie wherein others are for just consideration appointed to joyn with them as also between both these *Jurisdictions* and a third whereby the *King* hath a transcendent authoritie and that in all causes over both" (8,8,7). Finally, Hooker insists that in the Church of England all such judicial processes are governed by law, and kings bind themselves to use their jurisdictional power within the limits of the law (8,8,9).

The Members of the Church

Who were the members of the Church of England? On the one hand, the members of the church were first of all the English. In 1530 they were Catholic; in 1550 church structures had been reformed;

---

66. Thus universal power reaches "over all Courtes all Judges all Causes, the operation of which power is as well to strengthen maintaine and uphold particular jurisdictions ... as also to remedie that which they are not able to help and to redress ... " (8,8,4).

in 1555 they were mostly Catholic again; in 1560 Edwardian provisions were reinstated. The institutional church changed around the corporate body of the English Christians; the people at large adjusted more slowly. Yet by the end of the century to be "an English person was to be a member of the Church of England. The faith of the national church was, like it or not, the faith of the people of England for few could conceive of religious pluralism in society. Local parish churches, the primary focus of many people's religious loyalty, bore royal coats-of-arms and were the setting for a Protestant liturgy."[67] Yet again, within this single church there were differentiations of sympathies at least, and it may be useful to at least identify them along a spectrum of left and right of a defined center.[68]

The center can be stipulated as the Prayer Book Protestants. These were the majority of people who went along with the reforms more or less quietly. They might be those who accepted the Prayer Book as a strict norm and complained when clergy departed from it, or those who accepted it gradually and came to love it.

Left of this center were the Puritans, distinguished by the intensity of their religious fervor and the evangelical Calvinist cast of their doctrine and piety. They were a minority in the whole church, perhaps a faction within a given parish, or a given parish might be largely or even wholly Puritan in character.

Right of center were the conforming papists, people who remained Roman Catholic at heart, but who in various degrees and for a great variety of reasons conformed in varying measures to the activities of the Church of England. When "the services of the Church of England were the only ones on offer, and people sympathetic to Catholicism had to decide whether to attend them or do without liturgical provision altogether," they might compromise. Such people may have helped keep alive "a taste for ritual and liturgy" over against a triumph of Puritanism.[69]

Still further to the left were sectarian Protestants or Separatists. These would be those of a Puritan bent who could no longer remain in the Church of England and separated from it. Separation involved

---

67. Rosman, *Catholic to Protestant*, 92.
68. I draw this spectrum from Rosman, *Catholic to Protestant*, 65–73.
69. Ibid., 69.

implicit nonrecognition of the national church, and it was rare in the Elizabethan period.

And at the extreme right were the recusants whose loyalty to the Roman Church made them separatists on the right, that is, they refused the authority of and participation in the Church of England. Yet they were tolerated in the land and even at Court. But they were a very small percentage of the whole population. It is undoubtedly the case that one would find during an early period an analogous differentiation within the Lutheran and Calvinist churches as well.

Church Polity and Ministry

The polity of the church is a function of ministry, that is, polity differentiates, structures, and provides ministry, so that polity and ministry reciprocally entail each other. Hooker defines ministry as work in the church that "consisteth in doinge the service of Gods howse and in applying unto men the soveraigne medicines of grace ..." (5,76,10). The church is bound to perform certain ministries: administration of word and sacraments, prayers, spiritual censures, and so on. "Lawes of politie are lawes which appoint in what maner these duties shalbe performed" (3,11,20). Hooker recognizes a pluralism in polity among the churches. All people need language to speak, but they need not speak the same language. "Even so the necessitie of politie and regiment in all Churches may be helde, without holding anie one certayne forme to bee necessarie in them all" (3,2,1). But Hooker found it necessary to argue apologetically for the threefold structure of ministry found most clearly as early as Ignatius of Antioch and largely taken for granted thereafter, because it was challenged by the congregationalist principle and Calvin's church organization. Thus Hooker had to defend the lawfulness of what had always been in place in the church in England.

Scripture, ministry, and church polity. Scripture does say something about church organization and government, and Hooker appeals to a normative New Testament church. But he rejects the idea that scripture prescribes a detailed polity for all churches. In fact he revels in listing the many ways in which laws change in principle (3,10). Laws are constantly abrogated, in part repealed, or augmented as conditions warrant. "The nature of everie lawe must be judged of by the ende for which it was made, and by the aptnes of thinges therein prescribed unto the same end" (3,10,1). According to this axiom, given the changes in time and place and concrete needs of the community, neither God's being the author of a law, nor God's committing such laws to scripture, nor even the continuity of the end for which they are proposed, make laws unchangeable (3,10,7). They always need to be adjusted to new ends or by new means to fit the situation, and God provided human beings with reason and judgment to do just that. Citing Tertullian, he distinguishes between matters of faith and matters of outward order in the church: the rule of faith is stable, patterns of organization are changeable. Everyone instinctively knows "that the matter of faith is constant, the matter contrariwise of action daily changeable, especially the matter of action belonging unto Church politie" (3,10,7).

Relative to the laws of polity Hooker distinguishes certain formal principles which he calls the "principall and perpetuall parts in Ecclesiasticall politie." These are constant and necessary in God's church in contrast to the concrete provisions by which these formal principles are implemented (3,11,20). He notes four such stable principles requiring:

1. that ministers be differentiated to perform different functions;

2. that the clergy constitute a state of life established by God's word to which others are subject for their spiritual health;

3. that clergy were, are, and must be differentiated among themselves into at least two kinds, bishops and other ministers of word and sacrament;

4. that church polity itself demands a solemn admittance to the order of clergy. (3,11,20)

In contrast to these constants, he lists the wide range of variables: "times and places appointed for the exercise of religion; specialties belonging to the publike solemnitie of the worde, the sacraments, and prayer; thenlargement or abridgement of functions ministeriall depending upon those two principall before mentioned; to conclude, even whatsoever doth by way of formality and circumstance concerne any publique action of the Church" (3,11,20).

How do these two kinds of prescriptive structures, the one formal, a matter of principle, and unchanging, the other concrete, particular, and changeable, relate to the church's scriptures? Hooker responds explicitly: "Now although that which the scripture hath of thinges in the former kind be for ever permanent; yet in the later both much of that which the scripture teacheth is not always needfull; and much the Church of God shall always need which the scripture teacheth not" (3,11,20). At this point one has to rely on such God-given resources as natural law, reason, and common sense.

Clergy and laity. Hooker understood the whole church to be cleanly divided into laity and clergy (5,78,2).[70] Hooker clearly distinguishes the orders of ministry from various ministerial offices, functions, services that do not entail orders. Laypeople may be teachers, exorcists, readers, singers, and so on. They may even by their functions or training appear to be clergy and have been so called at a particular time. But they should not be confused with those ordained into clerical ranks. They resemble clergy and differ from the laity at large only functionally, and they cease being ministers when they cease ministering. By contrast, the ordination of ministers irrevocably ties them to the rank and body of clergy of which they become natural parts (5,78,10).[71]

Hooker displays a strong sacramental imagination as he characterizes the power of the ordained minister that utterly distinguishes the clergy from the laity. Secular rulers duly appointed have a derived authority given by appointment to office which God supports or upholds, but the authority of the minister is given by God and

---

70. Hooker sets up a framework for a discussion of the theology of ministry and ordination. A theology of ordination must deal with four things: first, the nature of ordained ministry as distinct from the exercise of ministry; second, the determination that "the onlie true and proper act of ordination is to invest men with that power which doth make them ministers by consecrating theire persons to God and his service in holie things duringe terme of life whether they exercise that power or no" (5,80,8); third, the distinction between ordination that makes a minister, and placing him in a parish or giving him a title or office. These last two points mark the essential difference from a congregational conception. Fourth, in considering past laws and customs, careful consideration should be given to the situations then and now (5,80,8).

71. These basic orders should also not be confused with offices such as "Deanes, Prebendaries, Parsons, Vicars, Curates, Archdecons, Chancelors, Officials, Commissaries and such other the like names" (5,78,12).

not by human beings (5,77,1). The power that is given to ministers "rayseth men from the earth and bringeth God him selfe down
from heaven"; "it giveth dailie the holie Ghost"; "it bringeth God
him selfe down from heaven, by blessing visible elementes it maketh
them invisible grace"; it disposes of the flesh and blood of Christ,
which in turn is the life principle of the mystical body of Christ, the
church itself (5,77,1). This power is given to the one ordained by
the Spirit, and so it is said *"Receive the holy Ghost,"* with the result
that the Holy Spirit becomes the empowering factor in ministry, an
abiding presence in the church through the minister (5,77,4; 5,77,8).
"Whether wee preach, pray, baptise, communicate, condemne, give
absolution, or whatsoever, as disposers of Gods misteries, our wordes,
judgmentes, actes and deedes, are not oures but the holie Ghostes"
(5,77,8).[72]

Hooker defended the division of the orders of ministry into three:
"It appeareth therefore how longe these three degrees of ecclesiasticall order have continued in the Church of Christ, the highest and
largest that which thapostles, the next that which presbyters, and
the lowest that which Deacons had" (5,78,5). He prefers the term
presbyter to priest, both for its own merits and because of Puritan
reaction against the term priest (5,78,2–3). As Hooker saw it Jesus
Christ established the order of presbyter with two levels: "some were
greater some lesse in power and that by our Saviors own appointment" (5,78,4). The apostles established the order of deacon (5,78,5).
Apostles were succeeded by bishops (5,78,9). For the three orders of
ministry to attain their goal God has ordered and structured them in
a hierarchical way, "appointing the lowest to receive from the neerest
to them selves what the influence of the highest yeeldeth" (5,76,9).

Presbyters. Presbyters are men ordained to that order of ministry,
and their responsibilities will be considered among the activities of

---

72. The power given in ordination is an indelible mark which puts the ordained
minister in a distinct rank or order within the church. To the ordained presbyter Christ
imparts a power over his mystical body and a power of calling forth Christ's own
body, and this "same power is in such not amisse both termed a kind of marke or
character and acknowledged to be indeleble. Ministeriall power is a marke of separation,
because it severeth them that have it from other men and maketh them a speciall *order*
consecrated unto the service of the most high in thinges wherewith others may not
meddle" (5,77,2).

the church. Here attention is drawn to Hooker's defense of absolute ordination, the quality of presbyters, and their support.

Hooker defends the practice of absolute ordination, that is, ordination without a tie to a parish and attachment to a particular congregation against a congregationalist conception of calling and ordination (5,80,3). "Presbyters and Deacons are not by ordination consecrated unto places but unto functions." By this Hooker means that ordination sets ministers apart, dedicates them to God, so that they are "severed and sanctified to be imployed in his service which is the highest advancement that mortall creatures on earth can be raised unto." This is not a temporary state that ceases with its exercise. "Whereas contrariewise from the place or charge where that power hath bene exercised wee maie be by sundrie good and lawfull occasions translated reteining nevertheles the selfe same power which was first given" (5,80,6). There is no canon or rule from church history that renders "ordinations at large" unlawful, and in fact the state of the church today requires them (5,80,11). The requirements are practical, that men be ordained on the basis of their qualities, at large and without title, and that bishops assign them where they are most needed (5,80,10).

Hooker addresses some of the major systemic problems facing the clergy at large ministering in the parishes and chapels across the whole church. The issues of the educational level of the clergy, the absenteeism from the parishes, and the holding of multiple incomes for various churches or titles prevailed in the Middle Ages, and church legislation in the late Middle Ages tried to address them, but with no great success. Hooker agrees that clergy should be educated, present to their charges, and not greedy for multiple incomes (5,81,2). But ideals must yield to practical necessities, and general rules and requirements must be such that they admit of particular cases, exemptions, privileges, where it would not be good to practice the normal rules (5,81,4). Surely the clergy should be learned. But if only the learned could be ordained, "the greatest parte of the people should be left utterlie without the publique use and exercise of religion" (5,81,5). Generally, candidates for ordination should be marked by "worthines as well for integritie and vertue as knowledg, yea for vertue more in as much as defect of knowledg maie sundrie waies be supplied, but the scandall of vitious and wicked life is a deadlie evell" (5,80,13). Surely ministers should be in residence, but of two evils one should chose the less. For example, the law provides for nonresidence of those who would study at the university to become learned ministers (5,81,6). In sum, Hooker balances church law against exceptions due to practical necessity and resists perfectionist interpretation.

Hooker urges the temporal support of the church. Given the role of religion in the commonwealth, he proposes the principle and axiom "that men are eternallie bound to honor God with theire substance in token of thankfull acknowledgment that all they have is from him" (5,79,1). This entails proper use of wealth and so on. It also means giving material support to the church in recognition of God's dominion and God's providence as the ultimate source of whatever wealth a person may have (5,79,1). Support for the church should aim at its solid foundation and its existence in perpetuity. Hooker refers to gifts of churches, the physical ornaments needed for the place and activity of worship, land to support the church, the practice of the tithe (5,79,3–9). "Thus therefore both God and nature have taught to convert thinges temporall to eternall uses, and to provide for the perpetuitie of religion even by that which is most transitorie" (5,79,10). Such things given to the church belong to God; they are not disposable by civil officials (5,79,14). Hooker is strong but not absolute in this principle, recognizing that there may be some situations in which church property, which is God's property, can be alienated (5,79,16).

Bishops. "A Bishop," according to Hooker, "is a Minister of God, unto whom with permanent continuance, there is given not onely power of administering the Word and Sacraments, which power other Presbyters have; but also a further power to ordain Ecclesiastical persons, and a power of Cheifty in Government over Presbyters as well as Lay men, a power to be by way of jurisdiction a Pastor even to Pastors themselves" (7,2,3). Bishops are of two kinds, "at large" and "with restraint": "At large, when the subject of their Regiment is indefinite, and not tyed to any certain place: Bishops with restraint are they whose regiment over the Church is contained within some definite, local compass, beyond which compass their jurisdiction reacheth not" (7,2,3). Given these definitions, Hooker proposes the following thesis: "This we boldly therefore set down, as a most infallible truth, That the Church of Christ is at this day lawfully, and so hath been sithence the first beginning, governed by Bishops, having permanent superiority, and ruling power over other Ministers of the Word and Sacraments" (7,3,1). He fleshes out the contention with historical considerations of the origin and superiority of bishops, how they relate to presbyters, and the nature of their jurisdiction relative to people and territory.

First, Hooker has a traditional view of the origin of the office of bishop. "The first Bishops in the Church of Christ were his blessed Apostles ... " (7,4,1). They were bishops at large, but they could also be or become bishops with restraint. The New Testament provides examples of both in Paul and James (7,4,1–2). Resident bishops were the successors of the apostles, even though apostles had no successors in apostleship (7,4,4). "The ruling superiority of one Bishop over many Presbyters, in each Church, is an order descended from Christ to the Apostles, who were themselves Bishops at large, and from the Apostles to those whome they in their steads appointed Bishops over particular Countries and Cities, and even from those antient times, universally established, thus many years it hath continued throughout the World" (7,5,8).[73]

Second, bishops enjoy a superiority over presbyters: "First he excelled in latitude of the power of order, secondly in that kind of power which belongeth unto jurisdiction" (7,6,1). As examples of superior spiritual power, Hooker points to "the power of ordaining both Deacons and Presbyters, the power to give the power of order to others, this also hath been always peculiar unto Bishops" (7,6,3).[74] The superior power of jurisdiction relates to the need for a governing authority in the community. He argues this authority from

---

73. Hooker does not regard this as an absolute church order, however, because "the absolute and everlasting continuance of it, they cannot say that any Commandment of the Lord doth injoyn. ... " It is "rather the force of custome, whereby the Church having so long found it good to continue under the Regiment of her vertuous Bishops ... then that any such true and heavenly Law can be showed ... " (7, 5, 8).

74. Hooker also mentions the power of consecrating virgins and widows, but not confirming, since presbyters have this power in some churches (7,6,2).

history: Ignatius of Antioch is a prominent precedent but Hooker also cites Calvin's recognition of the governing role of bishops in early Christian communities (7,6,9).

Third, Hooker draws on such historical examples as Ignatius and Cyprian to show that bishop and presbyters governed the church together with presbyters functioning as a group or college of counselors, consultants, and assistants, while at the same time remaining subject to the bishop and extensions of his authority (7,7).

Fourth, Hooker wanted to show that the organization of the church in its origins was not congregational, i.e., each particular congregation in each village did not have its own bishop; no congregation was autonomous; all related to a monoepiscopal center. He tried to demonstrate this by examining how the church spread through the cities and provinces of the Roman empire in such a way that, by God's providential design, Roman political organization influenced the church. "And how many soever these Parishes or Congregations were in number, which did depend on any one principal City Church, unto the Bishop of that one Church they and their several sole Presbyters were all subject" (7,8,2). The church's organization developed through cities, from "one city one bishop" to episcopal sees and dioceses: no independent churches but always higher structures of organization. As the church expanded numerically within the framework of Roman organization, the church developed structures of synods, metropolitans, primates, archbishops, patriarchs, that is, the preeminence of some bishops over other bishops.[75]

Deacons. "Deacons were stewardes of the Church unto whome at the first was committed the distribution of Church-goodes, the care of providing therewith for the poore, and the charge to see that all things of expense might be religiouslie and faithfullie delt in. A part also of theire office was attendance upon theire presbyters at the time of divine service" (5,78,5). Hooker defended the right of the deacons to preach if they were qualified to do so. Perhaps the most interesting aspect of Hooker's treatment of deacons lies in the way he develops a principle of functionality and meeting the needs

---

75. The question of the honor and privilege paid to bishops constituted a special question, and I will address it in the context of the relation of church to society.

of ministry from the apostles' act of creating this office: "Whereupon wee may rightly ground this axiome, that when the subject wherein one mans labors of sundrie kindes are imploied doth wax so great that the same men are no longer able to menage it sufficientlie as before, the most naturall waie to helpe this is by deviding theire charge into slipes and ordeining of underofficers, as our Savior under twelve Apostles seaventie presyters, and thapostles by his example seaven Deacons to be under both" (5,78,5).

The Activities of the Church

The category of the "activities of the church" houses the many facets of the external appearance or public face of the Church of England treated by Hooker. He produced such a thorough analysis of the church that collecting his considerations amounts to an expansive description of it, at least in formal rather than phenomenological terms. This gathering together of the many activities of the church also concretizes the functions of the orders of ministry described earlier.

The public face of the church. Hooker considers the public face of the church, in its external appearance through its buildings, its social celebrations, and its ceremonies.

Church buildings. The most obvious external manifestations of the church are its churches, and Hooker felt compelled to justify the existence and quality of these places of worship. For him, nothing appeared more obvious than that there be "places provided that the people might there assemble them selves in due and decent manner" (5,14,1). Solemn worship of God should take place in public as befits the role of religion in human society at large (5,11,1; 5,12,2). As Jews built their temples, so Christians from the beginning, when it was possible, built their churches and set them aside, dedicated to worship of God. He was utterly hostile to the phase of iconoclasm in the English Reformation. What was useful for worship and established by precedent should be preserved. Churches should be qualitatively such that they stimulate reverence and godliness, inspire a worshipful spirit. Their appearance should be worthy of their end which is public worship of God. Hooker thus reasons straightforwardly that "the service of God hath not then it selfe *such perfection of grace and comlines,* as when the dignitie of place which it wisheth for doth concurre" (5,16,1).

Church festivals. Hooker prefaces his consideration of religious feasts or festivals with a theology of time (5,69). It is simply fitting that there be feasts to remember and mark the times of God's visitation: "The sanctification of dayes and times is a token of that thankfullnes and a part of that publique honor which wee owe to God for admirable benefites" (5,70,1). Such festivals should give expression to religious joy, stimulate charity, and provide a certain rest from the cares of life that oppress the spirit. Of course religious festivals could be abused, but at their best they mix in graced proportion "praise, bountie, and rest" (5,70,2).

On church ceremonies. At the beginning of the *Book of Common Prayer* Cranmer had placed a brief rationale for the ceremonies preserved therein and an explanation of the criteria for their selection. No one, least of all Hooker, failed to notice the need for care and sensitivity in the matter of change in religious rite. Hooker devoted the whole of Book IV of the *Laws* to responding to various Puritan objections to the ceremonies which survived and flourished in the Elizabethan period. Early in Book V, however, he lays down some general constructive principles for their evaluation. First of all, as symbolic activities they must reflect what they point to or mediate, namely, God, and thus bear and command a certain religious reverence. Second, venerable traditions of things that have worked in the past should not be overturned without serious reasons. Third, however, the church can change things, and generally people should submit to the authority of the church in such matters. Yet, fourth, the principle of equity applies to all general laws; they always admit of exceptions and dispensations in certain concrete situations. Finally, and generally speaking, private opinion should not prevail over the collective wisdom and will of the church (5,6–10). These principle go a long way in explaining Hooker's rationale for the church's ceremonies.

Instruction in the faith. This section could be labeled "knowledge of God and doctrine." It concerns the first great function of the church, to receive, preserve, and mediate the revelation of God. The second will be to return to God through prayer our response of praise.

In the great dialogue between God and the earthly church these are the two fundamental movements: from above God's revelation, and from below human response in prayer (5,23,1).

The first of the two main functions and purposes of the church is to bear witness to what God has revealed. This revelation is contained in the scriptures, the word of God. All should know that "the word of God is his heavenlie truth touching matters of eternall life revealed and uttered unto men; unto prophetes and apostles by immediate divine inspiration, from them to us by theire bookes and writings. We therefore have no *word of God* but the Scripture" (5,21,2). The church witnesses and instructs people in this word of God by publishing the scriptures in written form, by explaining it through preaching sermons and teaching, and by the public and private reading of scripture (5,19,1). The reading of scriptures constitutes an integral part of liturgy: "We dare not admitt anie such forme of liturgie as either appointeth no scripture at all or verie little to be red in the Church" (5,20,5).

Forms of public prayer. In its second great function, the church facilitates and structures the public response to God in prayer. "Prayer" designates the central religious response required by all and at all times. It represents a work of the church both on earth and in heaven. Prayer in private is incumbent on all individually, but here Hooker deals with prayer as the public act of the church as a body or social entity (5,24,1). "Hooker makes public prayer synonymous with common prayer, a solemn service conducted in a house of worship, led by a virtuous, godly minister devoted to service."[76] In his view, the most important form of prayer is public ecclesial prayer, and by this he means prayer with a prescribed, uniform content. "But of all helpes for due performance of this service, the greatest is that verie sett and standinge order it selfe, which framed with common advise hath both for matter and forme prescribed whatsoever is herein publiquely don" (5,25,4). Such common prayer bears or carries the weakness of the individual into affective action. The form and rever-

---

76. Archer, *Richard Hooker*, 82. "In this context 'public prayer,' 'common prayer,' and 'liturgy' become synonymous, referring to the prescribed public service which Hooker takes pains to defend." Ibid.

ent solemnity of ordered prayer helps "that imbecillitie and weakenes in us, by means whereof we are otherwise of our selves the lesse apt to performe unto God so heavenlie a service, with such affection of harte, and disposition in the powers of our soules as is requisite" (5,25,1).[77]

The role of the presbyter is both to instruct and to lead in prayer. Hooker describes some of the specific tasks of the presbyter relative to prayer and instruction. In these functions one sees the need for his religious quality of life. He leads the community and prays for the community and his ordination is a sort of guarantee of his competence, a seal of his being chosen as God's instrument. As part of the whole objective ceremony the leader too must be such that he is conducive of a religious attitude to bear the community forward. "Vertue and godlines of life are required at the handes of the minister of God, not only in that he is to teach and instruct the people, ... but also much more in regard of this other parte of his function [to lead in prayer]. ... They are no fit supplicantes to seeke his mercie in behalfe of others, whose own unrepented synnes provoke his just indignation" (5,25,3).

Hooker devotes a chapter in the support of the litanies. He recounts the history of their origins and legitimates them by ancient precedent. There is no time when the petitions do not respond to the needs of someone in the church somewhere. "What one petition is there founde in the whole letanie whereof wee shall ever be able at any time to say that no man livinge needeth the grace or benefit therein craved at Gods handes?" (5,41,4). He comments as well on other specific prayers. Finally, Hooker was an advocate of music in public worship because of its power to support and reinforce religious and prayerful response. The criterion for church music revolves on

---

77. Targoff reminds us of the polemical background to Hooker on public prayer. Relative to the Puritan preference for extempore and spontaneous prayer, "Hooker argues for the effectiveness of the forms or texts of the Prayer Book themselves; secondly, in response to the puritan preference for private prayer, Hooker argues for the power of the collective utterance achieved only through public worship" (Targoff, "Performing Prayer in Hooker's *Lawes*," 276). Public prayer also responds to the problem stated by Paul at Romans 8:26: "for we do not know how to pray as we ought." Finally, public prayer plays a role in solidifying the nation-church or church-nation and thus fits Hooker's view of the role of religion in society and state. Ibid.

its ability to support prayer itself, the praise of God; superficial or ostentatious music would be unsuitable (5,38,1–3).

Sacraments. Hooker divides his treatment of the sacraments into three parts, a general sacramental theology and an explanation of baptism and the Lord's Supper in turn.

Sacramental theology. Hooker accepts the standard language of "visible signes of invisible grace," making the distinction between "theire force and theire forme of administration" (5,50,1–3). But he strongly resists the idea that sacraments *only* signify, or teach through the senses, and bear no mediation of union with God distinct from that of the Word (5,57,1). Rather Hooker strives for a certain ontological realism in his theological exploration of causality in the distinctively sacramental mediation of grace. This he does through a theological interpretation of the role of Christ and his incarnation.[78] Thus the background theology of the sacraments is the incarnational theology that supports the view of the church as the body of Christ which was considered relative to the nature of the church. Hooker does not *add* a theology of sacraments to his understanding of the church. Rather his ecclesiology is sacramental, and his view of sacraments flows out of conceptions of trinity, the incarnation of Christ, sanctification by the Holy Spirit and participation in Christ, all constituting a theological ontology of the church community. The realistic mediation of this grace through the administration of the sacraments flows from this construct (5,56,13).

The sacraments in Hooker's view are ceremonies established by God to indicate to human beings when God communicates saving grace to Christians and the distinctive character of that grace. They are moreover "meanes conditionall which God requires in them unto whome he imparteth grace" (5,57,3). Hooker cannot quite say that the sacraments are absolutely necessary for salvation, but they are necessary because of what they contain or mediate. "Neither is it *ordinarilie* [God's] will to bestowe the grace of sacramentes on anie, but by the sacramentes" (5,57,4). In other words, the saving

---

78. "And for as much as there is no union of God with man without that meane betwene both which is both, it seemeth requisite that wee first consider how God is in Christ, then how Christ is in us, and how the sacraments doe serve to make us pertakers of Christ" (5,50,3).

presence of God to the whole church as the body of Christ by participation is communicated to each person through the sacraments. The instrumental causal realism of Hooker's view appears when he refers to sacraments as "meanes effectuall whereby God when wee take the sacramentes delivereth into our handes that grace available unto eternall life, which grace the sacramentes represent or signifie" (5,57,5).[79]

Baptism. Hooker expands his exposition of baptism in polemical response to various Puritan positions, but his own position is straightforwardly traditional. On the one hand, ordinarily baptism is necessary for salvation (5,60,1). The ceremony itself of baptism is not the cause of saving grace, but neither is it a mere sign of regeneration; baptism is "an instrument or meane whereby wee receive grace, because baptisme is a sacrament which God hath instituted in his Church to the ende that they which receave the same might thereby be incorporated into Christ...(5,60,2). Hooker's realism thus stresses that something "happens" with baptism. Baptism is the "doore of our actuall enterance into Gods howse, the first apparent beginninge of life, a seale perhaps to the grace of *election* before received, but to our sanctification heere a step that hath not anie before it" (5,60,3). But, on the other hand, the necessity of baptism has to be understood according to the principle of equity, that is, as an economy that admits of exceptions. One has to expect that there will be cases in which one finds the inward life of baptism without the outward ceremony (5,60,5). He mentions the classical case of martyrdom among others.

In keeping with this tension of necessity and exception, Hooker defends infant baptism, that baptism be not restricted to a certain time and place, and in a case of necessity that anyone can baptize (5,61–62). But Hooker will not accept that the unbaptized child is condemned: he holds rather that the desire of parents for the baptism may be presumed to count in its favor, that "grace is not

---

79. Sacraments do not cause grace of themselves, but are instruments of God's power. Hooker states it this way: "with the outward signe God joyneth his holy spiritt, and soe the whole instrument of God bringeth that to passe, whereunto the baser and meaner part could not extend...where the instrument is without inherent vertue, the effect must necessarilie proceede from the only Agents adherent power" (6,6,11).

absolutely tyed unto sacramentes, and besides such is the lenitie of God that unto thinges altogether impossible he bindeth no man . . . " (5,60,6).

The Lord's Supper. In his treatment of the sacrament of the body and blood of Christ, the holy eucharist, Hooker turns almost immediately to the question of sacramental efficacy, or real presence, that proved to be so divisive in the Reformation on the continent. There is general agreement about a real participation in Christ by means of this sacrament, but what does that mean in more specific terms? (5,67,2).

Hooker responds to his own question in a manner that is both specific and Solomonic in its broad interpretation of other views. Working from the Aristotelian principle that "Everie cause is in the effect which groweth from it" (5,67,5), he states that "The bread and cup are his bodie and blood because they are causes instrumental upon the receipt whereof the *participation* of his boodie and bloode ensueth" (5,67,5). Therefore, just as the grace of baptism does not lie *in* the water itself, so too, "The reall presence of Christes most blessed bodie and bloode is not therefore to be sought for in the sacrament, but in the worthie receiver of the sacrament" (5,67,6). Thus Hooker tries to maintain sacramental realism and the efficacy of instrumental causality while at the same time transcending naive images of physicality. But at the same time he proffers these theological constructs within a framework of theological modesty, of not knowing exactly how the mediation of the dwelling in Christ is effected by the sacrament. He therefore seriously questions the vain and divisive contention over the question of exactly how God fulfills the promise of self-communication in Christ (5,67,6).

Hooker attempts a summary in five points of the efficacy of Communion which all should be able to hold in common: first, union with and participation in the whole person of Christ; second, sanctification by the Spirit of those so united; third, the communication to each of the force and virtue of Christ's sacrifice of his body and blood; fourth, this communion effects a real "transmutation" of the human soul "from sinne to righteousness, from death and corruption to immortalitie and life": fifth, a confidence in the face of all doubt that Christ's power can effect what he has promised (5,67,7).[80]

Non-sacramental rituals. Many of the ceremonies which were considered sacraments or had to do with sacraments in the church of the late Middle Ages are preserved in The Book of Common Prayer in nonsacramental form. Hooker comments upon them in his *Laws* as follows:

Confirmation. Hooker considered the rite of confirmation which he saw preserved in the church, not as a sacrament but as a "sacramentall complement" (5,66,6). He explains how historically the rite formed a part of baptism and gradually became a distinct ceremony administered by the bishop. Because of its antiquity and the function it plays of reinforcing faith, he sees a role for it (5,66).

Repentance. We saw earlier how Hooker distinguishes spiritual power from the power of jurisdiction. Spiritual power is given to those in orders; it is established by God and its effects are supernatural and divine; it descends from the head of the church, Christ.[81] Hooker also distinguishes between *inner* repentance, which is an inner virtue and which as a grace is given by God alone, and an *outer* or *external* or *public* repentance which refers to an ecclesial manner or discipline of dealing with sin in the community (6,3,1). Spiritual power or authority correlates with the public discipline of repentance.

How does this relate to rituals of repentance and forgiveness? To respond to this question, Hooker surveys the history of the church's dealing with sin and public repentance, and he finds that confession, especially public confession, is recommended by the fathers of the church. But he does not find a necessity for auricular confession, or that a sacramental confession was the only remedy for sin after baptism (6,4,13). By contrast, then, the practice of the Church of England includes, first, public confession. Each day's public prayer begins with a public acknowledgment of sin, with the expectation

---

80. Hooker also defends a number of eucharistic practices of the Church of England against Puritan objections. One is the bringing of Communion to the sick and to the dying. At no time is union with Christ as the principle of life more important (5,68,11–12).

81. Spiritual authority is "a power, which Christ hath given to be used over them, which are subject unto it, for the eternall good of their soules, according to his owne most sacred lawes, and the wholesome positive constitutions of his Church" (6,2,2).

that this puts words on the inner repentance of each person present. This is followed by the absolution pronounced by the minister alone (6,4,15).[82] Second, the church allows private confession and absolution but by no means requires it. Such a private confession and absolution is explicitly provided for as a possibility in "The Order of the Visitation of the Sick." Third, because the public confession can become routinized and careless, the church gives a solemn admonition about approaching the Lord's Table. And, fourth, ministers can exercise their spiritual jurisdiction by prohibiting notorious sinners from Communion (6,4,15). Hooker sees the declaration of absolution by the minister as completely within the power of the church's spiritual power to absolve sinners. But this should be understood exactly. The words of absolution do not effect forgiveness, for only God can forgive sin, but they truly declare it so.[83]

Hooker was not hostile to fasting and, typically, sees it in the light of a general principle of life. Set times of fasting "have theire ground in the law of nature" (5,72,1). The affections of joy and grief in sequence structure human existence itself. Fittingly, therefore, the Church of Christ as the school of life structures the life of its members with days of training in one and the other (5,72,2). Fasting serves to preserve the memory of the griefs of the past and the sin that caused them and, by contrast, to balance the spirit of festival with a certain order and control (5,72,18).

Marriage and other rituals. Marriage is a sacred and holy bond, the very basis of a society, and it should be celebrated and sanctified with religious ritual. Hooker's theology of marriage and the sexes, however, are medieval in many respects. He held the single state to be "a thing more angelicall and divine" (5,73,1). He also believed that women were inferior to men, made to be their "helper," and to be neatly subject to them in marriage (5,73,1–2). Apart from that,

---

82. See BCP, "An Order for Morning Prayer Daily throughout the Year."
83. "The sentence therefore of ministeriall absolution, hath twoe effects. Touching sinne it only declareth us free from the guiltines thereof, and restored into Gods favour: butt concerning right in sacred and divine mysteries, whereof through sinne wee were made unworthy, as the power of the Church did before effectually bind and retayne us from accesse unto them: soe upon our apparant repentance, it truely restoreth our libertie, looseth the chaines wherewith wee were tyed, remitteth all whatsoever is past, and accepteth us noe lesse, returned, then if wee never had gone astray" (6,6,5).

however, he held that the institution of marriage was a sacred state pertaining to the public order and thus should be publicly celebrated by the church. Ordination was another ritual which played a major role in the public life of the church, but which, as we saw, the Church of England declined to declare a sacrament.

The ceremony of The Thanksgiving of Women after Childbirth in The Book of Common Prayer had a history connecting it with ritual purity. But Hooker explains the ceremony as a celebration of the birth of a child, especially as an act in which "wemen after theire deliverance doe publiquelie show theire thankefull mindes unto God" (5,74,1).

The Book of Common Prayer contains orders for the "Visitation of the Sick" and "Burial of the Dead." Hooker describes the point of a burial service in direct terms: "The end of funerall duties is first to show that love towardes the partie deceased which nature requireth; then to doe him that honor which is fitt both generallie for man and particularlie for the qualitie of his person; last of all to testifie the care which the Church hath to comfort the living, and the hope which wee all have concerning the resurrection of the dead" (5,75,2).

In sum, the activities of the church were many, as the church fulfilled religion's role of being the spiritual foundation of society. The minister had a full life of active engagement with the people of his parish.

The Relation of the Church to Society

It remains to say something of the way the Church of England relates to society at large. A national church, whose head is the king or head of state, and which has the legal support of a parliamentarian act of uniformity, will also enjoy a close unity with society. There is little need to develop this at length save to show that Hooker's ecclesiology supports this unity at three levels: in principle, in fact through parish ministry, and at the upper end of society through the hierarchy.

In Hooker's view, social well being, the commonweal, depends on religion. Not only eternal but also temporal happiness is served by the delivery of the ministries of religion (5,76,title). Whatever distinctions between the social entities of church and civil government Hooker's Aristotelianism provided, they did not mean that religion and society were to be separated. Not only did they interact, they sustained each other symbiotically. Hooker's consideration of the nature of ministry lies on the premise that religion provides the basis of personal morality and of social well-being; it is the basis of a virtuous life and worldly peace, prosperity, and secular happiness. Religious values and God's grace are mediated to society by the church, and thus church ministry is key to the final health of society and state (5,76,1). The temporal good of all dominions hangs on religion and the church's ministry, so that "the Priest is a pillar of that commonwelth wherein he faithfullie serveth God" (5,76,1).

This plays itself out most concretely on the level of the parish church. The description of the church's activities, therefore, forms an integral picture of the overt religious dimension of society itself. The picture here does not differ radically in formal terms from that of the high Middle Ages. The church has been reformed, its power as an actor independent of the state may have been attenuated, but its role of mediating faith and divine grace to the whole social body has not changed.

What unfolds at the parish level is mirrored at the macro level of bishops. Bishops are often criticized for their involvement in civil affairs. Because of his conviction of the intimate relationship between religion and the running of society, Hooker sees no problem with civil and ecclesiastical functions being joined together in one person, and he gives a number of reasons and examples to make the case (7,15,3). Bishops assume civil responsibility because of necessity, or because of their talent they are specifically fit for the task, or public responsibility is imposed upon their position; these and other reasons may enjoin bishops to be engaged in civil society (7,15,7).[84] Hooker supports the honors that are bestowed on bishops because they deserve them (7,18,1). He lists a whole series of public benefits that accrue to society from bishops: they enhance the reputation of the nation abroad; the good they do is remembered and provides direction into the future; they act as spiritual consultants of kings on affairs of state; they support sovereignty beyond wisdom and valor with piety; they

---

84. In general Hooker does not argue that bishops ought always to be involved in secular affairs, but that they can be, that such involvement is neither unjust nor unlawful, and that sometimes bishops are called upon to be so engaged.

provide social structure and guidance for the people; they are models for the lower clergy (7,18,7–12). "Thus therefore Prelacy being unto all sorts so beneficial, ought accordingly to receive honor at the hands of all." Prelacy functions as "the temperature of excesses in all estates, the glew and soder of the Publique weal, the ligament which tieth and connecteth the limbs of this Body Politique each to other..." (7,18,12).

REFLECTIONS ON
HOOKER'S ECCLESIOLOGY

The reflections which follow underline certain features that characterize the ecclesiology of the Tudor Church of England as formulated by Richard Hooker. No deep logic governs either the choice or the order in which they are presented. Nor is there a limit to the observations that one could raise at this point. These reflections aim at situating Hooker and contributing to theological synthesis and construction; they seem to arise out of the data themselves. Hooker's ecclesiological method provides a good place to begin.

Hooker's Historical-Theological Method

Hooker approaches a modern method of ecclesiology in the way he combines the historical and theological in a single framework of inquiry and judgment. Booty believes that Hooker's method in theology and ecclesiology generally transcends his particular conclusions in importance. He defines that method as a style that combines concern for origins, tradition, and critical application. "The threefold authority, maintained in balance, is everywhere present. Scripture, tradition (church), and reason are brought to bear in such ways that truth is accented, truth which comprehends differing points of view as well as may be, given the exigencies of the time."[85] Along the same line Shuger defines the method of Hooker in terms of an integration of the social-historical aspect of the church with the theological. Hooker's *Ecclesiastical Polity* "relies on a rationalist and 'aggressively

---

85. Booty, "Hooker and Anglicanism," 232.

demystifying' historicism that calls attention to the contingent origins and coercive mechanisms of ecclesiastical polity. But within, alongside, or athwart (Hooker never explains the exact relationship) the church's 'external regiment,' the *Lawes* posits a visible mystical body of persons united by common agreement on the objects of their love: a community realized in antiphonal chant, sacramental participation, and pastoral care. Hooker views the church as primarily a house of prayer and sacramental worship."[86] The particular manner in which Hooker combined these features is quite striking in a theologian writing within the confines of the sixteenth century.

Continuity of the English Reformation with the Medieval Church

The account of the history of the development of the Church of England was organized around the Henrician Act of Supremacy, the Prayer Book, and the Thirty-Nine Articles. But a fourth factor was more important than all three, namely, the church that remained in place during the whole process. This consisted in the people, in their parishes, served by pastors, and governed by bishops. The church in each of these constituencies underwent change, but they were a continuous, living, corporate tradition.[87] The Church of England was not created out of whole cloth but shaped by a series of adjustments, some cutting quite deeply into a continuously subsisting corporate entity. But at the end of the sixteenth century, the institutions of the century before could still be found in something more than vestigial form. This is proved by the Puritan complaints. There were continuities in liturgy and organization. One of the reasons why the reformation of the English Church could go forward without a new code of canon law on the basis of relatively few acts of parliament was

---

86. Shuger, " 'Societie Supernaturall': The Imagined Community of Hooker's *Lawes*," 323–24.

87. Rosman reflects this premise when she writes: "In Elizabeth's reign theology was less a cause of contention than church organization and the exercise of authority. The circumstances of its creation meant that the Church of England had inherited institutional structures from the Catholic past. Successive monarchs saw no need to alter a well-established and reasonably effective machine." Rosman, *Catholic to Protestant,* 58.

that it could presuppose the old code, episcopal convocation, the episcopal system operative in the dioceses, and the ecclesiastical courts. "The English may increasingly have thought of themselves as a Protestant people, but only a minority accepted — or even understood — the details of Protestant dogma."[88] The point then pertains to the tension between continuity and change, sameness and difference. So pronounced is the tension in the case of the English Reformation that one could defend either side of the proposition that the church underwent radical change.

The View from the Parishes

Christopher Haigh views the Church of England from the perspective of the parishes, and from the broad angle of the basic Christian religious life practiced more or less fervently in the beginning and at the end of the reformations.[89] He locates the keynote of the Reformation insofar as it is Protestant in more or less radical internalization of a spirituality shaped by the doctrine of justification by faith; Christian faith in its Catholic form before the Reformation was a more or less morally conscious spirituality of religious practices. On this basis he offers the thesis that Elizabeth accomplished a political Reformation, one established in church polity, but the religious life of people in the parishes remained fundamentally constant. "For the Protestant Reformation was much less effective than the political Reformation had been: legislative destruction proved easier than evangelical construction" (288). Haigh admits that the Prayer Book was gradually accepted widely and "gained the legitimacy and the assumed efficacy of the mass book" (289). But this he interprets as a kind of reversion to a performance religion analogous to Catholicism, but in a center between the extremes of the old Catholicism and the new Protestantism. The great center was made up of "Parish Anglicans." In their conformity to the Book of Common Prayer, the godly Protestants viewed them as "papists and atheists" (289), and Catholics viewed them as Protestants. The parishes thus remained constant through the many reformations, and at the end of the sixteenth century, aside

---

88. Ibid., 92.
89. Haigh, *English Reformations*, 285. Cited in the text of this paragraph by page number.

from the papists and the godly Protestants, what remained was the great majority who formed parish churches which "were as they had always been: community centers, where people met God and their neighbors to mark seasons of the year and stages of life, to be reminded of duties and ask forgiveness for sins, to seek safety in this world and salvation in the next" (294). "While politicians were having their hesitant Reformations, while Protestants were preaching their evangelical reform, parish congregations went to church: they prayed again to their God, learned again how to be good, and went off home once more. That was how it had been in 1530; that was how it was in 1590" (295).

This thesis deserves more comment than it will receive here, for it raises a question that transcends the Church of England. What difference do the externals of church service and polity make relative to the Christian life? If it is more than Haigh admits, because of his extremely broad basis of comparison, still in a divided church this question still looms large for church leaders.

The Identity of the Church of England and Its Ecclesiology

The phrase implies the obvious: the historical is particular. The genesis and historical development of the Church of England was quite unique. From the beginning the Reformation in England concerned the church in the whole nation. It was not the church of Wittenberg or Saxony, and not the church of Geneva, but the church of a tight island nation with a strong monarchy. Unlike the Lutheran and Calvinist churches, no single reformer gave a founding spirit or insight to the Church of England. In those former cases deep thematic lines of definition pervade without being constricting and define without determining all the specifics. In both cases, the reformers themselves represent distinguishing points of departure and an overall charism for church development. By contrast, the Church of England owes its existence and character much more to the contingent events of history. Its formation was gradual by addition rather than organic growth of a more or less coherent originating spirit.

Reformation and revolution mean change, the former less radical with adjustment more continuous, the latter more radical with discontinuity more pronounced. One might argue which of the three

Reformations was the more radical, the German, the French Swiss, or the English, and responses would vary depending on the aspect or element of the church in question. But one has to admit a good deal of continuity between the Church of England at the beginning and at the end of the sixteenth century even while admitting radical change. The substance of the church in the people in their parishes, organized by diocese, priest, and bishop, was the thread of continuity. Because of its being contained within the nation, the development of the English Church over a period of sixty-five years is a classic case of both sharp interruptive change and a corporate subject remaining constant.

Distinctiveness of the Church of England: Change and Continuity in Liturgy

What was the center of gravity, the defining note, of the church which emerged from the English Reformation? Not the doctrinal-spiritual as in the Lutheran, nor the scriptural-organizational as in Calvin and Geneva. Whereas the need for autonomy and of escape from Roman authority and taxes forged a leading edge of change, perhaps one should locate the center of gravity in the liturgical. In Luther one cannot separate the doctrinal from the spiritual: the doctrine of justification governed Christian life completely. A doctrine of the church runs second to these concerns. In Calvin one finds a similarly intimate connection between the doctrine of the scriptural word of God and the church organization that mediates it. In analogous fashion, one might be able to make a case that the English liturgy encapsulated in the Book of Common Prayer, by providing the uniform pattern of worship, created a kind of "essential center" of the Church of England.[90] Such a case would begin with the premise that faith and

---

90. One can measure the distinctiveness of any given church in a variety of ways along spectra of different variables: doctrines, organization, ministries, relation to society. According to the last of these categories, the essential note of the Church of England is its English national character. Another category for comparison is liturgy, sacraments and forms of worship, including the vexing questions revolving around the eucharist which so divided sixteenth-century churches, namely, the mass as sacrifice or, more generally, the theological conception of the Lord's Supper, and the meaning of the doctrine of real or true presence. How great was the shift between each church of the sixteenth century and the theology and practice of the medieval period? A comparative study of worship would be very significant relative to this study. But far short of this,

worship of Jesus Christ constitutes the very basis of the church. And the gradual acceptance of the simplified English liturgy, so that it became the form of personal and national piety, gave it symbolic depth and unifying breadth. It also preserved a bond of unity with the past. "The English reform of worship differed from reform elsewhere partly through its emphasis upon continuity. Its concern, while purging received orders of worship of error and superstition, was to maintain that from the past which was of genuine value, or at least biblically permissible, not evil."[91] In explicit terms, that which was continuous with the past, if it was sound, edifying, and done in decent order, should be included.[92] One can see several logics simultaneously at work in this policy: attention to personal religious edification, to social solidarity, to doctrinal continuity. "Cranmer's concern to preserve continuity can be detected in the very structure of the Prayer Book, which seems to be patterned after the medieval liturgical library in its divisions: the Breviary (Morning and Evening Prayer), the Missal (Collects, Epistles, Gospels, and the Holy Communion), the Processional (the Litany), and the Manual (Baptism through Churching of Women)."[93] On this view, then, liturgical assembly and prayer, including a good deal of sacramental ritual, provide a substantial element to the distinctive character to the Church of England.

The Church of England as a National Church

The English Reformation began with the Act of Supremacy of 1534. That blunt statement needs all sorts of qualifications, but it serves to mark the threshold crossed by the withdrawal from Roman authority and institution, as well as the official wedding of church and state. Surely, on the one hand, the commixture of religion and society was already complete at the end of the Middle Ages and this merely confirmed it; but not, on the other hand, without some distinction of spheres which the Articles preserved. "Society, then, is one society, and the monarch's writ runs everywhere within it, though

---

consideration of worship within the church of England helps to define its distinctive character.

91. Booty, "History," 366.
92. "Of Ceremonies, Why Some Be Abolished and Some Retained," BCP, 18–21.
93. Booty, "History," 367.

always . . . subject to the critical authority of the word of God, which
the monarch himself does not have the authority to expound or
preach."[94] In the traditional battle between priest and prince over
investiture, this solution favors the monarch; the ecclesiology finds
its kinship in a broad family resemblance of the way things were
with Constantine, Justinian, and Charlemagne, in certain circumstances a deep and workable tradition.[95] But the union runs much
deeper because of England's strong monarchical government and
clear boundaries marking territorial identity. The degree to which
the church was drawn under the mantel of monarchy and parliament
was displayed in the nationalization of church land and possessions.
On the one hand, governmental agencies led the reform, not without the help of bishops and other religious figures such as Cranmer;
on the other hand, the church took on the character of a national
church.

Church as Public Social Agent

The national character of the Church of England accentuates its social relevance. Hooker argues forcefully against every reduction of
religion to the sphere of the personal relation of the individual to
God. In one neat text, he compresses an extended reasoning process into one sentence and a conclusion: "For I would know, which
of these things it is whereof we make any question, either that the
favour of God is the cheifest pillar to bear up Kingdoms and States;
or that true Religion publiquely exercised, is the principal mean to
retain the favour of God; or that the Prelates of the Church are they,
without whom the exercise of true Religion cannot well and long
continue? If these three be granted, then cannot the publique benefit
of Prelacy be dissembled" (7,18,1). What Hooker says of hierarchy,
when extended to the whole institutional church, posits an imaginative framework in which Christianity enjoys a symbiotic relationship
with society as a whole. This extends from the broad symbolic level
of sanctioning society and nation to the practical context of the institutional delivery of grace. This is the public church, not unlike the

---

94. O'Donovan, *39 Articles*, 100–101.
95. See Marshall, *Hooker and the Anglican Tradition*, 162–67.

framework of Aquinas, and it is so spontaneous a premise for Hooker that he can simply spell it out in a phrase, as in the quoted text. Note that in Hooker this intends no accommodation to culture or social reductionism of divine grace. The exact opposite is the case. As we saw, he has a high ecclesiology of the body of Christ. If the salt of the church does not maintain the flavor given it by the Word of God, then the whole function of the church to mediate God's values and grace to society would be vitiated.

Openness of the Church of England to Other Forms of Polity

This characteristic is found in the two other Reformation ecclesiologies presented in the last chapters. But the degree to which this point is made and consistency of its application may be distinctive in Hooker's ecclesiology. Most of the mainline reformers understood that the true church existed where the word was preached and the sacraments authentically administered, a principle that transcended institutional boundaries. This doctrine is found in the Articles; it is found in Hooker; it is official doctrine. Article 23 avoids naming the three orders of ministry to which the Church of England was thoroughly committed. The Articles were not indifferent to this order of ministry, which represented a sharp divergence from that of Calvin. But relative to the essentials, they simply asserted ministry of word and sacrament.[96] Why? The Church of England was committed in a time of religious conflict to openness to other systems, other polities, other divisions of ministry. This represented a larger principle which distinguished between the essential and inessential in church matters. Orders of ministry are subordinate to the inner life of the church, so that one had to be open to a pluralism of church polities in the wider church. This attitude was in some respects foreshadowed by Cyprian's episcopalism, which was open to the extent that it accepted differences within unity, but the English Church is much more deliberate and explicit about it, because responding to an actual situation of serious division in western Europe.

---

96. O'Donovan, *39 Articles*, 119.

The same openness operates in Hooker's ecclesiology when he does not argue to the exclusive polity of the church or for the normativity of his church's ceremonies or structures, but consistently argues to their lawfulness. It turns aside from thinking in exclusive or excluding terms. It reflects an internalization of the principle of *adiaphora*, that is, a distinction between the immutable and the mutable, the essential and the accidental, the necessary and the contingent, the important and the indifferent, and coupled these distinctions with a desire to be inclusive. This is not yet the "whole-part" principle which will be developed in the next section, but a reflection on the attitude of the Church of England that opens up to this principle.

The Idea of Via Media

The idea of a *via media* has frequently served as a maxim for pointing to one distinctive feature of the Church of England: between Rome and Anabaptism, between Rome and the Protestant churches, between Rome and the Puritans. It was pointed out that some historians and theologians resist the idea for good reasons. But if the phrase is not pushed to contain more than it can, if it is not construed as passive compromise but as indicating comprehensiveness and inclusive vision, it may still be a useful heuristic, that is, not a thesis but a lens for looking for distinctive elements. Hooker in some ways transcends this debate and offers a view of via media that is no compromise but a positive, inclusive vision, and these are some of its elements: (1) One transnational church, with many parts. This deeply internalized principle in Hooker negates every narrow framework of an exclusively right polity. (2) A national church, encompassing the nation, with a strong defense of supremacy: the latter provision is dated, the former is debated as meaningful in a pluralistic society. (3) A high body of Christ ecclesiology. (4) A sophisticated view of the relation of church to society and state. (5) Seeds for pluralism in ecclesiology within a single region. As a defender of uniformity, Hooker did not hold this view. The seeds, then, lie in his rationality and respect for historicity. One has to be impressed by Hooker's relatively irenic view of godly Protestantism or moderate Puritanism that polemically resists mainly its exclusivism and his modest argument for the *lawfulness* of the polity he defends, not its exclusive position.

PRINCIPLES FOR
A HISTORICAL ECCLESIOLOGY

We turn now to some principles formulated on the basis of the genesis of the Church of England. "Principles" refer to propositions exemplified in this case but generally applicable, and thus illuminating for the church and ecclesiology at any given time. This means that they were probably operative in the past as well, but the development of the Church of England exemplifies them in a clear way.

Church development cannot go backward. Mary's attempt at a restoration of the Catholic Church and its ultimate failure is instructive. Her anachronistic restorationism teaches the lesson that the church cannot go backward. This does not mean that had she acted more deftly and lived longer the Catholic Church could not have been reinstated. In many respects it was. The issue concerns the cost and the terms on which it was being reconstituted. Dickens comments that "Parliament would accept a return to the last years of Henry VIII but not a return to the Middle Ages."[97] It appears that somewhere in the course of the events of Henry VIII's reign, and then in the more radical changes that occurred with Edward, a threshold had been crossed. The church and society together were in the process of passing out of the Middle Ages and into a new era. A straight or literal restoration would not work; such a church would be out of joint, the way Donatism appeared as a dated, Cyprianic ecclesiology in a post-Constantinian period. A massive difference obtains between a *ressourcement* that reaches into the past to retrieve its treasures by interpretation and application, and an attempt at restorationism that ignores the differences of historical contexts and tries to reassert or reinstate the forms of the past onto the present without accommodation. Church development that goes backward is regression and will

---

97. Dickens, *English Reformation*, 288.

not last. The ambiguity built into Elizabeth's church was far more attuned to the situation at the time.

   The unity of the church in the modern period. Why was Henry VIII who had tendencies that favored tradition able to sever the connection of the Church of England from Rome? In the history of the competition of authority between popes and emperors and kings from the Gregorian reform until this time, it was not generally the case that national churches simply withdrew from papal authority. The relative ease with which Henry accomplished this seems to be a sign of the times. The possibility of division from the papacy was demonstrated during the Western schism: even though in that conflict England remained loyal to Rome, some nations were not united with the real pope, whoever he was. Beyond the economic forces and the desire for a male heir, one may suspect that larger historical and cultural forces were at work. Europe had grown more self-consciously differentiated. England had developed a strong national government; it was an autonomous nation. The English language was becoming settled into literary forms that strengthened the cultural and national bonds, and the printing press was allowing it to be read more widely. These translated into an ever stronger sense of national identity. If these partly define symptoms of early modernity in Europe, then this modernity is clearly reflected in the language of a differentiated unity of the entire church. Hooker recognized the necessity of a pluralism of church polities across the regions and societies of Europe. This was still quite definitely a time when one definably united community or society could not have a pluralism of churches within itself. That would come later. But across Europe at large modernity was beginning to define itself in terms of a pluralism of churches. In brief, Europe had reached a point where, if unity were defined as uniformity without self-conscious respect for differences, there could not be a united Christendom. Henry both helped create this situation and was carried along by it.

   On the distinction between the visible and invisible church. The formation of the Church of England provides an occasion for discussing the distinction between the visible and invisible church. This distinction, which Augustine introduced into the discussion of the church, became an important category in Reformation ecclesiology. For Augustine the primary meaning was gained with reference to the saved, the truly sanctified, within the large, mixed, empirical church on earth. The point was in contrast to a large social-historical entity which was the empirical church; within this outer church subsisted the secret, holy church made up of the sanctified elect and known only to God.[98] But in the period of the Reformation the distinction served another purpose, and thus took on a slightly different meaning. The invisible church basically designates the same people, but the point is to identify them as the true church precisely as differentiated from the empirical church in its institutional structure. It is offered as an explanation of where the true church was when the Roman Church as institution became corrupted and false; or where unity in the great church can be found now that the institution purporting to hold the whole thing together had lost its validity. Now the invisible church is the true church, not as the inner substance of the empirical church, but in some cases despite it. In any case, this inner, invisible, and true church accounts for the unity of the whole church and its continuity with the past.

The problem with this construct is that although it may work in principle, for to some extent it is theologically accurate to say that those truly united with God are invisible and cannot be known, it is too easy. It absolves a church, or its leaders and theologians, from having to deal theologically with pluralism. The whole construct rests on the supposition that unity in the sense of uniformity constitutes the normative ideal, and when one can no longer find it in the large institution, because of regional differences, one tries to save it on a spiritual or "purely" theological level. Who would deny that the church is the *congregatio fidelium* whose unity is constituted by the true faith of each believer and known only to God? The medieval canonists held this principle. But theology would have to become somewhat more nuanced to deal with pluralism and unity in a critical fashion.

---

98. I prescind here from consideration of the eschatological or triumphal church in heaven.

Divine support for human ecclesial institutions. Subsisting in
the recognition of a pluralism of churches across Christendom lies
the idea that the church is largely if not entirely a human institution,
but one whose human structures enjoy divine approval, support, and
sanction. While such structures enjoy divine blessing, they may be
changed in such a way that the new ones may also be ratified by the
will of God. This idea responds in part to some of the problems created by pluralism. Some of the reformers recognized this idea, some
more extensively or expansively than others, but none with more
clarity than Hooker. The issue frequently comes under the heading of
the divine institution of various structures or elements of the church,
where "divine institution" usually entails something unchangeable.
The two themes of openness to differences among the churches and
a concern for essential or dominical structures seem to collide. But
Hooker held them together on the principle that ecclesial structures
can be both human and divinely appointed, both lawful and open to
exceptions and changeable. The orders of ministry in the Church of
England are lawful, but not exclusively so. It would be difficult to exaggerate the depth and significance of this philosophical and religious
insight in a situation of pluralism. It will take the leadership of the
churches a good bit of time to catch up with Hooker on this point.

Whole-part tension. The ecclesiology of the Church of England
began to deal with this question in a nuanced way by its openness
to other church polities and ceremonies discussed in the second part
of this chapter. Implicitly this openness rests on a recognition of the
distinction between "whole" and "part" of the one great church. In
Hooker, the language of whole and part is spontaneous and unforced.
"In which consideration as the maine body of the sea being one, yet
within divers precinctes hath divers names; so the Catholike Church
is in like sort devided into a number of distinct societies, every of
which is termed a Church within it selfe" (3,1,14). In this respect
Hooker manifests an early modern consciousness within the church
of England, and he writes a historically accurate ecclesiology.

One can see the principle of a tension between whole and part
in various eras of the church. But in the West, since the Gregorian
reform, the dominant framework for understanding the church had
been simply one whole church over which the pope ruled as head

or overseer. With the Reformation and the division among churches, the perspective was changed, but in the *de facto* pluralism there remained a tendency to ignore a pluralism in principle. That is, to some extent each church saw and claimed itself to be the normative church.[99] But with the Church of England the principle passed to a new level of explicitness in the second millennium. The principle of a tension between whole and part as a real and unresolved tension and as the natural condition of the church was implicit in Jewel's *Apologie*. He says, first: "We believe that there is one Church of God, and that the same is not shut up (as in times past among the Jews) into some one corner or kingdom, but that it is catholic and universal, and dispersed throughout the whole world; so that there is now no nation which can truly complain that they be shut forth, and may not be one of the Church and people of God: And that this Church is the kingdom, the body, and the spouse of Christ; and that Christ alone is the prince of this kingdom; that Christ alone is the head of this body; and that Christ alone is the bridegroom of this spouse."[100] But, second, he explicitly excludes the possibility of one man having a universal superiority over the whole church. The apology rules out the universal jurisdictional authority of the bishop of Rome or pope.[101] Third, he appeals to the Cyprianic and Patriarchal paradigms of autonomous churches in communion with each other. And, finally, he applies all of this to the situation of a divided Christendom in Europe. By Hooker's time, the principle is axiomatic: All people need language to speak, but they need not speak the same language: "the necessitie of politie and regiment in all Churches may be helde, without holding anie one certayne forme to bee necessarie in them all" (3,2,1).

Hooker's whole-part theory and a conciliarist vision. Hooker's "whole-part" theory of the church combines the position stated in "The Bishops' Book" (1537), one church among many churches in the whole church, and elements of conciliarist theory.[102] Hooker's

---

99. I say to some degree because definitions of the church are open: wherever there is authentic word and sacrament.

100. Jewel, *Apologie*, 21.

101. Ibid., 21–23.

102. One of the principles of this conciliarism was that "the Church of Rome was not the catholic church but a member of the catholic church. Particular churches, including

"whole-part" theory of the church has to be understood within a
larger vision of the human race providing the context of ecclesiological thinking. He had a vision of common laws of nations that
were needed to promote stable interchange among all peoples (283).
Within this framework he shared conciliarist ideas in which the
whole body of Christians constituted the church. Councils represented a way of bringing the whole church in all its several parts
together to address issues pertaining to the whole. "Hooker saw the
church as the whole body of believers and the general council as
the only institution adequately representative of that church" (295).
Analogous to the English system of government, "the general council
was the parliament of the church" (295). Because of the change of
context to a pluralism of churches, however, Hooker's vision completely transformed late medieval conciliarism. His expansive view
of the unity of the human race included historicity and ingrained pluralism. "One God of infinite wisdom is revealed in nature, scripture,
history, and in the learning and wisdom of human beings in every
time and place. One truth must therefore complement and reinforce
another" (301). We can only live together by learning from one another in a community of churches; councils were a way of allowing
this to happen (301). Hooker in effect asks whether Christian reconciliation and unity are "even conceivable on any other than a conciliar
basis" (302). What Nicholas of Cusa perceived as in a distant land is
coming much closer in Hooker's imagination.

To draw the principle out is to recall the method of a historical
ecclesiology. The subject matter for an adequate ecclesiology must
be the whole church, that is, the great church, the whole Christian
movement. This is required by a *historical* ecclesiology, one that recognizes that the church cannot be narrowed down on the basis of
history to a segment of the church. But at the same time, one only
belongs to the whole Christian church from a specific standpoint,
that is, in and through a particular church. Therefore, ecclesiology
must always make explicit the tension that arises when one tries to

---

the church of England, made up the catholic or universal church which a general council
would represent" (Patterson, "Hooker on Ecumenical Relations," 291. Cited in the text
of this paragraph by page number).

deal with the whole church from a particular tradition. The imperatives for making this tension explicit will become more apparent with the consideration of the ecumenical movement and the resurgence of the value of unity in Christian consciousness. When historical consciousness becomes more generally internalized, it becomes more evident "that our universal communion in the truth of the gospel will not come about by the denial of denominational traditions, but only by the critical appropriation and sharing of them."[103]

---

103. O'Donovan, *39 Articles*, 10.

Chapter 4

Anabaptist, Baptist, and Roman Ecclesiology

This fourth chapter on the sixteenth century takes up two more distinct ecclesiologies in the Western church: a free church ecclesiology (based on the assumption that the Anabaptist and the Baptist share something in common), and early modern Roman Catholic ecclesiology. The description and interpretation of these actual ecclesiologies will then be characterized as broad types standing at opposite ends of a spectrum of conceptions of the church that marked the great church by the end of this extraordinary century. This typology will provide principles for historical ecclesiology at any given time.

The first two ecclesiologies considered here emerged as variants among the different churches that together made up the Radical Reformation. In order to contain the sprawling data of the Radical Reformation, an Anabaptist evangelical church has been chosen from the towns of Northern Europe to represent this tradition, that is, the early Mennonite Church. An analysis of the later but analogous Baptist Church that separated from the Church of England provides a complementary representative. The second distinct ecclesiology to be analyzed is the Roman Catholic as that was formulated at the end of the Council of Trent in the catechism that it commissioned. This short, schematic statement of the ecclesiology of the Roman Church does not show all the complex shifts in self-understanding that were mediated by the Reformation, by the exploration and discovery that opened up the world, by the Council of Trent itself that redefined doctrine in a polemical relation to the Protestant world and instituted considerable reform in church life, and by the new religious orders that were leading the Roman Church into the modern period. But this outline of an ecclesiology recapitulates the church of the

Middle Ages in the light of these shifts and helps define it for the future.

These four chapters on the sixteenth century represent fully one third of this two-volume work. No other century comes close to the importance of this one for the development of the whole church, especially in the West, as it moved into the modern period. The definitive introduction of radical pluralism into the life of the Western church, and therefore into the whole church, as distinct from the Eastern and Western churches living in relative isolation, marks a turning point in the church which church consciousness itself has yet to catch up with and fully embrace. This pluralism prompts the typology at the end of the chapter. It attempts to capture this ecclesiological pluralism at its two extremes with a framework that interprets it positively and constructively.

Logically this chapter unfolds in three steps: the development of the two ecclesiologies representing the left wing of the church, the consolidation of the right wing of the Western church, and a characterization of these two contrasting poles of the broad spectrum of ecclesiologies in schematic form. We turn now to Anabaptist ecclesiology.

ANABAPTIST ECCLESIOLOGY

The best way of representing Anabaptist ecclesiology involves examining the texts which gave expression to the order of these churches and defined in embryonic terms some of the foundational principles that guided the tradition into the future. But since this ecclesiology provides a clear alternative not only to the Church of Rome but also to the ecclesiologies considered in the last three chapters, it will be necessary at least to characterize the broad movement of thought and social flow out of which these churches emerged. The church as it appears in the writings of Menno Simons will make sense in the context of this current of religious energy.

The Radical Reformation

It must be understood that one cannot in a short space represent the history of this Europe-wide religious surge whose pluralism at times reached the boarders of chaos. This narrative, however, leans heavily on the comprehensive work of George H. Williams.[1] The strategy in what follows resembles a descent from great height: starting from a most general and abstract level with a definition of terms, the analysis moves "downward" in ever more specific reference to the concrete events that shaped the texts of Menno that will be analyzed.

One might assume from the perspective of the sociology of religion that, given a Reformation, it had to have a left wing. Luther released a tide of religious energy, and wherever new structures were built to restructure and contain it, there followed as well resistance and overflow. Once the promise of Reformation was set in motion, it had, like a flood, to fill in all the available religious fields of doctrine, practice, church government, and spirituality.

One way of defining an entity consists in distinguishing it through opposition to its counterparts. Thus Williams distinguishes the Radical Reformation from the Magisterial Reformation where the term "magisterial" plays a double role. First, it bears a reference to magistrates and indicates how the program of Luther, Zwingli, Calvin, and most obviously the Church of England were supported in various degrees by princes, electors, magistrates, and kings. This in turn gave a certain territorial base to the movement and a social legitimacy that enabled it to withstand various political and religious attacks. From the beginning or in their very genesis these movements related to the world of society and government in more or less friendly terms. Second, "magisterial" suggest the university and the academic *magister* who brought to the task of reformation extensive knowledge and learning.[2] The last three chapters bear eloquent witness to this dimension of the Magisterial Reformation: from Luther to Hooker theologians played leading roles and exercised authority within these movements. By contrast, the Radical Reformation advanced by and large apart from the territorial control of civil rulers and, frequently enough, in the face of persecution by them; it survived in small groups, houses, and conventicles by voluntary association; its leaders

---

1. George Huntson Williams, *The Radical Reformation*, 3rd ed. (Kirksville, Mo.: Sixteenth Century Journal Publishers, 1992). Referred to as RR.
2. Williams, RR, 9.

were often charismatic and may or may not have had an academic education.

How might one characterize the Radical Reformation as a whole, not as a contained entity, but as the diverse, heterogeneous tide that it was? Several qualities help to indicate that the parameters of this religious situation differ from those of the classic reformers. First, the Radical Reformation was carried forward by charismatic leaders who were multiple and diverse. Hundreds of leaders at various levels of influence, in different locales, with far-reaching influence or purely local significance, dealing with small groups or larger constituencies, all participated in and made up the Radical Reformation. Second, it would be too strong to say that the Radical Reformation was spread exclusively by itinerant leaders, but many of its leaders traveled, often because of their being exiled. The movement was enriched by the encounters of various leaders and their positive or negative influence on each other. The natural home of the Radical Reformation was not first of all the cathedral, university, or city hall, but the drawing room, the meeting place of an individual church, from which it might be carried to another place. Third, and as a consequence, one might say that the Radical Reformation advanced by trial and error, by attempted reform and either failure or success, or more likely something in between. The Radical Reformation cuts through apparent historical logic and dramatizes the nature of history itself with its display of arbitrariness and continency. Fourth, the Radical Reformation was religiously and morally intense: it gravitated toward single-minded piety that demonstrated itself in a strict moral life. It generated martyrs. The language of religious enthusiasm might overstate some manifestations of this religious seriousness, but it does not misrepresent.

Despite the great variety among representatives of the Radical Reformation, Williams is able to discern three broad groups that analogously share common themes: Anabaptists proper, the Spiritualists, and the Evangelical Rationalists.[3] The Anabaptists were the most prominent of the three because their doctrine of believer's baptism

---

3. Williams, RR, xxxiii–xxxiv; he reviews these distinctions again in the Introduction to the third edition of his work at pp. 14–18. See also George Huntson Williams, ed., *Spiritual and Anabaptist Writers* (Philadelphia: Westminster Press, 1957),

and re-baptism clearly set them apart from the churches that accept infant baptism. We shall see how this practice represents a deeper issue relative to the very nature of the Christian church. A second group of Spiritualists tended toward a more individualist interpretation of Christianity, less concerned with the institutions of doctrine, worship, or polity. And in the third group of Evangelical Rationalists Williams places such figures as Michael Servetus and Faustus Socinus, both of whom questioned the doctrine of the trinity as a result of the strong place they gave to natural piety and speculative reason alongside of scripture.[4]

The Anabaptists.[5] Besides being a part of the Radical Reformation, what defines an Anabaptist turns out to be complicated by the many points of view from which they may be seen, and especially the diverse values that color the vision. We can begin with the technical meaning of the name, not of their own design, but given them by outsiders. An Anabaptist literally is one who baptizes again, or re-baptizes people, as Cyprian did with converts baptized in schismatic

---

19–38. Williams further divides the Anabaptists into subtypes "Evangelical" and "Revolutionary": and he subdivides the Spiritualists into three groups: "Revolutionary Spiritualism," "Rational Spiritualism," and "Evangelical Spiritualism." I refer to this latter work as SAW.

4. Williams, SAW, 23–24.

5. The following works have been useful in the interpretation of the development and structure of Anabaptist and particularly Mennonite ecclesiology: Roland H. Bainton, "The Anabaptist Contribution to History," *The Recovery of the Anabaptist Vision: A Sixtieth Anniversary Tribute to Harold S. Bender*, ed. Guy F. Hershberger (Scottdale, Pa.: Herald Press, 1957), 317–26; Harold S. Bender, "The Anabaptist Vision," *The Recovery of the Anabaptist Vision*, 29–54; J. Lawrence Burkholder, "The Anabaptist Vision of Discipleship," *The Recovery of the Anabaptist Vision*, 135–51; Robert Friedmann, *The Theology of Anabaptism: An Interpretation* (Scottdale, Pa.: Herald Press, 1973); William Echard Keeney, *The Development of Dutch Anabaptist Thought and Practice from 1539–1564* (Nieuwkoop: B. De Graaf, 1968); Walter Klaassen, *Anabaptism: Neither Catholic nor Protestant* (Waterloo, Ont.: Conrad Press, 1973); Jacobus ten Doornkaat Koolman, *Dirk Philips: Friend and Colleague of Menno Simons, 1504–1568* (Kitchner, Ont.: Pandora Press; Scottdale, Pa. / Waterloo, Ont.: Herald Press, 1998); Cornelius Krahn, *Dutch Anabaptism: Origin, Spread, Life and Thought* (The Hague: Martinus Nijhoff, 1969); Robert Kreider, "The Anabaptists and the State," in *The Recovery of the Anabaptist Vision*, 180–93; Franklin H. Littell, "The Anabaptist Concept of the Church," *The Recovery of the Anabaptist Vision*, 119–34; *A Tribute to Menno Simons* (Scottdale, Pa.: Herald Press, 1961); *The Origins of Sectarian Protestantism: A Study of the Anabaptist View of the Church* (New York: Macmillan, 1964); John H. Yoder, ed., *The Legacy of Michael Sattler* (Scottdale, Pa.: Herald Press, 1973); N. Van der Zijpp, "The Early Dutch Anabaptists," *The Recovery of the Anabaptist Vision*, 69–82.

churches. Like Cyprian, the Anabaptists rejected the term because their theology showed they were baptizing for the first time. Perhaps more importantly, the Anabaptists denied infant baptism in principle. Thus their theology, which will be considered more carefully below, clearly distinguished them from the churches that embraced infant baptism.

But the technical definition of Anabaptism misleads when it overrides the pluralism of Anabaptist views or self-conceptions. Williams makes the point forcefully: "Almost as important in typological nomenclature might be such emphases in Anabaptism suggested by the adjectives communitarian, mystical, millennialist, separatist from the congregationally banned, conventionally Trinitarian (in terms of the *Apostolicum*), Christo-centric Unitarian (like such Germanic Anabaptists as Adam Pastor and Louis Haetzer), spiritualizing-conformist (David Joris), and proponents of the celestial flesh of Christ (Melchior Hofmann, Menno Simons)."[6]

Despite this wide-ranging diversity, as soon as groups of Christians refused infant baptism, they stood clearly apart from all the churches in place. The question of infant versus believer's baptism represented much more than either doctrine or sacramental practice in themselves, although both of these were involved. Beneath the Anabaptist movement lay a desire for the restitution of the church, and this meant reestablishing the church of the New Testament and the apostles. Surely seeds of such a primitivist impulse grew in Luther and Calvin, for raising up scripture as the ultimate and absolute norm for self-understanding implicitly moves in this direction. But the Anabaptists used the rejection of infant baptism and an insistence on believer's baptism to define the true church over against what was in place in a far more thoroughgoing way, in fact, against the Roman Church, society, and the other reformers as well. One can read this desire to recreate the apostolic church in the origins of the Anabaptist movement itself. The real issue was not the act of baptism but "a bitter and irreducible struggle between two mutually exclusive concepts of the church."[7] The rite of baptism

---

6. Williams, RR, 15.
7. Littell, *The Origins of Sectarian Protestantism*, 14. Cited hereafter as *Origins.*

became the visible dividing line between two fundamentally different ecclesiologies.

It will be helpful to draw out this difference in the broadest of terms because it defines the subject matter of this whole chapter. The difference Littell highlights reaches far; it separates two fundamentally different understandings of the church that in fact play out in different organizational systems. The one is the territorial church, a church coterminus with the state, or city-state, with a system of parishes that include all. The other is the conventicle, the voluntary association standing over against society, whether in contemporary Europe or the first and second centuries in the Roman empire, as outlawed and persecuted. The one is still the great church of Christendom, even in its pluralism, for each church claims to be the true church in a comprehensive way for all within varying territorial boundaries. The other has been mentally transported back in time and becomes again the early church, a struggling movement, finding a place in the interstices of society. A fundamentally new relationship with the world is at stake. The criticism by Anabaptism of the Magisterial Reform is that it stopped way short of the restitution of the apostolic church. In terms that will shed light on the history and texts considered in this presentation of Anabaptist ecclesiology, Littell makes this comment: "For working purposes, the Anabaptists proper were those in the radical Reformation who gathered and disciplined the 'true church' upon the apostolic pattern as they understood it. In a treatment of the Anabaptists, the doctrine of the church affords the classifying principle of first importance."[8]

The Brethren in the Netherlands. We can view the context of Menno Simons's ecclesiology in sharper detail in the light of the story of the community he joined. That story begins in Zurich, passes through Strasbourg, skirts Münster, on its way to the Netherlands and northern Germany.

The Swiss reform movement had its origin in Bible study groups and the leadership of Huldrych Zwingli. The Brethren began within Zwingli's movement as a radical faction preoccupied more with small groups of faith-filled Christians in the pattern of the earliest church

---

8. Littell, *Origins,* xvii.

than with the reorganization of the existing canton-wide church structures. This religious impulse came to a focus in baptism which the Brethren understood as the sacrament of faith with no equivocation. Debates between the radicals and the Zwinglians came to an impasse in the winter of 1524–25 and culminated in a meeting of the key leaders on January 21, 1525. At the home of Felix Mantz, Conrad Grebel, layman and chief leader of the group, re-baptized George Blaurock, a priest, who in turn baptized others present. This event is often considered the birthday of Anabaptism.[9]

Within a week the first Anabaptist conventicle or congregation was established in a village outside of Zurich, and the Anabaptist movement began to spread. But not without two serious problems: the first was persecution, which began almost immediately. In Zurich in 1525 "drowning was proclaimed as penalty for re-baptism, without trial or hearing."[10] The second problem concerned consistency and stability of doctrine. The years following 1525 involved many meetings of various groups in different locales in attempts to solidify the doctrine and practice of the movement. Nevertheless all sorts of different movements were identified as "Anabaptist."

Two years after the beginnings in Zurich, on February 24, 1527, "a number of brethren assembled at Schleitheim to discuss and draw up . . . a document which in due time became 'normative' at least for all the Swiss Brethren. The Seven Articles concern

1. baptism;

2. the ban;

3. the Lord's Supper;

4. separation from the world;

5. the office of shepherd;

6. the sword, that is, the relationship to civil authorities; and

7. the taking of an oath, forbidden for a disciple.

---

9. Williams, RR, 212–46 describes the rise of the Swiss Brethren; he cites at length Blaurock's reminiscence of the meeting in January 1525 at pp. 216–17. See also Littell, *Origins*, 12–18.

10. Littell, *Origins*, 17.

On all these points consensus was sought and given, for it was a voluntarily accepted *regula,* rather than a law dictated from above."[11] "It was particularly after the principles and practice of the movement had been laid down, in the so-called Schleitheim Confession ...that a local church life of an autonomous congregational type emerged."[12] Anabaptists expanded north into southern Germany, east into Moravia, and southeast into the Tyrol. Because this was a nonterritorial church consisting in small groups accepting believer's baptism, it was unaffected by regionally defined Catholic and Protestant boundaries. So it spread. In 1529 the Emperor decreed the death penalty for Anabaptists, a policy with which both Catholics and Protestants generally agreed, although it was unevenly enforced.

Strasbourg also figures in the story of the spread of the Anabaptism of the Swiss Brethren. Between 1529, when the celebration of the mass was outlawed, and 1534, when the church in the city was reorganized, Strasbourg served as a crossroads and a clearing house of the many fragments of the Reformation. Of special note in this mix is Melchior Hofmann, a prophet who moved spiritually in the 1520s through Lutheranism and a history of preaching in the north, to a literal form of imminent eschatology, and then to an acceptance of Anabaptist ideas. This last conversion occurred in Strasbourg in 1530. In that same year he was driven from the city and traveled north to Emden where he preached with considerable success. It was not long before he was again run out of town, as was the teacher he left behind. But Hofmann had baptized many and made his mark, as Obbe Philips would declare with reference to the Brethren in the Netherlands: "This was, in short the commencement of the first commission and became the beginning of the movement."[13]

11. Friedmann, *Theology of Anabaptism,* 128. The text of the Schleitheim Articles is found in Yoder, *Michael Sattler,* 34–43.

12. Van der Zijpp, "The Early Dutch Anabaptists," 69.

13. Obbe Philips, "A Confession: Recollections of the Years 1533–1536," SAW, 210. "On 23 April 1530 [Hofmann] escaped from the city [of Strasbourg] in haste and headed back to Emden, where he would soon father an Anabaptist congregation and thereby introduce the potent seed of Hofmannite (Melchiorite) Anabaptism into the moist soil of the Lowlands, long harrowed and tilled by Sacramentism and persecution." Williams, RR, 393.

Melchiorite apocalypticism contributed to the religious frenzy that led finally to the bizarre and bloody debacle in Münster in 1534–35. Catholic and Protestant alike portrayed this cataclysm as the natural outcome of the Anabaptist perversion, and its tangential relationship to the Brethren would be a constant embarrassment. Most significant for the tradition in the Netherlands was the baptism and ordination of Obbe Philips. In 1533 John Matthijs declared himself the emissary of Hofmann commissioned in the Spirit, and he in turn sent apostles of Christ to preach his message. Obbe Philips encountered two of these in the town of Leeuwarden and, along with others, was baptized. Also, the next day "at the suggestion of other brethren, and with the laying on of hands [they] laid upon us the office of preaching, [commissioning us] to baptize, teach, and stand before the congregation."[14] Eight days later Obbe's brother Dietrich (or Dirk) was also baptized by an apostle of Matthijs.[15] Not very long afterward the extremist views of Melchiorite Anabaptists began to beget violence. In March of 1534, the very apostles who baptized and commissioned Obbe Philips were arrested for demonstrating in Amsterdam and executed. In June of 1535 the divine kingdom of Münster, led briefly by Matthijs, came to an end in a bloody paroxysm. Thereafter and for the most part through the course of these events the Anabaptists of the Netherlands sought to dissociate themselves from the Melchiorites of Münster.

Menno Simons

Menno Simons was born in 1496 in the village of Witmarsum in present-day Netherlands. He was dedicated to the life of a priest early on and studied at a Franciscan monastery near his home town where he learned Latin and Greek, and read Tertullian, Cyprian, and Eusebius, but not the scriptures. He was ordained at twenty-eight in 1524 and assigned to the parish in Pingjum, next to his home, and after seven years was transferred to the parish of his upbringing, Witmarsum, where he served for five years.[16]

---

14. Obbe Philips, "Confession," SAW, 217.
15. Dietrich was later ordained or commissioned to preach by his brother Obbe.
16. Harold Stauffer Bender, "A Brief Biography of Menno Simons," *The Complete Writings of Menno Simons (c. 1496–1561)*, ed. H. S. Bender (Scottdale, Pa.: Herald Press, 1956), 4. Referred to hereafter as *Writings*.

Conversion. One of the most engaging aspects of Menno's life was his conversion to the Reformation movement. Menno himself gave an account of this protracted process.

It began with doubts about the eucharist. Early in his ministry, he wrote, "it occurred to me, as often as I handled the bread and wine in the Mass, that they were not the flesh and blood of the Lord."[17] To resolve the problem he decided to study the New Testament, an important decision because he was ignorant of the scriptures, fearing that "if I should read them, I would be misled" (RGF, 668). He did read the New Testament and discovered in the matter of the eucharist "that we were deceived" (RGF, 668). Just as importantly this incident impelled Menno to pursue the reading of scripture more deeply. The result: "I increased in knowledge of the scriptures daily, and was presently considered by some (not correctly however) to be an evangelical preacher" (RGF, 668).

A second event leading to an intellectual crisis over baptism occurred in 1531. As he records it: "Afterwards it happened, before I had ever heard of the existence of brethren, that a God-fearing, pious hero named Sicke Snijder was beheaded in Leeuwarden for being re-baptized. It sounded very strange to me to hear of a second baptism. I examined the scriptures diligently and pondered them earnestly, but could find no report of infant baptism" (RGF, 668). Moreover the Fathers' view that infant baptism cleansed them from original sin seemed to conflict with the scriptural role assigned to the "blood of Christ." He consulted further the opinions of Luther, Bucer, and Bullinger on infant baptism, but none corresponded to scripture: once again, "I realized that we were deceived in regard to infant baptism."[18]

A third major component in Menno's narrative about his conversion occurred in March 1535, but the events which lead up to it began with Melchior Hofmann's visit to Emden in 1530. This stimulated Melchiorite preachers in the North. In 1532 people advocating adult baptism appeared in Menno's parish. And two years

---

17. Menno Simons, *Reply to Gellius Faber* (1552), *Writings*, 668. This work of Menno will be referred to hereafter as RGF.
18. RGF, 669. "And so, my reader, I obtained a view of baptism and the Lord's Supper through the illumination of the Holy Ghost, through much reading and pondering of the scriptures, and by the gracious favor and gift of God; not by the instrumentality of the erring sects as it is reported of me." Ibid.

later Melchiorite preachers representing the experiment in Münster preached in Menno's village of Witmarsum.[19] Then, in March of 1535, envoys from Münster slipped out of the besieged city to rally Dutch Anabaptists to the rescue. Three hundred people, among them Menno's brother, successfully assaulted a fortified Cistercian abbey not far from Witmarsum, only to be later captured and slaughtered.[20] The event affected Menno deeply: it increased his revulsion for Hofmann's ideas; and the powerful witness of martyrdom for religious conviction both shamed him in his inauthentic Catholic situation and impelled him toward a ministry that would cut through the Melchiorite fantasy and nurture those who were confused.[21] In January of 1536 he resigned from his priesthood in the Roman Church.[22]

Anabaptist ministry. About a year after he left the Roman Church Menno was approached by a group of the Brethren and asked to assume the office of elder or bishop in the brotherhood. After some soul-searching, he accepted and was ordained in early 1537, presumably by Obbe Philips. His leadership would prove to be crucial because, on the one hand, the Melchiorite extremism continued after Münster, leading to confusion and disarray, and, on the other hand, Obbe Philips himself fell victim to disillusionment and left the brotherhood around 1541. Menno and Obbe's brother Dirk Philips became the leaders of the church still in the process of formation.

The next twenty four years of Menno's life were spent in ministry to the extended brotherhood of Obbenite, which soon became Mennonite, churches. From 1536 to 1543 he was based in Holland;

---

19. Menno writes: "I did what I could to oppose them by preaching and exhortations, as much as in me was. I conferred twice with one of their leaders, once in private, and once in public, but my admonitions did not help..." (RGF, 669–70). The siege of Münster by the bishop of Münster was begun in March 1534, and the city finally fell in June 1535.

20. Williams, RR, 581.

21. Here is Menno's testimony: "After this had transpired the blood of these people, although misled, fell so hot on my heart that I could not stand it, nor find rest in my soul. I reflected upon my unclean, carnal life, also the hypocritical doctrine and idolatry which I still practiced daily in appearance of godliness, but without relish. I saw that these zealous children, although in error, willingly gave their lives and their estates for their doctrine and faith. And I was one of those who had disclosed to some of them the abominations of the papal system." Menno, RGF, 670.

22. I have dwelt on these existential crises because elements in Menno's subsequent theology of the church correlate quite closely with some of these experiences.

from 1543 to 1546 in northwest Germany; and finally from 1546 to 1561 along the Baltic seacoast. Although he married in 1536 or 1537, much of his time was spent traveling and living clandestinely because, as an Anabaptist leader, he was wanted. Indeed, "the emperor himself, Charles V, was prevailed upon to publish a severe edict against Menno on December 7, 1542, which placed a price of 100 gold guilders on his head, and which further forbade giving aid or shelter to him in any way or reading his books."[23] Menno was never arrested, and he managed to write several book-length works as well as pamphlets. His style was never academic but somewhat sermonic and hortatory; he always related to the reader, frequently quite directly with phrases such as "Observe, reader" and "My brethren." But his principal task was leadership as he visited, encouraged, and animated congregations. He also exercised authoritative oversight, including the discipline and occasional ban, or excommunication, of leaders. In the last years of his life he became entangled in a controversy over the proper degree of severity of the ban which, in its divisiveness, was a source of sadness. He died in 1561.

Menno's Ecclesiology

A fair representation of Menno Simons's ecclesiology can be culled from the pages of his writings. These views are presented in a systematized framework quite unlike the style of this occasional writer who was usually addressing specific problems. The preceding sections provide the background and supply the imaginative framework needed to understand that the reality of the church being described here is quite different than the churches treated in other chapters. The referent of the term "church," when it is not the idealized theological reality, appears as the small, voluntary group that meets in houses, in the nooks and crannies of established society, and not ordinarily in the parish church.[24] Also, relative to structure, the suppositional bias leans toward informality, so that one will not find the complex organization found in Calvin or Hooker or the developed

---

23. Bender, "Biography," *Writings*, 17.
24. The word "church" in some ways is misleading in this respect, and Menno's preferred word for the church is "Gemeente" or community. Keeney, *Dutch Anabaptist Thought*, 145–48.

tasks of office with rights and duties described in a legal type of language. In various degrees, the Reformation churches examined up to now were built within a social framework that was in many ways continuous with the medieval church; the church Menno refers to is more like the church in the late first and early second centuries that was still in the process of forming itself.

Nature of the church and its members. A definition of the church and how Menno approached this common topic of identifying the "true" church provide a good place to begin.

Definition of the church. The church is "an assembly of the pious, and a community of the saints" who from the beginning believed in Christ and accepted his Word and followed his example led by his Spirit and trusting in his promise. "These pious people are commonly called Christians or the church of Christ, because they are born of Christ's Word by means of faith, by His Spirit, and are flesh of His flesh and bone of His bone . . . " (RGF, 734). The church should have the mind of Christ: the church imitates Christ, loves what Christ loves and hates what Christ hates (RGF, 738). Theologically this church goes back to the beginning, to Abel, Noah, Abraham and so on. But so too does the church of Antichrist, so that Menno has a vision of world history divided into light and darkness, the good and the evil (RGF, 735). This church is "of God" through Christ, which means it is from and dedicated to God just as, by contrast, the church of the Antichrist is of and for evil (RGF, 736).

True signs of the church. Menno proposes six true signs of the church:

1. Unadulterated, pure doctrine. The church is commissioned to preach faithfully what it received from Christ;

2. Scriptural use of the sacramental signs, that is, the baptism of believers and the celebration of the Lord's Supper;

3. Obedience to the Word. By this he means the pious Christian life: "The Lord says, Ye shall be holy, for I, the Lord your God, am holy" (RGF, 740);

4. Unfeigned, brotherly love. Disciples of Christ are known by their love for one another;

5. Bold confession of God and Christ, in the face of opposition and the world;

6. Oppression and tribulation for the sake of the Lord's Word. Persecution from the world or "the cross" naturally follows from testimony to the Word of God.

In sum: "We know for sure that where there is no pure doctrine, no pure sacraments, no pious Christian life, no true brotherly love, and no orthodox confession, there no Christian church is" (RGF, 752).

The ban could be included as one of the signs of the true church for it serves as the means by which some of the other true signs are maintained socially. Menno occasionally uses language that implies that the ban is an essential element of the church. The ban functions to keep the church holy, and as long as ministers do not practice the ban or punishment as scripture requires, the church will not measure up to what is required of it (RGF, 745). When those who transgress the Word "are known and then not excluded after proper admonition, but allowed to remain in the fellowship of their religion, then, in my opinion, she ceases to be the church of Christ" (RGF, 746). The visible church "must be sound in doctrines, sacraments, and ordinances, and irreproachable in life before the world, so far as man, who is able to judge only that which is visible, can see" (RGF, 747).[25]

The holiness of church and members. Menno describes the church as a holy community.[26] The true church is "a gathering or congregation of saints, ... namely, those who through true faith are

---

25. These signs generally and sometimes exactly correspond to the seven ordinances of the true church proposed by Dietrich (Dirk) Philips. The ban is listed explicitly by Dietrich Philips, and certainly Menno intends it implicitly. Its absence is actually surprising. Philips writes: "The *fourth ordinance* is evangelical separation, without which the congregation of God cannot stand or be maintained. For if the unfruitful branches of the vine are not pruned away they will injure the good and fruitful branches (John 15:6)." "Separation or exclusion must also be practiced for the reason that thereby the offender may be chastised in the flesh and be made ashamed, and so may repent that he may be saved in the day of the Lord Jesus (1 Cor 5:5)." Dietrich Philips, *The Church of God,* in SAW, 246, 247.

26. One could also approach this topic theologically through the sacrament of baptism. Believers' baptism presupposes the conversion and faith of those who come to the rite, thus assuring holiness of life at entrance into the community; the ban preserves the community in righteous belief and behavior. I will pick up these themes further on.

regenerated by God into Christ Jesus and are of a divine nature..."
(RGF, 667). These are congregations of the truly pious, made up of
members who are animated by Word and Spirit, and live lives of fasting and prayer, with blameless pastors and teachers who are chosen
and called by the same congregation into the service of the Lord and
not the world. "Wherever men conform themselves to the Spirit of
Christ, His Word, sacraments, ordinances, commands, prohibitions,
usage, and example, there the holy Christian church is found, as has
been heard, and there also the promise holds that the gates of hell
will not prevail against her" (RGF, 755).[27]

Menno ascribes to the preachers and congregational leaders responsibility for the holiness of the church. The church of Christ is
"begotten by sincere, pious preachers and Christians, who are ac-
tuated by the Spirit of Christ,... irreproachable in doctrine and life,
who in pure and faithful love seek their neighbors...." "They preach
the Word in the power of the Spirit, who as shining lights give light
before all men, and who with all their strength put their received
talent to work and make a great gain therewith to the treasure of
the Lord" (RGF, 736). What makes a church unholy? Menno spontaneously points to four things that correspond antithetically to his
ecclesiology: "frivolous doctrine of the preachers, the miserable infant
baptism, the unscriptural, idolatrous Supper, and the neglect of the
Lord's ordinance of the ban as practiced by the apostles" (RGF, 737).

Who then is the true member of the church? "If you want to be
a true member of the church of Christ, you must be born of the
Word of God; be Christian minded; bring forth Christian fruits; walk
according to His Word, ordinance, and command; die unto the flesh
and the world; lead an irreproachable life in the fear of God; serve
and love your neighbors with all your heart; confess the name and
glory of Christ, and be prepared for all manner of tribulation, misery,
and persecution for the sake of the Word of God and its testimony"
(RGF, 744).

---

27. This characterization of the church stands between and contrasts with those
Anabaptists who are "an assembly of people that have been misled by false prophets"
and a church of God that is openly and publicly recognized by society (RGF, 666). Such
churches are "of the world" and their comportment in every way reveals them to be "of
the world."

Organization of the church. The essential structure of the church can be reduced to four elements which Menno expresses negatively as lacking in other churches. They are (1) sound doctrine, (2) a self-supporting or nonsalaried ministry, (3) proper administration of the sacraments, and (4) a morally blameless life of the ministers. An authentic church must possess "a free, Christian doctrine, not hired nor sold for money, but urged by the Holy Spirit through brotherly love, a true use of the sacramental signs, according to the command, doctrine, and usage of Christ and His apostles, and an unblamable life and walk, led in love and fear of the Lord."[28] Relative to more established churches these four prescriptions allow for a good deal of further differentiation. The organization of ministerial tasks remains quite elementary and not as yet universally prescribed. Some of the most basic structures can be summarized as the institutions of scripture, the preacher, and the elder.

The encompassing authority of scripture. Scripture constitutes the first principle of universal authority. The whole of scripture, Old Testament and New Testament, are written for our instruction, admonition, and correction. Scripture is the "true scepter and rule by which the Lord's kingdom, house, church, and congregation must be ruled and governed. Everything contrary to Scripture, therefore, whether it be in doctrines, beliefs, sacraments, worship, or life, should be measured by this infallible rule and demolished by this just and divine scepter, and destroyed without any respect of persons."[29]

The calling and ministry of the congregational preacher and teacher. Menno gave clear instructions concerning the calling and

---

28. Menno Simons, "Brief and Clear Confession" (1544), *Writings,* 446. Cited hereafter as BCC. Menno describes the elemental structure of the church in another place as follows: "This constitutes the church in Christ: rightly to teach Christ's unadulterated Word in the power of the Spirit; to believe the same with all the heart and to practice it in all obedience; rightly to use the sacraments, such as baptism and holy communion, according to His own commandments and ordinance; to seek God from the heart, to fear Him, love Him, serve Him; to be born of God; to love one's neighbor, to serve him, comfort him, help and assist him; to avoid all false doctrine and the works of darkness; to mortify all carnal lusts that war against God's Word; to deny oneself and the world, to lead a pious, peaceful, chaste, sober, and humble life in righteousness according to the truth. In fine, to be of the same mind as was Christ Jesus!" Menno Simons, "Brief Defense to All Theologians" (1552), *Writings,* 537–38.

29. Menno Simons, "Foundation of Christian Doctrine," *Writings* 160. Cited hereafter as FCD.

responsibilities of the preacher and teacher of the congregation. The premise of these norms is that ministers are appointed in two ways, directly by God as with the prophets and apostles, and those others called through human agents (RGF, 644).[30] The following account refers to the second and ordinary way congregations appoint their ministers: first, calling is done by the church, not "by the world, but by the true Christians and obedient disciples of the Lord and His Word" (RGF, 644). In other words, Menno opposes the idea of magistrates or secular rulers appointing the ministers of the church. Second, the candidates for ministers should be of blameless doctrine and life. A minister must be holy and virtuous, and Menno proposes a whole list of required virtues (RGF, 646). Third, the purpose of ministry and preaching should be foremost in mind, together with the duties of the minister. Menno lists these duties as follows: "they should teach the Word of the Lord correctly, rightly use their sacraments, lead and rule aright the church of God, gather together with Christ and not scatter, console the bereaved, admonish the irregular, seek the lost, bind up the wounded, ban those that are incurable, without any respect of persons whether great or small; and solemnly watch over the vineyard, house, city of God, as the Scriptures teach" (RGF, 649).[31] While this passage suggests an almost omni-competent role of the congregational leader, Menno refers to a variety of different

---

30. "According to the Scriptures the mission and vocation of Christian preaching takes place in two ways. Some are called by God alone without any human agent as was the case with the prophets and apostles. Others are called by means of the pious as may be seen from Acts 1: 23–26" (FCD, 159). Every valid preacher of Christ and his Word has to have been called in one of these two ways. They do not appropriate this role of themselves but are called by God or by the church. And no one can succeed in this "high and holy office" except one who is enabled by the Spirit (FCD, 160–62). The basic principle is that the preachers are sent by Jesus Christ, as Christ was sent by the Father, and so they should be as like Christ as possible, as it were, extensions of Christ. The key text is John 20:21, "As my Father hath sent me, even so send I you" (BCC, 440). Ministers should be "those who are of one body, spirit, and mind with Him, even as He is one with the Father." BCC, 441.

31. In another place Menno sums up the many duties of the minister in three basic points. (a) Preachers, teachers, ministers are to teach and be exactly faithful in so doing with the teaching of Christ himself and the apostles. (b) Preachers are to "administer the sacramental signs conformable to the Gospel of Christ, namely, the baptism of believers, and not of infants, and the Supper under both forms." (c) Preachers are to be blameless and live morally upright lives. This is followed by a whole list of virtues. BCC, 441.

ministries: "the Holy Ghost has ordained in the house of the Lord bishops, pastors, and teachers, according to the precept of Paul who says, He gave some apostles, and some prophets, and some evangelists, and some pastors and teachers" all for the building up of the one body in the unity of the faith (RGF, 649). Thus one can expect some further differentiation of roles within each community. "In the fourth place, we should observe what kind of fruits they bring forth, for Christ says, I have chosen you and ordained you, that ye should go and bring forth fruit, and that your fruit should remain" (RGF, 650).

Ministers should be self-supporting, by their own farms or trade, "lest they be found selling the free Word of God which was given them without price, and living on shameful gain, robbery, and theft. Let all sincere and pious servants of Christ beware of this, and whatever they cannot earn by due labor and diligence will doubtlessly be provided for them as needed" by the members of the congregation (BCC, 442).[32] Ministers or preachers should "dispense, without pay, the precious Word of God, the word of eternal salvation and heavenly grace, which can be merited by no works nor paid for by money, even as we, by grace only, received it of God without price" (BCC, 446). This positive statement is accompanied by strong indictment of the ministry in other churches which is salaried, and he blames the objective, indolent, and immoral behavior of the ministers on the social structure of a salary which seems to undercut love of God and religious motivation by supplanting it with a desire for material gain.[33]

Elder. The exact structure of organizational authority in communities and more broadly uniting the communities together is not

---

32. Menno appeals to the early church for this view, the apostles and those appointed by them. "And as for the temporal necessities of life, the begotten church was sufficiently driven by love, through the Spirit and Word of God, to give unto such faithful servants of Christ and watchers of their souls all the necessities of life, to assist them and provide for them all such things which they could not obtain by themselves" (BCC, 443). In sum: self-supporting ministers, but supplemented by the congregation in all the necessities of their lives.

33. "I speak of your preachers in general, for they all enjoy such [ill-gotten] gain. Your doctrine, benefices, pensions, and rents are such an abomination before my eyes, that verily, brethren, I would rather be beheaded, burned, drowned, or torn into quarters by four horses than to receive for my preaching such benefices, pensions, and incomes." BCC, 445.

clear in the writings of Menno. It may be that they had not yet become uniform or standardized. But some principles are clear: first,
the leadership was lay, and the encouragement of the minister to
earn his own living protected ministry from professionalization and
the formation of a clerical caste. Second, ultimate authority lay in
the congregation as a whole, and they called the minister who functioned at the will of the Spirit as manifested in the community. Third,
the title "elder" signified an overseer in the community, but they
functioned at various levels. For example, on the one hand, Menno
writes to the elders in the congregations, and, on the other hand,
as a regional elder he communicates to the communities decisions
made on a broader level: "Dirk Philips our brother and I counseled
with the elders in the past in regard to this matter... and it was
resolved... how we would conduct ourselves in this matter according to circumstances."[34] It is clear that authority of the elders at both
levels was exercised with consultation in community.[35]

Mission of the church. The mission of the church does not always
find clear definition in ecclesiology because the notion of goals and
purpose lie deeply embedded in the nature of the church. But on
at least one occasion Menno addressed the issue quite directly. The
purpose of the church is to serve, thank, and praise God, and more
fully, it exists "for the purpose of hearing the Lord, of fearing, loving,
serving, praising, honoring, and thanking God sincerely" (RGF, 737,
also 742). The church exists in order that God in all God's works,
majesty, and love may be glorified. The optimum fruits or results
produced by the church are Christ-like people who conform to the
Word of God; the church strives to bring forth the fruits of Christ in
people who live the pattern of Jesus Christ (RGF, 738). One can read
in these statements a form of a classical spirituality of the imitation
of Christ.

Activities of the church. One has to assume that the community
assembled for preaching and prayer. But Menno's writings contain
no orders of worship or prescribed prayers. One must assume a great

---

34. Menno Simons, "Instruction on Discipline to the Church at Emden" (1556),
Writings, 1050.
35. See Littell, *Origins,* 91–95.

deal of local accommodation and pluralism in the assemblies of the different communities even as their situations differed. Relative to the activities of the church beyond preaching, however, Menno provides concise theologies of the sacraments, baptism and the Lord's Supper, and a good deal of reflection on the Christian life, especially the ban.

Baptism. Menno's theology of baptism consists in his justification for a rejection of infant baptism and an insistence on believer's baptism. But one should bear in mind the ecclesiological import of this whole discussion: the nature of the church is as stake.

Menno's theology draws directly from the New Testament.[36] Christ gave the command to go and baptize. But the command was to baptize those who believed. "Faith does not follow from baptism, but baptism follows from faith" (FCD, 120). Therefore, no baptism for children, because they do not and cannot have faith. To baptize children would be to pervert the sacrament and the will of Christ.[37] "This then is the Word and will of the Lord, that all who hear and believe the Word of God shall be baptized as related above" (FCD, 121).

The point is that grace is mediated through faith, and the effect of baptism is through existential faith. Menno stresses the actuality of religious faith against any objectification of it. But this means that the efficacy of the sacrament is not really mediated by the external sign, "but on account of the power and truth of the divine promise which we receive by obedience through faith" (FCD, 124). The reason why the baptism of children perverts the sacrament is that it reduces the regeneration to the immersion in water, rather than being the "inward change which converts a man by the power of God through

---

36. What is the "principal reason" why he opposes infant baptism and is willing to sacrifice his life for it? Because it is not in the New Testament or practice of the Apostles, and therefore it is not dominical. It is not part of the Word of God. If it were, he would follow it (FCD, 129). Or, more theologically: Baptism concerns regeneration and this has nothing to do with infants, "for regeneration as well as faith takes place through the Word of God and is a change of heart, or of the inward man, as was said above." FCD, 134. Also, CDC, 513.

37. Menno reacts against Luther for admitting infant baptism on the basis of some implicit faith; it is not possible for an infant to have faith; also against Bucer for reducing baptism to an introduction into the church. There simply is no testimony to infant baptism in the New Testament, and so the practice is a human invention. FCD, 126–27.

faith from evil to good, from carnality to spirituality, from unrigh-
teousness to righteousness, out of Adam into Christ" (FCD, 123).[38]
The sacramental sign, then, functions as outward sign of the inward
transaction negotiated through faith. "The seal in our consciences is
the Holy Ghost, but baptism is a sign of obedience, commanded of
Christ, by which we testify when we receive it that we believe the
Word of the Lord, that we repent of our former life and conduct, that
we desire to rise with Christ unto a new life, and that we believe in
the forgiveness of sins through Jesus Christ" (FCD, 125).

The Lord's Supper. In two deliberate texts Menno summarized his
theology of the Lord's Supper in four points and the two versions are
consistent. He makes his points in a straightforward manner. The
two accounts are combined here.

On the institution and nature of the sacrament: the Lord's Supper
is "a holy sacramental sign, instituted of the Lord Himself in bread
and wine, and left to His disciples in remembrance of Him" (CDC,
515). "It was also taught and administered as such by the apostles
among the brethren, according to the commandment of the Lord,
in which in the first place the Lord's death is proclaimed." "And it
also serves as a remembrance of how He offered His holy flesh and
shed His precious blood for the remission of our sins" (CDC, 515).
But the bread and wine are not the actual body and blood of Christ:
the sacrament is rather the memorial and sign of Christ's real life
sacrifice for our sins (FCD, 143–44).

As to the function of the sacrament, "it is an emblem of Christian
love, of unity, and of peace in the church of Christ" (CDC, 515). As
bread of many grains of wheat, we, though many, make up one body
in Christ. A meal of harmony and unity of all those in one Spirit of
Christ and one true faith. The action of the eucharist, then, is "not
only earnestly to show forth and remember His death, but also to

---

38. Menno summarizes his arguments against infant baptism as follows: (1) it is a
human rite, not found in the New Testament. (2) It is a perversion of the ordinance
of Christ, for only those who believe can be baptized. (3) It becomes a false security
when one hopes for salvation on the basis of a merely external rite and thus a harmful
superstition. (4) Christ has promised the kingdom to small children without baptism
(Mt 19:14; Mk 10:14; Lk 18:2). (CDC, 513–14. But Menno had a theology of sin which
differentiated it into "original," "actual," "lesser human frailties," and "the unforgivable
sin against the Holy Spirit." RFA, 563–66.

remember all the glorious fruits of divine love manifested toward us in Christ" (FCD, 144).

Regarding the purpose and use of the Supper, Menno says that "we have to observe that by the Lord's Supper Christian unity, love, and peace are signified and enjoined, after which all true Christians should seek and strive" (FCD, 145). That is, the love and unity of the Christian community are actualized in the celebration itself. The celebration involves an ethical mandate toward unity for all who partake in the one bread (FCD, 145). The ground of this mandate lies in an intimate union as a result of communion with Christ.

Who may participate in this sacrament? Menno holds that "none can rightly partake of this Supper except he be a disciple of Christ, flesh of His flesh, and bone of His bone..." (CDC, 515). "If you would be a proper guest at the Lord's table and would rightly partake of His bread and wine, then you must also be His true disciple, that is, you must be an upright, pious, and godly Christian" (CDC, 515). "Yea, as long as they err in doctrine and faith, and are in their lives carnal and blameworthy, they are by no means to be permitted with the pious to partake of the communion of the Holy Supper" (FCD, 150). Menno gets more meaning out of "do this in memory of me" than a literal interpretation of the elements actually being the body and blood of Christ. Christ ordained the Supper so that Christians could gather and commemorate their redemption in the sacrifice of Christ for the forgiveness of our sins. This existential character of participation in the sacrament also goes to real presence: Menno cites the New Testament text where Christ says that I am there where two or three are gathered in my name. This underlies the existential quality of the faith and love and regenerated life that is presupposed in the celebration of the sacrament (FCD, 146–48). The purpose of the Lord's Supper is communion of the pious and regenerated with Christ in union, peace, and unfeigned brotherly love constituting an existentially holy community (FCD, 142).[39]

---

39. Menno had strong feelings against the Roman Church's practice of the mass, and, considering it a work, he subjected it to the same critique as Luther. He also rejected transubstantiation and generally the objectification of the sacraments. It is possible to read in him a reaction formation against the objective kind of ritual ministry that he exercised for twelve years as a Catholic priest.

The Christian life, ethics, the ban. The high ideals of the Christian spirituality and life displayed in Menno's eucharistic theology, and which can be understood in the classical terms of the imitation of Christ, find a social reinforcement in the ban, or excommunication. From the outside, the ban appears as one of the identifying marks of this church; from the inside, Menno could not conceive of a true church without it. He considered this discipline three times in specific texts dedicated to it.[40] The first essay especially presents its theological logic in a straightforward way.

The concept of the ban rests on the premise that the community should be a morally upright body; it should display the fruits of regeneration. Menno begins his explanation of the ban with a characterization of the community in idealistic terms. The community of the regenerated is a community of love: "their works are nothing but brotherly love, one heart, one soul, one spirit; yes, one undivided body, fruitful, serving, and fellowshiping in Christ Jesus which is symbolized by the outward cup and the outward meal" (ACD, 411). If a morally upright community defines its premise, the principle governing the ban's logic says that the community helps the individual in his or her Christian life. The members of the community are "diligently to observe each other unto salvation, in all becoming ways teaching, instructing, admonishing, reproving, warning, and consoling each other as occasion requires . . . " (ACD, 411). The next point follows: if someone errs, one does not ignore him or her any more than one would ignore the person by the side of the road to Jericho. Rather one helps, out of love, by correcting the person. "Exhort him, rather, and seek by prayer, by words, and by deeds, to convert him from the error of his way, to save his soul, and to cover the multitude of his transgressions" (ACD, 412).

The crunch comes in declaring an unrepentant sinful person as outside the community and the avoidance of those who are separated or break off from the community. Following Paul's teaching, Menno says that one should have nothing to do with, one should

---

40. Menno Simons, "A Kind of Admonition on Church Discipline" (1541), *Writings*, 407–18 (This work will be cited hereafter as ACD); "A Clear Account of Excommunication" (1550), *Writings*, 455–85; "Instruction on Excommunication" (1558), *Writings*, 959–98.

avoid, those who were once part of the community but who have broken off from it, who "separate themselves from the body and fellowship of Christ, no matter whether it be father or mother, sister or brother, man or wife, son or daughter, no matter who he be, for God's Word applies to all alike and there is no respect of persons with God. We say, avoid him if he rejects the admonition of his brethren, done in sighing, tears, and a spirit of compassion and of great love..." (ACD, 412). In Menno's mind excommunication is ultimately self-excommunication: "no one is excommunicated or expelled by us from the communion of the brethren but those who have already separated and expelled themselves from Christ's communion either by false doctrine or by improper conduct" (ACD, 413). Correction is to be done gently and in love, so that the excommunication operates through shame when other gentler acts have failed. But when it comes to serious crimes such as apostasy, Menno insists that "you must shun the apostate in accordance with the Word of God, [and] take heed that while you shun them as diseased, foul, and unprofitable members unfit for the body of Christ, you yourselves may be found to be sound, fit, and profitable members in Christ Jesus" (ACD, 415). "Shunning" means "breaking of all social fellowship with impenitent and expelled persons."[41]

The ultimate purpose in all this is, as we saw with Calvin, the good of the community and of the persons involved. "There is nothing better to do with such than to cut them off with the knife of the divine Word, lest the others be corrupted and the ugly scurvy be transmitted to other sheep" (ACD, 414). Ideally, however, the next step should be welcoming people back. "But if he affectionately receives the admonition of his faithful brethren, confesses his fall, is truly sorry, promises to do better, and brings forth fruits worthy of repentance, then no matter how he has transgressed, receive him as a returning, beloved brother or sister" (ACD, 412).[42] The goal of

---

41. J. C. Wenger, *Writings*, 415, n. 4 It was the shunning of spouses and family members that became a bone of contention in the 1550s.

42. Some accused the Mennonites of a Pelagian perfectionism which Menno rebuts: they lie about his community who charge that "we expect to be saved by our merits and works; and that we boast to be without sin" (CDC, 507). He states clearly his doctrine of grace, his belief in justification by grace through faith: "we do not seek our salvation in works, words, or sacraments" (CDC, 504). Nor do "we boast of being perfect and

the process, then, is forgiveness, reconciliation, and reinsertion into the community. And the whole institution serves not only in actual cases but as a framework of spiritual authority generally encouraging righteous behavior.

Relation of the church to the world. Finally, how does the church relate to its environment, the world of society and its civil rulers? The very nature of this church as an organization in some measure places it over against the world. This can be seen in the rhetoric of the Christian life vis-à-vis the world, in the persecution the church suffers from the world, and in the church's expectations of civil rulers.

Boundary between church and world. Menno alludes to the strong boundary between the expectations of the Christian in contrast to life in the world in the language of the freedom of the Christian. "True enough, all things are pure to the pure, that is, to those who are not contrary to the Spirit and Word of God." Relative to those who are pure: "Since they themselves are pure, they will also use all lawful pure things purely: namely, in the fear of God, of necessity, with thanksgiving and moderation, to the praise of the Lord and to the service of their fellow men; to which end these things are created by God and given to the use of men. But all things forbidden by God, such as hypocrisy, getting mixed up with unfruitful works, conforming to the world, living in abundance, splendor, and idolatry; these are impure to the pure, that is, to the believing, obedient children of God. And they may never, according to God's will, be used by the pure, for the Spirit of God and the Word forbid it to them" (FCD, 183). Even this moderate statement of the Christian life and attitude toward the world cannot avoid conveying an attitude of distrust of the ordinary workings of society. The self-definition of the community or church over against the world could be more or less pronounced in different situations.

Persecution. But the Anabaptist church was persecuted, by Catholics and Protestants alike, for not conforming to the territorial pattern, and this reinforced a self-conception of the church against the world because the world hated the church. On the one hand,

---

without sins" (CDC, 506). Also, "we do not believe nor teach that we are to be saved by our merits and works. . . . We are to be saved solely by grace through Christ Jesus, as has been said before." CDC, 506

some churches had to assemble clandestinely or at night for fear of persecution.[43] On the other hand, those in the established churches encouraged them to come out in the open. But the call for openness promised only more persecution. While the church confidently debated issues publicly when occasion arose, pragmatically it had to avoid calling attention to itself (RFA, 572–76).

Role of civil rulers vis-à-vis the church. Menno's conception of the role of civil rulers relative to the church was rudimentary, clear, and consistent. "We publicly and unequivocally confess that the office of a magistrate is ordained of God.... And moreover, in the meantime, we have obeyed them when not contrary to the Word of God. We intend to do so all our lives. For we are not so stupid as not to know what the Lord's Word commands in this respect. Taxes and tolls we pay as Christ has taught and Himself practiced. We pray for the imperial majesty, kings, lords, princes, and all in authority. We honor and obey them" (RFA, 549). But, like Tertullian, Menno insisted that magistrates rule under the authority and judgment of God, and are to be obeyed only insofar as their commands or laws are not contrary to the Word of God (RFA, 551).

Menno also stressed the duty of magistrates to ensure social law and order: "you are called of God and ordained to your offices to punish the transgressors and protect the good; to judge rightly between a man and his fellows; to do justice . . . " (RFA, 551). It is God's law and that of scripture and the duty of magistrates and rulers that "without any respect of persons you judge between a man and his neighbor, protect the wronged from him who does him wrong."[44] In this situation these words translate into stopping the unjust persecution of his church. In fact, the magistrates are punishing the innocent and protecting the evil (RFA, 551–52). At one point, out of frustration, Menno asked that civil rulers make the judgment that his church was authentic and orthodox in the light of the scriptures.[45] Beyond that, however, the insistence on the part of the Anabaptist

---

43. Menno Simons, "Reply to False Accusations" (1552), *Writings*, 566–67. Cited hereafter as RFA.

44. Menno Simons, "A Pathetic Supplication to All Magistrates" (1552), *Writings*, 526. Cited as SAM.

45. "Next we request that your Noble Highnesses would examine in the light of God's Word that never leads astray, the living example of Christ, and the blameless

church that civil rulers perform their duty of preventing crime and ensuring public order and safety actually became a force that encouraged religious toleration and ultimately separation of church and state.[46]

BAPTIST ECCLESIOLOGY

We now focus attention on the formation of a church that bears a family resemblance to the Mennonites. The Baptist Church emerged out of the English Puritanism described in the last chapter in the context of the Church of England.[47] Some Puritans despaired of any further reform of the Church of England and sought separation from it. Some Separatism could be found in England in the course of the sixteenth century, predominately in London; and the movement of Robert Browne, who formed a theology of covenant and emigrated

---

piety of all the saints, as to what a genuine Christian looks like." SAM, 527; also SAM, 530 and FCD, 192.

46. This appears implicitly in the elementary character of the basic request: personal injury for religious convictions, especially true religious beliefs and practices, is a crime. See, for example, FCD, 117–20, 191–93. Kreider sums up the early Anabaptist views on civil government in ten principles. (1) The primacy of God's authority to the state's; (2) civil government ordained to protect the good and punish the evil; (3) uneven testimony on whether civil government was essential for all Christians; (4) agreement that Christians owe obedience to the state when not in conflict with Christian responsibilities; (5) division on whether a Christian could hold public office; (6) universal opposition to state sponsored or established churches; (7) dedication to nonresistance and refusal to bear arms; (8) refusal to swear civil oaths; (9) refusal to bring civil suits; (10) resistance to many civic policies and rituals. Kreider, "Anabaptists and the State," 189–93.

47. The following works have been helpful in the interpretation of the development and structure of the ecclesiology of John Smyth: Stephen Brachlow, "Life Together in Exile: The Social Bond of Separatist Ecclesiology," in *Pilgrim Pathways: Essays in Baptist History in Honour of B. R. White,* ed. William H. Brackney et al. (Macon, Ga.: Mercer University Press, 1999), 111–25; William H. Brackney, *The Baptists* (New York: Greenwood Press, 1988); James Robert Coggins, *John Smyth's Congregation: English Separatism, Mennonite Influence, and the Elect Nation* (Waterloo, Ont. / Scottdale, Pa.: Herald Press, 1991); Paul S. Fiddes, " 'Walking Together': The Place of Covenant Theology in Baptist Life Yesterday and Today," *Pilgrim Pathways,* 47–74; Keith L. Sprunger, *Dutch Puritanism: A History of English and Scottish Churches of the Netherlands in the Sixteenth and Seventeenth Centuries* (Leiden: E. J. Brill, 1982); Robert G. Torbet, *A History of the Baptists* (Philadelphia: The Judson Press, 1950); Michael R. Watts, *The Dissenters* (Oxford: Clarendon Press, 1978); B. R. White, *The English Separatist Tradition* (Oxford: Oxford University Press, 1971).

to Holland for a period, provided an example. But Separation became a movement in the early seventeenth century, and, more than any other single person, John Smyth provides the link from Puritan Separatism to the English Baptists.

The pressure for Separation increased dramatically in 1604, the year after James VI of Scotland became James I of England. Though nurtured in a Calvinist and Presbyterian milieu, he shocked English Puritans with a preference for the status quo of English episcopacy at the Hampton Court conference in January 1604. This was followed the same year by the king's confirmation of a set of canons for the regulation of the church that made public advocacy of Puritanism a crime. Smyth's and others' movement toward Separatism followed in the wake of this new set of circumstances. His active ministry as a Separatist leader lasted but a brief and turbulent period of time, and his views on the church constantly shifted. But Smyth's changes were "successive steps in one direction,"[48] toward a Baptist, congregational church polity that was radically simple and pure in form.

The strategy of this section consists in two stages of exposition: the first recreates the context of this ecclesiology through the history of the development of Smyth's career in church leadership and writing; this developmental sketch will set up a more analytical account in the next section which presents a holistic appreciation of the distinctive character of his ecclesiology.

John Smyth

John Smyth's brief career as a reformer and church leader was busy; he was a man in motion. These few pages indicate the direction his ministry and leadership took, as well as what may be considered stages in his developing ecclesiology.

Christ's College, Cambridge (1586–98).[49] Little if anything is known of Smyth before he arrived at Christ's College, Cambridge in 1586, and White guesses that he may have been born around 1570. During the course of his early studies Francis Johnson served

---

48. White, *Separatist Tradition,* 116.
49. W. T. Whitley provides a biography of Smyth in *The Works of John Smyth,* 2 vols., ed. W. T. Whitley (Cambridge: The University Press, 1915), xvii–cxxii. I refer to this volume as *Works* and to Whitley's biography as JS.

as his tutor. Johnson later separated from the Church of England and eventually led a Separatist church in Amsterdam; at Cambridge Smyth imbibed Johnson's Puritan sympathies.[50] He became a Bachelor of Arts in 1590 and continued studies, including the study of medicine, toward a Master of Arts. He was ordained by William Wickham, bishop of Lincoln, in 1594 upon his appointment as a Fellow of Christ's College, a position which he held from 1594 to 1598. Calvin's influence prevailed at Christ's College, and Smyth left there with a Puritan view of things.

Transition period (1598–1606). It is known that in 1598 Smyth was married, and Whitley thinks it possible that he took a position as a tutor before the year 1600 when he was appointed Lecturer to the Corporation of the City of Lincoln, "entrusted with the tasks of acting as chaplain to the mayor and preaching twice a week."[51] In the course of the two years in which he held this office he made some enemies and was forced out of the position in 1602 because of problems with his preaching. In 1603 he lost his licence to preach, but he also published some of his sermons in an effort to vindicate himself.

With the death of Elizabeth I in 1603 and the accession of James I, and especially in the light of the ecclesiastical canons of 1604, those with Puritan sensibilities had to reassess their position. Smyth moved to Gainsborough, a town within the Diocese of Lincoln, in 1603 and during this period practiced medicine, but this did not keep him from matters theological and ecclesiastical. In 1605 he published a work, also the fruit of his preaching, entitled *A patterne of true prayer:* it commented on the Lord's Prayer and also contained what might be called the first stage and point of departure of his ecclesiology.[52] His commentary on the petition "Thy Kingdom Come" proposes a definition of the church as the rule of God through Christ in the hearts of human beings: Christ is its head; it is subject to laws; its offices are the four proposed by Calvin with the addition of widows. Finally he accords to the magistrates the role of establishing

---

50. Watts, *Dissenters*, 41.
51. Watts, *Dissenters*, 41; White, *Separatist Tradition*, 117.
52. Smyth, *Works*, 67–247.

the church by law and protecting it.[53] In 1605, then, Smyth was still within the Church of England.

Gainsborough to Amsterdam (1606–8). In March of 1606 Smyth answered a charge that he had preached despite the bishop's prohibition. His defense indicates he was not yet a Separatist. Sometime between then and, at the latest, the autumn of 1607, when he describes himself as Pastor of the church at Gainsborough, Smyth made the move.[54] He entered fully into a discussion among likeminded ministers and laity of the diocese of Lincoln regarding separation. He became convinced that the situation was such that one had to choose to conform or to separate. In a letter written at this time Smyth proposes an ecclesiology that indicates a radical shift from 1605. Whitely summarizes it in four propositions: "Churches ought to consist of saints only. Each church ought to elect, approve, and ordain its own ministers. Worship should be spiritual and not limited by prescribed forms. Each church should be governed by a college of pastors."[55] This second stage of Smyth's ecclesiology provides a new basis or substratum that will remain constant amid the further changes.

In the course of 1606–7, then, a covenanted community was formed, and Smyth, having "renounced his ordination by Bishop Wickham, was chosen and ordained by the church at Gainsborough."[56] The church's membership transcended the town and drew from the surrounding region and met as well in the town of Scrooby. From this time onward, then, until the end of his life, Smyth will be the leader of this church. But his first task consisted in organizing it, and toward this end he produced and published in 1607

---

53. *Works*, 154–67. "Wherefore the Magistrates should cause all men to worship the true God, or else punish them with imprisonment, confiscation of goods, or death as the qualitie of the cause requireth." Ibid., 166.

54. White understands the transition as mediated by a period of intense reflection, the influence of Francis Johnson, and a meeting at which several people leaning toward Separation were present. *Separatist Tradition*, 120–24. Coggins, *Smyth's Congregation*, 32–41, describes the make-up of the initial congregation in detail.

55. Whitley, JS, lx. The letter is found in *Works*, 557–62.

56. Whitney, JS, *Works*, lxiv. It is not clear whether this one church had two leaders, Smyth and John Robinson, an associate of Smyth, also a former Fellow of Christ's Church, who would emigrate with Smith to Holland and settle with a community in Leiden, part of which formed the Mayflower expedition in 1620, or whether the two churches were already distinct in England. Watts, *Dissenters*, 42–43.

Principles and Inferences concerning The Visible Church.[57] Smyth elaborates this third stage in his ecclesiological thinking in a fairly ample church manual, as elaborate as Calvin's "Ecclesiastical Ordinances," but without the negotiations with civil magistracy. Also, he moves slightly away from Calvin's organization of ministry. This free and autonomous congregational church and the one in Scrooby "were organized as replicas of Johnson's congregation in Amsterdam."[58] Officers in the church were of two sorts corresponding to spiritual or temporal matters: bishops (also called elders) and deacons. The bishops-elders subdivided according to three distinct tasks: the pastor, the teacher, and the governor. The deacons, who deal with external matters and the works of mercy could be men, "or weomen deacons, or widowes." He also had room for prophets who were wisdom figures (PI, 258–62).

By 1607 it was also becoming clear that this Separatist Church would not have a peaceful future in England, and Smyth began making plans for the church to emigrate as a church. The most viable place for this seemed to be Amsterdam in the Netherlands, which offered a sizeable English population, religious tolerance, and even good relations within Calvinist lines of thinking. Also, Smyth's former tutor at Cambridge, Francis Johnson, led an English Separatist church that had been there since the 1590s. Thus, in 1608 Smyth's Separatist Church moved to Amsterdam.

Ministry in Amsterdam (1608–12). Smyth had four years of ministry for his church in Amsterdam, years which were also intellectually full.[59] Before the year he arrived was out, he had written another work further defining his ecclesiology by differentiating it from the Separatist Church already there and led by Francis Johnson.[60] Since he explicitly conceived this to be an adjustment of his

---

57. *Works*, 249–68. Cited hereafter as PI.

58. White, *Separatist Tradition*, 124.

59. Coggins gives a full account of these years with analyses of the relationships between the Separatist congregations and the development of Smyth's positions. Coggins, *Smyth's Congregation*, 43–114.

60. John Smyth, *The Differences of the Churches of the Separation, Works*, 269–320. The lengthy subtitle describes its contents: "A Description of the Leitourgie and Ministerie of the visible Church. Annexed: As a Correction and Supplement to a Litle Treatise lately Published, Bearing Title: Principles and Inferences, concerning the Visible Church." This work is cited as DCS.

prior ecclesiology, it may not represent a new stage of his thinking, but it contained three distinct developments.

First, Smyth expanded his idea of spiritual worship. This may be interpreted in contrast to the idea of public worship eloquently laid out by Hooker where the individual is often supported and buoyed up by common prayer and sacrament. For Smyth spiritual worship had its fountain in the Holy Spirit at work within the human spirit, and care had to be taken lest external helps quench the inner spirit (DCS, 276–77). But reading tends to function as an external prop and supplant the inner dynamism of spiritual worship, thus quenching the Spirit. Hence Smyth disallowed reading of scripture, not generally at liturgy, but as part of spontaneous prayer or worship. Second, he clarified and insisted that the "Presbytery is uniform consisting of Officers of one sort" with different names according to different tasks but not separate offices (DCS, 307). Third, he makes it clear that as the church calls the minister, the church can recall ministers, thus placing authority squarely in the congregation as a whole.[61]

In 1609, however, Smyth and his church took a step that warrants referring to a fourth stage in his developing ecclesiology. In the formation of his Separatist Church, Smyth had renounced his former ordination and had accepted ordination by his new covenantal community; now he doubted the validity of baptism received in the Church of England. He thus baptized himself anew, something he later regretted, and then baptized the members of his congregation. At the same time he rejected infant baptism. As the Anabaptists before him, he took the necessity of the actual faith of the one being baptized as an absolute prerequisite. This step more than any other broke his connection with the Puritans and established a doctrinal bond with the Anabaptists.

Also in 1609 and extending into 1610 Smyth entered into a conversation with the Waterlander Church which traced its ancestry to the Mennonites and shared his belief in believer's baptism. In the course of it he presented to them a series of twenty articles which

---

61. "The presbytery hath no powre, but what the church hath & giveth unto it: which the church uppon just cause can take away" (DCS, 315). Smyth also made it clear that his community would not accept outside help for its needy members: the community should assume full responsibility for its own.

functioned as a confession of faith.[62] But, in the end, these negotiations for a union failed. Moreover, the openness of Smyth to the Mennonite church caused a split within his own; those breaking away from Smyth saw in the Mennonites' laying hands on ordinands by ministers a kind of succession that would risk clericalism and the absolute authority of the congregation itself.

The fifth and final stage of Smyth's ecclesiology was formulated in 1611 in a work of one hundred propositions or theses entitled "Propositions and conclusions, concerning true Christian religion, conteyning a confesion of faith of certaine English people, livinge at Amsterdam."[63] It included a clear statement about the administration of baptism to believers and "not uppon innocent Infants" and the principle of religious freedom or the separation of church and state (PC, 745 and 748). Smyth was working on retractions and confirmations when he died in August of 1612.[64]

Coggins finds Smyth's lasting influence in his "congregational ideal." This underlay the original covenanted community, and was carried forward in the Baptist and Congregational traditions. "The congregational ideal, partly based on the Puritan understanding of the Bible and partly derived from the unique characteristics of the membership of the congregation, proved to be a powerful and enduring concept."[65]

Smyth's Ecclesiology

Although Smyth's ecclesiology is not presented here in systematic detail, this outline will indicate his central and distinctive positions within the framework used in the exposition of Menno's conception

---

62. *Works*, 682–84. Smyth shared not only believer's baptism with the Mennonites, but a rejection of the Augustinian doctrine of original sin and of Calvin's view of predestination. Watts attributes this break with Calvin to the influence of the Mennonites. Watts, *Dissenters*, 46.

63. *Works*, 733–50. I will cite this work hereafter as PC.

64. *Works*, 751–60. The connection between Smyth and the English Baptist tradition was completed by Thomas Helwys, a colleague of Smyth since the formation of the church in Gainsborough, who balked at the initiative of Smyth toward the Mennonites and, along with others, broke with him. In the winter of 1611–12 Helwys led his church back to England, establishing the first Baptist Church there, and "by 1626 there were some 150 General Baptists in England, gathered in churches in London, Coventry, Lincoln, Salisbury, and Tiverton." Watts, *Dissenters*, 50.

65. Coggins, *Smyth's Congregation*, 159.

of the church. This will highlight their similarities and the special features generated through the English tradition.

Definition of the church and its members. White sets a context for understanding Smyth's ecclesiology thus: "Just as the doctrine of the church dominated Smyth's theological thinking when he became a Separatist, so there can be no doubt that his understanding of the divine covenant dominated his concept of the church."[66] In this framework, then, Smyth defines the church as the company of the elect; the invisible communion with Christ is by Spirit and faith, and the visible church is a visible communion of saints (PI, 251). The church consists of "two, three, or moe Saincts joyned together by covenant with God & themselves, freely to use al the holy things of God, according to the word, for their mutual edification, & Gods glory" (PI, 252).

When Smyth speaks of the true church he intends the congregation. Three elements determine its authenticity: true matter, form, and properties. (1) True matter consists in the members who are the saints; they are "men separate from all knowne syn" and practicing the known will of God (PI, 253). (2) The true form, inwardly, consists in the presence of the Spirit, faith, and love. Outwardly, true form is found in the covenant: "a vowe, promise, oath, or covenant betwixt God and the Saints." The covenant defines the relationship with God and among the members (PI, 253–54). (3) The properties of the church are participation in the benefits of Christ's salvation through the means of salvation: word, sacraments, prayers, and ordinances from Christ. The properties also include participation in the powers of Christ: to receive new members, to preserve them within the community, and to cast out or excommunicate.[67] Smyth explicitly refers to this circumscription of the essential elements of the church as the restitution or reconstituting of the true, primitive, and apostolic church.

---

66. White, *Separatist Tradition*, 125.
67. PI, 254–55. "1. The true matter which are sayntes only. 2. The true forme which is the uniting of them together in the covenant. 3. The true propertie which is communion in all the holy things, & the powre of the L. Jesus Christ, for the maintayning of that communion" (DCS, 270). The church of Christ has the following powers given it by Christ: to announce the word, to administer the sacraments, to constitute and dismiss its ministers, and to excommunicate. FBC, 683.

It would be wrong to pass over the idea of "covenant" without reflecting on its theological depth. Smyth began his church in Gainsborough leading its members "into a covenant — a pledge between themselves and God 'to walk in all his ways, made known or to be made known unto them . . . whatever it might cost them.' "[68] Seen from below, covenant reflects the voluntary character of the church: Like the Anabaptist church, it "is a 'gathered' church, an association freely accepted and freely joined with; no compulsion or external influence is admitted to interfere with the freedom of the baptismal pledge."[69] But the act of covenanting and remaining in it is linked with the presence and activity of the Holy Spirit. Members of the church believed that covenanting "had formed them into an entirely unique, divinely blessed community by virtue of Christ's spiritual presence in their midst."[70] The concept of "covenant," therefore, cannot be reduced to a social idea of voluntary association, but has deep theological roots. Fiddes finds three distinct dimensions in Smyth's use of covenant. It refers, first, to the "covenant of grace" which God has made with human beings and angels for their salvation. It also refers to the agreement that God enters into with God's church or churches; a member of a church thus exists within this covenant.[71] Seen from above or theologically, then, a covenant theology of the church refers to God's eternal and cosmic salvific will and action into which the single covenanted community is drawn up and given its identity.

Organization of the church. Like Menno, Smyth accorded scripture an absolute authority, and he customarily cites scripture at every step along the way of an argument or statement of belief. Besides scripture's authority, two aspects of Smyth's understanding of church organization deserve to be highlighted, the offices of ministry relative to the whole congregation and his legitimation of offices in contrast

---

68. Brackney, *Baptists*, 32.
69. Friedman, *Theology of Anabaptism*, 132.
70. Brachlow, "Life Together in Exile," 116. According to Henry Ainsworth, the Separatist leader, those forming the church by a bond of covenant "are so built and coupled together by faith that they grow into a holy temple in the Lord, to be the habitation of God by the Spirit." Henry Ainsworth, *The Communion of Saints* (Amsterdam: 1607), 318–19, cited by Brachlow, 116.
71. Fiddes, " 'Walking Together,' " 52–55.

to the idea of succession. Both of these positions correlate with the nature of a "separating" church and sharply define the autonomy and authority of a congregational polity.

The two kinds of ministry. There are two offices in the church, bishops, or elders, and deacons, performing spiritual and temporal ministries respectively. Spiritual ministry in the church, "the preaching of the word, and ministerie of the sacraments, representeth the ministerie of Christ in the spirit" (PC, 746). Bishops or elders subdivide according to roles and types as pastors, teachers, and governors. Each should have the charism or excel in the quality needed for the specific task. Only then does ministry have its third sense, "the agreement undertaken and signed by church members when a particular local church was founded, and subsequently by new members upon their entering it."[72] The way of receiving ministers to office is by election, approbation, and ordination (PI, 256). This is performed by the whole church: "Ordination and so imposition of hands apperteyneth to the whole church as doth election and approbation" (PI, 258).

Most importantly Smyth emphasized the autonomy and authority of the congregation as a whole as the source of whatever authority the ministers might enjoy: this was always derivative. "The presbytery hath no powre, but what the church hath & giveth unto it: which the church uppon just cause can take away" (DCS, 315). The church as a whole has the power of elections which the presbytery does not. In the absence of elders, the church as congregation still has the power to admonish, convince, excommunicate, absolve, to pray, to preach, to sing psalms, to administer the sacraments.[73]

Smyth had a sense for a shared responsibility in the whole community. He speaks of the tasks or responsibilities of the ministers of the community with the language of care. The care of elders is

---

72. PI, 258–59; PC, 746. Relative to Francis Johnson's church, Smyth insisted "that there were not three types of elders, a pastor, a teacher, a ruling elder, but one who combined all these functions in one office." White, *Separatist Tradition,* 127; see DCS, 307–15.

73. DCS, 315. "An Eldership hath no powre Seperated from the Church: but as all powre floweth from the head to the body, & then to the hands through the body, which is first in the body before it come to the hands: So al powre Ecclesiastical or ministeriall is derived from Christ to the Church, & then through the Church to the Elders, which is first in the Church before it come to the Elders." Smyth, *Parallels, Censures, Observations* (*Works,* 437). Cited hereafter as PCO.

to direct and coordinate the public actions of the church; the care of prophets is consultation and wisdom; the care of pastors and teachers is to apply the word; the "cheef care of every mēber must be to watch over his brother in bearing one anothers burden, admonishing the unruly, comforting the feeble myned, admonishing the excommunicate, restoring them that are fallen" (PI, 261).

On succession and apostolicity. Smyth realized that the church he led had separated from a church built on succession, and he constructed an apostolic legitimation of the pristine church order that transcended it. He says directly that "there is no succession in the outward church, but that all the succession is from heaven..." (PC, 747). Outward forms do not establish the substance.[74] The gathering in faith and the covenant constitute the substance. "Unto whome the covenant & Christ is given, unto them al the promises are given, for al the promises are conteyned in the covenant, & in Christ.... But the covenant & Christ & al the promises, are given to the body of the church even to two or three faithful ones" (PCO, 389). He declares the point most clearly as follows: "We say the Church or two or three faithful people Seperated from the world & joyned together in a true covenant, have both Christ, the covenant, & promises, & the ministerial powre of Christ given to them, & that they are the body that receave from Christs hand out of heaven, or rather from Christ their head this ministerial powre."[75]

These two factors in the organizational structure of the church, namely, the orders of ministry and the revised view of apostolicity, draw together the specific dimensions of its congregational character and polity. All the major themes converge: covenant, vertical and direct legitimation by God in Christ, the small, free, gathered

---

74. But still the church should exist in order, and that order should "draw as neare the first institution as may be, in all things. Therefore it is not lawfull for every brother to administer the word and sacraments." PC, 747.

75. PCO, 403. At the end of his life, Smyth summed up his views on succession: "I deny all succession except in the truth: and I hold we are not to violate the order of the primitive church, except Necessitie urge a dispensation." Does this lead to splintering into many churches? It should not, for this would break "the bonde of love and Brotherhood in churches, but in these outward matters I dare not anie more contend with anie man but desire that we may follow the truth of Repentance, faith and regeneration, and lay aside dissention...." Smyth, *The Last Booke of John Smyth Called the Retractation of His Errours, and the Confirmation of the Truth.* (*Works*, 758).

community, the autonomy of the congregation, the powers of the congregation as a whole, the actuality or event quality of its existence, the intentional bonding of members in love. The very logic of a Separatist community, that is, the separating from the uniformity of the Church of England, enabled these elements of the church's existence to become accentuated.[76]

Mission of the church. Smyth does not frequently speak of the mission of the church in the teleological terms of organizational theory as, for example, in response to the question of its purpose in history. Such answers are found implicitly in the other areas of ecclesiology. For example, we have seen that the church exists for God's glory. "The visible church is Gods ordinance & a means to worship god in." "The true visible church is the narrow way that leadeth to life which few find" (PI, 252).

Activities of the church. What does Smyth's church do? This objective portrayal will not come close to representing the existential place of the church in the life of the small community it defined and that emigrated from England in order to find religious freedom. Consider, for example, the large role deacons would have in coordinating the adjustment of families to a new existence. But such formal activities as the assembly of the community, administration of the sacraments, and directives of the Christian life differentiated phases of its existence.

Assembly, preaching, and prayer. Smyth developed a theology of spiritual worship at some points in contrast to what he perceived to be going on in Francis Johnson's church. A significant principle urges that worship should be a purely spiritual response to God that is impelled by God in Word and Spirit and elicited from within. This stands in contrast to reliance on external helps that in some measure subtract from the purity of subjective response.[77] Thus in time of prayer, prophesying, and singing psalms, no books were to be used, not even scripture: "for whither we pray, prophesy or sing, it must be the word of scripture, not out of the book, but out of the hart."[78]

---

76. See White, *Separatist Tradition,* 129.
77. This is developed at length in DCS, 274–306.
78. DCS, 303. On the inner work of the Spirit constituting the essence of spiritual worship see DCS, 301.

A letter of a married couple in Smyth's congregation to their cousin captures the basic dynamics of assembly for worship: "We begin with a prayer; after read some one or two chapters of the Bible, give the sense thereof, and confer upon the same: that done, we lay aside our books, and after solemn prayer made by the first speaker, he propoundeth some text out of Scripture, and prophesieth out of the same by the space of one hour or three quarters of an hour." This is repeated by a second, third, fourth, and perhaps fifth speaker in the same manner as time allows. "This morning exercise beginneth at eight of the clock and continueth unto twelve of the clock. The like course and exercise is observed in the afternoon from two of the clock unto five or six of the clock. Last of all, the execution of the government of the Church is handled."[79]

The sacraments. Smyth's sacramental theology construes sacraments as external signs or pointers to what transpires essentially in and through the subjectivity of the believer. He describes the sacraments as such as outward signs that "doe not confer, and convey grace and regeneration to the participants, or communicants: but as the word preached they serve only to support and stirr up the repentance, and faith of the communicants till Christ come . . . " (PC, 746).

Applying this to the external rite of baptism he writes: "For baptisme is not washing with water: but it is the baptisme of the Spirit, the confession of the mouth, & the washing with water: how then can any man without great folly wash with water which is the least & last of baptisme, one that is not baptized with the Spirit, & cannot confesse with the mouth: or how is it baptisme if one be so washed."[80]

In Smyth's view "the outward baptisme of water, is to be administered onely uppon such penitent and faithfull persons . . . and not uppon innocent Infants, or wicked persons" (PC, 745). In a covenantal view the church is voluntary and an infant cannot enter it. Smyth held that "infants are conceived and borne in innocencie without

---

79. Cited in White, *Separatist Tradition*, 126–27; also found in Whitley, JS, *Works*, lxx-lxxi.

80. Smyth, *The Character of the Beast or the False Constitution of the Church*, *Works*, 567.

sinne, and that so dyinge are undoubtedly saved, and that this is to be understood of all infants under heaven" (PC, 735).[81]

Relative to the eucharist, Smyth defined the Lord's Supper as follows: "The Lord's Supper is an external sign of the communion of Christ and the faithful with each other through faith and love" (FBC, 683). His eucharistic theology and practice are summed up in this concise statement: "in the outward supper which onely baptized persons must pertake, ther is presented and figured before the eyes, of the penitent and faithfull, that spirituall supper, which Christ maketh of his flesh and blood: which is crucified and shed for the remission of sinnes (as bread is broken and the wine powred forth) and which is eaten and drunken (as is the bread and wine bodily) onely by those which are flesh, of his flesh, and bone of his bone: in the communion of the same spirit" (PC, 745–46).

The Christian life. The true church consists in the regenerate, the saints; and the regenerate are not capable of sin and hatred of others. The visible church, therefore, is called to be the outward sign of the spiritual church "which consisteth of the spirits of just and perfect men onlie, that is of the regenerate" (PC, 744). To achieve this Smyth expects the whole community to take up the task of admonition and excommunication. He worked out a system for admonishing and excommunicating with a rationale for each step analogous to Calvin and Menno, including casting officers out of their office (PI, 261–66). Smyth also acknowledged the ban. In fairly strong language he says "that persons seperated from the communion of the church, are to be accounted as heathens and publicans and that they are so far to be shunned, as they may pollute" (PC, 747). At the same time efforts should be made to win them back. Censure and excommunication enabled the community to keep the covenant with God and helped keep a soothing order in the community.[82]

Relation of the church to the world. It is difficult to measure the degree of contrast between the church and the world of society and state in Smyth's ecclesiology because, on the one hand, it

---

81. "Nullum esse peccatum originis, verum omne peccatum esse actuale et voluntarium...ideoque infantes esse sine peccato." Smyth, "The First Baptist Confession," *Works,* 682. Referred to hereafter as FBC.

82. White, *Separatist Tradition,* 130.

was a Separatist Church fleeing a society with an established religion, and, on the other hand, it professed a commitment to religious freedom or tolerance. In some measure the church in Smyth's view was self-contained. There should be no marriage outside the church community (PC, 749). Judgment in conflicts should be solved within the church and not by appeal to law or magistrates (PC, 748). The church should take care of its own needy members and not appeal to outside help: "in contributing to the Church Treasurie there ought to bee both a seperation from them that are without & a sanctification of the whole action by Prayer & Thanksgiving."[83] A relatively strong boundary between church and world lies implicit in the insistence that the true church also be a pure church. True visible churches may be pure or corrupt: in a pure church no visible or openly known sin is allowed; a corrupt church is one in which "one or more open knowne syn is tolerated" (PI, 267). But Smyth recommends no hostility to government and civil service. The office of magistrate is ordained by God for the good of humankind for the maintenance of order and justice; magistrates may please God in their calling (PC, 748).

Role of civil rulers vis-à-vis the church. Smyth at one time held that princes and civil rulers could erect visible churches in their dominions and "command all their subjects to enter into them" (PI, 267). But the assumption was that these were true churches. He then adopted the view that private persons could also found churches which, as autonomous, shared equal power with other churches. Private persons who founded a true church of God in obedience to Christ as king, priest, and prophet had "a Charter given them of Christ . . ." (PI, 267). The autonomy of the covenantal congregation finds legitimation in Christ.

From there Smyth moved to a position where he strongly asserted the separation of church and state. He proposed "that the magistrate is not by vertue of his office to meddle with religion, or matters of conscience, to force and compell men to this or that form of religion, or doctrine: but to leave Christian religion free, to every mans

---

83. DCS, 273; also 316–20 for detailed account of the handling of community funds.

conscience, and to handle onely civil transgressions, injuries and wronges of men against man..." (PC, 748).

Finally, Smyth came to accept a broad and positive view of human history that allowed him to break with a narrow view of predestination. God wills the salvation of all. God set up salvation through Christ before the foundation of the world, and "as god created all men according to his image, so hath he redeemed all that fall by actuall sinne, to the same end: and that God in his redemption hath not swerved from his mercie, which he manifested in his creation" (PC, 736). This represents a sweeping view of the economy of the salvation of Christ, although it is difficult to measure its exact dimensions in terms of today's questions. But one can see in this vision a dialectic between God's universal and particular will. White reads it in terms of covenant as a tension between the universal or everlasting covenant of God's grace and the covenant of a particular church. "In fact, it seems that for him, in the covenant promise of the local congregation the eternal covenant of grace became contemporary and man's acceptance of it was actualized in history."[84] This gives each particular church a rationale of sharing in a cosmic story: each is part of the broad covenant of God with humankind in general history.

An attempt to formulate what the ecclesiologies of Menno and Smyth share in common may properly conclude this portion of the chapter. A set of six interrelated convictions set the foundations of these ecclesiologies: the church is (1) an existentially authentic community, (2) made so by Christ's spiritual presence in the activity of the Spirit, (3) ratified in an ongoing covenant, (4) effected in a small congregation, (5) manifested by common discipline, so that (6) the whole church is constituted by these discrete and autonomous communities. All the other characteristics of a church, such as authority, ministry, sacraments, discipleship, ethics and other activities are to be understood in the framework established by these six qualities which determine their distinctive sense and valence.

---

84. White, *Separatist Tradition*, 128.

TRIDENTINE ROMAN ECCLESIOLOGY

Attention now moves to the Roman Church. The sixteenth century occasioned considerable development in the Catholic Church, if not in its large institutional structure, surely in its self-understanding and many procedural substructures.[85] At the outset, it is important to note the shift in the referent of the term church from Smyth's congregation to the Roman Church: when he petitioned the Waterlander Church for union, Smyth's Baptist Church listed thirty-two adults; the Roman Church still spanned all of Europe in a single organization and bureaucracy, even though large swaths of territory and people had withdrawn. To gain some minimal purchase on the ecclesiology of the Roman Church at this critical juncture of its history we turn to the Catechism of the Council of Trent. But this requires a word about the council that defined the Roman Catholic Church as it entered the modern period.[86]

The Council of Trent

Several factors have to be taken into account in situating the ecclesiology of the catechism. For example, a distinction of formal

---

85. Chapter 6 of CCH I presents an analysis of the ecclesiology of the church in the late medieval period. The analysis of the ecclesiology of the Roman Church just after the Council of Trent presented here assumes considerable continuity with that church in parish life and ecclesial organization. This account takes up where the earlier story left off.

86. I have used the following works in the interpretation of the ecclesiology of the Catechism of the Council of Trent: Giuseppe Albrigo, "The Council of Trent," *Catholicism in Early Modern History: A Guide to Research,* ed. John W. O'Malley (St Louis: Center for Reformation Research, 1988), 211–26; Robert Bireley, *The Refashioning of Catholicism, 1450–1700: A Reassessment of the Counter Reformation* (Washington: Catholic University of America Press, 1999); Yves Congar, *L'Eglise de Saint Augustin à l'Epoque Moderne* (Paris: Editions du Cerf, 1970); R. Po-chia Hsia, *The World of Catholic Renewal 1540–1770* (Cambridge: University Press, 1998); Hubert Jedin et al., *Reformation and Counter Reformation, History of the Church,* V, ed. H. Jedin and J. Dolan (New York: Seabury Press, 1980); Keith P. Luria, "'Popular Catholicism' and the Catholic Reformation," *Early Modern Catholicism: Essays in Honour of John W. O'Malley, S.J.,* ed. Kathleen M. Comerford and Hilmar M. Pabel (Toronto: University of Toronto Press, 2001), 114–30; John C. Olin, *Catholic Reform: From Cardinal Ximenes to the Council of Trent, 1495–1563: An Essay with Illustrative Documents and a Brief Study of St. Ignatius Loyola* (New York: Fordham University Press, 1990); John W. O'Malley, *Trent and All That: Renaming Catholicism in the Early Modern Era* (Cambridge, Mass.: Harvard University Press, 2000); Norman Tanner, *The Councils of the Church: A Short History* (New York: Crossroad, 2001).

ecclesiology from the actual condition of the church allows one to recognize that, while the church changed considerably, its formal self-understanding remained relatively constant. The health and vitality of the church on the eve of the Reformation varied in different regions of Europe, and there were many signs of religious vitality. Also, because the reforming measures of the Council of Trent did not take effect automatically, but in fact took many decades, the ecclesiology formulated at the end of the council may be taken as a point of departure or of reference for changes that would occur in the future. Because of the many continuities within the Roman Catholic Church at the end of the council with the late medieval church, one can relate the ecclesiology of the catechism as closely with the church prior to the Reformation as with the ecclesiology which would evolve in the course of the seventeenth century. Many things had changed since the end of the fifteenth century: the strength of nations and their power over the church locally, social and economic conditions, the opening up of new worlds to the East and the West, a shift in the scientific picture of the world, diffusion and internalization of the ideas and values of the Renaissance, and the extensive Reformation movement itself.[87] The world in Europe was changing, and relatively speaking the church had been radically altered. But the ecclesiology of the Council of Trent as synopsized in the catechism was as much a consolidation of the pre-Reformation Church, defined now in contrast to the Reformers, as it was a Reformed Catholic ecclesiology.

The Council of Trent was convoked by Pope Paul III and finally convened on December 13, 1545, twenty-eight years after Luther touched off the indulgence controversy. The council continued for eighteen more years through three periods (1545–47, 1551–52, 1561–63), including a temporary transfer to Bologna. By the time the council got under way confessional division in Europe had solidified and probably could not have been reversed. A number of different political and religious motives were at work in the principal actors. For example, the pope primarily wanted to stem the tide of the reformers, define the Catholic position on the theological issues they raised, as well as reform the church internally. But he was also wary

---

87. Birely, *Refashioning*, 8–15.

of the possibility of conciliarist feeling among bishops. The emperor wanted to win back Germany and believed reform of church abuses would foster his agenda.[88] Early on the bishops at Trent decided to deal with doctrinal matters and church reform at the same time, alternating between the two agendas, so that the major sessions passed both doctrinal decrees and the legislation of reform.

The first period produced doctrinal documents that went to the heart of issues raised by the Reformers: on scripture, including a statement on revelation and tradition, on original sin, and especially the "Decree on Justification." The legislation on church reform of the first period was not far reaching. The second period addressed doctrines and theology surrounding the sacraments. At the thirteenth session, the decree on the eucharist addressed the question of the real presence of Christ in the eucharist and proposed that the term "transubstantiation" "most aptly" designated that mystery.[89] When the council was suspended in April 1552, its agenda was far from over: its "doctrinal decrees embraced only a part of the disputed teachings, the reform decrees eliminated some but in no sense the most crying abuses, and they had no binding force, because they had not yet been confirmed by the Pope."[90] The third period, however, saw better attendance than the two earlier periods. Doctrinally, it continued work on the eucharist. The final session dealt with purgatory, the veneration of saints, the use of relics, images, and indulgences, all issues of common piety which were at the source of the Reformation movement.[91] In the end, church reform decrees "provided norms for

---

88. Jedin, *Reformation and Counter Reformation*, 465.

89. Council of Trent, Session 13, "Decree on the Most Holy Sacrament of the Eucharist," c. 2, in Norman P. Tanner, ed., *Decrees of the Ecumenical Councils*, II (London: Sheed & Ward; Washington, D.C.: Georgetown University Press, 1990), 697.

90. Jedin, *Reformation and Counter Reformation*, 479. Between the second and third period of the council, Paul IV (1555–59) tried to accomplish reform by his own efforts. "Paul created and sharpened two weapons: the Index of Forbidden Books and the Inquisition." Ibid., 486.

91. Much of what the Reformers referred to as superstition, Roman Catholics accepted as the religion of the people, what today would be called popular religion, but without too sharp a distinction between an elite and the uneducated masses in the performance of these practices, although understanding of them might differ. Trent displayed a desire for more control over these devotions and a reduction of excesses, but not a rejection of them. They were quite positive: "Catholic religious practices mediated not only relations among people and the divine, but also relations among people.

the nominations of cardinals and bishops, prescribed diocesan synods each year and provincial synods every third year, and insisted
that every bishop annually conduct a visitation of his whole diocese.
These decrees are the center of Tridentine Reform."[92]

The council was followed by a period of implementation and interpretation. Alberigo points to two lines of implementation, the one at
the periphery through the dioceses, the other imposed from the center. The former, with its regular synods and visitations was resisted;
the other more or less succeeded. "The publication of the Tridentine
Profession of Faith, of the Missal, of the Breviary, and especially the
Catechism provided appropriate instruments for affirming the ideal
of a uniform implementation of the decrees of the Council. This
ideal was strengthened by the nuncios and 'apostolic visitors' sent
from Rome."[93] This resulted, finally, in an overall interpretation of
Trent as providing a kind of Catholic integralism. As Rome reserved
to itself the interpretation of the decrees, it simultaneously promoted
"the uniformity and passivity of modern Catholicism" which was
quite different from the mood and intentions of the bishops at Trent
who expressly tried to avoid deciding debates within the church.[94]

The Council of Trent was a massive event in the history of the
Roman Church and of Europe, and an assessment of it rests on perspective and assumptions.[95] But the following principles provide one

---

Catholicism furnished means by which the faithful grouped themselves together and
served each other's social as well as spiritual needs. Indeed, distinguishing between the
two is artificial." After Trent new religious organizations were encouraged around the
Blessed Sacrament, the Virgin Mary, the rosary, and they flourished. "Across Catholic
Europe, penitential, Blessed Sacrament, and rosary groups became the dominant forms
of associational religious life." Keith P. Luria, " 'Popular Catholicism,' " 121–22, 123.

92. Alberigo, "The Council of Trent," 217. Another major reform was the provision
for setting up the seminary system for the training of clergy.

93. Alberigo, "The Council of Trent," 221.

94. Ibid., 222.

95. For example, John W. O'Malley does not read Trent as the major turning point
some have made it to be: "The status quo before the council was not so dark, and the
status quo after not so bright — nor so homogeneous" as, for example, Jedin paints it
(O'Malley, *Trent and All That*, 71). Part of O'Malley's evidence lies in the continuous
vital life of the church on the ground, for example, in the confraternities or pious associations alluded to in the analysis of the church in the late medieval period. They
flourished in the sixteenth century so that, despite corruption in high places, the religious life of the faithful went on uninterrupted. Although from the perspective of

[handwritten: ④ Catholics at Trent tried to figure out who they were]

such perspective. Because Protestants did not attend, it was a Catholic event that defined Catholic identity over against the Reformers. "The council thus was confined in jurisdiction as well as in representation to the Catholic world, and it functioned not as an instrument of reconciliation or reunion but as a body defining and legislating for those who remained in the Catholic fold."[96] This means, second, that emphasis lay in negativity; the doctrinal canons brought out the differences between the Roman Church and the Protestants, not what they shared in common. These two points closely tie the teachings of the council to its particular historical situation. Third, "the Council adhered to the principle of not deciding differences of opinion within Catholic theology."[97] The solidity of the synthesis thus conceals the pluralism. Fourth, on the broadest level, Trent made a great contribution to defining, solidifying, and preserving Roman Catholic identity in this tumultuous century on both the doctrinal and practical level of church life. The council eliminated "the most crying abuses on the diocesan and parochial levels and in the Orders, effectively strengthened the authority of the bishops, and gave priority to the demands of pastoral care."[98] Fifth, it also left some major issues unaddressed on the level of practical and theoretical ecclesiology. The Roman Curia was not reformed; the doctrine of the papacy and the relationship between bishops and the pope went unaddressed; and the overall doctrine and theology of the church were not elaborated. But, finally, Trent realigned the ministry of the church in the areas of "the training of priests, the duty of preaching the Gospel, the jurisdiction of bishops, and the obligation of residence for bishops and pastors."[99]

Luther these groups were riddled with works righteousness, they represent continuity in the church.

96. Olin, *Catholic Reform*, 28.

97. Jedin, *Reformation and Counter Reformation*, 470.

98. Ibid., 496. "We take so many of the decrees for granted, forming as they did a background to Catholic theology for so long that we easily forget what a striking achievement they are. They are rooted in medieval theology, indeed, yet they form a remarkable clarification and systematization of that theology." Tanner, *Short History*, 86.

99. Olin, *Catholic Reform*, 30. The central issue of the four, however, regarded the bishop. His authority was clarified; he was held to residency in his diocese; he was given responsibility for preaching and ministerial care in his diocese. The reform was

The last session also provided for the reform of the missal, the breviary, and the drawing up of a catechism for parish priests. The work on the catechism, initiated in a prior session, was to be given over to the pope and by his judgment and authority completed and made public.[100]

Ecclesiology of the Catechism of the Council of Trent

The Catechism of the Council of Trent appeared in September of 1566. Intended to be translated into various vernacular languages, it explicitly addresses pastors on the assumption that its message will be related through the parishes to people at large. Although it is not a work of the Council of Trent itself, it is directly authorized by the pope and indirectly shares a measure of Tridentine authority through the documents of the council that inform the catechetical teaching. The work is structured in four parts: creed, sacraments, the Decalogue, and the Lord's Prayer. The catechism represents a remarkable *summa* of the teaching of the Roman Church and the council in an English edition of six hundred pages.[101] What follows represents the church by distilling its teaching on the church from the explication of the creed and sacraments in a framework paralleling the one used for Menno and Smyth.

Definition of the church and its members. The catechism does not provide one clean definition of the church but many of them, so that the term church remains analogous. Most pointedly "church"

---

programmatic: the bishop was to undertake concrete measures to ensure the spiritual health of the diocese (Olin, *Catholic Reform*, 31). Charles Borromeo carried the Tridentine program forward in the archdiocese of Milan for two decades following the council, but generally his lead was not followed. See Hsia, *Catholic Renewal*, 106–10.

100. Council of Trent, Session 25, Decree on General Reform, chap. 21, Tanner, *Decrees*, 797.

101. *Catechism of the Council of Trent for Parish Priests*, trans. J. A. McHugh and C. J. Callan (New York: Joseph F. Wagner, 1923). This was not the only catechism available at the time, and more were written after it. But it possessed a certain distinct authority and a major function. Cited hereafter in the text as CCT. My title for this part of the chapter, "Tridentine Roman Ecclesiology," has a reduced "nominalistic" meaning according to its narrow reference to the *Catechism of the Council of Trent*, with occasional references to the council itself. A critical, substantive retrieval of Tridentine Roman ecclesiology would correlate a critical appropriation of the council's decrees with a social-historical analysis of the life of the church from below. This cannot be done here.

refers to "the assemblies of the faithful; that is, of those who are called by faith to the light of truth and the knowledge of God, that, having forsaken the darkness of ignorance and error, they may worship the living and true God piously and holily, and serve Him from their whole heart" (CCT, 97). The church differs from all other human societies because God founded it and called forth its members by the inner working of the Spirit (CCT, 98). Externally, the church appears as a visible "society of men on earth devoted and consecrated to Jesus Christ" and as such is not an object of faith. But it is an object of faith insofar as the "power which she possesses is not from man but from God" (CCT, 108).

Like Augustine the catechism has a sweeping, cosmic view of the church with levels of existence. *The church triumphant* "is that most glorious and happy assemblage of blessed spirits, and of those who have triumphed over the world, ... and are now exempt and safe from the troubles of this life and enjoy everlasting bliss" (CCT, 99). "*The church militant* is the society of all the faithful still dwelling on earth": militant because at war with the world, the flesh, and the devil (CCT, 99). The church militant contains two classes of persons, "the good and the bad, both professing the same faith and partaking of the same sacraments, yet differing in their manner of life and morality" (CCT, 99–100). The "Catholic faith uniformly and truly teaches that the good and the bad belong to the church ... " (CCT, 100). The *bad,* those cut off from God by sin, share a diminished class of membership: they are as "dead members ... attached to a living body" (CCT, 100). By contrast, the *good,* who are regenerate and united with God in grace, are not known; their union with God does not appear publicly.[102] In sum, the catechism has retained the three-leveled view of the church from Augustine.

The marks or signs of the true church. The signs of the true church are its four marks of authenticity: unity, holiness, catholicity, and apostolicity. Each is clearly defined.

---

102. This is Augustine's inner circle of those united with God in faith, hope, and charity, who in the ecclesiology of the Reformers make up the broad category of the invisible church that extends beyond confessional boundaries, but who in the view of the catechism only exist in the Roman Church.

Unity of the church: the unity of the church is defined both in institutional and in mystical or theological terms. Organizationally, the church "has but one ruler and one governor, the invisible one, Christ, whom the eternal Father 'hath made head over all the church, which is his body' (Eph 1:22–23); the visible one, the Pope, who, as legitimate successor of Peter, the Prince of the Apostles, fills the Apostolic chair" (CCT, 102). Theologically, Christ rules in the church by the Spirit; Christ is the invisible minister of the sacraments and source of grace. Also the Spirit holds the church together as a unity. As the human spirit holds together the human body of many parts, so too the divine Spirit holds together the mystical body of Christ (CCT, 104).

Holiness of the church: holiness consists in being set apart and attached to God. "The church is called holy because she is consecrated and dedicated to God; for so other things when set apart and dedicated to the worship of God were wont to be called holy, even though they were material" (CCT, 105). This set up the response to the question of how a church which contains sinners can be holy. Just as bad artists are still artists, so too "the faithful, although offending in many things and violating the engagements to which they had pledged themselves, are still called holy, because they have been made the people of God and have consecrated themselves to Christ by faith and Baptism" (CCT, 105). "The church is also to be called holy because she is united to her holy Head, as his body; that is, to Christ the Lord, the fountain of all holiness, from whom flow the graces of the Holy Spirit and the riches of the divine bounty" (CCT, 105). The church then causes holiness in its members by the mediation of grace: "the church alone has the legitimate worship of sacrifice, and the salutary use of the sacraments, which are the efficacious instruments of divine grace, used by God to produce true holiness" (CCT, 105). Holiness has thus been distinguished from morality or moral probity. In short, the church's holiness consists in its objectively being dedicated to and united with Christ the head and its function as the objective mediator of Christ's grace.

Catholicity of the church: catholicity means universality and this is interpreted here to mean amplitude and inclusiveness over time and space, ethnicity and class. "Unlike states of human institution, or the sects of heretics, she is not confined to any one country or class of men, but embraces within the amplitude of her love all mankind, whether barbarians or Scythians, slaves or freemen, male or female" (106). Also to this church "belong all the faithful who have existed from Adam to the present day, or who shall exist, in the profession of the true faith, to the end of time" (CCT, 106). Universality means further that no salvation can be found outside this church: "all who desire eternal salvation must cling to and embrace her, like those who entered the ark to escape perishing in the flood" (CCT, 106). The catechism assumes that something so universal must be true, while something local probably is not. "This (note of catholicity), therefore, is to be taught as a most reliable criterion, by which to distinguish the true from a false church" (CCT, 106).

Apostolicity of the church: apostolicity correlates neatly with succession. "The true church is also to be recognized from her origin, *which can be traced back* under the law of grace to the Apostles; for her doctrine is the truth not recently given, nor now first heard of, but delivered of old by the Apostles, and *disseminated* throughout the entire world" (CCT, 107, my emphasis) The dissemination and the tracing back imply historical mediation. "For the Holy Ghost, who presides over the church, governs her by no other ministers than those of Apostolic succession. This Spirit, first imparted to the Apostles, has by the infinite goodness of God always continued in the church" (CCT, 107).

Members. Members are constituted such by baptism which will be considered further on. But the catechism delineates members of the church from those who are not. These can be found in three classes: first, infidels, who are outside the sphere of the Christian faith; second, heretics and schismatics taken together, who cut themselves off from the faith, and belong as "deserters belong to the army from which they have deserted": and third, the excommunicated who are cut off by the judgment of the church and are only readmitted as members upon repentance (CCT, 101). Much more positively, the catechism depicts members as partakers in the communion of saints. This means that, in the unity of the Spirit, "whatsoever has been given to the church is held as a common possession by all her members" (CCT, 109). For example, all share in the fruits of the sacraments, baptism and the eucharist especially; all unite in the communion among the members in love and good works (CCT, 110). This makes the metaphor of the body of Christ a privileged symbol or name for the church: the unity and communion of many in their difference in the one head, Christ (CCT, 111).

Organization of the church. The organizational structure of the Roman Church is hierarchical. The institutional structure that developed over the centuries consists in offices and functions that are also sacred orders, in some cases bestowed by sacraments, into which one is called to serve. The discussion here is somewhat restricted to what the catechism says about candidates for official ministry, the power of orders, and a schematic outline of the large institutional structure. One could also represent the pyramid from the top down.[103]

Candidates for priestly ministry must display a holiness of life, possess a divine call, be moved by a right intention in seeking orders, and gain the competence in scripture, sacraments, and general theological knowledge in order to preach and teach the faithful (CCT, 318–20, 335–37). Prior to the seminaries mandated by the council, candidates for priestly ministry were trained by apprenticeship; the seminaries raised the level of the formation of ministers.[104]

The catechism deals with the question of the organization of the church broadly within the topic of the sacrament of Holy Orders because ordination bestows the power of orders and jurisdiction. "The power of orders has for its object the real body of Christ our Lord in the Blessed Eucharist. The power of jurisdiction refers altogether to the mystical body of Christ. The scope of this power is to govern and rule the Christian people, and lead them to the unending bliss of heaven" (CCT, 321). In turn, the duty of the priest is twofold: "The first is to consecrate and administer the Sacraments properly; the second is to instruct the people entrusted to him in all that they must know or do in order to be saved" (CCT, 336).

---

103. Official ministry in the church is performed by clerics, those drawn into the hierarchical structure. No mention is made here of the extensive "unofficial" ministry of laity in the confraternities or as individuals, nor does it deal with the extensive ministry of religious who were not clerics.

104. See the rather explicit directions of the council for the formation in seminaries of young people seeking ordination in Session 23, Decree on Reform, c. 18 in Tanner, *Decrees*, 750–53.

The sacred character of the organizational structure of the church appears at various junctures. For example, bishops and priests serve as "God's interpreters and ambassadors": they hold God's place on earth; they "exercise in our midst the power and prerogatives of the immortal God" (CCT, 318). The centrality of the system of priestly ministry appears in the view that "without it some of [the other sacraments] could not be constituted or administered at all . . . " (CCT, 317). It is theologically and sociologically noteworthy that the sacrament of orders impresses an objective seal or mark on the one ordained which brings with it the grace necessary to perform the duties of the office (CCT, 159, 323).

Finally, the catechism lays out the whole range of orders in an ascending pattern beginning with the reception of tonsure which enlists one into the clerical state of preparation to receive orders. A first largely ceremonial stage consists in the minor orders of Porter, Reader, Exorcist, and Acolyte. These are followed by major orders: Subdeacon, Deacon, and Priest. Ranks within the priesthood are also differentiated, mostly but not exclusively according to juridical power:[105] ordinary priest, bishop, archbishop, patriarch, and pope (CTT, 324–34). On the papacy relative to church government the catechism says that Christ "placed over his church, which he governs by his invisible Spirit, a man to be his vicar and the minister of his power. A visible church requires a visible head; therefore the savior appointed Peter head and pastor of all the faithful, when he committed to his care the feeding of all his sheep, in such ample terms that he willed the very same power of ruling and governing the entire church to descend to Peter's successors" (CCT, 104).

Mission of the church. The mission of the church appears in its definition: to communicate God's self-revelation in Christ, so that human beings may abandon ignorance and error for enlightenment, so that they may worship God in piety and holiness, and serve God from their whole heart (CCT, 97). The catechism holds up the image of the ark of Noah as a privileged symbol communicating the role of the church in history. In the symbolic manner of the ark, "God

---

105. Ordinarily the sacraments of confirmation and orders are conferred by bishops and not priests.

has so constituted that all who enter therein through baptism, may be safe from danger of eternal death, while such as are outside the church, like those who were not in the ark, are overwhelmed by their own crimes" (CCT, 107). The mission of the church, immediately and practically, is to draw people into itself. This follows from the conviction that there is no salvation outside the one universal institutional church, the only mediator of grace. Moreover, the church is the only "place" of true worship of God: "in the church of God only are to be found the true worship and true sacrifice which can at all be acceptable to God" (CCT, 108). Therefore, the mission of the church in history is to spread and envelope all peoples, of which in the age of exploration there were many more than previously thought. This understanding of the nature and mission of the church helps explain the extraordinary missionary activity that accompanied the movement of discovery and conquest begun in the sixteenth century.

Activities of the church. The religious activities of the late medieval church continued on into the sixteenth century. The Council of Trent did not undermine the devotional life of the parishes but encouraged the bishops to instruct the faithful "in matters relating to intercession and invocation of the saints, the veneration of relics, and the legitimate use of images...."[106] These activities constituted a substantial part of the religious life of the church. Under the heading of "activities," however, attention is directed to the catechism's view of the sacraments.

Assembly, prayer, and worship. The catechism gives the impression that the central acts of prayer and worship in the Roman Church, outside of home and family, revolved around the celebration of the eucharist and the sacraments in the parish church. This would be supplemented with a wide variety of devotions many of which were local. In fact the activities of the confraternities absorbed a good deal of the religious lives of church members in the cities and towns. But the Council of Trent's "emphasis on the parish as the privileged locus where Catholics would practice their faith... gradually eclipsed the preeminent role confraternities played in this regard in the late

---

106. Session 25, "On Invocation, Veneration, and Relics of the Saints, and on Sacred Images," Tanner, *Decrees*, 774–76.

Middle Ages...."[107] The catechism in laying down universal and essential matters connected with the sacraments reflects the council's concern for renewal of the sacramental life of the parish church. The aim in what follows is not to reproduce the extensive sacramental theology of the catechism, but to communicate the essential lines that it takes.

The sacraments. The catechism deals first with the sacraments in general, of which there are seven, before giving specific instruction on each one. "A sacrament is a visible sign of an invisible grace, instituted for our justification" (CCT, 143). It not only signifies or points to but actually accomplishes holiness and righteousness, not by its own power, but by mediating the action of Christ. All sacraments are analyzed in a scholastic manner as being constituted by matter (the material substance and actions) and form (the word of God specifying their divine intent). The objectivity of the sacraments means that the unworthiness of the minister does not destroy the validity of Christ's action in them (CCT, 155–56). This correlates with the fact that the church is made up of both good and bad members. People in the church should be convinced that "were even the lives of her ministers debased by crime, they are still within the church, and therefore lose nothing of their power" (CCT, 101).

Relative to baptism, the catechism presents pastors with a rudimentary but comprehensive theology of the sacrament, including definition, analysis in scholastic terms, the dispositions for reception, the effects of the sacrament, the elements of the ceremony, and an apology for infant baptism. The necessity of baptism extends to all, as well as to infants because of original sin, "so that unless they are regenerated to God through the grace of Baptism, be their parents Christians or infidels, they are born to eternal misery and destruction" (CCT, 177). A scholastic understanding of grace and the virtue of faith allow for a perception that, although infants do not believe with the assent of the mind, they are "established in the true faith

---

107. O'Malley, *Trent and All That*, 135. Trent passed a good deal of legislation that addressed the duties of parish priests, parishes, and parishioners with the goal of animating the religious life of the people through preaching, sacraments, and other spiritual ministry. Also, confraternities were bound to the bishop: he had the right to visitation, and they the duty to give an account to him of their administration. Council of Trent, Session 22, Decree on Reform, cc. 8–9, Tanner, *Decrees*, 740.

of their parents" and in the universal company of saints (CCT, 178). The effects of baptism include forgiveness of sin, regeneration, infusion of the virtues of faith, hope, and love, incorporation into the body of Christ and hence membership in the church.

Turning to the eucharist, although its celebration included a liturgy of the word, the emphasis of the treatment in the catechism rests on the elements of bread and wine, and the form of the sacrament which consists in the words of consecration in the eucharistic prayer.[108] Pastors are to instruct the faithful concerning the mystery of the real presence of Christ so that the whole Christ is mediated by the sacrament. By the mystery of transubstantiation "the substance of the bread and wine does not continue to exist in the Sacrament after consecration" (CCT, 235). The catechism explains why only priests can consecrate the elements, that only they should receive communion in both kinds, and why the eucharist may be considered a representation of the one sacrifice of Christ. Finally, the catechism teaches the extensive effects of the sacrament for the Christian life of individual and community, legislates that people must communicate at least once a year, and recommends frequent and even daily communion.

The catechism provides a forty-five page treatise on the nature and procedure of the sacrament of penance which plays a relatively large role in the sacramental life of the local community. Penance is constituted by the acts of the penitent and the formal absolution of the priest-minister acting in the name of Christ (CCT, 268–69). The effects of the sacrament are forgiveness and remission of sins committed after baptism, and thus, in the case of "mortal" sin that has from the human side killed one's relationship to God, restoration of justification and sanctification. The sacrament is considered necessary because "it is impossible to obtain or even hope for remission of sins by any other means" (CCT, 271). The catechism goes on to analyze the sacrament in detail according to each of its three parts as measured by these acts of the sinner: contrition, confession

---

108. But Trent sought to reestablish preaching in the churches by bishops and the parish priests. See Session 5, Second Decree: On Instruction and Preaching, and Session 24, Decree on Reform, c. 4, Tanner, *Decrees,* 667–70, 763.

of all serious sins to a priest, and satisfaction.[109] Satisfaction may be a mere token, or a more serious act of reparation to God for the sin committed, such as restitution in theft or public penance for a scandalous sin. The church also has the power of excommunication, but it is not highlighted because it is not the ordinary but the exceptional activity for handling serious, public sins, especially heresy.

The Christian life. The practice of the sacrament of penance plays a major role in the understanding and practice of the Christian life. It involves a firm, concrete sense of God's forgiveness, but binds this to the ministry of the priest quite explicitly: "no one is admitted to heaven unless its gates be unlocked by the priests to whose custody the Lord gave the keys" (CCT, 286). But also the whole character of the Christian community encourages a social concern. The idea of the communion of saints sets up a moral imperative for corporate responsibility and dedication to care of weaker members. "In fine, every true Christian possesses nothing which he should not consider common to all others with himself, and should therefore be prepared promptly to relieve an indigent fellow-creature. For he that is blessed with worldly goods, and sees his brother in want, and will not assist him, is plainly convicted of not having the love of God within him" (CCT, 112). While these are general statements of Christian solidarity, they also refer directly to the concrete life of the parish community.

Relation of the church to the world. Finally, relative to the relation of the church to the world, neither the council nor the catechism suggests a qualitative shift in the conception of the relationship of the church to the world that obtained in the late Middle Ages. The church and the world, in the sense of society and state, were either one or were partners. The church's participation in the exploration, settlement, and exploitation of new worlds was spontaneous and natural. When church and world were at odds it was a matter of fact and not principle.

---

109. Relative to the recognition of specific sins, the catechism contains an extensive section on the Decalogue where each of the ten commandments is analyzed in some detail thus providing an objective moral theology.

PRINCIPLES FOR
A HISTORICAL ECCLESIOLOGY

The development over the last four chapters has displayed a spectrum of ecclesiologies that have emerged with the Lutheran and Calvinist churches, the Church of England, the Anabaptist and Separatist movements, and the Roman Church. These ecclesiologies provided material for more general reflections and sets of principles with a wider historical relevance. The reflection and principles which follow attempt to typify the "two ends" of the spectrum of ecclesiologies generated in the sixteenth century under the titles "Free Church" and "Universal Institutional Church." The impulse for these types comes from Troeltsch's Sect and Church types.[110] But Troeltsch's types have been recast within the framework of a theological imagination, and the sociological language has been translated into ecclesiological principles.

A brief explanation of "types" as the category is used here will help clarify the limits and usefulness of their employment. Types are ideal; they represent something that does not exist; they are constructed abstractions. The types which follow begin with the ecclesiologies represented in this chapter, Mennonite and Baptist on one side, Roman Catholic on the other, but the specificity and concreteness of those ecclesiologies are left behind in the creative depiction of a coherent, abstract model. Types, then, are not true or false. Rather they function as reference points for comparison and contrast, as poles for identifying and measuring the degree to which various actual ecclesiologies compare with these admittedly arbitrary standards.[111] Types, then, do not stand alone for admiration, but are meant to work. They function in the measure in which they are used as points of reference in the comparison and contrast of elements within and among actual ecclesiologies.[112]

---

110. Ernst Troeltsch, *The Social Teaching of the Christian Churches* (New York: Harper Torchbooks, 1960), 331–43.

111. Thus one might legitimately complain, for example, that the "free church" type does not correspond to the ecclesiology of Menno Simons or John Smyth at a given point, or that the "universal institutional church" transcends or distorts Roman Catholic ecclesiology in certain respects.

112. Types are epistemologically tensive and ambiguous because simultaneously drawn from data yet constructed into ideal forms. This tension becomes dynamic when

The two types developed here are contrasting types; they are laid out in a five-point binary opposition or contrast to each other in order to emphasize that they are significantly different. But this does not mean that either one negates, cancels out, or invalidates the other. Neither set of qualities should be understood as exclusive or totalizing in the sense that it diminishes the merits of the other. Rather they define abstractly the two ends of the pluralism of ecclesiologies that emerged in the sixteenth century. They are imagined as lying at two ends of a spectrum in the sense that other ecclesiologies developed in the sixteenth century can be located "between them" in the sense of sharing various qualities of the "left" and/or the "right." These two different types of ecclesiology are proposed in their ideal form as both valid and autonomous. "Valid" means that they can be correlated with New Testament themes and/or be understood as developments from or in continuity with the New Testament period. They either have a basis there positively or they cannot be contradicted by the church as reflected in the New Testament. "Autonomous" means that neither derives from the other by corruption; neither is dependent on the other. Therefore, in contrast to accustomed Christian polemics, a historical ecclesiology from below recognizes a certain validity in the historical development and facticity of church organization at any given time. The universal societal church is not a deviation or corruption of the original free church, and the free church is not a deviation or corruption of the universal institutional church. With these presuppositions we turn to the free church type of ecclesiology.

The Free Church[113]

The principle of personal faith. The first quality of the free church rests in an implied theological supposition: the insistence on

---

it generates discussion. Types are useful when they promote conversation that yields self-understanding and understanding of the other.

113. The constructed character of the typology which follows can be demonstrated by comparison with other attempts to "typify" characteristic dimensions of "free church"

the fact that "true religion is always an intensely personal matter."[114] Faith ultimately defines one's personal relation to God, and no one can assume that responsibility for another. This attributes to each a serious responsibility for his or her faith relationship to what is taken to be ultimate truth and salvation. Implicitly this principle revolts against "nominal Christianity" as a contradiction of terms, and against every reduction of Christianity to mere external or objective observance. One stands personally in relation to God. On this basis both Luther and Calvin rejected the notion of "indirect faith," that is, not personally accepting doctrine from God or as God's word, but assenting to doctrine about God from the church as true, whether or not one understands it. If religion or Christian faith were to become so objectified that it lost this personal but not necessarily individualistic quality, Christianity itself would be lost. People with personal faith in God coming together constitute the church. This explains why infant baptism ill fits in this conception of the church. One can only be a conscious, free, and responsible member of the church.

The principle of voluntary association. This principle formed a kind of tacit presupposition of the Radical Reformation movement.

---

ecclesiology. Friedmann sees three essential qualities to Anabaptist ecclesiology: the church is (1) eschatological, a realization of the kingdom of God, (2) covenantal and voluntary, and (3) a restitution of the New Testament or apostolic church (*Theology of Anabaptism*, 121). Bender crystalizes the essence of Anabaptism in three points: (1) centrally and foundationally, existential discipleship or following Christ, (2) voluntary church membership based on conversion, (3) an ethic of love and nonresistance ("The Anabaptist Vision, 42–54). Littell joins together the elements of discipleship and an existential church community as reciprocally entailing each other ("The Anabaptist Concept of the Church," 123, 134). Klaassen sees two essential principles to Anabaptism: that the church be (1) an existential holy community, (2) that exists apart from the world (*Anabaptism*, 19–63). Keeney crystalizes the ecclesiology of Menno Simons and Dirk Philips in five principles: (1) a community of fellowship, (2) a restoration of the church reflected in the New Testament, (3) a visible community of the saved, (4) "a voluntary gathering of believers," (5) a holy fellowship without spot or wrinkle (*Dutch Anabaptist Thought*, 145–55). Relative to Baptist foundational principles, Torbet proposes four: (1) Scripture as the sole norm of faith; (2) baptism of believers, (3) priesthood of the faithful and autonomy of the local congregation; (4) religious liberty and separation of church and state (*History of the Baptists*, 15–34). Sprunger sees three essential principles operating in Francis Johnson's Separatist Ancient Church: (1) a covenanted community of people linked with Christ and one another into the future, (2) a separated community purified of the objectified rituals of the Prayer Book, (3) a community with common discipline. *Dutch Puritanism*, 55–60.
    114. J. S. Whale, (Cambridge: Cambridge University Press, 1955), 183.

It flows directly from the first point. If the church has its radical basis in personal faith in God, then it must be a voluntary association. As a free, autonomous community it cannot be controlled by the state, or by princes or kings or civil government. This free association has its foundation in its relationship to God. The logic moves from the freedom of faith and religion to the freedom of the church which is at the least the organization of people animated by that faith. A free church stands in revolt from an externally controlled church and asserts its autonomy given by God and exercised theonomously under God.

If the church is a free association, then the primary reference for the term "church" insofar as it is an organized community is the local church. Ordinarily the primary referent in this kind of ecclesiology is the parish church or congregation because the church becomes historically actualized in concrete congregations.[115] The distinction of Luther and Calvin between local congregation and universal church at this point takes a radical form. The universal unity of the church is cosmic or metaphysical, that is, it is ultimately explained by each church's unity with God and not by a universal institution or a historical succession. "Apostolicity" supposes that the New Testament church of the apostles is normative, and it means "to be true to the apostles," not to be standing in an unbroken line of ordinations.[116] It is also eschatological; it will be achieved at the end of time. Unity in this world can only be viewed in a moral and spiritual sense that urges communion between distinct independent churches without institutional or juridical bonds. On this principle, too, it is difficult to admit infant baptism. Being a member of a voluntary church means initiation on the basis of responsible choice.

The principle of spiritual interiority. The principle of spiritual interiority pushes forward the first principle of personal faith. It also radicalizes Luther's polemic against external structures and forms of Christian practice. It reflects a certain suspicion relative to the objective forms of religion: sacrament, ritual, cult, institutional practices.

---

115. In their origins such a church may take the form of a small, loose association as in the case of the gradual emergence of the New Testament Christian communities.

116. Littell, *Tribute to Menno Simons,* 24, and "Anabaptist Concept of the Church," 126–27.

The reason for this rests on the Christian conviction that God's Spirit works within the human person.[117] This explains or reflects Smyth's theology of prayer and worship. Faith, according to Dietrich (Dirk) Philips, is a spiritual rebirth, a being reborn, an inner conversion, a being born of God, an illumination of the human spirit, an inner love of God before all else.[118] The Spirit of God at work within the human spirit constitutes the essence of Christianity; all external mediations are merely instruments subordinated to this. Priesthood, hierarchy, sacraments, in some cases even the objective word of scripture are subordinated to the inner workings of the Holy Spirit and the attachment of the human spirit to God. The reason why discipline is considered to be a mark of the true church is that it in turn testifies to the active presence of the Spirit within the community and thus the actuality of the covenant.[119]

The head of the church, then, can be no other than Christ. Christ rules the community as it were "directly." From this point of view Jesus Christ appears as the transcendent and ever present head of the church, and not primarily as a historical figure who founded an institutional church. One finds no official hierarchical structure in the congregation, certainly not a vicar of Christ on earth that mediates the Lordship of Christ over the members of the church. The church is simply the community gathered in Christ by the Spirit. The church then is entirely lay; it is the *laos* or people of God, even though it may have charismatic leaders chosen through the Spirit.

Existentially holy community. Fourth, the principles already stated lead to the following quality or principle: the church is called to be an existentially holy community. The church achieves existential holiness as a community by the quality of the lives of its members. They lead subjectively ethical and holy lives. If there were no inner conversion, no real turning to God, there would be no church either.

---

117. The principle of interiority with reference to Menno is stated in contrast to the church as institution as follows: "Anabaptism rests ultimately on perpetual spiritual re-creation which derives its authority from the work of the Spirit among men thereby united, and not from ecclesiastical structure." Paul Peachey, "Anabaptism and Church Organization," *Mennonite Quarterly Review* 30 (1956): 217, cited by Littell, *Tribute to Menno Simons*, 28.

118. Dietrich Philips, "The Church of God," SAW, 234–37.

119. Brachlow, "Life Together in Exile," 119–22.

This contrasts with a holiness of objective forms: of doctrine, of sacrament, of priesthood, of tradition, of the word. Rather, holiness applies to the effects of these things in the life of the community itself existentially.

Therefore the church, which tends to be equated with a congregation or small group, does not understand itself as a mixed community. This church does not consist of sinners and saints, of good and evil, of pure and impure, not at least on any public level. Rather, this church endeavors to become a community of morally upright people. This explains or expresses why Menno Simons could not conceive of a real or authentic Christian church without the exercise of the ban. It structured socially the lives of church members in a common and fairly strict discipline. Their lives exemplify the effects of God in their lives. The ban means that when this discipline is flouted, one is excommunicated from the community, for the good of both the individual and the community. Thus what this ecclesiology may lose quantitatively in universality by finding its focus in the local community, it gains in quality, intensity, and seriousness of the Christian life and witness.

The church is a community of love, of effective love of one member for another and of all for all. Emphasis is laid on love of neighbor and especially care for the poor and less fortunate. This theme could achieve such an importance that it might lead communities into types of communistic communities or communes. Ulrich Stadler, writing in such a context, says that private property is theft.[120] From this point of view, the church looks back at the historical Jesus again not as a founder of an institution, but as the example of life. The ethics of this church is one of following Jesus, sometimes in actual poverty, but always in simplicity of life and humility.

Church indifferent to the world, society, and state. Although the church was divided at the Reformation, one of the remnants of Christendom lay in the close connection of church and society, the symbiosis of any given church with a given society, and uniformity

---

120. Ulrich Stadler represents a community that developed from the Swiss Brethren and withdrew from the world of society to an isolated rural existence based on communistic principles. See his "Cherished Instructions on Sin, Excommunication, and the Community of Goods," SAW, 278.

of church order. One does not yet find recognition of a pluralism of churches within one society. The free-church movement hastened the breakdown of the wedding of church and society by insisting on the right of pluralism of churches within a given society; the free churches promoted the recognition of the separation of church and state. But during the sixteenth century the Anabaptist churches were violently persecuted by Catholics and Protestants alike.

The attitude of this type of church to the world may be said to range from indifference to society, to separation from society and state, to hostility to the world. Certainly the world and society were dangerous to faith, and the ban meant separation from untrue Christians or those outside the community. Menno Simons demonstrates this with feeling in his explanation of the practice of excommunication and banning. The vision bears analogies with Tertullian's view of a thoroughly corrupted and idolatrous society; the church represents a minority group set off from the world or society and defined by a perfectionist ethic. Ironically, the world outside the church in the sixteenth century was no pagan Roman Empire but Christian society.

As distinct from the universal institutional church at the other end of the spectrum which involves compromise with the world, this church opposes any concession. In its noncooperation with society and the state, it often becomes pitted prophetically against it; it is against violence of all kinds, and in some cases refuses to recognize or allow its members to hold public office. This is done in the name of Christ. The two ecclesiologies studied here do not go to this extreme. But the tendency of the free church in its separation from the dominant established church is to constitute itself as a parallel society, much as the early church, and to define itself as either indifferent to or apart from or hostile to society. This hostility to the world sometimes translated itself into a militant attempt to transform the world, to absorb society into the Kingdom of God, and to set up a millenarian Reign of God. But in all cases, the church and the people in it belong to God and not to the world.

The Universal Institutional Church

The description of this theological type emerges out of an application of Troeltsch's church type to the Roman Church of the sixteenth

century and calling it a universal institutional church. While the ecclesiologies of Luther and Calvin share many of the qualities of the
free church theologically, in the end they too correspond sociologically to a church type according to Troeltsch. Better, they contain a
mixture of the qualities of both types. Most of the qualities of the
universal institutional type, arranged here to show a direct contrast
to the five free church qualities, will appear as either assumptions
or explicit qualities of the church described in *The Catechism of the
Council of Trent.*

The principle of institutionalization. The contrast to the principle of personal faith here is not impersonal faith. Rather it is a
question of the constitution of the church and of faith within that
church. Revelation points to a public phenomenon given for the
world. As a historical, human possession, to be preserved it must
be objectified in some form such as scripture and doctrines. The
church as an institutional society is the result of this objectification
and carries with it in history a tradition of doctrine and practice; the
institution is also a movement in history with a beginning and a
distinctive character that has been consistently developed over time.
People gather around a public confession of faith, and this gathering too becomes institutionalized because it constitutes the visible
historical society. Ultimately the church becomes identified with its
institutional structure.[121]

The church then is an objectively structured social phenomenon,
a visible society with a structure of leadership, offices, a law, and customs. This does not deny an inner life; but the church as church is
seen in its public, social and institutional character. People are not

---

121. Bellarmine's definition of the church illustrates this: "There is but one church,
and that one true church is the assembly of people gathered in the profession of the
same Christian faith and in the communion of the same sacraments under the authority of legitimate pastors especially of the one vicar of Christ on earth the Roman
Pontiff." He goes on to enumerate those whom the definition excludes; it does not
exclude sinners and those secretly unfaithful because the criteria are external. He continues: "we do not think any internal virtue is required but only an external profession
of faith, and communion in the sacraments which can be perceived by the senses. For
the church is a gathering of people that is as visible and palpable as the assembly of Romans, or the kingdom of France, or the Republic of the Venetians." Robert Bellarmine,
De Conciliis, et Ecclesia, De Controversiis: Christianae Fidei Adversus Haereticos,
II, Editio Prima Romana (Romae: Typographia Giunchi et Menicanti, 1836), Bk. III,
Chap. 2, p. 90.

viewed as constituting this church but as being continuously drawn into it as members through its public and objective forms. Members do not know all the subtlety of doctrines; they confess what the church confesses; indirect faith is believing on the basis of the church's witness and teaching. Infant baptism fits here because it is the public recognition of the entry of a person into the institution of his or her birth. Once the church is recognized as a social institution, it is not possible to contrast the inner life of the church and its objective institutional structure. These are two aspects of the same reality.

The principle of universality. The reason behind the principle of universality is closely related to the public character of revelation. Revelation is the truth from God and of God; it is for all human beings; and salvation depends on it. The church, then, tends to reach out to the whole of society; it should be coextensive with society. And because truth is one, the church tends toward uniformity. The church, then, is not the local congregation; the church is one large institution that is universal; it is the same in its form everywhere because local churches are simply parts or extensions of the one church. The theological basis of this unity is the oneness of Christ, revelation, faith, baptism, and love which the institution holds together. The institution defines the church not as bare institution but as the institutionalization of God-given grace. The catechism represents the pope as the head of one institution covering vastly different local regions.

Since this whole church is one and uniform, across time from the beginning and across societies in the present, the local congregation is precisely not autonomous. It is ruled or regulated by the central authority of the whole institution. Since the church is universal and meant to be coextensive with any given society in which it exists, it is precisely not a voluntary association. One is born into this church, as one is born into a nation, into Christian society, and one cannot find salvation outside it. Infant baptism makes perfect sense in this context. The voluntary principle appears as dissidence, as breaking the unity of the community, and thus as attacking the very truth of the revelation on which the unity is ultimately founded.

The principle of external sacramentality. The sacramental principle was enunciated clearly by Calvin. God could deal with each of us directly, as it were spiritually. But while in this world God has chosen to deal with us through this-worldly instruments. Thus the church is the instrument, the objective, public, historical means, for mediating God's salvation. The church itself is the objective, historical mediation to the individual's faith. This church has a structure and offices that enjoy a God-given authority: to rule or govern, teach, and sanctify. The sacraments are the ordinary means of this mediation along with preaching the objective word of God. The Spirit of God or grace is bound to word and sacrament. This is the sacramental principle: the Spirit is mediated through public external signs and not directly, interiorly, or spiritually without these public mediations which extend in history the appearance of God in Jesus. This intends no negation of the inner and the spiritual, but stresses the external institutions as the necessary, visible, and objective means of the communication of the Spirit.

The head of the church, then, is Christ; but Christ also has a visible vicar on earth. All institutions in this world need a head. Christ rules the community, but through the pope and not directly. From this point of view one looks back at Jesus Christ as transcendent Lord but also as founder of a historical church. This church is not simply lay; a strong distinction holds between the members and the offices or objective leadership structures that make up the public institution and the ministers who occupy those offices. In fact the church, as visible society, tends to be identified with the clerical class. Their authority is not so much charismatic, but juridical, pertaining to their office or role of leadership, and sacral, pertaining to the objective holiness of the church and their particular sacramental functions.

Objective holy institution. The holiness of the universal institutional church lies not so much in its members as in the objective institution itself and the elements that make up that institution. Holiness applies to what is of God, and these are God's words in scripture. The institution is founded by God; the doctrine it teaches is God's; the sacraments are God's instruments, and their saving grace does not depend on ministers. The catechism is explicit on this. The holiness of people, as individuals and as a whole community, is constituted by being in contact with this institutional sphere of grace by which God is historically mediated to them. Thus a clear distinction obtains between sacred office and the person who happens to exercise the office. The authority of the office holder is not ultimately due to personal qualities, nor is the minister's ability to mediate grace due to the minister's personal holiness. The ultimate ground of holiness is contact with God; it is not existential but depends on God's promise to be present to people in the institutions that God established.

The church then is precisely not an existentially holy community, something that proved itself to be historically impossible. The institutional church designates a mixed community, of sinners and saints, good and evil, pure and impure. Optimally, it consists in a community coterminous with the whole of society, and thus, apart from the lives of certain exemplary members, its general moral expectations are no better than that of the whole of society. What this church gains in universality, then, it necessarily loses in intensity of the Christian life at least statistically. People are not excommunicated except for serious public departures from church doctrine; they are not excommunicated simply for personal moral fault. People are still members of the visible and objectively holy church even if they are existentially cut off from God through sin but confess the objective doctrine of the church.

Effective love for the neighbor is still a Christian ideal in this church; but as a universal institution it is not *constitutive* of the church. In other words, a vast institution cannot be held together by such an actual and effective love the way a small congregational community could. Existential fellowship is less a requirement in a universal confraternity where unity is forged more by institution than by effective love. The love which binds the whole church together is more the communion among the churches within the same institution as seen in Cyprian and Augustine. From this point of view, the church looks back at Jesus less as an example of a life lived that actually binds people together, although this is not excluded, and more as the founder of an institution that unites, reconciles, brings people together.

The church as part of the world, society, and state. This church is defined as a visible social entity and hence as a part of the world and society. This does not necessarily mean that this church sees itself as a function of society and controlled by civil government. It may define itself as an autonomous, God-established institution and will thus stand over against society and the state when its own interests are at stake. This is what happened in the Gregorian reform. But it is still part of the world. In the tension of being of God but in the world, it is the aspect of the visible society in the world that receives most emphasis, but its relation to God gives it legitimation and autonomy.

Therefore this church is marked by the compromise that it makes with society and civil government. In fact its members live their lives within the world as members of society and leaders in government. In the Roman Church, only a few withdraw from the world and live apart from the world in cloistered existence. For the rest, the world of ordinary society may be dangerous, but this is combated by asceticism or discipline or self-control and not by flight. This describes the ideal. But in fact the institutional church is usually a support for social values and government policies; insofar as it is part of society, its members tend to accept the values and political policies of the place where it exists. Negatively, this compromise appears as a weakening of specifically Christian values; positively, it appears as inculturation and a leavening of society. Compromise means that the church and its members enjoy a peaceful relation with society and state and its members fully participate in all spheres of public life. Hooker describes brilliantly how Christians of this kind of church see religion as mediating the sacred ground and goal of all social life. The church as a whole has a message for society and in theory tries to exert influence on society. If the whole church found itself at odds with society, it could have a great impact because of its vast and even worldwide institutional power. In sum, this institutional church, if it is not coopted by society, can have great influence on society.

To conclude this chapter and the whole consideration of the sixteenth century, all five ecclesiologies sketched over the four last chapters symbolically represent a much broader pluralism in the actual affairs of the Western church. And this typology summarizes at its extremes the spectrum of five relatively clearly defined ecclesiologies that emerged in Europe in the course of that complex century. Their internal coherence and integrity dramatize the validity of pluralism itself. The church can never go back to a situation where Christian pluralism does not prevail. Nor should it. The typology demonstrates the positive value of living the Christian ecclesial life in different ways.

Part II

THE CHURCH IN THE MODERN PERIOD

Chapter 5

Modern Ecclesiology

While nothing can match the magnitude of the transformations in the church and ecclesiology in the sixteenth-century Western church, the transition to a modern method of theology and thus a modern way of thinking about the church represents another watershed. The turn to the subject that occurred in Western philosophy produced an echo in theology, and once that transition was made, there could be no going back to premodern ways of thinking, not at least without the risk of failing to communicate with a whole culture.

The modern ecclesiology described in this chapter draws from developments that occurred early in the nineteenth century. In terms of history the analysis jumps over two centuries, much as it leapt over the early Middle Ages, because what happened thereafter superceded in importance what went before. Although ecclesiology continued to develop during the seventeenth and eighteenth centuries and the ecclesiologies developed then bear some significance, the changes the church and its ecclesiology underwent in the nineteenth century were transformative. The Enlightenment and the French Revolution introduced new dynamics into church life, but more significant were the shifts in the method of the discipline of ecclesiology. The developments in the Western church in this century are often measured from 1815, the end of the Napoleonic period, to 1914, the beginning of World War I. During that period the church underwent a period of unprecedented expansion; its dialectical interaction with cultural forces in history and society altered its character in fundamental ways. One could say that the modern church, as distinct from the church in the early modern or Reformation period, took shape in the course of this century. But still deeper changes were occurring in intellectual culture and these spilled over into premises and methods for understanding the church as such.

Reflecting these historical dialectics, the first few decades of the century generated the two strongest representations of modern ecclesiology: the one, Protestant, was authored by Friedrich Schleiermacher; the Catholic, Johann Adam Möhler, authored the other.[1] These two ecclesiologies, both products of the Romantic revival after the Enlightenment, bear much in common despite their differences. Indeed, the whole century invites an interesting study in analogy as the two segments of the Western church, Protestant and Catholic, face the same historical, social, and cultural forces, that is, the same "world," and develop their responses.

This discussion of modern ecclesiology is divided into four parts. The first attempts to represent in a short space the development of the church in the course of the nineteenth century. It discusses alternatively in the Protestant and Catholic Churches developments in missions, postures toward the world, and the discipline of theology. This will help to retain a sense of the whole Western church. The second and third parts respectively present holistically the ecclesiologies of Schleiermacher and early Möhler. Part four collects some of the significant developments of this century and converts them into general principles and axioms for understanding the church as such.

THE NINETEENTH-CENTURY WESTERN CHURCH

The development of the church in the West during the nineteenth century can be called explosive. Although the next few pages do little more than point to that history rather than fully represent it, they provide the context and sources for the shifts in ecclesiology that

---

1. It should be noted that the history covered in this chapter runs far beyond these two figures who died in the 1830s. But their influence lived on, and the historical narrative will serve as a bridge to their impact on the twentieth century. A comparison between Adolf von Harnack, *What Is Christianity?* (Philadelphia: Fortress Press, 1986, orig. 1900), and Alfred Loisy, *The Gospel and the Church* (Philadelphia: Fortress Press, 1976, orig. 1902), would also generate insight into modern ecclesiology from a historical perspective.

accompanied it. Three foci or areas of development contain particular relevance for the self-understanding of the church and directly or indirectly contributed to ecclesiology. These areas are the expansion of the church through the missionary movement, the shifting relationship of the church to the world in the sense of culture, society, and state, and the discipline of theology of which ecclesiology forms a part.

The Missionary Movement

At the beginning of the nineteenth century the Protestant church was more or less contained within Europe, the British Isles, the Americas. The expansion of the Catholic Church in the sixteenth century and thereafter was carried forward to the East and to the Americas mostly by Spain, Portugal, and France. The church in the Philippines had been established through Mexico in the sixteenth century. In Africa Christianity remained for the most part in towns on the coast as mosquitos protected the interior. By the end of the century just about every country on earth had been touched, perhaps only slightly, by the expanding church. In terms of numbers and territory no expansion of the church equaled it. The way the missionary movement engaged the corporate imagination of Christians in the nineteenth century shared some of the qualities of the crusades in the Middle Ages.[2]

The reasons for this sudden and unprecedented expansion were many. A relative peace in Europe allowed its citizens to think of other things than war. The industrial revolution and expansion of trade supplied the means and instilled a desire for expansion. The onset of colonialism provided the structures. The vitality of Christian faith, coupled with a growing optimism about human existence and the course of history, induced a new corporate sense of Christian responsibility and an intense desire to communicate the faith in a new way and to all.

Mission history is fragmented. On the ground it consists of individual missionaries or small parties, sponsored by a sending society or a religious order establishing mission stations and working among

---

2. My main source for the history of missions is Stephen Neill, *A History of Christian Missions*, 2nd ed (London: Penguin Books, 1986).

peoples at preaching the gospel, translating the New Testament into the vernacular, establishing clinics, dispensaries, and schools, and finally winning some converts. The missionary movement then is the collection of these innumerable stories about individuals, or families, or bands of missionaries, by district and region, in province, state, and country, by area of the world: Far East, South East Asia, Oceania, South Asia, the Middle East, North, West, East and South Africa. But all these stories exist as part of a common Christian impulse to communicate, to encounter other people and convert them to the Good News of Jesus Christ. Thus together these individual narratives contribute to a collective story at the end of which the church, overwhelmingly European at the beginning of the nineteenth century, began the process of becoming a world church in a dramatically new way. This process would continue during the course of the twentieth century.

Protestant missions. The story of the Protestant missions revolves almost completely around mission societies, voluntary organizations designed to sponsor, send, and support missionaries to foreign lands. These societies began to be formed in England at the end of the eighteenth and their numbers grew in the course of the nineteenth century. They were many and varied, large and small, broadly or narrowly based; they could be confessional or cross-denominational or simply evangelical, unconnected with a particular church; they were supported by individual churches, denominations or synods, or simply individual Christians interested in supporting missions. They sent missionaries with different degrees of missionary formation beginning with none at all and ranging into training in ministry, theology, and professional or technical skills.

The main activity was preaching and communicating the Christian message. Bible translation was a major endeavor, and Protestants were leaders in this area. Schools were also a major strategy in missionary activity; elementary schools, secondary schools, and even eventual universities. This was a way of relating to elite members of a given population. Hospitals and other health work were typical of many missions. Missions might also support and run farms or agricultural institutions, or schools providing trade and industrial training, or publishing houses and printing presses. Various theories or theologies connected this developmental work to the ultimate goal of communicating Christian revelation.[3]

By the end of the century, when representatives of Protestant churches assembled in 1910 for the World Missionary Conference held in Edinburgh there was a palpable sense that the Christian mission would continue to intensify so that people actually envisioned the possibility that the whole world would be converted to Christ.

Catholic missions. Catholic missions also took on a new intensity during the nineteenth century and the church's unified structure offered tremendous support for a more coordinated effort. Roman Catholic missionaries were largely members of religious orders which functioned analogously to the Protestant mission societies, but under the auspices of a wider umbrella of an international organization and a united diocesan system. The Jesuits, suppressed in 1773, were restored in 1814 and many other religious orders of men and women were founded in the post-Napoleonic period: "the nineteenth century was richer than any other in the formation of new Orders and Sisterhoods specially devoted to missionary work or prepared to devote a large part of their resources to it."[4] Also, prior to 1850, Gregory XVI "prepared the framework within which the missionaries could be able to work by creating a large number of bishoprics and prefectures in all parts of the world."[5]

Problems with the missionary movement. A whole host of problems with nineteenth-century missionary activity, now clearly visible from a postcolonial perspective, are commonly admitted on all sides. First, missionaries inevitably inculcated a Western and even local European form of the Christian church. Second, the mission spread

---

3. Neill, *Christian Missions*, 216–17. Neill points out that events in the 1850s mark a new initiative in missionary activity among the Protestant churches. The English crown assumed colonial responsibility for government in India. China began to open up the interior of the country to foreigners, and Japan too became less resistant. In 1857 David Livingstone published his *Missionary Travels and Researches in South Africa* which was widely read and stimulated great interest. In the late 1850s the Second Evangelical Awakening in the United States was converted into mission responsibility and enthusiasm. New mission societies were created and the flow of missionaries from Europe and the United States was renewed. Ibid., 274–76. Since the nineteenth and twentieth centuries the majority of Protestant missionaries have been English speaking.

4. Neill, *Christian Missions*, 336–37.

5. Ibid., 338.

European divisions. In any given place there may have been personal friendships, but by and large these were exceptional. "It was taken for granted by the majority of Roman Catholics that the Protestants were the enemy."[6] Third, although the goal of missionary activity was to establish autonomous churches, the training of local ministers and clergy was slow to take off, and missionaries often harbored paternalistic attitudes and sets of Western norms which encouraged a protracted mission status for young churches.[7] Fourth, these now obvious failures concealed more difficult theological issues which gradually gave rise to the discipline of missiology. Theories of mission diverged; the ecclesiologies of the various sending societies and churches as well as cultural and educational situation of the host people account for the differences. But in the course of extensive missionary experience some common principles or at least strategic questions would emerge. Does one preach widely or establish schools for patient instruction? Should the missionary shed his or her Western dress? Western culture? But what in Western Christian practice is Western as distinct from Christian? Does the eucharist depend on grape wine? Which Chinese character for God really represents God? How should church order be accommodated to the reception of indigenous members, leaders, ministers, bishops? When and under what conditions should a new church be declared an autonomous church? These questions could be multiplied.[8] While for the most part missionaries transplanted their home churches, at the same time these searching questions relative to the nature and structure of the church were also being planted. The formal discipline of missiology came into existence during the nineteenth and early twentieth centuries in distinct Protestant and Catholic forms. But in both cases, missiology studied the church on the boundary with the world in the form of new cultures and societies,

---

6. Neill, *Christian Missions*, 369.

7. "Paternalism was perhaps the gravest weakness of all missionary work in the nineteenth century." They saw themselves building an indigenous church, but by and large they could not envisage it without themselves. Neill, *Christian Missions*, 362.

8. These questions were not new. They were raised by Mateo Ricci (1552–1610) and Roberto de Nobili (1577–1656), both Jesuit missionaries, in China and India respectively. The questions remain perennial.

and engaging in these issues helped to mediate a new and deeper historical consciousness.

Relationship to the World

This subheading refers to the way the church in Europe, Britain, and the United States interacted with the historical, social, and cultural forces of the nineteenth century. These forces consisted in, among other things, the carry-over of the intellectual culture of the Enlightenment and the reaction against it in Romanticism, the flourishing of critical history and generally an increasing sense of historicity, the growth of sciences, symbolized for example in the discovery of biological evolution, political forces released by the American and particularly the French Revolution in Europe, the gathering forces of the industrial revolution, and the emergence of political or democratic and economic liberalism. These forces also had a significant bearing on the discipline of theology which will be considered in the next section. Here the focus falls on some notable affects on general church consciousness. These common historical pressures had analogous effects broadly speaking in both the Protestant and Catholic branches of the Western church.

The French Revolution lies behind discussions of the relation of the church to society, state, and world in nineteenth-century Europe. This is a relationship that is unstable and fluctuating, qualities well illustrated in France. Before the revolution the Catholic Church in France enjoyed extensive privileges: it was wealthy and exempt from taxation; it enjoyed a monopoly in education and was led by a higher clergy drawn from the aristocracy. Monarchy and church were pillars of the *ancien régime*. With the revolution all this came crashing down. The revolutionary government reconstituted the church within the framework of a new French constitution. There followed a campaign of dechristianization during the Reign of Terror and a reestablishment of the church under Napoleon sealed with a concordat with Rome in July 1801. Two features of the concordat actually fostered attachment to Rome. One was the fact that the church had lost its property and its clergy was salaried by the state: this encouraged church leaders to look to Rome for leverage against state domination. The other was the power conceded by the concordat that the pope could demand the resignation of French bishops. The concordat gave the church in France a new life.[9]

The development of the churches in Europe during the course of the nineteenth century varied according to nation and principality on the one hand and church denomination on the other. Various movements marked church life in Britain: the Tractarian Movement, the movement of Social Christianity, the expansion of the Free Churches. The Christian church in North America underwent a spectacular growth in vitality, particularly in the United States. "In the U.S. the whole Christian macrocosm, dispersed in Europe among many nations, was to be transplanted into one country." Freed from European restraints against diversity or radicalism, after the American Revolution immigrant Christians "were free to experiment and to do whatever they wanted."[10]

Among the many elements that are new and distinguish the development of the Church in the West in the course of the nineteenth century, two have a particular bearing on the church and its self-understanding. One was an increasing reaction against modernity and a drift toward authoritarianism reflected in the segment of Protestantism called "fundamentalism." The Catholic analogue applied to the whole church as institution and is labeled from different perspectives as "ultramontanism," "integrism," or simply authoritarianism. In both cases the refuge in some form of pure dependence on authority can be read as reaction against a modernity which appeared not simply as anti-Christian forces at work outside the church but also, having entered the church, as a sort of virus attacking it from the inside. The other more positive common phenomenon across the churches was the recognition of the church's role in society. Social Christianity may be defined loosely as an anti-individualist interpretation of Christianity that sees the church playing a role in the amelioration of society and culture, but in a situation where

---

9. Alec R. Vidler, *The Church in an Age of Revolution* (London: Penguin Books, 1974), 11–21.

10. Vidler, *The Church in an Age of Revolution*, 235–36. At the end of the eighteenth century, regular religious practice was not high: less than 10 percent were churchgoers. But the Second Great Awakening changed that, and churches and missions flourished. Revivalism and church missions increased active church participation considerably. Ibid., 237.

now church and state are separate. It consisted in a reaction against the negative social effects of the rise of capitalist individualism in economics, industry, and commerce, a reaction against the poverty and inhuman living conditions of the agricultural and manufacturing poor. This accompanied the rise of socialism as a political economic theory and ran like a thread through the last half of the century in Europe, extended to North America, and reached a certain climax there in the Social Gospel movement. A brief depiction of both themes, first in the Protestant churches and then the Catholic Church, provides a lesson in social analogy.

Protestant. The development of the Protestant church in the course of the nineteenth century does not present a unified story. Each country in Europe has its church history; so too in Britain and North America. One could schematize the confessions, church orders, liturgies, and spiritualities of the churches according to some grid such as Orthodoxy, Evangelical Piety or Pietism, and Liberal Accommodation. Such a scheme would cut across denominations and nations and would thus tend to hide the complexity and the diversity among the Protestant churches.[11] And it is simplistic to reduce the alternatives of Protestant or Christian sensibilities to liberal and fundamentalist. This kind of digital thinking is tempting but completely misses the multiple thematics and options of the period. Despite the many other manifestations of a religious conservativism reacting against liberal trends of the nineteenth century, it is useful to note the appeal to an extrinsicist view of the way God's authority is mediated to the church in the view of fundamentalism.

"The term 'fundamentalism' derives from a Bible Conference of conservative evangelicals at Niagara in 1895. They took their stand upon 'five fundamentals': the inerrancy of the Scriptures, the deity of Jesus Christ, the Virgin Birth, the substitutionary theory of the Atonement, and the bodily Resurrection and imminent bodily Second Coming of the Lord."[12] These basic truths were then further developed in a series of tracts called *The Fundamentals*, published some years later, which expanded upon these fundamental truths of

---

11. Kenneth Scott Latourette, *A History of Christianity* (New York: Harper & Row, 1975), 1156.
12. Vidler, *The Church in an Age of Revolution*, 241.

FUNDAMENTAL

the church. Chief among them concerns the status of the Bible. "At the center of the fundamentalist opposition to liberalism was the question of the authority and inspiration of the Bible. For the fundamentalist, Christianity is irrevocably committed to the inerrancy of the Bible."[13] But the deeper dynamism of this fundamentalism can be considered in terms of authority. The desire for fundamentals and an unchanging essence and foundation of Christianity rests on a need for an authority that comes from outside the human situation and anchors it against the insecurity of being adrift in pluralism and change. This particular religious desire for authority is extrinsicist, that is, it sees God working not through natural processes, as does the liberal imagination, but supernaturally through intervention. Only such an action on the part of God can be salvific and guaranteed as such. To undercut this intervening and authoritative act of God is to undercut the essence of the Christian message.[14]

The second theme of social Christianity relates to the way the church came to the realization that it must play an independent part in social reconstruction. This received public attention in the Christian Socialist movement in England in the mid-nineteenth century.[15] During the course of the second half of the nineteenth century this social concern grew, became variously organized in different situations, and gradually took the form of the Social Gospel movement. The sources of these movements were:

1. organized labor and various labor movements;

2. the moral idealism of liberal theology expressed, for example, in the theology of Albrecht Ritschl;

3. the Bible itself when authors focused on the prophets, the teachings of Jesus on wealth and poverty, and an interpretation of

---

13. John Dillenberger and Claude Welch, *Protestant Christianity: Interpreted through its Development* (New York: Charles Scribner's Sons, 1954), 227.

14. Ibid., 228.

15. "The Christian Socialist movement of 1848–54 was in a sense born out of Chartism. John Malcolm Ludlow (1821–1911), Charles Kingsley (1819–75), F. D. Maurice (1805–72), Thomas Hughes (1822–96), and the rest, were a group of churchmen who realized that the Gospel of Christ must have something better to say to the working people of England than what the official church was saying." Vidler, *The Church in an Age of Revolution,* 95.

Jesus' message of the kingdom of God and its relevance for actual society;

4. the intensity of poverty and human suffering generated by the industrial revolution especially in the urban centers of manufacturing.[16]

The social gospel in the United States expressed itself in a wide variety of genres: in hymns, popular novels such as *In his Steps* by Charles M. Sheldon, the writings of various pastor-leaders such as Washington Gladden, political economists like Richard Ely, cultural animators like Josiah Strong, theologian-historians like Walter Rauschenbusch, exegete-theologians like Shailer Mathews, ethicists like Francis Peabody. It developed an explicit ecclesiology of engagement in the process of amelioration of the social order.[17] "The underlying principle of this new understanding of the gospel was the explicit and consistent recognition of the social nature of personal existence."[18] It made a permanent contribution to ecclesiology: "the ethical imperative of the social gospel, the emphasis on Christian social responsibility, the sharp criticism of any Christian ethics which deals only with 'individual morality,' the primary concern for the welfare of oppressed classes and races — these remain from the social gospel as an integral part of the Protestant witness. . . ."[19]

Catholic. The dynamics of the interaction between the Catholic Church and the world during the course of the nineteenth century also contained a drift toward authoritarianism and an increasing concern for social issues. It led as well to the development of a distinctive church culture. "This modern Roman Catholicism took the form of

---

16. Dillenberger and Welch, *Protestant Christianity*, 243–45. "The social gospel was a new application of the Christian ethic in response to the demands of a new historical situation. Conscience had to become 'social conscience.'" Ibid., 245. For coherent, insightful retrievals of the social gospel movement see William D. Lindsey, *Shailer Mathews's Lives of Jesus: The Search for a Theological Foundation for the Social Gospel* (Albany: State University of New York Press, 1997), and Darlene Ann Peitz, *Solidarity as Hermeneutic: A Revisionist Reading of the Theology of Walter Rauschenbusch* (New York: P. Lang, 1992).

17. See Roger Haight, "The Mission of the Church in the Theology of the Social Gospel," *Theological Studies* 49 (1988): 477–97.

18. Dillenberger and Welch, *Protestant Christianity*, 248.

19. Ibid., 254.

a counter-society, legitimated by a counter-culture, as a response to and in opposition to the emerging liberal culture and society which advanced with such apparent inexorability throughout those years."[20] It is not a Tridentine form, but new. A series of marks, qualities, and social behaviors will illustrate its character.

First of all, this church form defined itself against a variety of enemies. One was a spirit and movement of rationalism which directly attacked the faith and the church: "a self-proclaimed independence or autonomy believed to be enshrined in Luther's private judgment and in Kant's definition of Enlightenment" (358). It reacted against social differentiation of competencies, especially the separation of church and state. It is important to recognize how threatening this separation appeared to those used to the coincidence of church, society, and state. It was hostile to the paradigm of progress and organic development and had an apocalyptic view of a history run by the contrary forces of God and Satan.

Second and more positively, it idealized the Christendom of the Middle Ages where church and society were merged for the common good. The mind-set was restorationist and looked backward with nostalgia. Religious life was nourished by a vibrant set of devotional practices directed to Mary and Christ that offset political and social setbacks with supernatural patronage.

Third, on the social level the church created a set of Catholic associations which together provided a counterculture that protected Catholics from the contagion of modernity. "The new Catholic associations were at first grass-roots movements, almost always originating from below and often in response to threats to Catholic beliefs, values or liberties represented by advancing liberalism and/or anti-clericalism" (369). But a positive channeling of Catholic energy cannot be separated from the protective function of these associations: "The associations also had the purpose of promoting social contacts among Catholics, in the hope that they could thus be kept from infection by liberal ideas and sentiments" (371).

---

20. Joseph A. Komonchak, "Modernity and the Construction of Roman Catholicism," *Cristianesimo nella Storia* 18 (1997): 356. The following account of Catholicism in this period for the most part synopsizes this work and references in the text in this section are to pages of this careful study.

Fourth, on the ecclesial level authority was centralized: "One of the distinctive characteristics of the history of Catholicism in the nineteenth century was the increased centralization of Catholic life upon Rome and the figure of the pope" (371). During this period the pope gained the right to appoint bishops in France, and this became a pattern. But as the nations of Europe became more religiously secular, papal authority, originally sought as a political balance, was turned inward to become central control of the church itself. Vatican I and papal infallibility provided a symbol with considerable social power to define a kind of self-enclosed church.

Fifth, this control reached into intellectual life. It was exercised through the encyclical, textbooks in seminaries, and the standardization of the medieval synthesis into an integrist ideal. "Pius IX asserted that it was the role of ecclesiastical authority not only to oversee but also to direct theological developments" (374).

Finally, this church form stood in opposition to the world: the spirit of this Roman Catholic subculture was self-enclosed and hostile to the reigning cultural and political and economic spirit. But it was not passive, uninvolved, or privatistic. Leo XIII's *Rerum novarum* reflects a church which is aggressively countercultural and engaged in society.

This culture was shared by the whole church, analogously in each country, with a common hostility to the world: "a single interpretation of the challenge of modernity was everywhere considered to be applicable and normative by a Roman authority whose increasing control over local church life was itself a major element in the Catholic response to the challenge of modernity" (379).

In the United States the Catholic Church developed its own distinct version of the social gospel that ran parallel with the Protestant churches.[21] It emerged through the following stages. First, the

---

21. Paul Misner, *Social Catholicism in Europe: From the Onset of Industrialization to the First World War* (New York: Crossroad, 1991), tells the story of Catholic involvement in society in Europe. John T. McGreevy, *Catholicism and American Freedom* (New York: W. W. Norton, 2003), analyzes the interaction between Catholicism and Liberal Democracy in the United States from 1850 onward. The history of the Catholic social gospel movement in the United States is analyzed by Jay P. Dolan, *The American Catholic Experience: A History from Colonial Times to the Present* (Garden City, N.Y.: Doubleday, 1985), 321–46. The stages deployed here are drawn from his

working poor in industrial centers were largely Catholics who joined unions during the period of labor strife making the Catholic constituency largely loyal to the unions. A case in point were the Knights of Labor which reached its peak in the 1880s. Yet much of the clergy remained hostile to the unions for fear of socialism, or a commitment to the principle of private property, or reaction to a certain competitive religious aura of the union.[22] Second, a number of social activists, either priests or bishops, led the way in a progressive and socially liberal advocacy of labor and social reform. The most famous example is Father Edward McGlynn, an outspoken and politically engaged priest of the archdiocese of New York. Third, although the publication of *Rerum Novarum* did not immediately change Catholic social consciousness, still it authorized unionism, the rights of workers, and the social engagement of the church. Fourth, the progressive spirit of reform in the country during the course of the first two decades of the twentieth century gradually opened up Catholic consciousness. Finally, in the year 1919, the Catholic bishops of the United States published the "Bishops' Program of Social Reconstruction" which was the most "forward-looking social document ever to have come from an official Catholic agency in the United States."[23]

Theology

Theology as a discipline underwent extraordinary developments during the course of the nineteenth century up to the first world war. The two theologians studied in this chapter contributed significantly to that development in the early part of the century so that in some respects what follows them includes reactions to or the history of the effects of their thought. Although the brief space allotted to this history can contain little more than commentary on a list of names, we cannot do without it. The interpretation of the thought of these

account. It should be noted that parishes responded to poverty in a concrete or micro level of direct action. During this period some of the most basic parish agencies, like the St. Vincent de Paul Societies, were formed in each parish to help the poor, hungry, and sick.

22. This became a public debate within the church and finally the Vatican ruled that Catholics could belong to the Knights of Labor in 1888. Dolan, *American Catholic Experience,* 332–33.

23. Dolan, *American Catholic Experience,* 344.

theologians that follows is set within the perspective of its relevance for the self-understanding of the church.

Protestant theology. Christian theology in the period of the Enlightenment has been characterized as rationalist in spirit, scholastic in form, and moralistic in intent.[24] The philosophy and philosophy of religion of Immanuel Kant provided a kind of bridge connecting the outburst of Romantic creativity in theology with what had gone before. Kant undermined an objectivist ascent to God, solidified a turn to the subject, established philosophy as critical transcendental analysis, paradoxically established a rational basis for faith and even fideism in practical reason, and tied religion closely to morality. One can chart the developments in theology during the course of the nineteenth century with reference to the Kantian legacy.[25]

Friedrich Schleiermacher, whose ecclesiology will be analyzed at length, studied Kant seriously, drew deeply from him, and rejected some of his most basic contentions. Schleiermacher stands at the head of much of nineteenth-century Protestant theology. His ecclesiology represents a genuinely new understanding of the church when compared with the sixteenth century.[26] Hegel, Schleiermacher's contemporary in Berlin, also had a major influence on theology and ecclesiology, less in terms of a formal understanding of the church, and more in terms of situating the understanding of the church into a historicist framework. Thinkers like Ferdinand Christian Baur on Christian origins and the dynamics of the development of the church, and David Friedrich Strauss on Jesus placed the understanding of the church within a Hegelian framework of the dialectics of history and the context of a critical appreciation of faith and knowledge. Albrect Ritschl, drawing his inspiration from Kant, Schleiermacher,

---

24. Dillenberger and Welch, *Protestant Christianity*, 155.

25. Human thought, eminent philosophers and theologians, emerge out of history, that is, contemporary societies and cultures with their crises, dilemmas, languages, and applications. Linking these theologians diachronically does not, finally, explain their thought, but neither is it irrelevant.

26. Schleiermacher's "*Glaubenslehre* is dogmatics for a new age, not only by reason of its affinity with the subjective and historical turn in modern thinking, but also because it fully accepts the obligation to adjust its formulas to the current state of knowledge." Brian A. Gerrish, "Friedrich Schleiermacher," *Nineteenth Century Religious Thought in the West*, I, ed. Ninian Smart et al. (Cambridge: Cambridge University Press, 1985), 134.

and philosophers of value, proposed a theology-cum-ecclesiology of the kingdom of God that inserted the church squarely into the dynamics of social history.[27] Adolf von Harnack and August Sabatier provide two examples of liberal theology at the end of its run through the nineteenth century. Harnack's classic history of dogma and his widely read *The Essence of Christianity* relativize the structures of the church.[28] And Sabatier's views on religious authority seem to undermine prophetic discourse on the part of the institutional church.[29]

Some common themes or characteristics that embrace what was going on in nineteenth-century Protestant theology help to define a new post-Enlightenment framework for ecclesiology. The first and perhaps broadest move is the turn to the subject as a basis and source for theology. Although anthropology never assumes the role of an exclusive source, it provides a hermeneutical premise for interpreting scripture and the tradition of church confessions. The structure of theology, its fundamental method, has shifted.

Second, premises and assumptions from the Romantic reaction against Enlightenment thought become operative in theological reasoning and argument. Thinkers begin to regard human imagination as an epistemological resource that can go where pure reason cannot. Large metaphors such as organicity and growth become ways of understanding reality on a macro or cosmic level. Development is more than one thing after another; an optimistic attitude toward historical process reads teleology and even progress in the development.

It would be difficult to overemphasize the use of the metaphor of an organism and organic growth to understand the church in the Romantic period. "Organic models of history employ root metaphors taken from organic processes in order to understand historical experience."[30] Thus the history of Christianity and particularly the church

---

27. Albrecht Ritschl, *The Christian Doctrine of Justification and Reconciliation: Positive Development of the Doctrine* (Edinburgh: T & T Clark, 1900).

28. Adolf von Harnack, *What is Christianity?* (Philadelphia: Fortress Press, 1986).

29. Auguste Sabatier, *Outlines of a Philosophy of Religion Based on Psychology and History* (New York: Harper, 1957).

30. Bradford E. Hinze, *Narrating History, Developing Doctrine: Friedrich Schleiermacher and Johann Sebastian Drey* (Atlanta: Scholars Press, 1993), 9. The following

"should be understood as an organic process, since the church (as the kingdom of God on earth) is an organic community and because its organizing ideas (such as the kingdom of God) develop organically" (64). Some of the features of this image include construing Jesus and his teachings at the beginnings as a kind of seed for later developments. Thus an organic understanding allows for a constant unity and identity despite historical changes (66). The living character of organic unity allows for newness, change, as it interacts with what is outside itself over time; it retains identity as it adapts to its environment (67). It integrates biblical images such as the kingdom of God and the body of Christ. A living organism also holds together multiplicity in a unity: "each individual historical part — person, event, community, nation — has its own integrity as a part and each part must also be viewed as a reflection of a larger whole" (70). Finally, the metaphor of an organism leaves room for disease and thus a dialectic of critique and reform or return to health.

Third, when one fits the church into this broad scheme of history, it becomes intimately involved in historical process as a moral agent. This is less true of Schleiermacher who explicitly refused any reduction of Christian faith to morality. But in the ecclesiology of Kant, Ritschl, and Harnack the church is closely associated with corporate moral agency in history. Those who reacted against "liberal" theology unfairly read this theme as a flat-out reduction or collapse of religion into morality. A fairer appraisal would read it as a reaction against individualism.

Finally, when compared with the segment of the church whose concerns were more focused on preserving either orthodox doctrines or an affective evangelical piety, these theological developments would appear weak or compromising. From the perspective of Karl Barth's interpretation of Paul's Letter to the Romans, liberal theology appeared relatively thin in its appreciation of scriptural or ecclesial authority and the classical doctrines. Adjudicating this is one of the tasks of the twentieth century.

---

characterization of a social-organic understanding of the church drawn from Hinze, 62–76 refers to Schleiermacher.

Catholic theology. Thomas O'Meara characterizes Catholic theology of the Enlightenment as a textbook theology mediated through the metaphysical categories of Aristotle. It consisted in positive data collected from the tradition of the church, and expositions of doctrines through definitions, divisions of material, and elaborations in scholastic language. When the philosophy of Kant appeared, Catholic theologians attended to it and then shifted their interest to foundational questions of faith and reason and the epistemology of both. As scholasticism declined, and Protestant theology through Schleiermacher built on the Kantian turn to the subject and faith, Catholic theology found inspiration in Schelling's objective idealism as more congenial to the contemplative and sacramental imagination.[31]

Nineteenth-century Catholic theology did not follow the same route as Protestant theology; the Roman Church was not as pluralistic and, as a single institutional church, had an authority structure that became increasingly controlling after the restoration of the political order in Europe. A string of important theologians of the century might begin with Johann Sebastian Drey, founder of the Catholic Tübingen school of theologians. In the discipline of ecclesiology his most famous student and disciple was Johann Adam Möhler, whose early ecclesiology will be analyzed in detail. Although not as elaborated, his earliest ecclesiology runs along a track broadly parallel with Schleiermacher's. Among other things, Möhler proposed an organic, communitarian theory of tradition and development.[32]

But the creative period in Catholic theology which began in Tübingen was overshadowed by the Roman school of theology, especially its ecclesiologists who reigned from the period prior to

---

31. Thomas Franklin O'Meara, *Romantic Idealism and Roman Catholicism: Schelling and the Theologians* (Notre Dame, Ind.: University of Notre Dame Press, 1982), 65–68.

32. The problem of the development of dogma became a major issue in Catholic theology right up to the Second Vatican Council. How could a dogma develop? What is the structure of dogma that could allow such a development? These questions which were handled spontaneously in Möhler's thought became problematic thereafter. For example, John Henry Newman addressed the issue with his famous *An Essay on the Development of Christian Doctrine* (London: James Toovey, 1845). These theories provided a way in which theology could address historicity and gain some nuance in religious epistemology. See Mark Schoof, *A Survey of Catholic Theology: 1800–1970* (New York: Paulist Newman Press, 1970).

Vatican I right up to Vatican II.[33] Giovanni Perrone began teaching at the Roman College when it was given to the restored Jesuits in 1824. He begins a long line of teachers of the scholastic tract, *De Ecclesia,* which stretched well into the twentieth century: Carlo Passaglia, Clemens Schrader, John Baptist Franzelin, Domenico Palmieri, Camillo Mazzella, Louis Billot, Timotheus Zapelena. This scholastic ecclesiology closely reflected the increasing centralization of the authority of the church in the papacy.[34] Needless to say, the doctrine of the papacy and the infallibility of the pope commanded attention. Catholic scholastic thought received a boost when Leo XIII proclaimed a return of Catholic theology to Thomas Aquinas as its classical expression in *Aeterni Patris* of 1879 because it stimulated historical study of Aquinas. But historical retrieval was superceded by the exercise of authority against the modernist movement.[35]

In 1864 Pius IX condemned modern culture in the encyclical *Quanta Cura* and the "Syllabus of Errors." And in 1870 he presided at the First Vatican Council in which the infallibility of the pope was solemnly defined. The doctrine of infallibility of the pope had more symbolic power than programmatic efficacy: it was only explicitly invoked once after its definition. But it supplied an aura to the ordinary jurisdiction of the pope which included total direct power over every member of the church. The ecclesiology was not so much changed structurally as tightened into a knot of absolute authority. The power

---

33. See Yves Congar, *L'Eglise: De Saint Augustin à l'époque moderne* (Paris: Editions du Cerf, 1970), 428–35. T. Howland Sanks studies the ecclesiology of this protracted school longitudinally through the lens of church authority and its exercise in *Authority in the Church: A Study in Changing Paradigms* (Missoula, Mont.: The American Academy of Religion, 1974).

34. Gerald McCool analyzes the theology of Joseph Kleutgen, perhaps the leading representative of the Roman School in the mid-nineteenth century, as follows: theology was an Aristotelian science of the doctrines which were the object of faith. History provided the positive data of these beliefs, but history or historicity was not an intrinsic constituent of theology itself. Kleutgen had no sense of conceptual development and was blind to the plurality of conceptual frameworks for understanding. Theology was a unified discipline, and the scholastic form was its classical expression. *Catholic Theology in the Nineteenth Century* (New York: Seabury, 1977), 187.

35. Gabriel Daly, *Transcendence and Immanence: A Study in Catholic Modernism and Integralism* (New York: Oxford University Press, 1980), describes the striking contrast between the scholastic theology at the end of the nineteenth century and the presuppositions and methods employed by modernist thinkers. Daly's work is a thorough introduction to the theology of the movement.

of this authority was demonstrated in the fact that it completely knocked out the modernist movement with two blows, one ideological, the other programmatic.[36] The theological stroke consisted in another syllabus of errors entitled *"Lamentabili"* and the encyclical *Pascendi Dominici Gregis* of Pius X in 1907. They constructed and then condemned the heresy of modernism from the writings of theologians and exegetes. The practical exercise of authority consisted in setting up committees in every diocese charged with investigating and rooting out professors suspected of harboring or teaching modernist ideas. The condemnation of modernism thus mediated a dogmatic kind of fundamentalism and an enveloping authoritarianism that made critical thought during the twentieth century right up to Vatican II difficult and dangerous. Theology's mainstream lapsed into a predominantly centrally controlled textbook discipline.

If one limits one's consideration of nineteenth-century Roman Catholic ecclesiology to a consideration of the early Tübingen school and the emergence of the Roman school one sees a sharp contrast, a kind of reversal of direction from expansive learning in the Romantic age to a frightened introversion protective against modernity. The Tübingen school shared many of the qualities seen in nineteenth-century Protestant theology, and the analysis of Möhler's ecclesiology will show the degree to which his first extensive essay shares themes with Schleiermacher. But just as clearly the ecclesiology of the Roman school, which came to dominate the century mirrors the structure of the ecclesial consciousness of the leadership in Rome. An ecclesiology of a community becomes transformed into an ecclesiology of an integrist institution. The authority to which neo-orthodox theologians and even fundamentalists appealed against liberal theology was located in scripture; the authority which ultimately suppressed the modernist movement was the objective authority of a religious institution.

---

36. The modernist movement in the Roman Church tried to adjust Catholic teaching to modernity in the light of contemporary historical studies and philosophy; it flourished in France and England, also in Italy, and to some extent in the United States, and had allies in German liberal thought.

THE ECCLESIOLOGY
OF SCHLEIERMACHER

After this overview of the Western church during the nineteenth century *à vol d'oiseau,* we take up the more pointed subject matter of the chapter, the ecclesiologies of Schleiermacher and Möhler. As in earlier cases, these understandings of the church rose up out of history as it was filtered through the particular lives of these authors. It is imperative, therefore, to say something, however schematic it must be, about the life and vision of Schleiermacher. The influences on his formation and early intellectual work and particularly the structure of his dogmatic synthesis will help to situate his ecclesiology.[37]

Friedrich Schleiermacher

Schleiermacher was born in November of 1768. His father was a Reformed pastor who had encountered and been deeply influenced by the Moravian Brethren, and he enrolled his son in a Moravian school when he was still fourteen. The affective Jesus-centered piety of the Moravians made a deep impression on Schleiermacher over the course of his two years of residency. In 1785 Schleiermacher moved to a theological college or seminary of the Brethren. But in the end, his critical questioning and doubts regarding orthodox conceptions of the doctrines forced him to leave the seminary in 1787, and he took up studies at Halle University. Schleiermacher had already begun to

---

37. The following works have been helpful in situating and interpreting Schleiermacher's thought: Karl Barth, "Schleiermacher," *Protestant Theology in the Nineteenth Century: Its Background and History* (Valley Forge, Pa.: Judson Press, 1973), 425–73; James Duke and Francis Fiorenza, "Translators' Introduction," Friedrich D. E. Schleiermacher, *On the Glaubenslehre* (Chico, Calif.: Scholars Press, 1981); Jack Forstman, *A Romantic Triangle: Schleiermacher and Early German Romanticism* (Missoula, Mont.: Scholars Press, 1977); Brian A. Gerrish,. "Continuity and Change: Friedrich Schleiermacher on the Task of Theology," *Tradition and the Modern World: Reformed Theology in the Nineteenth Century* (Chicago: University of Chicago Press, 1977), 13–48; "Friedrich Schleiermacher," *Nineteenth Century Religious Thought,* 123–56; "From Calvin to Schleiermacher: The Theme and the Shape of Christian Dogmatics," *Continuing the Reformation: Essays on Modern Religious Thought* (Chicago: University of Chicago Press, 1993), 178–95; Thomas M. Kelly, "Schleiermacher and the Turn to the Subject," *Theology at the Void: The Retrieval of Experience* (Notre Dame, Ind.: University of Notre Dame Press, 2002), 11–49; Martin Redeker, *Schleiermacher: Life and Thought* (Philadelphia: Fortress Press, 1973); Stephen Sykes, *Friedrich Schleiermacher* (Richmond: John Knox Press, 1971).

read Kant in the seminary; at Halle he internalized Kant's work and studied as well classical Greek philosophy. After two years of courses and a period of private study Schleiermacher took his first theological examinations of the Reformed Church in 1790. For the next three years he acted as a tutor in the home of a wealthy family in Prussia.

The next major phase of Schleiermacher's life began with his assumption of the post of pastor at the Charité Hospital in Berlin in 1796. Prior to that he had taken his second theology examination in 1794, was ordained, and served as assistant pastor in a Reformed congregation for two years. Once in Berlin Schleiermacher entered the intellectual world of Friedrich Schlegel and the circle of literary and philosophical figures leading the way in the Romantic movement.[38] It was at the urging of his Romantic friends that Schleiermacher wrote and published in 1799 his *Speeches on Religion to Its Cultured Despisers*.[39] This work has a classic apologetic structure of appealing to those disaffected with Christianity by showing it to be the fulfillment of the very human ideals they espoused. To do this he used a Romantic style of writing and appealed to intuition, feeling, experience, imagination, nature, the infinite, the mystical, the "whole" to render Christianity intelligible and salvific: behind the objective language and institution lies the inner reality of religion which fulfills human aspirations, and its highest form is Christianity.[40]

Schleiermacher left Berlin in 1802 to take up ministry; in 1804 he went to the University of Halle as a lecturer and university preacher; and in 1806 he returned to Berlin. He was married in 1809 in the same month that he became minister at Trinity Church in Berlin,

---

38. This relationship is studied by Forstman, *A Romantic Triangle.* Schlegel and Schleiermacher became good friends and for several months in 1798 shared an apartment. Redeker, *Schleiermacher*, 30.

39. Friedrich Schleiermacher, *On Religion: Speeches to Its Cultured Despisers*, ed. and trans. Richard Crouter (New York: Cambridge University Press, 1988). Throughout the period that Schleiermacher was in Berlin and connected with the Romantic circle, he "was preaching regularly to an ordinary congregation in the Hospital chapel; what is more, he took his duties with great seriousness." Sykes, *Schleiermacher*, 8.

40. Redeker notes Schleiermacher's conception of the church in this early period: "the church is not an institution, not a structure for salvation in the traditional sense; above all it is not a hierarchical institution with sacral-magical authority. The church is rather a community arising from within the religious life as a completely free spiritual communion of truly pious men." *Schleiermacher*, 51.

and when the University of Berlin opened in 1810 "Schleiermacher was nominated Professor of Theology and first Dean of the Faculty."[41]

The *Speeches* of 1799 contain strata in Schleiermacher's formation that contribute to the definition of his mature theology. He had a love of philosophy, classical and modern, and his theology is mediated with philosophical categories. With Kant he had made the turn to the subject, but his phenomenology of the religious subject differed from that of Kant. Schleiermacher located contact with God in neither the intellect nor the will, but in "intuition" or "feeling." As he himself experienced with the Moravians, the human subject was inherently religious, and through philosophical analysis he established a philosophical basis for it. From the Romantics he borrowed language that distanced his transcendental analysis of religious experience away from the rationalism of the Enlightenment and joined it to the new optimistic humanism developing in the early nineteenth century.

Schleiermacher's master work, *The Christian Faith*, provides the source from which the ecclesiology which follows is drawn.[42] The first edition was published in 1821–22 and a second edition, including responses to criticisms, was published in 1830–31. Schleiermacher's ecclesiology is not free-floating; it was constructed as an integral part of his holistic understanding of the Christian religion. Moreover the method and form of this systematic dogmatics in no small part influence his understanding of the church.[43] As a consequence one should have at least a broad structural understanding of his theology to appreciate the ecclesiology within it. The following seven points are intended to lead into Schleiermacher's theological vision of Christian faith.

---

41. Sykes, *Schleiermacher*, 12.

42. Friedrich Schleiermacher, *The Christian Faith*, ed. H. R. Mackintosh and J. S. Stewart (New York: Harper & Row, 1963). This work will be cited as CF in the text by paragraph number and page.

43. And, vice versa, his views of the church influenced his dogmatics. For example, Schleiermacher supported the unified church set up by King Friedrich Wilhelm III in 1817, and he described his dogmatics as "composed with special reference to the Union of the two Protestant communions-the Lutheran and the Reformed" (CF, Preface to the Second Edition, xxiv; see Redeker, *Schleiermacher*, 187–93). In general, however, Schleiermacher did not favor unification based on legislation.

First, the basis of religion for Schleiermacher is religious self-consciousness or experience. Schleiermacher's terms for this experience, "piety" and "the feeling of absolute dependence," are technical categories carefully constructed through transcendental analysis that establishes religious experience as both inherently human or universal and realist in the sense that it is consciousness of a real relationship with God. This religious consciousness or piety is "immediate" in the sense of prereflective and thus prior to intentional acts of knowing and willing which reflect on it or react to its object.[44]

Second, however, this primal transcendental experience always and only comes to explicit consciousness in a mediated form; that is, it always becomes conscious through particular historical media. God-consciousness has its roots in a deep, primal consciousness of absolute dependence, but only comes to explicit reflective awareness together with a differentiated self-consciousness and world-consciousness. In other words, the experience of absolute dependence is not "an" isolatable experience but a dimension of experiences.[45]

Third, Jesus Christ is the historical source of the specific or distinct Christian religious experience. Historically, Christianity as an autonomous religion traces itself back to Jesus of Nazareth as its particular origin. Moving from Jesus, the Christian community, the church, has its foundations in Jesus as the source of Christian religious experience and is the community which carries this specific religious experience forward in history.

Fourth, Christian theology is reflection upon the distinctively Christian religious experience and as such has an ecclesial, descriptive, and historical character. "It is ecclesial in that it is rooted in the

---

44. For a neat unpacking of the layers of Schleiermacher's analysis of religious consciousness see Duke and Fiorenza, "Introduction," *On the Glaubenslehre*, 10–21.

45. The threefold differentiation of religious consciousness means that the doctrines of Christian faith can be interpreted in three ways: "as description of human states [self-consciousness], or as conceptions of divine attributes and modes of action [God-consciousness], or as utterances regarding the constitution of the world [world-consciousness]...." (CF, #30, 125). Ultimately, the second two are dependent upon the first, religious affections themselves. Schleiermacher uses this threefold structure of religious consciousness to create subdivisions of each of the major sections of his dogmatics.

Christian religious self-consciousness and is undertaken in the service of the church. It is descriptive in that it is to display in precise and coherent manner the content of Christian teaching. It is historical in that it must express that content in a form appropriate to the situation in which the church finds itself."[46]

Fifth, the structure of Schleiermacher's dogmatics after the extensive introduction has two major divisions, the second of which is divided again into two. The first large division finds its roots in the structure of Christian God-consciousness or feeling of absolute dependence: on the one hand, a dimension of Christian God-consciousness is common with that of all people; it is constitutive of the human as such. On the other hand, the specific element in Christian consciousness is the antithesis between resistance to or alienation from this God-consciousness and spontaneously accepting and living within it. This is the antithesis between sin and grace: sin is the absence, though never total, of God-consciousness which grace or God-consciousness fills. Correspondingly, the first part of the dogmatics deals with a broader common dimension of God-consciousness from which are drawn the doctrines of creation, the qualities predicated of God, and the world. The second major division or part of the dogmatics deals with sin and grace, and this is where specifically Christian theology begins. Sin is a universal condition, and the understanding of human existence in sin has corresponding implications for the doctrine of God as well. But grace or redemption overcomes sin, and this antithesis of sin and grace defines the essence of the specifically Christian experience of God-consciousness.[47]

In Schleiermacher's dogmatics, the explication of the Christian experience of grace is itself subdivided into two constitutive parts on

---

46. Duke and Fiorenza, "Introduction," *On the Glaubenslehre,* 3. "The theologian must therefore relate the consciousness of God distinctive to the Christian community, the stock of inherited statements expressive of that consciousness, and the patterns of thought current in the present age." Ibid.

47. Schleiermacher's dogmatics does not reduce Christianity to religion. The center of the dogmatics is not the introduction or the first part, but the second and specifically Christian part. Jesus Christ, therefore, is not an external occasion which awakens a generic experience of absolute dependence, and Christian doctrines are not reflections on a generic experience of absolute dependence. Rather Christian theology and doctrines are "reflections upon the distinctively Christian experience of redemption by Christ." Gerrish, "Continuity and Change," 38.

Jesus Christ and the church. The doctrine of Jesus Christ reflects on the Christian community's experience of his person and his redeeming activity as the source of the experience of grace. The doctrine of the church refers to the community which historically mediates the experience of Jesus Christ in history and thus is intimately connected with Schleiermacher's christology and theory of salvation.

Sixth, Schleiermacher's christology possesses a subtlety that is inevitably betrayed by short formulas. Given that caution, one might generalize in this way: Jesus of Nazareth is the Christ because, as the bearer of perfect God-consciousness, God was fully present and active within him during his earthly life. By communicating his God-consciousness historically to his disciples, and thus beginning the phylum of Christian God-consciousness, Jesus Christ remains active in history as the cause of Christian salvation.

Finally, then, and at this stage roughly, the church is the community of those who are saved by Jesus Christ because they actually experience Christ's salvation through the mediation of the church and by membership in it. Thus the doctrines of Jesus Christ and the church together fill out the Christian doctrine of salvation and grace.

This broad, sweeping introduction to Schleiermacher's ecclesiology is unavoidably dense. But it should at least succeed in showing that Schleiermacher was beginning a new thing in Christian theology. This constellation of method and content in turn led to a genuinely new understanding of the church.

The Ecclesiology of Schleiermacher

The ecclesiology of Schleiermacher occupies a substantial portion of his systematic theology. This condensed account of his ecclesiology will show how the church forms an integral part of his understanding of the very meaning of Christianity. It is not an appendix to his christology; Christian faith and salvation are intrinsically social phenomena. The order of Schleiermacher's discussion to some extent follows the pattern that has been used throughout this book.[48]

---

48. Brief accounts of Schleiermacher's ecclesiology can be found in Emilio Brito, "Pneumatologie, Ecclésiologie et Ethique Théologique chez Schleiermacher," *Revue des Sciences Philosophiques et Théologiques* 77 (1993): 23–51; Dennis M. Doyle, *Communion Ecclesiology: Vision and Versions* (Maryknoll, N.Y.: Orbis Books, 2000), 23–37;

Understanding the nature of the church. Just as Schleiermacher's ecclesiology forms an integral part of his christology and redemption theory, these doctrines provide the fundamental theological framework for understanding the church. The church mediates Christ's salvation in history. He specifies this understanding further with a general definition of the church, a schematic account of its historical origin, a theology of its origin, and the key theological construal of Christ and the Spirit as the foundation of the church.

Schleiermacher first defines the great church as the fellowship of believers; in it are all those who are regenerate, so that no one who has been converted to Jesus Christ is outside it. This whole church, however, has two degrees of membership, an inner fellowship and an outer fellowship: "the totality of those who live in the state of sanctification is the inner fellowship; the totality of those on whom preparatory grace is at work is the outer fellowship, from which by regeneration members pass to the inner, and then keep helping to extend the wider circle" (CF, #113, 525). This first definition of the church has no particular form of fellowship defining it: "every form, perfect and imperfect, that has ever been or that may yet appear, is included" (CF, #113, 525). The influence of Christ on the regenerate spontaneously elicits a fellowship: "no redeeming work can take effect on individuals without a fellowship arising." And the character of the organization has its norm partly in "the influence of Christ on individuals who thus become His instruments, and partly by His peculiar dignity, which is to be manifested in this organization over against the world" (CF, #113, 526).

Origin of the church. Historically and sociologically the church began with the historical appearance of Jesus.[49] The whole life of the expansive Christian community has a single historical point of origin

---

Eric G. Jay, *The Church: Its Changing Image through Twenty Centuries* (Atlanta: John Knox Press, 1980), 238–51; Trutz Rendtorff, *Church and Theology: The Systematic Function of the Church Concept in Modern Theology* (Philadelphia: Westminster Press, 1971), 110–60.

49. The Christian church properly so called is not part of a larger whole, and one should not say that the church existed from the beginning of the human race and remains the same to the end (CF, #156, 692). For Schleiermacher the church "only began with the personal action of Christ" (CF, #156, 693), so that faith in Christ is constitutive of the church; it is a thoroughly historical understanding of the church.

in the person of Jesus Christ. As people gathered around Jesus, one can say that he alone was the inner circle, and those attracted to his message formed the outer circle. As persons are converted to faith in and through the influence of Jesus Christ, they enter the inner circle or inner fellowship; they then begin to exercise influence on others, those in the world, or in the outer circle, and with their conversion the inner fellowship expands. Thus the church expands outward into history and the world.[50] This represents a historical sociological account of the origin of the church: a group formed around Jesus and then solidified in mutual interaction and cooperation; it mediated influence on others drawing them into the outer circle and then into the inner circle (CF, #115, 532–33).

To account for the church theologically Schleiermacher has recourse to two doctrines: election and the communication of the Holy Spirit. The doctrine of election addresses the origin of the church by looking backward and asking how it came to pass that some rather than others were called to the outer circle of the church and elected into the inner circle of faith and regeneration from out of the world.[51] The doctrine of the communication of the Spirit provides the ultimate principle of the unity of the church, fashioning a community into a divine organic reality: "the expression 'Holy Spirit' must be understood to mean the vital unity of the Christian fellowship as

---

50. "The Christian fellowship gradually expands as individuals and masses are incorporated into association with Christ. The general fact has been established that the new life of the individual arises out of the common life within the outer circle of which it lies. And this holds good also of the new life of the first disciples, when as yet the power of the inner circle was entirely confined to Christ. The origin of the Christian Church is thus the same thing as happens daily before our eyes." CF, #114, 529.

51. Under election Schleiermacher also discusses whether salvation is possible outside the church and responds affirmatively on the basis of Christ being sent for all. It follows then that, "if all in this fashion are included in the divine fore-ordination to blessedness, then the high-priestly dignity of Christ for the first time comes out in its whole efficacy — an efficacy which implies that God regards all men only in Christ." Thus, "if we take the universality of redemption in its whole range, ... then we must also take fore-ordination to blessedness quite universally; and ... limits can be imposed on neither without curtailing the other" (CF, #120, 560). In an analogy with Abraham's faith and obedience which was reckoned for his righteousness because of its effect on future faith in Christ, "we may also accept justification for Christ's sake before Christ, analogous to blessedness in sympathy with the future; and thus [we may also accept] scattered rudiments of the church, although not the Church itself." CF, #156, 695.

a moral personality; and this, since everything strictly legal has already been excluded, we might denote by the phrase, its *common spirit.* Accordingly, it should not really be necessary again to give the explicit assurance that by the phrase we mean to describe exactly what even in Scripture is called the Holy Spirit and the Spirit of God and the Spirit of Christ, and in our Church doctrine is also presented as the third Person in the Godhead" (CF, #116, 535). In other words, God continually constitutes the church as an inner sustaining force.

The Spirit and Christ. The key to Schleiermacher's theology of the church, however, lies in the connection between the constitutive formational role of the Spirit in the church and Jesus Christ. From the very beginning, the experience of the Spirit in the community of disciples was recognized as the Spirit of Christ. He explains how "after Christ's departure the disciples' common apprehension of Christ changed into a spontaneous prolongation of His fellowship-forming activity, and how it was only through this activity so related to the fixed apprehension of Christ becoming the imperishable common spirit, that the Christian Church arose" (CF, #122, 568–69). This statement combines historical realism and theological construction. It describes a passage from direct connection and dependence upon Jesus, to Jesus being mediated through the community. Thus the community becomes a more autonomous and spontaneous agent to preserving Jesus' God-consciousness, and the Spirit becomes the divine source of continuity and energy and solidarity of the community. The memory of Jesus is translated into imitation of him; this common activity is in each and in all and in each through the community; and this community or common life preserves the personal activity of Jesus Christ in history, and constitutes the common spirit of the Christian church (CF, #122, 568).[52] Thus when

---

52. Schleiermacher writes that the common identity of the church is one "because it all derived from one and the same source, namely, Christ; for everyone is conscious of the communication of the Spirit as being connected in the closest fashion with the rise of faith in him, and everyone recognizes that the same is true for all the others. For faith only comes by preaching, and preaching always goes back to Christ's commission and is therefore derived from Him. And as in Christ Himself everything proceeds from the Divine within Him, so also does this communication, which becomes in everyone

Schleiermacher defines the Holy Spirit with reference to the church,[53] he also makes precise the connection of the Spirit with Christ. The meaning of Spirit in the context of the church is not the Spirit as operative in creation, or in charismatic figures, or in the prophets, or even in the annunciation narrative.[54] Rather the meaning of Spirit in ecclesiology is bound to Christ so that the powers or effects of the Spirit within the Christian church are these: first, the Spirit in this sense is not found operative outside the church but is explicitly connected with Jesus Christ. Second, the Spirit is not an Arian Spirit, less than God, but God at work in the community. Third, the Spirit does not come from the outside as from the world, but operates within the human person. This follows the New Testament which describes the Holy Spirit as "a specific divine efficacious working in believers, though not one to be separated from the recognition of the being of God in Christ. The two things are strictly interdependent" (CF, #123, 570–72).[55]

Schleiermacher's theological understanding of the church can be synthesized in a series of direct propositions that barely contain this sweeping view: humankind is caught in the tentacles of sin which strangle consciousness of, and existence in relation to, God. Jesus Christ is a unique divine communication from outside the sphere of sin. Christ mediates redemption to this situation by communicating his God-consciousness through the church. Membership in the

---

the power of the new life, a power not different in each, but the same in all." CF, #121, 563–64.

53. "The Holy Spirit is the union of the Divine Essence with human nature in the form of the common Spirit animating the life in common of believers." CF, #123, 569.

54. The point of this distinction is not to deny the significance of these references relative to the Spirit, but to insist that in ecclesiology the Spirit is exclusively linked with Christic God-consciousness. Whereas the Spirit of God may be universally active, in the church the Spirit is always tied to Christ and Christian God-consciousness. The Christian church is a positive historical phenomenon.

55. "To recognize in our souls any leading of the divine Spirit which could not be brought into connexion with what Christ's words and life have conveyed to us as His way of acting, is to open the door to every sort of visionary fanaticism . . ." (CF, #124, 576). The point then for Schleiermacher is that *this* Spirit of God proceeds from Jesus Christ; it is not God as Spirit that descends miraculously on anyone or anywhere or can be claimed outside the church, but precisely the Spirit tied to Jesus Christ. CF, #123, 572.

church is defined by being set within the historical sphere of the influence of Jesus Christ. The experience of the Spirit and the influence of Christ mediated to members of the church are one and the same (CF, #124, 575).[56] Christ and the Spirit form the simultaneous and mutually implicating foundation of the church.

Mission of the church. The goal of the church as an organization is completely embraced within its mission which is intrinsic to the church's self-understanding and can only be understood theologically. The church continues Jesus' mission in history: "since the Divine Essence was bound up with the human person of Christ, but is now (His directly personal influence having ceased) no longer personally operative in any individual, but henceforward manifests itself actively in the fellowship of believers as their common spirit, this is just the way in which the work of redemption is continued and extended in the Church" (CF, #124, 577). The function of the church is to be the medium of the redeeming influence of Jesus Christ. The world, "so far as it is outside this fellowship of Christ, is always, in spite of that original perfection, the place of evil and sin. No one, therefore, can be surprised to find at this point the proposition that salvation or blessedness is in the Church alone, and that . . . the Church alone saves" (CF, #113, 527). One will appreciate this in the measure in which one recognizes the antithesis between the world and the dignity of Christ and the redemption he mediates (CF, #113, 527).

Schleiermacher's doctrine of the church provides a solid rationale for missionary expansion. Faith in the Christian church "contains the hope that the Church will increase and the world opposed to it decrease." He posits a gradual sanctification of the world as the Church grows and by "progressive domination" absorbs the unredeemed aspects of the world (CF, #113, 528). It was noted that Schleiermacher

---

56. "To us, however, not only is it certain that our participation in the Holy Spirit really belongs to the things which we are conscious of having had imparted to us by Christ, but also that in Christ everything derives from the absolute and exclusive power of His God-consciousness" (CF, #121, 564). God's presence and power in Christ rendered him sinless, which did not detract from his humanity but perfected it. So too, being dependent on God and conscious of it does not diminish human freedom but releases or liberates it.

accepted the possibility of salvation of all as the scope of the redeeming efficacy of Jesus Christ. At the same time he is quite clear in the
belief that Christianity is ordered to draw the other religions into
itself by conversion. "Now all other fellowships of faith are destined
to pass into the Christian fellowship..." (CF, #117, 536). "As regards those outside the Church, it is an essential of our faith that
every nation will sooner or later become Christian..." (CF, #120,
559). "Starting from the point that all other religious fellowships
are destined to lose themselves in Christianity, and hence that all
nations are destined to pass over into Christian fellowship, the common spirit of the Christian Church would then be the common spirit
of the human race" (CF, #121, 564).[57]

Organization of the church. Schleiermacher's ecclesiology unfolds in three parts: the origin of the church which has been
discussed, the organization of the institutional church alongside the
world, and the consummation of the church which contains his eschatology. We turn now to the second extended part. His method in
ecclesiology presents the church as existing in a twofold relationship,
to God and to the world. This double relationship accounts for essential, invariant elements in the church and elements that change or
vary with historical circumstance. "The fellowship of believers, animated by the Holy Spirit, remains ever self-identical in its attitude
to Christ and to this Spirit, but in its relation to the world it is subject to change and variation" (CF, #126, 582). The stable elements
have their roots in the Spirit of Christ, always one and the same;
and the variability comes from the world which is also inside the
church: thus one expects different forms of the church in different
times, places, nations (CF, #126, 583). The invariant elements of the
church are six: scripture, ministry of the word, baptism, the Lord's
supper, the power of the keys, and prayer in the name of Christ.[58]
Three of these structures are considered here as organizational, and

57. Schleiermacher believed that Christianity would in the course of history absorb
the world and all the other religions into itself: "This implies first of all that Christianity
has spread over the whole world, in the sense that no other religion survives as an
organized fellowship." CF, #157, 696.

58. All churches would admit that these three elements are constitutive of the
church: witness to Christ, living fellowship with Christ, and a communion of interaction among members. The six invariant structures represent these three elements

three will be treated as essential "activities of the church." The major significance of Schleiermacher's views on the variables in the church will become clear when they are discussed under the heading of the relation of the church to the world.

Holy scripture. Schleiermacher proposes his theology of scripture not as a propedeutic to faith or revelation, but as an ecclesiological doctrine, one pertaining to the doctrine of the church. Scripture is a constitutive dimension of the Christian church which is itself a body held together by Christian God-consciousness. This forges a tight synthesis of doctrines in which faith, revelation, and teaching are integrated into the life of the Christian community. Scripture's authority, therefore, is not outside the community or autonomous from the community but an authoritative source within the community. Against an exaggerated evangelicalism, he says that "The authority of Holy Scripture cannot be the foundation of faith in Christ; rather must the latter be presupposed before a peculiar authority can be granted to Holy Scripture" (CF, #128, 591; 591–94).

The authority and normativity of scripture works within the historical life of the community. The faithful preservation of the apostolic writings "is the work of the Spirit of God acknowledging His own products; He distinguishes what is to remain unchangeable from what has in many respects undergone transformation in the later development of Christian doctrine" (CF, #130, 602). The original expression of faith develops through an ongoing hermeneutical process like the reading of a classic: its fixed form in the New Testament must be "viewed as but one incident in a process which can only be fully vindicated through its ever-renewed confirmation as the Church perseveres in its task of inquiry, but otherwise is liable to correction" (CF, #130, 603).[59] How do the scriptures exercise

---

and reflect the prophetic, priestly, and kingly offices of Christ: scripture and the ministry of the word correspond to the prophetic office of Christ; the sacraments embody the priestly office of Christ; and the prayer in the name of Jesus and the power of the keys represented the kingly or governing function of Christ as head of the church (CF, #127, 589–91). Schleiermacher does not stipulate that each of these six elements must have exactly the same form in all churches.

59. The normativity of scripture operates in this tension: "For since the Spirit was poured out on all flesh, no age can be without its own originality in Christian thinking. Yet, on the one hand, nothing can be regarded as a pure product of the Christian Spirit except in so far as it can be shown to be in harmony with the original products; on the

their normativity? In his response to this Schleiermacher displays his sense of historicity: "the interpretation of Christian faith which validates itself in each age as having been evoked by Scripture is the development, suited to that moment, of the genuine original interpretation of Christ and His work, and constitutes the common Christian orthodoxy for that time and place" (CF, #131, 606).

Ministry of the word of God. At the center of church polity lies ministry of the word. Schleiermacher's frame of reference for the organization of the church is the congregation or perhaps the city or region, and his prescriptions are open to variations among different churches. His large formal definition of ministry is this: "Those members of the Christian fellowship who maintain chiefly the attitude of spontaneity perform by self-communication the Ministry of God's Word for those who maintain chiefly the attitude of receptivity; and this Ministry is partly an indeterminate and occasional ministry, partly formal and prescribed" (CF, #133, 611). This can be parsed in three points: first, as a matter of sociological principle, the dynamics of the community include active and passive members, "the spontaneous and communicative" and "the needy and receptive" (CF, #135, 618). In ministry "the relation of the spontaneously active to the receptive is a communication from the former to the latter," and "every such communication is a service and supply of the Word of God..." (CF, #133, 612). Second, the Spirit is always active in the community and cannot be limited or assigned tasks. Yet without a division of labor, the effects of the Spirit will not be delivered to the whole community (CF, #133, 614). But, third, the basis of all ministry is the priesthood of all believers. "This view, which forbids any sharp distinction between those who discharge the ordered Ministry and other Christians, we find in Scripture itself" (CF, #133, 613). These considerations yield the following thesis on the organization of the church: "There is in the Christian Church a public Ministry of the Word, as a definite office committed to men under fixed forms; and from this proceeds all organization of the Church" (CF, #134, 614).

---

other, no later product possesses equal authority with the original writings when it is a question of guaranteeing the Christian character of some particular presentation or of exposing its unchristian elements." CF, #129, 596.

Relative to the origin of the offices of ministry, Schleiermacher believed that Jesus directed an explicit ministry of teaching and preaching relative to outsiders (Mt 10:6ff), and this became an internal office of ministry since new members continually needed teaching and admonition. Then the apostles proposed a further division of official ministry in the deacons. The agent replacing apostles and appointing deacons, however, was the community itself.[60] Thus the two basic offices of ministry, "the main branches of the public Ministry," are teaching-preaching and service; the threefold division of bishop, presbyter, and deacon is an arbitrary development from this more primitive one (CF, #134, 615).

Schleiermacher lays down some broad principles for a well-ordered ministry. First of all, there can be any number of public ministries in the church, that is, different tasks for different people. Second, in principle, the distribution of ministries must be recognized as an act of the whole community: "it is the whole body that organizes the discharge of its functions and distributes these amongst its members" (CF, #134, 615). Third, at the center is the office of the ministry of the word: "the most spiritual Ministry of all — namely, the ordered presentation of the Word of God — keeps its place as the mid-point, from which all radiates out and to which all is in relation" (616). Fourth: "The public worship and service of the Church is in all its parts bound to the Word of God" (CF, #135, 617). Scripture and creed are the norms for all ministry and its content. Referring to Christian psalmody and hymns, Schleiermacher pronounces an axiom with wider relevance: "The more Christian poetry departs from these two basal forms and represents purely individual aspects of the religious life, the more its influence is confined to small coteries" (CF, #135, 618). In sum, relative to the organization of the church around the ministry of the word one can characterize the polity of Schleiermacher's church as congregational, calling for continual oversight

---

60. "It was the Apostles themselves, however, who proposed a division of this internal Ministry and left it to the whole body to transfer the ministry of serving tables to others; thus the teaching office became something entrusted to the Apostles by the community, just as the community had formerly transferred both offices combined to the new members of the Twelve" (CF, #134, 615). In this way Schleiermacher held that the office of the preaching-teaching ministry is established by Christ, but assignment to the office is a function of the community.

to make sure that preaching and worship and piety conform to the word of God, protective against clericalism and ecclesiastical distinction between ministers and those to whom they minister, an implicit doctrine of reception to balance authority, all in the name of unity in the Spirit (CF, #135, 618–19).

The power of the keys. The power of the keys is a "legislative and an administrative power, which is an essential effluence from the kingly office of Christ" (CF, #144, 660). This spiritual power refers "to the expansion and maintenance of the church, in the sense that it rests with the Church to decide who shall and who shall not be received into the Christian fellowship, and also who shall remain there or be expelled" (CF, #144, 661). This governing power consists in an extension of Christ's kingly activity, not in a literal way, since Jesus Christ was not a legislator or governor of a church, but analogously insofar as it is directed toward living a life patterned on Christ (CF, #144, 662). "The Power of the Keys is the power in virtue of which the Church decides what belongs to the Christian life, and disposes of each individual in the measure of his conformity with these decisions" (CF, #145, 662). Essentially this "power to bind and to loose" is the power of legislating and governing the church.

Schleiermacher does not locate this power in a particular office but in the community. Nor does he prescribe how the power itself is to be organized. He only provides some axioms or rules that qualify its exercise. (1) The power of the keys determines who is accepted to the ministry of the word, even though the ministry of the word in many respects overlaps with the power of the keys. For example, in the administration of the sacraments the ministry of the word includes the forgiveness of sins and this pertains to the power of the keys (CF, #145, 665–66). (2) The Office of the Keys does not reside principally in the body of ministers: this would result in clericalism. "Thus both legislative action and administration action derive ultimately from the congregation" (CF, #145, 667). (3) The whole congregation exercises this power in two ways: first, indirectly, "by ordering and distributing the offices to which legislation and judgment are formally assigned," and, second, by each individual and the whole group forming opinions and creating a climate of public opinion in the church. The exercise of this power has to be in line with human nature in union with the divine Spirit in any given time and place (CF, #145, 667). (4) It follows that "all legislative acts within the congregation are always subject to revision." Laws of one time may not apply nor be feasible in another time and may become injurious (CF, #145, 667–68). (5) Regarding excommunication, this administrative and disciplinary action must be used prudently and in a limited way; there is no such thing as complete excommunication (CF, #145, 668).

Activities of the church. Three of the activities of the church considered here are drawn from what Schleiermacher calls the invariant or essential elements of the church.[61] To these are added a reference to his ethics reflecting the social behavior of the community. Sacramental activity provides a good place to begin. This intends no slight to the main activity of the church of preaching the word of God around which the church is organized.

Baptism. Schleiermacher defines baptism in this way: "Baptism as an action of the Church signifies simply the act of will by which the Church receives the individual into its fellowship; but inasmuch as the effectual promise of Christ rests upon it, it is at the same time the channel of the divine justifying activity, through which the individual is received into the living fellowship of Christ" (CF, #136, 619). Because Christ himself enjoined baptism as an act of reception in the church, it is an action of Christ himself, and with it the process of Christian salvation begins (CF, #136, 619–20).[62] Baptism is an action not of the individual minister but of the church, and "the effect of the action does not depend on the intention being pure and unmixed, or on its always being definitely present to the mind of the person by whom baptism is administered" (CF, #137, 627).

Schleiermacher wanted to chart a middle course between an objectivity of the sacrament that so emphasizes the divine promise and minimizes human consciousness as to make it appear magical, and

---

61. In other words, these are institutionalized structures; I have introduced an implicit distinction between organizational structure and activity which is not Schleiermacher's.

62. Schleiermacher sought to accommodate the practice of believer's baptism and thus made it clear that baptism and regeneration do not always coincide exactly: sometimes faith and regeneration precede baptism and sometimes baptism precedes the act of faith chronologically; but both mutually enjoin the other. CF, #136, 623–24.

a subjective view that faith and regeneration need be tied to no external act whatsoever. In his view the act of the church is coordinated with the action of God within the person. Baptism is thus not merely an external act and not merely a subjective act (CF, #137, 632). He also reached a compromise between infant and believer's baptism. "Infant Baptism is a complete Baptism only when the profession of faith which comes after further instruction is regarded as the act which consummates it" (CF, #138, 633). Infant baptism is anomalous because it is administered in the absence of repentance and faith. On the one hand, baptism can be administered because "we have reason to count upon their future faith and their confession of it." This comes after instruction and consists in confirmation, which Schleiermacher takes to be integral to the sacrament of baptism, and not another sacrament or detached from baptism (CF, #138, 635–36).[63] On the other hand, as to the Anabaptists, he accepts their practice, and he also accepts their view that children who die without baptism are in the same position as children who die with baptism: there is no difference relative to their final salvation. He is prepared to enter into fellowship with Anabaptist churches if they recognize from their side the practice of infant baptism as he has explained it (CF, #138, 637–38).

The Lord's Supper. The doctrine of the Lord's supper rests both on scripture and the experience of Christian consciousness. Christians experience a strengthening of the spiritual life in partaking of the Lord's supper "for therein, according to the institution of Christ, His body and blood are administered to them" (CF, #139, 638). The origin of tradition of the Supper goes back "to the beginnings of the church, and to the Supper itself as Christ held it with His disciples" (CF, #139, 639). The need of the Lord's Supper lies in the demand that Christian piety and fellowship be nourished and strengthened against the inroads of "the world" (CF, #139, 638). And the efficacy of the sacrament consists in the strengthening of the relationship of

---

63. Infant baptism "does not straightway imply the possession and enjoyment of salvation but only a normal preparatory operation of the Holy Spirit" (CF, #138, 636). It brings the child not into the inner circle of regeneration but the outer circle of preparatory grace; its effects are suspended until the person really becomes a believer. For this reason confirmation is an integral part of baptism, and infant baptism only corresponds with Christ's institution when combined with confirmation. CF, #138, 637.

the individual to Christ and of the bond of the Christian members with each other. "Here, therefore, the two kinds of fellowship unite — that of believers with each other and that of each soul with Christ..." (CF, #139, 639).[64] He sees a relation between the Lord's Supper and confession of sin analogous to the relation between baptism and confirmation. As confirmation is the consummation of baptism, so too the Supper is the consummation of the confession of sin and absolution or church's declaration of forgiveness at the beginning of the communion service. "The confession of sin has no public ecclesiastical character save in relation to the Supper, and the wish to participate in the Supper cannot be otherwise expressed than through confession, for apart from sin there would be no need to renew our union with Christ" (CF, #141, 653). The antithesis of sin and Christic God-consciousness underlies this reciprocal relationship of confession of sin and union with Christ.

Schleiermacher recognized that the connection between the bread and wine and the body and blood of Christ is a contentious issue that cannot yield a common doctrine. He tried to strike a middle position between Roman Catholic transubstantiation, with its physicalist objective tendency, and the position that rejects any connection between the species and the spiritual participation in the flesh and blood of Christ, thus denying any reality to the sacrament (CF, #140, 644–51). Although he does not see any common position between Luther, Zwingli, and Calvin, agreement on the effects of the Supper is enough to bond the churches together. For example, the differences between the Lutheran and the Calvinist theories of the body and blood of Christ make a difference when one abuses the sacrament. But on the supposition of worthy participation,

---

64. "The one benefit of this participation is stated as being the confirming of our fellowship with Christ; and this includes the confirming of Christians in their union with each other, for the latter rests so entirely on their union with Christ that the union of an individual with Christ is unthinkable apart from his union with believers" (CF, #141, 651). The realistic effect of the sacrament is "a repeated nourishing of personal spiritual life out of the fulness of Christ's life" (CF, #139, 641). He describes this effect in terms that refer directly to the event of the supper: a group performing the same activity, becoming more closely united with Christ and with each other in so doing. This can happen in other ways too, but "the Lord's Supper is distinct from all else in this respect that in it the same result is bound up with this definite action, blessed and hallowed by the word of Christ." Ibid.

the differences disappear and do not justify separate existence (CF, #142, 657).

Prayer in the name of Christ. Schleiermacher's short treatise on prayer in the name of Jesus is ecclesiological and not a general theory of prayer, although one finds traces of the latter in it. His concern is the public prayer of the church and not private prayer of individuals. He also seems to limit the meaning of the term "prayer" to prayer of petition, that is, of asking something of God.[65] The two most important objects of the public and common prayer of the church are for good leaders and for unity as it moves into the future (CF, #146, 671). The standard, normative public prayer of the church in Jesus' name is "Thy kingdom come." It is prayer for the church that it realize itself into the kingdom of God, that is, expand and flourish, drawing more and more people into itself. Normative prayer is that which springs out of concern for the whole church and whose content keeps the condition of the church in view (CF, #146, 672). In the end, prayer in Jesus' name, that is, as the public prayer of the church and as constitutive of the church, must be interpreted in terms of its bearing on the kingdom, with which the church itself is intimately connected. "Hence such prayer can only share in the promise in so far as it stands in a close relation to the subject of the promise, i.e., in so far as the wishes laid before God can also be regarded as needs of the Church" (CF, #147, 675). This view stands in marked contrast to prayers of individuals for their particular needs or desires; these are best left on a personal or domestic level. "But public and common Christian prayers ought always to be representative of the pure type of prayer in Jesus' name, without bringing in subjects the connexion of which with the progressive development of the Kingdom of God is doubtful" (CF, #147, 675).

Ethics. Schleiermacher developed an extensive Christian ethics, a discipline integral to Christian self-understanding. Christian consciousness or piety expresses itself in thought and action, and as reflection on the first yields the dogmatics, reflection on the second

---

65. Relative to the past and present, God-consciousness takes the form of thankfulness and/or resignation. But relative to the future, human consciousness cannot avoid expectations, "and as long as this mental activity lasts, it is bound to combine with the God-consciousness and become prayer." CF, #146, 669.

yields Christian ethics. This Christian ethics is an ecclesial discipline: the church as the community of piety provides the ground and goal of Christian ethical reflection. Schleiermacher structured his ethics around the distinction between two spheres of Christian activity, the one concerned with the inner life of the church, the other the sphere of society. In each sphere he considered three kinds of activity: that which purified or restored human life, broadened or expanded it, or finally expressed or represented it.[66] Representational activity refers to actions which are self-constituting of the church itself. Some of the major topics of Christian community life include church discipline and reform, Christian family life, education, missions, patterns of home and public worship, and Christian virtues.[67] Relative to Christian behavior in society Schleiermacher considers criminal justice, war, education, business and labor relations, the arts.[68] Brandt concludes his analysis of Schleiermacher's ethics with the thesis that, far from being an accommodationist, he depicted the church as a transformer of society.[69]

3 KINDS

Relationship to society and world. Schleiermacher uses the relationship of the church to the world to set up a dynamic, tensive structure of mutual influence. Then, within this framework, he reconceives the distinction between the invisible and visible church. As he puts it: "The fact that the Church cannot form itself out of the midst of the world without the world exercising some influence on the Church, establishes for the Church itself the antithesis between

---

66. Brito analyzes the intimate relationship between Schleiermacher's ethics and his ecclesiology: the one (ethics) is a subset of the other (ecclesiology) and both are constituted by the impulse of the Spirit. One begins to see the breath of Schleiermacher's identification of the church with the kingdom of God and its reach into society when the ethics are factored in. "Pneumatologie, Ecclésiologie et Ethique," 24–35. See James M. Brandt, *All Things New: Reform of Church and Society in Schleiermacher's Christian Ethics* (Louisville: Westminster John Knox Press, 2001), 53 where he schematically represents the six spheres of ethical activity.

67. Brandt, *All Things New,* 92–105.

68. Ibid., 116–30.

69. Ibid., 116–18. "The transformative character of this theology of culture is now evident. The *Christian Ethics* promotes its vision of culture transformed by Christ by means of particular manifestations for each of the three kinds of action in the outer sphere: prophetic critique for restoring action; transvaluation of cultural goods for broadening action; and infiltration and permeation by the Christian spirit for representational action." Ibid., 130.

the *Visible* and the *Invisible* Church" (CF, #148, 676). The invisible
and visible church distinction is "existentialized" in the sense that it
appears as two dimensional fields or spheres in the church interacting
with each other. This dynamic framework allows him to combine a
theological and a historicist imagination in the statement of a whole
series of tensive principles and axioms that combine an ideal theological understanding of what the church should be with a concrete
realistic grasp of its limitations, in particular those relative to unity
and truth. Here more than anywhere else one sees the "modernity"
of Schleiermacher's ecclesiology. What follows attempts to digest this
rich teaching in three points: the framework, axioms regarding the
tension between unity and division, and axioms on truth and error.

Dialectical framework. The phrase "dialectical framework" is not
Schleiermacher's but interpretive of him, and it refers to a relationship between two factors constituting a unity by interacting with each
other in a dynamic but tensive relationship. Such is the relationship
between the church and the world. The "world" in Schleiermacher
is in one sense the world outside the church, and it often has a negative sense of resistance to the Spirit. But realistically the church is
in the world and the world is inside the church. Church and world
are distinct but related as two intertwined spheres. "Hence church
and world are not spatially or externally separate; at each point of
human life as we see it, wherever there is church, because there faith
and fellowship in faith are to be found, there is world as well, because there exist also sin and fellowship in universal sinfulness" (CF,
#148, 676).

Schleiermacher's distinction between the visible and invisible
church is structurally analogous. The visible church is the whole
church, the actual church as it exists; the invisible church is the totality of the effects of the Spirit within the church as a whole. The two
dimensions coexist in every individual, and in the whole community,
and mutually interact as antithetical or tensively related existentials,
analogous to the antithetical relationship between sin and grace, or
between whatever obstacle that may be placed in the way of the operation of the Spirit and the Spirit's salutary effects. "Thus the *invisible*
Church is the totality of the effects of the Spirit as a connected whole;
but these effects, as connected with those lingering influences of the

collective life of universal sinfulness which are never absent from any life that has been taken possession of by the divine Spirit, constitute the *visible* church" (CF, #148, 677). "The pure Church cannot everywhere be made visible; but it is necessary to treat of it separately as the peculiarly active element in the other" (CF, #148, 678). The six essential institutions of the visible church treated under the subheadings "Organization" and "Activities" are instruments of the invisible church, "the principal organs of the invisible Church, and most of all represent its forces at work within the visible" (CF, #148, 678).[70]

"The antithesis between the Visible and the Invisible Church may be comprehended in these two propositions: the former is a divided church, while the latter is an undivided unity; and the former is always subject to error, while the latter is infallible" (CF, #149, 678). The actual church always exists in an existential tension between the impulse of Christ and the Spirit to pure unity and truth, which is present within every Christian and in the church community as such, and at the same time the antithetical or limiting quality of either finitude or sin that accounts for division and error. The Spirit as the Spirit of unity and truth is the same everywhere, but every particular form or expression of it is divisive or in some measure erroneous. Moreover the two issues are closely related: what is error also divides, and what is really a defection from unity is also a defection from the truth. The two dimensions cannot be separated: the invisible church as a fellowship in unity and truth is mediated through the visible church (CF, #149, 679). Thus Schleiermacher systematically and conceptually builds the tension between the ideal and the actual into his ecclesiology: "the invisible Church is everywhere essentially one, while the visible is always involved in separation and division" (CF, #149, 680).[71]

---

70. The invisible church, then, is really a code word for the power of God, and the effects of the power of God within and at work within the church as a group of human beings united in their faith in Christ. It is God, then, that will give it the qualities of unity and truth; God is the active source of unity and infallibility, and God as active Spirit provides a direction into the future.

71. This tension is unrelieved: "That is to say, it is the common striving of all to recognize everywhere the same Spirit through what is outward, and draw it to themselves. But particular forms of outward expression, ideas no less than acts, which are the channels through which this one fellowship is mediated, are also in themselves the divisive element in the visible fellowship." CF, #149, 680.

Principles and axioms concerning unity and division. The seeds of separation exist in all people and groups. Historically these seeds combine in various groups and lead to actual separations among the churches. Yet in a state of separation, each part of the visible church remains a part of the invisible church as well, because it confesses Christ and lives in the Spirit. Thus every particular church has within it a movement toward reunion because the Spirit cannot wholly disappear from any part of the church. "Hence it is universally true that the Spirit unites, and that it is the fleshly mind that disunites" (CF, #150, 683). On this basis Schleiermacher proposes what is in effect a list of principles and axioms that reflect this tension of unity and division.

> "Whensoever separations actually occur in the Christian Church, there can never be lacking an endeavour to unite the separated" (CF, #150, 681).

> "The more the uniting Spirit pervades the mass and drives the worldly elements in it apart, the more these elements will lose their divisive force" (CF, #150, 682).

> "In the state of division each part of the visible Church remains a part of the invisible, for in it are found the confession of Christ and therefore also the activity of the Spirit" (CF, #150, 682).

> "The complete suspension of fellowship between different parts of the Visible Church is unchristian" (CF, #151, 683).

> "All separations in the Church are merely temporary" (CF, #152, 685).

> "No communion has the prospect of long life which seeks to base itself merely on divergent moral practice in the absence of relatively different doctrine, or conversely simply on certain peculiar doctrines in the absence of different ways of life" (CF, #152, 686).

> Christian loyalty to a specific denomination is conditional: "The essential thing is that each should love the special form of Christianity to which he adheres only as a transient form of the

one abiding Church, though a form that involves a temporary being of its own" (CF, #152, 686).

Proselytizing or promoting one's own church is only positive in reaction to a corrupt church and can never mean promotion of one's own church as an absolute end (CF, #152, 687).

Principles and axioms concerning truth and error. No actual element of human life can be fashioned in pure truth; all ideas and purposes are mixed with untruth and sin. Thus Schleiermacher lays down that "in every act of the religious consciousness truth is more or less infected with error" (CF, #153, 688). He attributes this to sin, but it also seems due to finitude as well. Yet it is equally true that no part of the church is completely devoid of "the action of the Spirit of truth" mediated especially through scripture and the ministry of the word (CF, #153, 688). This tension sets up another series of practical principles and axioms.

"As in every branch of the Visible Church error is possible, and therefore also in some respects actual, so also there is never lacking in any the corrective power of truth" (CF, #153, 687).

"No definition of doctrine, then, even when arrived at with the most perfect community of feeling, can be regarded as irreformable and valid for all time" (CF, #154, 690).[72]

"All errors that are generated in the Visible Church come to be removed by the truth which never ceases to work in it" (CF, #155, 691). Error is attached to the truth, and as the Spirit takes possession of the whole of a church, the influence of error should gradually diminish.[73]

---

72. This principle, reflecting historical consciousness, has constructive supports for discerning and interpreting past theological expressions: "No one can be bound to acknowledge the contents of such presentations as Christian truth except in so far as they are the expression of his own religious consciousness, or commend themselves to him by their scriptural character." CF, #154, 690.

73. "What is innermost in every truly regenerate life is simply the whole truth of redemption; and it is solely as limited to this domain that we affirm the infallibility of the invisible Church." CF, #149, 678.

To conclude, this synthetic and abbreviated account of Schleiermacher's ecclesiology does not do justice to its subtlety. But it is enough to show the shifts in thinking which modernity wrought. The same forces will be seen at work in Möhler.

THE EARLY ECCLESIOLOGY OF MÖHLER

Möhler's ecclesiology almost appears as an anomalous oddity in the history of modern Catholic thought. While his early work has classic qualities, it appeared within a specific period of historical opportunity.

Johann Adam Möhler

Möhler was born in 1796 in Württemberg.[74] He was sent to the Lyceum in Ellwangen in 1813 for philosophical studies. In 1815 he entered the theology faculty in Ellwangen, and when it moved to Tübingen in 1817 to become the Catholic theological faculty at the university Möhler transferred with it. After one year he went to the Catholic seminary in Rottenburg and a year later was ordained a priest in 1819. This was followed by a year of pastoral work in a parish. From early on people recognized that Möhler was gifted

---

74. These works have been helpful in situating Möhler's ecclesiology: James Tunstead Burtchaell, "Drey, Möhler and the Catholic School of Tübingen," *Nineteenth Century Religious Thought in the West*, II, ed. Ninian Smart et al. (Cambridge: Cambridge University Press, 1985), 111–39; [Yves] M.-J. Congar, "L'Esprit des Pères d'après Möhler," *Supplément à la Vie Spirituelle* 55 (1 April 1938): 1–25; "Sur l'Evolution et l'Interprétation de la Pensée de Möhler," *Revue des Sciences Philosophiques et Théologiques* 27 (1938): 205–12; Peter C. Erb, "Introduction," Johann Adam Möhler, *Unity in the Church or The Principle of Catholicism: Presented in the Spirit of the Church Fathers of the First Three Centuries*, ed. and trans. Erb (Washington, D.C.: Catholic University of America Press, 1996); R. W. Franklin, *Nineteenth-Century Churches: The History of a New Catholicism in Württemberg, England, and France* (New York: Garland Publishing, 1987), 78–183; Michael J. Himes, *Ongoing Incarnation: Johann Adam Möhler and the Beginnings of Modern Ecclesiology* (New York: Crossroad, 1997); "'A Great Theologian of Our Time': Möhler on Schleiermacher," *Heythrop Journal* 37 (1996): 24–46; Bradford E. Hinze, "The Holy Spirit and The Catholic Tradition: The Legacy of Johann Adam Möhler," in *The Legacy of the Tübingen School: The Relevance of Nineteenth-Century Theology for the Twenty-First Century*, ed. Donald J. Dietrich and Michael J. Himes (New York: Crossroad, 1997), 75–94; Hervé Savon, *Johann Adam Möhler: The Father of Modern Theology* (Glen Rock, N.J.: Paulist Press, 1966). Möhler's work, *Unity in the Church*, will be cited as UC by part, chapter, paragraph number and page with reference to the Erb edition.

intellectually, and after a year of parochial work he began teaching classical languages at a *gymnasium* and then was a tutor in church history. In the Spring of 1822 the Catholic theological faculty at Tübingen offered him a position as lecturer in church history and also canon law. But before taking up his post he was to spend a year preparing himself by study and by traveling to various universities in order to meet and learn from the experts in his field, both Protestant and Catholic. In 1823 he began lecturing at Tübingen, including courses in canon law each summer from 1823 to 1825. Such are the bare facts of Möhler's education.

But these data do little in themselves to situate the work to be analyzed, *The Unity of the Church,* published in September or October of 1825. For that, one needs to back up and consider three lines of historical energy, ranging from the general to the particular, that converged in the genesis of this work: the Catholic renewal under the force of Romanticism, the Tübingen school, especially the influence of Drey, and Möhler's own concomitant intellectual work that fed into the construction of *Unity.*

Möhler began to formulate *Unity* almost twenty five years after the publication of Schleiermacher's *Speeches.* Catholic theologians for some time had been reading the Romantic thinkers and drawing inspiration from them. Ideas usually associated with Schleiermacher in Protestant theology had counterparts in Catholic thinkers during the first quarter of the nineteenth century: a turn to the subject and making religious experience the basis of theology; the church as less an institution and more a community of people sharing a common religious life; the Holy Spirit as a kind of soul of the church. These ideas were in circulation in the Catholic Romantic movement prior to Möhler.[75]

Möhler encountered these ideas up close at Ellwangen and then Tübingen, not in his textbooks, which were objective, deductive scholastic manuals, but in the person of Johann Sebastian Drey. Drey was deeply influenced by both Schelling and Schleiermacher, although he formulated his ideas in a Catholic framework. Already

---

75. Himes, *Ongoing Incarnation,* 15–27.

in 1812 Drey advocated a renewal of theology along Romantic lines.[76] In 1819 Drey published his own outline of the structure of theology analogous to Schleiermacher's.[77] The point, then, is that the forces of the general Romantic revival in Germany were readily available to Möhler through Tübingen and Drey specifically. When he took his "study trip" before taking up his lecturing, he had a rich apperceptive background for an enthusiastic reception of new ideas.[78]

Still more proximate to the content of *Unity* is the work that engaged Möhler at the same time that he was designing and writing it. His intellectual activity during the years from 1823 to 1825 consisted in published essays, reviews of the works of others, and initial drafts of ideas that found their way into *Unity*. He was also lecturing in canon law. On the one hand, analyses of this work and of sketches that served as drafts of *Unity* show that his thinking developed during this brief period.[79] On the other hand, he was reading the early Fathers with Romantic lenses and finding material that confirmed an organic view of the church as community. But during the summers he was lecturing in canon law which focuses attention on the institutional aspects of the church. Himes reads Möhler's view of the church in the work leading up to *Unity* as containing a tension between two foci contending for primacy: the church as institutional

---

76. Johann Sebastian Drey, "Toward the Revision of the Present State of Theology," in Joseph Fitzer, *Romance and the Rock: Nineteenth-Century Catholics on Faith and Reason* (Minneapolis: Fortress Press, 1989), 62–73.

77. Johann Sebastian Drey, *Brief Introduction to the Study of Theology with Reference to the Scientific Standpoint and the Catholic System* (Notre Dame: University of Notre Dame Press, 1994). In this work Drey portrays the church as the subject matter of theology insofar as it is the community as bearer of the religious experience that provides the data for the discipline. See Himes, *Ongoing Incarnation*, 38. Schleiermacher's work is *Brief Outline on the Study of Theology* (Richmond: John Knox Press, 1966).

78. Himes shows in a pointed way how Schleiermacher influenced (Möhler's *Unity* ("Möhler on Schleiermacher," *Heythrop Journal*, 24–31). So obvious are the influences of Schleiermacher and Schelling on Möhler that Erb feels obliged to underline the Catholic ecclesiology that he had absorbed (Erb, "Introduction," 19–21). By emphasizing its Catholic character Erb undercuts a dismissal of Möhler's early work as a mere reflection of outside forces.

79. See Himes, *Ongoing Incarnation*, 50–72 and Erb, "Introduction," 40–50. Erb finds in Möhler's earliest lectures "an eighteenth-century view of the church as a religious institution, maintaining a specific doctrine, system of worship, and constitution, and characterized by its universality, holiness, infallibility, and unity in truth." Erb, "Introduction," 31.

structure and the church as community with an inner spiritual life animated by the Spirit. *Unity* would try to resolve that tension. Möhler's ecclesiological writing did not end with *Unity in the Church*. In 1832 he published *Symbolism*, an extensive analysis contrasting Catholicism and Protestantism.[80] In this work Möhler pulls back considerably from positions taken in *Unity*; indeed, the whole spirit is different. In some respects he came to disparage his earlier work.[81] His pneumatocentrism is replaced with a christocentrism; he draws sharper distinctions between the Catholic Church and other churches. Some commentators draw the connection between this later work of Möhler and the emergence of the Roman school of ecclesiology.[82] Attention is focused exclusively on Möhler's early ecclesiology because it better reflects the influence of modernity and, as such, it became influential later in the twentieth century. Möhler's relatively short theological career ended with his death in 1838.

The Early Ecclesiology of Möhler

Möhler's *Unity in the Church* has a straightforward structure seen in the table of contents: the first of two parts treats the unity of the "Spirit" of the church; the second treats the unity of the "body" of the church. Each part has four subsections or chapters, divided into paragraphs. But Möhler did not intend a comprehensive ecclesiology. This representation of his thought does not follow exactly the order of his presentation. The book begins with and finds its center of gravity in the Spirit. He says he could have begun with Christ who promised and sent the Spirit. But he "did not wish to discuss what might

---

80. The full title is descriptive of the content of this work: *Symbolism: Exposition of the Doctrinal Differences between Catholics and Protestants as Evidenced by Their Symbolical Writings,* intro. by Michael J. Himes (New York: Crossroad, 1997).

81. The shift from *Unity* to *Symbolism* and the thematic contrast of these two works are striking; Möhler abandoned at certain points particular construals of Schleiermacher and his own earlier language. Himes analyzes at length Möhler's journey between the two works and the resultant differences between the two positions in *Ongoing Incarnation,* 152–334. See also Philip J. Rosato, "Between Christocentrism and Pneumatocentrism: An Interpretation of Johann Adam Möhler's Ecclesiology," *Heythrop Journal* 19 (1978): 46–70 passim; and Hinze, "The Holy Spirit and the Catholic Tradition," passim.

82. "Möhler begot Passaglia; Passaglia begot Schrader; Passaglia and Schrader begot Scheeben and Franzelin." Yves Congar as cited by Peter Riga, "The Ecclesiology of Johann Adam Möhler," *Theological Studies* 22 (1961): 564, n. 5.

reasonably be assumed as already known ... " (UC, Preface, 77). The point of the book is to explain the role of the Spirit in the church, and for this reason it is often described as a pneumatocentric ecclesiology. But this is a correct designation only if it is construed as nonexclusive of the constitutive role of Christ in the founding and being of the church. This pneumatocentrism is a matter of emphasis and weight on the role of the Spirit in the Church.[83] The ecclesiology of Möhler contained in this book is laid out here according to the pattern used to present Schleiermacher's ecclesiology.[84]

The self-understanding and nature of the church. Möhler's most straightforward definition of the church does not appear until the second part: "The church is the external, visible structure of a holy, living power, of love, the body of the spirit of believers forming itself from the interior externally" (UC, 2.1, 209). Less than complete, this formulation at the beginning of his treatment of the "body" of the church undercuts a separation between a visible and an invisible church. It also declares the integral unity of the theological account and the organizational account of the church. These are two reciprocally related dimensions of one single church, its internal life and life principle and an external materiality and structure. If either is lacking, there is no church. "If, then, the church is to be viewed as the external production of an inner forming power, as the body of a spirit creating itself, it is by all means necessarily this institution through which and in which true faith and true love are preserved and perpetuated. *One* common, true *life* forms itself through the totality of believers as a result of two factors: a spiritual power and its external organic manifestation" (UC, 2.1.49, 211–12).

Did Jesus found the church? Möhler does not develop at length the origin of the church in the explicit terms implied by this question. The result is that one can say that in one sense Möhler did conceive of Jesus intentionally founding a church, but in another sense this

---

83. Technically speaking, since there is only one center of a circle, Möhler's ecclesiology is not Spirit-centered but, like Schleiermacher's, his ecclesiology is elliptical, that is, controlled by two centers, Christ and the Spirit.

84. Summaries of Möhler's ecclesiology can be found in Doyle, *Communion Ecclesiology*, 23–37; Riga, "The Ecclesiology of Johann Adam Möhler," 563–87; Rosato, "Between Christocentrism and Pneumatocentrism," 46–70; Gustav Voss, "Johann Adam Möhler and the Development of Dogma," *Theological Studies* 4 (1943): 420–44.

conception is not fully accurate and misrepresents Möhler's early ecclesiology. Several of Möhler's texts seem to describe Jesus founding the visible church in its offices. The church forms a tradition of the life-praxis of truth, stemming from the source Jesus Christ, each generation connected historically back to the source (UC, 1.1.6, 93). "Christ chose the Twelve Apostles from the multitude of his disciples. They were to proclaim his teaching throughout the whole world and to have general oversight over his believers" (UC, 2.1.50, 213). "The thought of an invisible church founded on earth by Christ is so completely opposed to Christianity, however, that only the visible church was assumed by Jesus Christ, by his apostles, and by the early church. This church was always present as a fact as far back in time as we go" (UC, 2.1.49, 211). This appears to portray Jesus as setting up the church during his earthly ministry. But contextually these texts are making other points, and in the broader context of Möhler's conception of the church the idea of Jesus setting up an objective church as an external historical act does not fit. The external is always a function of the internal, so that no formal church could exist without the internal principle of God as Spirit enlivening human hearts. Therefore, granted this external action of Jesus Christ as the material source and foundation of the church, Möhler's whole attention immediately focuses on the Spirit's role in the church. Because no formal church can exist without the inner work of the Spirit, Möhler's ecclesiology leads him to consider the historical origin of the church in the event of the communication of the Spirit.

Supporting this view of the priority of the Spirit Möhler writes: "If we say merely that the Church is a so-called construction, we leave the impression that Christ had, so to speak, *ordered* his disciples *together* without arousing in them an *inner* need that brought and holds them together, that the Church existed before believers, since they first became believers in it, that the church was above all something different from believers, something aside from them" (UC, 2.1.49, 209).[85] He goes on to say that these inner dispositions are gifts of the Spirit. It may be that one could say cautiously that Jesus

---

85. Perhaps this bestowal of the Spirit was concomitant with Jesus' interaction with his disciples. But the principle stands: no church without an inner communication of the Holy Spirit.

founded the church in an external or *material* sense, but in terms of public history, the *formal* constitution of the church occurs for Möhler with the gift of the Spirit at Pentecost. "Inspired by *one* Spirit, the apostles proclaimed in living speech and in all locations what they had received in living speech from the Lord. Wherever a congregation was founded, they established the same doctrine through the same Holy Spirit, because without this Spirit the foundation of a Christian church is not possible. Thus, in the whole church, in all her expansion, one and the same doctrine must be sounded forth as the utterance of one inner religious life, as well as the expression of one and the same Spirit" (UC, 1.2.9, 99).[86]

The Spirit as constitutive of the church. The Holy Spirit constitutes the church in history. The metaphor behind the role of the Spirit in the church is organic, that is, the inner life principle of a living thing. "Together all believers form an organic whole. By the different communication of one and the same Spirit according to the different needs and characteristics of each person, all are directed to each other and are, together, members completing one another.... Since the same Spirit reveals itself in all true believers and since it is the same at all times, it establishes only peace, joy, and unity" (UC, 1.3.26, 143). The Spirit of God relates to the historical church like the inner spirit and the outer body in a human person. Möhler spells out this analogy in quite explicit terms. "The spirit of a human being is, above all, the enlivening, animating principle. The Spirit comes to self-consciousness and manifests this in that it shapes a bodily organism. By the destruction of the body the human spirit itself loses its earthly being. It is the same with the Christian Spirit: [if it had no body,] it would only wander about erringly in dubious, uncertain appearances.... The human spirit works and is further active through the orders, organs, and functions of the body. In a like manner the Spirit ruling in the church begets organs for its activity.... The active power given to believers by the Holy Spirit

---

86. See the discussion of this point by Himes, *Ongoing Incarnation*, 130–34, 261–63. He supports the idea that for Möhler in *Unity* Pentecost represents the foundation of the church, to the point of relativizing the temporal and external priority of forms established during Jesus' lifetime. Ibid., 263.

forms the visible body of the church, and...the visible church preserves and bears the higher power granted to it and communicates it" (UC, 2.1.49, 212).

Möhler sets up a kind of symbiosis between the individual and the community. "Each specific individual has the inner Christian life principle, the inner power of faith, only from the totality, and in this way the believers together form a unity from the apostles throughout all time. Likewise, the true expression of inner faith, true doctrine, can also be held and determined only by the totality; that is, with regard to the determination as to what true doctrine is, a Christian is directed to the totality of all contemporary believers and to all earlier believers as far back as the apostles" (UC, 1.2.10, 102). Möhler thus justifies a certain form of "indirect faith," that is, of the individual's faith being dependent on the community. "The individual believer as an individual could err, but never if that individual clung to the totality, to the church." Not because of agreement of many, but "because the totality of gifts of the Holy Spirit is in the totality of believers" (UC, 1.2.10, 103).

Functions of the Spirit relative to Catholic concerns. The Spirit has several functions in Möhler's ecclesiology and responds to several problems that have been of particular concern in the Catholic Church since Trent. Among them are the unity of the church, revelation, truth, tradition and its relation to scripture, doctrine, particularly in the nineteenth century the question of development of doctrine.

To begin with unity: the church needs a principle of unity. "If all individual members were active without the special activity of each individual being determined by *one* moving principle, they would be involved in a wild activity destroying every single member of the whole in the same way. The constant law for the common organism is the image for the church body: an unconstrained unfolding of the characteristics of single individuals that is enlivened by the Spirit so that, although there are different gifts, there is only one Spirit" (UC, 1.4.35, 166). But in this unity each individual is respected: "Although the Catholic principle binds all believers into one unity, the individuality of each is not suspended, for each individual is to continue as a *living* member in the whole body of the church" (UC, 1.4.35, 166).

The Christian's knowledge of truth through faith is also mediated through the love engendered by the Spirit in the church. As Möhler states it, "true faith, true Christian knowledge, has its beginning in the Holy Spirit and the communication of the Spirit through the bond with the church" (UC, 1.1.4, 87). "It is the basic principle of the church that the individual's Christian life and through this life the individual's Christian knowledge has its source in the influence of the church community enlivened by the Holy Spirit" (UC, 1.1.6, 92). The point Möhler makes here concerns the existential interdependence of faith's knowledge and the life of love within the community that mediates this faith-knowledge: "this knowledge was formed out of the life of the church and each of the two — knowledge and life — in its own way drew closer to the other" (UC, 1.1.6, 92).

The Spirit also plays a role in the interpretation of scripture, as it did in its inspiration: "the biblical words are revelations of the Holy Spirit, but they are only understandable to the person to whom the Spirit has already communicated itself" (UC, 1.2.8, 97–98). On this basis Möhler understands the way scripture must be interpreted in the church: the church explains the Bible because "the letter is not the Spirit itself but is only an expression of the Spirit, and if one has obtained this Spirit in the church's life, one will understand the expression" (UC, 1.2.8, 97).[87]

Möhler's view of tradition combines Christ's teaching, or the word of the gospel, and the Spirit, to form a broad, existential-historical notion of tradition. Tradition consists in the community itself as a whole, living in history and passing on its life into the future.[88] Tradition includes oral and written teaching being handed down to successive generations. And it is important that tradition be seen as stretching backward continuously to the apostolic period where it

---

87. A fuller account of the view of revelation that underlies these conceptions lies beyond the scope of this presentation.

88. For a concise account of Möhler's organic view of tradition and development of doctrine see John E. Thiel, *Senses of Tradition: Continuity and Development in Catholic Faith* (New York: Oxford University Press, 2000), 63–67. Möhler's view of tradition as the active life in history of the whole community resembles the social existential view of Maurice Blondel in his work *History and Dogma*. See *The Letter on Apologetics and History and Dogma* (New York: Holt, Rinehart and Winston, 1964), 219–87.

gains the specificity of its content (UC, 1.2.12, 107). But tradition cannot only be understood in terms of external doctrines; it constitutes the inner identity of Christianity and church. God's presence as Spirit supplies the inner ground and power of tradition. "The divine power, active and forming itself in the church from the church's beginning, is the same throughout all time and binds in essence the last generation with the generation of the first century (The church, then, to this degree, knows no past, and the past here with the future loses its meaning, and both are dissolved into an eternal present.) As a result the belief of one specific generation and of each individual believer is only a new structure and form of this same divine power" (UC, 1.2.12, 108).

Möhler sets up the unity of scripture and tradition with the principle that there can be no appropriation of the external word of scripture without the internal testimony of the Spirit. Scripture addresses believers, that is, "those who had already received the Spirit from the community of believers and with it the evangelical doctrine." Thus, the living gospel carried in tradition — which Möhler also refers to as the living truth of the gospel or simply the living truth — "always preceded the written gospel and went along with it, even after the authors of the Holy Scriptures had passed away" (UC, 1.2.14, 113). It follows that one is not to think of scripture and tradition as separate sources of revelation.[89] Scripture and doctrine are one in the Spirit, and scripture is to be read in the spirit or light of church doctrine (UC, 1.2.15, 117). Möhler proposes a number of theses that bind scripture and tradition together functionally. (1) "Tradition is the expression of the Holy Spirit giving life to the totality of believers." (2) "... Scripture is the first member in the written tradition." (3) "Scripture was created out of the living tradition, not vice versa" (UC, 1.2.16, 117). (4) Scripture is not given to believers without tradition; tradition is not given to believers without scripture. "They proceed in one another and live in one another"

---

89. "The Holy Scriptures are not thought of as something different from the living gospel, nor the living gospel, the oral tradition, as something different from the written Gospels, as a different source. As both were the word and doctrine of the Holy Spirit and both were given by the apostles to the believers, so both forms of the word were viewed as belonging fully together and in no way separable." UC, 1.2.15, 114.

(UC, 1.2.16, 118). And the Spirit, everywhere operative and always the same, provides the ground within the believing community for the sameness of meaning and truth across time and differences.

Möhler's theory of the development of doctrine employs the notion of the Holy Spirit, within an organic community, expressing itself from within as it moves through time. "Just as the divine Spirit did not disappear with the apostles, but is always present, so the apostolic doctrine never disappears but is always present with the Spirit at all times" (UC, 1.2.10, 100). The Spirit bears and communicates the word or teaching of Christ, but in an existential way, so that the grounding truth of tradition lies in the living gospel. The Spirit provides the principle of the inner life of the organic community as in a moral person. Tradition is the continuous historical life of this community, and the Spirit, as the principle of its identity and continuity across time, generates relevant new forms or structures or doctrines. The Spirit which testifies to the truth of given doctrines in one period is the same Spirit which testifies in a later period (UC, 1.2.13, 109–10). A doctrine is a true Christian doctrine if it was always present to the church "at least in seed." "Thus what first came at a later time is not Christian, since everything Christian was given at once with the divine Spirit that always had to express itself. Therefore, the basic principle: nothing except what is transmitted" (UC, 1.2.13, 110).

The common key to Möhler's theory of revelation, truth, tradition, and development lies in the turn toward existential, lived truth. "Christianity does not consist in expressions, formulae, or figures of speech; it is an inner life, a holy power, and all doctrinal concepts and dogmas have value only insofar as they express the inner life that is present with them.... Since doctrinal concepts, dogmas, and the like, are explanations of a *specific* inner life and inner life is to be made firm by them, they are not matters of indifference but highly necessary." But Christianity consists not in knowledge, but "a new divine life given to people...." (UC, 1.2.13, 111). Development then occurs through tradition: "tradition contains these successive unfoldings of the higher seed of life by protecting the inner unity of life itself" (UC, 1.2.13, 112). Once unity in the Spirit is presupposed, Möhler seems to tolerate a broad range of developments and pluralism or differences, antitheses, within the community. "Thus it is possible and always necessary that believers, always holding fast to the true nature of the antithesis, reflect the infinity of the possible developments in the Christian religion, and thus preserve and activate life through the free play of many individuals moving in harmony" (UC, 1.4.46, 198).

The church as constitutive of salvation. Each Christian achieves his or her salvation through the church. The church of the Spirit is the mediation of Christ: "Just as we experience nothing historically [*historisch*] of Christ without the Church, we experience him in ourselves only from and in the church" (UC, 1.1.7, 94). The church thus constitutes the salvation of each Christian. But Möhler seems to go further to say that the church constitutes salvation as such, so that the church mediates the salvation of all who are saved. Salvation involves a cosmic community of participation in God the author of all reality, and reconciliation with God through Christ's mediation constitutes the church: "With the reconciliation and the union reestablished with God by Christ, reconciliation and union with all the reconciled is given, and thus the community of all. In this unity of our life with all the redeemed we are first conscious of true union with Christ, just as we are of unity with God in the harmony of our individual life with the universal life. Thus our true reconciliation through Christ is actually and essentially linked with our community with him in community with the totality of the redeemed" (UC, 1.3.31, 154–55). This constitutive role is modified by a consideration of conscious awareness. Möhler seems to say that all who are saved are part of the church, whether they know it or not: "although redemption is so closely tied to the community of believers, it is not said that the person who does not know and understand the community in the way described — indeed this is the case with many in the church — is not redeemed. We often *live* the truth without being conscious of it and are thus often better off than with our twisted concepts. I only emphasize here the union between the two that St. Paul and the early church with him expressed in the most specific way" (UC, 1.3.31, 155). The church, then, is the cosmic community of the saved, the whole body of Christ, and not limited to the empirical church in history.

The mission of the church. The mission of the church is to continue to communicate in history true knowledge of God in faith and thus salvation. There is no true knowledge of God without revelation, that is, special revelation (UC, 1.4.36, 168). And therefore no true knowledge of God outside the church. This is so because pure knowledge of God requires a pure and holy soul. "This soul only God can give; it does not exist outside the church. For this reason no pure knowledge of God is possible without [outside] it" (UC, 1.4.38, 173). Similarly, the church is the only place where the Spirit of God can be surely encountered. "Before the time of Christ the Spirit ... descended only haltingly and sporadically, here and there, on individuals. As a result no common, spiritual, or religious life could be established: everything was a special and peculiar case" (UC, 1.1.2, 84). But with the communication of the Spirit on the apostles and the church, the Spirit would never leave, never come again, but "would continually be present" (UC, 1.1.2, 84). The mission or task is to share the truth of revelation in the life of the Spirit. The Spirit is now bound to the Christian community and the "task entrusted to the church is to communicate this Spirit to God's creatures so that all members who receive it are made alive" (UC, 1.1.2, 84). He quotes Irenaeus to the effect that there is no salvation outside the church because no truth outside of the Spirit which is now bound to the church. But he also admits that the Spirit can work directly on people. But when it does "the individual penetrated by it would feel irresistibly drawn to kindred spirits," and hence the church (UC, 1.1.3, 86).

The organization of the church. A mere glance at the table of contents of *Unity in the Church* would show that the Möhler's frame of reference is the large, transnational Roman Catholic communion. The unified organization of the body of the church consists in the higher clergy, so that he deals with unity in the bishop, the metropolitan, the unity of the total episcopacy, and in the pope.

The bishop. Möhler accepts the account of Clement of Rome relative to the origin of the office of bishop. Christ appointed apostles as missionaries, and they set up bishops as their successors, so the apostolic office would not cease to exist. The local communities solidified around the bishop who provided a secure bond of unity of life and teaching. This historical event has a priori logic: "Without a determined, ordered, and continual teaching office one could not in any way think of a continuing tradition, which, as we heard, is fully necessary to demonstrate the identity of the higher consciousness of the church through all moments of its existence" (UC, 2.1.50, 213–14). "The fact that the apostles appointed leaders, bishops, and priests everywhere and installed them in their positions is undeniably proven by the history of the early church" (UC, 2.1.51, 215).

Möhler insists on the objectivity of the office. "What is primary is not the person of the bishop as such, even if considered as having the greatest doctrinal capabilities, but the bishop's quality as the center of the unity of all" (UC, 2.1.50, 214–15). The bishop does not function as merely an extension of the faithful. The bishop emerges out of the community, and because he is "to exhibit the love of all in a living image, all must be active in his selection" (UC, 2.1.52, 220). But the bishop enjoys an objective office appointed by God and does not function at the behest of the people. "Although the bishop is . . . an offspring of the congregation who chose him, he does not act on the orders of the people. His office is not an arbitrary one, arising out of human agreement. It is positive [that is, historically given] and of divine origin. . . . We have noted that the apostles themselves installed bishops everywhere, and therefore it is a divine law by which the office of bishop is founded" (UC, 2.1.52a, 221). This office is an organ of the body of Christ that cannot be changed (UC, 2.1.52a, 222).[90]

Möhler has a curious thesis on the development of the exercise of episcopal authority. Originally the bishop was "not raised above the others, since he was understood as one with the congregation, and it was not considered aside from him nor he aside from it." Thus he exercised authority in a "communal manner" in the presence of the congregation. But this changed in the course of time, and Möhler attributes the sociological shift not to the bishop but to the people and

---

90. Möhler supports the priesthood of all the faithful, but not in such a way that it removes the distinction between clergy and laity. The church is structured into orders, or organs of the body, by God through Christ. This distinction therefore should be seen in terms of "a distinction of gifts in the church upheld by the Holy Spirit." UC, 2.1.54, 225.

illustrates it in the case of Cyprian. Möhler sees a certain "fall" of the people as they ceased to be the holy community of earlier days. "The bishop now was no longer chosen out of the highest unitive activity of love working in *all* Christians. Rather, he always related more to the congregation as the law does to a person in whom disposition is weak and unholy. . . . The bishop now evermore entered a position in which he must indicate and fulfill what is and should be, rather than what his presence had earlier expressed." As a result the congregation and the bishop became increasingly distinct in their relation to each other (UC, 2.1.55, 226–27). "It was not characteristically the bishops who raised themselves up, but the people who sank, and as a result the bishops obviously appeared higher and more powerful than earlier" (UC, 2.1.55, 228).

Möhler proposes a high, mystical-organizational theology of the bishop. The bishop as it were personifies the unity of believers and their love for one another. As such he is the living symbol that realizes the actual union of the congregation or local church. He has learned from Ignatius of Antioch: "Since the bishop is the personified love of the congregation and the center of all, the person who is bound to him is in community with all, and anyone who is separated from him has withdrawn from the Christian community of all and is separated from the church. . . . This center is therefore so necessary that without it congregational union is unthinkable, and the concept of a church is so determined that a united people is one in one bishop. Two bishops in a congregation are as impossible as two centers of a circle; one of the two cannot be the center" (UC, 2.1.52, 218–19). "A communal religious act without him is, therefore, impossible" (UC, 2.1.52, 219).

The metropolitan. The place and function of the metropolitan bishop developed historically. But it would be a mistake to reduce the place and function of the metropolitan to these contingent historical relationships. "Christianity's inner forming impulse, which knows nothing of any isolation or separation, is thus the true basis for the union of the metropolitanate. The Church body forms itself organically from the interior outward as the structure of an inner, active power, not from the exterior inward in the manner of stones and all inorganic materials" (UC, 2.2.56, 231). The role and status of the metropolitan follows as a corollary of the premise of the organic character of the church as it expanded beyond the individual congregation into groups of churches. The development was both spontaneous and evolutionary. The metropolitan is the center of a group of neighboring bishops and it plays a centering and coordinating function. And the natural organizational means for this was the synod. "In the gatherings to ordain a new bishop, without doubt, they held counsel regarding other broader ecclesiastical matters as well, and when bishops came together for such purposes, their gatherings were expressly called synods" (UC, 2.2.59, 235). In contrast to Pseudo-Dionysius, who saw hierarchy descending from above, Möhler describes an ascending pattern of organic grouping. "Just as the bishop acted in the center of the priestly *corona* (as it is said) and was surrounded by the people, so did the metropolitan act in the counsel of bishops, surrounded by the presbyters" (UC, 2.2.59, 237).

The unity of the total episcopacy. All the bishops together form a corps or college of bishops as a unifying structure. Möhler is still thinking within the framework of organic development. From the beginning, communities stayed in communication with each other through bishops. But at a certain stage, in the middle of the third century with Cyprian, the development reached a new stage where the communication among bishops became the universal structure of the episcopate. Thereafter the transgeographical corps of bishops became a structure of the unity and solidarity of the church. It was not so in the beginning, except in seed; it had to develop; but what developed did so according to the essence of the church.

Cyprian wrote of this one unified episcopacy, in which individual bishops have a part but with responsibility for the whole, in his *Unity of the Church.* "Each bishop is an offspring, resting on a divine institution, of a specific group of believers contingent in and for itself [the local church], and by this the totality of bishops is a total product of all believers, completely indivisible and one, as the believers themselves are, whose unity the bishops present" (UC, 2.3.63, 245). A bishop is a bishop by being a member of the episcopacy. "For as little as one could be a bishop without being made a member of the whole body, so little could he remain a bishop if he was robbed of this association" (UC, 2.3.65, 251).

Unity in the primate. "The visible church lacks the keystone if it remains in the pattern described above; the unity of the episcopate and of all believers in it must represent itself in one church and one bishop: he is the living center of the living unity of the whole church" (UC, 2.4, 255).

The grand vision of the unity of the whole church in the papacy combines the necessity stemming from the organic character of the church's unity and historical development. "In a complete organism, as in the universal whole, individual parts are organic so that each member is seen as a type of the whole, and the power forming the whole repeats its basic form within individual parts" (UC, 2.4.67, 255). In this view, the whole church needs a bishop primate, for without it the unity of all the bishops would not itself be represented in a living image (UC, 2.4.67, 256). Yet this was not the condition of the church all at once; it had to develop historically. According to the law of development, papal primacy cannot be proven before the time of Cyprian when the unity of the church as a whole in the episcopacy first became evident. The primacy is not a concept but a reality; it only became historically manifest after the time of Cyprian (UC, 2.4.68, 257). "Thus, before a personalized image of the unity of believers could truly manifest itself, this unity on which further development followed had to be present" (UC, 2.4.68, 258). At an early period "there could still be no indubitable facts demonstrating the primacy of a church" (UC, 2.4.69, 261). "The further development and outward formation of the primacy belongs to the later period" (UC, 2.4.70, 262).

The activities of the church. Möhler offers a rather general discussion of worship and the sacramental principle. His reflections unfold within a context of unity and diversity in forms of worship. At this point one sees how far Möhler is from being concerned about the details of a sacramental theology or developing a practical manual for church practice. He offers rather a theological theory of worship. In it he compares formal worship in the church to doctrine as expressions of inner faith or piety: "Just as doctrine is the inner faith of the church grasped in concepts, so worship in its most significant aspect is faith reflecting on itself in significant signs" (UC, 1.4.47,

198]. There is thus a parallelism between doctrine and worship, and Möhler exhibits a concern for unity and diversity in each.

Common worship requires public symbols. Such public symbols externalize the inner religiosity of the community, render it public, so that it can then bend back in common appropriation, nurture, and self-expression. Such is the sacramental principle. What, Möhler asks, is the role of physical symbols in a spiritual religion such as Christianity?[91] "Christian religiosity is necessarily a common religiosity. We do not know of an unmediated activity of finite spirit. Symbols, like the word, mediate inner movement. They are not only the unifying point of all but are also the organ through which the interiority of the one flows out into totality and back from it again. This holy symbolism is an expression of unspeakable discovery" (UC, 1.4.47, 200).[92]

Möhler describes the nature of the church's sacraments in very general terms. The sacrament combines inner and external form. The external form is necessary. But the truth and efficacy of the sacrament does not lie in the external form, so that those who try to recreate the external forms of apostolic times miss the point.[93] Sacraments, then, are symbols that make present and actualize what they symbolize. He injects his view of sacraments with realism. "It is fitting that what [Christ] left behind for the continual use of his believers be highly valued: symbol and context, signifier and signified, belong together as sacrament. The bread does not merely signify

---

91. "There is a powerful religiosity in us. We are compelled to develop this reflex until our whole religious characteristic has revealed itself in it as in doctrine. We believe that such religiosity is not truly alive in us if we do not find it fully expressed again externally. It is good that this is so. If we meet our productions again, the religious power that produces the symbol is awakened and reproduced." UC, 1.4.47, 199.

92. "Christianity greatly rejoices in symbols. This is already evident in that Christ offered the highest to believers in the form of a symbol, namely, *himself.*" "When Christ gives his believers the Holy Spirit, he breaths upon them. When he wishes to teach them humility in his school, he washes their feet." UC, 1.4.47, 200.

93. "Such individuals already indicate their imprisonment to the external since they look upon worship as something external which can be accepted or rejected. They think that one is celebrating the Lord's Supper as Jesus and his disciples did since one has no external form. But one only does as they did if one has the inner form and not if one avoids this or that external form. And what does such a person do other than declare the form of one time to be that of all times, and thus in fact forces all into one form." UC, 1.4.48, 201.

him; it is him. We do not merely remember him; he is present, he is in us, and we in him. Baptism does not merely signify purification; true baptism is purification itself. Even if the symbols, which the church begets out of inner need, do not possess this power, they nevertheless gather believers together around them, are together an organ and expression of life, and 'where two or three are gathered in my name (Christ), there am I in the midst of them'" (UC, 1.4.47, 200).

Möhler applied his theory of development to the emergence of sacraments. Regarding what was given to the church by Jesus and the apostles Möhler says that "little was required by them, and their requirements were not at all times the same. Little was directly prescribed. Everything was to be an externally free expression of the religious. In time this expression *had to develop in itself according to need* and only that was to be considered as a proper goal which was not brought in from the external but was the result of the inner working in the external. The apostles were employed in building up inner Christianity" (UC, 1.4.48, 201).

Möhler's conceives of development as both free and open as it moves through history but internally controlled by the organic inner principle of religious life. "We must concede that, on the one hand, there is a drive toward an evolution of symbols and, on the other, a restriction, but on the whole a progressive expansion" (UC, 1.4.48, 202). The restriction is the inner essence and religiosity of the community. No external limits were placed on the church, so that earlier external forms determined later forms. In fact the church very freely borrowed external forms from outside itself, from Judaism or Paganism, even prayer forms, so long as "a Christian idea could be bound with them" (UC, 1.4.48, 202). "All the external worship practices that he handed down, the Supper, Baptism, and so on, Christ took from Jewish practices already in use" (UC, 1.4.48, 203). How is this possible? "The principle of unity stood above forms, and in all its movements it resulted in nothing other than expressing *one* spirit in the many forms" (UC, 1.4.48, 203).

This openness in development in different historical contexts gives rise to the idea of pluralism in sacramental forms and other forms of worship, or unity amid difference in worship. The basic intuition is that the one Spirit provides the unity of inner form and it tolerates large differences, so that one should not become fixated on small or paltry things or external forms. "Indeed, such minds wished to place spiritual unity in chains, narrow its general recognition with *contingent* external limits, constraining it with many stipulations and, wherever they found spiritual unity, endangered it whether by replacing it with another or curtailing it. If for the sake of exterior unity anyone destroyed or did not further internal unity, such acts would not only be laughable but unanswerable" (UC, 1.4.48, 203). "Every desire for unity in external worship that did not thus freely develop from this same Spirit itself or was not established by this same inner need by necessity or by acknowledged appropriateness, was turned aside as inadmissible and unenlightened. Yet the greatest freedom existed in unity" (UC, 1.4.48, 205).

To conclude this representation of Möhler's early ecclesiology: it may bear noting again that his ideas have been forced into a framework not his own. Recognizing this helps to clarify both what he was not and what he was doing in this early work. Möhler did not set out to develop in any explicit way the relation of the church to the world or society, ecclesial ethics, or a whole range of topics indigenous to an adequate ecclesiology. But this arrangement of his ideas shows by implicit comparison with other ecclesiologies how the fundamental metaphor and the framework he used for understanding the church entailed a thorough revision of Catholic ecclesiology. For example, Möhler's attention to the inner life of the church animated by the Spirit represents a significant contrast with the emphasis on the external institution found in the Catechism of the Council of Trent and developed by Bellarmine. Relative to the Roman Catholic understanding of the church that was in place at the time, Möhler represented a conceptual revolution. Such a radical turn-about on that foundational level calls in turn for a rethinking of all the standard topics in a more comprehensive and practical ecclesiology. This was not to happen during the nineteenth century.

PRINCIPLES FOR
A HISTORICAL ECCLESIOLOGY

We move now to the level of broad interpretation. It should be quite obvious to anyone who has read up to this point that something new and distinctive is going on in these two representatives of modern ecclesiology. Highlighting distinctive themes in the ecclesiology of one or both of these authors will confirm this general conclusion and provide principles for ecclesiology as it moves forward in the modern period. The premise here is that one cannot go back, or, if one attempts a *ressourcement* by retrieving the past, the past will always be brought forward into the new world of the present. This view of things contains an implicit judgment that the return to the premodern self-understanding proposed by the Roman school of theology was not really adequate to the times, or faithful to the gospel in a modern context.

Modernity binds Schleiermacher and Möhler together. No one can miss the remarkable parallels that run through the ecclesiologies of Schleiermacher and Möhler. They appear especially striking when placed against the background of the sharply different ecclesiological options that emerged in the sixteenth century. There are, of course, basic commonalities which unite Christian churches provided by faith itself: one Christ, one Baptism, one Spirit, one set of scriptures, one Creed. But what begins to bridge the differences between Protestant and Catholic ecclesiologies laid down so clearly during the sixteenth century on a historical level is modernity itself as this was carried by the history of Europe and reflected in the literature of the period. Newton, the French revolution, European politics, Kant, Friedrich Schlegel, Schelling, and others lay behind these two ecclesiologies. Schleiermacher's is a Protestant ecclesiology, and Möhler's is a Catholic ecclesiology. Yet it is plain that these two constructive ecclesiologies are approaching each other. Surely there remains considerable differences between these two thinkers, and the task at this juncture is not to explore but simply to highlight them. More significant is the fact that Schleiermacher and Möhler share in the same post-Enlightenment Romantic renewal. Surely there are multiple lessons in that.

Similarities amid differences. A symmetry between these two ecclesiologies appears at several foundational areas. The approach to understanding the church involves historical reconstruction and uses the framework of a religious community of believers understood in organic terms of growth and development. The church in both is a fellowship or communion among Christians themselves and with God as mediated by Christ and the Holy Spirit. The Holy Spirit is the principle of divine life within the community. The Lord's Supper is a primary representation of this unity in Christ and fellowship in the love poured out by the Spirit. The image of the body of Christ in its organicity is favored. In all this the church plays an intrinsic role in the Christian economy of salvation.[94] The clearest explanation of the differences between these two ecclesiologies lies in the referents of their ecclesiologies: Schleiermacher's church has the congregation as its primary unit, and in this respect his ecclesiology shares some qualities of the free church type; Möhler's church is the universal institution. While both of these basic types operate as fundamental frames of reference, they are finely developed and nuanced. For example, although Schleiermacher's church is a voluntary association, and he was attentive to its proper size so that it could remain a community, he also appreciated church structures, and theologically he shared a high ecclesiology where the church was not the result of faith but the mediator of faith. Although for Möhler the church is an organic, interpersonal community; still, a universally united episcopacy and then papacy were essential organic developments of this living community. The contrast between these two ecclesiologies appears wide when it is viewed from the perspective of the concrete churches they intend and the fundamental imaginative frameworks of interpretation. But today's pluralistic culture forces distinctions about what is essential and allows recognition that both may be valid rather than competitive.

---

94. Doyle, *Communion Ecclesiology*, 26–28. "Möhler's ecclesiology in *Unity* shares much with that of Schleiermacher. As opposed to the medieval juridical view, it emphasizes a spiritual communion among human beings with God. As opposed to scientific rationalism, it is mystical and transcendent and sacramental. In line with Romanticism, it finds a grounding in religious experience. It is organic, dynamic, and historically conscious. It values unity as the broker of a legitimate diversity, not as its oppressor." Ibid., 32.

Schleiermacher exemplifies a method in ecclesiology from below. Schleiermacher defines the method of ecclesiology in a manner corresponding to what was stipulated at the head of this work. Several characteristics urge the designation. Schleiermacher does not appeal to Jesus as the founder of a universal structure for the Christian community nor to the New Testament as providing such a charter. His turn to experience entails the premise that church structure emerges from the community itself. Möhler's pneumatocentrism also encourages this view; the church formally began at Pentecost; structures developed organically. Schleiermacher's ecclesiology exhibits a sense of historicity and a critical appreciation of historical sources: one must appeal to the history of the church to understand the church; theological statements about the church cannot be separated from a critical historical imagination. A theological or dogmatic conception of the church separated from the actual historical church would be empty ideas; a reductionist historical or sociological portrayal of the church would not be church at all.[95] The data for constructing the self-understanding of the church, therefore, consist in the confessional statements of actual churches. This broad sense of historicity, which itself took different forms and continued to develop in the course of the century, represents an irreversible turning point in modern theology and a breakthrough in ecclesiology because so many other considerations are rooted in it.

Schleiermacher presents a "high" ecclesiology within the context of a historical conception of the work of Christ. One of the advantages that Schleiermacher's ecclesiology enjoys over that of Möhler is comprehensiveness and completeness. Since it is part of his systematics, he has related ecclesiology to other parts of his theology and draws out fairly clearly how the church relates to the work

---

95. "If the attempt were made to set forth the self-identical and invariable element in Christianity in complete abstraction from the historical, it would scarcely be distinguishable from the undertaking of people who imagine that they are expounding Christianity when in point of fact what they offer is pure speculation. And if anyone tried to present solely the variable in Christian history in complete abstraction from the self-identical, his aim would apparently be the same as that of people who, penetrating no further than the outer husk of things, permit us to see in the history of the Church nothing but the complex and pernicious play of blinded passion." CF, #126, 585.

of Christ. The "height" that the statement attempts to define re-
lates to the intrinsic connection between the person and work of
Jesus Christ and the role of the church in history. Jesus Christ in
Schleiermacher's view is the climax of God's dialogue with human
beings in history. God was active in Jesus in so perfect a way that his
God-consciousness completely enveloped and perfected his freedom.
Jesus' saving activity consisted in mediating that God-consciousness,
communicating it to others to form disciples who formed a church.
"The church, in which Schleiermacher detects a 'being of God' analogous to the being of God in Christ, is the locus of Christ's continuing
influence and the historical means by which the Kingdom of God
must be extended and the divine election consummated."[96] Since
the church is the very medium through which this Christian God-
consciousness is communicated, it is constitutive of the salvation
wrought by Jesus Christ in history. And the mission of the church,
its purpose or goal, is to continue this mediation outward into the
world and forward in history. The church *is* the playing out in history
of God's salvation in Jesus Christ.[97]

Schleiermacher wrote in his dogmatics that the distinction "between Protestantism and Catholicism may provisionally be conceived thus: the former makes the individual's relation to the church
dependent on his relation to Christ, while the latter contrariwise
makes the individual's relation to Christ dependent on his relation
to the church" (CF, #24, 103). Many commentators have indicated
that in the terms of this maxim Schleiermacher's ecclesiology can be
construed to be much closer to the Catholic conception than to the
Protestant. But it seems even clearer that such is the case because
Schleiermacher is closer to Calvin on this issue than to Luther. We
have seen the interpretation of Calvin's ecclesiology that gives Book

---

96. Gerrish, "Friedrich Schleiermacher," *Nineteenth Century*, 144.

97. It does not follow that there is no salvation absolutely speaking outside the
church; but it does follow that there is no Christian salvation outside the church.
While much of what is said in this generalization concerning Schleiermacher is not at
odds with the ecclesiology of Möhler, the following difference stands out: Möhler had
a mystical view of the church. He believed that the church unites one with Christ and
that the unity with Christ of all the saved formed them into a spiritual community.
This led him to understand the church as a community transcending history and as
constitutive of salvation of all who are saved. See UC, 1.3.31, 154–55.

IV of the *Institutes* a considerably more important place in his overall scheme than an anti-climax to his christocentrism. In Calvin too the medium in history, indeed the sacrament in history, for actualizing God's grace and will is nothing else than the church. Schleiermacher is an heir of Calvin here.[98]

In the tension between community and office community enjoys a primacy. This thesis implicitly contains two propositions: that there is a tension between the institutional and communitarian dimensions of the church, and that in such a tension the communitarian commands a higher value. That such a tension exists has been displayed in the whole course of the history of the church and its ecclesiology. Schleiermacher's ecclesiology implicitly recognizes and deals with it; but in Möhler the polarity and tension between these two dimensions assume a great deal of importance. For the prominence of the organic metaphor for understanding the church correlates with the living interplay of a community and places it in center stage. Organicity signifies unified interaction of living forces. It stands in contrast to static structure, permanent but dead, or unchanging formal relationships. The sociological distinction between society, which is a formally determined, objective structure, and community, which is a group considered in its subjectivity as living and in motion, correspond with and reinforce the organic metaphor. To develop the organic metaphor still further with twentieth-century knowledge, the principle of sameness and definition is an inner determinant, a programmed code which allows for growth and change, and not an external structure that confines. But what is key to the lasting value of this distinction is the dialectical tension between these two dimensions. This means that neither pole can be absent, that the tension cannot be resolved, that whatever primacy be maintained, it does not mean the elimination of the other pole.

But Möhler clearly emphasizes the primacy of the communitarian character of the church. While both agree on this, Möhler's emphasis may be understood as a reaction against the intrinsic danger

---

98. But not only here. Gerrish affirms and Himes concurs that Schleiermacher's dogmatics are thoroughly influenced by Calvin's *Institutes* in its "churchly character," its consistent reference to "Christian religious affections," and its "scientific character" of systematic precision. Gerrish, "From Calvin to Schleiermacher," 185 and passim.

within a massive, institutionalized transnational church which defines its unity precisely in objective universal terms. The danger is to reduce the referent of the term church to its institutional form. This was indeed the tendency following the Council of Trent as seen in the catechism it mandated. The church is a visible society easily becomes the visible institutional structure of offices. The refusal to separate an invisible and visible church, a good instinct, led in a direction toward emphasizing the primacy of the institution as the bond of church unity, which is potentially problematic. At an extreme this would reduce the church's religious mediation to an objective function, whereas in Schleiermacher's congregationally based ecclesiology this never appears as a danger. Be that as it may, whereas Möhler implies no denial whatsoever of the necessity and importance of objective institution, community and intersubjective relationships enjoy a primacy. The rationale for that primacy will be discussed in what follows. But at this point it is important to see how Möhler's pneumatocentrism fits into the pattern. The Spirit lives in the community by being the gift to each member of it. Thus the Spirit animates the whole community as its divine life-giving force. The dynamic character of the action of the Spirit in human life and history becomes prominent. The active presence of the Spirit in the community makes the church a living, changing community interacting with the world. This is of course what the church has always been and done, but it has rarely been raised up with such clarity.

Office and institution emergent from and dependent upon community. The primacy consists in the subjective community being the source of the objective institution and the telos or purpose of the institution's function. Institution does not create community in early Möhler; rather community creates institutions. Institutions arise historically out of the community of disciples. And the point of institution is to sustain and maintain community.

The metaphor of organicity has resurrected some of the fundamental insights about the nature of social institutions that were at work in Marsilius of Padua and underlay conciliarism. This can be seen when organicity is applied to church organization not simply as governmental structure but more generally as ministerial structure.

The offices of ministry in the framework of the primacy of community appear as creations of the community. The community creates those offices of ministry that the situation demands, and responds to basic needs of the community with consistent ministry. The point here is not to read the representative democracy of Marsilius into Möhler, which would be clearly wrong. It is rather to trace the direction in which the focus on the primacy of the organicity of the community leads. That direction points toward a functional understanding of offices that emerge within the organism in order for it to respond to its inner needs and environmental demands. Offices are created by the community, not placed upon it from outside itself. The purpose and goal of such creation arises from the mission of the church and the means needed to accomplish it. This understanding is not reductionistic and in no way cuts church institutions from God's will or intentions. The Spirit of God within the community and Jesus at its origins provide the explicit link between the structure and performance of the church and God's will in a way that does not undercut human freedom but augments it. The practical implication of this conception is that the church can never lack the resources for reforming or creating church ministries in a way that allows the church to meet its pastoral needs at any given time or place.

Making basic sense out of the distinction between visible and invisible church. Schleiermacher makes modern sense out of the distinction between a visible and an invisible church. This distinction begins with Augustine: the church within the church, the elect and sanctified "dove" distinct within the larger empirical church. It continuously appears in different guises along the history of ecclesiology and takes on different meanings when employed to meet new situations. In conciliar theory it frequently means the communion of all Christians in faith as distinct from institutional structure. The distinction is interpreted in widely different senses: sometimes it is taken as a separation, as though there were two churches. At other times it appears paradoxical: what would an invisible church be? Roman ecclesiology rejects the distinction as used by the Reformers because it was used to undercut the hierarchical structure and authority of the transnational institutional church.

Schleiermacher retrieves the categories of the visible and invisible church as a purely theological distinction. The invisible church is the divine dimension of the church, the effects of grace or of the work of God as Spirit within the empirical organization. This formulation cannot be understood as dividing the church into parts or separating the invisible off from the church as organization. It respects Augustine's conception but without making the elect or sanctified a group set apart. In fact, the dimensions of the visible and invisible church are also at work in a single individual person. In associating the invisible church with the effects of divine presence to the church, Schleiermacher has clarified the union and distinction of the divine and human dimensions of the church. Visible and invisible elements dialectically interact in the life of the church.[99]

Relation to the world as an important category. The category "world" in Schleiermacher's ecclesiology is complex; it contains much of the depth and richness that one finds in St. John's gospel. Many take the term "world" to refer to the range of reality outside the church: the world exists outside the church. But Schleiermacher rejects that usage, for the world is also inside the church as a dimension of it, and there is no church outside the world. Moreover the world inside the church, while it sustains the church as the field in which it exists, also has a dimension of being resistant to the influence of God as Spirit. The term "world" refers to the sum total of elements that are not caught up in the Spirit of Christ, "human nature in the whole extent in which it is not determined by the Holy Spirit..." (CF, #126, 583). The "world" is thus a symbol that refers to history that has not been reached by Christianity; it refers to natural historical limitation and diversity in human beings; it also refers to sin which resists conversion. The world is the natural and historical "prime matter" which is made church by the influence of the Christian Spirit as form. Thus the world will always influence the church, and the church will influence the world by mediating Spirit

---

99. Schleiermacher's conception is compatible with Catholic uses of the image of the body of Christ, the idea of the Spirit animating the church, and a sacramental view of the church. Schleiermacher has turned the distinction into something generally useful, but the terms "visible" and "invisible" will always get in the way.

and Christian God-consciousness to it. A mutual tension and reciprocal influence of the church on the world and the world on the church also represents a dialectical interaction that is going on within the church itself. The mission of the church in this light is to penetrate the world with its God-consciousness and all that accompanies it. The church is called to mediate the effects of God's presence as Spirit to human history and society within itself and beyond itself.

Pluralism among the churches and within the church as necessary in principle. Schleiermacher's historical consciousness allowed him to recognize that pluralism within the great church was necessary. This historical consciousness is expressed in the tension between the church and the world, the invisible power of God's grace and its limited and resistant reception in finite and sinful human subjects. In this situation pluralism is not merely a negative necessity but a positive asset. Where all is limited, no single manifestation or arrangement commands the field, and diverse arrangements can mediate more than any single form. Thus the several maxims that Schleiermacher developed to accommodate diversities which otherwise would ground divisions should not be regarded negatively as concessions or compromises with the world. There is no existence of the church outside the world. His formulas recognizing that all truth is limited, contingent, and mixed with error render the idea of pluralism a positive value. More truth is contained in a pluralistic set of doctrines about the transcendent Christian reality than any single formula could contain.[100] Schleiermacher's maxims, then, are not superficial accommodations but a careful, subtle, and realistic set of principles that will ultimately serve as the implicit basis for the ecumenical movement in the next century.

Defining the shift in modern ecclesiology: historical consciousness. In an effort to define the threshold over which understanding of the church passed in the modern theology represented by Schleiermacher, Brian Gerrish turns to his view of dogmatics and the question of the development of doctrine. Doctrines develop, and the church develops with the doctrines for the doctrines are functions of the

---

100. There were seeds for the recognition of pluralism sown in the sixteenth century, especially among churches in different nations. But Schleiermacher represents a leap forward in historical consciousness.

church's historical God-consciousness. Dogmatics is a historical discipline consisting in reflection on the church's present, although not unconnected with knowledge of the church's past. This involves a new conception of the nature of the church. "For the church appears, no longer as the divinely instituted custodian of infallible truths, but as a social phenomenon caught up in historical flux."[101] "Doctrines, like the church (or rather *with* the church), are also in constant movement and change. The old absolutes of Protestant orthodoxy give way before a thoroughly historicized conception of the church's teaching" (43). Doctrines are not permanently fixed pronouncements to be affirmed or denied; rather they are functional propositions related to the life of the community at a particular stage of its career. The *traditum* of tradition is not a static thing that is handed down, but a living corporate consciousness that both hands down and is handed down. Gerrish quotes Karl Barth for an antithetical view: "'The church can only deliver [the message] the way a postman delivers his mail; the church is not asked...what it makes of the message'" (44). With Schleiermacher, by contrast, the church community is the ambassador, not the postman, of Christ. Dogmas and creeds and confessions become subjects of constant reinterpretation in the light of contemporary knowledge of reality. Understanding of faith develops as "part of the life of the church, which itself is not a legislative institution, but a living organism brought into being by Christ and still guided by his presence" (45). If one were to put a name on what happened here, it could be called an internalization of historical consciousness.[102]

Expanding the shift in modern ecclesiology laterally. The historical consciousness entailed in the sense of historical development and the necessity of making the church relevant to the world at any given time also applies laterally across different cultures. The Spirit

---

101. Gerrish,"Continuity and Change," 41. References in the paragraph are to pages in this essay.

102. It would not be difficult to draw an analogous portrait of the potential significance of Möhler's early ecclesiology over against a more authoritarian conception of the church. But there are major differences between Barth's neo-orthodoxy and the premodern role of the institutional authority of the church in the ecclesiology of the Roman school.

is the principle of unity within the differences generated by historical development across time. The Spirit is also the principle of unity
among the churches in different regions and across the boundaries of
denominations at any given time. It will take some time before this
insight is collectively internalized as in, for example, the ecumenical movement, but its seeds are latent in the organic ecclesiologies
of Schleiermacher and Möhler. A reflection of Congar brings this to
the surface: "Just as the Holy Spirit actualizes the deepest and most
decisive unity of the church not through external boundaries and
laws but by way of an internal, vital inclination, which orients souls,
through love, in the direction of communion and unanimity: so too
the same Holy Spirit actualizes correct belief and unity in the same
faith less by way of boundaries and external formulas than by an internal, vital inclination of the souls in which it works, directing them
toward the same truths and the same life's work. This is surely the
foundational idea of Möhler in *Unity*."[103] From the Fathers Möhler
learned that life in the Holy Spirit was unified in the power of love;
life alienated from the Spirit is egoistic, divisive, fragmented, and ultimately heretical. Through interchange and familiarity across the
external boundaries of the churches Christians began to recognize
that since life in other churches was marked by love it must unfold
in the Spirit. Thus the differences and divisiveness between churches
must come from culture and not the Spirit. During the course of the
twentieth century this lateral application of historical consciousness
and an expanded appreciation of the role of the Spirit within the
church would be gradually internalized.

---

103. Congar, "L'Esprit des Pères d'après Möhler," 6.

Chapter 6

Twentieth-Century Ecclesiology: The World Council of Churches, Vatican II, and Liberation Ecclesiology

How would one characterize the twentieth century? A simple list of major events can evoke a sense of rapid, momentous change that characterized this relatively short period of time. It has been called the century of death: two world wars, several genocides, and a development of such an awesome technology of human destruction that mere reflection upon it causes anxiety. These weapons can now be "home made." It was a century of a quantum increase in exploration and knowledge: relearning the size of creation in terms of time and space, the complexity of physical reality, and the intricacies of life itself. Pictures of the planet from outer space have altered the perspective of human self-understanding. Medical science pushed back the median age of death, presided over an explosion of human population, and witnessed new world-threatening pandemics. New technologies have united the race as never before and thereby show us our differences: radio, cinema, air travel, television, the World Wide Web. Perhaps the most striking development of all has been a new sense of historicity mediated by the sheer rate of change.

Every attempt to represent the development of ecclesiology across such a century requires decisions about what to raise up and explanations of why it is chosen and how it should be represented. Despite the somewhat arbitrary character of these decisions, naming these choices at the outset as the biases or hypotheses that govern the next two chapters will at least clarify their unfolding. Three common threads with respect to the development of Christian ecclesiology run through both of these chapters and will focus the interpretation at the end. The first is that twentieth-century ecclesiology betrays a growing consciousness, appreciation, and organization of pluralism. Pluralism here means a form of unity that respects diversity or, inversely, the recognition of unity amid difference and plurality. The second overarching thematic which the data will illustrate is that the church internalizes and acts out in new ways its symbiotic relationship with the world. Third, the ecumene, or whole world, both in geographical terms of the five continents and human terms of the secular sphere of human activity, progressively becomes the horizon for understanding the church.

Six areas of development, subject matters, or events have been chosen to illustrate these developments, the first three of which will be presented in this chapter. The first is the ecumenical movement and its most significant achievement, the creation of the World Council of Churches. Nothing like this had ever existed before, and its relevance for ecclesiology is direct and immense. The second is the protracted event of the Second Vatican Council and the forces it released into the Roman Church and beyond. The third section then discusses the ecclesiology found in liberation theology with special attention to basic ecclesial communities. Chapter 7 will round off the ecclesiological developments at the end of the millennium. First we turn again to the ecclesiology of the Eastern churches which has been left unattended since the narrative of historical developments into the late Middle Ages. The Orthodox churches have been influential in the development and life of the WCC and a representation of Eastern ecclesiology can have a major role in a constructive ecclesiology for our time. Second, the world-wide spread of pentecostal churches will be represented as introducing yet another new form of church structure. Third, the chapter will then present in abbreviated form the already schematic ecumenical ecclesiology presented in the document *Baptism, Eucharist and Ministry* of the Faith and Order Commission of the World Council of Churches.[1] The process which generated this document began in the preparations for the World Conference at Lausanne in 1927 a half century earlier.

---

1. *Baptism, Eucharist and Ministry*, Faith and Order Paper 111 (Geneva: World Council of Churches, 1982). This work is cited hereafter as BEM.

Taken together, these six topics over these two final chapters provide a broad witness to the ecclesiology as it developed across the twentieth century and as the church begins its third millennium.

THE ECUMENICAL MOVEMENT
AND THE WORLD COUNCIL OF CHURCHES

The ecumenical movement refers to the massive consciousness and momentum within the churches in which "Christians have learned to accept with equal sincerity both the underlying unity of faith in Christ which has never been lost and the seriousness of the differences by which the Christian communions are kept in separation."[2] This movement is much wider than those events leading to the development of the World Council of Churches, but the WCC was its most significant achievement. After a review of that development, this first part of the chapter will focus on the ecclesiological status of the WCC and how a constructive sense of pluralism became integrated into common Christian consciousness.

The Ecumenical Movement and Genesis of
the World Council of Churches

A variety of different initiatives concretized a general will to overcome the divisions in the church. The creation of the World Council of Churches was both a part of this ecumenical movement and its most dramatic manifestation.

The ecumenical movement. Kenneth Scott Latourette reiterates the common view that "The World Missionary Conference, Edinburgh 1910, was the birthplace of the modern ecumenical movement."[3] That date provides a formal reference point for developments beginning earlier and flowering thereafter. For example, the Evangelical Alliance, at which "800 Christian leaders assembled from the

---

2. Stephen Charles Neill, "Plans of Union and Reunion: 1910–1948," in *A History of the Ecumenical Movement: 1517–1948*, 4th ed., ed. Ruth Rouse and S. C. Neill (Geneva: World Council of Churches, 1993), 445. The history of the ecumenical movement and the genesis of the WCC presented here is largely dependent on this compendium produced by a team of historians. The work is cited hereafter as HEM.

3. Kenneth Scott Latourette, "Ecumenical Bearings of the Missionary Movement and the International Missionary Council," HEM, 362.

United States and Canada, England, Scotland, Ireland, Wales, France, Switzerland, Holland, Germany, and Sweden" was founded in 1846 in order to promote unity among different Christian groups.[4] Missionaries and missionary societies met frequently in the course of the nineteenth century. Other conferences were motivated by the conviction that cooperation in missions depended on churches "at home" confronting their differences directly. The nineteenth century saw formulas and programs of prayer for unity among the churches.[5]

A good number of different kinds of Christian activity carried the ecumenical movement forward in the first half of the twentieth century. Christian lay movements, that is, formal Christian groups which like some missionary societies were not churches, were organized both nationally and internationally. The YMCA, the YWCA, and the Student Christian Movement or SCM were missionary in character and carried the ecumenical spirit.[6] Already in 1902 the Methodist Church in Canada proposed a process that would move through stages to bring together in a single church Methodists, Presbyterians, and Congregationalists. The United Church of Canada was finally inaugurated in 1925.[7] Another form of ecclesial union developed within denominations with such entities as "The Baptist World Alliance," "The Lutheran World Federation," "The International Congregational Council."[8] Other types of ecumenical cooperation among churches developed locally into national councils of churches. Churches also cooperated in various common projects such as publishing or supporting Bible societies.[9]

Special note has to be made of the early influence of interdenominational movements such as the Student Christian Movement.

---

4. Ruth Rouse, "Voluntary Movements and the Changing Ecumenical Climate," HEM, 318–24, at 319.

5. Ibid., 338–49.

6. Ruth Rouse, "Other Aspects of the Ecumenical Movement: 1910–1948," HEM, 599–612.

7. Stephen Charles Neill, "Plans of Union and Reunion: 1910–1948," HEM, 454–58. This essay reviews a great variety of different kinds of church unions, or federations, or reunions that occurred during the first half of the twentieth century. Another influential church union was the Church of South India which brought together churches with an episcopal polity and those without. Ibid., 473–76.

8. Ibid., 613–20.

9. Ibid., 620–40.

The SCM communicated the idea of unity which respected diversity. Because it was interdenominational, participants came together for common activities while remaining loyal to their particular denominations and confessions. This demonstrated at the same time a kind of unity that might be attained as well as a way toward it. "In essence it was the idea of a movement in which the churches would give of their riches, not give them up; would share their heritage, not surrender it."[10] This seminal notion represents a crucial step in the direction of a recognition of the positive character of pluralism.

The genesis of the World Council of Churches. One may also take The World Missionary Conference as the start of the long process, interrupted by two World Wars, leading to the formation of the World Council of Churches. The ordinary way of telling this extraordinary story proceeds through the stages marked by a succession of World Conferences; these conferences and the organizations and committees which planned them and oversaw their implementation provided the vehicle by which the WCC was founded.[11] These conferences were sponsored by two movements with distinct but overlapping concerns: the Faith and Order movement and the Life and Work movement. Both held world conferences in the 1920s and again in 1937. At these last meetings they agreed to sponsor and be subsumed into a World Council of Churches which first met and constituted itself in Amsterdam in 1948.

"Edinburgh 1910 summed up and focused much of the previous century's movement for uniting Christians in giving the Gospel to the world."[12] In the course of it, Charles H. Brent, an American

---

10. Rouse, "Voluntary Movements," HEM, 343.

11. But one should not overlook the leadership and tenacity of two or three generations of leaders who carried this movement forward. Unfortunately, in this brief space, I cannot list or introduce these leaders with the exception of a passing reference to the names of one or other of them. W. A. Visser 't Hooft, in his *The Genesis and Formation of the World Council of Churches* (Geneva: World Council of Churches, 1982), tells this story with an intimate knowledge that pays tribute to the leaders who made it happen.

12. Latourette, "Ecumenical Bearings," HEM, 355. Also the International Missionary Council, founded in 1921, grew out of the Continuation Committee of this conference and went on to become an influential force cooperating with Faith and Order and Life and Work in the formation of the WCC. Without this umbrella organization young churches in the developing world were in danger of isolation and divisive splintering. Ibid., 402.

Episcopalian missionary bishop in the Philippines, gave a speech in which he insisted that the issues of doctrine and church structure had to be addressed by the churches. Brent himself took on the project and brought a proposal for an international conference on Faith and Order to his own Episcopal Church in the U.S. In 1912 a deputation was sent to the Anglican Churches of Great Britain and Ireland. By the time of the outbreak of World War I the idea had been put before most of the churches of the world. After the war the leadership shifted "to a body representative of the Anglican, Lutheran, Orthodox, Reformed, and other Churches of Europe and America."[13]

The roots of the Life and Work movement reach into the Social Christianity described in the last chapter as well as a deep concern for international peace and the role of the church in promoting it. In 1914 Nathan Söderblom was elected archbishop of Uppsala. With the outbreak of the war he issued an appeal for peace in the name of the church and began to lead the churches in an effort to help bring it about.[14] After the war, at a conference held in 1919 Söderblom promoted his idea for "an Ecumenical Council of the Churches which should be able to speak on behalf of Christendom on religious, moral, and social concerns of men."[15] The churches had to have such an organ to address the world. Thus at a Conference at Geneva in 1920 Söderblom proposed an ambitious ecumenical program, the movement called Life and Work was created to carry it out, and committees were put into place to begin the work of planning an ecumenical conference as a step to a council.[16]

But this call by Söderblom was anticipated by the Orthodox Church of Constantinople. The Holy Synod of 1919, no doubt inspired by the League of Nations, heard a proposal for a League of Churches and studied the matter. In January 1920, in an encyclical

---

13. Tissington Tatlow, "The World Conference on Faith and Order," HEM, 410. During the war, in 1916, a North American Preparatory Conference was held at which were decided the subjects that should be considered by the World Conference. Ibid., 414.

14. Nils Karlström, "Movements for International Friendship and Life and Work: 1910–1925," HEM, 519–30.

15. Ibid., 533.

16. Ibid., 535–39.

letter to all the churches, the Church of Constantinople formally proposed the formation of a League of Churches.[17]

The Universal Christian Conference on Life and Work which met in Stockholm in August 1925 consisted in more than 600 delegates from 37 countries. It discussed the unity of the church and its role in addressing various social issues. Perhaps the main contribution of Stockholm was the event itself: it made a significant impact on the participants and through them on the churches. Differences were encountered and reckoned with across confessional boundaries and theologies. The subject matter of a single faith and its bearing on society transcended divisions. Moreover, the Conference "affirmed in unmistakable terms the responsibility of the churches for the whole life of man. In doing so, it brought to focus the manifold and scattered endeavors of generations."[18]

Meanwhile planning for Faith and Order also went forward, and in 1927 at Lausanne the first World Conference of Faith and Order assembled with just over 400 delegates including staff from a broad representation of churches and continents, less from Asia than from Europe, Africa, and North America.[19] The "Final Report" of the Lausanne Conference is a remarkable short document which in six chapters sums up basic agreements and the world of differences among the represented churches. The preamble announces a common confession of faith in Jesus Christ. From there it moves on to document (1) the call to all Christians to unity; (2) the church's evangelical message for the whole world; (3) a concise definition of the church as the communion of believers in Christ, called by God's will to be the instrument for the preached word and work of God's Spirit in history. This church has (4) a common faith based in scripture and creed; (5) a structured ministry which in fact is divided roughly according to three types: episcopal, presbyteral, and

---

17. Visser 't Hooft, *Genesis and Formation*, 1–6.

18. Nils Ehrenström, "Movements for International Friendship and Life and Work, 1925–1948," HEM, 549–50. See "Message: Universal Christian Conference on Life and Work: Stockholm, 1925," in Michael Kinnamon and Brian E. Cope, eds., *The Ecumenical Movement: An Anthology of Key Texts and Voices* (Geneva: WCC Publications; Grand Rapids: William B. Eerdmans, 1997), 265–67. This work is cited hereafter as *Anthology.*

19. Tatlow, "The World Conference on Faith and Order," HEM, 421–25.

congregational; and (6) a ministry of sacraments, principally baptism and the eucharist.[20] Each short description of what is shared
in common is accompanied by explanations of where the divisions
lie. The fundamental pattern of this document is followed in later
ones in the course of the century culminating in the document BEM
of 1982.

Continuing committees kept the momentum of these conferences
alive. But in 1930 the committee of Life and Work reconstituted
itself as a permanent organization and gave itself the name "Universal Christian Council for Life and Work." This marked another
significant step toward the formation of a council of churches.[21]
Thereafter, with the rise of totalitarian regimes in Europe and Russia, the question of the role of the church became more pressing and
both movements planned conferences in 1937: Life and Work met at
Oxford, after which Faith and Order met in Edinburgh.

"Oxford, the second of the Life and Work conferences, moved away
from the classical liberalism of Stockholm 1925 in favor of a social
ethic informed by such theologians as Reinhold Niebuhr and Karl
Barth."[22] The church is called to become involved in social life by
addressing the values of the gospel to these key problems: national
life, race, the issues of society. The report urges ecumenical unity
without which its message to society will not be effective. The conference was convinced that "lack of unity conflicts seriously with
the ultimate and supreme purposes of the church. These purposes
are and must remain to proclaim the gospel of God's love in Jesus
Christ to all mankind, to administer the sacraments, to fulfill the
Christian ideal of fellowship and to guide the souls of her children
in the ways of holiness."[23]

---

20. Lucas Vischer, ed., *A Documentary History of the Faith and Order Movement 1927–1963* (St. Louis: Bethany Press, 1963), 27–39. Cited hereafter as DHFOM.

21. Visser 't Hooft, *Genesis and Formation*, 24–26.

22. Kinnamon and Cope, *Anthology*, 268.

23. "The Oxford Conference on Church, Community and State, 1937," *Anthology*, 268–77, at 274. The report bears out the reflection that "during the 1930s Life and Work was becoming more 'theological,' while Faith and Order was becoming more 'practical.' This convergent development was an important factor in bringing the two movements together." Visser 't Hooft, *Genesis and Formation*, 37.

The "Final Report" of Edinburgh, 1937 contains a descriptive ec-clesiology, which follows the path laid out by Lausanne ten years earlier. In addition it sketches three quite different kinds or types of unity: a federation of churches involving cooperative actions, an in-tercommunion of churches in which churches recognize the others as true churches, and a corporate or organic union in which churches come together to form a united church. The report then points to various key factors which promote and provide obstacles to each of these forms of unity, such as the likeness or lack of it between church confessions, patterns of sacramental worship, church orders or polities and structures of ministry. In so doing it maps the com-plexities of ecumenical discussion and approaches to unity.[24] Not least among them is the principle which William Temple, archbishop of Canterbury, announced in his sermon at the opening service of the conference: "We are here as representatives of our churches; true, but unless our churches are ready to learn one from another as well as to teach one another, the divisions will remain. Therefore our loy-alty to our own churches, which have sent us here, will not best be expressed in a rigid insistence by each upon his own tradition."[25]

Perhaps the most important acts of both of these conferences were to approve the formation of the World Council of Churches. Through a whole series of various meetings, loosely coordinated through a network of leaders who attended them, various ecumenical organi-zations lurched forward toward the decision to form the WCC. But a meeting from July 8 to 10, 1937, in London at Westfield College of the "Committee of Thirty-five" who represented the main ecu-menical organizations proved to be a turning point. It proposed "a World Council of Churches as a permanent organ of the churches for the accomplishment of their common ecumenical task. The Council was defined as 'a body representative of the churches and caring for the interests of Life and Work and Faith and Order respectively.' "[26] This proposal was submitted to both of the conferences of 1937 just

---

24. "Final Report of the Second World Conference on Faith and Order," DHFOM, 40–74.

25. William Temple, "Sermon at the Opening Service," *Anthology*, 20.

26. Willem Adolf Visser 't Hooft, "The Genesis of the World Council of Churches," HEM, 702.

reviewed, and they approved the plan and appointed seven persons to form the Committee of Fourteen to design and implement it.[27] They began work almost immediately. The elements of a constitution were designed at a meeting in Utrecht in 1938.[28] The first assembly was planned for 1941 but was interrupted by World War II. It finally happened in Amsterdam in 1948.

The Self-Definition of the WCC relative to the Church and the Churches

"The opening service of the Assembly took place in the Nieuwe Kerk at Amsterdam on Sunday, 22 August 1948. 147 Churches in forty-four countries were represented by 351 official delegates. . . . On the morning of Monday, 23 August 1948 the World Council of Churches came into existence."[29] After confessing unity in Christ and division among the churches, the Assembly stated its intention in forming the WCC: "But Christ has made us His own, and He is not divided. In seeking Him we find one another. Here at Amsterdam we have committed ourselves afresh to Him, and have covenanted with one another in constituting this World Council of Churches. We intend to stay together. We call upon Christian congregations everywhere to endorse and fulfill this covenant in their relations one with another. In thankfulness to God we commit the future to him."[30]

The statement of purpose shows clearly that the WCC is not a church, and surely not a static institutional entity, but a framework for the churches to network and face common issues together. "There is but one Lord and one Body. Therefore we cannot rest content with our present divisions. Before God, we are responsible for one another. We see already what some of our responsibilities are, and God will show us more. But we embark upon our work in the WCC in

---

27. Ibid., 703–04. Faith and Order approved the plan conditionally.

28. At Utrecht, the plan "elaborated at Westfield College was used as a starting point, and three problems were discussed in greater detail: the authority of the Council, its doctrinal basis, and the way in which representatives to the Assembly and the Central Committee should be chosen." Visser 't Hooft, *Genesis and Formation*, 48. The plan met the conditions stipulated by Faith and Order.

29. Ibid., 719–20.

30. "Message," First Assembly of the WCC, *Anthology*, 21

penitence for what we are, in hope for what we shall be."[31] The reports accepted by the Assembly give explicit voice to the two major ecclesiological concerns of the twentieth century: the inner demand for unity that appreciates distinct traditions and the relevance of the church for the world. These two issues reinforce each other. The church is virtually united in its belief in its "vocation to worship God in His Holiness, to proclaim the Gospel to every creature." The church has also been "set apart in holiness to live for the service of all mankind." But differences appear in the sphere of "the relation between the Godward vocation of the Church in worship and her manward vocation in witness and service" and in the "nature of the Church's responsibility for the common life of men and their temporal institutions."[32]

The ecclesiological status of the WCC. The question of the ecclesiological status of the WCC had been implicit in its planning and formation from the beginning: it received explicit attention and an answer in a meeting held in Toronto in 1950.[33] This short document defines the WCC, clarifies what it is not, and formulates the assumptions underlying its existence.

"The WCC is composed of churches which acknowledge Jesus Christ as God and Savior.... The Council desires to serve the churches which are its constituent members as an instrument whereby they may bear witness together to the common allegiance to Jesus Christ, and cooperate in matters requiring united action. But the Council is far from desiring to usurp any of the functions which already belong to its constituent churches, or to control them, or to legislate for them, and indeed is prevented by its constitution from so doing.... The Council disavows any thought of becoming a

---

31. "Report of the First Assembly of the WCC," II, #31, DHFOM, 81. "We bring these, and all other difficulties between us into the World Council of Churches in order that we may steadily face them together." Ibid., #30, DHFOM, 81.

32. "Report of the First Assembly of the WCC," II, #16–20, DHFOM, 78–79.

33. "The Church, the Churches and the World Council of Churches: The Ecclesiological Significance of the World Council of Churches," a document received by the Central Committee of the WCC at Toronto, 1950, DHFOM, 167–76. The document is also found in *Anthology*, 463–68. It is cited in the text as "Toronto" from DHFOM. Visser 't Hooft drafted this text which then underwent some revisions at the Toronto meeting. He gives an extensive analysis of its development and content in *Genesis and Formation*, 70–85.

single unified church structure independent of the churches which have joined in constituting the Council, or a structure dominated by a centralized administrative authority."[34]

"Toronto" lays out what the WCC is not and does not do: it is not a superchurch and has no ecclesial authority of its own; does not negotiate church unions; is not based on a single ecclesiology; does not relativize any given ecclesiology or declare all ecclesiologies equal; does not define the character of church union. All of these matters are understood in different ways by the member churches ("Toronto," 169–71).

The positive approach to the nature of the WCC proceeds through the suppositions underling it and what it does. The most basic of many assumptions supporting the WCC asserts that a common faith serves as its bond of unity. The WCC stands on what unites the churches, not what divides them. Member churches thus "recognize in other churches elements of the true church," and they are substantial and constitutive: faith in Jesus Christ, a valid baptism, life in the Spirit, etc. "They are a fact of real promise and provide an opportunity to strive by frank and brotherly intercourse for the realization of a fuller unity" ("Toronto," 174). Several things derive from this basis: recognition of a common headship of Christ, and a common faith that the church on a theological level is one in Christ, which in turn legitimates conversation and cooperation. "The member churches enter into spiritual relationships through which they seek to learn from each other and to give help to each other in order that the Body of Christ may be built up and that the life of the churches may be renewed" ("Toronto," 175).

In sum, the WCC is not a church but is an ecclesial institution and instrument that must be understood in the context of the wider ecumenical movement. It is a vehicle of the churches and for the churches that enables their networking. It should be understood functionally but not "merely" functionally; nor at this point should it be regarded "substantially," as in an autonomous integral and undivided organism. It is rather a means for enhancing the integral life

---

34. "Report of the First Assembly of the WCC," taken up and cited in "Toronto," 167–68.

of each church and the whole church and the mission of each church and the whole church.

Elements of a Pluralistic Understanding of the Church

A growing sense of pluralism, which signifies the positive, constructive insight that unity and diversity can coexist and be mutually enriching, is foundational to the ecumenical movement. But in itself this conviction merely defines formally an arena for understanding and negotiating multiple forces and vectors. The insight allows for infinite concrete variations; each church will have its thresholds and limits. This issue was discussed at the Third Assembly of the WCC in New Delhi in 1961. And in 1990 a subcommittee of the WCC issued a report on the wider religious pluralism within which the Christian church must now situate itself.[35]

"New Delhi" defines the unity of the church as follows: "We believe that the unity which is both God's will and his gift to his church is being made visible as all in each place who are baptized into Jesus Christ and confess him as Lord and Savior are brought by the Holy Spirit into one fully committed fellowship, holding the one apostolic faith, preaching the one Gospel, breaking the one bread, joining in common prayer, and having a corporate life reaching out in witness and service to all, and who at the same time are united with the whole Christian fellowship in all places and all ages in such wise that ministry and members are accepted by all, and that all can act and speak together as occasion requires for the tasks to which God calls his people" ("New Delhi," 144–45). The text goes on to develop this fulsome and compacted description phrase by phrase.

The report also states forthrightly that the unity just described subsists within diversity: "We are clear that unity does not imply simple uniformity of organization, rite, or expression" ("New Delhi," 145). The fellowship and unity of the whole church which is created by the Holy Spirit does not imply "a rigid uniformity of structure,

---

35. "Third Assembly of the WCC: Report of the Section on Unity," DHFOM, 144–63. This report is cited in the text as "New Delhi" from this source; it is found in an abbreviated form in *Anthology*, 88–92. "Religious Plurality: Theological Perspectives and Affirmations, 1990," is found in *Anthology*, 417–20; it is cited as "Religious Plurality."

organization, or government. A lively variety marks corporate life in the one Body of one Spirit" ("New Delhi," 148). Moreover, the deepest problem and most serious obstacle to effective unity consists in different understandings of the nature of ministry, church organization around ministry, and the "validity" of the ministries of other churches. A good example is the contrast between the insistence upon and the nonacceptance of episcopal ministry among the churches ("New Delhi," 149–50).

"New Delhi" then proposes some principles for dealing with diversity in the context of the unity bestowed by the Spirit which should prove to be important for understanding the church. First, relative to doctrinal bases for unity, "two useful distinctions may be made — that intellectual formulations of faith are not to be identified with faith itself, and that *koinonia* in Christ is more nearly the precondition of 'sound doctrine' than *vice versa*" ("New Delhi," 155). Second, the situation of diversity within a unity impelled by the Spirit and the love of God exerts pressure "on the limits of our own inherited traditions" and urges a certain "theological necessity of what we may call 'responsible risk'" ("New Delhi," 154). Third, relative to intercommunion, we must consider whether there are certain situations "when intercommunion is possible even before full union is achieved" ("New Delhi," 153). "Moreover, if we reversed the usual order of discussion and focused on Eucharistic action — what God does and calls us to do at the Lord's Table — rather than (first of all) on Eucharistic administration — i.e., the problem of valid ministry — we might find a clearer way to the heart of an adequate sacramental doctrine" ("New Delhi," 157). The practical demands of ecumenical association are forcing these principles to the surface.

Finally, one can read in the New Delhi report a development in the understanding of the ecclesial status of the WCC beyond "Toronto," one that moves in the direction of a more substantial ecclesial status while still falling well short of understanding it as a church. To a certain extent "Toronto" regarded the WCC as an objective institution formed by the member churches. Here a more social-existential view sees the WCC as not other than the lives of the churches which sustain it: "It is the churches in continuing council. It is not over or apart from the churches but next to them at all times" ("New Delhi,"

161). Here the meaning of the term "council" shifts slightly from a common secular meaning of a federation or league understood in objective, juridical terms and begins to approach an ecclesial sense of a synod of the churches. "We should speak of the Council as 'we' rather than 'it' or 'they'" ("New Delhi," 161). The usage even approaches a sacramental understanding of this institution for it is "an instrument of the Holy Spirit for the effecting of God's will for the whole church, and through the church for the world" ("New Delhi," 161). The problem of finally defining the status of the WCC is that it is a first in history and has no exact generic predecessors.

In the course of thirty years after the Assembly in New Delhi in 1961, a new sense of an interreligious pluralism began to affect the understanding of the Christian church. "Religious Plurality" was produced by a WCC subunit on Dialogue with People of Living Faiths Consultation in 1990.[36] The document has an implicit trinitarian structure which treats the world's religious pluralism from a Christian perspective of the creator, Jesus Christ, and the Spirit and adds notes on interreligious dialogue.

God as creator: people of all times and places have interacted with God. Religious pluralism is caused by the various ways in which God relates and interacts with people and the richness and diversity of human beings themselves. The conviction that "God as creator of all is present and active in the plurality of religions makes it inconceivable to us that God's saving activity could be confined to any one continent, cultural type, or groups of peoples" ("Religious Plurality," 418).

Christology and religious plurality: "We find ourselves recognizing a need to move beyond a theology which confines salvation to the explicit personal commitment to Jesus Christ" ("Religious Plurality," 419). "The saving presence of God's activity in all creation and human history comes to its focal point in the event of Christ" (Ibid.) But how the saving mystery of Christ is available to people outside the Christian sphere we do not understand.

---

36. The text is a product of a four year process of study. The conference that produced the document included participants from the Orthodox, Protestant, and Roman Catholic Churches. The document is a landmark for a new level of an appreciation of pluralism and its impact on Christian self-understanding as church.

The Spirit and religious plurality: the Spirit of God is and has been at work in the living faiths of other peoples, so that we can learn about God in dialogue with other religions ("Religious Plurality," 420).

The report concludes that dialogue will assume a new importance in the church and "result in the deepening of our own life of faith" ("Religious Plurality," 420). It enriches our knowledge of ultimate truth, transforms the way in which theology is to be done, and together with a common praxis of liberation provides a new basis and source for theology.

To conclude: measured by the ecumenical movement and the creation of the WCC, the development of especially mainline Protestant ecclesiology across the twentieth century was remarkable. It is difficult today to imagine how separate the churches were from each other at the turn of the twentieth century.[37] Much of this separation was gradually overcome by mutual recognition of each other by the churches and a common openness to the world.

THE ECCLESIOLOGY OF VATICAN II

The Second Vatican Council (1962–65) was a major event in the history of the Roman Catholic Church and not without impact on all Christians. Karl Rahner compared its significance to the council of the apostles in Jerusalem because it marked a turning point, a transcendence of the Gregorian and even the Constantinian church by an acceptance of responsibility for being a world church.[38] Vatican II provides the first official and comprehensive ecclesiology at a conciliar level in the history of the Roman Catholic Church. The tight synopsis of that ecclesiology which follows is prefaced by a brief account of the ecclesiological events leading up to it; it is followed by an account of its aftermath in the final decades of the twentieth century.

The Catholic Church prior to Vatican II

The question of what led to Vatican II does not elicit a clear answer. The reasons for the ambiguity are more obvious. On the one hand,

---

37. Ehrenström, "Movements," HEM, 593.
38. Karl Rahner, "Towards a Fundamental Theological Interpretation of Vatican II," *Theological Studies* 40 (1979): 716–27.

clear lines of continuity can be drawn between the ecclesiology in place before Vatican II and the content of the council itself; it is the same church. On the other hand, the changes in direction are astonishing. From another perspective, despite the suddenness of the change contained in Vatican II when compared with the ecclesiology of the first half of the century, one can still find green shoots of promise growing in various movements within the church during that period.

The ecclesiology in place can be measured by what was taught at the Gregorian University right up to 1960.[39] The doctrines of the infallibility and the universal jurisdiction of the pope were in place after 1870. Understanding the church proceeded in two large steps: an apologetic approach established the divine nature of the church through historical and philosophical reason; on that premise a dogmatic method argued from the authority of God revealing and of the church teaching through magisterial statements about itself.[40] The hierarchical structure of the church was established as such by God through Jesus, a historical and theological premise proven by citation of New Testament texts. The keystone of the hierarchy was Peter and his successor popes. Once these theological principles were in place, however, the analysis became heavily sociological or political and legal. Theologically, the Spirit of God was the soul of the church, and the power of the Spirit was mediated by a hierarchical ministry with divine authority. This juridical authority held the church together as an institution and may "not undeservedly be called the soul of the church."[41]

The modernist crisis in the Roman Church at the turn of the century augmented an institutional concern for integrity of doctrine in

---

39. T. Howland Sanks, in *Authority in the Church: A Study in Changing Paradigms* (Missoula, Mont.: Scholars Press, 1974), 102, after his study of the successive ecclesiologists at the Gregorian in the period between Vatican I and Vatican II, says that the ecclesiology remained relatively constant. The Gregorian theologians were important because they set the trend for the ecclesiology taught around the world.

40. Sanks, *Authority in the Church*, 92, n. 2, commenting on Timotheus Zapelena, the Jesuit ecclesiologist at the Gregorian whose work *De Ecclesia Christi* was republished six times up to 1954–55 and used in courses up to 1961. Ibid., 91.

41. Sanks, *Authority in the Church*, 66, citing Domenico Palmieri, a Jesuit ecclesiologist of the Roman School in the late nineteenth century. In other words, both the Holy Spirit and juridical authority were referred to as the soul of the church.

every form of teaching. After it, close institutional oversight of theologians made creative thought difficult. Pius XI's response in 1928 to the invitation to join the ecumenical movement indicates the degree of ecclesiocentrism that characterized early twentieth-century Roman ecclesiology.[42] This encyclical gives the ecclesiological rationale for standing aside from the movement: only one true church exists and this is synonymous with the Roman Church. Christian unity consists in membership in the Roman Church and the submission of all Christians to the authority of the pope. Rome "cannot on any terms take part in their assemblies, nor is it anyway lawful for Catholics either to support or to work for such enterprises; for if they do so they will be giving countenance to a false Christianity, quite alien to the one church of Christ" (MA, 8). In the end, "the union of Christians can only be promoted by promoting the return to the one true church of Christ of those who are separated from it, for in the past they have unhappily left it" (MA, 10). Regarding membership, the encyclical states that "in this one church of Christ no man can be or remain who does not accept, recognize and obey the authority and supremacy of Peter and his legitimate successors" (MA, 11).

The most authoritative twentieth-century ecclesiological teaching in the Catholic Church prior to Vatican II was *Mystici Corporis Christi*.[43] This encyclical letter grew out of extensive writing on the Pauline concept which peaked with the work of Emile Mersch in 1933.[44] Yves Congar summarizes the content of the encyclical as follows: the church is the *body* of Christ, signifying the church as visible organization that is one, visible, hierarchically organized, with distinct members including sinners; of *Christ*, who is founder and head, and who sustains the church's mission by his command and by his Spirit who is the soul of the church; this body is *mystical*, which means that the notion of body is more than a pure metaphor

---

42. Pius XI, *Mortalium Animos*, Encyclical on Religious Unity (January 6, 1928), in *The Papal Encyclicals 1903–1939*, ed. Claudia Carlen (Wilmington, N.C.: McGrath Publishing Co., 1981), 313–19. Cited as MA.

43. Pius XII, *Mystici Corporis Christi*, On the Mystical Body of Christ (June 29, 1943), in Carlen, *The Papal Encyclicals*, 37–63. Cited as MCC.

44. Emile Mersch, *The Theology of the Mystical Body* (St. Louis: B. Herder, 1951).

pointing to a moral union, and not a physical union, but a mystical union constituted by God and God's grace.[45]

While the root metaphor is theological, and the whole concept appeals to piety, when it is absorbed into the framework of Vatican I the result is narrowly ecclesiocentric. The body of Christ is identified with the Roman Catholic Church (MCC, 13), the institutional authority structure becomes divinized (MCC, 65), membership is restricted to Roman Catholics (MCC, 41), and baptized Christians who are not Catholic are related to the true church by no more than "an unconscious desire and longing" (MCC, 103).[46] Vatican II will retreat considerably from these positions.

The positive resources for the renaissance appeared less in doctrinal form and more in movements and programs occurring in Europe.[47] The liturgical movement began as a Benedictine revival of liturgy in the nineteenth century; it was nurtured by biblical and historical research and a desire to make the liturgy a living bridge between the institutional church and the interior life of the faithful, the "hierarchical" and the "communitarian." Eucharistic piety stimulated by Pius X fed both the liturgical movement and the theology of the mystical body. In first half of the twentieth century this movement encouraged liturgical reform.[48] Another movement, often referred to as *ressourcement*, consisted in return to the sources of the church in scripture and the Fathers.[49] These provided a new perspective of salvation history for understanding the church, as well as

---

45. Yves Congar, *L'Eglise: De saint Augustin à l'époque moderne* (Paris: Editions du Cerf, 1970), 470.

46. On church membership the encyclical refers back to Boniface VIII and appropriates the doctrine of submission to the pope contained in his encyclical *Unam Sanctam.* (MCC, 40). "They, therefore, walk in the path of dangerous error who believe that they can accept Christ as the Head of the church, while not adhering loyally to his Vicar on earth" (MCC, 41).

47. Congar, *L'Eglise,* 461–69, surveys these positive developments. The history of developments in Catholic ecclesiology up to and including Vatican II with special reference to the laity is recounted by Paul Lakeland, *The Liberation of the Laity: In Search of an Accountable Church* (New York: Continuum, 2003), chaps. 1–3.

48. Pius XII addressed liturgical reform cautiously in his encyclical *Mediator Dei,* On the Sacred Liturgy (November 20, 1947), and thus gave the movement prominence.

49. For example, Henri de Lubac's *Catholicism: Christ and the Common Destiny of Man* (San Francisco: Ignatius Press, 1988, original 1937), is a dialogue with the Fathers of the church.

images and language for describing it that transcended neoscholasticism. The biblical movement received authoritative encouragement with the encyclical of Pius XII, *Divino Afflante Spiritu* (1943). Still another movement which provided a stimulus to the thinking of Vatican II were the various lay organizations that came under the general heading of Catholic Action. These activities could take many different forms and engage different groups or classes of people, such as students, workers, and so on. This movement was stimulated by Pius XI. "As did Leo XIII and Pius X before him, but with new force, Pius XI invited the laity to take their part in the mission of the church or in its apostolate."[50] This commission and participation were understood to be grounded in baptism, confirmation, and spiritual charisms. This activity of the laity took hold and became a topic of concern which constantly needed to be addressed. Finally, the ecumenical movement was generating great interest despite official neglect. Many theologians were deeply involved and committed to its goals so that, by the eve of the council, the obvious success in the formation of the WCC meant that the ecumenical movement could no longer be ignored.[51]

But these movements do not amount to a social explanation of the calling of the council. The early 1950s, with Pius XII's encyclical *Humani Generis* (1950) and the repression of several theologians connected with a progressive *nouvelle théologie* including Congar, held no promise for a reforming council. One must, therefore, ultimately credit the new pope, Angelo Giuseppe Roncalli or John XXIII, for summoning Vatican II. He announced the council on January 25, 1959, less than three months after he was elected pope, and it appears that the decision to hold a council was entirely his.[52] In fact

50. Congar, *L'Eglise*, 467.

51. No Catholic theologian was more committed to the ecumenical movement than Yves Congar. For an overview of his early involvement see Alberic Stacpoole, "Early Ecumenism, Early Yves Congar, 1904–1940," I and II, *The Month* (January and April 1988): 502–10, 623–31.

52. "The calling of a new Council was, then, the fruit of a personal conviction of the pope, one that slowly took form in his mind, was strengthened by others, and finally became an authoritative and irrevocable decision during the three-month period after his election to the pontificate." (Giuseppe Alberigo, "The Announcement of the Council: From the Security of the Fortress to the Lure of the Quest," *History of Vatican II*, vols. I–III, ed. G. Alberigo and J. Komonchak [Maryknoll, N.Y.: Orbis Books

the Catholic Church was hardly prepared for such a council because in the wake of the anti-modernist repression public discussion of the issues involved in the vital movements was curtailed.

What were John XXIII's reasons for calling the council? On the occasion of announcing the council he assigned it these two aims: first, "the enlightenment, edification, and joy of the entire Christian people," and, second, "a renewed cordial invitation to the faithful of the separated churches to participate with us in this feast of grace and brotherhood, for which so many souls long in all parts of the world."[53] It appears, then, that the ecumenical issue was a prime motive for the council, a discussion of unity among all Christians. But these aims were not really well worked out in his mind. "The clarification and fuller conception of the shape and aims of the Council would be achieved by Pope John during the ensuing months and years and would also be affected by the broad debate that followed upon the announcement."[54]

A Synopsis of the Ecclesiology of Vatican II

We turn now to the content of the council's ecclesiology. It is important to insist at the outset that the Second Vatican Council should not be viewed only as a set of documents; it was also an event, and appreciation of the whole event affects the interpretation the documents. For example, by the end of the second session conciliar theologians came to realize that the council was a genuinely free and dynamic clash of ideas and opinions, the spirit of John XXIII that the council was to be a true *aggiornamento* had taken hold, and a real dialectic of papal leadership and conciliar autonomy defined the proceedings.[55]

---

and Leuven: Peeters, 1995–2000], I, 13. This work is cited hereafter as HVII by volume number and page.) One should not discount the many social factors of which Roncalli, with his wide experience, was very aware: an increasing pressure of intellectual culture on church positions, an isolation of the church from world movements including the ecumenical movement, the beginnings of globalization in the post–World War II period, the interactions of the world's religions.

53. Alberigo, "The Announcement," *HVII*, I, 15, quoting the pope's redaction of his words as distinct from the doctored official version.

54. Ibid., 16; also 34.

55. Giuseppe Alberigo, "The Conciliar Experience: 'Learning on Their Own,'" HVII, II, 583; "Conclusion: The New Shape of the Council," HVII, III, 491–96

Moreover, the whole Catholic world was watching through aggressive media coverage. Having said that, this synthetic interpretation has to deal with the council as a set of texts. In so doing it follows the formal outline used throughout this work. By contrast, the council's documents are not systematically arranged, although they deal mostly with various facets of the church. The "Dogmatic Constitution on the Church" contributes the pattern of the whole tapestry, but it too is not without seams. This outline of yet another interpretation of this intricate and still contested ecclesiology is designed to serve the purpose of this comparative ecclesiology, namely, to lay distinct ecclesiologies in schematic outline alongside each other for implicit comparison and contrast, and to demonstrate how all ecclesiology changes in response to the times. In other words, the goal here is not to portray this Roman Catholic ecclesiology in the magnificent complexity of its balanced trajectories.[56]

The nature and organization of the church. A good place to begin is at the center. The "Dogmatic Constitution on the Church," *Lumen Gentium,* defines the church theologically in terms of its commanding theological metaphor and organizationally in terms of its orders of ministry. All the other topics after these two add more nuance and complexity to these basic conceptions.

Theological self-understanding. The theological image of "the people of God" commands a privileged place in this ecclesiology. The council does not completely abandon other images such as the "body of Christ" or the "temple of the Holy Spirit," but it dedicates a chapter in *Lumen Gentium* to "the people of God" (LG, 9–17). This

---

56. References and citations of Vatican II are drawn from *The Documents of Vatican II,* ed. Walter M. Abbott (New York: Herder and Herder & Association Press, 1966). The documents are cited by the abbreviations of their Latin titles as follows: "Dogmatic Constitution on the Church" (*Lumen Gentium,* LG), "Constitution on the Sacred Liturgy" (*Sacrosanctum Concilium,* SC), "Pastoral Constitution on the Church in the Modern World" (*Gaudium et Spes*), "Decree on Ecumenism" (*Unitatis Redintegratio,* UR), "Decree on Eastern Catholic Churches" (*Orientalium Ecclesiarum,* OE), "Decree on the Bishops' Pastoral Office in the Church" (*Christus Dominus,* CD), "Decree on the Appropriate Renewal of the Religious Life" (*Perfectae Caritatis,* PC), "Decree on the Apostolate of the Laity" (*Apostolicam Actuositatem,* AA), "Decree on the Ministry and Life of Priests" (*Prebyterorum Ordinis,* PO), "Decree on the Church's Missionary Activity" (*Ad Gentes,* AG), "Declaration on the Relationship of the Church to Non-Christian Religions" (*Nostra Aetate,* NA), "Declaration on Religious Freedom" (*Dignitatis Humanae,* DH).

chapter uses the genre of the history of salvation or the economy of God's saving dialogue with human beings in history, and this gives the image a supple openness. The church is one, and the referent of this ecclesiology is the Roman Catholic Church, yet the people of God is often defined quite broadly: "God has gathered together as one all those who in faith look upon Jesus as the author of salvation and the source of unity and peace, and has established them as the church..." (LG, 9).[57] The image of the people of God, which could be interpreted as in line with the idea of the *congregatio fidelium* of the medieval canonists, also acknowledges and reinforces the place of the laity in the church. But this restoration of the priesthood of the faithful should not be understood in competitive terms; the church also remains a hierarchical structure (LG, 10–11). The whole church, the whole people of God, is filled with the Holy Spirit and shares in the prophetic office of Christ (LG, 12). Such language empowers the laity with responsibility in a new way.

The council used another effective theological image for the church: the church "is a kind of sacrament or sign of intimate union with God, and of the unity of all mankind" (LG, 1). When this language, which appears in several texts and contexts (LG, 48; AG, 1, 5; GS, 42), joins the historicist perspective of "the people of God," it creates a dynamic imperative and appeal that the church make itself a concrete historical sign of the values of the kingdom of God and the reign of God manifested in Jesus' ministry.

---

57. People belong to the "people of God" "in various ways": beyond the boundaries of the Roman Church are all those who believe in Christ, and beyond them the whole of humankind are creatures of God and called to salvation by grace (LG, 13). Vatican II taught that the unique church of Christ cannot be collapsed into or identified with the Roman Church without remainder. Rather the true or whole church "subsists in the Catholic Church," and "many elements of sanctification and of truth can be found outside of her visible structure" (LG, 8). The council also enumerates the substantial foundational elements constituting the church which all Christians share: faith, attachment to Christ, symbolized and effected in baptism, and a community animated by God as Spirit (LG, 15; also UR, 13–23). For a discussion of the contested phrase, *subsistit in,* of LG, 8, see Edward Schillebeeckx, *Church: The Human Story of God* (New York: Crossroad, 1990), 189–95; Francis A. Sullivan, "The Significance of the Vatican II Declaration That the Church of Christ 'Subsists in' the Roman Catholic Church," *Vatican II: Assessment and Perspectives. Twenty-five Years after (1962–1987),* ed. René Latourelle (New York: Paulist Press, 1989), II, 272–87.

Organization of ministry. One should distinguish the church as a community of faith from its institutional structure, but one cannot separate these two dimensions that constitute a single church (LG, 8). Accordingly, the people of God is also a structured hierarchical institution. The offices of the pope, bishop, priest, and layperson, with the addition of the religious life of the evangelical counsels, make up the hierarchical structure of authority and the organization of its ministries.

1. The pope. "In this church of Christ the Roman Pontiff is the successor of Peter, to whom Christ entrusted the feeding of his sheep and lambs. Hence by divine institution he enjoys supreme, full, immediate, and universal authority over the care of souls. Since he is pastor of all the faithful, his mission is to provide for the common good of the universal church and for the good of the individual churches. He holds, therefore, a primacy of ordinary power over all the churches" (CD, 2).[58]

2. The bishop (LG, 18–29; CD). Vatican II's teaching on episcopacy is extensive and nuanced. First, by ordination and then administrative appointment a bishop is "the visible principle and foundation of unity in his particular church," the diocese (LG, 23). The bishop's office symbolically and juridically embodies Christ's role of prophet, priest, and king. His ministry is to preach and teach; to lead worship, administer the sacraments, and especially preside at the liturgy; and to govern, administer, and rule the local church.

---

58. Vatican II's ecclesiology emphasizes the place and role of the bishops in the church, while subsuming into itself the teaching of Vatican I on the papacy which said: "Wherefore we teach and declare that, by divine ordinance, the Roman Church possesses a pre-eminence of ordinary power over every other church, and that this jurisdictional power of the Roman pontiff is both episcopal and immediate. Both clergy and faithful, of whatever rite and dignity, both singly and collectively, are bound to submit to this power by the duty of hierarchical subordination and true obedience, and this not only in matters concerning faith and morals, but also in those which regard the discipline and government of the church throughout the world." Vatican I, "First Dogmatic Constitution on the Church of Christ" (*Pastor Aeternus*), 3, in Norman P. Tanner, ed., *Decrees of the Ecumenical Councils: II, Trent to Vatican II* (Kansas City: Sheed and Ward; Washington, D.C.: Georgetown University Press, 1990), 813–14. This doctrine, far more than infallibility, sets the Roman Church apart from all others.

Second, the bishop also belongs to the college or group of bishops.[59] As a member of this group, but not as an individual, a bishop shares in the oversight and governing of the universal church. The head of the college is the bishop of Rome, and the college does not act apart from the head. Thus the bishop's office and ministry contain a doubly tensive relationship. On the one hand, the bishop is autonomous in relation to the local church, but under the pope's jurisdiction; on the other hand, in relation to the whole church, the bishop is a member of a college which shares a universal responsibility, but as a body which has the pope as its head.

Third, the council legislated that the bishops of a nation or region should form themselves into episcopal conferences which could offer cooperative support and action to face the needs of the church in a particular territory (CD, 37–38).[60]

3. The priest (LG, 28; PO). The priest derives his priesthood from the bishop's fullness of priestly power.[61] Priests, then, are cooperators with bishops, as it were extensions of their bishops, but constitute one priesthood with their bishop. The priest preaches the word of God (PO, 4); he administers the sacraments, and especially presides at the eucharist (PO, 5). The priest prays the official prayer of the church on behalf of people and the world (PO, 5). In the name of the bishop, the priest exercises leadership and authority in the parish community, is responsible for Christian education in the parish, and ministers to groups in the larger secular community, especially the poor (PO, 6).[62]

4. The layperson. Vatican II gave considerable attention to the laity precisely as an order of distinct status in the church, with

---

59. The council employs the language of a communion ecclesiology: "In and from such individual churches there comes into being the one and only Catholic Church" (LG, 23).

60. An episcopal conference is "a kind of council in which the bishops of a given nation or territory jointly exercise their pastoral office . . . " (CD, 37).

61. Bishops "handed on to different individuals in the church various degrees of participation in this ministry" (LG, 28).

62. PO, practically speaking, describes the ministry of the diocesan priest dealing with the parish community. It attends less to priests of religious orders or those engaged in other ministries. Thus, for the most part but not exclusively, it describes the priest as cultic minister.

distinct responsibilities but less correlative power or authority. The laity are discussed under the heading of the members of the church.

5. The religious (LG, 43–47; PC). Vatican II's discussion of religious life in the Western church emphasizes that it "is not an intermediate one between the clerical and lay states" (LG, 43). Rather, both priests and laypeople may live the life of the evangelical counsels of poverty, chastity, and obedience which, broadly speaking, define religious life. *Perfectae Caritatis* deals less with the nature of religious life than the need and some guidelines for renewing it. One must understand the amazing variety in the different forms of religious life that crisscross the diocesan structures to animate church life. Vatican II urged, first, a return to the sources of Christian life generally and the "original inspiration behind a given community," and then an adjustment and adaptation to the present time and the needs of the apostolate (PC, 2). One of the strongest calls of the council to adjust to the modern world was addressed to religious.

Unity of the church. Vatican II's positions on the unity of the church are also filled with tensions. Church unity is addressed in two distinct contexts: the one has to do with the recognized pluralism of life within the Roman Catholic institutional structure; the other has to do with unity among the churches on the ecumenical level. The question of ecumenism comes up in the context of the relation of the church to its environment.

The decree *Orientalium Ecclesiarum*, however, provides a case study for understanding how significant diversity and pluralism can obtain within the one Roman Church. The council endorses pluralism in principle: "For it is the mind of the Catholic Church that each individual [Eastern Catholic] Church or rite retain its traditions whole and entire, while adjusting its way of life to the various needs of time and place" (OE, 2).[63] The idea of a "rite" transcends liturgical rubrics: as a social category it includes distinctiveness "in liturgy, ec-

---

63. Even more strongly, members of Eastern Catholic Churches should know that "they can and should always preserve their lawful liturgical rites and their established way of life, and that these should not be altered except by way of an appropriate and organic development" (OE, 6).

clesiastical discipline, and spiritual heritage" (OE, 3). These church traditions are subsumed into the governing authority of the Roman Pontiff, but this is understood to be an example of where the Petrine ministry guarantees and protects the autonomy and equality of these traditions from lateral pressures (OE, 3; LG, 13). These churches, the council insists, "fully enjoy the right, and are in duty bound, to rule themselves, [and] each should do so according to its proper and individual procedures . . . " (OE, 5). In principle and in large measure in fact, therefore, the Roman Church according to Vatican II is pluralistic.

The members of the church (LG, 30–38; AA, GS, passim). Vatican II proffered extensive, progressive teaching on the laity. The documents frequently and forcefully assert that everything pertaining to the "people of God" applies to the laity. All members of the church "cooperate in the common undertaking" of its saving mission with their charismatic gifts and service (LG, 30). "But the laity, too, share in the priestly, prophetic, and royal office of Christ and therefore have their own role to play in the mission of the whole people of God in the church and in the World" (AA, 2). The council emphasizes responsible, active participation in the playing out of the church's mission, and the authorizing grounds for this commission lie in baptism, confirmation, and participation in the eucharist (LG, 11). Some of the language is quite forceful and striking: "For by its very nature the Christian vocation is also a vocation to the apostolate.[64] No part of the structure of a living body is merely passive but each has a share in the functions as well as in the life of the body. . . . the member who fails to make his or her proper contribution to the development of the church must be said to be useful neither to the church nor to himself" (AA, 2).

This is probably the most forceful official statement ever made by the Roman Church about the active ministerial role of the laity. On the one hand, the council taught that these ministries are au-

---

64. The term "apostolate" refers to the activity carried on in and by the church in different ways through its members for the attainment of its mission of "spreading the kingdom of Christ everywhere for the glory of God the Father." After the council in many places the term "ministry" replaced the term "apostolate."

tonomous: "The laity derive the right and duty with respect to the apostolate from their union with Christ their Head" (AA, 3). On the other hand, it is clear that these ministries come under the supervision of the clergy (AA, 24). On the one hand, the special competence of the laity is for the witness of Christian values in the secular sphere (AA, 2, 5, 7, 13). This premise is prominent in the teaching of the council on the relation of the church to the world. On the other hand, it is clearly stated that the competence of lay ministry extends "both in the church and in the world, in both the spiritual and the temporal orders" (AA, 5). The laity have a right and sometimes an obligation to express an opinion regarding the good of the whole church. This is to be facilitated "through agencies set up by the church for this purpose" (LG, 37). This refers to various associations of the laity reminiscent of the fraternities and to parochial and diocesan pastoral councils which are to be set up in a way that gives the members of the church at large a voice in the governance of the church (CD, 27). The council also urged training centers for formation of the laity in the apostolate (AA, 28–32).

The goal or mission of the church. Vatican II constantly refers back to the mission and goal of the church. This becomes explicit in the consideration of missionary activity. The church has as its goal and purpose the perpetuation of the work of Jesus Christ in history. This entails preaching the gospel and establishing communities where God will be glorified and the values of the gospel actualized (AG, 1). Rather than being accomplished once and for all, this mission represents an ongoing task which has a double aspect: *ad intra*, the preaching and animation of the life of the community, and *ad extra*, the church's reaching out beyond its borders to those who are not Christian (AG, 6). *Ad Gentes* addresses traditional missionary activity *ad extra*, but not without significance for understanding pastoral activity *ad intra*. Relative to missionary activity, the council envisages this in terms of planting indigenous and autochthonous churches (AG, 6). No major advance at this point.

But *Ad Gentes* does contain some distinctive teachings relative to the nature of the church itself. First of all, it affirms clearly that "The pilgrim church is missionary by her very nature" (AG, 2). This entails the view that the church bears a missionary character always and wherever it is.[65] It also means that all members of the church internalize this same missionary character: all Christians are missionaries (AG, 4). The active responsibility attached to membership predicated of all the laity becomes more focused with the symbol of mission.

A second development relative to the mission of the church becomes more apparent in *Gaudium et Spes* but should be mentioned here. In the discussion of the church's relation to the modern world, the term "world" takes on a cultural meaning. The world of modernity to which the church also has a mission does not exist beyond its boarders in far-off places; it is the world in which the church exists in the West. When the church is recognized as intrinsically missionary, and the world, as other than the church, is conceived as the very context in which the church exists, the dynamic missionary character of the church becomes directed as well to secular society. This theme is played out in *Gaudium et Spes* and it will be considered further on with respect to the relation of the church to its environment.

Third, classical missionary themes relative to historical context and cultural difference become internalized in the general consciousness of the church. Vatican II shows a new consciousness of the implications of being a world church. The mission of the church unfolds differently in different parts of the world, in different circumstances, conditions, situations of the people being addressed. The word "inculturation" does not appear in Vatican II, but the process of adaptation to culture and with it a new level of historical consciousness assume explicit importance (AG, 6, 22, 26).

In sum, the affirmation of the missionary character of the church possesses a dynamic and even activist understanding of the role of the church in the world and in human history.[66]

Activities of the church. The activities of the church are many, directed inside and outside the church, ranging from the personal

---

65. Thus, for example, even an "established" church in its own inner life is missionary.

66. Various reasons account for this: the recognition that the church should have been more influential in preventing the two world wars, secularization in Europe and the desire to regain influence in society, the example of the Life and Work movement and then the World Council of Churches, the increasing speed of historical development throughout the world after World War II.

and social behavior of its members (ethics) to a wide variety of specific tasks. In this consideration the focus falls on activity *ad intra*, specifically worship as represented in the "Constitution on the Sacred Liturgy" (SC), one of the most important of the whole council.[67]

The work of redemption unfolds principally in and through the celebration of the eucharist, which in Catholic liturgy includes the reading of scripture and the preaching of the word. "The liturgy is thus the outstanding means by which the faithful can express in their lives, and manifest to others, the mystery of Christ and the real nature of the true church" (SC, 2). This ecclesiology realistically portrays the presence of Christ in the church in the sacraments, "especially under the eucharistic species" (SC, 7) and also in the administration and celebration of the other sacraments: in his word read in the scripture, in the power of the person of the minister. Liturgy, therefore, "is a sacred action surpassing all others. No other action of the church can match its claim to [sacramental] efficacy, nor equal the degree of it" (SC, 7).

The liturgy "is the summit toward which the activity of the church is directed; at the same time it is the fountain from which all her power flows. For the goal of apostolic works [ministry] is that all who are made sons of God by faith and baptism should come together to praise God in the midst of his church, to take part in her sacrifice, and to eat the Lord's supper" (SC, 10). The claim is pointedly high: the eucharist is the achievement of the twofold goal of all apostolic activity — "the sanctification of men in Christ and the glorification of God" (SC, 10).

The council itself did not accomplish the liturgical reform. Rather it mandated the reform and provided some general guidelines for its undertaking. These addressed the eucharist, the other six sacraments, devotions, the divine office, liturgical practices, the liturgical year, liturgical music and church art.[68] The reform was to be thorough

---

67. It may be important simply to note that the Roman Church has become a huge organization whose activities in the modern period have become diverse and complex on the level of the parish, diocese, national or regional, and international levels. What the church does varies throughout the world. Focusing on liturgical activity represents a radical cutting to the core of ecclesial activity.

68. The norms and guidelines for the liturgical reform are extensive. They call for careful historical research into texts and rites (SC, 25), study of scripture as the

and taken seriously: bishops were to set up their own liturgical commissions and institutes for instruction (SC, 44). Strong directives were given that training in liturgy should be made available to all classes in the church from historical, spiritual, pastoral, and legal perspectives (SC, 14–20).

Changes in liturgical practice are extremely sensitive issues. The significance of this aspect of the council is the decision itself to undertake a thorough reform of the liturgy. In fact, this resulted in two major changes that significantly impacted church consciousness: the translation of the liturgy from Latin to the vernacular and the shift of the priest at the eucharist from facing the altar with his back to the people to the other side of the altar facing the people. The impact of these two changes in the parishes was dramatic.

Relation of the church to the world. Perhaps the council's most surprising move was to redefine the church's relation to the world, in this case, the specifically modern world. The decree *Gaudium et Spes* is so rich and influential that it continues to encourage new interpretation and cause debate. In dealing with the relationship of the church to the world outside it the discussion moves to an interpretation of how the church redefined itself relative to modernity, and then considers in order its new relationship as a religion with society, with fellow Christian churches, and with other religions.

The relation of the church to the specifically modern world. The "world" refers to the sphere of history and society and culture. The world in this sense is the creation of human beings and an expression of the human spirit (GS, 53–55). The world possesses an autonomy relative to the church which stems from God's own creativity; "created things and societies themselves enjoy their own laws and values" (GS, 36, 34–36). In principle the church and world are not in a competitive or adversarial relationship, except where sin prevails. Although Christ and the Spirit are broadly at work in the world, sin also distorts the world as it should be (GS, 37–38). Church and world,

---

source for symbolic meaning and prayer (24), care that the participation of the laity is promoted (30–31), attention to the educative character of liturgy (33) and to preaching (35.2), encouragement of Bible services (35.4), more use of the vernacular (36.2), adaptation to different regions, peoples, and cultures (37–38), provision of periods for experimentation (40.2).

therefore, are mutually related and intertwined: the church exists in the world, and because its members come from the world the world impacts the church; inversely, the church exists for the world and the human project, as its vocation is to be a leaven or soul or spiritual principle for human existence. Thus "the earthly and the heavenly city penetrate each other" so that there should be a "mutual exchange and assistance" (GS, 40). The world bears resources for the church (GS, 44).

The contribution to ecclesiology comes at this point, and it is thoroughly modern. The church exists for the world. The mission or goal of the church is to bring to bear on the human project the gospel message, values, and grace of God revealed in Jesus Christ. The church's message is not bound to a particular time or place or culture, but "can enter into communion with various cultural modes, to her own enrichment and theirs too" (GS, 58). But this means that the church has to understand each culture and each generation so as to be able to respond to the perennial questions in the language intelligible to them (GS, 4). This new relationship affects the elementary spirituality implicit in the Christian life: privatization is disallowed, the Christian way entails engagement with the world.[69] It also affects the self-understanding of the Christian church. The church and its doctrine have constantly to be reinterpreted through a correlation with the world and its various cultures. Thus the council invites theologians "to seek continually for more suitable ways of communicating doctrine to men of their times. For the deposit of faith or revealed truths are one thing; the manner in which they are formulated without violence to their meaning and significance is another" (GS, 62). This amounts to a stunning reconception of the church in relation to the contemporary world, as distinct from the medieval (*devotio moderna*) and early modern periods right through

---

69. The council rejected the view of those "who think that religion consists in acts of worship alone and in the discharge of certain moral obligations, and who imagine they can plunge themselves into earthly affairs in such a way as to imply that these are altogether divorced from the religious life. This split between the faith which many profess and their daily lives deserves to be counted among the more serious errors of our age.... The Christian who neglects his temporal duties neglects his duties toward his neighbor and even God, and jeopardizes his eternal salvation" (GS, 43).

the nineteenth (*Syllabus of Errors,* 1864) and early twentieth centuries. Promulgated at the end of the council, this decree formed a new context for understanding the basic dogmatic constitution on the church. In this way, at least on a broad symbolic and affective level as distinct from the juridical, *Gaudium et Spes* became the principle document of Vatican II.[70]

The relation of the church to civil government, other churches, and other religions. The council addressed three other crucial relationships to the world outside itself. It is important to note the essential teaching in each case even though it cannot be developed at proper length.

First, Vatican II's doctrine of religious freedom has to be understood against the background of modern European history and the persistent idea of "Catholic nations." The subject, religion, refers to those "internal, voluntary, and free acts whereby one sets the course of his or her life directly toward God" (DH, 3). And religious freedom is understood as "immunity from coercion in civil society" (DH, 1). "This Vatican Synod declares that the human person has a right to religious freedom" (DH, 2). That is, no one can be forced to act contrary to his or her beliefs, or restrained from acting in accord with them. To many for whom the separation of church and state defines a way of life, this may seem obvious. But this doctrine contains many social consequences with major significance in some societies and for the whole church as well.[71]

Second, with Vatican II the Roman Church joined the ecumenical movement. "This sacred Synod, therefore, exhorts all the Catholic faithful to recognize the signs of the times and to participate skillfully in the work of ecumenism" (UR, 4). The council recognized the movement as a work of God and vowed that the Roman Church, joined with other churches, would "go forward without obstructing the ways of divine Providence and without prejudging the

---

70. This is a contentious interpretation. But few interpretations of the deeper and broader significance of Vatican II are not. It is interesting to underline the fact that Vatican II (GS, 62) endorses the distinction between faith and its expression made by the WCC at New Delhi in 1961. See supra, p. 380.

71. Herminio Rico, *John Paul II and the Legacy of Dignitatis Humanae* (Washington, D.C.: Georgetown University Press, 2002), draws out the meaning of this teaching and how it fared during the papacy of John Paul II.

future inspiration of the Holy Spirit" (UR, 24). As to the actual unity and possible communion that could presently be enjoyed with other churches, the council defined the relationships differently according to the degrees of closeness in theology, polity, orders, and sacraments, and this was symbolized by distinctions of designations of other churches precisely as "churches," or "communions," or "communities." Relationships were judged closest with Eastern Orthodox churches with whom the Roman Church was willing to enjoy full communion on the basis of how things stood before 1054 (UR, 14–18; OE, 26–27). Relationships with Western churches were rooted more fundamentally in the basics of a common faith, commitment to Christ, baptism as a sacramental bond of unity, but with major differences relative to authority, sacraments, and orders of ministry.

But the major significance of this commitment to the ecumenical movement lies in the changed attitude and actions it represents, for example, to enter into formal dialogues, to cooperate in ecclesial projects, to pray *together,* and generally to be open to appreciation of the other (UR, 4). This included as well changes in the way theology was learned and taught, that is, ecumenically, involving a search for more mutually accommodating languages and recognizing a hierarchy of truths in which substantive matters are not confused with accidentals (UR, 5–12). Perhaps most important of all is the recognition of a legitimate pluralism, mentioned earlier with respect to the Eastern Catholic churches, but also extended to the Eastern Orthodox churches; the principle enshrined in this advocacy of pluralism has a relevance that has yet to be fully exploited (UR, 14–18).

Third, Vatican II's text on the relation of the church to the world's religions may appear somewhat underdeveloped in the light of the discussion at the beginning of the twenty-first century (NA, 1–5). It does little more than underline the spontaneously religious character of human existence and calls for deep respect for the religions of others. It also measures the closer relationship between Christianity and Islam than with other world religions, and an intimate relationship with Judaism. It insists upon the unity and solidarity of the human family as the context for cooperation and interchange between the religions. As such it reflects again the new openness of the church to the world of human history.

THE AFTERMATH OF VATICAN II

At the end of the Second World War the Roman Church began to expand rapidly, and in the wake of decolonialization the development of the church on the perimeter relative to the Roman center became more self-conscious. Vatican II provided a significant stimulus to this expansion. The documents of Vatican II and the history leading up to it yield a fairly coherent synthesis of the ecclesiology of the Roman Church.[72] But it would be much more difficult to synthesize developments within the whole church after the council because of regional variations. But the Catholic Church also underwent some changes that affected the communion as a whole. For example, since the council a quantum shift has been occurring because of the diminishment of the church in the developed West and the rapid growth of the church among developing nations. Perhaps more important was the self-consciousness accompanying this expansion. In an age of rapid communications the Catholic Church became more recognizably pluralistic than ever before. While the whole church was held together as a unity by visible, well-traveled popes and the exercise of juridical and disciplinary authority by the Vatican, the forces of difference remained acutely felt. Because of this regional pluralism, a description of the church in the decades after Vatican II must remain on a somewhat abstract and formal level. What follows describes it in terms of its organization, goals, members, activities, and relationship to the world.[73]

---

72. Such a synthesis would contain some tensions between different factions within the church which have left their marks in the documents.

73. Alberigo observes that postconciliar Christianity has been able to recognize a "power or energy [in the council], and to distinguish the living substance from the accidentals that are lifeless..." (Giuseppe Alberigo, "The Christian Situation after Vatican II," in *The Reception of Vatican II*, ed. G. Alberigo et al. [Washington, D.C.: Catholic University of America Press, 1987], 13). Alberigo is clear about the framework for judging the council: it has to be read in epochal terms, and not merely in response to a contemporary entrenched Vatican bureaucracy, or the twentieth century, or Vatican I. The vision of John XXIII projected the church opening itself up to a new era (Ibid, 15–16). If this is so, then the effects of Vatican II will not have run their course in the few years or decades after it. Rather these will gradually take hold after the restorationist impulse has run its course.

Collegiality

The main, formal ecclesiological move of Vatican II in organizational terms consisted in defining the nature and function of the episcopate in a way that integrated it with the papal power defined at Vatican I. Collegiality is the term which best summarizes how episcopacy was conceived: bishops as a *collegium* exercise corporate responsibility for the whole church together with its head, the pope. Two structures, episcopal synods and episcopal conferences, provide the main institutional vehicles for the exercise of this collegial, episcopal authority and responsibility. Of the two, episcopal conferences proved to be more effective. Several synods were summoned after Vatican II with varying degrees of preparation and importance. They do not teach directly, however, but through and with their head, the pope, and the popes exercised control over their published results.

Episcopal conferences are explicit groupings of national or regional bishops who work together to address issues proper to their regions. They both decentralize a highly centralized church, and they add support to bishops who are isolated in their regions and lack resources as individual bishops. For this reason they may also seem to undermine the formal authority of the center and the autonomy of individual bishops, and thus there has been a certain tension between these conferences and the Vatican both theoretically and practically regarding the handling of specific local issues. But these tensions between the center and the periphery, and between Western Christianity and Christianity in non-Western cultures may be salutary. A certain degree of institutional power at both ends may work for the good of the whole church.

Other developments in the government or self-understanding of the church included the official joining in the ecumenical movement. This led to many official dialogues in which the church participated on the local, regional, and universal levels. A second development relates to the center of gravity of the self-understanding of the church. The whole council in various decrees emphasized the significance of the local church and thus promoted a certain self-consciousness about it.[74] The idea of the whole church was differentiated into a

---

74. On the significance of the "local church" for ministry and inculturation see Joseph A. Komonchak, "Ministry and the Local Church," *Proceedings of the Catholic*

new awareness of the distinctiveness of each parish, diocese, and especially regional or national church. Another significant development consisted in an increasing demand on the part of local churches for a reform of the Vatican curia or bureaucracy because it is perceived to interrupt the free flow of interchange between the papacy and the bishops.[75]

Priority of Mission

The conception of the mission of the church carries with it the deepest convictions about the place of the church in history and beyond, that is, eschatologically. This understanding evolved considerably after Vatican II beginning with new convictions expressed in the council that grace and salvation are common outside the church. Reflection has led at some points to reversals of former conceptions. What is the church for? The realization of the kingdom of God. To whom does the church address itself? To the whole world in all its dimensions. Who are its agents? God, for it is God's mission; but under the leadership of the hierarchy all the laity are asked to participate in this mission. Moreover, they are called to do so in collaboration with other churches and other religions. What is the principle strategy? Not simply proclamation, but also and perhaps primarily witness and dialogue with all willing to listen.[76]

These developments in the theology of the mission of the church and its missionary activity represent a profound reorientation of the understanding of the church that obtained before the council. By a kind of reversal the church is reconstrued "inside out": in place of a certain ecclesiocentrism, the church is understood as being for the world.[77] As a religious symbol "mission" portrays a deep sense that the church is sent by God and is meant to reflect God's project in the

Theological Society of America 36 (1981): 56–82; "The Local Realization of the Church," *The Reception of Vatican II*, 77–90.

75. John R. Quinn, *The Reform of the Papacy: The Costly Call to Christian Unity* (New York: Crossroad, 1999).

76. Peter C. Phan "Proclamation of the Reign of God as Mission of the Church: What for, to Whom, by Whom, with Whom, and How?" *In Our Own Tongues: Perspectives from Asia on Mission and Inculturation* (Maryknoll, N.Y.: Orbis Books, 2003), 32–44.

77. Johannes C. Hoekendijk, in his influential *The Church Inside Out* (Philadelphia: Westminster Press, 1966), makes this missiological point forcefully. In the

world. This gets played out historically, in this world, in service of God's values as they have been revealed in Jesus' ministry and leads to the conviction that evangelization and work for humanization cannot be separated. Work for the material welfare of poor people is not simply a preevangelization but a kind of evangelization in itself, an evangelization by praxis. The building up of human life in every form, when done on the basis of Christian motivation, is part of the ministry of evangelization. And evangelization itself may be considered also as a form of humanization. In short, one can distinguish, but one cannot separate communication of the gospel from an overall concern for the humanization of people in all its dimensions. All the authors who emphasize the significance of the symbol of mission for understanding the church today share this basic conception. The church continues Jesus' ministry in the world today; this mission comes from God; and this mission must be interpreted in historical terms, just as the identity of Jesus was revealed in and through his public life and ministry.[78] This theme of "mission" will be illustrated more pointedly in the liberation ecclesiology described in the next section.

Members

After Vatican II major ecclesiological developments touched the two principle categories of membership in the Roman Church, the clergy and the laity. These developments should be understood against the wide backdrop of significant church growth outside the West and diminishment of numbers in Europe and North America.[79]

---

ecumenical atmosphere after Vatican II his thought had an impact on Catholic mission theory.

78. José Comblin, *The Meaning of Mission: Jesus, Christians, and the Wayfaring Church* (Maryknoll, N.Y.: Orbis Books, 1972), 1–23; Roger Haight, "'Mission' as the Symbol for Understanding the Church Today," *Theological Studies* 37 (1976): 620–49; "The 'Established' Church as Mission: The Relation of the Church to the Modern World," *The Jurist* 39 (1979): 4–39; Jon Sobrino, *The True Church and the Poor* (Maryknoll, N.Y.: Orbis Books, 1984), 253–301.

79. On May 25, 2004, Sean O'Malley, archbishop of Boston, announced the closure of 65 out of the archdiocese's 357 parishes, about 18 percent, due generally to parishes in the red, buildings in need of repair, demographic changes, and an aging corps of priests (*New York Times*, May 26, 2004, A14). While North American Catholicism, fueled by immigration, has been growing since Vatican II, patterns of full participation in the church in terms of weekly church attendance have shifted significantly. Interpretation of these developments in terms of numbers alone, then, would be quite deceptive.

On the one hand, relative to clergy, the numbers of clergy are increasing where the church is on a growth curve as in, for example, Africa. Africa has been advancing toward a goal of an all African clergy. Although new seminaries are being opened, the numbers can scarcely remain commensurate with church growth. On the other hand, the developed West has experienced a sharp loss in the number of priests among the diocesan clergy and the religious orders, and the shrinking number of women in apostolic orders has led some sociologists of religion to predict that they will be virtually extinct in the foreseeable future.[80]

In a movement parallel to the loss of professional ministers who were clerics or religious Western churches saw an equally remarkable rise of the laity, a virtual flood of lay ministers who have taken the places of priests and sisters in parishes and chaplaincies, as spiritual counselors, teachers, organizers, and administrators.[81] One can vaguely discern a pattern here that moves in a direction opposite to the one by which the original offices of ministry were developed in the early church. Then, ministers moved from being largely defined by charismatic inspiration and talent to becoming more routinized into offices and more professionalized as ministerial orders. Today, in the churches of the developed Western churches, ministry is moving away from being the exclusive task of the clergy or professional ministers and being diffused back into the community in the hands of multiple lay ministers with a variety of talents and expertise.

Liturgy

The activities of the church and the congregations are many. The center of vitality of the actual church is the parish. The quality of parish life varies because of the many factors that have to come together.

---

80. See, for example, Helen Rose Ebaugh, *Women in the Vanishing Cloister: Organizational Decline in Catholic Religious Orders in the United States* (New Brunswick: Rutgers University Press, 1993).

81. Relative to the church in the United States, Thomas F. O'Meara, *Theology of Ministry* (New York: Paulist Press, 1999), develops the theology of ministry with special reference to the ministry of the laity; William V. D'Antonio et al., *Laity, American and Catholic: Transforming the Church* (Kansas City, Mo.: Sheed & Ward, 1996), studies the laity sociologically; Philip J. Murnion and David DeLambo, *Parishes and Parish Ministers* (New York: National Parish Life Center, 1999), gives a profile of the laity working in the parishes.

In North America, where the various reforms initiated by Vatican II were consciously implemented and participation by the laity in the corporate ministry of the parishes increased, the quality of religious life became more intentional and more services were offered.

Attention has been called to the significant impact on Catholics of turning the altar around so that the priest faced the people and translating the Latin liturgy of the Roman Rite into the vernacular of each place or linguistic group. A certain amount of liturgical experimentation around the world was also permitted. But over time, as in the case of the Elizabethan Book of Common Prayer, more and more Catholics were socialized into a liturgy that was both more controlled, as experimentation was curtailed, but more indigenously adapted to each region.

Relation to the world

The single most influential message of Vatican II was carried most explicitly in the Pastoral Constitution on the Church in the Modern World: it defined the church in relation to the world and symbolized an open attitude of dialogue with and service to the human family. It also conveyed a concrete, historical outlook that forced attention on what was actually going on around the world. Three major social and theological movements emerged after the council which can be directly traced back to the lines of force released by *Gaudium et Spes:* one is a new concern for social justice that lay beneath liberation theologies; a second is an overriding concern for inculturation; and a third exists in the community at large as the question of the relation of the church to other religions and is expressed ecclesially in various forms of interreligious dialogue.

The following section will discuss liberation theologies which contributed new dimensions to ecclesiology and church structure. But it should be noted here that liberation theology helped mediate a deep shift in church consciousness. Since the nineteenth century the Roman Church had been developing an explicit social teaching, and concern for society consumed a considerable part of the church's energy and activity. But through Vatican II and especially as mediated by the liberation theology which developed first in Latin America during the 1960s, the church came to a new consciousness of how this concern for justice was not a necessary addendum to faith but an intrinsic and essential dimension of Christian faith itself.[82] For many this concern for justice was acted out through basic ecclesial communities.

Second, the historicist outlook of *Gaudium et Spes* and the general concern for local churches around the world displayed in the council led to an increasingly deeper awareness that the church as such was intrinsically bound to no single culture, but had to be born anew in every distinct culture in which it could be expected to survive and be effective in its mission. This profoundly historicist insight was accompanied by an experience that is demanding: on both the theoretical and practical levels the church in each region or culture has to be reconstructed in order authentically to be appropriated. This project which is currently going on all over the Roman Catholic world sets up new themes and dimensions in the tensions between the center and the periphery of the church politically and theologically.

Third, the world to which the church relates is religiously pluralist, and frequently religion so saturates the culture which the Christian church must address in a language that is comprehensible that dialogue with the world's religions has become inescapable. Moreover, such cohabitation has led increasingly to the Christian experience of the positive value of other religions for the salvation of their faithful. This experience has steadily become more widespread since Vatican II. In various non-Western regions and through immigration to the West, Christians are rubbing shoulders with and marrying people of other faiths. This is both putting pressure on the formulations of previous teaching and inviting new ecclesial initiatives.

---

82. The following texts of the Synod of Bishops, Second General Assembly (November 30, 1971), had considerable influence in the Catholic Church at large: "Action on behalf of justice and participation in the transformation of the world fully appear to us as a constitutive dimension of the preaching of the gospel...." "For unless the Christian message of love and justice shows its effectiveness through action in the cause of justice in the world, it will only with difficulty gain credibility with the men of our times." *Justice in the World,* #6 and #35, in Joseph Gremillion, ed., *The Gospel of Peace and Justice: Catholic Social Teaching since Pope John* (Maryknoll, N.Y.: Orbis Books, 1976), 514 and 521. J. Bryan Hehir, "Church-State and Church-World: The Ecclesiological Implications," *Proceedings of the Catholic Theological Society of America* 41 (1986): 54–74 shows how Vatican II and this synod moved Catholic social teaching from being inseparable but extrinsic to the nature of the church to something internal and intrinsic to the essence of the gospel message itself and hence ecclesial ministry.

The idea of interreligious dialogue forms a new background for understanding the church and coalesces with ideas of the mission of the church just outlined. In the past Christianity was often communicated with the accompaniment of the sword. It is generally agreed today that force cannot qualify as a Christian mode of evangelization, that any imposition of Christianity on human freedom contradicts the very truth it seeks to communicate. Dialogue, then, seeks to guarantee a form of communication of the gospel that respects and preserves the freedom of other people. Also, on the basis of a respect for the experiences of other religions, this strategy entails listening. The policy of dialogue does not rule out conversion in either direction. But the feeling is that, in accordance with the doctrine of grace, conversion is ultimately in the hands of God and is not the explicit goal of the Christian participant in the dialogue. When that is not stipulated or manifest, the situation becomes tainted by mistrust, and dialogue itself is impaired or impossible. The immediate goal is to communicate, to bear faithful witness to, to be a sign and sacrament of the content of Christian faith, and to listen to what God is doing in other religions.

LIBERATION ECCLESIOLOGY
AND BASIC ECCLESIAL COMMUNITIES

The rise of liberation theologies exemplifies many of the themes portrayed abstractly in the previous section. During the course of the last third of the twentieth century liberation theology burst on the world scene and had a major impact on the church's self-understanding and organization. Liberation theology interprets the Christian message and the church from the perspective of those who suffer from systemic social, political, and cultural oppression, most pointedly due to racism, sexism, and social-economic exploitation. The depth and breadth of liberationist concern among the churches on every continent cannot be represented adequately in a short statement. What follows, therefore, uses the strategy of representing the movement by one example of it, in this case the liberation theology which emerged in Latin America in the 1960s. This analytical portrait attempts to portray this theology and ecclesiology in a description broad enough for it analogously to represent black liberation theology and feminist liberation theology as well.[83] The movement of establishing basic ecclesial communities accompanied the appearance of liberation theology in Latin America, and it would be hard to establish clearly whether one was prior to the other in logic or historical development. These BECs bear pointed analogies with ecclesial phenomena outside the Latin American and Catholic context in which they are presented.

This compressed account of liberation ecclesiology, after a brief analysis of its historical genesis in Latin America, revolves around two foci. The first concerns the logic of liberation theology itself and how this theology, when it was applied to the church, transformed the self-understanding of the very nature and mission of the church. The second turns attention to organizational structure, and how basic ecclesial communities represent for some churches — such as the Roman Catholic Church whose parish congregations can be excessively large — a more effective organizational unit for making God's word and sacrament relevant to actual everyday life.

Development of Liberation Theology

The period after the Second World War witnessed a good deal of realignment among nations around the world. Even though most nations in Latin America were independent since the nineteenth century, the decolonialization after the war created a sense of nationalism and progressive nation building. Catholic Action, in groups analogous to those among youth, university students, and workers in Europe, stimulated engagement in social issues and movements. But

---

83. Two classic works here are James H. Cone, *Black Theology and Black Power* (New York: Seabury Press, 1969), and Elisabeth Schüssler Fiorenza, *In Memory of Her: A Feminist Theological Reconstruction of Christian Origins* (New York: Crossroad, 1983). Black liberation theology, womanist theology, and feminist liberation theology are not generally associated with new ecclesiological organization but have had significant influence on the reform of existing structures. There are notable exceptions to this rule, such as Rosemary Radford Ruether's *Women-Church: Theology and Practice of Feminist Liturgical Communities* (San Francisco: Harper & Row, 1985). It will become apparent further on in this chapter and the next that basic ecclesial communities, small Christian communities, and more generally pentecostalism have enhanced the role of women in the churches.

the Second Vatican Council itself provided the single most important impulse leading to liberation theology. The phrase "liberation
theology" does not appear in the council. Yet every major theme of
liberation theology can be found implicitly or explicitly in the overall
teaching of the council.[84] More specifically, the Decree on the Missionary Activity of the Church and the Pastoral Constitution on the
Church in the Modern World provided the theory and mandate that
the church turn to the concrete world of particular societies and apply
the message of Christ to each particular context and situation. The
earliest liberation theologians studied in Europe, but they returned to
Latin America to write a theology responsive to the poverty and oppression of their societies and the creative energy of their cultures.[85] A
major public marker for the expansion of the liberationist movement
among the churches, however, was the Second General Conference of
Latin American Bishops (CELAM) held in Medellín in 1968.[86] The
documents of this conference commit the Latin American Church
to the institutionally violated poor of the continent. After this meeting writings under the explicit title of liberation theology began to
appear in Latin America. The movement and its theology flourished
during the course of the 1970s and the 1980s and spread extensively
throughout the world.

Deep Logic and Basic Principles of Liberation Theology

In an attempt to differentiate elements in liberation theology that
have a bearing on its ecclesiology, it is helpful to distinguish between

---

84. Segundo Galilea, "Latin America in the Medellín and Puebla Conferences: An
Example of Selective and Creative Reception of Vatican II," *The Reception of Vatican II*,
59–73; Gustavo Gutiérrez, "The Church and the Poor: A Latin American Perspective,"
The Reception of Vatican II, 171–93.

85. Two major initiators of liberation theology, always working with others, were
Juan Luis Segundo, whose *A Theology for Artisans of a New Humanity*, 5 vols.
(Maryknoll, N.Y.: Orbis Books, 1973–75), was first published in 1968, and Gustavo
Gutiérrez, whose *A Theology of Liberation: History, Politics and Salvation* (Maryknoll,
N.Y.: Orbis Books, 1973), was first published in 1971. Gutiérrez is regarded as the
father of Latin American liberation theology.

86. Conferencia General del Episcopado Latinoamericano II (1968: Bogotá and
Medellín, Colombia), *The Church in the Present-Day Transformation of Latin Amer-
ica in the Light of the Council / Second General Conference of Latin American Bishops*
(Washington, D.C.: Secretariat for Latin America, National Conference of Catholic
Bishops, 1970).

a deep logic that underlies this theology and some of its major principles which continually operate as axioms and criteria of judgment. Liberation theology, of course, is theology, that is, an understanding of faith and of reality in the light of faith. But this theology has such a symbiotic relationship to a movement of Christian faith and praxis seeking social justice that it is unintelligible without recognition of this as its source.[87]

The deep logic of liberation theology. A good number of fundamental insights and convictions, either from the Enlightenment or the historical consciousness that was generated in the nineteenth century, can be seen at work in liberation theology. Three in particular help to explain what is going on in it and how it carries forward themes from Vatican II.

The formal structure of a common human experience that Edward Schillebeeckx calls a negative experience of contrast applies to and clarifies the dynamics of liberation theology.[88] Such a negative experience of contrast is negative because it reacts against a situation or event that is perceived as negative or wrong: this experience may be quite forceful and approach outrage or scandal: "this should not be!" But such an experience entails more than passively being affected by the negative. As a complex, dialectical experience, a negative experience of contrast contains an implicit recognition of what is positive and should be, for one could not really appreciate the negativity as negativity without a horizon of appreciation of what should be. Moreover, an implicit desire to right the wrong, to negate the negativity, accompanies the affective dissonance of this moral insight and

---

87. The following works have been helpful in tracing these outlines of liberation theology: Comblin, *The Meaning of Mission;* Ignacio Ellacuría, *Freedom Made Flesh: the Mission of Christ and His Church* (Maryknoll, N.Y.: Orbis Books, 1976); Ignacio Ellacuría and Jon Sobrino, eds., *Mysterium Liberationis: Fundamental Concepts of Liberation Theology* (Maryknoll, N.Y.: Orbis Books, 1993); Gutiérrez, *A Theology of Liberation;* Roger Haight, *An Alternative Vision: An Interpretation of Liberation Theology* (New York: Paulist Press, 1985); Alfred T. Hennelly, *Liberation Theology: A Documentary History* (New York: Orbis Books, 1990); Juan Luis Segundo, *The Community Called Church* (Maryknoll, N.Y.: Orbis Books, 1973), *The Sacraments Today* (Maryknoll, N.Y.: Orbis Books, 1974); Sobrino, *The True Church and the Poor.*

88. Schillebeeckx, *Church,* 5–6; Roger Haight, "The Logic of the Christian Response to Social Suffering," *The Future of Liberation Theology: Essays in Honor of Gustavo Gutiérrez,* ed. Marc H. Ellis and Otto Maduro (Maryknoll, N.Y.: Orbis Books, 1989), 139–53.

outrage. Although such a logic is implicit in many everyday moral appreciations of common events, contrast experiences can be profound and may lie at the basis of fundamental human conversions. When the situation involved is massive and social, as in the holocaust, and when a large percentage of a population shares this experience, it can unleash powerful social energy. Such was the growing consciousness of the poverty in Latin America. People could no longer appreciate human destitution as willed by divine providence, nor even simply as "the way things are": rather it came to be recognized as a systemic or socially institutionalized practice of violence, with historical causes and human responsibility behind them. Surely the Christian message has something to say about this situation.[89]

Another deep logic that suffuses liberation theology expands the element of desire for change and the impulse toward action contained in a negative experience of contrast. The church must address social human degradation; reaction against dehumanization has to be part of its fundamental mission. Such reflections lead to the recognition that the mission of the church in history has to be thought of in more intentional and dynamic categories: the church is a project in history.[90] To be a Christian involves being part of God's project in history. The mission of the church still remains primarily one of evangelization, but this is subsumed into a larger framework of being the agent of God's values and intentions for all humankind in history. The church, then, exists under a divine mandate to midwife the kingdom of God in history, not just ecclesial history, but common human history. This interpretation does not work against the religious liberty of all, but is to be measured against individualism as engaging all Christians in a corporate responsibility to be concerned with society and its structures, against a passive Christianity as involving a social

89. This deep logic is found throughout the course of the history of the church. For example, liberation theology and ecclesiology share a close analogy with the theology of the Social Gospel despite some large differences in historical context. See T. Howland Sanks, "Liberation Theology and the Social Gospel: Variations on a Theme," *Theological Studies* 41 (1980): 668–82 for a comparison between the charter texts of Gustavo Gutiérrez and Walter Rauschenbusch. This experience underlies the text of the Latin American Bishops Conference in Medellín of 1968.

90. This foundational conviction supports the theology of Juan Luis Segundo; it finds its most explicit statement in works of spirituality, such as *The Sacraments Today* and *The Christ of the Ignatian Exercises* (Maryknoll, N.Y.: Orbis Books, 1987).

ethical impulse and imperative, and against privatization as a view of Christianity that does not legitimize oppressive social structures. The church, by representing the values of the kingdom of God, subverts institutions which hold human freedom and dignity captive; the church is dedicated to liberation where and in the exact measure that social institutions suppress human freedom from flourishing. The mission of the church is God's mission as revealed in the praxis of Jesus to liberate freedom from the inner constraint of sin and the external results of sin in social structures that victimize.

A third deep logic of liberation theology lies implicit in this notion of God's project in history and consists in its embrace and adaptation of a historical consciousness. The church and its mission are tied together because immersed in history: the church is a historical reality with a historical project. This means that it cannot be understood apart from, because it does not exist apart from, its particular time and particular place. The church refers primarily or in the first instance to the concrete organization of people who exercise their Christian faith in history by responding to their place and situation in history.[91] In the interchange with that time and place, the church is meant not merely to take on the elements of the host culture but rather to be reborn and reincarnated within that culture. The further implications of this paradigmatic experience and insight into the demand for inculturation will be drawn out further below.

Some principles of liberation ecclesiology. A number of theological and ecclesiological principles have their basis in the fundamental logic just outlined and have become the hallmarks of liberation theology. An enumeration of several of them will help fill out the theological context for basic ecclesial communities.

The first and perhaps best know of these principles announces a preferential option for the poor by the church. Although the phrase was not used at Medellín in 1968, it was acted out by the Conference as the bishops across the continent of Latin American dedicated the

---

91. Of course, what is called a deep logic of liberation theology is the premise of this whole work. But it was not always so in Roman Catholic ecclesiology, and it is interesting to see how this sense of historicity made its way into Catholic consciousness through Vatican II and its application to distinct historical situations such as that of Latin America.

church to the concerns of the masses of poor people held in captivity by the structures of society and the economy.[92] The partiality of the church for one segment of society is the partiality of the true neighbor as illustrated in Jesus' parable of the Good Samaritan and the man who fell victim on the road to Jericho (Lk 10:28–37); it is peculiarly the option of the rich, not against them, unless they profit from others' suffering. Since in Latin America the vast majority of people were "the poor," such an option constituted a mandate for inculturation.

The far-reaching implications of a theology of and for "the people" is explained by Gustavo Gutiérrez in terms of the premises for the method of theology. On the assumption that modern theology has its base in the experience and faith praxis of a community, when that base is preeminently the poor, the fundamental theological question shifts. The basic question does not revolve around the problem of God, as in apologetics, for the object of the discipline. The grounding problematic is the "nonperson," the negation of human life, and the question of how so many can be systemically disregarded as persons in what ostensibly is a Christian continent. The Christian theologian in Latin America must explain what salvation means to the poor, a task which demands considerable reinterpretation of what was normally preached. The same can be said of liberation theology generally no matter who make up its primary constituency. Such explanation does not aim at enabling acceptance of an intolerable situation but at energizing subjects with the creative power of the Spirit of Christ for combating human suffering.

The effort to make the idea of salvation relevant and credible to the poor and those who suffer requires that it be reappropriated in historical terms. The theological imagination has to be yanked away from mythic or theoretical accounts of redemption and its mediation to the individual through worship and sacrament, to be sublated or subsumed into a historicist context where word and sacrament bestow the power of life. In the theology of Ignacio Ellacuría this entails

---

92. A full account of this principle which suffuses liberation theology is found in Gustavo Gutiérrez, *The Power of the Poor in History* (Maryknoll, N.Y.: Orbis Books, 1983).

not simply a construal of the historical effects of the salvation of individuals who so experience conversion that they respond to the poor. It means the historicization of salvation itself, although not without eschatological hope. Salvation includes the salvation of history, the redeeming of patterns of behavior by institutions that victimize and the creating of institutions that set human beings free.[93]

The shift of imaginative consciousness to a salvation that consists in history itself requires in its turn a translation of the gospel, the very message of Jesus Christ, into historical terms. Such a new consciousness entails a historical consciousness in a sense that is somewhat different than the theoretical framework of a general principle. Here historical consciousness refers to the necessity of understanding and explaining the gospel to people by using concrete and existential language and referents. The conceptual language of theology must be shown to be applicable, to refer to things that can be experienced in personal but especially social life in the community. Here historicity correlates with a certain pragmatism of being able to direct the one who understands back to life so that what is said can act as a guide. Theology, no matter how theoretical and critical, becomes intrinsically conjoined with ethics and thus practical.

Finally, the principle of functionality can be deployed here to summarize the logic and principles of liberation theology and show how they come to bear on ecclesiology. The principle of functionality understands ecclesial structures as a function of the church's mission: they arise to organize and canalize the inner finality of the church; their validity and viability rest on successfully enabling the church to carry forward the mission of Jesus Christ. Newly realized exigencies of the mission of the church will require new structures or adjustments in old ones. If this principle is set within the context of the logic and principles of liberation theology, it helps to explain the role and function basic ecclesial communities came to play in liberation ecclesiology.

---

93. The point is made forcefully by Ellacuría throughout his book, *Freedom Made Flesh*; see also his essay, "The Historicity of Christian Salvation," *Mysterium Liberationis: Fundamental Concepts of Liberation Theology*, ed. I. Ellacuría and J. Sobrino (Maryknoll, N.Y.: Orbis Books, 1993), 251–89, and Kevin F. Burke, *The Ground Beneath the Cross: The Theology of Ignacio Ellacuría* (Washington: Georgetown University Press, 2000).

Nature and Qualities of Basic Ecclesial Communities (BECs)[94]

The movement of basic ecclesial communities in the churches of
Latin America and other parts of the world could be a church-
transforming phenomenon. It consists in the creation of a new
political or organizational substructure in the church below that of
the parish and under the umbrella of the parish. A basic ecclesial
community is an intentional community, one whose size permits the
members to know each other. The description of them which follows
is drawn from the experience in Brazil where they are an important
phenomenon linked with the movement that correlates with liberation theology. It has to be noted, however, that as a phenomenon
BECs have taken on a large variety of types or styles.

A generalized portrait of BECs that correlates with liberation theology would include some of the following features. The "base" of such
basic communities refers not only to their small size which makes
them a kind of primal unit, but also to "the base" as the popular level
of society where BECs flourish among the poor in the countryside or
urban periphery. BECs are proactive rather than passive; they spontaneously include extensive ministry of the laity. Because of the lack
of clergy, BECs can be good examples of what a particular church
might look like when the concept of ministry is expanded to include
the laity as Vatican II instructed. They live on lay leadership, and yet
have kept lines of communication with the larger church, both verti-
cally through the parochial-diocesan structure and horizontally with
other BECs forming something of a movement. These communities
could be seen as analogous to early Christian communities where
basic ministerial functions are reemerging from the communities as
such prior to the absorption of ministry into controlling offices. But

---

94. Sources for this account of BECs are the following: Marcello deC. Azevedo,
Basic Ecclesial Communities in Brazil: The Challenge of a New Way of Being Church
(Washington, D.C.: Georgetown University Press, 1987); Leonardo Boff, "The Base
Ecclesial Community: A Brief Sketch," *Church: Charism and Power* (New York: Cross-
road, 1985), 125–30; *Ecclesiogenesis: The Base Communities Reinvent the Church*
(Maryknoll, N.Y.: Orbis, 1986); Pablo Galdámez, *Faith of a People: The Life of a Basic
Christian Community in El Salvador, 1970–1980* (Maryknoll, N.Y.: Orbis Books, 1986);
Sergio Torres and John Eagleson, eds., *The Challenge of Basic Christian Communities*
(Maryknoll, N.Y.: Orbis Books, 1981).

they are in solidarity with the parish and diocese and, if they are to flourish, enjoy the support of the hierarchy.

BECs generally operate out of a sense of mission, and many are organized around a faith consciousness that includes common concerns of everyday life and social issues. Thus the idea of mission in the sense of addressing the world provides many BECs with a unifying direction of their energy, perhaps with a quite specific focus for social action. Scripture plays a major role in the spirituality and assembly of these communities. Many communities have built into their common practice reflection on the scripture and its application to daily life thus making it a formal element of their existence. In socially conscious BECs scripture nourishes a critical, prophetic consciousness that demystifies in the light of Jesus and the values of the kingdom of God structures that might otherwise appear "natural" or the way things have to be. In this way BECs internalize the theological ideas that the church should be the sign and agent of the kingdom of God and the relevance of salvation for historical existence. This means that these small "churches" empower Christian existence in active, Christian subjects, and this manifests itself in concrete ways. Galdámez, a pseudonym for a pastor whose life was endangered at the time of his writing, testifies that in his BECs this meant forming cooperatives to support small business in the community, or groups to support families victimized by alcoholism or family abuse. In a liberationist conception of human existence these activities can be manifestations of grace and salvation; they are agents of humanization that help release freedom from captivity into creativity.

Small Christian communities in Africa. The idea of a basic ecclesial community is analogous. What has been described here are BECs which have become part of and helped structure the same movement that gave birth to and is reflected in liberation theology. But a BEC might also be centered in reflective prayer based in scripture, or be essentially a liturgical community. In some parts of Africa, where the dominant concern of second-generation church communities is inculturation, the language of liberation might be less prevalent, but the equivalent of BECs have become an official pastoral strategy of the church under the designation of "small Christian communities."

In 1973 the bishops in East Africa committed their churches to making the formation of small Christian communities the cornerstone of their pastoral leadership. This called for a new conception of the church: present parish structures were too large; new structures had to be adopted "so that the life of the church is incarnate in the life of the people by building up a witnessing people."[95] The aim of these communities is to make Christianity operative in the daily lives of people. It calls for adjustments such as a new emphasis on training the laity and a reorientation of clergy in the direction of collaboration (Lwaminda, 96–99).

Generally SCCs fall within the pastoral strategy of the parish in Eastern Africa. The rise of SCCs is "partly a Catholic response to the mushrooming indigenous churches and also an answer to those Catholics who were leaving the church to join indigenous churches" (Nasimiyu, 183). Healey surveys twelve SCCs in Kenya, Tanzania, Uganda, and Zambia with which he is personally familiar. Their pastoral engagement varies considerably from concern with social issues to providing ministries within the community or parish. The ministries of SCCs in two Kenyan dioceses examined by Nasimiyu deal with catechetics, expectant mothers, burial, alcoholism, Bible study, the poor, public health, healing, ecological issues, and consciousness raising (188–96). The assessment of these church organizational structures is positive: "the SCC is the place where the church can express itself in a meaningful Christian communion and also the place for pastoral evangelization and the development of lay ministries. In

---

95. Peter Lwaminda, "A Theological Analysis of the AMECEA Documents on the Local Church with Special Emphasis on the Pastoral Option for Small Christian Communities," *The Local Church with a Human Face,* ed. Agatha Radoli (Eldoret, Kenya: AMECEA Gaba Publications, 1996), 91. AMECEA is the umbrella group of the Catholic bishops of East Africa: Association of Member Episcopal Conferences in Eastern Africa. Other works on small Christian communities are Joseph G. Healey, "Twelve Case Studies of Small Christian Communities in Eastern Africa," in *How Local is the Local Church? Small Christian Communities and Church in Eastern Africa,* ed. Agatha Radoli (Eldoret, Kenya: AMECEA Gaba Publications, 1993), 59–103; John Mutiso-Mbinda, "Ecumenical Challenges of Small Christian Communities and the African Synod of Bishops," ibid., 120–35; Anne Nasimiyu-Wasike, "The Role of Women in Small Christian Communities," ibid., 181–202. These authors are cited by name and page.

Eastern Africa SCCs are truly today's new way of being church from the bottom up. They are a kairos for the Catholic Church in Eastern Africa" (Healey, 96). Ecumenically, they offer one of the best possibilities of encountering other Christian churches on a local, village level. According to Mutiso-Mbinda, although SCCs are the ideal way of renewing the parish by making it "a community of communities" (133), they are vulnerable to becoming fundamentalist or pentecostal if they do not have well-trained leadership (129, 133).

Nasimiyu writes from the perspective of women in the church in Africa. Her research on the ground leads her to the conclusion that SCCs enable women to assume a voice in a patriarchal culture. Women outnumber men in SCCs at about three to one. But the office of chairperson will almost inevitably be given to a man, if there is one available (186). Yet the numbers and work of women gradually earn them authority. In sum, the SCCs are a central arm of the parishes for addressing issues that enhance human life in African, and despite a very strong patriarchal culture, "African women are becoming prominent in the church, especially in the SCCs" (Nasimiyu, 200).[96]

The ecumenical movement, the formation of the World Council of Churches, the Second Vatican Council and the energy it released in liberation ecclesiologies, and the search for new, smaller patterns of church organization were all major movements within the church community in the twentieth century. We turn to an attempt to formulate some of the significance of these events into practical, reflective statements for the self-understanding of the church.

---

96. In the Catholic Church in the United States the ecclesial structures analogous to BECs are also called small Christian communities, and they have generated considerable ministerial energy and written reflection. A short bibliography of small Christian communities would include: Bernard J. Lee et al., *The Catholic Experience of Small Christian Communities* (New York: Paulist Press, 2000); Thomas A. Kleissler et al., *Small Christian Communities: A Vision of Hope for the Twenty-First Century* (New York: Paulist Press, 1997); James O'Halloran, *Signs of Hope: Developing Small Christian Communities* (Maryknoll, N.Y.: Orbis Books, 1991); Robert S. Pelton, ed., *Small Christian Communities: Imagining Future Church* (Notre Dame, Ind.: University of Notre Dame Press, 1997); John Paul Vandenakker, *Small Christian Communities and the Parish: An Ecclesiological Analysis of the North American Experience* (Kansas City, Mo.: Sheed & Ward, 1994).

PRINCIPLES FOR
A HISTORICAL ECCLESIOLOGY

Two broad characteristics in Christian consciousness have been nurtured during the course of the twentieth century: historical consciousness and social consciousness. Historical consciousness refers to a self-conscious appropriation of the consequences of historicity. Everyone shares in such a consciousness in some degree, but at different depths of appreciation. For many at the end of the twentieth century, living in history means that everything, every person, institution, idea, and value, has a particular existence, and its meaning is intrinsically influenced by its time, place, and circumstances. In itself, this consciousness need not entail relativism; it may still allow convictions of timeless truths and continuity of intrinsically human values. But not in such a way that truth and value stand still. One finds it far more difficult, if not impossible, to claim that particular institutions from the past are unchanging or willed by God in their past forms, that church institutions cannot or do not change like all other finite human institutions. Change and difference, as these appear in the simple comparison between the church today and the church in any premodern period, constitute the intrinsic nature of finite temporal existence. Our most primitive experience, that which is closest to the ground, bears the character of a narrative: nothing exists and no perception can take place that does not come from a particular somewhere and is not headed forward into the future. The historical consciousness that arose in the church across the missionary and ecumenical movements, and characterizes our new experience of ourselves as one humanity in one world, has forced distinctions between what is essential and what is peripheral in ecclesial existence.[97] A historically conscious ecclesiology today must be modest, cannot be absolutist, must be open to the world and to other churches.[98]

---

97. The category of the "adiaphora" of the ecclesiology of the Church of England in the sixteenth century became in the ecclesiology of Vatican II a "hierarchy of truths." Both reflect a historical consciousness.

98. There are some churches which do not share these characteristics at all. But it still remains incumbent on an integral ecclesiology to account for these churches in its own self-understanding.

Social consciousness refers to a recognition of the degree to which social conditions influence opinions, attitudes, knowledge, and convictions of any group of people. Just when the ecumenical movement was taking off in the late 1920s, H. Richard Niebuhr wrote his *The Social Sources of Denominationalism* which showed how little doctrine and how much concrete elements of the ethos of churches were responsible for identity and division.[99] The World Council of Churches itself provides a grand testimony to differences that are all deeply rooted in social system and tradition. Of course, when such living ideas and convictions are lifted out of their social matrices and manipulated and juggled and mixed together with others, as appears to be the case in various ecumenical statements, the result can be portrayed as shallow compromise. Each tends to say: "No truth and no ecclesiology can approach the integrity and authenticity of my community." It is only in an expanded horizon of mutual relationships that one can begin to internalize the social construction of reality and the social and cultural relativity of all knowledge.[100] The process of acknowledging and facing this issue was going on within the church throughout the twentieth century. This process is far from over; it will never be completed. But the depth of what is involved here entered a new phase in the last third of the twentieth century as the churches began to address their status within the family of world religions.

Against the background of how Christian consciousness developed in the course of the twentieth century, attention is directed to the formulation of some lessons and principles that were mediated or represented in the ecumenical movement, the formation of the World Council of Churches, the extended event of the Second Vatican Council, and the emergence of liberation theologies.

The unity of the whole church is an essential quality. Today, only a unity in difference can be achieved, and such unity is of more value than uniformity. Perhaps the most important lesson for

---

99. H. Richard Niebuhr, *The Social Sources of Denominationalism* (New York: World Publishing, 1972, originally 1929).

100. Karl Mannheim, in *Ideology and Utopia: An Introduction to the Sociology of Knowledge* (New York: Harcourt Brace, 1985, originally 1936), explains these basic concepts in a straightforward way that rejects relativism.

ecclesiology internalized during the course of the twentieth century concerned the value and the quality of the unity of the church. This was learned through a contrast experience. The divisions among the Christian churches are not simply scandalous: they also seriously compromise the mission of the church to the world, both the world of those who are not Christian and whom the church addresses through its missionaries, and the world of Christian Europe, in which the church had little leverage in preventing two world wars. The reaction against such division on the enormous scale of the ecumenical movement across the whole century dramatically affirmed the intrinsic necessity of making unity in Christ and the Spirit visible, tangible, organizational, real. It could no longer remain on the notional level of a common name or a common set of doctrines; it had to be actualized in some organizational form. But this unity could only be achieved within the context of the newly internalized historical and social consciousness. This modern framework, in turn, both allowed the unity to take form and changed the character of the unity that was possible and thus sought: it had to be a unity within differences. What united the churches must transcend them and thus allow for real differences among them. Unity has to be pluralistic. While this may seem a cliché today, it is, like historical consciousness, appreciated at different levels and with various boundaries. It is striking, in fact, how little the cliché is reflected in church behavior.

Existential community in Christ holds priority over doctrinal agreement. This is a statement of the relative importance of different levels of community and communitarian bonds. It does not declare a contentious thesis, as in a competitive, zero-sum game, where to grant priority to one factor minimizes the importance of another, in this case, doctrinal expression. In fact, friendship in Christ completely transcends doctrinal agreement, and every Christian with friends in other churches knows this to be true. But while no one participating in the ecumenical movement could fail to recognize it, the assertion by no means removes the ambiguity involved. Pluralism requires fairly nuanced concepts of faith and belief in which a common faith can brook real differences of expression or practice, and where distinctions are made between what is essential and what is not. But each community has its own thresholds of toleration and a center of gravity that will be offended by deviations from its particular norms for what is essentially Christian. Each community will have its own traditions which make up a real part of their genuine identity. Yet each is able to find or grant that other churches participate in true Christian faith. In the course of the twentieth century, therefore, the church, in the sense of each church that participated in the ecumenical movement, reassessed the quality and character of its own faith in such a way that it grasped the center or core of Christian faith, distinguished this from accidentals, peripheral material, and contingent forms of expression, possessed a natural inclination to preserve those elements of its tradition that were identity-defining even though they were not essential to the Christian faith, and were willing in some measure to live with others who lacked those particular elements for the sake of a broader unity. If this is an accurate description of a substantial body of Christians and Christian churches, it represents a major ecclesiological development. In the light of these basic principles, the future life of the whole church could take on a new open character.

The key to this principle lies quite deeply embedded in an understanding of the epistemological structure of Christian faith and an internal appropriation of a strategy that is based on it. The epistemological structure was stated by the WWC in "New Delhi" (1961) and at Vatican II (1965): the content of faith exceeds what doctrine can put into words.[101] This allows for a recognition of and a learning from the teaching and practices of other churches. The strategy consists in explicitly focusing on that which unites churches, that is, the common substance of faith. This cannot be done by ignoring differences; but it must be done sometimes in spite of differences and at other times rejoicing in them.

The deliberately vague phrase "communion ecclesiology" opens up a creative imagination for ecclesiology in our time. Communion ecclesiology is a category that contains or highlights several potentialities that came to fruition in the quest for unity as well as other events of the century. Several impulses in the course of the

---

101. See supra, pp. 380 and 398–99.

twentieth century have nurtured a trend toward communion ecclesiology.[102] "Communion" as applied to church and ecclesiology can mean a number of quite different things. These reflections are limited to filling the category with some of the developments and insight mediated by the nature of the WCC and the dynamics of Vatican II. The development of the World Council of Churches required considerable self-transcendence and trust in God as Spirit at work in the church at large on the part of the member churches; it entailed open reliance on a common faith and on the other churches. The result is a form of communion ratified by membership in a common institution. The WCC is not a church, but it represents a form of actual communion. Various levels and meanings of communion run through Vatican II: a new emphasis on the local church allows one to view the whole church as a communion of churches under one head; the idea of a *collegium* of bishops, each with his local responsibility for his own church and, as member of the college, a responsibility for the church at large, supports the notion that the whole church is a communion. Commonly expressed in both the WCC and Vatican II, despite major differences, is a sense of the whole and of being in communion with the whole in a fellowship or community of a single faith. This is enabled by some form of institution that encourages and supports that communion. The role of jurisdiction, however, differs greatly in these two examples and distinguishes these forms of communion. But the new thing in all of this is the sense of communion itself that can absorb the dialectical tensions it entails: the corporate self-identity and local autonomy it presumes, the acceptance of a sense of being responsible to other churches in a way that recognizes a measure of authority of the others with whom each particular church

---

102. Dennis Doyle, in *Communion Ecclesiology: Visions and Versions* (Maryknoll, N.Y.: Orbis Books, 2000), surveys the field of communion ecclesiologies from a Roman Catholic perspective in the twentieth century but reaching back as well to Schleiermacher and Möhler. So many different ecclesiologies are included under the umbrella that one may lose sight of the relevance of the category. One such relevance, I suggest, lies in a creative theological imagination: the phrase allows one to imagine a variety of ecclesiological possibilities relating to unity and organization. Communion ecclesiology most typically characterizes the Eastern churches, and their ecclesiology will be considered in the chapter that follows.

shares communion, and the willingness to give the larger unity some institutional form.

The size of the basic unit of churches has to be adjusted to accommodate the religious needs of the people. Communion ecclesiology, which among other things suggests that the greater church is a communion of more basic ecclesial units, has opened up a space for new attention to the local church. This applies less to churches already congregational in their polity, and more to churches defined as larger units as, for example, the Roman Catholic Church, the Orthodox churches, or the Anglican Communion. Empirically and sociologically, the place where individual Christians actually encounter the church is in the local congregation, especially or most explicitly in its gathering for worship. The Christian may belong to a large church, but for the most part he or she lives in a parish or congregation, so that this place of assembly provides a first existential referent for the meaning of church. A new centering of the imagination on the parish or congregation in ecclesiology need not in any way undercut the status and importance of larger ecclesiological units. Quite on the contrary, communion ecclesiology is intrinsically relational and interactive; the relationship between lower and higher communions in organizational terms is primarily intended to support and enhance the existence of the lower with the support and resources of the higher. The primary purpose is not control. This line of thinking could open up more lines of continuity and communication between the mainline communions or churches and congregational or free churches.

Ecclesiology today must explicitly attend to the relation of the church to the world that constitutes its environment: inculturation. All organizations must adapt to their environment or cease to exist. All Christian churches are inculturated in some culture. The Christian churches always accommodate the cultures and societies in which they exist sooner or later. These statements are all more or less true because they reflect the laws of history. The question today has to do with self-conscious appropriation of these principles and making them operative in a church's life. For inculturation is a matter of degree and sometimes this involves painful choices on the part of congregations or the leadership of larger churches. Sometimes a missionary church in one place is really still inculturated in another culture foreign to the one in which it exists. The principle of the need for inculturation is becoming more obvious in the churches, but this will not make it easier to implement. Since inculturation points to a radical process of rethinking identity and practice in indigenous categories and symbols that are not Western, this process can be difficult, slow, and politically and culturally charged. But more and more Christians are becoming aware of its necessity. It is an issue which practically speaking all Christian churches share in common.

No adequate ecclesiology today can ignore the issues of justice that prevail in society. Another consistent theme in the development of twentieth-century ecclesiology takes up again the problem of the relation of the church to the world. This generalized problematic takes many different forms. One consists in the manner in which the church exerts a public influence on society and government in matters of social justice. Beginning with Constantinian legitimation and support, and continuing through the Middle Ages, the church had direct bearing on societies and governments. By contrast, the modern period exhibited a growing autonomy of nation states and civil institutions that filtered out in various degrees the influence of the churches. One can read the Christian social movements in Europe in the nineteenth century, the Social Gospel in the United States, the Life and Work movement, and Catholic social teaching along with *Gaudium et Spes* as representative of a desire that Christian faith and values have an impact on national and global social life. That influence must be expressed and acted out on the basis of new social and cultural principles. The questions are the same: what does the language of salvation, reconciliation, justice, and peace mean when Christian European nations continually go to war among themselves? Or on their poor citizens? This demand for relevance to the world has spawned a new political or liberation theology that is not premised upon a competition between civil and religious authority in their proper sphere. It must be granted that these two authorities can indeed see things differently and be at odds over concrete social issues. But this new political theology grants the autonomy of secular rule and seeks to address to a freedom civilly guaranteed the transcendent values of the *humanum* as that is religiously perceived from the perspective of Christian revelation. A dominant theme in the ecclesiologies of the WCC and Vatican II and its aftermath affirms that Christian faith is relevant for life in this world and that the church exists to mediate those values to society at large.[103] Liberation movements and their theologies put these deeply Christian and ecclesiological convictions into practice.

As a corollary to a concern for social justice, the functioning ecclesiology of all Christian churches is challenged by the fundamental equality of men and women. Feminist liberation theology has raised this issue as an irreversible, universal concern; it will be felt as a challenge by all churches in various ways and different degrees. This is due partly to the patriarchal character of the origins of the church, including its constitutional scriptures, and partly to current patriarchal cultures and social arrangements. Given the phenomenon of globalization, few patriarchal societies in the future will ultimately be able to hide. Obviously this issue commands a large body of literature and will continue to occupy the churches in the future. But the issues can be stated sharply. On the one hand, the Christian churches are built on religious values that have direct bearing on discrimination against any group. On the basis of the fundamental dignity of all human persons created by a personal God in love, one would expect the Christian churches to be a leading voice in promoting the equality of women in society. On the other hand, this issue defines an area where the credibility of the church as a witness to its own message before the world is at stake. Some churches are meeting this challenge from the gospel better than others.

In an increasingly "globalized" world of interdependence of peoples and heightened, self-conscious identity, Christian mission must become formally dialogical. The concepts of contextualization and inculturation are modern or postmodern depending on the radicality with which they are understood. These processes were announced as premises of the method of ecclesiology underlying this

---

103. In a Christian Europe of the sixteenth century, it was hard for most Christians to identify with Anabaptist ecclesiology, which saw the church standing apart from and being severely critical of what was then a Christian society. Today, however, in an increasingly secularized and pluralistic Western Christianity, Anabaptist ecclesiology takes on a new relevance.

work. Thus across the length of the life of the church one can see the church entering into dialogue with the social, political, and cultural world in which it settled and taking on indigenous qualities, styles, and ways of proceeding. This could very well have happened imperceptibly. But in a globalized and pluralistic world, differences are noted. Especially from the period of the missionary movement in the nineteenth century, cultural differentiation became more apparent to general consciousness as the social sciences began to document it and epistemology began to explain it. In the postcolonial developments after World War II, nationalism and self-definition went hand in hand, and this extended to the definition of Christian identity. In the course of the twentieth century the church has become a world-church in a qualitatively new way. The majority of Christians in the world today no longer live in the developed West, that is, in Europe and North America. Formerly missionary churches, dependent on the West especially, have become dynamically developing churches, and in a foreseeable future they will have a much greater impact on the life of the whole body. The principles of pluralism, of unity amid difference, will be continually tested in new ways.

The global church in the twenty-first century is gradually internalizing two genuinely new qualities. The first is the self-conscious need for inculturation. In today's Christian world, where the intellectual community resides on the boundary between modernity and postmodernity, all churches express a demand that Christian doctrine and theology, worship and moral ideals be integrated into the social and cultural threads that define the life-patterns of a particular people. The second is the recognition in various degrees across the churches of the validity of other religions and the way they are embedded in their home cultures. The outreach of the church to these cultures and religions cannot be imperial; it can only be made through dialogue in a conversation geared on a first level to mutual understanding. The churches are gradually shedding many aspects of a former absolutism and learning humility before a God active outside the Christian sphere.

To conclude: two principles contain a depth and breadth that can summarize what happened in the course of the ecumenical movement that led to the formation of the World Council of Churches and the event of Vatican II and its aftermath including liberation theology. The first was the profound, corporate realization that the divided church absolutely needed some form of institutional unity in order for it adequately to perform its divine mission in history. This conviction was generated in the massive contrast experience of the scandal given by division and competition among the churches around the world and the impotence of the churches in the face of Christians killing each other in two world wars. This was no mere political insight, but a religious experience of infidelity to God's intent for the church. The second was the modern or postmodern recognition that the only unity that could be achieved is one that entailed differences. In the course of the ecumenical movement and against the odds of its being able in any measure to succeed, this conviction matured into a positive or constructive conviction and not a mere concession to finitude and sin. The plurality and differences in the unity that we seek is a blessing to rejoice in and be glad. But this principle is never learned once for all and must be internalized over and over again.

Chapter 7

Twentieth-Century Ecclesiology: Orthodox and Pentecostal Ecclesiologies and BEM

Surely the ecumenical movement, the formation of the World Council of Churches, and the Second Vatican Council dominated the arena of ecclesiological development during the first two thirds of the twentieth century. But they by no means exhausted this phenomenal period; other movements have taken off and will be major factors for the world church in the future. The context in which these developments have unfolded included many events of a worldwide social and geopolitical character. Beneath them, by slow steady increment, the "size" of the planet continued to decrease, and the interdependence of peoples gradually increased along with a consciousness of being one human race. The new technologies made those with education and position neighbors to all human beings. The new mobility of more and more peoples has made the world cosmopolitan and more complex as the population of the planet continues to grow.

In this context we turn again to the Orthodox Church, which represents an ecclesiology that is as distinct from those outlined thus far in this comparative ecclesiology as it is rich in its retrieval of early patristic theology. Relative to the spectrum of ecclesiologies presented in chapter 4, Orthodox ecclesiology shares a position on the right side of the axis along with the Roman Church. And if some churches in the Anabaptist and free church tradition have settled into ecclesiological positions closer to the center, a new left belongs to pentecostalism. It will be analyzed as representing a distinct, free form of ecclesiology. Finally, the chapter presents an interpretive synopsis of the ecumenical ecclesiology presented in the Faith and Order document of the World Council of Churches: "Baptism, Eucharist and Ministry."

ORTHODOX CHRISTIANITY:
THE ICONIC ECCLESIOLOGY OF JOHN ZIZIOULAS

The ecclesiology of the Orthodox Church is intimately connected with the basic doctrines of Christianity which were formulated in the patristic period. These doctrines in their turn directly shape a spirituality, so that ecclesial life, worship, and ecclesiology reinforce each other in an insoluble whole. This holistic interconnectedness suggests an approach to this ecclesiology that integrates it into the wider spirituality of this church and thus communicates its theological comprehensiveness. We begin, therefore, with a simple historical indication of the many independent and dependent Orthodox churches which make up the communion. The next section outlines the spirituality of Orthodoxy in the broadest terms of trinitarian doctrine and how these doctrines form a kind of framework for ecclesiology. These broad strokes are designed to provide an apperceptive background for the analysis of the ecclesiology of one noted Orthodox theologian. This gives a neat counterpoint of doctrinal generality and a specific exemplification of it. Eastern Orthodoxy has not held a general council in the modern period, and there is no commonly formulated ecclesiology. But there is broad agreement on the fundamental level at which it is represented here, and Zizioulas's ecclesiology has been both widely read and accepted as representative of Orthodoxy.

The Orthodox Church in the Twentieth Century

The Orthodox Church today consists of a variety of different churches which share the broad lines of a common ecclesiology and canonical tradition and which are, for the most part, in communion with each other. Communion among the churches is of the essence of this ecclesiology. Recognition of how many autonomous churches make up the Orthodox Church enables an appreciation of its unity and plurality across nation and culture.[1] One can think of these churches quite

---

1. The historical data and the broad characterization of Orthodox theology and ecclesiology that follow are drawn principally from John Binns, *An Introduction to the*

arbitrarily as existing in three large groups: those associated with the Eastern Mediterranean, Arab lands, and the Muslim religion; those assembled in the Soviet Union during the twentieth century; and relatively new churches that are the product of recent missionary activity or immigration.[2]

Among the first group, the oldest and most prestigious church is the Patriarchate of Constantinople. Among the Orthodox churches it enjoys primacy after Rome since the early patristic conciliar period. But in 1923 the greater part of the Greek Orthodox Christians were expelled from Turkey so that the constituency of the patriarchate was greatly reduced. But its position of primacy in the Orthodox Church is of major significance. The most important in terms of numbers and power within this group is quite distinct from the Muslim world: the Church of Greece. This church closely identifies with the Greek nation and its cultural identity, but its jurisdiction overflows the nation to the North into the Balkans. It is a well-developed church with schools and seminaries for its clergy.

Other churches in this group are the Patriarchate of Alexandria, which is relatively small since most of the Egyptian Christians are not Orthodox because they did not accept the Council of Chalcedon. The ancient Patriarchate of Antioch covers the territory of Beirut

---

Christian Orthodox Churches (Cambridge: Cambridge University Press, 2002) [JB]; John Meyendorff, *The Orthodox Church: Its Past and Its Role in the World Today*, 4th rev. ed. (Crestwood, N.Y.: St. Vladimir's Seminary Press, 1996) [JM]; *Living Tradition: Orthodox Witness in the Contemporary World* (Crestwood, N.Y.: St. Vladimir's Seminary Press, 1978) [JM2]; Ronald Roberson, *The Eastern Churches: A Brief Survey* (Rome: Edizioni Orientalia Christiana, 1999) [RR]; Timothy Ware, *The Orthodox Church* (London: Penguin Books, 1997) [TM]; Hugh Wybrew, *The Orthodox Liturgy: The Development of the Eucharistic Liturgy in the Byzantine Rite* (Crestwood, N.Y.: St. Vladimir's Seminary Press, 1996) [HW].

2. The churches described here are Chalcedonian. In christological terms, on the Antiochene and Alexandrian side of the Chalcedonian compromise are respectively the Assyrian Church of the East which retained the "two nature" language associated with Antiochene theology and six Oriental Orthodox churches which share Cyrillian language in christology ("the one incarnate nature of the Word of God") and are in communion with each other. These are the Armenian Apostolic Church, the Coptic Orthodox Church, the Ethiopian Orthodox Church, the Syrian Orthodox Church, the Malankara Orthodox Syrian Church, and the Eritrean Orthodox Church. These churches reject the respective designations "Nestorian" and "Monophysite," and more and more their christological positions are being recognized as "orthodox" so that differences from Chalcedonian belief are considered more matters of terminology than faith (RR, 15–41).

and Syria and the Patriarch resides in Damascus. The Patriarchate of Jerusalem has responsibility for Orthodox Christians in Israel and Jordan, but these are few. The particular responsibility of this church is care of the holy places. The Church of Cyprus has been autocephalous since 431 when the Council of Ephesus declared it so. The Church of Sinai is also considered an independent church even though it "consists basically of just a single monastery, St Catherine's, at the foot of the Mountain of Moses in the Sinai peninsula (Egypt)" (TW, 135).

The second group of Orthodox churches are those which existed either in the Soviet Union or under other communist regimes. Most of these churches will remember the twentieth century as one of persecution. This is most true of the Patriarchate of Moscow or the Russian Orthodox Church, by far the largest of all Orthodox churches. The repression of this church by the state had various stages, most severe of which was the period from the Bolshevik Revolution up to 1943. In that year, with the advance of Germany into Russia, Stalin allowed a revival of church life in a controlled way, but this was followed by persecution under Khrushchev between 1959 and 1964. Since the fall of the Soviet Union the Russian Church has been relatively free to develop its ecclesial infrastructure again. One of the more serious problems involves sorting out the churches in the Ukraine where in this newly independent state there are distinctions between Catholic Orthodox, an autocephalous Orthodox Church divided in two, and the Orthodox Church that remains under the jurisdiction of Moscow.

The many other churches of Eastern Europe each have their own history under distinct regimes in the course of the twentieth century. Each government controlled or repressed the church in varying degrees, or in some cases suppressed church life. A list of these churches helps to convey the complexity of Orthodoxy and the degree to which the century was one of serious persecution for the largest portion of these Christians: the Church of Albania, the Church of Bulgaria, the Orthodox Church of the Czech Republic and Slovakia, the Church of Finland, which is under the Jurisdiction of the Ecumenical Patriarch, the Church of Georgia, the Church of Macedonia, the Church of Poland, the Church of Romania, the Church of Serbia.

The third group of Orthodox churches is no group at all but all the rest. "In the past Orthodoxy has appeared, from the cultural and geographical point of view, almost exclusively as an 'Eastern' Church. Today this is no longer so. Outside the boundaries of the traditional Orthodox countries there now exists a large Orthodox 'dispersion,' with its chief center in North America, but with branches in every part of the world" (TW, 172). The Orthodox Church in the United States has grown considerably with immigration, but this has led to divisions among churches along ethnic or national lines. Thus the Orthodox Church in America is not a single united church of the whole nation under its metropolitan, because other Orthodox churches coexist with it. Orthodox churches have also been established in Africa, principally in Uganda and Kenya whose churches are associated with the Patriarchate of Alexandria, in Western Europe, and in the Far East where Orthodox churches exist in China, Japan, and Korea. The Orthodox Church is now a world church.

Doctrine, Spirituality, and the Framework of Ecclesiology

Across the large canonical, organizational, and cultural variations among these churches, they share a common spirituality that transcends the differences and keeps them in communion.[3] Orthodox ecclesiology is unintelligible apart from the classical Christians doctrines formulated in the patristic period. An attempt to characterize that spirituality in the objective terms of basic doctrines, therefore, will set the stage for this distinctive ecclesiology. What follows leads into the specific religious framework needed for appreciating Zizioulas's ecclesiology.

Central to all Orthodox self-understanding is the doctrine of the Trinity. This doctrine, which functions as a name for God, characterizes the immanent life of God but more importantly represents the cosmic narrative of how God acted and still acts in history. Holy God is absolutely transcendent and not available to human knowledge,

---

3. "Regardless of the age in which he lives or his status in life, when the Orthodox Christian enters a church [building] he feels instinctively that he is in the presence of Heaven, that the Kingdom of God is already here; he knows that Christ is there in the spiritual communion of his Body and his Blood, in the Gospel read by the priest, and in the prayers of the church." JM, 182.

except that God enters into relationship with human beings. The doctrine of the Trinity remains so central because it characterizes the very nature of the transcendent God as divine being reaching into history for human salvation. Everything religious transpires within this framework of the trinitarian economy of salvation.

The incarnation of the Word of God, the Son, constitutes the saving address of God to the world and human beings in it. The incarnation of the Son entails two truths bearing a foundational, ontological character. The first affirms that very God has assumed as God's own a human nature, and thus human nature as such, and in so appropriating human nature God has bestowed the quality of divinity on it; God not only ratified humanity with a divine love, but made it "of God" or possessive of the quality of divinity. Such is the meaning of the descent passage of Paul in Philippians 2 (JM, 177). Human nature, and with it materiality itself, has been drawn up into the divine sphere by a personal self-communication of God, and that embrace has transformed its quality of otherness from God, not to mention sin and defect. The second holds that the Incarnation of the Son thus alters the situation of humanity relative to the transcendence and unknowability of God: God has made God's self available in Jesus Christ so that a way is open to a knowledge of God that is as it were "direct" in and through the Son.[4]

The Holy Spirit plays a major role in Orthodox spirituality and ecclesiology, for the Spirit actualizes what was accomplished by Jesus Christ in each person and in the community of believers. The Spirit effects in the rest of human beings what occurred in Jesus Christ by inspiring and bringing about in each case identification with and participation in the incarnation. Salvation is sanctification and even deification. "This deification is realized when we become members of the Body of Christ, but also, and especially, by the unction of the Spirit when the latter touches each one of us: the 'economy of the Holy Spirit' means precisely this, that we are able to enjoy communion with the one and truly deified humanity of Jesus

---

4. "Direct" but not immediate, for Jesus Christ, as approached by human beings, is precisely the sacrament or icon of God who mediates God to history and responds to the human quest for God. In all of this the discussion of the final reaction of Orthodoxy against iconoclasm is significant. See CCH, I, 288–90.

Christ throughout history from the time of the Ascension to the final Parousia" (JM, 177).

Orthodox theology takes this narrative of what God did for human salvation and construes it as the ongoing activity of God. This initiative of God in history, although it occurred definitively or eschatologically in the event of Jesus Christ, continues in present history. The church has to be understood as part of that history in dynamic terms. From the time of the Ascension and Pentecost the church became the historical medium embodying Christ through whom deification in Jesus Christ becomes publicly available in history. Human beings can participate in the redemptive work of Christ through the sacraments: "by dying and rising again with Christ in baptism, by receiving the seal of the Spirit in confirmation, by becoming members of the actual body of Christ in the eucharist, and finally by making progress in every greater knowledge...."[5] The understanding of the church, therefore, from the beginning finds its place in the all embracing theology of history. The role of the church in history is to make God present and known in the world, not only in the sacraments and the Word, but also through the Spirit in the lives of church members.

When we turn to consider the nature of the church, still in the broadest possible framework, it becomes apparent that in the contrast between ecclesiology from above and from below, this is ecclesiology from above.[6] It leans toward the mystical and theological in the sense that the theological imagination always draws the historical dimension of the church up into the doctrines of Christ and the Holy Spirit: the church is considered as the image of Trinity, the

---

5. JM, 174–75. "This 'deification' in Jesus Christ is available to us through Baptism and the Eucharist: the Incarnate Word communicates to us the divine life and transforms our whole being from inside." Ibid., 186.

6. By "from above" I mean especially a structure of the theological imagination that does not on methodological principle ascend to God through the finite and this-worldly, but one that moves in the opposite direction to illumine and interpret finite reality by a construal of God's presence and activity within the finite which transforms empirical reality into a form of divine reality as symbolized by the doctrines (See the discussion in CCH, I, 17–55, esp. 18–25). An example of this way of thinking is illustrated in this observation of Meyendorff relative to church unity: "If we...understand church unity as basically a eucharistic and therefore eschatological reality, our attitude will be different from that which considers the Church as immanent in the world, so that its destiny is determined by the secular goals of mankind." JM2, 139.

body of Christ, and an ongoing Pentecost. The church is icon of the Trinity; the church is "extension of the Incarnation, the place where the Incarnation perpetuates itself": the church is the place in history of the indwelling of the Holy Spirit.[7]

Characteristically, this deeply theological way of understanding the church bestows on it a certain objective character that allows language bearing a meaning that transcends empirical observation and sometimes contradicts it. Considerations of the unity of the church, its catholicity, its organization, its holiness all share in this theocentric or mystical point of view. The church transcends its members; it is essentially constituted by God out of human beings and not an intentional human community. The church is one with a oneness that transcends the divisions among Christians and churches.[8] "We must not say that because Christians on earth sin and are imperfect, therefore the Church sins and is imperfect; for the Church, even on earth, is a thing of heaven, and cannot sin."[9]

Monasticism. Monasticism continues to play an important role in the Orthodox Church. "Without monasteries it is hard to see how the life of the church could be maintained" (JB, 107). These institutions exist in a variety of forms in towns, in cities, or in secluded places far off from society as on Mount Athos in Greece, the spiritual center of Orthodoxy. They have assumed a symbiotic relationship to the church at large through a variety of functions. Monks fully and carefully celebrate the liturgy in these communities and set the example for the churches. They are places of prayer, study, and basic instruction in theology and spirituality. Monasteries have "a role in providing the future leaders of the church, especially since only monks can be consecrated as bishops" (JB, 108).[10] Monasteries

---

7. TW, 239–45, citation at p. 241.

8. "Christian unity is a unity with Christ in the Holy Spirit, and not a unity among men which has been lost at some time in the past. This unity belongs to the One Church, which cannot be divided by human controversies. Men cannot divide God and his Truth, and then restore them to unity." JM, 201.

9. TW, 244. The mystery of the church is that sinners are transformed into something other than themselves, the Body of Christ. Ibid.

10. "According to Orthodox tradition, clergy are divided into two types: married clergy and monks. The decision is made at ordination, and since a monk cannot marry, this has the consequence that marriage has to precede ordination." JB, 108.

also provide places of pilgrimage and centers of hospitality and thus nurture the popular faith.

Eucharistic liturgy. The liturgy of the Orthodox Church is a product of historical development. As in the West a major development occurred toward the end of the fourth century when the custom of receiving communion at each liturgy ceased and the eucharistic celebration changed its character: the ritual took on a life of its own as a symbolic, allegorical drama of the Christ event carried out by the clergy in which the laity participated but more passively. This is exemplified in Chrysostom's liturgies and sermons (HW, 60–66). Development was deeply affected by the iconoclast crisis and its resolution.[11] During the fourteenth century development reached a certain term. Although church buildings varied, they frequently followed the basic pattern of the Greek cross and the basilica; the "sanctuary came to be completely shut off from the sight of the congregation by a solid screen," and the order of the liturgy was stabilized (HW, 145–47).

Wybrew so contrasts the liturgies of the Western and Eastern churches that those of Roman Catholics, Anglicans, and Protestants appear cut from the same simple, transparent, and participatory pattern exemplified in Justin Martyr's *First Apology*. Against this backdrop, Orthodox liturgy appears opaque and heavy with formality and choreographed symbolism. The church building itself is iconic, an image of heaven on earth: "the lower portion of the nave signifies the visible world, [and] the dome, and still more the sanctuary, are images of heaven, where the triune God is worshiped by angels and archangels and the whole company of heaven" (HW, 4). The church encompasses the altar and the ceremony with the dome of heaven and surrounds the worshipers with iconic representations of the company of saints (JB, 57–59). The liturgy itself has two faces:

---

11. As people received communion less frequently and the service became less a meal and more a dramatic action subject to various symbolic interpretations, a mystagogical approach in line with Dionysius the Areopagite interpreted the rites as drawing people into the heavenly sphere even as Christ is the descending incarnate one. An approach recommended by Jesus' words, "Do this in remembrance of me," refers to the whole rite as a drama and finds in the actions various parallels to the life of Jesus. These symbolic paths explore various aspects and layers of meaning in the fundamental mystery of the human encounter with the divine in the service. JB, 51–54.

the one is the public interchange between the clergy and the choir, the other is the invisible and inaudible work of the clergy in the sanctuary which is separated off from the nave by the screen. Since the whole service depicts the earthly ministry of Jesus, his death, resurrection, and ascension, although few participate by receiving communion, "all can do so by contemplating the saving mystery of the incarnation, passion, and glorification of the Lord" (HW, 10–11).

The liturgy "is the meeting of God and humanity, and at it the nature of the church is most clearly seen and experienced" (JB, 40). This is so because the church is a communion that is effected by a sharing of the life of God communicated in Christ and through the Spirit. This reality of the church "becomes an event when the liturgy is celebrated," so that church "is created, sustained and visibly present at the Eucharist, or Liturgy, or Communion" (JB, 40). It will be shown in the ecclesiology of Zizioulas how the constitutive relation of the eucharist to church explains some points of its organization, for example, why bishops are autonomous and equal, why the whole church is present in any local church, why the size of congregations tends to be small (one celebration on a given day), why wider organization of the church is less essential, why despite divisions in organizational structures there can be communion (JB, 41–43).

Two fundamental principles can be evoked to sum up the general framework of Orthodox ecclesiology: the one stipulates the unity, catholicity, and autonomy of the local church; the other is communion among the churches. Again, the theological character of these foundations of ecclesiastical organization is noteworthy. At the heart of Orthodox ecclesiology, as well as the conception of the Christian life, is the eucharist. In the celebration of the eucharist the reality of Christ being present and constituting the Body of Christ is actualized in a unique and privileged way. This grounds the idea that the whole or total church, the *fullness of the reality of God's presence in Word and Spirit, is present in every local community where people gather around a bishop and the eucharist.*[12] "The local

---

12. JM, 193; JM2, 84. The referent of the term "local church" developed from the one congregation in a city to the diocese.

churches, however, are not mere isolated units living in separation from each other: they are united by the *identity* of their faith and their witness to the truth" (JM, 193). This identity expresses itself in episcopal consecrations when several bishops from surrounding churches attend them, in meetings such as synods or councils, and in communion between churches. But the communion between the churches constituting their unity should not be thought of in organizational and administrative terms but in theological terms of faith and the power of the Spirit. Communion is also balanced by the fact that ultimately a local church is not subject to authority from outside itself. "In the Orthodox Church . . . no power can exist by divine right outside and above the local eucharistic community, which corresponds today to what we call the diocese" (JM, 193). The only visible criterion of truth, then, does not lie in an external office, but in an internal consensus that finds expression in synod, council, or more generally communion. But this consensus is not outside the local church or above it but an expression of common accord among the churches. These themes take on specificity and more detail in the Orthodox ecclesiology developed by John Zizioulas.

Some Foundational Categories in John Zizioulas's Ecclesiology

John Zizioulas was born in Greece in 1931. His doctorate in theology was completed at the University of Athens. He was a professor of theology and worked with the Commission on Faith and Order at the World Council of Churches before becoming Metropolitan of Pergamon, representing the Ecumenical Patriarchate. The analysis of his ecclesiology which follows draws mainly from his *Being as Communion*, a collection of his major essays, because it concisely combines a historical retrieval of the early Fathers, systematic construction, and ecumenical sensitivity into a holistic, foundational portrayal of the church.[13]

The ecclesiology of Zizioulas differs from the Western tradition in method and content. In order to respect that difference, at the risk of some repetition, this ecclesiology is presented in two stages.

---

13. John D. Zizioulas, *Being as Communion: Studies in Personhood and the Church* (Crestwood, N.Y.: St. Vladimir's Seminary Press, 1997. Orig. 1985). This book is referred to as BC in the text.

The first stage provides an overview or systematic description of this ecclesiology in the terms of the essential categories that Zizioulas uses to characterize it. This will serve as a glossary of the terms of his distinctive theological method and language. The second stage presents this ecclesiology according to the template that has been used throughout this essay.

An understanding of Zizioulas's theology might begin with a consideration of his epistemology. Several terms could be used to characterize the approach or method of Zizioulas's theology: sacramental, theophanic, meta-historical, symbolic, mystagogical, iconic.[14] He addresses Christians, presupposes basic beliefs, and appeals to the transcendent experience implied in them. In contrast to a historicist imagination that attends to historical causality and continuity, Zizioulas discovers transcendent reality as a presence within history and the finite. A liturgical sensibility and an iconic imagination allow an appreciation of God's presence in the material world.

The very basis of Zizioulas's understanding of all things is the Trinity. "Trinity" represents less a doctrine about God and more a substantive pointing to the reality of God. "It would be unthinkable to speak of the 'one God' before speaking of the God who is 'communion,' that is to say, of the Holy Trinity. The Holy Trinity is a *primordial* ontological concept and not a notion which is added to the divine substance..." (BC, 17).

The Trinity shows itself in the economy of salvation, and ecclesiology is built upon this divine trinitarian economy. "The fact that man in the church is the 'image of God' is due to the *economy* of the Holy Trinity, that is, the work of Christ and the Spirit in *history.* This economy is the *basis* of ecclesiology, without being the *goal* of it" (BC, 19).

Zizioulas's ecclesiology, therefore, unfolds within the large cosmic-historical framework of creation and redemption in which both

---

14. Zizioulas characterizes his ecclesiology as "theophanic" and "meta-historical." He also cites Yves Congar on Eastern ecclesiology generally as saying that it resembles the theology of the fathers and of the liturgy as embodying the idea of "a 'showing,'or a manifestation of invisible heavenly realities on earth. The result is a conception of the church that is principally sacramental or iconological." BC, 171, n. 1.

Christ and the Holy Spirit have essential roles. Against a christocentric or christo-monistic understanding of the church, he provides an essential function for the Spirit as constitutive of the church. "What I mean by 'constitutive,'" he says, "is that these aspects of pneumatology must qualify the very ontology of the church. The Spirit is not something that 'animates' a church which already somehow exists. The Spirit makes the church *be.* Pneumatology does not refer to the well-being but to the very being of the church" (BC, 131–32). Zizioulas thus posits distinct reciprocally related and coordinated roles of Christ and the Spirit relative to the church's ontological grounding: If pneumatology is constitutive, the institution of the church is changed: it is instituted by Christ and constituted by the Spirit. "Christ *in-stitutes* and the Spirit *con-stitutes*" (BC, 140).

Perhaps at the very center of Zizioulas's ecclesiology lies the eucharist: the church has a eucharistic foundation and structure. But this entails a number of insights and qualities of the church which also need to be noted. First in importance has to be the primal iconic character of the eucharist itself. The Eastern church "lives and teaches its theology liturgically; it contemplates the being of God and the being of the church with the eyes of worship, principally of eucharistic worship, image of the *'eschata' par excellence*" (BC, 19). Two things are going on in this formula: on the one hand, an iconic appreciation emerges out of the attitude of worship; and the eucharist is the central act of Christian symbolic or sacramental worship which engages this openness to transcendence.[15] On the other hand, the eschatological or ultimately real to which Zizioulas refers is not simply the "not yet" that will be realized in the future at the end of a historical process, but "a state of existence [which] confronts history already now with *a presence from beyond history.* In the latter case an 'iconic' and liturgical approach to eschatology is necessary more than it is in the former. It is the understanding of eschatology as this kind of *presence* of the Kingdom here and now" that is intrinsic to eucharistic assembly (BC, 174, n. 11).

---

15. Along the way, Zizioulas reminds his readers that eucharist itself is to be "understood properly as a community and not as a 'thing'" (BC, 13). It is Christ communicating himself personally to a concrete community.

Once the church is viewed primarily as a eucharistic community, other characteristics follow. These five have continual relevance. First, the primary referent for the church is the local church in the sense of the episcopal church. This stems from the earliest period when the church was first constituted as a eucharistic community and the whole church of a given locality assembled as such.[16] Second, the church, constituted by the Spirit, has an epicletal character. This means that the presence of the Spirit cannot be simply presumed, but must always be implored through prayer. The church is the body of Christ as event of the Holy Spirit and not simply as organizational structure. As in the eucharist, the Spirit is always petitioned in prayer. This means that "the church *asks to receive from God what she has already received historically in Christ as if she had not received it at all,* i.e., as if history did not count in itself" (BC, 185). Third, catholicity is realized in the *local* church. Zizioulas strongly insists on the geographical locality defining a eucharistic community and thus the basic church. To have catholicity or inclusiveness one must have a congregation in a local place where people come together. This is the gathering catholic church (BC, 256–57). Catholicity means that "each eucharistic assembly should include *all* the members of the church of a particular place, with no distinction whatsoever . . . " (BC, 247). Fourth, universality as distinct from catholicity refers to openness to other churches. The local churches should be in communion with other churches. Structures enable this universality, but "utmost care must be taken so that the structures of ministries which are aimed at facilitating communion among the local churches do not become a superstructure over the local church" (BC, 258).[17]

---

16. The theological grounding of the episcopal local church as the basic unit of ecclesiology is the eucharist in which the community is in touch with ultimate reality, the *eschata*. "The *anamnesis* of Christ is realized not as a mere re-enactment of a past event but as an *anamnesis of the future*, as an eschatological event. In the eucharist the church becomes a reflection of the eschatological community of Christ, the Messiah, an image of the Trinitarian life of God" (BC, 254). More will be said further on to justify the diocesan unit over the parochial.

17. One can gain an insight into Zizioulas's iconic style of reasoning at this point. "The *nature* of God is communion" (BC, 134). This involves no priority of persons over the oneness of God, but "the one substance of God coincides with the communion of

Fifth, institutionally, the bishop occupies the central position in the organization and ministry of the church. "In the case of the local church the 'one' is represented through the ministry of the bishop, while the 'many' are represented through the other ministries and the laity" (BC, 136). Among the many functions of the bishops, two stand out. On the one hand, the bishop stands at the head of the eucharistic community. The church as "the eucharistic community must both always be *local* and always have the priority over against a universal unity in our ecclesiological thinking" (BC, 237). On the other hand, the bishop, as the visible center of the unity of the local church as eucharistic community, is the vital bond of unity with the other churches (BC, 238).

These methods, presuppositions, and categories share a fundamental consistency; together they make up the grammar and logic of Zizioulas's ecclesiology. The discussion now turns to a representation of this ecclesiology according to the pattern adopted for this book.

The Ecclesiology of John Zizioulas

Zizioulas's ecclesiology does not fit as neatly as others into the now standard pattern of exposition. But using that framework will allow a more expanded treatment of some of the themes already noted and provide a schema that will enable an implicit comparison with Western ecclesiologies.

Theological understanding of the nature and goal of the church. Zizioulas understands the church in the light of the economy of the Trinity. In this theology the doctrine of the Trinity is not adjusted to a conception of the world and cosmos. Rather Trinity is the framework that contains and shapes Zizioulas's understanding of all reality. In his theology of the Trinity "the contribution of each of these divine persons to the economy bears its own distinctive characteristics which are directly relevant for ecclesiology in which they

---

the three persons" (BC, 134). "In ecclesiology all this can be applied to the relationship between local and universal church. There is one church, as there is one God. But the expression of this one church is the communion of the many local churches. Communion and oneness coincide in ecclesiology." BC, 134–35.

have to be reflected" (BC, 129–30). Within this trinitarian perspective, he proposes the Body of Christ as the primary and governing image for the church. But for him this requires a certain emphasis on the Holy Spirit to set the proportions right. No christology without pneumatology. "The Holy Spirit, in making real the Christ-event in history, makes real *at the same time* Christ's personal existence as a body or community. Christ does not exist *first* as truth and *then* as communion; he is both at once. All separation between christology and ecclesiology vanishes in the Spirit" (BC, 111).

How do Christ and the Holy Spirit relate in forming the theological foundation of the church? The role of the Son in the economy of the Trinity is to become incarnate, to become history. Thus the principle itself of the economy belongs to the Son and is christological (BC, 130). The role of the Spirit, and that of none other, is to liberate Christ from the particularity of history, Judaism, Palestine, the first century, and to make Jesus the Christ of all history and beyond it. This involves, first, adding eschatology or transcendent finality to the incarnation: "The Spirit makes of Christ an eschatological being, the 'last Adam'" (BC, 130). Second, the Spirit makes Christ a corporate personality, the basis of human communion. "Pneumatology contributes to christology this dimension of communion" (BC, 131). "The church is *constituted* in and through eschatology and communion. Pneumatology is an ontological category in ecclesiology" (BC, 132).[18]

Zizioulas's pneumatological ecclesiology leads him to an accent on community and communion. Many of the hard edges of institution and organization, as in authority and jurisdiction, are softened and become more pliable when community and communion guide the imagination.

Organization and polity. It will be instructive to begin this schematic description of the organization and polity of the church with a remarkable paragraph of Zizioulas which illustrates at once

---

18. "Thus the mystery of the church has its birth in the entire economy of the Trinity and in a pneumatologically constituted Christology.... For this reason the mystery of the church is essentially none other than that of the 'One' who is simultaneously 'many' — not 'One' who exists first of all as 'One' and *then* as 'many,' but 'One' and 'many' at the same time." BC, 112.

his iconic theological imagination, his dependence on the Fathers, especially Ignatius of Antioch, and the eucharistic character of his ecclesiology; it also defines the four orders of ministry and thus the organization of the church. The structure of the eucharistic assembly is the structure of the church. Turning his imagination to an early eucharistic assembly, he writes: "we can see that in the center of the *synaxis* of the 'whole church' and behind the 'one altar' there was the throne of the 'one bishop' seated 'in the place of God' or understood as the living 'image of Christ.' Around his throne were seated the presbyters, while by him stood the deacons helping him in the celebration, and in front of him the 'people of God,' that *order* of the church which was constituted by virtue of the rite of initiation (baptism-chrismation) and considered the *sine qua non* condition for the eucharistic community to exist and express the church's unity" (BC, 152–53). This is not an argument for a church structured by four orders of membership; it is a "showing" of the church as it is meant to be across history in the economy of salvation.

Each of the four orders of ministry have a role: "Thus the particular ministries of (a) the laity, (b) the deacons, (c) the presbyters and (d) the bishop, clearly evidenced with St. Ignatius, became the indispensable ministries of the church in her relation *ad intra* . . . " (BC, 221). He explains the role of each and their indispensability by their being relationships that structure the whole.

Bishop. The bishop binds together the one and the many on the most fundamental level. The bishop is much more prominent than the "first" in any broader level of organization. The jurisdiction of the bishop in the local church is implied throughout. "In the case of the local church the 'one' is represented through the ministry of the bishop, while the 'many' are represented through the other ministries and the laity. There is a fundamental principle in Orthodox ecclesiology going back to the early centuries and reflecting the proper synthesis between christology and pneumatology. . . . This principle is that the 'one' — the bishop — cannot exist without the 'many' — the community — and the 'many' cannot exist without the 'one' " (BC, 136–37). These ontological principles are played out canonically by the prescription that there can be no episcopal ordination without a community or outside a community; no episcopacy without a community attached to it (BC, 137). Nor can the many exist without the one: there is no baptism, which is an act of the community, without a bishop, nor any ordination without a bishop (BC, 137).[19]

Presbyter and priest. Presbyters in the Ignatian scheme were the counselors of the community and of the bishop who was the head. They remain such in the episcopal local church. But Zizioulas also describes the priesthood as it developed in the early centuries and which correlated with the parish community. The idea of priest is one of mediator.[20] Thus the term priest symbolizes the following: "as Christ (the only priest) becomes in the Holy Spirit a community (His body, the church), his priesthood is realized and portrayed in historical existence here and now as a Eucharistic community in which his 'image' is the head of this community offering *with and on behalf* of the community the eucharistic gifts. Thus the community itself becomes priestly..." (BC, 231).

The order of the priest then is relational; it designates a "place" in the community that is specific and personal. There is no community without such a particular order, and this order is distinct from other orders. In sum, priesthood is a place in the community (BC, 231–32).[21] Because ordination and the order are relational, if someone

---

19. "The Orthodox Church...has opted for the view that the concept of the local church is guaranteed *by the bishop* and not by the presbyter: the local church as an entity with full ecclesiological status is the *episcopal diocese* and not the parish. By so doing the Orthodox Church has unconsciously brought about a rupture in its own eucharistic theology" (BC, 251). The solution to this problem would be the creation of small episcopal dioceses which would more exactly correspond with eucharistic communities. BC, 251, n. 6.

20. "Thus the ordained person becomes a 'mediator' between man and God not by presupposing or establishing a distance between these two but by *relating* himself to both in the context of the community of which he himself is part. It is in this way that the gradual application of the term *priest* was extended from the person of Christ, for whom alone it is used in the New Testament, to the bishop, for whom again alone it was used until about the fourth century." BC, 230.

21. The category of "place" is iconic. Zizioulas draws it from Ignatius where he speaks of the bishop as being "in the place of God" (Letter to the Magnesians, 6, 1; 3, 1–2; Letter to the Trallians, 3, 1; BC, 152–53). This "place" in the community is assigned by ordination, and as such it is iconic of the transcendent order it reflects when viewed in the context of the eucharist. BC, 229–30.

leaves the community, "he ceases to be an ordained person" (BC, 233).[22]

Deacons. Deacons bear the gifts of the world to the eucharist in order to bring them back to the world (communion) as new creation (BC, 222).

Laity. The laity, too, constitute an order in the church and more will be said of that under the heading of members.

We saw that in Zizioulas's view the church is an icon of God, of the Trinity. It is so as a structured, relational community. Ministry is relational; authority is relational; the community is a relational entity in the sense that it is constituted by the divinely appointed orders that put people in relation to each other. This is a key move: it removes ordination and ministry from the realm of a power given an individual so that it becomes describable only as a set of relationships. "If ordination is understood as constitutive of the community and if the community being the *koinonia* of the Spirit is by its nature a *relational entity*, ministry *as a whole* can be describable as a complexity of relationships within the church and in its relation to the world" (BC, 220). The problem of authority in ministry is "solved" because it is by definition relational, i.e., not a power of a person or an office over many. As relational, "authority establishes itself as a demand of the relationship itself. Thus the church becomes *hierarchical* in the sense in which the Holy Trinity itself is hierarchical: by reason of the *specificity of relationship*" (BC, 223). Hierarchy and authority consist in relationship not power (BC, 224).[23]

---

22. But Zizioulas also explains a return that does not require a new ordination because the community recognizes what it had done earlier (BC, 234–36). In the early church the parish gradually emerged as a eucharistic community. Why is that not a church? Zizioulas responds that it is not a church because it is centered on a presbyter leading the eucharist and not a bishop. And this "destroyed the image of the church as a community in which *all* orders are necessary as *constitutive* elements" (BC, 250). In other words, in a priest-centered eucharistic community all the orders were not present because the council of presbyters and the bishop were not included.

23. Ministry as relationships constitutive of the community responds to the classic dilemma in understanding ministry from Catholic and Protestant perspectives: is ministry a power or grace of an individual that is passed along with ordination, or is ministry a possession of the community which is delegated to the person ordained? Zizioulas combines both perspectives in a structured, relational community.

What has been said up to this point refers to the local-episcopal church. But this church also exists in communion with other churches. What is to be said of the institutions that reflect and in some measure structure this communion? Zizioulas spontaneously appeals to the Trinity: God is a communion of persons. "The *nature* of God is communion" (BC, 134). This means that "the one substance of God coincides with the communion of the three persons" (BC, 134). "In ecclesiology all this can be applied to the relationship between local and universal church. There is one church, as there is one God. But the expression of this one church is the communion of the many local churches. Communion and oneness coincide in ecclesiology" (BC, 134–35). Communion is constituted with the church itself; the Spirit constitutes each church and the church as a communion, a being in communion with other communities. There can be no institution that constitutes that communion prior to the existence of the local church itself. No institution exists "which derives its existence or its authority from anything that precedes the event of communion." Communion "cannot be self-sufficient or self-explicable or prior to the event of communion; it is dependent on it" (BC, 135).

How do these principles apply to the question of the larger polity structures in the Eastern church, to the offices of metropolitan and patriarch? In Zizioulas's view these are organizational structures. That is to say, metropolitan structures do not constitute larger church units in a proper sense. "As the principle of *the essential equality of all bishops* became a basic feature in Orthodox canon law, neither the metropolitans nor the patriarchs ever reached the position of heads of *particular ecclesial units* representing structures *above* or *besides* the episcopal diocese" (BC, 252). Some problems were created when the autocephalous church arose in the nineteenth century. This refers to "the Orthodox Church in each nation . . . governed by its own synod without interference from any other church" which "has its own head (patriarch, archbishop or metropolitan)" (BC, 253). These sometimes absorb the autonomy or authority of the individual diocesan bishop. But the bottom line ecclesiologically is that "utmost care must be taken so that the structures of ministries which are aimed at facilitating communion among the local churches do not become a superstructure over the local church" (BC, 258). Orthodoxy knows no "super-local eucharist or a super-local bishop. All eucharists and all bishops are local in character — at least in their primary sense" (BC, 258). "In a eucharistic view of the church this means that the local church ... is the only form of ecclesial existence which can be properly called church. All structures aiming at facilitating the universality of the church create a *network of communion of churches, not a new form of church*" (BC, 258). "This is not to deny that there is only *one* church in the world. But the oneness of the church in the world does not constitute a structure besides or *above* the local churches" (BC, 258, n. 15).[24]

Relative to ecumenism, world-confessions, and a recognition of other churches, Zizioulas simply avers to the pervasive hostility of the Orthodox Church to intercommunion with other non-Eastern churches. Moreover, since a church must actually bind people together, and this can only happen in a physical locality, he does not recognize confessional unities as churches. World federations or synods of confessionally similar churches are not really churches but come under the notion of ecclesial networks which may in fact be quite useful (BC, 259–60).

The members of the church and their relation to the world. What follows synthesizes into a concise statement ideas which in other ecclesiologies were drawn out in greater detail: the activities of the members of the church, especially their sacramental and ethical stance, the conception of the relation to the world and its implication for the Christian life that is promoted in a particular ecclesiology.

In Zizioulas's ecclesiology, apart from a developed sacramental theology which is not considered here, the sacraments of baptism and the eucharist have a direct bearing on the nature of the church community and institution. For Zizioulas, baptism is the assigning of a "place" for a person within the community. Baptism and confirmation are thus a form of ordination making a person a member of a particular order, in this case of the eucharistic community and

---

24. He thus implicitly rules out in principle the unity of the Roman Catholic Church and the network of the WCC, as well as synods and councils: these have ecclesial significance, but they cannot be regarded as forms of *church* properly so called. BC, 259.

a layperson (BC, 216). A layperson is not a negative order, as in "nonordained." Rather the rites of baptism and confirmation constitute an act of assigning a person to a particular order in the community thereby creating the community itself. Ordination in the case of baptism "is the act that *creates community* which thus becomes understood as *the existential 'locus' of the convergence of the charismata* (1 Cor. 12)" (BC, 217).

The eucharist mediates another aspect of the church's foundational structure. We have already seen how the assembly of people for the eucharist is also an act constituting the church, not in an efficient-causative sense, but in the sense of iconic participation. "In the eucharist, therefore, the church found *the structure of the Kingdom,* and it was this structure that she transferred to her own structure" (BC, 206). The elements of this structure revolve around Jesus, his death and victory over death, and his becoming the Christ whose body is made up of people, where many become one, and where they are assembled around Christ like the apostles. The Spirit is present and at work in all of this, so that the church offers communion in the life of the Trinity and becomes the body of Christ (BC, 209). The eucharist continues to structure the church. The eucharist "provided the early church from the beginning with (a) the basic concept and framework of her structure, and (b) the context for a perpetuation of this structure in history. This leads to a real synthesis between the historical and the eschatological dimensions of the church's existence without the danger of 'institutionalization.' For the eucharist is perhaps the only reality in the church which is *at once an institution and an event;* it is the uniquely privileged moment of the church's existence in which the Kingdom comes epicletically, i.e. *without emerging as an expression of the historical process, although it is manifested through historical forms*" (BC, 206).[25]

---

25. Zizioulas's iconic imagination thus allows for a synthesis between the historical and the theological that does not remove the tension between history and the eschata, between the concrete, worldly, and finite and the eternal, final, and really real. This synthesis is a practical possibility, because "the kingdom of God is always present *with a structure*" (BC, 205). There must be a tension between institution and event with

Finally, relative to the relation of the church to the world, Zizioulas envisages how "the world is *assumed* by the community and referred back to the Creator" (BC, 224). "The church relates to the world through and in her ministry by being involved existentially in the world. The nature of mission is not to be found in the church's *addressing* the world but in its being fully in *com-passion* with it" (BC, 224). The key is the eucharistic character of ministry: these ministries are channeled through the head of the community, the bishop or head of the eucharistic community, and they are always varied according to time, place, need: "the church must always have a *variety* of such ministries *ad extra,* according to the needs of the time and the place in which she exists" (BC, 225).

In sum, Zizioulas represents Eastern Orthodox ecclesiology in an iconic mode that synthesizes the historical and the theological into a sacramental view of the church as the body of Christ charged with the Holy Spirit. It is a communion ecclesiology, with the episcopal eucharistic community as its foundational unit. Its mission is to mediate God's trinitarian salvation in history now and into the eschatological future.

PENTECOSTAL ECCLESIOLOGY

"According to the well-known statistician of Christianity, David Barrett, there were an estimated 74 million 'Pentecostals / Charismatics,' or 6 percent of the world's Christian population in 1970. In 1997 he estimated that this figure had reached 497 million or 27 percent of the Christian population, more than the total number of 'Protestants' and 'Anglicans' combined, and only twenty-seven years later. Barrett projects that according to present trends the future is likely to rise to 1,140 or 44 percent of the total number of Christians by 2025. Pentecostalism is therefore fast becoming the dominant

---

no collapse on either side. The Spirit is present in the community, but there can be no community without structure. Moreover the kingdom of God is always "centered on Christ surrounded by the apostles. And this implies again a structure, a *specificity of relations,* a situation in which the relations within the community are *definable,* and they are definable not arbitrarily but *in accordance with the eschatological nature of the community.*" BC, 205.

expression of Christianity and one of the most extraordinary religious phenomena in the world of any time."[26]

This arresting statement means at least that pentecostalism cannot be ignored as a form of church and thus an ecclesiology. Yet the ecclesiology of the stunningly dynamic movement does not readily reveal itself. Pentecostalism is intrinsically a loose and embryonic form of church that tends to become something other than itself when it takes on stable, institutional structures. Much of the writing about pentecostals has been social scientific: historical, sociological, psychological, and anthropological. Narrative and descriptive rather than theological analyses provide the common pattern in introductions to pentecostalism. The following three-part interpretation adopts a theological perspective building on the social; it will, first, define and describe its origins, second, indicate its spectacular expansion throughout the world and some of the reasons for it, and, third, present typical pentecostal structures or patterns of social existence that are found in analogous forms in most pentecostal churches.[27]

---

26. Allen H. Anderson, "Introduction: World Pentecostalism at a Crossroads," *Pentecostals after a Century: Global Perspectives on a Movement in Transition, Journal of Pentecostal Theology, Supplement Series* 15, ed. Anderson and Walter Hollenweger (Sheffield, U.K.: Sheffield Academic Press, 1999), 19. This work will be cited in the text as AA. Other works used in this interpretation of Pentecostal ecclesiology are: R. Andrew Chestnut, *Born Again in Brazil: the Pentecostal Boom and the Pathogens of Poverty* (New Brunswick, N.J.: Rutgers University Press, 1997) [RAC]; André Corten, *Pentecostalism in Brazil: Emotion of the Poor and Theological Romanticism* (New York: St. Martin's Press, 1999) [AC]; Harvey Cox, *Fire from Heaven: The Rise of Pentecostal Spirituality and the Reshaping of Religion in the Twenty-first Century* (Reading, Mass.: Addison-Wesley Publishing, 1995) [HC]; Walter J. Hollenweger, *The Pentecostals: The Charismatic Movement in the Churches* (Minneapolis, Minn.: Augsburg, 1972) [WH]; Philip Jenkins, *The New Christendom* (Oxford: University Press, 2002) [PJ], "The Next Christianity," *The Atlantic Monthly* 290 (October 2002): 53–68 [PJ2]; David Lehmann, *Struggle for the Spirit: Religious Transformation and Popular Culture in Brazil and Latin America* (Cambridge: Polity Press, 1996) [DL]; Cecília Loreto Mariz, *Coping with Poverty: Pentecostals and Christian Base Communities in Brazil* (Philadelphia: Temple University Press, 1994) [CLM]; David Martin, *Pentecostalism: The World Their Parish* (Oxford: Blackwell, 2002) [DM]; Karla Poewe, ed., *Charismatic Christianity as a Global Culture* (Columbia: University of South Carolina Press, 1994) [KP]; Vinson Synan, *The Holiness-Pentecostal Tradition: Charismatic Movements in the Twentieth Century*, 2nd ed. (Grand Rapids: Eerdmans, 1997) [VS].

27. I want to underline the fact that the pentecostal churches do not lend themselves to the analytical style that has been adapted in volume two of this work. The primary reason is that a pentecostal church rests on the rock-bottom basis of actual religious experience. This leads Harvey Cox to state quite clearly that "the movement

The Origins of Pentecostalism

Analysts do not define pentecostalism in a neat formula. But the intelligibility of the statistics such as those at the head of this discussion demand reference to a more or less specific phenomenon. On the one hand, we are not discussing here pentecostalist influences and practices, such as speaking in tongues, that have influenced mainline churches, for example, the Catholic charismatic movement. On the other hand, some churches may be on the boundary between a mainline denominational church and a pentecostal church. Included among the pentecostals are African independent or initiated churches. A definition must be specific enough to capture a real similarity of type and open enough to include great differences. One such working definition is this: "the pentecostal movement is ... a movement concerned primarily with the *experience* of the working of the Holy Spirit and the *practice* of spiritual gifts" (Anderson, AA, 20). Those who study pentecostalism constantly stress these counterpoints: diversity around the world, but a similar, identifiable, analogously embodied common identity.[28]

Some of the qualities of pentecostalism will help add some substance to this broad abstract designation of a common identity. To begin, how does pentecostalism relate to fundamentalism? Although pentecostals adhere to many of the fundamentals of fundamentalism, they are quite different, and there is no reciprocity.[29] Although

---

looks and feels quite different to outsiders than it does to insiders" (Cox, AA, 10). Cox's own interpretation of pentecostal Christianity (HC) adopts a narrative genre and an anecdotal style that fits the subject matter, and he folds in the analytical, theological interpretation along the way. The strategy here has to be more abstract and it is adopted with a hope that the generalized level of the analysis not be understood narrowly or restrictively. This maxim seems to apply: whatever one says about pentecostalism, the opposite may also be true.

28. "Pentecostal churches all over the world, in the most diverse cultures and societies, exhibit astonishingly similar patterns of growth, use similar techniques of oratory and proselytization, and similar forms of organization and leadership, and also resemble each other strongly in their ritual practices" (DL, 8, also 222). Karla Poewe calls pentecostalism, or Charismatic Christianity, a global culture which transcends national, ethnic, racial, and class boundaries (KP, xii)

29. In 1928 the World's Christian Fundamentals Association went on record at their convention in condemning the pentecostal movement as fanatical and unscriptural and disavowing all fellowship (VS, 208). The comparison which follows is drawn from Russell P. Spittler, "Are Pentecostals and Charismatics Fundamentalists? A Review of American Uses of These Categories," in KP, 103–16.

both may be reactions to developments in Protestantism in the nineteenth century, they have separate historical origins. Although they share similar views on the status of scripture, fundamentalism rejects speaking in tongues and expectations of physical healing. The sharpest divergence, however, may be located in a style of cognitive spirituality. Fundamentalists "major" in doctrines, pentecostals in religious affections (HC, 14). Fundamentalist Christians argue theologically in defense of creeds. "Pentecostals give testimonies. The one goes for theological precision, the other for experiential joy. There is a profound difference between the cognitive fundamentalist and the experiential pentecostal" (KP, 108). Pentecostals are less associated with political conservativism than fundamentalists. "On balance, the pentecostals turn out to be more restorationist, less aware of the course of Christian tradition, less polemic, collectively less antimodernist, more oriented toward personal charismatic experience, less politically involved, as much or more socially involved, . . . more ecumenical and less dispensational, and perennially less theologically sophisticated" (KP, 113–14).

André Corten analyzes pentecostalism as a kind of emotionalism; it so integrates emotions into religion and religious experience that emotion constitutes its basis. "Millions of Brazilians have been swept up in this emotional fervor for the last ten or twenty years. They do not go to meetings where people exchange words (as in the BECs); they go to services where people sing the praise of God, and where people 'speak in tongues' " (AC, 26). Especially the poor, those crushed by suffering, are drawn up into a corporate experience of jubilation, enthusiasm, and divine elation. The defining elements and practices of pentecostalism, speaking in tongues, singing, healing, being slain in the Spirit, these have their foundation in emotion.[30]

Hollenweger attributes the growth of pentecostalism in the developing world and its ability to overcome racial, social, and linguistic

---

30. Corten's social-psychological analyses would be good examples of reductionism if they were taken as adequate in themselves. The social scientist, writing *about* pentecostalism as an objectified phenomenon, as distinct from an insider's theological account, risks serious misunderstanding when the portrait is construed as an explanation. The reservation extends to the whole of this social-historical section. The presentation of the method of this work in CCH, I, 17–66 is particularly relevant at this point.

barriers to its oral character. He summarizes this orality in this way: "The oral quality of pentecostalism consists of the following: orality of liturgy; narrative theology and witness; maximum participation at the levels of reflection, prayer, and decision making, and therefore a reconciliatory form of community; inclusion of dreams and visions into personal and public forms of worship that function as a kind of 'oral icon' for the individual and the community; an understanding of the body-mind relationship that is informed by experiences of correspondence between body and mind as, for example, in liturgical dance and prayer for the sick."[31]

The story of the origin of the modern pentecostalist revival has achieved a parabolic character that serves as a common reference for bringing out some of its classic qualities. The rise of American pentecostalism is tied to two preachers and a place: Charles Parham, William H. Seymour, and the Azusa Street Mission in Los Angeles.[32] Parham was a preacher and Bible teacher who became convinced that speaking in tongues was the only definite sign of baptism of the Spirit and this should become part of Christian worship. Seymour was a black preacher who sat in on Parham's classes at a new Bible school in Houston in 1905. Seymour learned from Parham that baptism in the Spirit was a new empowerment beyond the forgiveness of sanctification (WH, 23–25). In 1906 he was invited to Los Angeles to preach by the pastor of a black holiness church, and he came with Parham's doctrine of speaking in tongues as evidence of baptism by the Spirit. When his first sermon, based on Acts 2:4, "All of them were filled with the Holy Spirit and began to speak in other languages, as the Spirit gave them ability," was not accepted by the church, Seymour began to preach in the home of a member of the congregation. During such a meeting on the night of April 9, 1906,

---

31. Walter J. Hollenweger, "The Pentecostal Elites and the Pentecostal Poor: A Missed dialogue?" KP, 201.

32. The story of Azusa Street is told by Synan, SV, 84–106, and Cox, HC, 45–65. The events leading up to Azusa have a prehistory. Synan provides a review of nineteenth century revivals and various holiness churches that form part of a pervasive style of Christian spirituality and the background of what came to be known in the twentieth century as the pentecostal movement (VS, 1–83). David Martin underlines the connection between pentecostalism and Methodism and the evangelical revivals or "awakenings" leading up to the twentieth century. DM, 7–11; also WH, 21.

"Seymour and seven others fell to the floor in a religious ecstasy, speaking in tongues" (VS, 96). News of this event spread quickly in local evangelical circles, incited great curiosity, so that new space was acquired in an abandoned two-story frame building and former church at 312 Azusa Street. Interest grew still further when the *Los Angeles Times* wrote a front page article on April 18, 1906, headlined in tiers: "Weird Babel of Tongues, New Sect of Fanatics is Breaking Loose, Wild Scene Last Night on Azusa Street, Gurgle of Wordless Talk by a Sister" (VS, 84). By the summer of 1906 "people of every race and nationality in the Los Angeles area were mingling in the crowds that pressed into the mission from the street" (VS, 99).[33] The Azusa Street revival "continued unabated, day and night, for three more years" (VS, 102), and Seymour published a four page newspaper entitled *The Apostolic Faith* to extend its influence; by 1908 it reached 50,000 subscribers (HC, 101). Over the course of those years it was visited by many preachers who later spread pentecostalist spirituality and founded churches, denominations, or foreign missions. Although pentecostal practices had already been in place, the Azusa Street revival "is commonly regarded as the beginning of the modern pentecostal movement" (VS, 104), because it focused attention of preachers and served as a catalyst for generating new energy.[34]

---

33. Parham was invited to Los Angeles and arrived there in the summer of 1906, but he rejected the Azusa Street revival, some think for reasons of race. "In retrospect the interracial character of the growing congregation on Azusa Street was indeed a kind of miracle. It was, after all, 1906, a time of growing, not diminishing, racial separation everywhere else" (HC, 58). In reaction to a good deal of criticism of his ministry on racial grounds, Seymour began to think that "it was not tongue speaking but the dissolution of racial barriers that was the surest sign of the Spirit's pentecostal presence and the approaching New Jerusalem." Ibid., 63.

34. Who is the father of the modern pentecostal revival? While most point to Seymour, some identify with Parham. For example, at the Assembly of God Web site one reads: "The beginning of the modern pentecostal revival is generally traced to a prayer meeting at Bethel Bible College [founded by Parham] in Topeka, Kansas, on January 1, 1901. While many others had spoken in tongues previously during almost every period of spiritual revival, most researchers agree it was here that the recipients of the experience, through study of the scriptures, came to believe speaking in tongues is the biblical evidence for the baptism in the Holy Spirit" (Http://ag.org/top/about/history.cfm) But currently Parham is recognized as having been a racist, and his role in the foundation of the movement is being minimized. See Walter J. Hollenweger, "The Black Roots of Pentecostalism," in AA, 33–44.

The Expansion of Pentecostalism

The extent to which the experience at Azusa Street directly or indirectly sent ripples around the world is remarkable.[35] Gaston Barnabas Cashwell of North Carolina traveled to Azusa Street, was baptized in the Spirit, and became the apostle of pentecostalism in the American South. Thomas Ball Barratt of Norway received a pentecostal experience in New York in 1906 before he had a chance to travel to Los Angeles; back in Oslo in December he celebrated the first modern pentecostalist meeting in Europe. William H. Durham of Chicago, a disciple of Seymour, assumed leadership of the movement after 1910 and was responsible for sending missionaries to Canada, Italy, and South America.[36] Luigi Francescon became a pentecostal at Durham's church in Chicago and began churches in Argentina and Brazil in 1909–10. Daniel Berg and Gunnar Vingren, Swedish immigrants to the United States, became pentecostals in South Bend in 1909 and took up a missionary ministry in Brazil founding the Assemblies of God there. Willis C. Hoover, a Methodist missionary in Chile, read an account of the pentecostal experience in 1907 and became the father of Chilean pentecostalism. Pentecostalism in South Africa was initiated by John G. Lake who had received baptism in the Spirit through the ministry of Charles Parham and began his mission in 1908. Pentecostalism reached Russia through the ministry of Ivan Voronaev who was baptized in the Spirit in New York in 1919 and soon returned to Russia with his family. Azusa Street had a direct link to Korea in Mary Rumsey, who had received the gift of tongues there in 1907 and, after working in New York, arrived in Korea as a pentecostal missionary in 1928. An offshoot of Azusa Street lies indirectly behind some pentecostal churches in Nigeria.

"In recent years, the greatest quantitative growth of pentecostalism has been in sub-Saharan Africa, South East Asia, South Korea and especially in Latin America" (Anderson, AA, 25). The spread of

---

35. The following list summarizes Synan's larger digest of some of the known examples of the international impact of the Azusa Street revival at VS, 129–42.

36. But Durham broke with Seymour on a theological point that seemed to undercut baptism in the Spirit by maintaining that no sanctification was needed after the "finished work of Christ." This controversy split pentecostalism in two, roughly along Calvinist and Wesleyan-holiness lines. See HC, 62–63; VS, 149–52.

pentecostalism in Latin America has been extraordinary: some analysts predict that "if current rates of growth continue, five or six Latin American countries will have non-Catholic — mostly Pentecostal — majorities by 2010. In several other nations the non-Catholic percentage of the population will have reached 30 to 40 percent" (HC, 168). In Africa, the pentecostal movement unfolds in the independent churches which are sweeping the continent. "In addition to the several thousand denominations, ranging in size from a few thousand to millions of members, there are also innumerable unaffiliated congregations. At present rates of growth, by the year 2000 these churches will include more members in Africa than either the Roman Catholic Church or all the Protestant denominations put together" (HC, 246). The rapidity of the growth of pentecostalism in Korea is symbolized by a few single, full-service communities. "For many years now, the largest Christian congregation in the world with an estimated 800,000 members in 1995, has been a pentecostal one, the Yoida Full Gospel Church in Seoul, Korea" (Anderson, AA, 27).

Many factors rather than any single reason combine to help explain this historical, religious phenomenon. From a theological perspective it is hard to doubt the power of God as Spirit within this huge phenomenon. The effects of the Holy Spirit correlate with the affects of the pentecostal churches. From a social perspective, the most important can be located on the levels of the religious and psychological (empowerment), the cultural (inculturation), and the organizational (church structure).

First, on the level of individual persons, pentecostalism readily adapts to elements of indigenous religions, such as ecstatic engagement with the world of the spirit, appeal to the miraculous, and social discipline. All of these help connect it with individual persons and empower them. An example frequently cited lies in empowerment of the family, where both husband and wife are strengthened in themselves and in their roles. They gain a new prestige. "Pentecostalism . . . helps forward this domestic reconciliation by locating the evil outside the self, in the demonic powers, and it claims to have the spiritual resources to counter these powers" (David Martin, KP, 86).

Second, pentecostalism possesses the ability readily to inculturate itself wherever it is. "In varying degrees, pentecostals in their many and varied forms, and precisely because of their inherent flexibility, attain an authentically indigenous character which enables them to offer answers to some of the fundamental questions asked by indigenous peoples. A sympathetic approach to local life and culture and the retention of certain indigenous religious practices are undoubtedly major reasons for their attraction, especially for those overwhelmed by urbanization with its transition from a personal rural society to an impersonal urban one" (Anderson, AA, 217).

The way pentecostal healing has taken a shamanistic form indigenous to Korean culture provides an example that illustrates the point perfectly. If a " 'shaman' is one whose power comes directly from the supernatural world rather than through the medium of a traditional ritual or body of esoteric knowledge," then certain pentecostal practices of healing in Korea involve "a massive importation of shamanic practice into Christian ritual" (HC, 224–225).[37] The issue is also particularly sensitive with respect to the independent churches in Africa and is intrinsic to the issue of inculturation itself. Can a Christian shamanism be explained theologically?[38] Pentecostalism raised for the whole Christian world the issues of the limits and boundaries of inculturation, and they are perennial.

Africa offers another critical example of inculturation. The Legio Maria church in Africa combines conservative elements of Catholicism, such as the Latin mass and rituals, and charismatic experiences

---

37. "In traditional Korean society the shaman (*mudang*) served as a link between ordinary people and the spirit world, which was populated by numerous gods, ancestors, and spirits. Through rituals and offerings shamans can control the spirit world, transforming malevolent spirits into protective spirits, perform healing and exorcisms, and bring about concrete benefits for individuals in this world" (Mark R. Mullins, "The Empire Strikes Back: Korean Pentecostal Mission to Japan," in KP, 92). Mullins adds that shamanism has been a major component in the growth of pentecostalism in Korea and illustrates this with specific church pastors and their churches.

38. Cox answers yes in terms of primal spirituality: "Pentecostalism in Korea, and elsewhere, while tapping into a very ancient spiritual cosmology finds itself, paradoxically, on the leading edge of both Christian theological reflection and Western medical research. In so doing it is evidently fulfilling the first condition for the success of a new religious movement: it is helping people recover vital elements in their culture that are threatened by modernization" (HC, 228). The idea of primal spirituality will be invoked again further on.

of healing, exorcism, prophecy, glossolalia, dream interpretation, and visions. It began among the Luo in western Kenya, and these features, together with its openness to polygyny, help account for its ability to attract members. It is the largest independent Catholic church in sub-Saharan Africa.[39]

A third factor that enables pentecostalism to spread rapidly lies in its congregational mobility. The single, broad identity of pentecostalism defined by similarities of doctrine, worship style, and ministerial structure, is fluid and open. For example, it contains independent churches or congregations of various sizes and denominations or unities with which distinct congregations or churches are affiliated. Affiliation means allegiance to a superior pastor or authority structure that legitimates the individual pastor who at the same time retains his own congregation. But congregations may change affiliation or strike out on their own without being considered schismatic because they remain members of the pentecostal family (DL, 126–27). It also offers relatively easy access to church leadership based not on education but on charismatic effectiveness. "It is with this wider range of promises and services, and this reduced set of formal and professional demands, that the pentecostals have swept through large sectors of Latin American society" (Martin, KP, 81, 77–78).[40] If one counts independent churches, that is, small chapels and prayer groups that are not affiliated, pentecostalist churches are innumerable.

Facilitating the expansion of pentecostalism, too, is the formation of denominations. Hollenweger has discovered phases in the process by which a free, independent pentecostal movement or congregation gradually evolves into a denominational church. He charts the development unfolding in four stages of increased organization of roughly

---

39. This church is analyzed by Nancy Schwartz, "Christianity and the Construction of Global History: The Example of Legio Maria," KP, 134–74.

40. "The Evangelical Churches are portrayed as a single movement in which ordination is, so to speak, transferable, and a pastor's departure to form a rival establishment is not a sign of fundamental disagreement ... " (DL, 123). Although there are often direct links between pentecostalism in North America and various parts of the world, its resources in Latin America "are not primarily dollars or even itinerant television evangelists, but vast numbers of Latin American pastors, some full-time, many part-time and unpaid. The real resource is local commitment in structures so fissiparous that there is no question of some control from abroad." Martin, KP, 77.

twenty-five years each. As an established denomination the church may possibly become a member of the World Council of Churches. Then, in a revival of the pentecostal spirit, a group may split off to become a new independent pentecostal church.[41] The process is of some interest to ecclesiology.

The Assemblies of God in the United States is a case in point. In 1914 around 300 pentecostalist pastors and laymen assembled from twenty states and some other countries as well for a "general council" in Hot Springs, Arkansas. They listed five reasons for their gathering: the need of doctrinal unity, conservation of the work, interest in foreign missions, the possibility of chartering churches under a common name, and the need for establishing a Bible training school. "A cooperative fellowship emerged from the meeting and was incorporated under the name 'The General Council of the Assemblies of God.' Most of the delegates had little desire to form a new denomination or sect, and they structured their organization to unite the assemblies in ministry and legal identity while leaving each congregation self-governing and self-supporting."[42] The Assemblies of God went on to become the largest pentecostal church in the U.S. "The type of government adopted by the new church was essentially congregational, whereas the earlier southern groups had developed strongly episcopal forms. In general the Assemblies of God represented the 'Baptistic' type of pentecostal church while the older ones were of the 'Methodistic' type."[43] The Assemblies of God developed a creed or declaration of faith and in fact explicitly rejected the World Council of Churches (WH, 514–17).

The Assembly of God Church in Belém, Brazil passed from being a group of charismatic churches to a denominational church. During a twenty-five year period, the pastor-president "transformed a once loosely organized charismatic church into a bureaucratic religious institution. In its theological and musical training programs, bureaucratic division of labor, and profound concern for civil status

---

41. Walter J. Hollenweger, "Crucial Issues for Pentecostals," AA, 186–88.

42. *Http://ag.org/top/about/history.cfm*

43. VS, 155. Also the formation of the Assemblies of God effectively ended the interracial character of the pentecostal movement. With some exceptions denominations of pentecostal churches became largely segregated. Ibid.

the AG now resembles its mainline brethren more than it does the independent pentecostal denominations of the slums" (RAC, 129–30). This church will provide an example of the organization of a pentecostal denomination.

The Ecclesiology of Pentecostalism

As a sweeping, pluralistic, loosely defined movement, pentecostalism does not provide a single developed systematic theology with a locus on ecclesiology. This effort at constructing an ecclesiology, therefore, resembles the strategy of volume 1 of this work: it constructs from various elements a type of church which, when formalized in the categories of a now familiar template, displays an abstract ecclesiology.[44] This highly interpretative effort will at least show that pentecostalism provides a new, distinct way of "being church" for an increasingly large number of Christians in the twenty-first century.

Self-understanding and mission. "The Church is the body of Christ, the habitation of God through the Spirit, with divine appointments for the fulfilment of her great commission. Each believer, born of the Spirit, is an integral part of the General Assembly and Church of the First-born which are written in heaven (Eph 1:22–3; 2:22; Heb 12:23)."[45] The pentecostal community is the place where one encounters Jesus Christ in the Spirit and thus finds salvation. It is also the agency through which the message and the encounter is spread

---

44. The following theological works have been helpful in guiding the theological dimension of this ecclesiology: Simon Chan, "Mother Church: Toward a Pentecostal Ecclesiology," *Pneuma: The Journal of the Society for Pentecostal Studies* 22, 2 (2000): 177–208 [SC]; Donald W. Dayton, *Theological Roots of Pentecostalism* (Metuchen, N.J., and London: The Scarecrow Press, 1987) [DD]; Veli-Matti Kärkkäinen, *An Introduction to Ecclesiology: Ecumenical, Historical and Global Perspectives* (Downers Grove, Ill.: InterVarsity Press, 2002) [VMK]; Steven J. Land, *Pentecostal Spirituality: A Passion for the Kingdom* (Sheffield, U.K.: Sheffield Academic Press, 1993) [SL]. Kärkkäinen comments on "the lack of writings on ecclesiology" in pentecostalism and credits the Roman Catholic-Pentecostal Dialogue for stimulating it. "Pentecostal ecclesiology is of an ad hoc nature which leaves much room for improvisation. Since most pentecostals emphasize the spiritual, thus invisible, nature of the church, much of their writing has been on ecclesiastical polity that is characterized by the restorationist desire to go back to apostolic times" (VMK, 73). A fully developed ecclesiology written in the pentecostal tradition is Miroslav Volf, *After Our Likeness: The Church as the Image of the Trinity* (Grand Rapids: William B. Eerdmans, 1998).
45. Statement of Fundamental Truths (1916) of the Assemblies of God, U.S.A., in WH, 515.

abroad through missionaries. At the foundation of the community lie certain doctrines, whether written down and stated formally or embedded in language and practice, which are similar to those of other churches but which come together and take on a distinctive meaning through pentecostal usage.

The doctrine of scripture is a good example. "Pentecostals live with the Bible. They read it every day and know many passages by heart. The words of the Bible are woven into their prayers and writings" (WH, 321–22). The phrase, "the Bible says," seals convictions and ways of life. "For the pentecostals the mere existence of a verse in the biblical text confers upon it a validity in itself with direct relevance for their everyday life. In the place of an elaborate, learned apparatus brought to bear on the text and its context, we find an open-ended set of moral prescriptions bolstered by a repertoire of ready-made decontextualized quotations" (DL, 181–82).

Four basic doctrines can be taken as defining in an inclusive way the character of pentecostal experience and its theological roots. The first is the doctrine that Jesus Christ is savior as it is simply stated in John 3:16; the second is that he baptizes in the Spirit as witnessed in Acts 2:4; the third is that Christ heals as stated in James 5:14–15; and the fourth is the second coming as recorded in 1 Thessalonians 4:16–17. This fourfold pattern expresses "clearly and cleanly the logic of pentecostal theology" (DD, 21). These four elements are all linked together to form a distinctive structure of experience that applies broadly across the wide varieties of pentecostalism.(DD, 22). These four christological themes thus represent "the basic *gestalt* of pentecostal thought and ethos: Christ as Savior, as Baptizer with the Holy Spirit, as Healer, and as Coming King" (DD, 173).

Eschatology plays an important role in pentecostal vision of reality. The pentecostal movement began in an atmosphere of expectation of the parousia and second coming of Jesus. The whole movement uses a language of imminent expectation which can be read in the typical titles of pentecostal journals or magazines: *The Bridal Call, I Come Quickly, Maranatha, The End-Time Messenger.* A vague scenario of the end time finds expression in categories such as these: rapture, tribulation under the antichrist, the return of Christ and the millennial kingdom, the resurrection of the dead for the final judgment, destruction of the earth and a new creation of heaven and earth, with God all in all (WH, 415). The hymns speak of the nearness of the end time; sermons look at current events to find the signs of the times. Heaven and hell are real places and very practicably available to all. When pentecostal experience is actualized as in worship, it is a participation in the transcendent kingdom of God in the sense of Zizioulas, a participation in the reality of the kingdom beyond history, the *eschata,* an experience of transcendence, something beyond the self (SL, 98).[46]

But, finally, the doctrine of the Holy Spirit provides the central focus of pentecostal faith; the experience of the Spirit as this is recorded in Acts 2:1–4 stands at the beginning as the paradigmatic Christian experience, so that baptism of the Holy Spirit is an experience analogous to this first, primal Christian experience (WH, 321–52). The doctrine of the Spirit as this is embodied in a spirituality forms the foundation for a theological understanding of the church. Pentecostalism offers "a dynamic, enthusiastic type of spirituality to the modern church" (VMK, 70). More specifically, the Spirit as experienced in worship often supplies the implicit referent for ecclesiology. In other words, the church actualizes itself most fully in the worshiping assembly. Just as the "category of experience is essential to understanding the spirituality of pentecostals, and thus their worship" (VMK), so too assembly for worship is the key to the theological understanding of the church. The assemblies of pentecostals for worship "are designed to provide a context for a mystical *encounter,* an experience with the divine. This encounter is mediated by the sense of the immediate divine presence.... The gestures,

---

46. Cox makes eschatology one of the three main ingredients of primal spirituality and shows how prophecy and millennialism appeal to basic or primal hope (HC, 82–83, 111–22). Pentecostalism as religion or church rests on an elementary mood, "what might be called a 'millennial sensibility,' a feeling in the pit of the cultural gut that a very big change is under way" (HC, 116). This is related to the negative contrast experience explained in the last chapter relative to liberation theology, for pentecostalism appeals to the same constituency: it is religion for the poor and the suffering, though not exclusively so. "Pentecostalism has become a global vehicle for the restoration of primal hope. The movement started from the bottom. A partially blind, poor, black man with little or no book learning outside of the Bible had a call" (HC, 119). "Things have to change." "Things are changing." "Things will be different." Analogous to basic faith, primal hope looks to the future with expectancy: it has to.

ritual actions, and symbols all function within this context to speak of the manifest presence."[47] This base of the Spirit-filled assembly gives rise to various foundational theological constructs for characterizing the theological understanding of the church. Two of these are "charismatic fellowship" and the Spirit-filled community.

The idea of a charismatic fellowship provides Kärkkäinen with what he takes as a basic model for the church. The fellowship is constituted by the Holy Spirit; it is formed by a common experience of the Spirit that draws people into the body of Christ. As distinct from an ecclesiology of the word (Protestant) or of the eucharist or cultic activity (Catholic), a distinctively pentecostal ecclesiology revolves around a community gathered in the Spirit. Because it is a community gathered by the Spirit it is essentially dynamic and charismatic, with an active, participatory laity. But charismata are not stressed at the expense of structure and institution.[48] This understanding of the church entails empowerment of individuals with the Spirit, active participation of people in worship, participation of laity in church ministry and in the world, experience of charismatic actions of God, restoration of apostolic signs: healing, miracles, prophecy, speaking in tongues, and inculturation into the values and meanings of a people (VMK, 77–78).

The image of the Spirit-filled community, not far from the former image, builds on the concept of "ecclesial pneumatology," that is, the idea that we are united to Christ and God by the Spirit. But the Spirit is not merely encountered by the individual: "Spirit-baptism is first an event of the church prior to its being actualized in the personalized Spirit-baptism" (SC, 180). The encounter with the Spirit is an ecclesial encounter, making the church the place where the Spirit

---

47. Daniel E. Albrecht, "Pentecostal Spirituality: Looking through the Lens of Ritual," *Pneuma* 14, 2 (1996): 21. Cited by VMK, 70–71. Kärkkäinen comments on "emotionalism" as the way this experience of contact with God appears to the outsider. It is part of a tradition of experiential religion. "This type of worship is often accompanied by singing in tongues, applause to the Lord, the raising of hands and the shouting of loud 'amens' and 'hallelujahs.'" VMK, 71.

48. VMK, 74–76. Kärkkäinen is dependent here on Peter Kuzmic and Miroslav Volf, "Communio Sanctorum: toward a Theology of the Church as a Fellowship of Persons," unpublished paper read at the International Roman Catholic-Pentecostal Dialogue, Riano, Italy, May 21–26, 1985.

is encountered. This does not deny that the Spirit is present more generally in creation and in history. But the church is the privileged place where the Spirit is to be found (SC, 198). The doctrine that accents this is the ascension: "Christ is no longer bodily present and the only 'bodily' presence of Christ in the world is the church, his body. . . . The Spirit takes the place of Christ's physical absence in the church, thus making the church the 'temple of the Spirit,' the special locus of the Spirit's presence" (SC, 199).

This ecclesial pneumatology resulting in a Spirit ecclesiology is accompanied by four distinctive qualities that are typically pentecostal. First, the church is a dynamic inclusive community, not narrowly homogeneous, but like Seymour's community it unites people across barriers. Second, it is a healing community where the power of God in Christ reaches to the body. "Prayer for healing of the body, mind and spirit must be a regular part of the church's *liturgical* life" (SC, 188). Moreover, it is especially "in the eucharistic event when the action of the Spirit is particularized. In short, the holy communion should be the best occasion for prayers of reconciliation and healing to take place" (SC, 189). Third, the Spirit actualizes the truth of Christ in the community so that people actually encounter transcendent truth and it becomes a dynamic character of the community itself. Fourth, this makes the community an eschatological community insofar as it lives in the presence of transcendent, eschatological reality. The church in its members encounters that which is beyond history, and this becomes acted out in history (SC, 184–96).

Organization. Pentecostal churches vary from small, informal congregational gatherings to highly structured denominations. The Assemblies of God Church in Belém, Brazil provides an example of a highly structured church. Chestnut describes the church holistically in this way: "At the apex of the administrative pyramid, decision-making power is concentrated in the hands of the pastor-president. At the ample base, common members involve themselves in the daily activities of the church through a wide range of low-level offices and positions. . . . [This] critical mass of members feel as though they are an integral part of the church through active engagement in the plethora of church activities and organizations" (RAC, 130).

The hierarchy according to office in a state or on a regional level of organization has a pastor-president who presides over the State Convention of the Assemblies and is responsible for administrative and financial matters. This is constituted by over 200 church leaders of various ranks and is controlled by the pastor-president. "Pastors and evangelists based at the Central Temple and its appendage, [the seminary], constitute the pastoral elite. As salaried clerics, pastors and evangelists manage the affairs of the mother church, such as directing administrative departments, teaching at the seminary, visiting congregations in the interior of the state, and performing the ecclesiastical rites of communion, marriage, baptism, and burials" (RAC, 131–32). The church has eleven departments that coordinate activities: Administration, Evangelization, Finance, Pastoral Counseling, Spiritual Counseling in Hospitals, Works, Social Assistance, Media and Culture, Planning and Technical Support, and Music" (RAC, 134). Below the pastor-president are pastors, evangelists, and presbyters, deacons, auxiliaries, and helpers. Other individual congregations have analogous officers but the names and functions may vary (DL, 120).

The spinal cord of the regional church is a core of full-time ministers and administrators who direct the churches. Leading each congregation are paid pastors, co-pastors, and assistant pastors. The social status of the minister is likely to be on more or less the same level as members of the congregation, unlike educated Catholic priests among the poor in Brazil. But the structure is authoritarian and the minister establishes his authority and preaches in a didactic way (DL, 190). Under the pastors are a large body of volunteers. Above the unpaid workers are deacons who "have the job of organizing day-to-day church life: communion, the church premises, discipline, choir practice, youth groups and hospital visiting. Still unpaid, the *diacono* appears to be a crucial figure between the fully-fledged, salaried *pastores* and the other grades" (DL, 124). The first level of those beneath the deacons consists in a large band of full members of the church who are active workers in church ministry; a second level are those who attend church services regularly and frequently; and a third are those in an outer circle who attend church occasionally. The church as an organization communicates with its members through the volunteer workers, elders, and missionaries who actively reach out to those outside the church in order to draw them in. At a church service, the workers are publicly available to coordinate the actions of the whole assembly while the evangelist or pastor leads the group. Generally speaking, high numbers, close to 80 percent, participate in church organizations on the congregational level (RAC, 135). Both those who hold some church office as well as those who only participate in ecclesiastical activities derive a new sense of dignity from these activities (RAC, 140–41).

The education of the ministers in pentecostal churches varies from very little to more and more. It is likely to be higher in denominations which have established seminaries because they prize various levels of training of their ministers in church management, Bible and preaching, or more general education including Christian theology. There are a good number of university-level opportunities for the training of pentecostals in North America and various levels of training in developing countries (DL, 129–31).

Members. "It is generally agreed that the pentecostal growth in Latin America is concentrated among the poor. Available data in Brazil and elsewhere broadly confirm this" (DL, 210).[49] Martin describes what pentecostalism does for the poor in Latin America: "It takes those marooned and confined in the secular reality by fate and fortune, and offers them a protected enclave in which to explore the

---

49. Cecília Loreto Mariz compares and contrasts the way basic ecclesial communities and pentecostals relate to the culture and context of the poor in Brazil. Using this relation to the poor as a common reference point, she provides a good contrast between the assumptions, world views, and pastoral goals and strategies of these two ecclesiologies. Although they seem to share in common at least the small size of their basic units, their approach to and success among the poor and their popular cultures are vastly different (CLM, 61–80). David Lehmann contrasts the two this way: "the one is concerned very seriously with theology, the other cares little for theology; the one is little concerned to draw boundaries around its membership, the other does so with great care, as if drawing the frontier of an ethnic group; the one insists that the path to belief lies through rational analysis, the other rejects such an idea and accepts only the fulminating descent of the Holy Spirit; the one minimizes ritual in favor of belief, form in favor of content, the other continually recreates ritual and equates belief with an emotional state and an array of practical prescriptions for everyday life; the one insists on the indissoluble connection between religious belief and political commitment, the other rejects such a connection totally. . . . It is hard to believe that both are appealing or responding to the same needs, desires, frustrations and alienations of the mass of poor people whose adherence they seek . . . " (DL, 6).

gifts of the Spirit, such as perseverance, peaceableness, discipline, trustworthiness, and mutual acceptance among the brethren and in the family. Real and fictive fraternity are mutually supportive. The believers, nearly two-thirds of them women, link themselves together in chains of mutual encouragement. They sing and pray by the hour because that sacred time tells of their discovery of themselves as of infinite value, not in the eye of the law, but in the eye of the Author of all law" (DM, 71). Pentecostalist ministers may have no political agenda, but pursue "a particular kind of personal transformation, and their language is couched in personal stories and imagery rather than in abstract propositions" (DM, 167). But this is not intrinsic to pentecostalism, and ministers are taking a new look at the causes of human suffering.

Relative to Brazil, but with relevance beyond, pentecostalism has an appeal to women, since they form a majority in these churches. Pentecostal churches preach stable households and enhance the public image and identity of women. Although pentecostal churches preach Paul on subordination of wives to husbands, dwell excessively on sexual propriety, and support female subordination in the public sphere, at the same time "the detailed attention paid to the family, especially the nuclear family, has the effect of enhancing women's self-image as mothers, since so many of them are alone as heads of their households" (DL, 133).

Finally, the number of middle-class pentecostal churches is growing in both the developed and developing worlds. These churches tend to be separated from churches of the poor and occasionally embrace a gospel of wealth (Hollenweger, AA, 188–90).

Activities. Pentecostal churches may engage in a number of activities within the congregation. Churches offer counseling and a range of other services as seen in the departments of AG, Belém. The discussion which follows, however, focuses on ritual and liturgy, the ceremonies of the assembly. This is described in terms of a number of standard pentecostal practices arranged at the discretion and according to the style of the pastor or preacher. Whether or not what happens constitutes a formal liturgy, one can expect a set of recognizably Pentecostal elements that are more choreographed than they may appear.[50] The distinctive elements of the congregation's services have the function of setting the boundaries of this particular church and foster a sense of identity in the members. The new pentecostal churches seem to mirror the process in the earliest Christian communities of forming ritual for the first time; it entails creative inculturation (DL, 136–39). In fact, Boff's phrase, ecclesiogenesis, applies more cogently to new pentecostal churches than to BECs.

Preaching. Cox describes pentecostal language critically and sympathetically as a language of religious enthusiasm; especially in the period after Azusa Street, it overflows with accounts of wondrous happenings and plainly miraculous events. For the outsider these events are incredible on the face of it and so seem to discredit the testimony. Harvey Cox recommends staying with the prose and appreciating the genre on the basis of the actual experience it articulates. Pentecostalist preaching generally does not consist in critical, analytical representation; communication proceeds not be argument but by narrative. Its at times seemingly fantastical hyperbole translates the emotional depth and the power of what is recalled. In every case religious language is symbolic; in the mechanisms of pentecostal writing and preaching the symbolism works in a distinctive way: the language represents wondrous events, and the wondrous events symbolize the pervasive, dynamic presence of the Spirit which is the heart of the matter. What spread from Azusa Street and continually draws people in is not a doctrine but an experience (HC, 67–72). The style of preaching aims at direct communication of a spiritual and moral message that edifies. The language does not convey historical-critical exegesis of the Bible, but uses free association of ideas and applications to the present. The characters in the biblical story provide examples to be imitated or metaphors or metonyms with immediate application to what is going on in the world today. The whole

---

50. "The preacher leads the service on his own initiative: if there is a liturgical sequence it is certainly not as precisely codified as that of the Catholic Mass or an Anglican service" (DL, 136). Participant observer Cox writes: "In each of the churches the worship followed the pattern I have now learned to expect in pentecostal churches: high-amperage music, voluble praise, bodily movement including clapping and swaying, personal testimonies, sometimes prayers 'in the Spirit,' a sermon full of stories and anecdotes, announcements, lots of humourous banter, a period of intense prayers for healing, and a parting song." HC, 6.

message is a free, creative assembly of story and application (DL, 179). Another style of preaching, typical of some black pentecostal churches, takes of the form of an emotional, repetitious, rhythmic dialogue with the congregation. It frequently builds toward corporate congregational religious experience.

Tongues. Speaking in tongues, or glossolalia, is a gift of the Holy Spirit and manifestation of baptism of the Spirit. However it is ritualized it consists in a kind of ecstatic possession in which, by the power of the Spirit, a person speaks in what appears as gibberish or in foreign and unlearned languages. A classic text authorizing the practice forms part of the description of the archetypal pentecostal experience: "And they were all filled with the Holy Spirit and began to speak in other tongues, as the Spirit gave them utterance" (Acts 2:4). Cox analyzes what is going on in this phenomenon as another manifestation of primal spirituality that gives it cogent, public meaning: think of glossolalia, dreams and trances, prophecy and millennialism "in the broader perspective of religious history, as the recovery of primal speech (ecstatic utterance), primal piety (mystical experience, trance, and healing), and primal hope (the unshakable expectation of a better future), then their contemporary reemergence becomes a little less baffling" (HC, 83).[51] These transcendentals that lie beneath and structure the religious character of human existence are tapped directly by what on the surface may appear to be bizarre practices. This applies specifically to speaking in tongues. Pentecostals today understand that tongue-speaking is basic, apophatic language, "a way for individuals within a faith community to pray without the limitations of verbal speech. They see it as a bonding device, tying people together in a beloved community. They see it as a radically democratizing practice, enabling even the least educated persons and not just the trained preacher to speak out" (HC, 95).

Music. No other sensation can lead as directly to feelings as music; what is seen needs interpretation, while music often interprets itself.

---

51. Pentecostalism "has succeeded because it has spoken to the spiritual emptiness of our time by reaching beyond the levels of creed and ceremony into the core of human religiousness, into what might be called 'primal spirituality,' that largely unprocessed nucleus of the psyche in which the unending struggle for a sense of purpose and significance goes on" (HC, 81). Cox's treatment of the logic of these seemingly direct encounters with God as Spirit and the gifts is particularly enlightening. HC, 81–138.

It is not surprising, then, that "music is not an incidental part of worship but provides its substance."[52] Comparing pentecostalism itself to the "logic" of jazz, Cox notes how "the message of the Bible is taught, sung, and celebrated with heartfelt enthusiasm. The basic chords, as it were, are there. But the message is delivered with what might be called 'riffs,' with a free play of Spirit-led embellishment and enactment" (HC, 147). Analyses of inspiration and participation demonstrate how close and revealing the analogy is. Music also helps explain further how pentecostalism, by taking on the music of each culture, can be as embedded in it as American pentecostalism is in black culture.[53] Corten, in his secularizing style, ties the use of music to the emotions: "The singing produces, especially when it is prolonged, a rise in the emotional climate. Its repetitiveness becomes hypnotizing . . . the singing contributes to turn the service into an 'event'; at times it is merely decor; at other times it polarizes emotion" (AC, 41). "The faithful who attend a service leave charged with 'an event,' just as one leaves the theater. The faithful do not leave with the single gratification of an accomplished duty, but with the impression that they attended/participated in an event" (AC, 43).

Satan and demonology. Pentecostalist churches generally believe in a personal principle of evil, the devil. The Christian life is not simply a battle against the flesh or the evil within us, but also against the external powers that surround. "We believe in the personality of the Devil, who by his influence and power brought about the downfall of man and now seeks to destroy the faith of every believer in the Lord Jesus Christ."[54] Here the language of the preaching of pentecostals can become quite literal so that it is difficult to determine in various cases the exact content of the beliefs (WH, 377–84). Cox finds some

---

52. Cox, HC, 148. Cox's treatment of the function of music is built around an extended analogy between jazz and pentecostalism which successfully helps to draw one into the worship of this church. These comments are dependent on his "Music Brought Me to Jesus," HC, 139–57.

53. The analogy with jazz also illustrates the difference between "classical" pentecostalism and domesticated versions created by various accommodations or appropriations of its features by other churches. "Charismatic" movements in the mainline churches should be distinguished from this "type" of church. See Cox, HC, 150–53; Spittler, KP, 104.

54. WH, 377, citing the "Doctrinal Basis" of the Assemblies of God, Australia.

writing on demonic spirits and the powers of darkness obsessive and frightening (HC, 281–87).

The presence of the devil pervades pentecostalism and is seen in doctrine, practical church membership, and ritual. Explicit belief in a personal devil is frequently a doctrine in the pentecostalist creed. Because of the practical pervasiveness of the devil to all of life's decisions, one has to be perpetually on guard, and the church provides that protection. Many churches provide regular or weekly rituals of exorcism (DL, 139). Oral Roberts's dualism is sharp and clear: "God is a good God, and the devil is a bad devil. God's will for you is good (health, riches, well-being); the devil's will for you is bad (sickness, poverty, depressions). Therefore make your choice for the good, for God!" (WH, 363).

Exorcism, healing, and miracle. "The attitude of individual pentecostal groups to the healing of the sick by prayer in general, and to the healing evangelists in particular, varies a great deal. On the whole one can say that the more recent and more enthusiastic groups look with favor on the healing evangelists. On the other hand, the older pentecostal groups have gone to some trouble to keep the healing evangelists at a distance" (WH, 357). The language of exorcism and healing looks for overt miracles by the power of God overcoming the evil spirits. "Whatever your sickness and its cause may be, you know that it is an oppression by Satan, a work of the devil. Put your trust in Jesus Christ, who has come to destroy the works of the devil and to set free the oppressed, and you will be healed" (WH, 358). Generally speaking, if healing fails, it is because of unbelief and not the will of God. The theology of this practice links the immediate presence and relevance of Jesus Christ, as he is depicted in the gospels, to the situation today. As Jesus cured in the New Testament, so Jesus cures today by the same power, as invoked by the minister and through the faith of the believer (WH, 368).[55]

---

55. Hollenweger calls attention to the extensive criticism of the "flamboyant healing evangelists" and their division of the world into the sphere of God and the demons, while at the same time recognizing the necessity of a "sober healing ministry" by which the church manifests Christian concern for the body and for health. Walter J. Hollenweger, "Crucial Issues for Pentecostals," AA, 178–83.

Cox explains the practices of healing and the expectation of miracle once again according to the logic of "primal piety" (HC, 82, 99–110). Primal piety lies beneath belief and practice as an elementary desire for a wholeness given from outside the self that can only be accomplished by a power that transcends the self. It reflects what theologians from Augustine to Tillich assumed was a desire to be, to not cease being, but to be absolutely. The symbol of salvation gains its meaning from this basic desire. This exigency for wholeness explains why religion and healing, especially miraculous healing, can merge. Primal piety or desire for salvation overrides creed, commandment, and liturgical form. Grounded in a prerational level of the human, healing ritual, however chaotic it may appear, is sacramental: it puts people in "direct" contact with this saving power of the Spirit, and they go back to it whether or not it works at any given time.

Sacraments. Relative to baptism, the conception of baptism of most pentecostals is close to that of the Baptists. The doctrine of the Assemblies of God is stated this way: "The ordinance of baptism by a burial with Christ should be observed as commanded in the scriptures, by all who have really repented and in their hearts have truly believed on Christ as Savior and Lord. In so doing, they have the body washed in pure water as an outward symbol of cleansing, while their heart has already been sprinkled with the blood of Christ as an inner cleansing. Thus they declare to the world that they have died with Jesus and that they have also been raised with him to walk in newness of life."[56] While most pentecostals would accept this form of Pauline language, there may be significant differences in the way baptisms are performed ranging from indoor to outdoor ceremonies performed in rivers or lakes.

"There is no fully developed eucharistic doctrine in the Pentecostal movement. When statements are made about the Lord's Supper, it is interpreted on Zwinglian lines as a memorial of Jesus' death. But there is a clear and well-developed pattern of eucharistic *devotion and practice*" (WH, 385). The Assemblies of God, U.S.A. article of faith on the Lord's Supper is as follows: "The Lord's Supper, consisting of the elements, bread and the fruit of the vine, is the symbol expressing

---

56. Statement of Fundamental Truths (1916), Assemblies of God, U.S.A. WH, 514.

our sharing the divine nature of our Lord Jesus Christ; a memorial of his suffering and death and a prophecy of his second coming; and is enjoined on all believers 'until he comes' " (WH, 515). But the pattern of how the Lord's Supper is commemorated may vary considerably in frequency and in the physical deployment of the ritual. Generally it would not compete with mediations or expressions of the power of the Spirit in the community and assembly. Some pentecostals also follow literally the mandates of foot washing in the New Testament and take it as a sacrament, while others do not (WH, 395–96).

Ethics. Pentecostal communities, if they are at all structured, emphasize a variety of disciplinary practices. The following are examples, not universal prescriptions. Churches look for some form of observance of a reflective or less active reverence for the Lord's day. Pentecostal churches may forbid military service, caution against vices, and urge a narrow sexual ethic. Ethical rigorism varies according to particular churches and cultures (WH, 399–412). In Brazil, all pentecostal churches "impose a complete prohibition on alcohol and tobacco, and a variety of controls on sexual behavior....These are constitutive elements of the liminality which demarcates the community, but *evangélicos* also see the rules as setting them apart from the world of irreligion, or simply from 'the world,' drawing boundaries between the world of darkness and the domain of light, and between believers and unbelievers" (DL, 201).

Tithing, or giving 10 percent of one's income to the church, is recommended by some or may even be required: in some denominations it is a condition for full membership in the church. In Brazil all pentecostal churches practice tithing: "members are expected to give 10 per cent of their income on a regular basis" (DL, 203). Also some pentecostal churches preach the gospel of prosperity where conversion to Christ leads to material well-being or wealth (DL, 208).

Relationship to the world. The pentecostalist feature of being less politically conscious or involved is rapidly changing. Politically conservative pentecostals have organized in the United States, while others write what approaches a pentecostal liberation theology (HC, 295–96). Pentecostals have been deeply engaged in political processes in Latin America on both the far right and on the left. The major example from the right is General Efrain Ríos Montt, the former pentecostal Sunday school teacher who came to political power in Guatemala in 1982. "Ríos Montt recast the battle against leftist rebels as a holy war pitting his Christian soldiers against the atheistic forces of evil" (RAC, 145). On the left, Carioca Benedita da Silva, whom the Holy Spirit cured of breast cancer, is a woman pentecostal who was elected to the Brazilian congress in 1986. "As both congresswoman and senator from the Workers' Party, da Silva has championed the cause of dispossessed African Brazilians, workers, women, and favelados" (RAC, 146–47). A wide variety of witnesses to a social concern and need for political action is appearing among various pentecostalist churches in many different parts of the world. They engage in political programs not just to help victims but also to change social structures. This sometimes takes on the language of liberation theology. It also expands on the idea of healing to include liberation from oppression (Anderson, AA, 210–16).[57] Chestnut estimates that the great bulk of pentecostals are situated somewhere in the center, but leaning politically to the right.

In sum, pentecostalism provides a new, free-church movement in ecclesiology. Here the church's dynamic character as event is almost preecclesiological in any academic sense. Institution is closely aligned with charism. Independent congregating assemblies and individual churches beneath denominational superstructures seem anachronistically to embody a first-century form of embryonic churches in a process of formation. Pentecostalism thus forms the new left wing of ecclesiology, one that goads the other churches to be more responsive to their constituencies.

---

57. Pentecostalism and liberation theology share the idea that salvation includes effects on material life in this world. In liberation language this pertains to social, economic, and political liberation of historical existence, and in pentecostalism it applies to healing. But some pentecostal theologians are also extending the idea of healing to the social condition of existence [Miroslav Volf, "Materiality of Salvation: An Investigation in the Soteriologies of Liberation and Pentecostal Theologies," *Journal of Ecumenical Studies* 26 (1989): 448, 454–57, 460–64]. An example is Eldin Villafañe, *The Liberating Spirit* (Grand Rapids: Eerdmans, 1993), who writes from a Hispanic perspective. Consider as well the proposal for a black British liberation theology from a pentecostalist base by Robert Beckford, "Black Pentecostals and Black Politics" in AA, 48–59. Lee Hong Jung explains the necessity and rationale for "de-shamanizing" Korean Pentecostalism and creating a *minjung* liberation theology from a pentecostal perspective in "*Minjung* and Pentecostal Movements in Korea," AA, 138–60.

BAPTISM, EUCHARIST, AND MINISTRY

Baptism, Eucharist and Ministry is an ecumenical statement developed by the Faith and Order Commission of the World Council of Churches and published in 1982.[58] Given the representations of Orthodox and pentecostal ecclesiologies, this document strikes a middle position on the spectrum of ecclesiologies. BEM is also known as the Lima Document since the meeting of the commission that finally ratified it was held in Lima, Peru. The Faith and Order Commission promotes the goal of visible unity among the Christian churches. This can only be achieved on the basis of things held in common, and thus some fundamental agreement on baptism, eucharist, and ministry (Pref, viii)

This document evolved over a fifty year period beginning with the first Faith and Order Conference held at Lausanne in 1927. "The material has been discussed and revised by the Faith and Order Commission at Accra (1974), Bangalore (1978), and Lima (1982)" (Pref, viii). A draft of the statement was circulated after the WCC's fifth assembly in Nairobi in 1975. Roman Catholics were involved in the evolution of the text; Orthodox churches reviewed the document; it also drew upon the experience of bilateral and multilateral conversations among churches and some church unions across confessional lines (Pref, viii)

The doctrine of the document is ecumenical. It aims both at reconciling historical controversies and divisions, and addressing current contextual issues. It has input from virtually all confessional traditions. But it does not propose a complete theological development of these three areas of ecclesial life. Rather it focuses on those aspects related to the problems of mutual recognition leading to unity. The main text proffers major areas of theological convergence; the commentaries that accompany the text deal with differences that have been or are still to be overcome (Pref, ix)

The spirit behind the document was a sense of the possibility of a breakthrough in ecumenical relations, and it was sent to all the

---

58. *Baptism, Eucharist and Ministry*, Faith and Order Paper No. 111 (Geneva: World Council of Churches, 1982), is cited in the text as B or E or M with reference to paragraph number of the specific section.

churches for official and authoritative reaction and response.[59] The document has its critics, of course. But even one of the more severe, who from a distinctive perspective considers it fundamentally wrongheaded, also refers to it as a "unified, impressive, perhaps classical work."[60] The order in which the document presents the three topics has been changed in this account.

Ministry

This is the most complex of the three topics for it engages significant areas of division. The structure or outline of the presentation assumes a great importance. The treatise has six parts. The first characterizes or defines the church holistically as the whole movement of the people of God who are followers of Jesus Christ, in a community animated by God as Spirit, with a mission to evangelize or address the world with the gospel. The Spirit generates a pluralism of gifts and a pluralism of churches with different orders of ministry. The next five sections focus on the nature of ordained ministry and various forms and orders of ministry. Significantly this document centers on the threefold order of ministry (bishops, presbyters, and deacons) as the dominant pattern that all should regard as historically central without quite making it normative. It addresses apostolicity and then the act of ordination. It closes with the question of the mutual recognition of ordained ministries across denominations.[61]

The statement combines a historical with a theological perspective in its definition of the church. The church is (a) the whole movement of the people of God who (b) are followers of Jesus Christ, (c) in a community animated by God as Spirit, (d) with a mission to evangelize or address the world with the gospel. (e) The Spirit generates a

---

59. Responses have been gathered together by Max Thurian, ed., *Churches Respond to BEM*, vols. 1–6, Faith and Order Paper Nos. 129, 132, 135, 137, 143, 144 (Geneva: World Council of Churches, 1986–88). These were followed up by a final report, *Baptism, Eucharist and Ministry (1982–1990)*, Faith and Order Paper No. 149 (Geneva: WCC Publications, 1990). Analysis of those responses exceeds the limits of this work.

60. Markus Barth, "BEM: Questions and Considerations," *Theology Today* 42 (1986): 490–98, at 95 and 98.

61. Like Calvin, the treatise addresses three basic questions: (1) The nature of ordained ministry (without an extensive discussion of authority or jurisdictional powers), (2) the offices of ministry, (3) the meaning, act, and conditions for ordination. See especially the account of Calvin's "Ecclesiastical Ordinances,' supra pp. 97–99.

pluralism of gifts and a pluralism of churches with different orders of ministry. (f) The differences among the churches' orders of ministry raise the question whether some common understandings of church order can be determined (M, 1–6).

Recognizing a need for some common language among the churches at this point BEM lays down some definitions of charism, ministry, ordained ministry, and the title priest. These are straight-forward. It stays close to scriptural language and consistently reaches back to origins. Ministers are those who are publicly responsible in the church; the church has never been without them. It examines the notion and the historical role of the twelve and the apostles. It remains sensitive to the possible split between ordained ministers and laity: ministers are functions of and in service to the community (M, 12). Their chief responsibility consists in assembling and building up the community by word and sacrament, and guiding and leading its mission. "Since the ordained ministry and the community are inextricably related, all members participate in fulfilling these functions" (Commentary on M, 13).

The document has a nuanced view of the authority of the ordained minister. This is not portrayed as a possession but a gift that involves a responsibility toward the community and that cannot be exercised without the cooperation of the community. Thus reception and relationship are built into the gift. The appeal is to the New Testament and the example of Jesus (M, 15–16).

Relative to ordained ministry and priesthood (M, 17), the document affirms Jesus as the unique priest, the church as a priesthood, and the priesthood of believers in such a church, but it also says that an ordained minister can be called a priest because he or she does priestly things. This paragraph, important for the recognition of priests by some Protestant churches, is accompanied by a practical commentary. Relative to women in the church, the document simply says that all churches have to reflect on inclusion in the church. As more and more churches promote ordination of women ministers, this has to be studied by the churches (M, 18).

"Ministry" carefully attends to church structure, the orders of ministry, ordination, and the exercise of these charges. It supports the distinct ministries of bishops, presbyters, and deacons (M, 19–25).

The New Testament witnesses to a pluralism of church structures or polities: it "does not describe a single pattern of ministry which might serve as a blueprint or continuing norm for all future ministry in the Church" (M, 19). But the threefold structure became the universal pattern of ordained ministry in the second and third centuries. Recognized too is that this structure, where maintained, has undergone change; and other alternative ordained ministries "blessed with the gifts of the Holy Spirit" have been introduced; "nevertheless the threefold ministry of bishop, presbyter and deacon may serve today as an expression of the unity we seek and also as a means for achieving it" (M, 22). Every church needs some form of *episcopé* to express unity and church order. The threefold order needs various reforms in different churches. But it challenges those churches which do not have these orders with the question whether the value of unity might warrant their acceptance of it. Finally, three guiding principles for the exercise of ordained ministry generally are underscored: ordained ministry must be *personal* to mediate God as personal, *collegial* so that ministry remain a common task representing the concerns of the community, and *communal* so that it be rooted in the community (M, 26–27).

"Ministry" also outlines the functions of each of the three offices of ministry. Bishops preach, administer sacraments, exercise oversight, represent unity, lead the mission of the church, relate the church to its area and to the wider church, and are responsible for the transfer of ministerial authority, i.e., ordination. Presbyters serve as ministers of word and sacrament in the local eucharistic community, teachers, preachers, and ministers of pastoral care, and exercise responsibility for discipline and order in the congregation. Deacons represent the church's ministry to the world, take care of administrative responsibilities inside the church, and may be elected to governance (M, 28–31). The document also recognizes other charisms in the church, both those of a stable kind and those of prophets and leaders in times of crisis (M, 32–33).

Turning to apostolicity and succession in apostolic ministry, "Ministry" breaks the identity and necessary dependence of these concepts with simple episcopal succession, while at the same time not undermining the strong recommendation that episcopacy be adopted (M, 34). "The primary manifestation of apostolic succession is to be found in the apostolic tradition of the church as a whole" (M, 35). Apostolicity, then, is predicated of the church, and it is accomplished through several mechanisms: "orderly transmission of the ordained ministry" expresses this continuity, and those churches without such an orderly transmission should examine it. Succession of bishops is another expression of the apostolic character of the churches. But churches without episcopacy have other ways of maintaining apostolicity, through ordinations and general preaching of the gospel (M, 37–38).

Ordination itself receives a good deal of attention (M, 39–50). Ordination "denotes an action by God and the community by which the ordained are strengthened by the Spirit for their task and are upheld by the acknowledgment and prayers of the congregation" (M, 40). Its origins lie in the laying on of hands in the New Testament period. The act of ordination is described ritually and theologically with the pattern of the early church in the background: ordination takes place in a context of worship, perhaps eucharistic worship, and involves an invocation of the Spirit, a laying on of hands, a community activity that links ordination to a bestowal of the Spirit.

The document also considers the conditions for ordination. Ordination follows a call or vocation, discerned in prayer, and authenticated in the community. Ordained ministers may be professional ministers salaried by the church or people with other occupations. They must be trained in the study of scripture, theology, spirituality, and prayer, and during this period the call may be tested. The document takes a stand against reordination after a minister takes some form of leave of absence (M, 48). Disciplines governing the conditions for ordination may differ among the churches and are not grounds for division. Nor should there be grounds for discrimination among candidates for ordination (M, 45–50).

Can the churches recognize the ordained ministries of other churches? All churches should be willing to examine their forms of ordained ministry and be prepared to renew their understanding and practices. Crucial is the idea of the apostolic succession of bishops: those without episcopacy are asked to consider it as a powerful expression of apostolicity; those with episcopacy should recognize other expressions and means of apostolicity that ground authentic ministries. Ordination of men and women has to be worked out. "The mutual recognition of churches and their ministries implies decision by the appropriate authorities and a liturgical act from which point unity would be publicly manifest" (M, 55). "The common celebration of the eucharist would certainly be the place for such an act" (M, 55).

Baptism

BEM describes the origin of Christian baptism as being rooted in the ministry of Jesus both historically and theologically. It then passes to a characterization of the meaning of the sacrament, using largely scriptural and theological language. A third section describes how baptism must be understood in close conjunction with Christian faith, and the fourth contains a statement on three major practical problems concerning baptismal practice among the churches: first, infant baptism and baptism of believers; second, the related rituals of baptism, chrismation, and confirmation; and, third, the mutual recognition of baptism across denominational lines. The statement concludes with some considerations on the celebration of baptism.

"Christian baptism is rooted in the ministry of Jesus of Nazareth, in his death and in his resurrection" (B, 1). The treatment of baptism and the other topics is historical-theological, that is, it combines a theological imagination with a genetic historical approach to the origins and development of the institutions. Five meanings or functions of the sacrament typify a theology of baptism. Baptism mediates a participation in Christ's death and resurrection. This implies a theology of sin and grace entailing conversion, pardon of sin, and cleansing, and this in turn points to the ethical dimensions of the sacrament. Baptism mediates the gift of God as Spirit, and by uniting a person to Christ it incorporates the person into the body of Christ, the church. Baptism thus helps account for the unity of the church. Finally, baptism provides a sign of the kingdom of God in this world and a promise of it in the next (B, 2–7). "Baptism" dwells on the sacrament's close link with faith, not just an act professing faith, but also the ongoing attitude of Christian faith which represents a constant grace. "The life of the Christian is necessarily one of continuing struggle yet also of continuing experience of grace" (B, 9). Continuous growth in faith also joins the effects of baptism with personal sanctification and ethical responsibility.

The treatise takes up three practical areas of conflict among the churches that need some sort of resolution (B, 11–16). On baptism of infants and of believers it proposes that both systems have a coherent logic and both may be tolerated by all the churches. It proposes some norms, however: baptism is to be celebrated publicly in the context of the community; re-baptism is disallowed (B, 11–13). On the distinctions between baptism, chrismation, and confirmation, all Christians agree that baptism involves water and the gift of the Spirit, and this gift of the Spirit may be ritually signified in different ways in different churches. On the mutual recognition of baptism across denominational lines it says: "Mutual recognition of baptism is acknowledged as an important sign and means of expressing the baptismal unity given in Christ. Wherever possible, mutual recognition should be expressed explicitly by the churches" (B, 15).

When it comes to the celebration of baptism, "Baptism" contains some practical advice about the administration of baptism while recognizing pluralism. For example, as a public community celebration baptism ordinarily should be performed by an ordained minister. The basic elements of the rite are enumerated: "the proclamation of the scriptures referring to baptism; an invocation of the Holy Spirit; a renunciation of evil; a profession of faith in Christ and the Holy Trinity; the use of water; a declaration that the persons baptized have acquired a new identity as sons and daughters of God, and as members of the Church, called to be witnesses to the Gospel" (B, 20). In sum, BEM proffers a concise theological treatise on baptism which attends to ecumenical problems. It is straightforward but measured and nuanced.

Eucharist

BEM begins its theology of the eucharist with a description of the historical and theological origin of the sacrament in the testimony of Paul to the tradition, and in the theological reconstruction of its association with Jesus before his passion. It then characterizes the meaning of the eucharist descriptively as the gift of Christ to us

through the power of the Spirit which has these defining characteristics: it is a ritual of thanksgiving to God, a memorial or anamnesis
of Jesus, constituted by an invocation of the Spirit (*epiclesis*), constituting a communion of the faithful among themselves, by being
a meal symbolizing the kingdom of God. The third part is a brief
indication of the major elements of a eucharistic celebration and
some points of consensus among the churches or theologians concerning what occurs theologically and practically in the ceremony:
celebrant or president, real presence, frequency, variations in certain
understandings of the elements.

Typically, the method of "Eucharist" proceeds "from below." Its
opening paragraph relates the eucharist back to Jesus's meals with
disciples. In the earliest church the practice developed into "the
central act of the church's worship" (E, 1).

The attempt to express the meaning of the eucharist in a short
space moves through stages. The eucharist is defined as follows: "The
eucharist is essentially the sacrament of the gift which God makes
to us in Christ through the power of the Holy Spirit. Every Christian receives this gift of salvation through communion in the body
and blood of Christ. In the eucharistic meal, in the eating and drink-
ing of the bread and wine, Christ grants communion with himself.
God himself acts, giving life to the body of Christ and renewing each
member" (E, 2).

This definition is filled out with four essential characteristics. The
eucharist is a rite of thanksgiving as in the prayer of blessing at meals.
"Thus the eucharist is the benediction (*berakah*) by which the church
expresses its thankfulness for all God's benefits" (E, 3). The eucharist
is also an anamnesis or memorial of Christ, the "the memorial of the
crucified and risen Christ . . . " (E, 5). This anamnesis of Christ corresponds with the content of the reading of scripture and the preached
word at the eucharist (E, 12). The doctrine of real presence is recalled without any endorsement of a particular theological construal
of it: "the eucharistic meal is the sacrament of the body and blood of
Christ, the sacrament of his real presence" (E, 13).

BEM's theology of the eucharist is pneumatological. The invocation of the Spirit or *epiclesis* is stressed in this treatment because
"[t]he Spirit makes the crucified and risen Christ really present to us

in the eucharistic meal . . . " (E, 14). "It is in virtue of the living word of Christ and by the power of the Holy Spirit that the bread and wine become the sacramental signs of Christ's body and blood" (E, 15).

The eucharist constitutes a communion of the faithful (E, 19–21). It provides one of the bonds holding the church together. In the eucharist one finds theological grounds for conceiving the whole church within the local assembly. Eucharist entails reconciliation and thus social-ethical responsibility. "As participants in the eucharist, therefore, we prove inconsistent if we are not actively participating in this ongoing restoration of the world's situation and the human condition" (E, 20).

Finally, the eucharist is described as a meal of the kingdom (E, 22–26). It symbolizes the final banquet. It contains ethical imperatives such as inclusiveness: as Jesus addressed publicans and sinners and had table-fellowship with them during his earthly ministry, so Christians are called to solidarity with the marginated (E, 24).

BEM also addresses practical issues in the celebration of the eucharist. It mixes theological reflection and practical suggestion in an attempt to bridge the gaps in practice and recognize differences in the ways of celebrating the eucharist. The document urges frequent, that is, weekly eucharistic services. But it also avoids many sticking points. For example, the word "mass" is not used; nor is the ritual called a sacrifice; nor are terms like "transubstantiation" or "consubstantiation" used.[62] Priests are mentioned but played down as only one term for the ordained minister.

BEM, in sum, is an effort at a consensus statement. As such it was and remains a working document. On the one hand, it cannot be expected that all Christian churches would accept all of its provisions. On the other hand, when it is taken seriously within a framework of a Christian imperative to seek unity, it should be useful and challenging.

---

62. In its commentary on the doctrine of real presence, "Eucharist" acknowledges a history of various attempts at theological explanation (E, Commentary on 15). The effect is the suggestion that no single explanation may be considered essential to the doctrine of real presence.

PRINCIPLES FOR
A HISTORICAL ECCLESIOLOGY

The three ecclesiologies that have been sketched in this last chapter can be envisioned as representing two ends of a spectrum of ecclesiologies that moves from right to left and includes a negotiated centrist position. While so imagining them accomplishes little, at least it illustrates something that has come to light in the course of this work: no center or absolute norm for how the church is to be arranged exists. As a historical reality the church corresponds to no Platonic form. Yet no church holds that the church exists outside of any norms or criteria for authenticity. The topic of what such criteria may be lies outside the boundaries of this work. But tentatively laying out the lessons of history in the form of some principles for a constructive ecclesiology contributes to the discussion of such norms. What follows are theses that suggest some of the lessons and principles derived from Orthodox and pentecostal ecclesiologies and the effort of the World Council of Churches to sketch aspects of the church held in common.

An iconic imagination enables ecclesiology to recognize and constructively integrate the dynamic tensions within the church. Orthodox ecclesiology as represented by Zizioulas embodies a number of tensions that help define a method of ecclesiology from below and whose relevance the history of ecclesiology has demonstrated. He posits a tensive relationship between a christological and a pneumatological framework for understanding the church. The one tends to stress the autonomy of institutional form as derivative from Jesus; the other tends to combine an ontological and functional understanding of institution flowing from a Spirit-filled community. Zizioulas teaches us that ontology and functionality do not have to be antithetical: they are two aspects of the historical church. Zizioulas calls repeatedly for explicit attention to be given to the tension between history and eschatology, which can be translated roughly into a dual appreciation of the church as a historical community which bears iconically transcendent reality. According to the maxim of Edward Schillebeeckx: one reality in two languages.[63] This church, therefore,

---

63. Edward Schillebeeckx, *Church: The Human Story of God* (New York: Crossroad, 1990), 210–13.

has to be approached simultaneously with a symbolic or iconic imagination and historical criticism. The dogmatic dimension, however, is not extrinsically authoritarian or literal, but operates from inside faith's commitment with a mystagogical or transcendent lens: faith encounters the transcendence named in the doctrines. The transcendent reality mediated by the church, therefore, does not blind one to historical finitude or corruption but criticizes them. The church has aspects that orient attention *ad intra,* and an impulse relating the church *ad extra:* these have to be coordinated and balanced. Finally, the iconic character of the church also reflects what was laid down as a premise of this work, that the church is essentially constituted by two relationships, to God and to the world. The point is that these two relationships intersect and continually qualify each other as in a dialectical historical process. The double relationship itself essentially defines the iconic character of the church. Zizioulas's own ecclesiological construction embodies a synthesis of the sacramental and liturgical center of gravity and a Western historicism. Ecclesiology from below intends to preserve this tension.

The Orthodox Church provides an example of communion ecclesiology that has functioned since the earliest period of the church. In the domain of church polity and organization, from a certain perspective Eastern Orthodox ecclesiology is the oldest in the Christian tradition. The church first took shape in the Eastern Mediterranean region and Asia Minor. This ecclesiology retrieves the language of Ignatius of Antioch and also Cyprian who present the bishop and the local church as the basic unit of ecclesiology. Communion ecclesiology in Zizioulas can be read as a retrieval of the ecclesiology of these fathers and a reinterpretation of it for a world church. The bishop and local church represent the basic unit and these units are held together primarily by a unity of faith through communication. The communication is downward to parochial eucharistic communities, laterally with other episcopal churches, and upward with heads of national churches or patriarchs, and worldwide through communions of communions.

The combination of the iconic and historical imaginations found in Orthodoxy as represented by Zizioulas gives new depth to the expression of the whole-part dialectic that emerged most clearly in the sixteenth century. There the tension tended to find its meaning in a historical and spatial sense of the whole church spread abroad and the local church of district, territory, or nation. But the local church is also the whole church theologically; unity, holiness, catholicity, and apostolicity can be predicated of the local church, so that the local eucharistic community, which sociologically is where Christians assemble, can also be understood as the basic unit of the church theologically. This opens up many lines of communication among churches, including especially the free congregational churches.

Pentecostal churches exemplify the need of the church to address itself to the religious needs (primal spirituality) and cultures of particular peoples. All ecclesiologies appeal to the New Testament for the authority of the polity and validity of various practices. But the church in the New Testament is pluralistic and in motion; it bears witness to early practices but provides no proof texts for particular institutions. It does not represent a "finished" church polity, but a church that is institutionally fluid, open, precisely in the process of formation. No ecclesiology surveyed in this book approaches the church in the New Testament in institutional terms as closely as pentecostalism. Pentecostal churches exemplify the "event" character of the church; they make church happen.[64] The church is most fully church when people actually gather and function as church. Pentecostal ecclesiology, when it is considered abstractly, favors communitas over structure:[65] in the measure in which this church becomes more institutionalized, it tends to be less itself. Although it does not neglect structures, they must promote charism. It is probably true that pentecostal churches inevitably become more institutionalized as time goes on; or they may have a steady turnover in their constituency. But when they exist alongside more structured churches, they press home lessons that are already known but have to be continually retrieved: the gathered congregation is the existential, historical, and faithful church-in-act.

---

64. The point does not imply that other churches lack this quality. But pentecostalism's stress on experience of the Spirit within corresponds with much of the language of the experience of the Spirit found in the New Testament.

65. The distinction and tension between communitas and structure is described in CCH, I, 127.

Some of the principles involved in this truism are obvious. The church has to inculturate if it is to communicate with and express the religious desires of the people it addresses and serves. The church is only faithful to God's word when it successfully makes that word available to people. A church will only have an impact on a community when it becomes part of that people's culture. There will always be debates in theory and practice about Christ and culture: what is the proper characterization of this relationship? When does this particular practice compromise the revelatory word of the gospel? But difficulty of resolving these questions cannot blunt the absolute need for the gospel to become incarnate in the spirituality of individuals and the cultures of peoples.

The tongues of Pentecost can function as a symbol of pluralism: the unity expressed in diverse languages. Frank Macchia uses the symbol of the pentecostal tongues of the Spirit to point to the unity in the Spirit and the diversity of the witness that characterizes the New Testament and the church in the period of its formation. He cites Karl Rahner as a principal proponent of the idea: "All of us 'know' in the Spirit of God something more simple, more true, and more real than that which we are capable of knowing and expressing in the dimension of our theological concepts."[66] Building on this Macchia says it "is only when language, culture, and theological tradition are relativized by the all-encompassing mystery of God's Spirit that they can be affirmed in all their diversity as vehicles for expressing the communion of a free humanity with a free and self-giving God" (FM, 14). Tongues thus have an iconoclastic function because they symbolize an experience of God as Spirit that spontaneously "recognizes the relative worth and beauty of every language of faith represented but democratizes them all by locating their absolute significance in their role as witness to the unspeakable grace of God" (FM, 14). Pentecostal tongues "do not abolish the diversity of expression but unite them as a polyphonic witness to the one

---

66. Karl Rahner, "On the Theology of the Ecumenical Discussion," *Theological Investigations* 11, *Confrontations I* (New York: Seabury Press, 1974), 38, cited by Frank D. Macchia, "The Tongues of Pentecost: A Pentecostal Perspective on the Promise and Challenge of Pentecostal/Roman Catholic Dialogue," *Journal of Ecumenical Studies* 35 (1998): 12. Cited in the text as FM.

gospel" (FM, 15). Macchia picks up the fact that the earliest Christian movement was pluralistic, and that this became constitutive of the church by its incorporation into the New Testament canon of scriptures. The symbol of tongues, therefore, finds its setting within the context of the plurality of communities that are represented by the scriptures. "Tongues as an eschatological sign symbolize a search to actualize a unity in the midst of an ever-expanding diversity" (FM, 16).

BEM only has an authority which, theologically, reflects God's initiative found in Christian origins and, practically, in the measure that the several churches recognize it. What is going on in BEM? Is it a "least common denominator" ecclesiology which, as such, would be the ecclesiology of no church? Is it an assembly of elements and provisions which has been arrived at by negotiation? In this case, since each element would be borrowed from one tradition or church but not others, the result would reflect the defining tradition of no single church. Is BEM a twentieth-century synthesis hammered out by church leaders, which weaves together foundational principles of ecclesiology drawn from the common sources of scripture and the traditions of the churches, that can elicit agreement of most but not all because in the long run it is an arbitrary construction?[67] All of these characterizations of BEM minimize the authority of this document. Is there a way of characterizing BEM more positively as an example of constructive ecclesiology that has intrinsic authority and thus some normative value? Can it be described in a way that displays a more than merely expedient character?

No answer to that question is feasible outside the context of historical and social consciousness. With those premises in place, one way of approaching this consists in turning to the reasons and motives that initiated and then guided the long process of producing BEM. What motivated the process of seeking to define the ecclesial unity Christians share and what goals were sought? That process arose out of a negative experience of contrast shared by enough Christians to stimulate a world movement. The unity we profess is not manifested historically in the church, so that together the churches

---

67. Barth, "BEM: Questions and Considerations," 496.

demonstrate against the Christian message. Ultimately missionary cooperation will falter without addressing differences; the Faith and Order conferences and then the Commission within the WCC cannot assemble Christians without addressing differences. These early insights were accompanied by the strategic principle that the way of constructively addressing differences lay in defining what Christian churches share in common. The goal was never the unity of a single church, but the unity of the faith to which the many churches, while remaining many, were to give common witness.

But unity has its demands. The tendency of all churches in the conversation is to say "we have the formula for unity." Each party wants to say that the unity of the church's witness to faith is found in [my interpretation of] the Word of God, or in [my understanding of] the apostolic witness. But such formulas for the church cannot be imposed; all churches have to take part in the conversation. The New Testament and twentieth-century Christian experience agree on the premise that faith appeals to freedom, that faith itself and the unity it impels cannot be commanded by human authority, that common self-understanding and organization must be a function of conversation.[68] Such conversation produced the BEM document. The fact that that conversation went on since preparations for Lausanne (1927) lends seriousness but not finality to this document. This document's authority lies in the ongoing concern for the process, and the fact that it provides a temporary bridge for communication and interchange. BEM links the churches in discussion. The normative character of BEM does not refer to its ability to be imposed on any church, for it cannot. But churches can discover a normativity in it according to the measure that they recognize it as a vehicle for the ongoing conversation and the pursuit of historical unity commanded by God.

---

68. The contingent and arbitrary character of ecclesial organizations cannot be overcome; this is the intrinsic nature of historical reality. But this experience can be offset or mitigated by the strength of the imperative for Christian unity that the New Testament and early tradition emphasize so strongly. In other words, Christians *must* write such documents, *must* create unifying institutions, and *must* recognize the ministry of others churches. The questions each church has to pose relate not to what keeps them apart as distinctive, which is a given, but to how they can find a way to participate in this public witness to one faith.

BEM, as an outline for a transdenominational ecclesiology, performs a positive function for all the churches. Can one conceive a transdenominational ecclesiology which, while not being the ecclesiology of any single church, still provides a normative function for all Christian churches? A positive response to this question requires at least some indication of why such a construct might be needed and how it would perform such a function.

The factors pointing to a need for such an ecclesiology include much of the positive energy that flowed into the ecumenical movement. In several respects Christians are entering into a "transdenominational era." The phrase tries to capture developments within the Christian church that are analogous to those found operative in the process of globalization. The gradual unification of the planet and growing interdependency of peoples both relativize local structures of existence and generate self-conscious insistence on difference and maintenance of identity. These social-historical forces provide lived corporate existence with a dialectical structure in which these three elements, interdependency, relativization, and reassertion of identity, reinforce and intensify each other. Analogously, the Christian church now exists in a shrinking world in which one finds multiple religious traditions among which the Christian movement is one. On this level of the pluralism of religions one can discern a need for a conversation that reflects on the nature of the Christian community as a whole, as differentiated from other religions. Reciprocally, within the Christian community itself, a common Christian identity appears more distinctly or in sharper relief against the background of religious pluralism than when it is viewed as a self-contained ecumenical movement. Both the multiplicity of religions and the multiplicity of Christian churches and their divisions have in some degree relativized denominational identity and correspond with a new relative ease with which people can change ecclesial affiliation or membership. More and more Christians are able to distinguish their particular churches and communions from the inner nature of Christianity itself: they are not identical with or reducible to each other. As in the process of globalization, this does not mean that denominations are displaced or abandoned; in fact they may become significantly more important because less taken for granted and more passionately cherished for the identity they provide. But they are deabsolutized, recognized as a matter of religious freedom and choice, so that transition from one church tradition to another is not only thinkable but also sometimes attractive. In sum, the fluidity and the pluralism within the large Christian church, which can only increase as the center of gravity of the church shifts to the developing world, suggests a need for constant definition of that which Christians share in common.[69]

Transdenominational ecclesiology points to the task of all Christian churches to consider the nature of the Christian church as a whole. Such ecclesiological reflection includes but transcends the boundaries of the particular church or tradition of any given community or theologian. The premises for such reflection consist in many of the principles to which the history of ecclesiology gives constant witness: that real theological and historical unity characterizes the whole Christian movement; that the church attaches a high value on a public ecclesial witness to this unity; that no Christian church exhausts or contains without remainder ecclesial self-understanding or witness; that unity must be pluralistic in such a way that life-giving traditions or denominational identities be preserved; that ecclesial organizational structure and relation to the world are constantly shifting; that defining the common nature of the church, therefore, will escape every essay because it is a constant and shared task that is always in process. On these premises, and with these conditions and provisos, a transdenominational ecclesiology can serve a positive function similar to the WCC itself, which is not a church but an ecclesial institution with a valued ecclesiological function. A conscious dedication to the construction of a transdenominational ecclesiology will help fashion a common framework and common language for

---

69. I agree with Stephen Sykes's negative critique of the effort to establish an "essence of Christianity" insofar as that quest was or is construed as reductive of the full life of the churches. See his *The Identity of Christianity: Theologians and the Essence of Christianity from Schleiermacher to Barth* (Philadelphia: Fortress Press, 1984). While the efforts of BEM may seem from a limited perspective as analogous, the premises and goals differ greatly. BEM is, like a type, precisely not an ecclesiology of any church but an abstraction; the process of constructing it is filled with dialectical tensions between what is and what can be. Its authority lies in its mediation of the word of God that relativizes human institutions and "religion" so that the human person can be free to recognize the word of God in the other churches.

the ecumenical conversation, interaction with society and the world, and interreligious dialogue. Such an ecclesiology as an ongoing discipline also helps preserve Christian unity and identity in an inclusive and nondivisive way. As a discipline it remains a function of and in service of the churches and provides witness to the wider world.

In sum, BEM challenges the whole Christian church to try to understand the church as a whole, in a way that follows an integral method transcending an ecclesiology formed by committee, that preserves the pluralism of traditions, and so represents the whole that each individual church can recognize its inner authority.

Conclusion

Ecclesiology in the Twenty-first Century

A work such as this admits of no real conclusion. The historical survey merely brings the discussion up to the present; the future presses in. It may be helpful, nevertheless, to put in words the obvious issues that must occupy the church and the churches in the immediate and perhaps long-term future. Three such issues among many seem both large and lasting.

The present historical situation sets the stage for these issues. The Christian church in both its Western and Eastern branches is entering a distinctly new period of its history as the churches in the developing world grow in numbers and strength. Africa is becoming a largely Christian continent; the church is expanding in a number of sectors in Asia; Latin America, long a Christian sphere, is undergoing a significant changes in its ecclesial shape. The Orthodox Church will take on new contours in North America, Africa, and East Asia. The process of globalization is deeply affecting the church. New theologies of mission are being designed and new agendas for the churches are appearing, or taking on more radical forms. It is not necessary to predict particular political shifts within the churches in these regions or how they will relate to the more established churches of the Greek and Latin successions. But one can point to these three issues that will command attention because they do so already.

First, new demands for inculturation are being heard from all parts of the world. What is new in them is the dissatisfaction with what has been done up to now; it is not sufficient. In worldwide communions, such as in Roman Catholicism and less so the Anglican communion, this demand for inculturation sets up center-periphery tension. Sometimes Europe and/or North America represent the pole of the tension vis-à-vis the other continents, and it is felt with new force in this postcolonial period. It affects all churches which have relationships across national and cultural frontiers. Questions that before could be simply labeled "syncretistic" are not so easily dismissed. It seems that a new level of historical and cultural consciousness is arising spontaneously and will not be put off by an authority that comes less from the gospel and more from a different culture.

Second, the demands for inculturation carry with them the requirement that Christian consciousness and its theology revisit the attitudes of the church toward other religions. Cultures outside the West broadly construed are frequently shaped by religions that closely and deeply define the intertwined systems of value and meaning. Churches have to reflect and take theological stock of how they relate to these deep and newly vital traditions. This is no easy task since this problem goes to the heart of Christian self-understanding, and different churches, like different theologians, have different perspectives on the issue. This is not the place to deal at any length with this far-reaching christological and ecclesiological issue, but neither can it be minimized in any projection of the agenda of the church for the future. It is so basic that it tacitly influences all other issues.

Third, the church has to develop some commonly accepted formulas for how to implement the growing conviction that the churches have to consciously and formally accept pluralism as a characteristic of being in the world. No one can doubt the principle that unity can only be maintained across societies, nations, and cultures by welcoming differences. But these are usually conceded on peripheral not central matters, on accidental rather than substantial truths or practices. Emotion and confusion run wild here. How can differences relative to sexual behavior, for example, cause people to forget or override the profound bond of unity that the Spirit forges in faith's attachment to Jesus Christ? Of course, what is important for some may be trivial for others in matters of authority, doctrine, ethical norms, and moral practices. But for the churches to remain in communion with each other, or even in touch with each other, attitudes, conceptual frameworks, and church law will have to be fashioned in a way that allows churches to find in others what they share in a common transcendent faith despite serious differences.

BEM models a desire, a set of premises, and a strategy for engaging these issues. A fitting conclusion to this work would be a more fully developed constructive ecclesiology that appeals to the threads of the tradition of the church which are held in common, is schooled in the principles and axioms of historical and comparative ecclesiology, and is built upon the common faith in Jesus the Christ and God as Spirit.

Index